DATABASE PROCESSING:
Fundamentals, Design,
Implementation

SECOND EDITION

DATABASE PROCESSING:
Fundamentals, Design,
Implementation
SECOND EDITION

David M. Kroenke

 ® SCIENCE RESEARCH ASSOCIATES, INC.
Chicago, Henley-on-Thames, Sydney, Toronto
A Subsidiary of IBM

Acquisition Editor	Terry Baransy
Project Editor	James C. Budd
Compositor	Graphic Typesetting Service
Illustrator	Michael Rogondino
Text Designer	Judith Olson
Cover Designer	Barbara Ravizza

Library of Congress Cataloging in Publication Data

Kroenke, David.
  Database processing.

  Bibliography: p.
  Includes index.
  1. Data base management. I. Title.
QA76.9.D3K76 1983   001.6'442   82-10676
ISBN 0-574-21320-1

Originally published under the title, *Database Processing: Fundamentals, Modeling, Applications*.

10 9 8 7 6

Contents

Preface

Many changes have occurred in the more than five years that have passed since *Database Processing* was first published. These changes are of two fundamental types. First, people have learned how to better manage and use database technology. Five years ago, companies were still wrestling with databases, and the horror stories that accompany the introduction of new, major technology were common. Such stories are far less common today. Professionals have gained a better understanding of the capabilities of database technology, and the expectations for databases have become more realistic. In many cases, large corporations have given up the idea of a single, integrated corporate database. Rather, several databases exist with clearly defined interfaces. This situation is unlikely to change in the future because the move away from a single database was prompted as much by the limitations of people and organizations as by the limitations in technology.

During this same period of time, the quality of products and services from DBMS vendors has improved significantly. Database software has become more reliable and easier to use, and utility programs for database maintenance have been improved. Also, the vendors themselves have developed more realistic expectations of the capabilities of their products. Vendor documentation and training have been improved as well. All in all, the interval from 1977 to 1981 has been a period of consolidation in database processing. No dramatic technological changes occurred; businesses had time to catch their breath.

In 1981 this situation changed. Several vendors announced database management systems based on the relational data model. Until these announcements, relational database processing had been the favored child of academicians, but had seen little practical application. Early relational products had unacceptable performance. In the last two years, performance has been improved. Major manufacturing organizations have tested relational DBMS products and have found segments of their workload that can be processed with acceptable performance. Further, improvements in development staff productivity have been incredible. Using a relational DBMS, one company found application development productivity improvements to be greater than 100 to 1.

Thus, by late 1982 the situation was this: established DBMS products are used to manage large databases having heavy workloads and stringent performance requirements. New relational DBMS are starting to be used to manage small to medium databases with moderate workloads and where the need for flexibility and rapid response to new requests is essential. Some large companies are maintaining two databases: one is an operational database processed by an established, high-performance DBMS product. This database contains the up-to-the-minute data. The second database contains information for management and is maintained by a relational DBMS product. The data is less current; perhaps it is refreshed from the operational database overnight, but processing is flexible.

NEW REQUIREMENTS FOR STUDENT KNOWLEDGE

In my opinion, changes in requirements for database education have paralleled changes in industry. There has been a period of consolidation, followed by a need for practical knowledge regarding relational processing. As the number of DBMS products has dramatically increased, knowledge of any particular DBMS has become less important and a broader knowledge of fundamental concepts has become more important. For example, students need to know enough database technology to evaluate its application in a given situation, to participate in database design, and to understand implementation concerns such as control of concurrent processing, recovery, and security. Further, students should know and observe the ways that application programs interface with DBMS products. It is less important that they know the ins and outs of any particular DBMS product. Today, this latter knowledge is readily available from vendors or from within the companies that use a particular product. What is not readily available in industry is a broad understanding of the technology.

At the same time, relational database technology is seeing practical application. In 1977 relational discussions centered on normal forms and theoretical languages. These subjects had little to do with putting the products out the door, and most students were unable to utilize such knowledge. Today, graduates can be expected to design relational databases and to use relational languages such as Structured Query Language (SQL) in a practical setting. Knowledge about these issues will be most relevant to the graduate's career.

STRUCTURE OF THIS TEXT

This edition of *Database Processing* is organized to reflect these changes. It also reflects my own learning concerning the teaching of database models. In 1977, I taught database models to future practitioners without a clear notion of why I was doing it. Database models seemed important. Today, I believe that database models are important to the practitioner primarily as design tools. The CODASYL DBTG model, the relational model, and other models discussed in Chapters 5 and 6 can be used to facilitate database design. Using models to group and characterize DBMS products remains useful, but in my mind such a use is of secondary importance. Thus the change in subtitle from *Fundamentals, Modeling, Applications* to *Fundamentals, Design, Implementation* reflects a change in philosophy as well as content.

The first four chapters of this edition (Part I) present introductory and fundamental concepts. Chapter 1 defines database processing and compares and contrasts it to file processing. Chapter 2 presents an overview of the development of a database application. This chapter concludes with a short case adapted from my consulting experience. Students may find the ending of this case unsettling. If so, ask them to rewrite history. What would they have done? I am indebted to Steve Guynes of North Texas State University in Denton for the idea of the new Chapter 2. Steve suggested the need to give students a view of the forest before plunging into the trees.

Chapter 3 presents input/output processing and will be a review for students who have studied computer organization. A new section has been added on meta-access methods such as the virtual I/O used by IBM's System/38. Chapter 4 combines Chapters 2 and 3 of the first edition. The fundamental organization of this chapter was suggested by Lt. Col. Robert J. Tufts, United States Air Force. Colonel Tufts provided many other valued suggestions as well.

Chapters 5 through 10 (Part II) concern database design. Chapter 5 surveys the design process and introduces a case that will be used throughout the balance of the text. Also, Chapter 5 surveys database models and suggests ways such models can be used as design tools. According to the process described, database design has two phases. During the first phase, or logical database design, a DBMS-independent design is developed. This design reflects only requirements; it is not biased by the weaknesses or peculiarities of any DBMS product. Chapter 6 discusses such designs and presents a design tool called the *semantic data model*, which was developed by Michael Hammer and Dennis McLeod. Dr. McLeod, of the University of Southern California, has kindly reviewed this material.

Physical database design, or DBMS-dependent database design, is the subject of Chapters 7 through 10. At this point the path of discussion forks. Although we need to consider designs for different DBMS products, we cannot consider a design for every product. Instead, we consider physical design for two important categories of DBMS products, namely, products based on the relational data model and products based on the CODASYL DBTG model.

Chapter 7 presents concepts of the relational model, and Chapter 8 presents relational design strategy and criteria and develops a relational design for an application discussed in Chapters 5 and 6.

Chapter 9 presents concepts of the CODASYL DBTG model, and Chapter 10 presents DBTG design strategy and criteria and develops a DBTG design for the same application in Chapters 5 and 6. Thus students will be able to compare and contrast the two models for the same design application.

Chapters 11 through 14 (Part III) consider database implementation. First, Chapter 11 discusses the functions of a DBMS product and focuses particularly on the control of concurrent processing, backup and recovery, and security. Then, Chapter 12 implements the relational database design developed in Chapter 8 using the relational DBMS product *SQL/DS*. Chapter 13 implements the DBTG design developed in Chapter 10 using the DBTG product *IDMS*. Finally, Chapter 14 discusses database administration.

There are many important DBMS products besides SQL/DS and IDMS. The discussion of these systems does not imply an endorsement. I chose these particular ones because I believe they are effective and popular systems, and that students who understand them will be able to transfer this understanding to other DBMS products. There is simply insufficient space in this text to discuss all of the excellent products that exist. Further, knowledge of many such systems adds little to the students' overall understanding of database concepts and technology. For balance, however, three additional DBMS products, namely, DL/I, TOTAL/IMAGE, and MicroRIM, are discussed in the appendix.

A NOTE ON PUNCTUATION

This text brings together material that is not normally published under the same cover. Punctuation standards differ widely among sources. As a consequence, developing a standard for punctuation has been difficult. For example, the literature of the relational model uses the underscore to connect words, e.g., ORDER_NUMBER. The DBTG model uses the hyphen to connect words, e.g., ORDER-NUMBER. Furthermore, computers today support upper- and lower-case letters, whereas many models that were developed several years ago do not. The result is chaos.

Alice Lescalleet, who copy edited the manuscript, has done a superior job in bringing this material together and establishing as consistent a punctuation standard as possible. She has established general rules regarding punctuation and then modified those rules where necessary to introduce students to the punctuation that is normally associated with a given topic. In general, files, records, and relationships will be shown in all capital letters, e.g., ORDER and ORDER-ITEM. Fields (alias data-items, attributes, and columns, depending on context) will be shown in initial capitals, e.g., Item and Line-item. As of this date, DBMS products do not allow lowercase letters, however, so when discussing a particular product all names (including fields) will appear in capitals, e.g., ITEM and LINE-ITEM (in an IDMS schema). Furthermore, for DBTG or other COBOL-oriented material, hyphens will be used as connectors. For relational or entity-relational material, underscores will be used as connectors.

If you do not follow all of this notation, do not worry. Realize that differences in punctuation exist, and that such differences have no conceptual significance.

To my knowledge, this punctuation problem has been unaddressed to date. I thank Ms. Lescalleet for her courage and patience in addressing this problem and for correcting so many of my errors.

ACKNOWLEDGMENTS

Many people have helped in the preparation of this manuscript. Besides those already mentioned, I thank reviewers Barbara Beccue, Illinois State University; H. L. Capron; Roger Knights, independent consultant; Christopher W. Pidgeon, California State Polytechnic, Pomona; Richard W. Scamell, University of Houston; and Barbara A. Springer, Intel Systems Corporation.

Additionally, I thank the following individuals who reviewed the first edition and suggested changes: James D. Brainerd, Ferris State College at Grand Rapids, Michigan; Norman D. Brammer, Colorado State University; Robert Grauer, University of Miami; Susan Hinrichs, Missouri Western State College; Mary E. S. Loomis, University of Arizona; Sham Navathe, University of Florida; Frank J. Pisacane, Quinnipiac College, Hamden, Connecticut; Michael J. Powers, Illinois State University; Leonard Shapiro, North Dakota State University; and Oebele G. Van Dyk, State University of New York at Oswego. Additionally, Doris Gottschalk Duncan, Golden Gate University at San Francisco, provided advice and assistance during early discussions regarding second edition content.

Dr. Doug Cashing of Saint Bonaventure University, New York, reviewed and answered questions in the first draft of this edition, and provided many helpful comments as well. Additionally, thanks to Glenn Smith of James Madison University, Harrisburg, Virginia, for developing the comprehensive Instructor's Guide that accompanies this edition.

Thanks to the students at North Seattle Community College and those at Seattle University who so enthusiastically enunciated opportunities for improvement in the first draft of this edition. Dr. Kyu Y. Lee of Seattle University kindly created a way for me to classroom teach this material.

Dr. Donald R. Deutsch, Chairperson of the ANSI X3H2 Committee, provided materials and insights for the preparation of Chapters 9 and 10. Also, Darryl Olson of Boeing Computer Services read, reviewed, and suggested improvements for the relational material. Thanks as well to John Cullinane and Cullinane Corporation personnel for assistance in the preparation of material for Chapter 13, and to Wayne Erickson of MicroRIM for assistance with material in the appendix. Further, I thank Marilyn Bohl of IBM for her friendship and assistance over the last seven years.

Finally, a special thanks to the personnel at SRA. Terry Baransy in particular has been patient and supportive during more ups and downs and crises than

I'm sure he cares to remember. Thanks also to Jim Budd and others at SRA for their tireless effort and diligence.

TO THE STUDENT

The next few years will likely see the application of database technology in wider and wider spheres. Databases will become more prevalent on micros, and, with nonprocedural languages, end-user programming will become a reality. Conceivably, in the future all data management will employ database technology. Consequently, the knowledge you gain in this class will constitute an important part of your professional expertise. Best of luck!

David M. Kroenke
Mercer Island, Washington

1

Introduction

In the early 1970s, database processing was considered an esoteric subject, of interest only to the largest corporations with the largest computers. Today, database processing is becoming an information systems standard. In some computers, such as the Hewlett-Packard 250 and the IBM System/38, all data is organized into databases; files, as individual entities, do not exist.

The change to database processing has occurred largely because of economics. As you will see, database processing favors people at the expense of computers. Programmers and other users of data can be more efficient and effective with database processing - they can accomplish more within a fixed amount of time. On the other hand, database processing requires more computer resources than traditional processing does. Main and peripheral storage and central processing unit (CPU) cycles are required by the database processing program.

In the last ten years the cost of labor has been increasing steadily. Even worse, management has encountered great difficulty acquiring and keeping competent systems development personnel. Meanwhile, the cost of computers has decreased dramatically. As *Computerworld* puts it, "The computer industry has developed the equivalent of a $2.50 Rolls Royce that gets 2,000,000 miles per gallon."

Thus, simply stated, people have become more expensive as machines have become cheaper. In parallel, database processing has offered the potential for trading people resources for machine resources. The result has been a substantial increase in the number of database applications. By all standards, these trends are likely to continue. Conceivably, files as independent entities might disappear entirely; perhaps in another ten years all commercial data processing will become database processing.

WHAT IS DATABASE PROCESSING?

Database technology allows an organization's data to be processed as an integrated whole. It reduces artificiality imposed by separate files for separate applications and permits users to access data more naturally.

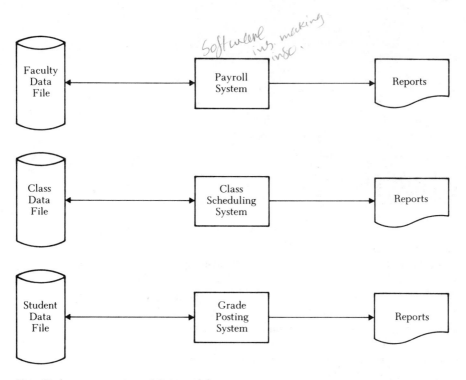

Note: Each system contains a definition of data.

Figure 1-1   Three File Processing (Pre-Database) Systems

To appreciate this concept, consider the three systems shown in Figure 1-1.
These are *file processing systems*; they are predecessors of database systems.
With file processing, each file is considered to exist independently. The payroll
system in Figure 1-1 processes only the faculty data file; the class scheduling
system processes only class data; and the grade posting system processes only
student data. These systems are effective in that they produce checks, schedule
classes, and record grades.

But, suppose someone wants to know the salary paid to each instructor who
teaches a class scheduled by the class scheduling system. To obtain this information, a new program must be written to extract data from both the faculty
and the class data files. Unfortunately, there is no guarantee that these files are
compatible. The faculty data file might be written in COBOL binary format,
whereas an incompatible PL/I record format might be used for the class data
file. If so, one file must be converted to the format of the other, and then the
extraction program written, tested, and run. This process will take time. Users
may decide (as many have) that responses to new requirements or one-of-a-kind
requests are so long in coming that they are not worth requesting.

In some cases, conversion entails so much effort to eliminate incompatibility that it simply cannot be done within a reasonable cost. This leads to the situation where the user knows that needed information is "in the computer" but seemingly no one can get it out.

Figure 1-2 shows a database processing system. The files in Figure 1-1 have been integrated into a database that is processed indirectly by the application programs. The payroll, class scheduling, and grade posting systems can perform their old functions, but the programs call upon the database management system (DBMS) to access the database. The DBMS is a complex and usually large program that acts as a data librarian. It stores and retrieves data. Observe that for the DBMS to perform its function, it stores not only data, but also a description of the format of the data.

The faculty, class, and student data in Figure 1-2 can be processed as an integrated whole. Since the files have been created by the DBMS, all of the data is compatible. Further, the DBMS may have features to enhance integrated processing. For example, a faculty record can be logically "tied to" several class records to represent the relationship between teacher and class. Thus database processing is integrated processing.

ADVANTAGES OF DATABASE PROCESSING

Data integration offers several important advantages. First and foremost, *database processing enables more information to be produced from a given amount of data*. Data is recorded facts or figures; information is knowledge gained by processing data. When data is physically partitioned as shown in Figure 1-1, information can be derived from faculty data, from class data, and from student data. However, information cannot be derived from a combination of faculty and class data. For example, information can be gained about average faculty salaries, but not about the average salary of faculty teaching the course DAT104. Computing this average would require data from two of the separated files. Thus partitioning data limits the combinations of data to be processed and hence the amount of information that can be obtained.

In contrast to Figure 1-1, the database in Figure 1-2 does not partition the data. Derivations can be made from combinations of faculty and class data, or class and student data, and so forth. The average salary of faculty teaching course DAT104 would be readily obtained. Thus the primary reason why people develop databases is to obtain more information from a given amount of data. They do this by removing artificial partitions.

Another important advantage of database processing is the elimination or reduction of data duplication. In the file processing systems in Figure 1-1, some student data is apt to be recorded in both the class data file and the student data file. In the database, it need only be recorded once. Elimination of duplication saves file space, and to some extent, can reduce processing requirements.

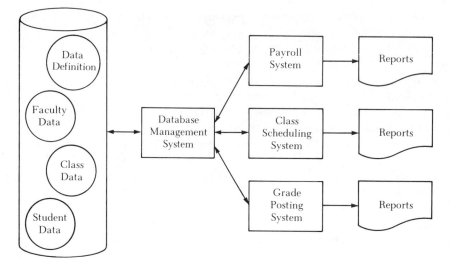

Figure 1-2   A Database Processing System

The most serious problem of data duplication is that it can lead to a lack of data integrity. If student data is recorded in two places, it is possible to change the data in one place but not in the other. Data items then disagree with one another.

A common result of a lack of data integrity is conflicting reports. Perhaps nothing is more aggravating to management or more embarrassing to the data processing staff than to be confronted with computer reports that disagree. Users soon learn to distrust all computer-generated output.

Creation of program/data independence is a third advantage of database processing. In Figure 1-1, programs interface directly with files. Each program must contain a description of the format of the files it uses. Thus the structure of files will be distributed across programs. This distribution creates problems when a file is changed. For example, if the Zip Code field is expanded to nine digits, all programs that access a file containing Zip Code will need to be modified, even if those programs do not use Zip Code.

For the database application in Figure 1-2, however, application programs will obtain data from an intermediary, the DBMS. Consequently, the application programs need not contain data structure. Only the DBMS will need this structure. With this architecture, to convert to nine-digit Zip Codes, only the DBMS and those programs that use Zip Code will need to be changed. Programs not using Zip Code will be independent of this change.

Consider another example. Suppose a new field is added to a database record. In this case, the database description will be modified to include the new field, but application programs that do not require the field will be unaffected. Consider a third example. Assume a new disk device or technique for processing a file becomes available. In the database example, only the database description (and possibly the DBMS) need be changed. Such program/data independence is exceedingly valuable to companies maintaining hundreds of programs and files.

Another advantage of database processing is better data management. When data is centralized in a database, one department can specialize in the maintenance of data. That department can specify data standards and ensure that all data adhere to the standards. When someone has a data requirement, he or she can contact one department instead of many file maintenance groups. Furthermore, centralization of data management leads to economies of scale. One person working full time on data problems can be more efficient than 20 people working one-twentieth of their time on the problems.

Database processing creates another type of economy of scale. Since there is only one DBMS processing a shared database, improvements made to the database or to the DBMS will benefit many users. In contrast, improvements made to payroll or another file processing system benefit only the users of that system. Thus more money and more analyst and programmer time can be spent improving the database application than could be spent on any single file processing application. Benefits such as a more useful design or better performance will result. Also, since most organizations buy or lease their DBMS, this economy of scale means that more money can be spent on the DBMS. Consequently, expensive (and sophisticated) DBMS systems become cost justifiable. They possess features that are simply not affordable in file processing applications.

Figure 1-3 shows the long range average cost curve for a typical business enterprise. As activity size expands, the average cost of the activity usually falls (point A in the figure). Beyond that point, however, the average cost begins to rise. This curve pertains to data processing as well as to other business activities. For data processing, the vertical axis represents the cost per transaction. The transition from file processing to database processing and the attendant economies of scale occurred on the left-hand (decreasing) part of this curve.

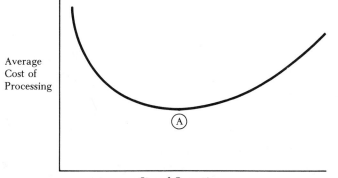

Figure 1-3 Long Range Average Cost Curve of Typical Business Activity (Database Processing Included)

Some databases, however, have grown so large that they have passed the point of minimum cost. When the database becomes this large, many companies decide to divide the database into several databases. Then, the economies of scale just discussed apply to each of the smaller databases. Each of these operates on the decreasing portion of its own long range average cost curve.

When a database is divided in this way, the new, smaller databases can all reside on the same computer or they can be placed on different computers. If these databases reside on different computers, they are called *distributed databases.* The simultaneous processing of such distributed databases is exceedingly complicated. Many of the problems of distributed database processing are unsolved. Consequently, we will not consider distributed database processing in this text. See references [7], [8], and [13] for more information.

Figure 1-4 summarizes the advantages of database processing. Actually, these advantages may not be fully experienced in every system. We will find later that there can be good reasons for data duplication in a database, and that program/data independence is not as independent as we might like.

File processing diehards will say that file processing can accomplish all of the advantages in Figure 1-4. Strictly speaking, they will be right. Attaining these objectives with file processing, however, will be exceedingly difficult and require application programmers to write sophisticated and complicated data management code. This large burden will increase errors in programs and make them difficult to maintain. If, on the other hand, the DBMS is properly selected and used, it will provide these services for the programmer and enable the advantages in Figure 1-4 to be realized in a timely and cost-effective manner.

DISADVANTAGES OF DATABASE PROCESSING

A major disadvantage of database processing is that it can be expensive. The DBMS may cost as much as $100,000 to buy. Furthermore, this expense is often

---

More Information from the Same Amount of Data
New Requests and One-of-a-Kind Requests More Easily Implemented
Elimination of Data Duplication
Program/Data Independence
Better Data Management
Affordable Sophisticated Programming
Representation of Record Relationships

Figure 1-4   Advantages of Database Processing

akin to the tip of the iceberg. The DBMS may occupy so much main memory that additional memory must be purchased. Even with more memory, it may monopolize the CPU, thus forcing the user to upgrade to a more powerful computer. Conversion from existing systems can be costly, especially if new data must be acquired.

Once the database is implemented, operating costs for some systems will be higher. Sequential processing of payroll, for example, will never be done as fast in the database environment. There simply is too much overhead.

Another major disadvantage is that database processing tends to be complex. Large amounts of data in many different formats can be interrelated in the database. Both the database system and the application programs must be able to process these structures. This means more sophisticated programming. Application system design may take longer, and highly qualified systems and programming personnel are required.

Backup and recovery are more difficult in the database environment. This is because of increased complexity and because databases are often processed by several users concurrently. Determining the exact state of the database at the time of failure may be a problem. Given that, it may be even more difficult to determine what should be done next.

Even the failure of just one application program may pose serious problems. If program A modifies several records and then fails, it may be necessary to roll back (or eliminate) A's modifications. If this is done, program B, which read the records after modification but before they were rolled back, may have invalid data. This problem is considered in detail in Chapter 11.

A final disadvantage is that integration, and hence centralization, increases vulnerability. A failure in one component of an integrated system can stop the entire system. This event is especially critical if, as is often the case, the operation of the user organization depends on the database.

Figure 1-5 summarizes the major disadvantages of database processing. These disadvantages should be weighed against the advantages discussed in the previous section. We will discuss in the next chapter a systematic technique for

---

Expensive
   Database Management System
   More Hardware
   Higher Operating Costs
Complex
Recovery More Difficult
Increased Vulnerability to Failure

Figure 1-5 Disadvantages of Database Processing

analyzing these advantages and disadvantages and for developing a database application.

COMPONENTS OF A BUSINESS DATABASE SYSTEM

A business database system is a collection of five components that interact to satisfy business needs. The five components are hardware, programs, data, people, and procedures. We will consider each of these in turn.

Component 1: Hardware

To date, database systems do not require any special type of hardware. Database processing, however, does involve special programs and overhead data. Thus database applications often require more hardware: more main memory, a faster CPU, and more direct access storage.

In 1982, several vendors announced new products called *database machines*. These machines are special purpose computers that perform database processing functions. As shown in Figure 1-6, the computer processing the application program sends requests for service and data over a channel to the database machine. The machine processes the requests and sends results, data, or messages back to the main computer. Thus database processing can be performed simultaneously with applications processing.

At this writing, the true effectiveness of these machines is unknown. If substantial processing efficiencies can be obtained at a reasonable cost, then data-

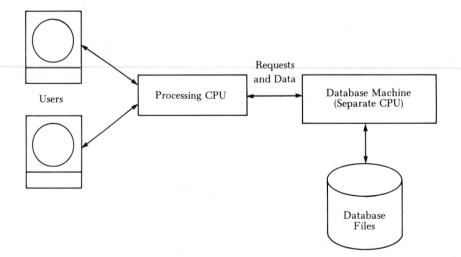

Figure 1-6 Schematic of Processing with Database Machine

base machines will likely become important. Until then, however, it is safe to say that, in general, database applications do not require special hardware.

Component 2: Programs

Several types of programs are used in database processing systems. Figure 1-7 shows the approximate relationships of the major types. Online processing requests or transactions are provided by users at terminals. The requests are sent to the processing computer over communications lines.

The requests are received and routed by the *communications control program* (CCP). This program has several important functions. It provides communications error checking and correction, it coordinates terminal activity, it routes messages to the correct next destination, it formats messages for various types of terminal equipment, and it performs other communications-oriented tasks. The CCP is an important and complex program.

The CCP routes online input to the next level of programs. This level contains *application programs* (AP) as well as database *utilities*. The application programs satisfy specific needs like order entry, inventory accounting, billing, and so forth. They are tailored to a specific business need.

Figure 1-7 shows batch inputs to application programs. This data is not processed online via a communications system. Rather, the data is collected into groups

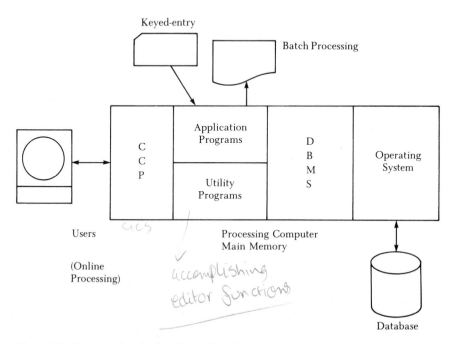

Figure 1-7 Programs Involved in Typical Database Processing

or batches and submitted as a batch to the application program. An example of batch processing is weekly payroll. All employee records for the week are gathered together and processed as a unit. Batch data is not processed by the CCP; instead, it is routed directly to application programs. This figure illustrates that database processing need not be online processing. Certainly, much online processing is done, but batch processing is also common.

The utility programs are provided by either the DBMS or the hardware vendor. These programs provide a wide variety of services. Query/update utilities provide generalized retrieval and update of the database. Since this is a generalized interface, many users can employ the query/update utility for many different purposes. Since no application program is involved in this mode, programmers are not required. This frees programmers for other activity and gives users greater control over the timing and processing of their requests. Other utility programs enable users to define and obtain reports with minimal programmer involvement.

Still other utilities create and maintain the database. Most vendors provide programs to generate database structure, to unload or reload database data, to reformat and clean up database files, and so forth.

First, the general structure of the database is defined. (More will be said about this in the next section.) Then data is loaded into the database. For normal processing, the DBMS receives data and stores it for subsequent processing. Both the application and utility programs call on the DBMS to provide database service. This system acts as a sophisticated data librarian. The DBMS allows application programs and utilities a wide variety of access strategies. It also enables these programs to have different views of the same data so that applications can use data in a format that is familiar and useful to them.

The DBMS also has features to provide security over data; the tools provided ensure that only authorized users can obtain authorized data. Also, the DBMS controls concurrent processing and includes features to provide backup and recovery. More will be said about these important functions in Chapter 11. The DBMS functions are summarized in Figure 1-8.

The final type of program involved in database processing is the *operating system*. This set of programs controls the computer's resources. For example, the DBMS itself does not do input/output. Rather, it sends requests for input/output services to the operating system. These programs, in turn, cause the service to be performed.

All programs are controlled by the operating system. Further, transfers of messages between programs are processed by the operating system. In a sense, you can view the operating system as the glue that holds all of the other programs together.

In most installations, only the application programs are written by the inhouse data processing staff. The CCP, the utilities, the DBMS, and the operating system are generally supplied by vendors. Usually the operating system is supplied by the hardware vendor, and in many cases, the CCP and the DBMS are

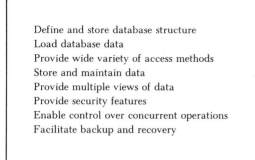

Define and store database structure
Load database data
Provide wide variety of access methods
Store and maintain data
Provide multiple views of data
Provide security features
Enable control over concurrent operations
Facilitate backup and recovery

Figure 1-8   Functions of the DBMS

also procured from this source. However, it is also common for the CCP and the DBMS to be obtained from independent software vendors.

In this book we will be primarily concerned with the DBMS and application programs that use it. At times, we will also consider utility programs. The operating system and the CCP are important programs, but they are generally discussed in other courses. Consequently, we will consider them only peripherally in this book.

Component 3: Data

A database is a *self-describing* collection of *integrated files*. The database is self-describing because it contains, within itself, a description of its structure. Database processing differs from file processing in which the structure of the files is distributed across the application programs as previously discussed. Program/data independence is possible only because the database is self-describing.

According to standard usage in the computer industry, *bits* are grouped into *bytes* or *characters*, *characters* are grouped into *fields*, and *fields* are grouped into *records*. A collection of *records* is called a *file*. It is tempting to continue this progression by stating that files are grouped to form a database. This statement, however, would be false. A database is more than a collection of files; it is a collection of *integrated* files. Another way of saying this is that a database is a collection of files and relationships among records in those files.

For example, suppose a bank groups customer, checking, and savings files together. If this grouping contains none of the record relationships, it is not very useful. It is also not a database. To be a database, we need to add two ingredients. First, we need to add relationships among the records. Then we will know, for example, that a given checking record corresponds to a particular customer. The second ingredient needed is a description of the data; this will make the collection self-descriptive. Once we have a self-descriptive collection of integrated files, we have a database.

Another difference between file processing data and database data concerns the term *file*. For file processing, the records in a file are usually grouped together physically. A file of customer records will be located on a given tape volume or on contiguous cylinders of a disk. Thus the logical grouping of customers and the physical collection of customer records are the same.

For database processing, the logical collection of customer records probably does not exist as a physical collection. One customer record may be in one file on one disk device, and another record in another file on another disk device. The DBMS may spread records across various storage media. Thus, in database processing, there are *logical files*, or collections of records having meaning to users, and *physical files*, or collections of records on physical devices.

The records of physical files are really just containers for data. A 2000-byte physical record may contain several logical records of different types. For example, a physical record may hold a customer record, two checking records, and three savings records. These records may be completely unrelated. Realize, therefore, that with database processing, the terms *file* and *record* may each have two different meanings.

Processing databases Database records can be processed in a wide variety of ways. Records can be accessed *sequentially* within a file, *randomly* by value of a field, or by *relationship* to other records. Sequential processing of database records can result in surprises. Unless the DBMS is told otherwise, the records will be presented in whatever order is convenient to the DBMS. This may appear to be nonsensical to the application. To prevent this situation, the DBMS may be instructed to provide records in a particular order, say, for example, in ascending order of customer number. However, this feature is not available on all DBMS. If unavailable, the application program would be forced to extract the records in the DBMS's nonsensical order and sort them externally.

A *key* is a field that is used to identify a record. Customer number, vendor name, part number are examples of keys. For database processing, keys can be *unique* or *nonunique*. If unique, a value of the key identifies only one record. Social Security Number is a unique key. The number 500-00-0001 identifies one and only one individual. Customer number and part number are more examples of unique keys.

(Actually, Social Security Numbers may not be unique, even though they are supposed to be. Because of a variety of human errors, some Social Security Numbers are held by more than one person. In fact, one such number was retired because over 1100 people were using it! [74] We will assume for examples in this text, however, that Social Security Numbers are unique.)

A nonunique key identifies a group of records. Credit limit is a nonunique key. The value $1000 identifies all those customers having a credit limit of $1000.

There are likely to be many. Other examples of nonunique keys are Zip Code and customer name.

Application programs can access records by key value in any order. If the key is unique, the DBMS identifies the qualifying record for processing. If nonunique, the DBMS provides the records one at a time. In a typical sequence, the application program would ask the DBMS for the first record having the key value, then for the next record, and so forth until there are no more qualifying records. Thus the records are processed sequentially within key value.

A third way to process database records is by relationship. For example, customer and checking records are related. Application programs may ask the DBMS to use this relationship to find all checking records for a given customer, or to find the customer record for a given checking record. Many other possibilities exist, as you will see in Chapter 4.

Three views of data   In a database system a variety of forms, or views, of the data are defined. One such view is called the *schema*, or *conceptual view*. This is the complete, logical view of the data. The term *logical* means the data as it would be presented to a human. In fact, the data may be stored on the files in a completely different form.

The schema describes all of the data in the database. For a bank, the database schema might include the customer, checking, savings, loan, and credit records (Figure 1-9). It would be undesirable from a control standpoint to allow every

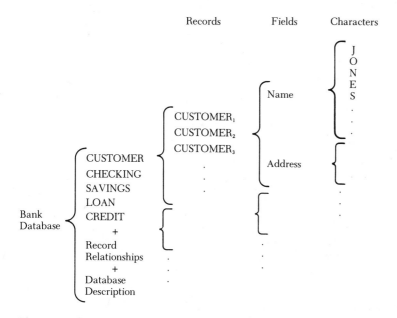

Figure 1-9   Composition of Bank Database

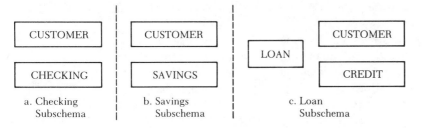

Figure 1-10   Example Subschemas for a Bank Database

application program to access all of this data. The bank would not want the checking programs, for example, to have access to loan data.

To restrict access to the database, companies define another type of view called a *subschema*, or *external view*. The subschema defines a subset of the schema to be seen by a given application program or user. The bank, for example, may define a *checking subschema* that contains the customer and checking records, a *savings subschema* that contains the customer and savings records, and a *loan subschema* that contains the customer, loan, and credit records. See Figure 1-10. A program that invokes the checking subschema will see only customer and checking records. All other database records will be invisible to that program.

Note there will be more than one subschema, and subschemas can overlap. Subschemas can also reorganize the schema. Fields can be renamed or reordered, and sometimes new or modified relationships can be defined. The particular capabilities depend on the DBMS used. You will see examples in Chapters 12 and 13.

A third view of the data is called the *internal*, or sometimes, the *physical view*. This is the form of the data as it appears to a particular processing computer. It describes how data is physically arranged and how it is allocated to files.

Each of these views must be defined before the database can be processed. Usually, the database administrator (see next section) writes the conceptual and external views. Often the internal view is created automatically by the DBMS when the database is defined.

The ability to have multiple views of the data is very convenient. It means that external views can be tailored to the needs of the application. Even though the data is centralized and shared, it can appear to each user in a format that is familiar and useful to him or her.

Figure 1-11 summarizes the three views of data. Again, the essential concept to understand is that database processing offers a variety of views of the same data.

Component 4: People

People are the fourth component of a business database system. *Clientele* are the people for whom the system is developed. The clientele of an airline res-

Type of View	Description
Schema (Conceptual)	Complete logical view of the data
Subschema (External)	Subset or transformation of schema
Physical (Internal)	Appearance of data to computer

Figure 1-11   Three Views of Data Supported by Database Processing

ervation system are the people who take flights. The clientele of a payroll system are employees. Clientele do not usually have an active role in database system development or use, and we will not generally be concerned with them.

Users are people who employ the system to satisfy a business need. The users of an airline reservation system are the clerks who make reservations at a video display terminal (VDT). The users of the payroll system are payroll administrators, clerks, and business managers.

Operations personnel run the computer and associated equipment. Typically, the operations department includes machine operators, data control personnel, and data entry people.

Systems development personnel design and implement the database system. They determine requirements, specify alternatives, design the five components of the system, and manage systems implementation. The design of the database structure or *schema* (more on this in later chapters) is an important function of these people. Systems development personnel include systems analysts, application programmers, and systems programmers (those people who support and maintain the operating system, the CCP, the DBMS, and other similar support programs).

The final category of people in database applications is *database administration (DBA) personnel*. A database is a shared resource. As such, its design and use must be managed with a view toward all users, considered collectively. (Sometimes called the *user community*.) The function of the DBA staff is to serve as a protector of the database and as a focal point for resolving users' conflicts. The DBA should be a representative of the community as a whole, and not of any particular user or group of users. In this role, the DBA must arbitrate the processing rights and responsibilities of each user.

This book is oriented primarily toward systems development people. However, it is important for development people to know the roles and needs of users, operations, and DBA. Therefore, these people will be considered from time to time, particularly in Chapter 14.

Component 5: Procedures

The final component of a business database system is procedures. Both users and the operations staff need documented procedures for normal conditions.

The users need to know how to sign on to the system, how to use the terminals, how to provide data, and so forth. They also need procedures that ensure they do not interfere with one another.

At the bank, users share the same customer record. This sharing provides for elimination of duplicated data and for better data integrity. However, sharing also creates problems. When a customer closes a checking account, a user in the checking department cannot automatically delete the customer record. The customer may still have savings or loan accounts. Thus users need procedures that provide for orderly processing of the shared data.

Computer operations personnel also need procedures. They need to know how to start and stop the database applications and how to perform backup. Further, if there are special operating instructions such as mounting certain disks or the like, these instructions need to be documented as standard procedures.

Every system fails at some point, and when a database system fails, both users and operations personnel need procedures describing what to do. These

1. Hardware
   Standard
   Database Machines
2. Programs
   CCP
   Application
   Utility
   DBMS
   Operating System
3. Data
   Bits, Bytes, Fields, Records, Files, Database
   Database Records and Files
   Physical Records and Files
   Primary and Secondary Keys
   Record Relationships
   Multiple Views
4. People
   Clientele
   Users
   Operations
   Systems Development
   Database Administration
5. Procedures
   Procedures for Normal and Failure/Recovery for:
      Users
      Operations
   Database Management Procedures for DBA and Others

Figure 1-12   Five Components of a Business Database System

procedures are especially important for database processing because so many applications are dependent on the database. Users need to know what to do during the failure, what data to save, and what transactions can and cannot be processed during the failure. When the system is returned to operation, users need to know what to do to resume processing. For example, how can a user tell how much work needs to be redone? Also, how much of the data gathered during the failure needs to be input before new transactions can be processed? All these issues need to be considered in developing user recovery procedures.

Such procedures are also important for computer operations. When the database system fails, operations personnel need to know what to do. What action should be taken to identify the source of the problem and to get it corrected? What needs to be done to minimize damage to the database? Who should be called? Once the problem is corrected, how should the database be restored? How is rollback or rollforward (see Chapter 11) to be performed? These actions need to be carefully thought out and documented during the design and implementation of the system. Waiting until the error occurs is far too risky.

Every business is a dynamic activity, and business needs will change. For a database system, however, change must be made very carefully. A change made to benefit one user may be detrimental to users in seemingly unrelated departments. Consequently, changes to the database need to be made with a communitywide view. Procedures must be defined and documented to control change to the database. The DBA provides a forum for change, and the users need to be told how to use this forum to facilitate changes they need. Figure 1-12 summarizes the five components of a business database system.

SUMMARY

Database processing is integrated processing. Advantages over file processing are more timely information, more information, less data duplication and hence better data integrity, program/data independence, better data management, and economies of scale. Disadvantages are cost, complexity, difficult recovery, and increased vulnerability to failure.

A business database system has five components. Database systems often require more *hardware* than file processing systems. A separate CPU is used for database machines. Several types of *programs* are used: the communications control program, application programs, utilities, the database management system, and the operating system. The *data* component is complex. Records can be related to one another, they can be accessed in several ways, and a variety of views of data are supported.

Important *personnel* in database systems are the clientele, users, operations personnel, systems development personnel, and the database administrator. These groups need *procedures* for normal and failure/recovery activities.

It may seem strange to find a discussion of people and procedures in a text about database processing. Perhaps you feel that only database design, only technical issues about data relationships and the like, and only the development of database-oriented application programs should be discussed in a text like this. Certainly, these issues are important, and in fact, they comprise the bulk of these pages. You should realize, however, that knowledge gained from systems development courses applies to the development of systems that use DBMS. Also, even though the majority of this book is concerned with the data and program components, the other components, especially people and procedures, are vitally important.

GROUP I QUESTIONS

1.1   Explain the difference between a database system and a file processing system.

1.2   Summarize the advantages of database processing.

1.3   Summarize the disadvantages of database processing.

1.4   When would a company be likely to divide the database into several databases?

1.5   Do database systems require special hardware? Do they ever use any special hardware? When?

1.6   Name and discuss the major categories of programs involved in database processing.

1.7   Define database.

1.8   Explain the meaning of the term *self-describing*.

1.9   Explain the meaning of the term *integrated files*.

1.10   Is a database a collection of files? Why or why not?

1.11   Define nonunique key and give an example.

1.12   Explain three different views of database data.

1.13   Briefly describe the job responsibilities of each of the following database system personnel:

   a. clientele

   b. users

   c. operations

   d. systems development

   e. administration

1.14   Describe the types of procedures needed by database

   a. users

b. operations

c. administration

1.15 Give an example of a database with two database files, at least one unique secondary key and one nonunique key.

GROUP II QUESTIONS

1.16 How would you explain the advantages of database processing to the board of directors of a company? Assume these people know very little about data processing.

1.17 How should a company decide if the benefits of database processing justify the extra costs?

1.18 Summarize the impact of database processing on security. What aspects of security become easier? What aspects become more difficult? How can security be improved when using database processing?

1.19 Is it possible that two bank tellers could attempt to withdraw the last $1000 from an account at the same time? Could two different people each receive the $1000? How can this be prevented?

1.20 Briefly describe actions that should be taken during failure/recovery. Discuss responsibilities (if any) for clientele, users, operations personnel, systems development staff, and database administration personnel.

2
The Database
Development Process

The study of database processing involves learning the intricacies of file processing, data structures, database models, and the like. Students often have difficulty relating these abstract concepts to the commercial business world. What do linked lists (a data structure) have to do with business users? Or, what do multiple keys have to do with sales and marketing? Since it is easy to get lost in technical details, we need to have perspective—to see the forest before we examine the trees. Otherwise, the relevancy of the technology may never be understood.

To gain such perspective, this chapter presents an overview of the database development process. We will discuss the prime activities involved in developing a database system, and see how database processing allows systems developers to meet the needs of business people more effectively. We will also illustrate this process with a case study.

To initiate your learning of database technology, we will discuss the first two stages of development—specification and evaluation—in detail. The discussion of these topics is intended to provide a perspective on how database systems originate. These two stages will not be discussed after this chapter.

The two remaining stages of systems development—design and implementation—will only be introduced in this chapter. In fact, since it is the purpose of the entire book to teach database design and implementation concepts, it would be premature to describe details in Chapter 2. Therefore, in this chapter, insofar as design and implementation are concerned, you should strive to understand the nature of activities that must occur. Do not expect to learn the details; they will be addressed throughout this text.

OVERVIEW OF THE DATABASE DEVELOPMENT PROCESS

Developing a business database system is just like developing any other business computer system, *only harder* (because the database will be shared). Figure 2-1 lists the major stages of the development process.

```
 1. Specify Requirements
        Include problem definition and feasibility assessment
        Specify detailed requirements
 2. Evaluate Alternatives
        Specify alternatives
        (one or more may involve database processing)
        Select one alternative
 3. Design
        Specify and order hardware
        Design program logic
        Design data structure (schemas, subschemas)
        Design procedures for users and operators
        Define user organizational structure
 4. Implementation
        Install and test new hardware
        Code and unit test programs
        Convert data
        Document procedures
        Train users
        Test in parallel
```

Figure 2-1   Stages of Database Project Development

Stages of database development

The first stage is the same for both file and database processing. During this stage, the problem is defined, the feasibility of a computer-based solution is examined, and the system requirements are specified in detail. In stage 2, alternatives for meeting the users' needs are examined and one of the alternatives is selected. It is here, in stage 2, that the subject of database processing should first occur. If it is to be used, database technology will be one of the alternatives to be discussed.

Once the alternatives have been evaluated, the project continues into the design stage. Here, hardware is specified and ordered, programs are designed (or ordered from vendors), and, assuming a database alternative is selected, the structure of the database is developed. Procedures for operations and user personnel are also designed, and the organizational structure and job functions of users are developed.

Once design is complete, the system is implemented. This phase involves installing and testing hardware, coding and testing computer programs (or, installing them if they are purchased), compiling database structure definitions, converting data, documenting procedures, and training personnel. Finally, the system is tested in parallel with the existing system, and users and operations activities are converted to the new system.

A warning

A common violation of this process occurs when the development staff starts out to build *a system that uses database technology*. That's getting the cart before the horse. Instead of developing a database-oriented system, the staff should begin to build a system, of whatever type, that meets the users' needs. Such a system may turn out, after evaluation, to employ database technology. Then, again, it may be a file processing system or some other type of system.

To be effective, the development team must be free of solution biases. They need to concentrate on building the system that best meets needs as defined by the users. Unfortunately, since there is fashion in information systems just as there is fashion in clothes, developers must fight the temptation to be the first on their block with a "whatever" database system. Vendors, by the way, have long since learned how to use fashion to manipulate systems development people. Far too many database management systems have been purchased before anyone knows how they might be used.

SPECIFICATION STAGE

The prime task to be accomplished during the specification stage is to determine what the users want the system to do. Since determining user needs can be expensive, this stage is usually divided into two phases, shown in Figure 2-2.

Problem definition and feasibility study

The first phase is short and inexpensive; its purpose is to determine, in an approximate, rough-cut way, if a computer-based system makes any sense. Usu-

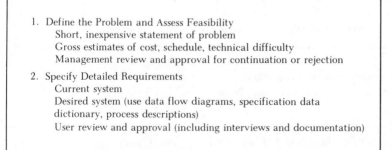

1. Define the Problem and Assess Feasibility
   Short, inexpensive statement of problem
   Gross estimates of cost, schedule, technical difficulty
   Management review and approval for continuation or rejection
2. Specify Detailed Requirements
   Current system
   Desired system (use data flow diagrams, specification data
   dictionary, process descriptions)
   User review and approval (including interviews and documentation)

Figure 2-2 Two Phases of Systems Specification

ally, only a small team is involved. Depending on the size of the project, perhaps two or three experienced people will develop the initial problem definition and feasibility statement. These people may perform this task on a part-time basis.

The goal of this study is to establish rough boundaries of the problem and to head off a potential disaster. To do this, the problem is defined in general terms, and the desirability of meeting the users' needs with a computer-based system is examined. To assess feasibility, the project team develops gross estimates of the costs, schedules, and technical difficulty of completing the project. These estimates are examined in light of potential benefits to determine if a computer-based system makes any sense.

For example, the approximate cost of hardware might be twice the most optimistic value of the solution. Or, the approximate date of completion might be two years after the company is required to meet a federal regulation. Or, a significant advance in the state of the art may be required to solve a small problem. The risk inherent in attempting a computer-based solution may not be worth the effort. In any of these cases, the computer-based solution to the problem does not make sense.

Once the team has defined the problem and made gross estimates of the costs, schedules, and technical difficulty, the results are presented to management. Sometimes the project team issues a feasibility statement to management for approval. In other cases, the team submits estimates of costs, schedules, and technical difficulty, and management decides on feasibility. Either way, it is management that decides if the project continues, not the data processing organization.

Clear communication is critical. Management is unlikely to approve a project communicated with incomprehensible writing or speaking, missing data, or poor logic. Management must clearly understand what is being communicated. *Further, systems developers should assume the responsibility for good communication.*

Management will review the preliminary phase work and decide either to continue the project or to look for other, non-computer-based ways of satisfying the users.

Specifying detailed user requirements

If the decision is to continue with a computer-based system, then the developers determine, very specifically, what the users want the system to do. Extensive, time-consuming, and expensive interviews are conducted with future users of the system in order to develop this specification.

The project team   At this point, a project team is formed. The people who have done the preliminary work usually become team members, as do other system developers and perhaps future users. Ideally, each major organization that will use the system has a representative on the team. This arrangement ensures that user interests are considered at each stage and generates interest among the user organizations. If the users must contribute employees to the project for a period of time, they will be more interested in the outcome of the project.

The project team should be headed by a relatively senior person who has a great deal of systems development experience and good rapport with users. The team should be sponsored by a top-level executive and should periodically report to him or her. The size of the team depends on the size of the organization, the project, and the number of user departments involved. Roughly, it should be from three to a dozen or so people.

The first task of the project team is to establish the scope of their effort and define their responsibilities. Establishing scope helps to ensure that members know and agree with what they are to do. A project team may flounder for weeks or even months if it lacks clear direction.

Contacting users   Users have *the* critical role in the specification phase. Since the system is being developed for users, the requirements must come from *them*. The users must be interviewed to determine what is to be produced, and they determine when the specification is complete and documented satisfactorily. Thus the bulk of the work in this phase is interviewing users and documenting findings. The team must contact every type of user of the system firsthand. This can be a sizable task; there is, however, no substitute.

There are many strategies for defining and documenting user needs. The traditional strategy is to interview users individually, and then to document, in ordinary English, the user needs. The result of this traditional process is a large tome of requirements that is seldom understood in its entirety.

Recently, new procedures have been developed for determining and documenting user requirements. These procedures allow users to be interviewed in groups, and they use graphical tools to portray the results of the interviews. These tools greatly reduce the size of the requirements documentation, they increase the comprehensibility of the requirements specification, and they set the stage for effective database design. Because of these advantages, we will discuss the new procedures in this chapter. See either [35] or [63] for further information.

Understanding and documenting the existing system   A problem is a perceived difference between what is and what ought to be. Therefore, to specify requirements for a new system, both the existing system and the desired changes to that system need to be documented. One useful way of documenting these learnings uses data flow diagrams, a data dictionary, and process descriptions. We will consider each of these tools in turn.

A data flow diagram (DFD) is a graphic tool that shows how data and the processes that change data are connected. DFDs are sometimes said to be a picture of the system from the standpoint of the data. A simple example is

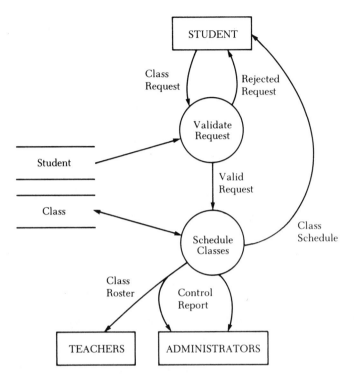

Figure 2-3   Example Data Flow Diagram (DFD)

shown in Figure 2-3. In this diagram, a square or rectangle represents entities outside of the system, a circle or bubble represents a process within the system, one or two straight lines represent a file of data, and arrows represent the flow of data. Data items are named alongside arrows. The DFD in Figure 2-3 illustrates the flow of documents among students, teachers, and administrators during class scheduling.

Although DFDs can be developed by interviewing users one at a time, a more effective approach is to interview users in groups. For the DFD in Figure 2-3, a group of scheduling personnel could be interviewed, a group of teachers, and so forth. During the interview, the project team members can draw the draft DFD on poster paper for all to see. If any user disagrees with the DFD, he or she can express the disagreement while the DFD is being prepared. Having users provide checks and balances in this way improves the quality of the DFD. Also, interviewing in groups saves time.

For the DFD to have any meaning, the items that flow between processes must be defined. This is done in the *specification data dictionary*. This dictionary describes the content of each data item shown in the DFD. The dictionary for the DFD in Figure 2-3 is shown in Figure 2-4. Finally, the logic of

Data Item		Content
Class Request	IS	Student name + Student number + REPETITIONS OF 　Class name + 　Class number + 　Section number
Rejected Request	IS	Class request marked "REJECTED"
Valid Request	IS	Class request of current student in good standing
Class Roster	IS	Class name + Class number + Section number + REPETITIONS OF 　Student name + 　Student number + 　Student grade level + 　Enrollment status
Control Report	IS	Date + Time + Count of processed requests + Count of rejected requests + Count of valid requests + Count of closed sections
Class Schedule	IS	Student name + Student number + REPETITIONS OF 　Class name + 　Class number + 　Section number + 　Class time + 　Class location + 　Class instructor name

Figure 2-4   Sample Specification Data Dictionary for DFD in Figure 2-3

For each class request, do the following:

1. Get requester's student data from the Student file.

2. If no such data:
   2.1 Mark request "REJECTED."
   Return request to student.

3. If student status is other than "GOOD":
   3.1 Mark request "REJECTED."
   Return request to student.
   3.2 Otherwise (request valid):
   Mark request "VALID."
   Send request to Schedule Classes process.

Figure 2-5   Process Description for Validate Student Process

each process needs to be delineated. This can be done with structured English, pseudocode, flowcharts, or any other similar technique for presenting logic. These descriptions are called *process descriptions*. The structured English process description for the Validate Student Process is shown in Figure 2-5.

For a complex system, several levels of DFDs would be needed. Each of the processes in Figure 2-3 would be expanded into a DFD of its own, and some of these might be expanded again to a third level. For a complex system, four or five levels may be needed. However, process descriptions are only developed for the bottom or fundamental processes. See [34] for more information on this topic.

After the existing system is documented, the developers then determine what the users want. This can be done while the documentation of the current system is being produced, or it can be done in a second phase. The same three tools (or their equivalent) are used, that is, the DFD, the specification data dictionary, and the process descriptions are developed and documented for the new system.

User review   Users review this documentation for accuracy and completeness. The users may disagree with one another about desired capabilities. If so, the team needs to identify the areas of disagreement, and then facilitate changes to obtain agreement among users for a single, consistent set of specifications. These specifications become the blueprints of the new system. Again, it is the users, not the development team, who determine when the specifications are accurate and complete.

The process of developing system specifications is no different for a database system than for any other system. The system development methodology and procedures that you have already learned apply. You may wish to consult [35] or [65] for more information on this process.

EVALUATION STAGE

The second stage of the database development process is evaluation. The purpose of this stage is to determine, in a general way, the best approach for meeting the users' needs. A variety of alternatives are identified and examined, and one is selected. If requested by management, a cost/benefit, or return on investment, study is done. Finally, a project plan is developed that specifies major tasks for systems development. This plan documents major tasks, including which parts of the system are to be developed in-house, which are to be developed out-of-house (if any), and which are to be procured from a vendor.

As shown in Figure 2-6, the evaluation stage typically has three phases: identifying alternatives, selecting an alternative, and developing the project plan. Each of these phases will be considered in turn.

1. Identify Alternatives
      Hardware
      Programs
      Data
      Procedures
      People
2. Select an Alternative
      Subjective analysis
      Cost/benefit or return on investment analysis
      Combination
3. Develop Project Plan
      Alternative selected
      Support environment
      Major tasks

Figure 2-6   Phases of the Evaluation Stage of Systems Development

Identifying alternatives

At this stage of the systems development process, the project team identifies alternative sets of hardware, programs, data, procedures, and people that will satisfy the users' requirements. We will consider data and programs first, and then the three remaining components.

Data   There are usually several data alternatives. For example, the system can utilize either file processing or database technologies. If file processing, then sequential, random, and indexed sequential alternatives could be considered. If database processing, the scope of the database, or databases, needs to be determined. For example, for a retailing company, the database might contain only customer and order data, or it might contain customer, order, backorder, inventory, and other data. The retailer might decide to have several files, to have a single database, to have files and a database, or to have two or more databases.

If one or more of the alternatives involves database technology, the team would probably prepare preliminary database designs showing record types and relationships. Several different alternatives might be identified.

Programs   Both systems and application programs need to be considered. With large or new systems, the operating system must be chosen. Further, if a database alternative is being considered, the DBMS to be procured is also part of the alternative. (DBMS are so expensive to build that, for nearly every situation, it is impractical to consider in-house development.)

As you will learn in this course, DBMS products fall into three broad categories. Some are based on the CODASYL DBTG data model, some are based on the relational data model, and some are based on other data models. Therefore, the development team might first examine the requirements and determine which data model best meets the needs. Then, the team would evaluate DBMS products that are based on that particular model.

Other considerations apply, however. Some DBMS products operate on only one or two types of hardware; if the hardware cannot be changed, the DBMS selection must be constrained to compatible systems. Also, some DBMS products are limited in the amount of data they can process, or in the speed with which they can process it. These considerations limit the number of DBMS alternatives to be considered.

In addition to the operating system and the DBMS, alternatives concerning application programs may need to be specified. What language will be used to write the programs? Will high-level, nonprocedural languages be used? Can some programs be written by the users after the system has been implemented? What role, if any, will the DBMS-provided query/update utilities play? At this stage, no attempt is made to make detailed decisions. Rather, only the features and facilities that will be needed are identified.

Hardware   If the system requires a new computer, hardware alternatives need to be identified. Typically, however, the hardware is already in place, and developers do not have the luxury (and responsibility) of this decision. Additions or modifications to hardware are frequently made, however.

If a database alternative is considered, more main memory, a faster CPU, and more online storage may be needed. DBMS vendors can provide some advice on what will be required. This advice is always suspect, however, because the vendor is biased. Current users of a DBMS product can often provide better advice about the amount of hardware that will be needed.

As mentioned in Chapter 1, there are currently a few special purpose computers that do database processing exclusively. Called *database machines*, these computers operate as back-end processors between the applications CPU and the data. If the development team considers a database machine, then this hardware would be part of the alternative.

Procedures   Procedures usually take only a minor role in the specification of alternatives. They are considered when different styles of system use necessitate different types of hardware or programs, or different data designs. For example, suppose a retailing company's marketing department makes sales forecasts by analyzing five years of historical sales data. There are several procedures for accessing this data. The data can be stored on tape and processed in batch mode. It can be stored on tape, and portions of the data staged to online devices for online access as it is needed. A third alternative is to store all of the data online at all times. Each of these alternatives requires different amounts and types of hardware and possibly different DBMS features.

A purist would say these are not differences in alternatives, but in requirements. The purist would demand that the users decide which style of access they want. The problem is that the users may not know. They may say that they want online access to all data providing it does not cost too much. If the issue is an important one, the developers must identify an alternative system to meet each of the requirements.

People The final component of a system alternative is people. If database technology is used, a vital issue to be addressed is who is to be the database administrator (DBA), and what is that person (or group) to do. A draft of responsibilities, or alternative responsibilities, should be developed.

Broadly speaking, the function of the database administrator is to protect the database and to ensure that it is structured and used so as to provide maximum benefit to the community of users. Three primary functions are involved. First, the database administrator manages data activities. The DBA negotiates processing rights and responsiblities with users. The goal of this function is to minimize conflicts such as one user deleting another user's data.

The second DBA function is to control the structure of the database. This is sometimes referred to as *database configuration control*. As time passes, requirements will change, and users will want to change the database structure (as opposed to changing database values). Such structural changes need to be made carefully; changes made to benefit one user can detrimentally impact another. The DBA meets with users and ensures that changes are made on an orderly and acceptable basis.

Finally, the DBA is the manager of database resources. The DBMS, associated utilities, special purpose hardware, if any, and other resources are under the control of the DBA. As vendors announce new features, or new products, the DBA evaluates these products and recommends their use when appropriate. Also, if users have performance-related problems, the DBA will change resources or acquire new ones, if needed.

The DBA position(s) (a staff of several people may be needed) are not created and filled until database design and implementation have been accomplished. The DBA activity, however, must be considered during the discussion of alternatives. Initially, there may be resistance to the idea. Since the DBA is required for a successful database project, discussions of DBA responsibilities need to be started early. Also, the cost (and benefits) of the DBA staff should be part of the alternative evaluation.

Selecting an alternative

Once the alternatives have been identified, the next task is to select the best one. As shown in Figure 2-7, several styles of selection are used.

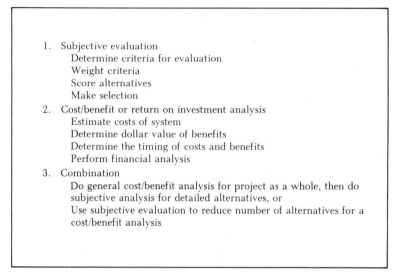

1. Subjective evaluation
   Determine criteria for evaluation
   Weight criteria
   Score alternatives
   Make selection
2. Cost/benefit or return on investment analysis
   Estimate costs of system
   Determine dollar value of benefits
   Determine the timing of costs and benefits
   Perform financial analysis
3. Combination
   Do general cost/benefit analysis for project as a whole, then do
   subjective analysis for detailed alternatives, or
   Use subjective evaluation to reduce number of alternatives for a
   cost/benefit analysis

Figure 2-7   Techniques for Selecting an Alternative

Subjective evaluation   One method is to subjectively evaluate the relative costs and benefits of each alternative and to make an intuitive decision. This approach is the cheapest, the quickest, and probably the most frequently used. Results of this approach vary depending on the difficulty of the decision, the quality of intuition, and luck.

For example, a retailing company might subjectively evaluate data alternatives for an inventory project. They might consider the advantages and disadvantages of a database containing customer, order, inventory, and accounting data, and compare these to the advantages and disadvantages of a database having only a portion of this data—say, order and inventory data. These two alternatives could then be compared to an alternative with all of this data stored in separate files.

To perform these analyses, the project team would gather data, talk with users, perhaps talk with other companies having similar problems, and make a decision. The decision would probably be made by a consensus of key data processing and management personnel.

Once a company has decided on a database approach, a subjective analysis could be used to determine which DBMS to purchase. One way to do this analysis is to identify criteria for comparing alternatives and weight the criteria according to their relative importance. Then, each DBMS is subjectively scored on these criteria by team members and others who have special knowledge or interest in the project. A total score is determined for each alternative. The alternatives with the highest scores are then subjected to the detailed analysis.

Database System
Meets Retrieval Requirements
Meets Update Requirements
Meets Security Requirements
Recovery
Simplicity
Ease of Use
Format Convertibility
Program/Data Independence
Cost
Operating Effectiveness
Operating Efficiency
Documentation
Vendor Support
Growth Potential
Size
Training

Figure 2-8   Possible Criteria for Preliminary Evaluation

Figure 2-8 shows example criteria for evaluating a DBMS. This list is by no means exhaustive, and some of these criteria may not be important to an organization. The cost criteria should not be detailed cost estimates but rather subjective assessments from high to low. There should not be too many criteria. If there are 5 alternatives and 15 criteria, each judge has to make 75 ratings. At one every two minutes (allowing time for research), this rating process requires

Criteria	*Weight*
Retrieval	20
Update	20
Security	5
Recovery	10
Ease of Use	20
Cost	10
Operating Efficiency	10
Vendor Support	15
Total Points	110

Figure 2-9   Example DBMS Evaluation Criteria

2 1/2 hours to do. Figure 2-9 shows criteria and weightings used by one company for the selection of their DBMS. Figure 2-10 presents a sample evaluation form.

An easy and inexpensive way to gather data about commercial database systems is to interview current users. The project team should find out names of organizations that have used the DBMS under consideration and ask them to score the systems against the criteria. Another source is product survey publications such as those published by Datapro and Auerbach, and a third source is consulting firms specializing in database applications. Experienced opinions should be obtained, but they should not supplant the opinions of the project team members who know the organization and requirements.

Operating effectiveness and efficiency are probably the two hardest criteria to evaluate. Benchmarks and simulation are two analytical techniques that can be used to assist the evaluation. A benchmark is just a trial run using data similar to what will actually be used. The project team designs a database and runs the system to observe performance and cost. Supposedly, a judgment can then be made regarding the operating feasibility of the system.

Benchmarks have not been highly successful in the database field. Unfortunately, a meaningful benchmark can only be made with a full-sized database. Building such a database is tantamount to implementing the system, so it is not often done. Another problem is that benchmarks tend to measure the knowledge of the project team instead of the performance of the DBMS. If the team understands the DBMS well, benchmark results tend to be good; if not, the benchmark results tend to be poor.

Simulation of the proposed system can produce more accurate operating predictions. If the simulation incorporates a good model of the database system, as well as of the communications control program, the operating system, and the hardware, then the results can be useful. However, good simulations are expensive to develop and difficult to produce. In reality, simulations are seldom worth the trouble they take.

Criteria	Alternatives						
	1	2	3	4	5	6	7
Retrieval	——	——	——	——	——	——	——
Update	——	——	——	——	——	——	——
Security	——	——	——	——	——	——	——
Recovery	——	——	——	——	——	——	——
Ease of Use	——	——	——	——	——	——	——
Cost	——	——	——	——	——	——	——
Operating Efficiency	——	——	——	——	——	——	——
Vendor Support	——	——	——	——	——	——	——

Figure 2-10   Sample Alternative Rating Form

Generally, unless there are serious questions about the ability of the system to meet a requirement, benchmarks and simulations are not advisable. A better investment of time and money would occur by interviewing more users of the DBMS under consideration.

Cost/benefit analysis   Another technique for selecting an alternative is to estimate all the costs of the project and compare them to the dollar values of the benefits. If the benefits do not exceed the costs in a reasonable period, then the project should be discontinued or redesigned.

We have used the phrase *in a reasonable period* because it conveys the essentials of cost/benefit analysis. Actually that phrase is weighted by implications and to explain them we will have to take a short diversion from database systems into the world of capital investment analysis.

In the early days of data processing, information systems were exempt from the analysis typically made of other capital expenditures. Computers were new, almost magical, and a lot of money was invested without regard to the return on the investment. Those days are nearly gone. Increasingly, information systems projects must be justified on the basis that money invested will generate sufficient benefits not only to cover the costs of the investment but also to create an acceptable rate of return.

Management's position is something like this: Suppose the organization has $500,000 to invest. It can develop a new database application, or it can add to its manufacturing plant. If the rate of return on the database system is 2 percent and that on the manufacturing plant is 22 percent, then it should buy the plant and forget the database. DP enthusiasts object to this line of argument. They make remarks like "without the database system the firm won't survive" or "all manufacturing will suffer." If these remarks are true, then the rate of return has been incorrectly computed at 2 percent. Rate of return, then, is a corporate yardstick for determining the worth of an investment.

This means that to evaluate database alternatives we need to compute the rate of return for each and choose the alternative with the largest return. This alternative can be taken to management and its rate of return compared with the rate for other investment opportunities.

To calculate the rate of return we must use a concept called *present value*. Essentially the idea is that a dollar today is worth more than a dollar next year. A dollar today can be invested at 15 percent at a bank and be worth $1.15 a year from now. To determine the present value that will be equivalent to a dollar a year from now, we need to know how much money could be invested at 15 percent to yield a dollar in a year. Tables and computer programs are available to do this. The present value of $1 a year from now is 86.96 cents at 15 percent. This means 86.96 cents invested at 15 percent will yield a dollar in a year. The present value of a dollar at 15 percent two years from now is 75.61 cents.

To determine the present value of a string of expenses and receipts we simply apply the present-value factors. Figure 2-11a shows the calculation of present

Year	Expense	Receipt	Net	5 Percent Present Value Factor	Present Value
0	10,000	0	– 10,000	1.0000	– 10,000
1	0	5,000	5,000	.9524	4,762
2	2,000	10,000	8,000	.9070	7,256
3	8,000	6,000	– 2,000	.8638	– 1,728
				Net Present Value	290

a. Present Value of an Investment at 5 Percent

Year	Expense	Receipt	Net	10 Percent Present Value Factor	Present Value
0	10,000	0	– 10,000	1.0000	– 10,000
1	0	5,000	5,000	.9091	4,546
2	2,000	10,000	8,000	.8264	6,611
3	8,000	6,000	– 2,000	.7513	– 1,501
				Net Present Value	– 344

b. Present Value of an Investment at 10 Percent

Figure 2-11 Example Rate of Return Calculations

value, at 5 percent, for an initial investment of $10,000 with a variety of expenses and receipts in succeeding years. In Figure 2-11a, if the net present value were zero, that would indicate the discounted benefits could be expected to match the costs; the project would earn exactly 5 percent. Since it is positive, the project can be expected to earn more than 5 percent. Figure 2-11b shows the calculation of present value at 10 percent. Here the net present value is negative, indicating that the project can be expected to earn less than 10 percent. A linear interpolation approximation yields an interest rate of 7.3 percent.

This method can be used to evaluate database processing alternatives. The costs and the dollar values of the benefits must be determined for each alternative, and the present value computed at some interest rate. The alternative with the highest net present value is identified. The rate of return for that investment can be determined by interpolation as in the previous example. (Actually, there are a myriad of programs available to accomplish this task; one of them should be used.)

To use this technique for systems alternatives, all we have to do is determine the costs of development and operation, as well as the dollar values of the benefits, and then compute the rate of return for each alternative. Unfortunately, this is the tough part. How do we determine all of the costs and quantify the benefits? For example, what is the dollar value of having a report on time instead of ten days late or with no errors instead of with three minor ones? There are no hard and fast answers to these questions, and you will probably discuss them at length in a systems development course. For now, the following brief guidelines may help you understand this process.

1. *Attempt to avoid a consistent bias*. If some costs are overestimated and others are underestimated, the errors tend to cancel one another out. This is not true if costs or benefits are consistently overestimated or underestimated.

2. *Ignore inflation*. Inflation should affect alternatives equally, and it should affect costs to the same degree as benefits. Generally, attempts at predicting inflation have not been successful. Since inflation usually does not make a significant difference, it should be ignored.

3. *Consider every possible cost*. Figure 2-12 presents common sources of costs of a database system. Expenses in all of these categories should be considered in performing the cost/benefit analysis.

4. *Consider the timing of costs*. Not all developmental costs will be incurred at the onset. Most likely, the database application will be implemented in stages, so the calculation of present value should consider that some development costs will occur immediately, but others will occur later. The same statement applies to operating expenses.

5. *Determine a dollar value of every benefit of every requirement*. Every documented requirement has at least one benefit. The project team must determine all benefits and put dollar values on them. Sources of benefits are shown in Figure 2-13. Savings obtained by benefits in all of these categories should be considered in developing the cost/benefit analysis.

Development Costs	*Operating Costs*
Database Study	DP Personnel
Program Expenses	User Personnel
Hardware Expenses	Computer Time
One-Time Training	Hardware Maintenance
Data Conversion	Software Maintenance
Data Capture	Data Maintenance
Facilities Preparation	Backup
Program Conversion	Recovery
Program Creation	Recurring Training
Database Generation	Communications Expenses
Testing	Paper/Cards
Documentation	Electrical, Etc.
Design	Documentation

Figure 2-12   Sources of Database System Costs

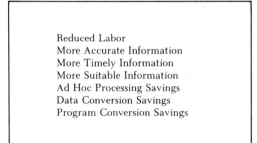

Reduced Labor
More Accurate Information
More Timely Information
More Suitable Information
Ad Hoc Processing Savings
Data Conversion Savings
Program Conversion Savings

Figure 2-13   Sources of Benefits of Database Processing

6. *Consider the timing of benefits.* Benefits will occur as the system is implemented. Not all benefits will start the day the implementation starts (or finishes). The time of occurrence should be accounted for in the present-value calculation.

Combination of subjective and cost/benefit analyses   A third approach for selecting an alternative is a combination of the first two. A subjective analysis could be done to select the two or three best alternatives, and then a detailed cost/benefit analysis made to select the best one.

Alternatively, a cost/benefit analysis could be done for gross estimates of the costs and benefits of the project without concern for the alternative selected. This analysis would assure management that a financial disaster will be avoided. After the project has been analyzed for financial desirability, then the particulars of the alternatives are analyzed subjectively. Thus, given that a database system makes financial sense, the team would determine the particular DBMS, the scope of the data, and other parameters by subjective evaluation.

Project plan

The results of the evaluation stage of systems development are documented in the project plan. Components of this plan are listed in Figure 2-14. As shown,

Alternative Selected
Definition of Major Tasks
Task Dependencies
Task Labor Estimates
Project Schedule

Figure 2-14   Components of a Project Plan

this plan describes the alternative selected and indicates the tasks to be accomplished to develop the system.

At this stage, tasks are stated in broad terms such as: procure hardware, install and test DBMS, design schemas, and so forth. The purpose of developing this plan is not to identify every action that needs to be accomplished, but rather to indicate major activities.

Once the major tasks are defined, dependencies among tasks are determined. For start-to-end tasks, task A (installing hardware) must be completed before task B (installing DBMS) can begin. For end-to-end tasks, neither task C (test DBMS) nor task D (validate test data) can be completed until both are completed. Finally, for start-to-start tasks, both tasks E (validate programs) and F (validate procedures) must begin at the same time. Once task descriptions and dependencies are determined, they can be assembled into a project plan.

At the same time, estimates are made regarding the amount of labor needed for each task. These estimates, together with the task schedule, provide guidelines as to the amount and timing of labor needed. Further, schedule bottlenecks are identified and eliminated. For more information on this process, see [29].

Management review

After the evaluation stage has been completed, management reviews the team's conclusions and recommendations and issues directions. The directions can confirm conclusions drawn by the project team and authorize initiating work on the design stage. Other possibilities are for management to direct the team to consider another alternative, or to redo the analysis, or to reschedule tasks and reformulate the project plan.

Sometimes, when management is discouraged with either the costs or schedule of development, the users are asked to prioritize requirements. The users may be asked to identify requirements that are mandatory, nearly mandatory, and optional. Also, users may be asked to determine which requirements can be deferred for a period of time, and which cannot.

After the prioritization has been done, management will ask the project team to repeat the evaluation stage for a subset of the requirements. This effort will result in another project plan, with another set of costs and schedules. The prioritization may be iterated several times until management is satisfied or the project is canceled.

For example, customer service may specify that they need direct access to all customer purchases for the last two years. If this requirement necessitates an upgrade of the CPU (more channels are needed to handle increased volume of direct access data) to meet this requirement, management may decide that the requirement is not worth it. Under pressure, the users may agree that they can live with two months of direct access purchase data. Given this fact, the development team would respecify the amount of hardware needed and the attendant costs.

DESIGN AND IMPLEMENTATION

We have not yet discussed enough database technology to describe design and implementation in detail. Therefore, we will discuss these stages more broadly than we have discussed specification and evaluation stages. In reading this section, your primary goal should be to learn the basics of database design and implementation.

Database design

Two major tasks are accomplished during the design of a database-oriented system. One task is to define the database structure, and the other is to design the application programs.

Considering the first task, a two-phased process is often used. First, the logical structure of the database is developed. In this context, the term *logical structure* means a DBMS-independent database design. This design is then transformed in the second phase into a design that conforms to the limitations and peculiarities of a given DBMS product.

The logical design can be specified in a variety of ways; Figure 2-15 shows one technique, called a *data structure diagram*, or DSD (also called a Bachman diagram after Charles Bachman, the man who invented it). The single/double arrow notation is used to express relationships among records. It will be explained in Chapter 4. The DSD only shows the relationships among records; the content

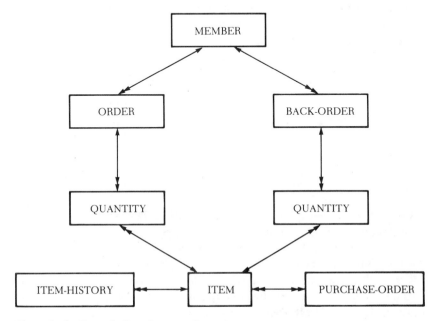

Figure 2-15   Example Data Structure Diagram

of these records must be documented in the data dictionary. This is done by expanding the specification data dictionary to include field types, lengths, and so forth. The expanded data dictionary is called the *design data dictionary*.

To describe record relationships, you need to know what possibilities exist. We will discuss this topic in Chapter 4. Also, other ways of expressing logical database designs will be discussed in Chapters 5 and 6.

Once the logical structure has been defined, it is transformed into physical form that conforms to the features of the DBMS to be used. Thus the logical structure is mapped into the data description facilities provided by the DBMS product. Depending on the application and the DBMS, this mapping can be difficult and complex, or simple and straightforward. We will discuss this process further in Chapters 5, 8, and 10.

Programs are designed in parallel with development of the logical database structure. A variety of techniques can be used. Again following the work of Page-Jones [65], the program structure charts are developed, interface descriptions are written, and functions of major program modules are defined. See also [35] and [63]. Programs for database processing will be shown and discussed in Chapters 12 and 13.

As the design of the database and the application programs is completed, final specifications are developed on any needed changes to hardware. The hardware is ordered during this stage (or even earlier if the specifications are specific enough) so that it will be available during implementation.

Concerning procedures, facilities for database security and control must be designed. A plan is developed to ensure that only authorized users can make authorized access at authorized times. This plan utilizes features of the operating system and the DBMS, as well as controls designed into application programs. Backup and recovery procedures need also to be designed.

Finally, functions of the database administrator are finalized. The office of the DBA is organized, job descriptions are written, and qualifications of future DBA personnel are defined.

This is a quick overview of database design. We will return to this topic in Chapters 5 through 10, after we have discussed fundamental concepts in Chapters 3 and 4.

Database implementation

The last stage of the systems development process is implementation. During this stage, hardware is installed and tested, programs are coded and tested, data is converted, procedures are documented, and users are trained. A parallel test with the old system completes this stage.

Several aspects of this process are unique for database systems. First, before data can be converted, the database design must be coded using the language and other facilities provided by the DBMS vendor. Just as with programs, several runs may be made to remove syntax errors. DBMS data descriptions will be illustrated in Chapters 12 and 13.

Once the structures are compiled, a test database is constructed. This is done to test the accuracy of the database descriptions as well as to provide a facility to test application programs. One difficulty that must be surmounted in a database implementation is that when testing several programs, one program may make changes to the test data that interferes with another. Thus test activity must be well planned and coordinated. This fact usually means testing is slower than for file processing systems.

Often a new database system involves a large number of application programs that concurrently process the database. As a result, the testing task may be very large. If 50 different programs access the database concurrently and an error develops, it can be hard to trace the source of the error. Consequently, a carefully prepared and coordinated test plan is mandatory. This plan should indicate how programs are to be tested independently (sometimes called *unit test*), and how programs will be aggregated and tested as a whole (called an *integrated test*).

Procedures for the users and operations personnel are documented during this stage. Users need to know how to accomplish their job function using the new system. They also need to know what to do in the event the system fails, and how to resume processing when the system is restored.

Operations personnel need procedures for backing up the database as well as procedures explaining action to take in the event of a system failure. Operations recovery procedures also need to be developed. Operations activities are often more complex for a database system than for a file processing system. Consequently, well-documented procedures are even more important.

After procedures have been documented, users and operations personnel need to be trained. Experience has shown that simply delivering the procedures document to these people is inadequate. Without some type of training, they may not be able to read the procedures. Also, the users will have questions and misunderstandings, and these necessitate training sessions. Sometimes the cost of training is reduced by using audio and video tape.

The final phase of implementation is a parallel test with the old system. In theory, results from the old system are compared with the new. The theory breaks down when the old system and the new are appreciably different. The existing system may be so chaotic that its results are unreliable; more commonly, the existing system is so primitive as compared to the new system that results of the old and new systems will be difficult to reconcile.

In reality, then, parallel testing is sometimes difficult. The reconciliation of new and old results can be time-consuming and expensive. This fact should not be construed to mean that parallel testing cannot be done for a new database system. Rather, it means that testing will probably take longer than is anticipated, and that the idealistic goal of a complete parallel test may require compromise.

SPECIFICATION STAGE FOR SUNSHINE GARDEN SUPPLY

The previous sections of this chapter have provided an overview of the general process for developing a database-oriented system. The discussion of design and implementation stages will be extensively amplified in the remainder of this book. The specification and evaluation stages, however, will not. Therefore, we will consider them in greater detail in the remainder of this chapter. Specifically, we will consider the experience of one company: Sunshine Garden Supply.

Sunshine Garden Supply is a cooperative that sells seeds and garden supplies by mail order. The term *cooperative* means that the company is owned by its customers. At the end of the year, profits are distributed to customers in the form of refunds. Each refund, or dividend, is a percent of the total amount purchased by a member during the year. For example, assume profits are 10 percent of sales. If a customer orders $500 worth of merchandise during the year, his or her refund will be $50.

In 1980, Sunshine was operating a file processing system to maintain member names, addresses, and other member data, to record member purchases, and to produce dividend checks at the end of the year. They also had file processing systems to account for inventory, to prepare accounts payable checks, and to process the general ledger. All these systems operated separately.

In late 1980, several problems were brought to the attention of Sunshine's senior management. To assess the situation, management scheduled a meeting of the managers of all Sunshine departments, to include Marilyn Jasper, the Director of Data Processing.

Many issues were discussed in the meeting, which became quite lengthy. After about four hours, when it seemed that no consensus was going to develop, Marilyn Jasper volunteered the resources of the data processing department to conduct a study to define and document the problems. She also said they would estimate the costs, schedules, and technical difficulty of developing computer-based systems or adjustments to a computer-based system in order to solve the problems. This proposal was just what was needed at this point in the meeting, and the group enthusiastically accepted her offer.

(Marilyn made this offer because she believed that some of the problems were going to result in data processing projects, and she wanted an opportunity to conduct a problem definition and feasibility study. She knew the earlier the data processing staff was involved, the better.)

Sunshine's problem definition and feasibility study

Marilyn and one of the data processing employees, Bob Harris, talked with the accounting, order processing, purchasing, and membership departments the next week. As they worked, they developed the data flow diagram shown in Figure 2-16.

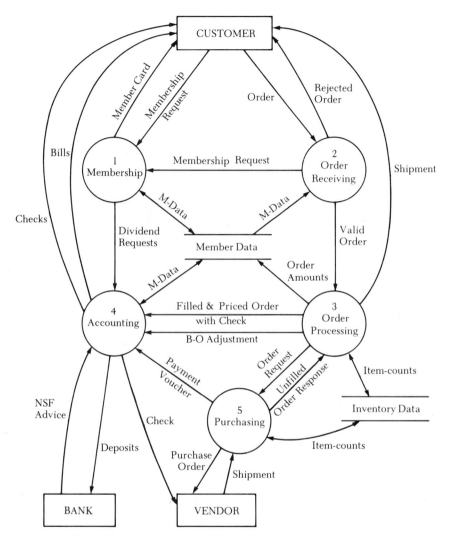

Figure 2-16 DFD for Sunshine's Existing System

Sunshine's data flow diagram   There were five major processes at Sunshine; each process occurred in a separate department. The membership process established or adjusted (address change, for example) membership data (M-Data) and computed dividends at yearend. The order receiving process opened the mail and accepted or rejected orders. A process description for order receiving is shown in Figure 2-17.

Order Processing filled and priced orders. Clerks accessed an online inventory file to determine stock levels, and filled as much of an order as they could. The order was priced, and picking slips (a document telling the warehouse

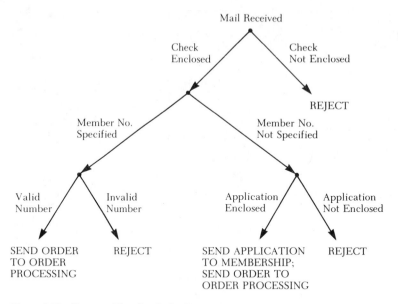

Figure 2-17 Decision Tree for Order Receiving

personnel what to pick from inventory) were generated. Shipments were sent to customers, and a copy of the filled and priced order and the customer check were sent to Accounting.

If an item needed to be backordered, the order was marked "BACK-ORDERED," and a backorder request sent to Purchasing. Once the backordered item was received, or it was determined that the item would never be received, Purchasing would return a backorder response to Order Processing. Order Processing then either shipped the items and sent a backorder adjustment to Accounting, or notified Accounting (using the same form) that a refund was due. Accounting had several functions. They requested the preparation of and mailed all checks. Accounting also generated bills to customers when necessary (bad check, underpayment, etc.), and processed payment adjustments when substitutions or cancellations occurred in lieu of backorders. When payment problems developed with members, Accounting modified member status so that Order Receiving would accept no more orders from that member.

Finally, Purchasing generated purchase orders to vendors and sent vouchers for payment to Accounting. They modified inventory counts when shipments arrived, and ordered goods for filling backorders.

Problem definition As the team developed this data flow diagram, they identified the three groups of problems shown in Figure 2-18. One group concerned the *member master data*. Since only order totals were kept in the member file,

---

1. Member Master Data
    a. Marketing and customer service cannot determine which customers have ordered which products.
    b. Sunshine has too little control over member master records; possibility of computer crime.

2. Order Processing
    a. Customer Service takes too long to determine the status of backorders.
    b. Some backorders are lost.
    c. Order Processing finds it difficult to cancel backorders.
    d. For newly arrived stock, new orders sometimes processed before backorders.
    e. Labor costs of order processing too high.

3. Cash Management
    a. Checks not cashed until order is validated, filled, and priced. Sunshine loses two or three days' interest.
    b. Refund checks sometimes sent to customers before order checks clear the bank. If the order check is returned NSF (not sufficient funds; that is, it bounces), members have a refund on a bad check.

Figure 2-18   Problems of Sunshine, 1980

the marketing department was unable to determine which members were buying which products. They needed this information to plan marketing strategies and to provide better input to the purchasing department.

Also, customer service wanted a history of product purchases. Recently, a pesticide that Sunshine had been selling was determined to be defective and dangerous. Sunshine notified all members of this fact, but would have preferred to know precisely which members had purchased the pesticide so they could take more definitive action.

The accounting department had another problem with the master file. Sunshine had been severely criticized in the last audit because of a lack of control over member records. The auditors stated, and quite accurately according to accounting, that anyone in the membership, order processing, or accounting departments could change any field of the member record. Since the purchases-to-date data was used as a basis for computing dividends, this meant that Sunshine employees could effectively give themselves or their friends any dividend they wanted.

The second group of problems concerned *order processing*. First, customer service complained it was just about impossible to determine the status of backorders. A backorder could be in the order processing department, it could be in purchasing, or it could be in shipping. Some were even misplaced and lost. Also, when backorders were found in purchasing, customer service would try to determine if purchasing had ordered the items, to determine when the items would arrive, and to add time for processing. Most of this information was unreliable.

Often members would give up, purchase the items from another source, only to have the goods arrive from Sunshine a week or two later. Further, when customers did cancel backorders, Sunshine had trouble cutting through the confusion to stop the backorder. In these cases, straightening out payments was a nightmare.

Another problem occurred when backordered stock arrived. To reduce the number of backorders, arriving stock was placed immediately into inventory. New orders, however, were processed faster than backorders, and new orders sometimes depleted the stock of items before backorders were processed. This meant that backorders were delayed further until another shipment of the item was received. Another way of stating this problem is that Sunshine wanted FIFO (first in, first out) order policy; with backorders, however, they sometimes had a LIFO (last in, first out) order policy.

Sunshine had tried holding backordered items out of the inventory until the backorders were processed, but this holdback caused problems, too. Namely, more backorders were generated for items that were actually in stock but not yet shown to be in the inventory.

A third problem was that the cost of processing an order was too high. Part of this problem was caused by inefficiency in processing backorders. Additionally, however, costs were high because order clerks were required to manually price orders. They would determine if items were in inventory, and if so, price them. Then, a copy of the priced order would go to Accounting, and a picking slip would go to the warehouse for shipping. This procedure took time. Also, sometimes errors were made. These errors would be detected by the accounting department, which would send the order back to Order Processing for correction. All in all, many labor hours were being wasted.

The third group of problems concerned *cash management*. Sunshine required that all orders be prepaid. Thus checks would arrive with orders. However, the checks stayed with the orders until they had been filled and priced. Since pricing might take two or three days, Sunshine was losing interest on this money.

Second, prepayment required customers to price orders. Many customers, however, made pricing errors. As long as these were relatively minor, Sunshine would simply adjust them via the dividends at yearend. However, if the member was owed more than $50 (possibly because of a pricing error, but more usually due to a discontinued item or a canceled backorder), Sunshine would send the member a refund check. Since refund checks were sent as soon as Sunshine determined they needed to be sent, the refunds were sometimes made before the member's check cleared the bank. If the check was returned for not sufficient funds (NSF), Sunshine essentially had made the member a loan. In most cases this was accidental, but the credit department knew of one construction project whose landscaping had been partly financed this way.

Project	Cost ($)	Schedule	Level of Technical Difficulty
Control of Master Data	35,000	6 months	Easy
Member/Order History for Marketing	150,000	1–3 years	Medium to difficult
Automated Backorder Processing	85,000	1.25 years	Easy—medium
Automated Pricing	70,000	1 year	Easy—medium
Integrated History, Backorder, Pricing System	Not estimated	Not estimated	Not estimated
Cash Management (Procedural changes only)	Less than 5,000	1 month	Easy

Figure 2-19   Costs, Schedule, Technical Estimates for Sunshine's Problems

Feasibility study   Marilyn and Bob documented the problems listed in Figure 2-18. Then, they investigated the cost, schedule, and technical difficulty of computer-based solutions. Their findings are summarized in Figure 2-19.

Concerning member master data, they concluded that changes to the existing member master system could readily be made to improve control. Some of the application programs could be changed to restrict the users' views of the data. These changes, coupled with a new system of account numbers and passwords, should satisfy the needs of accounting and the auditors.

Marilyn estimated these changes would cost about $35,000 including labor and computer time, and could be done in six months (less if the priority of other data processing projects was reduced). There were no significant technical difficulties in this project.

Matching products to members, however, appeared to be a major project. One problem was that Sunshine kept no computer-sensible records of orders. To satisfy marketing, such records would have to be kept. Further, it appeared that these records were to be accessed in a variety of ways. Some people wanted to access orders by order number, some by member number, and some by product number. Further, marketing wanted to do special mailings to members in specified geographic locations who had purchased certain products.

To round out the list of difficulties, different groups wanted the data kept for different periods of time. At the maximum, marketing said they wanted records kept for five years. The team thought this would require substantial increases in Sunshine's computer storage capability.

Because of the vagueness of the requirements at this point, Marilyn and Bob were reluctant to estimate costs, schedules, and technical difficulty. Still, they realized management needed some information, so they guessed as best they could. (They explained in their written and verbal reports that they were guessing, and why.)

They figured that at least $150,000 would be required to develop a minimal capability for keeping computer-sensible orders. More, possibly much more, would be required to meet all of the marketing needs they knew about. They figured they could do something in a year, and a lot in three years. They figured that the technical difficulty would be medium to very difficult, depending on the specific requirements to be met.

On the backorder problems, a simple solution would be to develop a system that maintained records of backorders. Customer service could access these records to determine backorder status. Also, Purchasing could use this system to determine what and how much to order. Further, when shipments arrived, the system could be used to determine, exactly, how many items to withhold from inventory for backorders. Such a system would solve most of the problems.

The pricing needs could be met by extending the current inventory system used by Order Processing. That system was used to extract items from inventory when the clerks prepared the picking slips for the warehouse. The programs could be changed to compute the retail price of the items withdrawn, and even to accumulate order totals for the Order Processing personnel. These computations would substantially increase the flow of work.

The cost, schedule, and technical estimates of the backorder and pricing systems are shown in Figure 2-19.

As Marilyn and Bob examined these problems, they observed strong interrelationships. Developing a computer-sensible order would help both marketing and order pricing. Also, if order processing could be tied to an automated backorder system, then the labor needed to process backorders would be reduced. Further, if the order processing system were connected to the purchasing/accounts payable system, then Purchasing could make quicker and better decisions about what and how much to backorder. This system would reduce the size of the inventory and could generate substantial cost savings.

Marilyn and Bob decided to identify the integrated alternative, but not to guess at costs, schedules, and technical difficulty. Instead, they deferred this issue until more was known about the requirements. As they explained to management, this issue did not need to be resolved at this point, anyway. The cost, schedule, and technical estimates for the integrated system would all be higher than for separate systems. Therefore, if management believed the separate systems were infeasible, they would certainly view the integrated system as infeasible. On the other hand, if management viewed the separate systems as feasible, then the next step would be to specify detailed requirements. This specification would provide the team with the data they needed to make estimates on the integrated alternative. Therefore, no action was needed on the integrated alternative at this time.

The team discovered the cash management problems could readily be solved. In fact, only changes in manual procedures were required. Order Processing could separate checks from orders as they were received. The order number would be written on the check, and the check would go directly to Accounting and then to the bank. The amount received would be written on the order. When the filled and priced order was received in Accounting, the record of payment would be matched against the order.

The problem of refunds on bad checks could be solved by holding refund checks for a period of ten days. If bad checks were returned, the refund check could be pulled and destroyed. Since neither of these solutions involved data processing, the changes were made by the user departments.

Management review and approval

Marilyn and Bob documented the problems and alternatives they identified and submitted these, along with the DFD, to Sunshine's Data Processing Steering Committee. Marilyn and Bob briefed this group on the results. They concluded their presentation by recommending that Sunshine invest the time to specify detailed requirements without attempting to choose among any of these alternatives.

They justified this recommendation as follows: A conservative estimate of the benefits of developing the minimal systems to solve control, marketing, back-order, and pricing problems was well in excess of the estimated $305,000 cost. The schedules, although not pleasant, were feasible. No significant technical problems needed to be surmounted to develop the minimal systems. Therefore, it made sense to proceed to determine requirements.

Further, it would be necessary to determine detailed requirements for the systems, regardless of the alternative eventually chosen. Therefore, as long as the separate system alternatives were feasible, it made sense to continue the project. A decision on separate vs. integrated alternatives could be made later.

This recommendation seemed sound to the steering committee, and it was approved.

SUNSHINE'S DETAILED REQUIREMENTS

At this point, Marilyn appointed Bob as the project leader and assigned a junior analyst, Karen Potter, to the project. At the same time, Marilyn excused herself from the project so that she could attend to her other responsibilities. Also, an experienced order clerk was assigned full time to the project.

The team spent the next five weeks interviewing users in the membership, order receiving, order processing, accounting, purchasing, customer service, and marketing departments. They determined that their understanding of the present system was accurate (as summarized in Figure 2-16), and they made every effort to determine new features the users wanted. After two weeks, the team produced the first of a sequence of DFDs. The highest level DFD is shown in Figure 2-20.

No changes from the DFD in Figure 2-16 were proposed for the membership or accounting departments. However, the customer service and marketing departments were added to the new DFD. These departments were to share files as shown in Figure 2-20.

Once they agreed on the first level DFD, the project team proceeded to expand or explode each of the processes. For example, the explosion for the Order Processing function is shown in Figure 2-21. Each process is numbered as $3.n$ since Order Processing is numbered 3 in the DFD in Figure 2-20. Similar DFDs were constructed by exploding the other first-level processes. The team

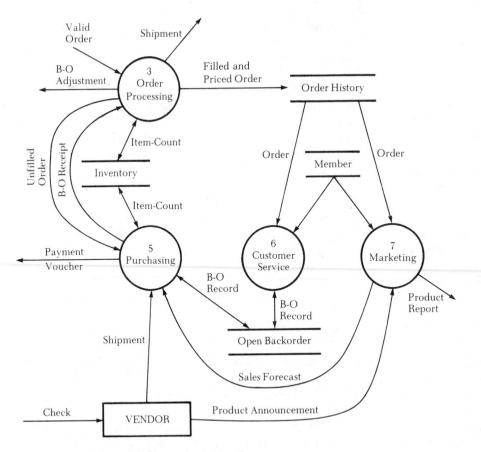

Figure 2-20 Modified DFD for Sunshine's New Systems

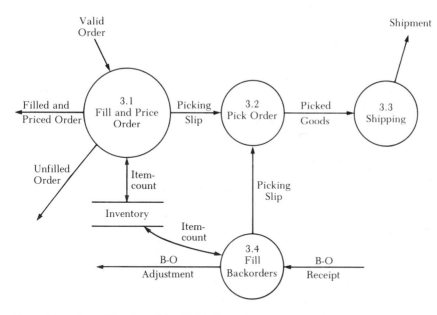

Figure 2-21 Second Level DFD for Order Processing

believed that some of the second-level DFDs were too general, so they exploded them to the third level. After these DFDs had been documented, the team reviewed them with the users and made changes as necessary.

The particulars of these DFDs require considerable explanation and are not essential for our discussion here. Suffice it to say that the DFDs were prepared, a specification data dictionary was developed for every data item that appeared on any DFD, and process descriptions were written for each of the bottom-level processes. All these specifications were reviewed with the users and modified until the users were satisfied. At this point, the project moved onto the second stage of systems development—evaluation.

EVALUATION AT SUNSHINE

Once the requirements specification had been reviewed and approved by the users, Bob and Karen began to identify alternatives.

Sunshine alternatives

The team investigated alternatives for each of the five components. They considered data first, and then hardware, programs, procedures, and personnel.

Data Alternative	Degree of Integration
File Processing	ORDER, MEMBER, BACKORDER, PRICING, INVENTORY, PURCHASING, ACCOUNTING files totally separate.
Limited Database	ORDER, MEMBER, BACKORDER, PRICING, INVENTORY integrated. PURCHASING and ACCOUNTING files separate.
Full Database	ORDER, MEMBER, BACKORDER, PRICING, INVENTORY, PURCHASING, ACCOUNTING files completely integrated.

Figure 2-22   Alternatives for Sunshine's Data

Data   When they examined the data component, they determined a key issue was the degree of integration. On one hand, the new systems could be developed separately using file processing; and at the other extreme, the new systems could be totally integrated, with all data in a single database. There was also at least one feasible alternative between these extremes (see Figure 2-22).

Hardware   Sunshine already had a computer, and when the team considered the hardware component, Marilyn told them that they could propose additions to this system, but that it was simply infeasible to consider switching computers. Marilyn said that she would support a change only if the team could convince her that it was absolutely required. She added that she didn't see how this could be the case.

Reluctantly, Bob and Karen agreed. Although they would have liked to consider changing computers, they did not see that this would be essential. Their mainframe computer was supplied by a large and popular vendor, and the support was basically good. System programs were sometimes difficult to manage, but basically the hardware was effective. Also, Sunshine had one of the smaller mainframes of the vendor's line, so they had a great deal of upward mobility.

Programs   Considering programs, there was only one real issue. Did Sunshine need a DBMS, and if so, which one? Clearly, if they selected the file processing alternative, no DBMS would be needed. Either of the integrated alternatives, however, would necessitate purchasing a DBMS.

To find DBMS alternatives, the team talked with their hardware vendor and they talked with other companies who were already using DBMS on hardware similar to Sunshine's. Also, they investigated advertisements; they went to a free seminar hosted by an independent DBMS vendor; and they attended a DBMS workshop held by the local chapter of DPMA (Data Processing Management Association). They were amazed at the number of alternatives they found, as well as the complexity of the issues involved.

Some people thought it was essential to have a CODASYL-compatible system; others thought this was entirely unimportant. Some people said that relational systems were the only alternative to consider and that Sunshine should utilize this technology as soon as possible. Others said that relational systems were great in theory but that they were not yet practical. Relational systems were fantastic for small problems, but not for the amount of activity that Sunshine would have.

Some vendors said database machines were very important; others said this was only advertising fluff. Some people told them to avoid inverted file systems because they were exceedingly slow. Others told them to use inverted file systems because they were exceedingly fast. (At this point, the project team didn't even know what an inverted file system was.)

Some people advised the Sunshine project team to acquire a DBMS that could run on several different types of hardware; this would allow the possibility for a change to another brand of hardware if Sunshine ever decided to make such a change. Others said that the best systems were provided by hardware vendors themselves. Still others told them to acquire a DBMS from an independent source, but only if the vendor had concentrated its development efforts on a single type of hardware. The confusion raged on and on.

Luckily, Karen had taken a database course in college. She was able to help Sunshine sort through this confusion and to narrow their choices to three systems. One was based on the CODASYL model and was a linked-list-based system. Another was based on a model of its own and was an inverted list system. The third was based on the relational model, it was new, and no one was certain what data structures it used. See Figure 2-23.

	Data	Programs	Hardware	Procedures	People
1.	Separate	File processing	Existing	Separated	Existing
2.	Limited integration	A. CODASYL DBMS	Upgrade	Member/Order management	Informal DBA
		B. Relational DBMS			
		C. Inverted list DBMS			
3.	Full	A. CODASYL DBMS	Upgrade	Centralized data management	Formal DBA
		B. Relational DBMS			
		C. Inverted file DBMS			

Figure 2-23 Sunshine's Alternatives

Procedures and people The procedures and people required for the new systems depended on the degree of integration. If all data was to be integrated into a database, then Sunshine needed a strong database administration (DBA) function. This person, or group, would determine which users could do what to which data, and would control changes to the structure of the data. Such control would imply strong, central management of the data.

If only the member and order data was integrated, then a weaker DBA function could be allowed. The order, membership, customer service, and marketing departments could agree on a person or group of people to control and protect the database, but the function would be less formal than for the totally integrated database.

If file processing was selected, then there would be no need for a DBA, and procedures could be separate. Figure 2-23 summarizes these alternatives.

Sunshine alternative selection

Sunshine's project team considered several ways to select among the alternatives in Figure 2-23. Although, in theory, they believed a return on investment analysis was the best way of proceeding, they didn't think it was appropriate for Sunshine. Since most of the benefits would be intangible, the team did not believe they could put realistic dollar values on them. Better customer service, better market forecasting, quicker response to backorder problems, and the like were simply not quantifiable in dollars. Consequently, they believed a return on investment analysis was inappropriate. In fact, because the team would be guessing at the value of benefits, they would really be doing a subjective analysis, even though their analysis would have quantitative trappings.

Marilyn told the team that the decision to omit a rate of return analysis applied to this system only. For other, future systems, the data processing department would continue to perform, or at least to consider, rate of return studies.

Therefore, the team decided to do its own subjective analysis, to estimate costs and schedules, and to propose one of the alternatives to management. Management could then determine if the costs of the project appeared justifiable in light of the intangible benefits and in light of whatever other investment opportunities Sunshine had.

Sunshine's subjective analysis The first decision the team needed to make was whether to use file or database processing. The team discussed this issue for some time, and prepared the list of advantages and disadvantages shown in Figure 2-24. Of the advantages listed, the major one was the flexible processing for marketing. The marketing analysts wanted to be able to examine the data in many ways, and they wanted to be able to make unusual and one-of-a-kind queries. Such flexible processing would be possible with database processing since records would be integrated, record relationships would be represented,

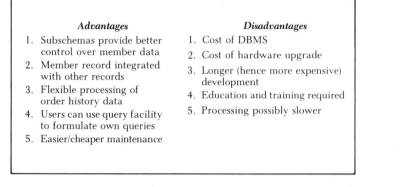

Advantages	Disadvantages
1. Subschemas provide better control over member data	1. Cost of DBMS
2. Member record integrated with other records	2. Cost of hardware upgrade
3. Flexible processing of order history data	3. Longer (hence more expensive) development
4. Users can use query facility to formulate own queries	4. Education and training required
5. Easier/cheaper maintenance	5. Processing possibly slower

Figure 2-24   Advantages and Disadvantages of Database Processing at Sunshine

and the marketing users would have a query facility they could use without data processing involvement.

The prime disadvantage was cost. The DBMS would be purchased, more hardware would be acquired, and development would be extended and therefore more expensive. On the other hand, maintenance would be easier with database processing so some of the expense should be recouped in reduced maintenance. Still, the team did not believe all of the additional expense would be recovered.

The project team decided they would propose a database alternative to management and explain the intangible benefits of this technology. If management believed the system was going to be too expensive, they could back down to the file processing system.

The next issue the team addressed was the scope of the database. The team saw little advantage of integrating all of Sunshine's data. The major problems could be solved without integrating purchasing or accounting data. Therefore they proposed that the new system would include only member, order history, backorder, inventory, and pricing data. Later, after the initial system had been developed, other data could be added to the database, if appropriate.

Finally, the team needed to decide which DBMS to purchase. They talked with the DBMS vendors again and called five companies that were using each system. The relational product was so new it was difficult to find five companies that had used it. When the team did find users, they discovered that the product was employed as an auxiliary to another DBMS—almost as a sophisticated report writer. Although the vendor promised great things to come, Sunshine decided to find another product.

Between the two remaining systems, Sunshine decided on the CODASYL product. They made this decision because the users of this product raved about it. They said it performed just as promised, that vendor support was good, that the documentation was clear and accurate, and that enhancements to its capability were made regularly. Although users of the other product were also satisfied, they did not rave about it to the same degree. The project team considered the fact that the product was compatible with the CODASYL model to be beneficial but not essential. The team decided on alternative 2A—the CODASYL DBMS.

Sunshine's project plan After the team had made the alternative selection, they developed a project plan. Rather than present the details of that plan, we will summarize the cost and schedule aspects as shown in Figure 2-25. The DBMS vendor had quoted a price of $205,000 for the DBMS with the features that Sunshine needed. Further, $65,000 of additional hardware would be needed.

In addition, the team estimated that approximately 4.5 labor-years would be needed to design and build the system. The total cost of this labor (including overhead) would be $225,000. Finally, they estimated that $15,000 of miscellaneous expenses would be required. The team did not include machine time as a cost of this project. Sunshine had available time on their system, and the marginal cost of using this time was low.

Concerning schedules, the team proposed that from two to three people be assigned to the project, depending on the stage of development. The calendar time needed to complete major tasks is listed in Figure 2-25. The total schedule time needed would be 18 months.

Costs	
DBMS purchase price	$205,000
Hardware upgrade	65,000
Development labor	225,000
Miscellaneous expenses	15,000
Total costs	$510,000

Schedule *(Elapsed time for project, in months)*	
Training	1
Design	6
Building (development and test)	6
Conversion	1
Miscellaneous	2
Total elapsed time	18

Figure 2-25 Costs and Schedules for Sunshine's Alternative 2A

Sunshine's management review The project plan was documented in more detail and presented to management. The steering committee members wanted to know how the plan would change if the team developed a file processing system. Marilyn responded that the $205,000 would be saved, along with about $50,000 in labor. Thus the database alternative was about twice as expensive as the file processing alternative.

Management was astounded at this fact. They asked questions like, Why do we need this capability? Is it worth it? Are we spending an extra $255,000 for a nice-to-have but unnecessary system?

The committee was unconvinced that the advantages of database processing were worth this expense. Therefore, they directed the team to reexamine the file processing alternative, and to explain again, if appropriate, why Sunshine needed a database system.

We're not going to describe what happened next. Instead, what do you think? Is database processing justifiable for Sunshine? Are the advantages sufficiently great to justify the extra costs? How should the project team proceed? If you were a member of this team, what would you do? Hopefully, at the end of this course, you will be prepared to answer these questions.

SUMMARY

This chapter has surveyed the systems development process as it pertains to database technology. Four stages of systems development were described: specification, evaluation, design, and implementation.

During specification, the problem is defined, a feasibility analysis is made, and, if appropriate, the users' requirements are defined and documented. One technique for documentation uses data flow diagrams, a specification data dictionary, and process descriptions.

The specification stage of a database project should be no different than for a file processing project. In fact, the technology to be used for meeting the users' needs ought not even to be addressed at this stage.

During the second stage—evaluation—alternative ways of meeting the requirements are identified. Then the project team evaluates the alternatives and recommends one to management. Styles of evaluation are subjective analysis, cost/benefit analysis, or a combination of the two. The evaluation stage is completed by preparing a project plan detailing the approach to be taken, the support environment, major tasks, and a project schedule.

During the design stage, all five components of the business computer system are designed; and during implementation, the five components are constructed and tested. As far as the people component is concerned, the organizational structure is designed. Also, during implementation, people are hired and trained. The project is completed by testing the new system in parallel with the old.

This chapter considered the first two stages—specification and evaluation—in detail. These stages will not be further discussed in this text. However, the last two stages—design and implementation—were only introduced. Design and implementation will be considered again and again in the remainder of this text. If you have gained an overall perspective of how a database system is developed, and if you are familiar with the topics you need to learn, you have accomplished the goal of this chapter.

GROUP I QUESTIONS

2.1   List the four stages of systems development and explain what activity occurs during each step.

2.2   How does database systems development differ from file processing systems development?

2.3   Describe a common violation of the systems development process as it pertains to database technology.

2.4   Name and describe the two phases of activity that occur during the specification stage of systems development.

2.5   Name three dimensions of system feasibility.

2.6   Who has responsibility for clear communications with management?

2.7   What should be the composition of the requirements-stage project team?

2.8   Describe four sources of user requirements.

2.9   What is the danger of using computer jargon during user interviews?

2.10   What is the purpose of a data flow diagram?

2.11   Name three documents that make up the system specification.

2.12   Draw a data flow diagram of the systems development process as described in this chapter.

2.13   Who is the ultimate authority in deciding when the requirements are complete and accurate?

2.14   What are the five components of a system alternative? List two considerations for each component.

2.15   What is the function of the database administrator?

2.16   Describe the process of subjective evaluation.

2.17   Explain the concept of present value and show how it can be used to perform rate of return analysis. How can such analyses be used to choose among alternatives?

2.18   What are the components of a project plan?

2.19   Name and describe two major tasks for design of a database system.

2.20   Name and describe the major tasks for implementation of a database system.

2.21 Why did Marilyn Jasper volunteer data processing labor to define Sunshine's problems?

2.22 Examine Sunshine's data flow diagram in Figure 2-16.

   a. Which processes read member data? Which processes use member data?

   b. Which processes issue checks? Which processes authorize check issuance?

   c. What is the difference between an order and a valid order?

2.23 Summarize Sunshine's problems. Which problems had a computer solution? Which did not?

2.24 How did data processing personnel assess the feasibility of computer-based solutions to Sunshine's problems?

2.25 Do you agree with the logic the project team used concerning feasibility of the integrated alternative?

GROUP II QUESTIONS

2.26 Do you agree that database technology should not be considered until the second stage of systems development? Is there ever a case where it makes sense to describe database technology as a requirement?

2.27 Is it ever justifiable to skip the consideration of feasibility? Do you agree with the approach Sunshine took toward feasibility? Should Sunshine's feasibility evaluation have been more extensive? Less?

2.28 Identify a current user of a database project. Ask that person if they were interviewed during the requirements stage. If so, what was the process like? Did the user feel satisfied at the time? Why or why not? Does the user feel satisfied today?

2.29 Expand the data flow diagram in Figure 2-3 by exploding each process into subprocesses. Use your local university as an example.

2.30 Interview the manager of a data processing operation. Has that person ever done a cost/benefit or similar analysis? If so, what happened? If not, has that person ever known of a cost/benefit analysis being done? Interview a senior level manager of a local company. Has that person ever done a cost/benefit analysis on any business alternative? Has that person ever done a cost/benefit analysis on any computing alternative? Why or why not? How did either (both) work out?

2.31 Develop a Sunshine data alternative other than the ones developed by the Sunshine project team. Subjectively analyze your alternative in relation to the alternatives in Figure 2-23.

2.32 Do you think that Sunshine needs a database system to solve their current problems? How would you respond to the directive that Sunshine's steering committee gave the project team?

I
FUNDAMENTALS

The next two chapters present fundamental material in the study of database systems. Chapter 3 considers input/output processing and file organizations. Direct access storage devices and their operation in conjunction with channels and the CPU are discussed in some detail. Sequential, indexed sequential, and direct file organizations are explained, and their advantages and disadvantages are compared.

Chapter 4 discusses data structures commonly used in database processing. Three types of lists—sequential, linked, and inverted—are defined and applied to the representation of trees and networks. Also, the application of these lists for representing secondary keys is discussed.

The purpose of these chapters is to establish a vocabulary of structures and processing methods that will be used throughout the book. When we say in later chapters, for example, that the database system IDMS represents one-to-many relationships using linked lists, the reader will understand the terms *one-to-many* and *linked lists* and know the advantages and disadvantages of this design.

3
Input/Output Processing and File Organization

The purpose of this chapter is to present the concepts of input/output (I/O) processing that we need for study and analysis of database systems. We will discuss not only the activities of moving data to and from main memory, but also the characteristics of I/O devices and data organization on those devices.

I/O processing is a key factor in database operation and performance. When a terminal user requests information from the database, the request is transmitted through a communications network to main memory (input). After receiving this input, the database system either obtains data from or transmits data to one or more secondary storage devices (input and/or output). Finally, the database system sends a message back to the user via the communications network (output). Consequently, to understand and evaluate some aspects of database system design, we must first understand how input and output are accomplished.

This chapter is divided into five sections. The first concerns the characteristics of secondary storage devices that are important in database systems. The second section describes typical formats of data on these devices, and the third discusses I/O activity—how the user's program interacts with the operating system to accomplish I/O tasks. File organization, or the way data is arranged and accessed, is the subject of the fourth section. Finally, the last section describes a new type of *virtual* I/O.

SECONDARY STORAGE DEVICES

Peripheral devices can be divided into two broad categories: sequential and direct access. Sequential access devices require that records be processed in sequence; for example, the fourth record must be processed before the fifth. Direct access devices do not have this requirement. Records can be processed either sequentially or at random. This means, for example, that the fifth record can be processed after the tenth. The term *direct access* is used to indicate that it is possible to access any record directly without accessing any preceding or succeeding records.

Sequential devices

Typical sequential devices are card readers, printers, punches, typewriters, VDTs and other keyboard devices, and tape units. With the exception of tape units, these devices are used in the database environment to obtain instructions or data from the user or to transmit data back. Tapes are used by a DBMS primarily to hold archive copies of the database. They serve as backup in case of a system failure or provide a starting point if the database system is shut down for an extended period.

As a general rule, sequential devices do not have a significant impact on the design or performance of a database system. Therefore, we will not consider them further. (As indicated in Chapter 1, however, sequential processing is commonly done via the DBMS. Even though this type of processing is sequential, the DBMS uses direct access devices. In fact, quite often the DBMS accesses records randomly, but presents them to the user in sequential order.)

Direct access devices

The most common type of direct access storage is conventional, or hard, disk. Other types include floppy, or soft, disks (also called diskettes), drums, and mass storage devices.

Disk   A disk pack is mounted inside a disk unit (Figure 3-1). Data is recorded on the surfaces of a disk in concentric circles, or *tracks*. The number of surfaces

Figure 3-1   IBM 3350 Disk Unit

on a disk pack as well as the number of tracks on a recording surface depend on the type of disk. The IBM 3350, a disk unit used with larger IBM systems, has 16 disks per pack, 30 surfaces per pack (the top and bottom surfaces are not used), and 555 tracks per recording surface.

Data is read from or written to a disk by read/write heads. In most disk units, the heads are attached to access arms that can move to position the heads at any track on the recording surface of a disk. When the access arms are fixed in a position, data can be read from or written to one track on each recording surface. The collection of these tracks is known as a *cylinder*. Note that the 3350 has 555 cylinders, and each cylinder has 30 tracks. A disk pack and the read/write heads of a smaller disk unit are shown as an example in Figure 3-2.

Not all disk units have movable read/write heads. Some units such as the Burroughs 9372 have fixed heads. Fixed-head units have one read/write head per cylinder and consequently are more expensive than movable-head units of a similar size. They may be faster, however, because no time is spent moving the read/write heads to the correct track. Some disk devices even have a combination of fixed heads on some cylinders and movable heads on others.

Generally, fixed-head devices have closer tolerances (the head is closer to the surface of the disk), and have greater capacity for a given surface area. Also, they usually have fewer maintenance problems because the environment is controlled and the pack is not subject to physical handling.

Disk packs can be removable or permanently mounted. If removable, inactive data can be removed from the system by replacing the disk pack. This frees the disk unit for other data. If the pack is permanently mounted, the data must be copied to tape or other media to be removed.

Some units, called *data modules*, enclose both the disk pack and the read/write heads in a sealed cartridge. Data modules generally have very long times

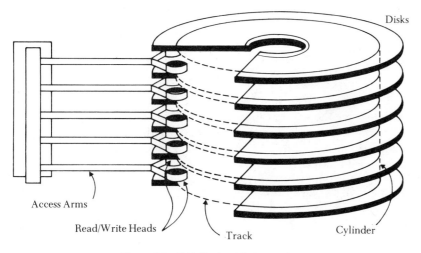

Figure 3-2   Disk Pack with Access Arms

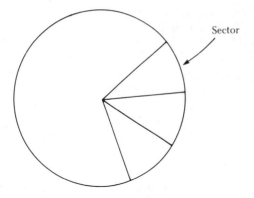

Sector

Figure 3-3 Sector of a Disk Surface

between failures because the environment is closed. Some data modules are removable and others are not.

The term *sector* is sometimes used when describing locations on a disk pack. A sector is just a pie-shaped section of a disk surface (Figure 3-3).

Sectors can be given IDs, and a particular location on a track can be specified by its sector ID. Almost all disk units hold the same amount of data per sector on a small track near the center of a disk as that on a large track near the outside of the disk. The reason for this is that it takes the same amount of time for a sector on a small track to pass the read/write heads as it takes for a sector on a large track. Thus, to keep the data transfer rate constant, there must be an equal amount of data per sector on every track.

Disk I/O time requirements   The time required to transfer data to or from a disk consists of the time to position the read/write head at the correct location on the disk plus the time to actually transfer the data. Positioning the read/write head involves moving the access arm to the correct cylinder (not applicable for a fixed-head device) and waiting for the record to revolve under the read/write head.

The time required to move the access arm, sometimes referred to as *access motion time*, depends on the distance the arm must move. If the arm is already over the correct cylinder, the time is zero. The time required to move the IBM 3350 access arm one cylinder is 10 milliseconds (ms); to move all 555 cylinders takes 50 ms; and the average move time is 25 ms.

Rotational delay, or the time required for the correct data to revolve under the read/write head, depends on the distance the disk must revolve. At best, it is zero (when the head is over the required data); at worst, it is the time required for one complete revolution of the disk. The average of these times is often used for timing purposes. The maximum rotational delay for the IBM 3350 is 16.8 ms; 8.4 ms is the average used for timing purposes.

Data transfer rate is the time required to move the data from a device to main memory or from main memory to the device. It depends upon the speed of the device as well as on the amount of data to be transferred. The IBM 3350 transfers 1.198 million 8-bit bytes per second.

The *disk control unit*, or simply *control unit*, is a device that manages the activities of one or more disk units. It directs a disk unit to move the access arm, to search for certain records, and so forth.

Considerations for database applications

Considerations for database applications   Access motion time, rotational delay, and data transfer rate, then, are the major time factors when transferring data to or from disk devices. In general, there is little the designer of a database system can do to minimize data transfer time. About all that can be done is to obtain a faster device. There are, however, strategies to reduce access motion time and rotational delay.

First, as mentioned in Chapter 1, DBMS usually store several logical records within a single physical record. Therefore, where possible, logical records that tend to be processed together should be stored in the same physical record. If so, all of the logical records can be obtained with one I/O operation.

Second, consider access motion time. Assume that it is desired to sequentially write a physical file that requires three cylinders on a particular type of disk. There are many ways that records can be allocated to the disk pack. One way is to write a record on the first track of the first cylinder, then move the access arm to the second cylinder, write a track of records, move to the third cylinder, write a track, move back to the first cylinder, and so forth. If there are N tracks per cylinder, this procedure requires $3 \times N$ moves of the access arm.

A second way of allocating the records is to write a track of records on the first track of the first cylinder, then write a track of records on the second track of the first cylinder, and so on, until all N tracks on the first cylinder have been written. Then the access arm is moved to the second cylinder and the process repeated. This procedure requires only two moves of the access arm and consequently is much faster. Generally, sequential data sets are allocated in this way.

Unfortunately, the access pattern for database applications is seldom sequential; it is usually a mixture of sequential and random. There is a rule that can be drawn from this sequential example, however: *when possible, records that tend to be processed sequentially should be allocated to the same cylinder.*

This rule requires several explanations. By "records that tend to be processed sequentially" we mean records that are processed in a sequential pattern at least some of the time. If they are processed in several sequential patterns, it is desirable to accommodate the one used most frequently.

Further, it is not a simple task to determine whether records are being processed in a pattern. There are several approaches, however. Sometimes the application dictates that there will be a pattern. For example, requests for data about an order may frequently be followed by requests for line items on that order. In this case, both the order and line-item records should be stored on the same cylinder.

In Chapter 13, you will see how the IDMS database designer can communicate, via the database description, the need to keep logical records close together. Here, "close together" means in the same physical record, or on the same cylinder.

A final consideration, which pertains to rotational delay, is that *records should be ordered on a track in the order in which they tend to be processed*. For example, if there are three records, say, A, B, and C, and if they tend to be processed in the order C, B, A, then they should be ordered on the track C, B, A. This allows the order C, B, A to be processed in one rotation instead of two, as would be required if the records were ordered alphabetically (Figure 3-4).

Now that you understand these considerations, you should know that database experts are currently debating how they should be applied. Many people believe that these considerations should only be used in the design of the DBMS. They think that users and database designers (as opposed to DBMS designers) ought not to have any control over the physical placement of data. If database designers do obtain control over the physical placement of data, maintenance of the database becomes much more difficult.

On the other hand, some experts believe that database designers must have control over the physical placement of data—especially when high performance is required. The response to this is that the short run advantages of better performance are lost by increases in maintenance costs over the long run. Take

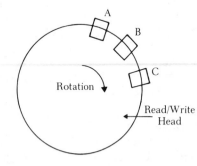

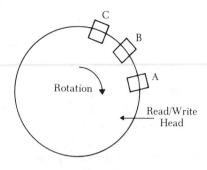

a. Records can be processed in the order C, B, A, in less than one rotation.

b. Processing of records in the order C, B, A requires two rotations. First record C is processed, then one rotation occurs, then record B is processed, then one rotation occurs, then record A is processed.

Figure 3-4 Effects of Record Order

Figure 3-5   Floppy Disk

your choice. Both of the DBMS presented in Chapters 12 and 13 allow a limited degree of control over the physical placement of data.

Other direct access hardware   In addition to conventional, hard disk storage units, three other types of direct access media are commonly used. One is called a *floppy disk*, or sometimes just *floppy*. This media is similar to hard disk storage units, but floppies have only one disk instead of a stack of them. Further, this disk is flexible, hence the term *floppy*.

The arrangement of data on a floppy is very similar to that on the disks previously described. One difference is that floppies, because of their design, contain less data. A typical floppy has two surfaces with 70 tracks per surface and 7680 bytes per track. The total capacity is just over a million bytes. Also, the times for access motion, rotational delay, and data transfer are considerably longer for floppies. Figure 3-5 shows a floppy disk.

Another commonly used direct access media is called a *drum*. A drum is a cylinder that can have data recorded on its outer surface. The tracks on a drum are circles around this surface, as shown in Figure 3-6. Each track has its own read/write head, so there is no access motion and hence no delay for moving

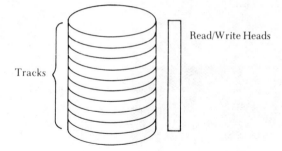

Figure 3-6 Drum (Fixed Read/Write Heads)

the access arms. Drums were more prevalent in the past than they are today. Newer, faster, greater capacity disks have replaced many of them (Figure 3-7).

A final type of direct access device is actually a hybrid, or combination of tape and disk technology. Figure 3-8 shows a *mass storage device*. Data is stored on small rolls of magnetic tape and then moved or staged to direct access devices when needed. After the data is processed, it is moved from disk back to the small rolls of tape. The capacity of this unit and similar units manufactured by other companies is typically in the range of 400 *billion* bytes. Thus mass storage devices provide very large capacity, direct access capability.

The cost per byte of stored data is less for a mass storage unit than for the several pure direct access devices required to yield the same capacity. The disadvantage is that the data must be staged from tape to disk and back. This staging, however, is automatic; it requires no human intervention.

Device	Access Motion Time (ms)	Average Rotational Delay (ms)	Data Transfer Rate (ms/byte)	Capacity (Mbytes)
IBM 3350 (Movable Heads, Removable Disk Pack)	Avg. 25	8.3	0.0008	317
Burroughs 9372 (Fixed Heads, Nonremovable Disk Pack)	None	20.0	0.0048	9.9
IBM 2303 (Drum)	None	8.6	0.0032	3.9

Figure 3-7 Summary of Direct Access Performance Characteristics

Figure 3-8   IBM Mass Storage Device

DIRECT ACCESS DATA FORMATS

The formats of data on certain IBM direct access devices are described in this section. The formats used with these devices are discussed because they are typical and because these devices are commonly used in database applications. This discussion is not meant to imply an endorsement for any particular manufacturer's product.

Key and no-key formats

The format of data depends on whether the records are written with or without keys. Here, the term *key* means an identifier that is external to the record (not embedded) and which the operating system uses to access a particular record. Embedded keys that are not used by the host operating system to access records are not included in this definition of key. Such keys are discussed in the section "Direct File Organization" that appears later in this chapter.

Figure 3-9 features the no-key format. The index point is a special mark on the track that indicates the start of the track. Note that a track is a circle; the two index points shown are actually the same point. The G's in this figure represent gaps in the data on the track that are necessary for correct timing of activities.

To illustrate the use of these gaps, suppose the control unit of the disk is searching for the start of a track. When the index point is detected, a signal is

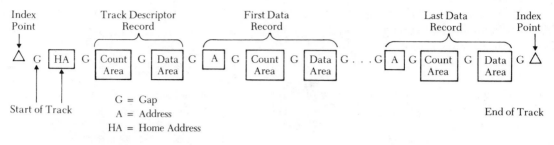

Figure 3-9   No-Key Data Format

sent from the disk to the control unit; the control unit then performs certain activities and responds with a signal to the device to read the next field (home address). While these actions occur, the disk is rotating. When the device receives the signal to read home address, the disk has already rotated past the index point. Consequently, there must be a gap between the index point and the home address. Other gaps are necessary for similar reasons. They are of different lengths, depending on the length of delay between the processing of the data fields.

The home address area as well as the count and data areas of the track descriptor record are used by the system to specify the address of the track (cylinder and track numbers), whether the track is operative or defective, and if defective, which alternate track has been used as a replacement. These data fields normally concern the operating system but not its users.

The next three groups (A, count area, and data area) constitute one data record. These groups repeat on the track for each data record. The A field is a 2-byte address marker that enables the control unit to sense the beginning of a record.

The count area is pictured in detail in Figure 3-10. The flag field is used by the system to indicate the condition of the track and other information used by

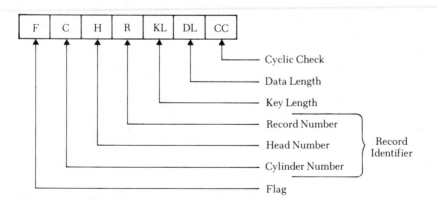

Figure 3-10   Count Area

the control unit. The cylinder number (2 bytes), head number (2 bytes), and record number (1 byte) form the unique record identifier. KL is the key length, which is always zero for the no-key data format. DL is the length of the data area that follows. The cyclic check field is used to check for errors in reading and writing.

The important concept here is that the unique record identifier and the length of the data area precede each data record. The control unit knows exactly how much data to read from the count area because the area is always 11 bytes long. It refers to the DL field in the count area to obtain the length of the data area. Thus the control unit has the length of a data area before reading it.

The data format of keyed records is very similar to that of no-key records. The only differences are that a key area precedes the data area of every data record and the key-length field in the count area is not zero. It contains the length of the key area (Figure 3-11).

Fixed block architecture

Recently, vendors (notably IBM) have developed a new disk type based on *fixed block architecture* (FBA). These devices do not use the record formats shown in Figures 3-9 through 3-11. Rather, data is stored in fixed-size containers or blocks. The IBM 3370, for example, stores data in 512-byte blocks. Data is packed into these fixed-size containers like furniture is packed into shipping crates.

The IBM 3370 (an FBA device) has two sets of read/write heads per disk pack. Since these heads can operate simultaneously, data can be processed much faster. However, data that appears to the programmer to be stored contiguously (physically next to each other) may in fact be stored by the two sets of heads on completely separated parts of the disk. Thus, with these devices, a logically sequential file may not be physically sequential at all.

With traditional devices it is possible to access records by physical position. The cylinder, track, and record number can be used to identify a record. With fixed block architecture this is no longer possible. Instead, blocks are accessed by block number; this number is translated into a physical location. Again, blocks having sequential numbers may not necessarily be physically contiguous.

Consequently, when data is stored on fixed block devices, programs have no control over the physical location of data. This lack of control can result in

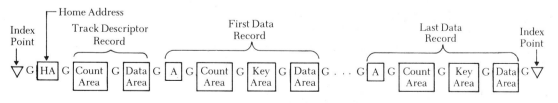

Figure 3-11   Key Data Format

inefficiencies. On the other hand, separating programs from knowledge of physical data locations creates device independence. Data can be moved from one device to another without any impact on programs.

Track capacity

The number of records that can fit on a direct access device depends on the size of the device, the length of the records, and whether or not the records have keys. The IBM 3350 has 19,069 bytes per track. As we see from Figures 3-9 and 3-11, not all of this space is available for data records. Assuming the length of all records is constant, the number of records per track can be calculated using formulas supplied by the manufacturer.

Another, simpler method is to refer to a table like the one in Figure 3-12. This particular table is intended for use with an older IBM disk device, the IBM 3330. Tables are available for each type of disk device; the designer would use a table for the device type to be used to store the file or database.

As an example of the use of this table, suppose an application has 3150-byte records with keys. Look under the "With Keys" column and find the row that has a minimum less than or equal to 3150 and a maximum greater than or equal to 3150. In this case, it is the third row down and the table indicates that three records can fit on a track. If the records did not have keys, then we would use the "Without Keys" column and determine that four records could fit on a track.

The database designer uses a table like the one in Figure 3-12 when determining the record length of files to be used by the DBMS. To minimize wasted

Total Bytes per Record				Records per Track
Without Keys		With Keys		
Min	Max	Min	Max	
6448	13030	6392	12974	1
4254	6447	4198	6391	2
3157	4253	3101	4197	3
2499	3156	2443	3100	4
2060	2498	2004	2442	5
1746	2059	1690	2003	6
1511	1745	1455	1689	7
1328	1510	1272	1454	8
1182	1327	1126	1271	9
1062	1181	1006	1125	10

This table is taken from IBM publication GX20-1920,
3330 Series Disk Storage Reference Summary (40).

Figure 3-12   Track Capacity Table for IBM 3330

disk space, the designer should pick a length close to the maximums in Figure 3-12. Thus, for a 3330 device, the designer might pick 6440, or 4252, or some other length close to the maximum (the DBMS may impose other constraints, such as the record length must be a multiple of 4). In Chapter 13, you will see how this calculation is communicated to IDMS (a DBMS) via the IDMS Device Media Control Language.

File record formats

As Figures 3-9 and 3-11 show, there is a considerable amount of overhead information for each data record. One way to reduce this overhead is to make the physical records longer by grouping several logical records into one physical record. This process is called *record blocking*. For example, suppose the logical data records are 100 bytes long. Any number of them can be appended together. If we group eight, we form a block of records that is 800 bytes long. Record blocking reduces the amount of overhead information per track, and consequently reduces the total amount of space required for the file. It also increases the complexity of the I/O task. Either the application program or the system must block the records before writing them and deblock them when reading.

In addition to being *blocked* or *unblocked*, records are *fixed length* or *variable length*. Consequently, there are four basic record formats: *fixed unblocked*, *fixed blocked*, *variable unblocked*, and *variable blocked*. With each of these formats, records may or may not have keys.

To see how each of the record formats could be represented on IBM direct access devices, consider examples where there are three records with keys 100, 200, and 300. In each of these examples, if the records did not have keys, then the key fields would be omitted.

Fixed unblocked   If the records are fixed unblocked, each record has count, key, and data areas and appears as shown in Figure 3-13. (The address marker field has been omitted for clarity.)

Fixed blocked   If the records are fixed and blocked three per block, the block will have one count field and one key field. The key field for the block contains the value of the highest key in the block (Figure 3-14). Also, within the block, key fields precede the records as shown.

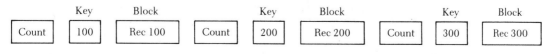

Figure 3-13 Fixed Unblocked Format

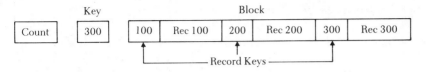

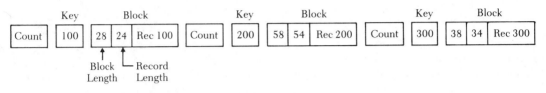

Figure 3-14 Fixed Blocked Format

Figure 3-15 Variable Unblocked Format

Variable unblocked Assume record 100 is 20 bytes long, record 200 is 50 bytes long, and record 300 is 30 bytes long. If the records are unblocked, they appear on the track as shown in Figure 3-15. Two control words, or 8 bytes, have been added to each data area. The first word holds the total length of the block in bytes (for example, 20 for record 100 plus 8 for the two control words). The second word holds the total length of the record (20 plus 4 for the record-length control word).

Variable blocked When variable-length records are blocked, the programmer must specify the maximum length of the block. The operating system then fits as many whole records into the block as possible. Records are not split across blocks unless the programmer indicates that this is permissible, in which case a *variable spanned record format* is used.

Assume the records have the same lengths as in the variable unblocked example, they are not spanned, and only the first three fit in the first block. They appear on the track as shown in Figure 3-16. The key field is assumed to be 5 bytes long. The first word of the block holds the total block length. The first word of each record of the block holds the record length (for record 100, it is 20 for data length plus 5 for the key plus 4 for the record-length word).

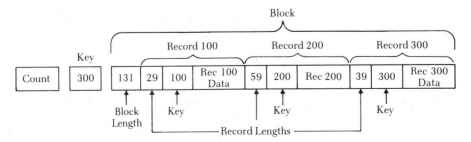

Figure 3-16 Variable Blocked Format

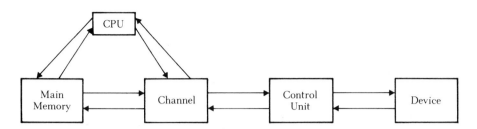

Figure 3-17 I/O Processing Components

INPUT/OUTPUT PROCESSING

Computer systems I/O processing is described in this section. This leads to a discussion of CPU/channel overlap and the importance of buffering for sequential processing.

The CPU, channel, control unit, device, and main memory are the major components used for I/O tasks (Figure 3-17). The CPU instructs the channel to transfer data to or from main memory. The channel obtains data from the control unit and moves it to main memory (read) or moves data from main memory and sends it to the control unit (write). The control unit orders the device to read or write data in accordance with the commands of the channel.

The channel is actually a small computer that can operate independently of the CPU. It performs its function of transferring data by executing small computer programs known as channel programs. These programs are supplied by the operating system and are completely separate from the application programs written by users.

The order of activities (Figure 3-18) can be summarized as follows: The CPU processes a user's application program to a point where some I/O activity is required. It then builds a channel program, using special instructions known as channel commands, and signals the channel. The channel translates the chan-

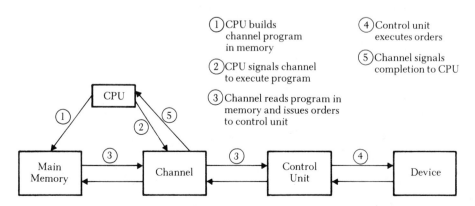

Figure 3-18 CPU/Channel Coordination

nel program into orders that it issues to the control unit. Such orders may direct the control unit to find a particular disk address and transfer data to or from that location. When the channel has finished executing its program, it signals the CPU that the I/O is complete. The CPU can then continue executing the user's program. The CPU may be idle while the channel is operating, or it may be performing tasks for the other jobs in the machine.

To understand the processing controlled by a channel program, consider an example that requires the channel to read record 2 from track 8 of cylinder 5 into the main memory location at address 21000. The channel program, which consists of general commands plus operands to make the command specific, appears as follows:

Command	*Operand*
SEARCH ID EQUAL	05082
READ DATA	21000

The first command causes the channel to signal the control unit to look for a count area that holds the record identifier (cylinder, head, record) 05082 (Figure 3-18). The control unit in turn directs the device to move the access arm to cylinder 5 (if necessary), use the read/write head for track 8, and read all count areas until the one with 05082 is found. If no such count area is found, the control unit signals an error.

The next command causes the channel to signal the control unit to send it all of the data in the next data area on the track. This is the data area immediately following the count area with record identifier 05082. The channel transfers the data it receives from the control unit to memory location 21000.

There are other channel commands to search on the key field, as opposed to the count field, and to read count and data, or read count, key, and data, as opposed to read data. Also, there are several write commands and even a form of "GO TO" command.

Note that when the CPU directs the channel to find a particular record, the search is restricted to the control unit and the device. It is not necessary to read an entire track into main memory and search the track. Rather, the control unit either finds the record on the disk or signals an error to the channel.

As mentioned previously, when the channel is executing a channel program, the CPU may be idle. To fully appreciate this concept, assume a program requires execution of subroutines A, B, and C. Further assume subroutine C requires a record from a peripheral device. The activities of the CPU and channel are depicted in Figure 3-19. The channel is idle when the CPU is operating, and the CPU is idle when the channel is operating.

Now, assume the CPU can request data before it is needed. For example, suppose the CPU instructs the channel to read the record before it begins execution of subroutine A. In this case, the CPU starts the channel but does not wait immediately for completion. Instead, it executes subroutines A and B and then checks to determine if the I/O is complete. If so, it can immediately

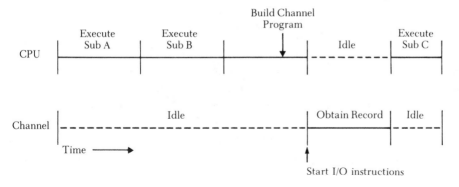

Figure 3-19   CPU and Channel Activities with No Overlap

process subroutine C. If not, it must wait, but the wait is shorter than it would have been without the preprocessing before execution of A. The CPU and channel activities are presented in Figure 3-20. Note here that the CPU never idles; the record is already in memory by the time it is required. This type of processing is sometimes called *overlapped processing* because of the parallel or overlapped operation of the CPU and the channel.

Overlapped processing is usually unknown to persons who have programmed at the COBOL level but have not programmed at an assembler-language level. With the latter, it is possible to issue a request for I/O without waiting. The CPU can be directed to perform other activities not involving the requested I/O while the channel is operating.

Processing with multiple channels   Larger computer systems have several or even many channels. All of these can operate simultaneously. In such a system, however, not all channels can be allocated to all devices. The designer of the hardware configuration must consider typical processing workloads to

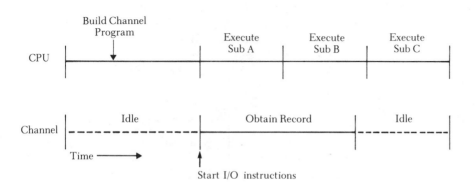

Figure 3-20   CPU and Channel Activities with Overlap

determine which devices to connect to which channels. If the channel connections are incorrect, bottlenecks may develop while several applications wait for the same channel.

Also, because not all channels can be connected to all devices, the computer operations staff may have to perform a juggling act to move data to the available devices, channels, and so forth. Further, reducing channel and device contention among different jobs becomes quite important. This becomes even more important (and difficult) when there are several CPUs sharing the same direct access devices. And you thought computer operations were trivial!

FILE ORGANIZATION

In Chapter 1 we mentioned that DBMS must interface with the operating system to perform I/O. More generally, any program, whether a DBMS or not, must do this. The portion of the operating system that does I/O is often referred to as the *data management access methods* (or just *access methods*). Figure 3-21 shows the relationship of the operating system user (DBMS or application program), the access methods, and the channel. The access methods build the channel programs discussed in the previous section.

Numerous access methods have been developed. Each has a particular *file organization* and *access technique* (or techniques). Strictly speaking, the file organization is the structure of the file; the access technique is the way the file structure is manipulated. Commonly, however, this distinction is not made, in which case file organization describes not only structure but also access technique. We will use the latter, more common definition.

You need to understand three types of file organization: sequential, indexed sequential, and direct. Sequential file processing is used by DBMS for producing journal files and archive database copies, as will be discussed in Chapter 11. Indexed sequential files, as such, are not used by DBMS. The *techniques* of indexed file processing, however, are used. To explain, no DBMS processes the database using the operating system's indexed sequential file organization. Many DBMS, however, create their own version of indexed files. So, if you learn indexed sequential file processing, you will accomplish two objectives in one reading: you will learn a type of file processing, and also you will learn a technique used by the DBMS itself. Finally, direct organization, or a variant

Figure 3-21 Access Method Interfaces

closely akin to direct organization, is used by all DBMS to organize the database itself. Therefore, learning direct organization will help you to understand how DBMS products operate and will facilitate your understanding of DBMS performance issues.

These three types of file organizations have a multitude of different names. Often, people in industry use acronyms when referring to these file organizations. SAM is used for sequential access method, ISAM (pronounced I-SAM) stands for indexed sequential access method, and DAM or more commonly BDAM (B-DAM) stands for (basic) direct access method.

Whether or not these particular acronyms are used, every modern operating system will provide the types of capability described under these names. Strive to get to underlying concepts if you have trouble communicating with a particular vendor using these terms.

Sequential file organization

Sequential file organization is the simplest of the three file organizations to be discussed. Records are written to a file in sequence. Once a sequential file is created, records can be added at the end of the file. It is not possible to insert records in the middle of the file without rewriting the file. Also, it is generally not possible to modify an existing record without rewriting the file. Records are usually read in sequence. With some systems, however, it is possible to start this sequential reading at any record location; there is no requirement to start reading at the beginning of the file.

Because the access pattern is sequential, it is often possible for the system to anticipate I/O activity. In the case of a sequential read, for example, when the user's program requests, say, record 10, the system can request the channel to read record 11 next. Thus, when the user's program requests record 11, it may already be in main memory. This technique is known as *anticipatory buffering*.

Consider a sequential file with fixed-length 100-byte records blocked three per block. Suppose there are two buffers, or areas of main memory for holding records, labeled A and B. When the file is processed, the activities in Figure 3-22 take place.

The first action is to instruct the channel to fill both buffers. As soon as the user requests the first record, the system must ensure that buffer A has been filled and wait if necessary. Once it is filled, the system passes record 1 to the user. When the user requests records 2 and 3, they are already in the buffer and are simply passed to the user.

When record 4 is requested, the contents of buffer A are no longer needed. Therefore, the system requests that buffer A be filled with the next block. Then the sytem checks whether or not buffer B is filled and waits if necessary. When B is filled, record 4 is passed to the user. Execution continues in this way, alternating buffers.

User's Program	System Response
Open the file	Request channel to fill buffer A with block 1 (records 1–3). Request channel to fill buffer B with block 2 (records 4–6).
Read record 1	Wait for buffer A to be filled if necessary. Send record 1 to user.
Read record 2	Send record 2 to user. (It is already in the buffer.)
Read record 3	Send record 3 to user.
Read record 4	Request channel to fill buffer A with block 3 (records 7–9). Wait for buffer B to be filled if necessary. Send record 4 to user.
Read record 5	Send record 5 to user.
Read record 6	Send record 6 to user.
Read record 7	Request channel to fill buffer B with block 4 (records 10–12). Wait for buffer A to be filled if necessary. Send record 7 to user.

Figure 3-22   Anticipatory Double Buffering

The savings that can be realized by anticipatory buffering are illustrated in Figure 3-23. Note the large amount of parallel processing of the CPU and the channel. The CPU never waits in this example. If the processing of records were faster than shown in this figure, however, the CPU might have to wait for the channel.

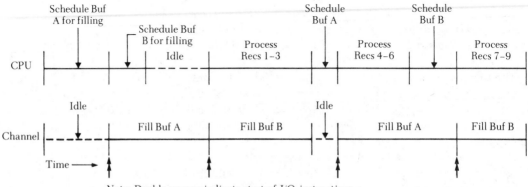

Note: Double arrows indicate start of I/O instructions.

Figure 3-23   CPU/Channel Activities During Anticipatory Buffering

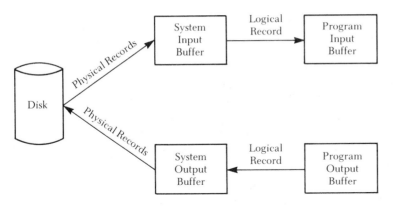

Figure 3-24 Physical and Logical Record Movement

Writing a file involves essentially the same techniques as reading. The system blocks the user's records and, when a buffer is full, schedules it for output. Then it switches to the second buffer, blocks the user's records in it, and schedules it for output when full. At this point, the system must check to be certain the write of the first buffer is completed. If not, it must wait. Once the write is complete, it switches buffers and continues.

Figure 3-24 shows the relationships of input and output buffers and the record areas within a program. The access methods move physical records (blocks of logical records) into the input buffers. Then, logical records are deblocked and moved into the program input record area. On output, the reverse occurs. A record is moved from the program output record area and blocked in a system buffer. When a block is full, the output to the file is initiated, and another output buffer is used to block the outputs.

There is considerable moving of data between the buffers and the user's area. Techniques such as *exchange buffering* or *locate-mode processing* are available to reduce this movement. Basically, these techniques allow the user to process data in the buffer. In the case of a read, when the user requests a record, the system passes the address of the record in the buffer. The data is then referred to in the buffer. In the case of a write, the system passes to the user the address of an area that is to hold the new record. The user then creates the new record in that area.

Indexed sequential file organization

The indexed sequential file organization allows both sequential and random processing. Sequential processing can start at the beginning of the file or at any other record in the file. Random processing is accomplished by specifying the key-field value for the desired record. This record is found via indexes.

Nearly every business-oriented computer supports some form of indexed sequential processing. From the application program standpoint, these forms appear very similar. Internally, however, the file structures and processing methods differ substantially. Therefore, consider the following discussion as an example; the particulars will vary from one computer to another.

Also, this discussion presents the actions taken by the operating system. Application programs are not involved with the details that follow. Rather, the application program issues a command to read a particular record, or insert a new record, or whatever. Finding space, updating indexes, and so forth are all done by the operating system. The only user responsibility beyond writing the application programs is to allocate space for the files and indexes. Unfortunately, with some systems, this itself can be a cumbersome task.

Indexed sequential files are composed of three areas. The *prime area* contains records of the file. When the file is created or reorganized, all records reside in the prime area. Records in the prime area are in order by key. The second area of an indexed sequential file is the *overflow area*. Records are placed in the overflow area when additions to the file cannot be fitted into the prime area. The *indexes* are located in the third area of an indexed sequential file. These indexes are used to locate a particular record for random processing.

File indexes   To understand the processing of an indexed sequential file, consider an example that has fixed unblocked records. Suppose four records fit on a track. Figure 3-25 depicts the first five tracks of the file. Note that each record has a unique key and that records are in order by key.

Suppose it is desired to read record 79. One way to access this record is to sequentially read the records in the file until record 79 is found. This may be a very slow process. A faster way of finding record 79 is to use the track index (Figure 3-26). The track index contains the value of the highest key on each track. To locate the track that contains record 79, it is only necesssary to find

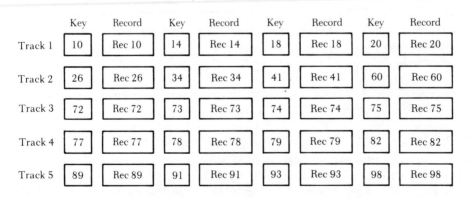

Figure 3-25   Five Tracks of an Indexed Sequential File

Track Number	Highest Key on Track
1	20
2	60
3	75
4	82
5	98

Figure 3-26 Track Index

the first track that contains a record with a key greater than 79. In this case, that is track 4. The highest key of track 3 is 75, and the highest key on track 4 is 82. Therefore, if record 79 exists, it must be on track 4. Consequently, the next step is to read track 4 to find record 79.

Using the track index does not eliminate sequential searching; it just reduces the magnitude of the task. Instead of searching a large file of records, we are able to search a table that points toward the desired record location.

If the file is large, the track index is long. To reduce the search time on the track index, another index, called the *cylinder index*, is created. This index shows the highest key on each cylinder. Now to find a given record it is necessary to search the cylinder index to find the cylinder containing the record. Then the track index for that particular cylinder is searched to find the track containing the record. Then that track is searched to find the record. For brevity, Figure 3-27 assumes there are only five tracks per cylinder. In common practice, there are more, depending on the device. Recall, for example, that the IBM 3350 has 30 tracks per cylinder.

If the file is large, even the cylinder and track indexes may not be enough. For example, if the file has 5000 tracks of data and resides on a 3350, there could be 5000/30, or 167, entries in the cylinder index. (Actually, both the track index and the cylinder overflow areas take up space on the cylinder. This means that not all 30 tracks can hold data. More likely, 25 tracks would hold data so there would be 5000/25, or 200, entries in the cylinder index.)

When the cylinder index is large, it may be desirable to break the cylinder index into parts and create a master index on the parts of the cylinder index. For example, the cylinder index may be broken into parts having 20 entries each. The master index has the highest key in each part.

To find a particular record, it is necessary to search the master index to find the correct cylinder index, to search that cylinder index to find the correct track index, to search the track index to find the correct track, and finally to search the track to find the desired record (Figure 3-28). If necessary, this process can be continued, creating several levels of master indexes. It is sometimes desirable to create and store small indexes in main memory to speed up processing.

Cylinder Index

Cylinder	Highest Key
1	98
2	184
3	278
.	.
.	.
.	.

Track Index for Cylinder 1

Track	Highest Key
1	20
2	60
3	75
4	82
5	98

Track Index for Cylinder 2

Track	Highest Key
1	107
2	122
3	148
4	163
5	184

Track Index for Cylinder 3

Track	Highest Key
1	201
2	210
3	223
4	259
5	278

Assume desired record has key value 248.

1. Search cylinder index to find correct cylinder. Cylinder 2 has highest key of 184; cylinder 3 has 278. Therefore, cylinder 3 must contain the record.

2. Search track index for cylinder 3 to find track. Track 3 has highest key of 223; track 4 has 259. Therefore, track 4 must contain the record.

3. Search track 4 for the desired record.

Figure 3-27 Search of Cylinder and Track Indexes

Indexed sequential file processing When an indexed sequential file is created, all records are written into the prime area in sequence by key. The indexes are generated at this time. We have already studied the way records can then be retrieved from the file. The process of updating an existing record (sometimes referred to as *replace* or *update-in-place*) is similar to the retrieval process. The indexes are used to find the desired record, and the new record is written on top of the old one.

A deletion from the file is also straightforward. The indexes are used to find the desired record, and a special mark is inserted into the record to indicate that it has been deleted. However, subsequent attempts to access this record will not automatically result in an error. The program that performs the access must check for the special mark that indicates deletion.

Insertions to an indexed sequential file are quite troublesome because the key order of the file must be maintained. To illustrate, assume that it is necessary to insert record 55 into the file depicted in Figure 3-25. The only way that key

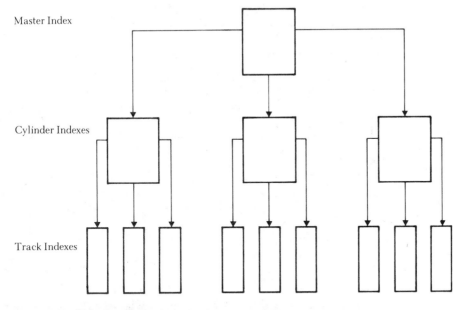

Figure 3-28 Index Structure

sequence can be preserved is for record 55 to replace record 60 on the file. But what happens to record 60? Clearly it is undesirable to put 60 on top of 72, put 72 on 73, and so on, completely rewriting the remainder of the file. The answer is that record 60 is put into an overflow area and pointers are set up to ensure that record 60 can be found during subsequent processing. Doing this requires extension to the track index. If we compare Figure 3-29 with Figure 3-26, we see that two words have been added to each index entry. The first word holds the highest key in the overflow area for this track. The second word holds the address of the first overflow record or is null if there is none. This address might have the format: CCHHR, where C is the cylinder number, H is the head or

Track Number	Highest Key on Track	Highest Key in Overflow	Address of First Over- flow Record
1	20	20	Null
2	60	60	Null
3	75	75	Null
4	82	82	Null
5	98	98	Null

Figure 3-29 Complete Track Index

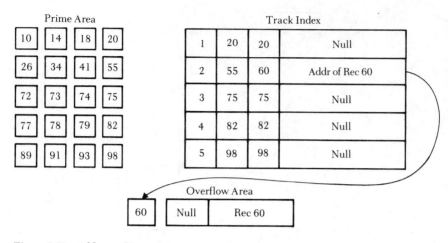

Figure 3-30 Addition of Record 55

track number, and R is the record number on the track. Alternatively, the address could be a block number and displacement (offset) into the block where the record starts.

When record 55 is inserted into the file, it replaces record 60, which is written into the overflow area, and the track index is modified accordingly. The results of these operations appear in Figure 3-30. Note that a new field has been attached to record 60 in the overflow area. This field is used to point to the next record in the overflow area. In this case, it is null.

Now suppose record 24 is to be inserted into the file. A key value of 24 is greater than the last key on track 1, but less than the first key on track 2, so the record could be inserted in the overflow area of track 1. Doing this, however, would change the Highest-key-in-overflow field in the track index. This strategy is undesirable because it would require a change in the cylinder index and possibly in higher indexes. Consequently, records must be inserted in such a way that the Highest-key-in-overflow field need not be changed. To ensure this, record 24 is added to track 2 rather than track 1. All records on track 2 are moved over one place, and record 55 is bumped into the overflow area. The file now appears as in Figure 3-31. Record 55 is the first record in the overflow area, and a pointer (address) to record 60 has been added to record 55.

If record 57 were to be added to the file, it would be inserted in the overflow area and the address in record 55 would be modified to point to record 57 (Figure 3-32). The prime area and track index would remain the same.

Although we have not shown it here, there are actually two types of overflow areas. One is a cylinder overflow area, which receives overflow from tracks on one particular cylinder. One cylinder overflow area exists for each cylinder in the file. The second type is the independent overflow area. This area receives overflow from any track whose cylinder overflow area is full. Records from

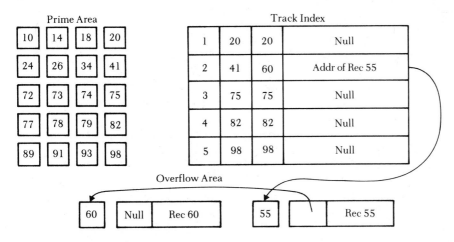

Figure 3-31   Addition of Record 24

different tracks can be intermixed in this overflow area. The pointers attached to the records allow the system to maintain the correspondence between records and tracks.

It should be clear from this discussion that insertions in indexed sequential files are indeed troublesome! Note, too, that if there have been many insertions, it usually takes a long time to find a record. At that point, no file operation is efficient. Imagine the time required to process a list of 50 overflow records, half of which are in the independent overflow area and half in the track overflow area. Processing of these records would be especially slow if the records were positioned alternately on the two areas and the areas were on different cylinders, thereby causing the access arm to move back and forth.

There are two ways of reducing the magnitude of the insertion problem. One is to create a certain percentage of dummy records when initializing the file. Then insertions can be made on top of the dummy records, or records that are displaced can be moved onto the dummy records. The second way is to periodically reformat the file. Reformatting entails creating a new file with all records correctly sequenced in the prime area. The operating system vendor usually supplies such reformatting utilities.

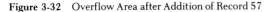
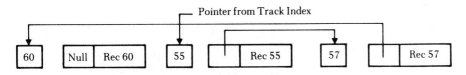

Figure 3-32   Overflow Area after Addition of Record 57

Direct file organization

Direct or random file organization is primarily used for random processing, although sequential reading is possible. Direct organization differs from indexed sequential in that records are in no particular order on the file. Thus sequential reading may present records in apparently nonsensical order. The programmer has greater flexibility with direct than with indexed sequential, but the programming task is more complex.

Direct organization is the fundamental organization of almost every database. DBMS usually do their database I/O using direct organization. Typically, when other features such as indexes are needed, the DBMS provides them on top of the operating system's direct access methods.

Records are identified in one of several ways. One method is to specify the *relative track* and *relative record number* of a desired record. Relative track means track number relative to the start of the file. Relative record means record number relative to the start of the track. A second method of identifying a record is by *relative track* and *key* (in this case, records must have keys). A third method is by *relative block address;* this is the block number (physical record number) of the desired record relative to the start of the file. The last way is by *physical address*. This could be the actual cylinder, head, and track record number on the device, or it could be a block address and displacement with the block (FBA devices). In general, physical addresses change if the file is moved to another volume or device.

Unlike indexed sequential, where each record is identified to the system by its key, direct organization does not support any particular correspondence between record content and file address. It is left to the programmer to establish a way of correlating records to file locations.

Address computation   Perhaps the easiest way of addressing records is to use a field or portion of a field as a relative block address. For example, suppose an inventory file has records with Part-number fields. If part numbers are unique, say if they start with 1 and run consecutively in steps of 1 up to the number of parts in the inventory, then the part number can be used as the relative block address of the record in the file. Unfortunately, such part numbers are very rare. What can be done is to create a second part number that does meet these conditions. This is really not an effective solution, however. Keeping account of the correspondence between part numbers can be a nightmare.

Another approach, sometimes referred to as a *hashing scheme,* is to perform some sort of arithmetic operation on a field of the record and to use the result as an address. For example, in a file of students, each record may have a student number. If these student numbers do not start with 1 and run consecutively in increments of 1, they are not suitable for use as addresses. Addresses can be created, however, by using only the last few digits of the student number. This is sometimes referred to as the *division/remainder method* because taking the last few digits is equivalent to dividing by a number and using the remainder.

For example, taking the last five digits is equivalent to dividing by 100,000 and using the remainder.

The problem with a hashing scheme is that the generated addresses may not be unique. Students with numbers 4363570 and 8263570 will both have address 63570. This situation is referred to as a *collision*, and the resulting addresses, 63570, are called *synonyms*.

There are techniques for processing synonyms, but even so, it is always desirable to minimize them. Analysis of the records may show that the last five digits are not the best ones to use. Perhaps using the second, fourth, and last three digits would lead to fewer synonyms.

Digit analysis is a way of selecting digits to use for addressing. For example, a representative sample of the records in the student file can be collected. Counts of the number of times each digit appears in each position can be made and tabulated. The results for a hypothetical sample of size 1000 are shown in Figure 3-33.

Analysis of this table indicates that positions 1, 2, 4, and 5 are not suitable because the digits tend to be clustered in those positions. Positions 3, 6, 7, 8,

Digit Position

Digit	1	2	3	4	5	6	7	8	9
0	400		105			50	100	180	10
1		100	100		100	150	120	200	130
2		300	98	400		75	99	80	60
3			95		150	75	105	75	240
4		300	102			200	80	140	105
5	600		102		400	180	102	75	80
6		100	80			80	100	40	130
7			98	600	350	140	98	150	80
8		200	120			40	101	10	105
9			100			10	95	50	60

Figure 3-33 Results of Digit Analysis of 1000 Records

and 9 appear to be the best choice. This analysis is inconclusive, but deriving
and following some guidelines is probably better than guessing. A more thor-
ough analysis would examine the correlation between positions as well.

Another type of hashing scheme is *folding,* in which a key is split into parts.
The parts are added, and the sum or part of the sum is used as an address.
Folding can be combined with the division/remainder method. The parts of the
key are added together and the sum is divided by a number; the remainder is
the calculated address. This scheme is generally effective because every character in the key participates in the hashing calculation. See Figure 3-34.

A third approach for addressing a direct file is to use a cross-reference list or
table. The table has keys in one column and file addresses in another (Figure
3-35). To find a record, the key column is searched for a match on the desired

Key:	412483	Key:	715823408
Add:	412 + 483	Add:	715 + 823 + 408
		Divide sum:	1946/1000
Address:	895	Address:	946

a. Folding   b. Folding with Division/Remainder

Figure 3-34   Hashing Methods for Addressing Records

Key	Address (Relative Block Type)
123	1
241	8
618	6
723	4
1841	5
1981	2
2318	7
2742	3
.	.
.	.
.	.

Figure 3-35   Cross-Reference Table

key value. If a match is found, the address is taken from the corresponding address column. That address may be any one of the four types mentioned at the start of this section. The indexes of an indexed sequential file are an extension of this concept.

A variation of this technique is often used in database systems. Consider a database of employee information. Assume there are three database record types: employee SALARY, employee PERSONAL data, and employee CHILD. Further, assume all three types reside on the same physical file with one database record per physical record. Also, assume the physical records are unblocked so there is one physical record per physical block. This means that relative block addresses are also relative record addresses.

Figure 3-36 shows the relationships of the SALARY, PERSONAL, and CHILD records. To find employee information, the database system maintains a cross-reference table like that in Figure 3-37. The first column has Employee-number, the second the relative block address of the physical record containing the

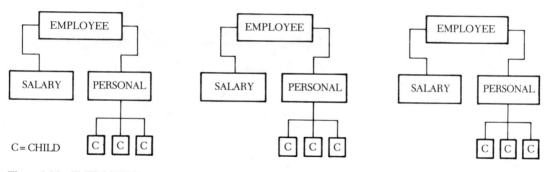

Figure 3-36   EMPLOYEE Data Structure

Employee-number	SALARY Record Address	PERSONAL Record Address
100	4	12
130	5	9
180	11	6
240	8	7
260	3	2
300	10	1

Figure 3-37   Employee Cross-Reference Table

SALARY record for that employee, and the third the relative block address of the PERSONAL record.

The cross-reference table for the CHILD records is within the PERSONAL records. The first 200 bytes of each PERSONAL record contain personal data and the last 40 bytes contain space for up to ten 4-byte relative block addresses of CHILD records. One such record is shown in Figure 3-38. In this example, then, part of the cross-reference table is carried with the data.

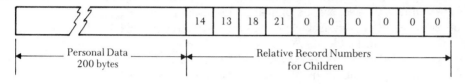

Figure 3-38　PERSONAL Record

Direct file processing　Because of the flexibility inherent in direct file organization, there are many ways to process such files. A method that typifies processing using hash addressing schemes is illustrated here. Another method not using hash addressing is discussed in Chapter 4.

Consider a database of fixed-length student database records. One database record is contained in one physical record, and the file is unblocked. Assume there are 16,000 database records to be processed randomly by student number. The division/remainder method is to be used to generate relative block addresses. Finally, assume the file is to be 80 percent full, which means that the total size of the file will be 20,000 records. The reason for having 4000 unused records will soon be evident.

Assume student numbers have six digits. One way to create a relative block address from a student number is to divide the student number by 20,000 and take the remainder. The result will range from 0 to 19,999. Since we want addresses from 1 to 20,000 we will add 1 to this remainder. This procedure will generate synonyms, so it is necessary to find a method for processsing them. We establish the following rules:

1. To insert a record:
    a. If the calculated address is empty, insert the record at that address.
    b. If the calculated address is full, do not insert the record at that address. Increment the calculated address by 1. Repeat steps *a* and *b* up to 10 times.
    c. If steps *a* and *b* have been repeated 10 times and the record still has not been inserted, print the message FILE TOO DENSE and stop.
2. To find a record (for retrieval, updating, or deletion):
    a. Read the record at the calculated address.
    b. If this is the desired record, stop. If not, increment the calculated address by 1. Repeat steps *a* and *b* up to 10 times.

c. If steps *a* and *b* have been repeated 10 times and the record has not been found, print the message RECORD NOT FOUND and stop.

These rules assume that empty or unused records can be identified. One way to indicate empty records is to insert a special mark into the first byte of each one before any records are loaded. The mark must be one that cannot be confused with valid data. A bit combination that does not have a character representation may be a good choice. When a record is deleted, this special mark can be inserted into the record.

The purpose of the limit of 10 repetitions is to prohibit searching all the way through the file. Such searching would be extremely expensive. This means that the file cannot be 100 percent full because if the last empty record number is, say, 18,000, and the generated address for a record is 5, the empty record will not be found. We accept this situation because we do not want to read from record 5 to 18,000 to find the record.

The number 10 is arbitrary here. We could say 15 or 20, but this could result in slower processing. Note that if the message FILE TOO DENSE is written, it means that too many synonyms have been generated in one area. The file should be made larger and the address computation modified.

Actually, for this type of processing, 80 percent density is high; 60 percent might be more realistic. Note that the fewer synonyms there are (or the better the hashing scheme is), the more dense the file can be.

An algorithm to load the file is presented in Figure 3-39. This algorithm assumes three files: a sequential file containing the student records to be loaded (STUDENT), the direct file to be loaded (DIRECT), and a report file (REPORT). The algorithm has four procedures.

LOAD-PROCEDURE is the high-level module that calls the other three procedures. The DOWHILE statement causes PROCESS to be performed repeatedly while both EOF-STUDENT and DENSITY-FLAG are 0. If either one of these variables is not 0, then PROCESS is not to be performed. If either variable is 0 the first time, PROCESS will not be performed at all.

INITIALIZE opens the files and formats the direct file with 20,000 dummy records. Such formatting is usually required to establish a direct file. Also, during this process, the special mark will be placed in the dummy records. INITIALIZE also sets flags to 0 and reads the first record. If no student records are found, an error message is generated.

PROCESS attempts to load the record. First, the RBA (relative block address) is calculated, and then a flag that indicates successful insertion is set to 0. Next, up to 10 attempts are made to find a place for the record. The DO loop will be processed until a record is inserted, or up to 10 times.

This algorithm wraps around the file; if RBA becomes larger than 20,000, it is set back to 1. This would occur, for example, if the initial address were 19,999 and the last two record positions were already full. In this case, RBA would be 19,999, then 20,000, then 1, and so forth.

```
    BEGIN LOAD-PROCEDURE
        DO INITIALIZE
        DO PROCESS WHILE EOF-STUDENT = 0 AND DENSITY-FLAG = 0
        DO WRAPUP
    END LOAD-PROCEDURE
    BEGIN INITIALIZE
        OPEN STUDENT, DIRECT, AND REPORT FILES
        FORMAT DUMMY RECORD
        DO FOR I = 1 TO 20,000
            WRITE DUMMY RECORD TO RECORD I ON DIRECT FILE
        END-DO
        DENSITY-FLAG = 0
        EOF-STUDENT = 0
        READ STUDENT RECORD; AT END SET EOF-STUDENT = 1
        IF EOF-STUDENT = 1
            THEN WRITE "NO INPUT DATA" TO REPORT FILE
        END-IF
    END INITIALIZE
    BEGIN PROCESS
        RBA = Remainder (STU-NUM / 20,000) + 1
        SUCCESS-FLAG = 0
        DO FOR I = 1 TO 10 WHILE SUCCESS-FLAG = 0
            READ RECORD RBA FROM DIRECT FILE
            IF RECORD RBA IS UNUSED (STILL IN DUMMY FORMAT)
                THEN WRITE STUDENT RECORD TO RECORD RBA ON DIRECT FILE
                    SUCCESS-FLAG = 1
                ELSE RBA = RBA + 1
                    IF RBA GREATER THAN 20,000
                        THEN RBA = 1
                    END-IF
            END-IF
        END-DO
        IF SUCCESS-FLAG = 1
            THEN READ STUDENT RECORD; AT END SET EOF-STUDENT = 1
            ELSE DENSITY-FLAG = 1
        END-IF
    END PROCESS
    BEGIN WRAPUP
        IF DENSITY-FLAG = 1
            THEN WRITE "FILE TOO DENSE" TO REPORT FILE
            ELSE WRITE "LOAD COMPLETE" TO REPORT FILE
        END-IF
        CLOSE STUDENT, DIRECT, REPORT FILES
    END WRAPUP
```

Figure 3-39 Algorithm to Load a Direct File

If the record is successfully inserted, the next STUDENT record is read, and assuming there is more data, PROCESS will be repeated. If the record was not successfully inserted, the density flag is set to 1. This will terminate the loop on PROCESS.

The last procedure, WRAPUP, writes the correct termination message and closes the files.

Finding a particular student's record is similar to the loading process. Figure 3-40 presents an algorithm to find the record for student SN. This algorithm is written as a procedure to be invoked by another program. The outputs of the algorithm are a success flag and the desired record (if found).

This algorithm does not stop when an unused record is encountered as we might expect. For example, when searching for the record of student 003456, the RBA is 3457. Suppose 3457 and 3458 are occupied by records other than 003456, but 3459 is empty. If 003456 were present, wouldn't it be in location 3459? Can we therefore conclude that 003456 is not in the database?

```
BEGIN FIND-PROCEDURE (SN)
/Note: SN is the Student-number to be found.  It is input to
this procedure from the calling procedure./
RBA = Remainder (SN / 20,000) + 1
STOP = RBA + 10
IF STOP GREATER THAN 20,000
     THEN STOP = STOP - 20,000
END-IF
SUCCESS-FLAG = 0
DOWHILE SUCCESS-FLAG = 0 AND RBA NOT = STOP
     READ RECORD RBA FROM DIRECT FILE
     IF RECORD RBA CONTAINS SN
          THEN SUCCESS-FLAG = 1
          ELSE RBA = RBA + 1
               IF RBA GREATER THAN 20,000
                    THEN RBA = 1
               END-IF
     END-IF
END-DO

/Note: At this point, if success flag = 0, the record does not
exist.  Otherwise, the record containing SN is in main memory.
The application program can now process SN./
END FIND-PROCEDURE
```

Figure 3-40   Algorithm to Find a Hashed Record

The answer, of course, is no (otherwise the algorithm would be in error, and we wouldn't ask this question). Position 3459 could have been occupied when 003456 was inserted in the database but afterwards deleted. This means 003456 may be in a position past 3459. Consequently, we must examine all 10 candidate records before concluding a record is not in the file.

The hashing scheme shown here is a simple one. It can be expanded in several ways. If records are blocked, several synonyms can be stored in the same block. In this case, records are stored away from the calculated address only when the block becomes full. This strategy can reduce the number of extra reads. Another extension uses a hash function to generate the first location but then uses linked lists (see next chapter) to represent alternate locations. This approach is used by several database systems, notably TOTAL and IMAGE. A good summary of hashing can be found in [58].

Comparison of file organizations

In this section we have discussed sequential, indexed sequential, and direct file organizations. None of the three organizations is uniformly superior to the other two; each has its advantages and disadvantages as summarized in Figure 3-41. The analyst must determine which organization best meets the needs of a given situation.

VIRTUAL INPUT/OUTPUT

Since the development of sequential, indexed sequential, and direct file organizations, computer architectures and operating systems have been created that extend I/O processing capabilities beyond these basic capabilities. One type of new capability combines file processing techniques and provides capabilities to manage libraries of files. Since systems of this type extend traditional capabilities, we will term them *meta-access methods*. We will discuss IBM's VSAM as an example of such a system.

Another new development in file processing greatly separates programs from physical file locations. For this type of processing, the operating system stores records in whatever locations happen to be convenient. The concept of a file as a physically contiguous group of records disappears entirely. Not only logical but also physical file records are intermixed on the devices, and records in the same file may reside on several different volumes. The application program never knows the actual physical location of the data. We will call this type of processing *virtual input/output*, and also discuss it in this section.

Virtual storage access method

The *virtual storage access method* (VSAM) is a set of operating system programs that combines sequential, indexed sequential, and direct file processing under a common umbrella of services. See Figure 3-42. Additionally, VSAM

File Organization

	Sequential	Indexed Sequential	Direct
Advantages	Simple, easy programming Double buffering for I/O overlap commonly available Variable-length and blocked records easily accommodated Optimal use of peripheral storage space	Can update in middle of file Can insert in middle of file Can process both sequentially and randomly	Can update or insert in middle of file Programmer has control over record allocation Less system overhead than with indexed sequential
Disadvantages	Cannot insert in middle of file Cannot update in middle of file (in general)	Processing may be slow Unique keys required Periodic reorganization required Variable-length records difficult to process	Address calculation required Program must do own blocking, deblocking Variable-length records nearly impossible to process

Figure 3-41 Summary of File Organizations

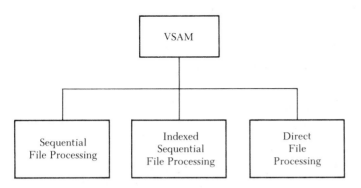

Figure 3-42 VSAM Meta-Access Method

creates independence between programs and devices. Application programs need not be concerned with characteristics of the device on which the file resides. VSAM will make necessary conversions.

Key— one specific field within each record of field.

A VSAM *entry sequenced data set* (ESDS) is created sequentially. Insertions are made only at the end of the file. With one exception, ESDS files are equivalent to sequential files as discussed in the last section. The exception is that indexes can be defined on ESDS files so that records can be located by either unique or nonunique key.

A VSAM *key sequenced data set* (KSDS) is functionally equivalent to an indexed sequential file. Both sequential and direct processing are possible, and insertions can be made in the middle or at the end of the file. Also, alternate indexes can be defined so that records may be located by supplemental unique or nonunique keys. Internally, KSDS files are organized differently from the indexed sequential files discussed previously and provide better space utilization.

VSAM's *relative record data sets* (RRDS) are functionally equivalent to direct files as discussed in the previous section. The file is organized as a collection of fixed-length buckets of data; each bucket is addressed by its relative position in the file. As with direct processing, no keys or indexes are provided by the operating system. The application program must make the conversion from logical content to relative record position.

In addition to these I/O capabilities, VSAM also provides an extensive cataloging service. This service can greatly simplify the management of large libraries of files. VSAM provides capabilities that fall between those of typical file organizations and those of database management. A VSAM library contains many different files just as a database does, but the relationships among the files are not represented.

Because of the catalogs, VSAM is able to take over many space management functions (the allocation of indexes, for example, in an indexed sequential file) in behalf of the user. Consequently, the use of VSAM considerably simplifies the user's job control language. Also, VSAM provides improved security.

Thus VSAM provides device-independent support for all of the three fundamental file organizations. A particular file, however, must be organized in just one way. In addition, VSAM provides extensive file library management services. VSAM has considerably more capability than a simple file organization method, yet not as much capability as a DBMS. Hence the term *meta-file organization*.

Other vendors provide products similar to VSAM. These systems can be very effective when requirements necessitate the management of large numbers of files, but when record relationships need not be represented.

Virtual input/output

Virtual I/O eliminates the concept of a physical file. Programs define and access logical files (collections of logical records), but these files are not associated with any particular physical file or location. With virtual I/O, only the operating system knows where or how data is physically located.

As a consequence, application programs cannot process records directly by relative block number or physical address. Instead, programs access records by their arrival sequence or by key. Thus an application program can access the first record stored, the next record stored, the last record stored, and so forth. The operating system will determine the volumes and the addresses on the volumes where those records happen to reside.

Similarly, one or more fields can be defined as a key. Records can then be accessed by key value. Again, however, the physical location of the data is unknown to the application program. To understand this concept more fully, consider the IBM System/38, which employs virtual I/O in its operation.

All programs and data in the System/38 are assigned a virtual address. This address has no physical meaning; it is simply a positional identifier. Addresses are specified by 48-bit numbers; they range from 0 to 281 trillion. A file is assigned to a 16-million-byte *segment* of this virtual address space. If the file is smaller than 16 million bytes, a portion of the address space is unused.

The address space is divided into 512-byte blocks called *pages*. A page of the virtual space can reside in main memory, it can reside on FBA direct access devices, or it can be unused. (Note that the length of System/38's pages and the length of blocks on FBA devices are the same.) If unused, the page does not physically exist anywhere. It is simply a virtual location that has been assigned to the file, if the file ever grows large enough to need it.

In Figure 3-43, file records are assigned to pages and locations within pages. Thus record A may be assigned to page N, bytes 0 through 100. Record B may be assigned to page N, bytes 300 through 400. Record C may be assigned to page M, bytes 200 through 400, and so forth.

When a record is needed, the System/38 obtains the record's virtual address and then determines if the page containing the record is in main memory (using, by the way, a hashing function). If not, the system brings the record into main memory.

This processing is transparent to the application program. The application program does not and cannot know either the virtual or the physical address of the record.

Virtual I/O file processing   Records are stored, or assigned to the virtual address space, in the order in which they are created. (Again, this implies nothing about the physical location of the data.) However, records can be accessed according to two types of *access path*. *Arrival sequence* processing means that the records are accessed according to their order of creation. Records can be accessed sequentially from first to last, or from last to first. They can also be accessed directly, by creation number. Thus the 10th record created can be accessed, or the 1768th record, and so forth.

Records can also be accessed in *key sequence* in either ascending or descending order. Also, the record having a particular key value can be accessed, or

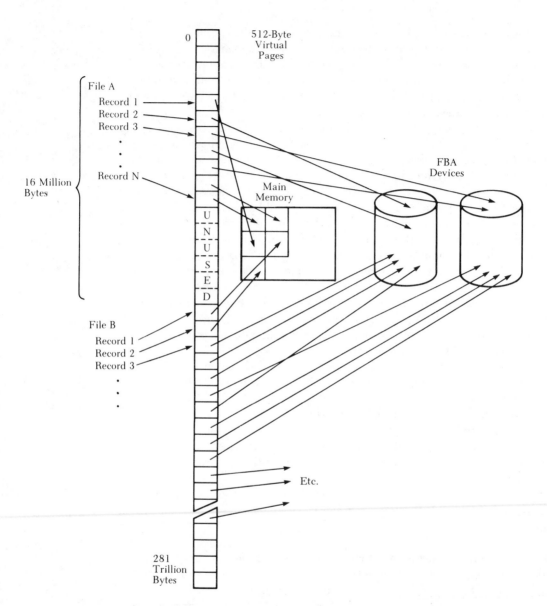

Figure 3-43 Virtual I/O Addressing

the record just prior to a key value or just after a key value can be accessed. Furthermore, one record can be accessed randomly, and records beyond that record accessed sequentially. Keys can be either unique or nonunique.

Keys in the System/38 are a group of one or more fields. For example, the key of a CUSTOMER record could be Customer-number. However, if customers have divisions, and each division has a record, then the key might be the combination of Customer-number and Division-number.

When keys are combinations of fields, the System/38 allows access by a portion of the key. For example, a program could access the first record for a given Customer-number, and then access all records for divisions of that customer. This method is called a *generic search* since it is a search for all records having a given property (the same Customer-number).

Using a concept called a *logical file*, the programmer can have multiple access paths to the same data. Thus the same file can be accessed in sequence by arrival position, in sequence by key, directly by arrival number, or directly by key or a portion of a key.

The System/38 uses these virtual I/O capabilities to provide a novel, interesting, and apparently useful style of database management. Since it is novel, however, discussions of it are inappropriate in an introductory database text such as this one. If you want further information, see [49] and [50].

By eliminating the concept of a physical file, virtual I/O represents a major extension of input/output processing. Most likely, this capability, or one similar to it, will form the foundation of I/O processing in operating systems of the future. We may expect someday that all operating systems will allow users to view data as they define it, but will store data in files (or, ultimately, on different computers) in a format and location that has nothing whatsoever to do with the logical format.

SUMMARY

This chapter has presented the fundamental concepts of I/O necessary for understanding database processing. We have discussed direct access devices, data formats, I/O operations, file organizations, and two new styles of file management.

The most commonly used direct access device is the conventional, or hard, disk. The time to process I/O requests on such a device has three components. Access motion time is the time required to move the access arm to the correct cylinder. Rotational delay is the time for the correct data to revolve under the read/write head. Data transfer time is the time needed to move the data between the disk and main memory.

The design and operation of disk devices imply considerations for DBMS processing. First, data that tends to be processed together should be located on the same cylinder. Second, physical records should be recorded on the disk in the same order in which they are used. Finally, if possible, data that is used together should be located in the same physical record.

There are a variety of data formats. The count, key, and data format is commonly used on IBM devices. There are gaps between each of these areas for timing purposes. Where possible, record length should be established so that physical records just fill up the track. Four record formats are common: fixed unblocked, fixed blocked, variable unblocked, and variable blocked. Fixed block architecture (FBA) is a new data format in which only fixed-length blocks are recorded on the disk devices.

Channels are small computers that transfer data between main memory and I/O control units. Channels can operate simultaneously with the CPU; throughput will be increased by maximizing this simultaneous activity. Anticipatory buffering with sequential files is one way of gaining such simultaneity.

There are three common file organizations: sequential, indexed sequential, and direct. Sequential files store data in the order in which it is written. Insertions can only be done on the end. To delete, modify, or insert in the middle of a sequential file, the entire file must be rewritten.

Indexed sequential files allow both sequential and direct access processing. Records can be inserted, deleted, and modified regardless of their position in the file. Indexes are created by the access method to allow direct retrieval by key value.

Direct files are collections of buckets or containers for data. Usually, direct records are addressed by their relative position. The application program must make the correspondence between relative position and key value. Sequential processing of a direct file is possible, but, unless the application program makes special provisions, the records will appear in no particular order.

Two types of file organizations have been developed that supplement these three fundamental types. Meta-access methods provide not only file organization and processing capability, but they also provide catalog and other services to assist in the management of large numbers of files. VSAM is an example of such a meta-access method. Virtual I/O is a style of file processing in which the concept of a physical file is eliminated. Instead, the operating system allocates records to whatever physical devices and locations it deems appropriate.

Group I Questions

Use the following data for questions 3.1 through 3.5:

The ABC 2000 disk drive has 300 cylinders per pack, 10 surfaces, and 20 tracks per cylinder. The average rotational delay is 10 ms, the time to move the access arm to an adjacent cylinder is 5 ms, and the average time to move the access arm to any cylinder is 10 ms. The time to transfer one byte of data is 0.001 ms. The ABC 2000 has 10,000 bytes per track.

3.1   A sequential file with 9000 records resides on an ABC 2000. Ten records can fit on a track. How many cylinders are required to hold the data? What is the total access motion time to read the file sequentially?

3.2   If the file in question 3.1 has records that are 900 bytes long and start at the beginning of the pack, how long will it take to read the entire file? Assume one-half rotation is required for each record.

3.3 Suppose four records fill a track of an ABC 2000 in the order ABCD.

    a. What is the largest the records could be?

    b. If one-half of the accesses of these records is in the order BCDA, one-fourth in the order BDCA, and one-fourth in the order ADCB, what is the average rotational delay?

3.4 Suppose a formula for computing the length of the number of records on an ABC 2000 is:

$$\text{Length} = 100 + (40 + RL + KL) \times NR$$

    where   RL = record length
               KL = key length
               NR = number of records

    a. How many bytes will ten 300-byte nonkeyed records occupy?

    b. How long will fifteen 200-byte keyed records be? Assume the keys are 20 bytes long.

3.5 For the data in question 3.4,

    a. How many 200-byte, nonkeyed records can fit on a track?

    b. How many 200-byte records, with keys of 20 bytes, can fit on a track?

    c. If there are to be exactly eight nonkeyed records on a track, how large can the records be?

    d. If there are to be exactly eight records with keys of 10 bytes, how large can the records be?

3.6 Suppose fifty-six 100-byte records or eleven 1000-byte records will fit on a track of a disk. How many cylinders does it take to hold five thousand 100-byte unblocked records? How many cylinders does it take to hold the same records blocked 10 per block? Explain the difference.

3.7 Suppose a file contains 100-byte fixed-length keyed records. If the first six records of the file have keys A, B, C, D, E, and F, sketch the layout of the first track for the following formats:

    a. Unblocked records

    b. Records blocked two per block

3.8 Sketch the track layout for the records in question 3.7 if the records do not have keys.

3.9 Suppose a file contains variable-length records. The first six records have keys and lengths as follows:

A	200
B	10
C	45
D	110
E	90
F	35

Assume the key field is 10 bytes long, the maximum block size is 300 bytes, and the records are not spanned.

a. Sketch the layout of the first track if the records are unblocked.

b. Repeat *a*, but assume the records are blocked.

3.10 Suppose an indexed sequential file has 12 unblocked fixed-length keyed records, arranged 3 per track. If the key of the first record is 5, that of the second is 10, and so on, by increments of 5, sketch the prime area. Sketch the track index.

3.11 For the file described in question 3.10, sketch the prime and overflow areas after each of the following actions occurs:

a. Record 22 is inserted.

b. Records 22 and 16 are inserted.

c. Records 22, 16, and 21 are inserted.

3.12 Under what conditions is it desirable to put the cylinder index and its associated track indexes on the same cylinder?

3.13 If the STUDENT file considered in this chapter is 60% dense, how many records should the file contain?

3.14 How must the hashing scheme be modified for the STUDENT file if it is 60% dense?

3.15 What modifications are required to the hashing algorithms in this chapter if the STUDENT file is 60% dense?

3.16 If records A, B, and C are synonyms, which record should be closest to its calculated address? How should the input file be sorted prior to loading the file?

3.17 Describe applications for which sequential, indexed sequential, and direct organizations are appropriate.

3.18 Describe applications for which sequential, indexed sequential, and direct organizations are not appropriate.

3.19 Explain the term *meta-access method*. What features does a meta-access method have that an access method does not?

3.20 Explain how VSAM differs from sequential, indexed sequential, and direct access processing.

3.21 Explain the term *virtual address*. Under what conditions can a virtual address be assigned but unused?

3.22 What is access by arrival sequence? Name an application for which this type of access would be useful.

3.23 Explain how keys can be composed of several fields. Describe an example. For your data, give an example of a generic search.

Group II Questions

3.24 Discuss the tradeoffs between a fixed-head unit with nonremovable disks and a movable-head unit with removable disks. How might a data center decide how many of each type to have?

3.25 Where should the most active data be located on a disk?

3.26 Outline a method by which a database system can search for a pattern in the user's access. Describe how this information can be used to optimally allocate data to secondary storage.

3.27 What would be the effects of eliminating the count area from records in a file?

3.28 Determine a formula for computing the number of keys per track in terms of gap length, key length, record length, and so forth.

3.29 Explain the advantages and disadvantages of spanned records.

3.30 What techniques besides anticipatory buffering can a program employ to know what data to preprocess?

3.31 In the multiprogramming environment, why worry about CPU/channel overlap for just one application?

3.32 Design a method other than the one described in this chapter for handling insertions in an indexed sequential file.

3.33 Construct a hashing scheme different from the one described in this chapter.

3.34 Describe in detail a procedure to select the best digits for a hash address.

3.35 Describe in detail methods for evaluating the merits of two hashing schemes.

3.36 Explain how the index of an indexed sequential file can be considered an extension of cross-reference-list addressing on a direct file.

3.37 Describe a method for processing synonyms that is different from the one described in this chapter.

Projects

A. Write a program to block and deblock fixed-length records using two buffers. Your program should have a write module that passes records one at a time to a blocking module. This module receives the records, blocks them, and, when a buffer is full, writes it and then switches buffers. When there are no more records, the write module should signal end-of-file in some way, and the blocking module should insert a special character at the start of the next record and write the last buffer. Your program should have a read module that calls a deblocking module for the records. The deblocking module fills the buffers and passes one record at a time back to the read module. When a buffer is empty, it reads the next block and switches buffers.

B. Do project A, but for variable-length unspanned records. Assume the maximum block size is 1000 bytes.

C. Do project B, but for variable-length spanned records.

D. Write a program to create and process an indexed sequential file of STUDENT records. Assume the records have a 6-byte Student-number, which is the key, a 20-byte Name field, and a 4-byte Major field. You should load the field, dump it sequentially, and then randomly insert, delete, replace, and read records. Finally, dump the file sequentially. Be sure your program can detect efforts to insert a record that is already on the file, or to delete or replace one that is not on the file.

E. Write a program to create and maintain a direct file of STUDENT records. Assume the records have a Student-number field (6 bytes), a Name field (20 bytes), and a Major field (4 bytes). Create 100 records on the direct file and use a hash addressing scheme on the Student-number field. The file is too dense if a record cannot be inserted in one of the 10 records past its calculated address. Insert, delete, read, and replace records. Be sure your program can "wrap around" the file, and can detect efforts to insert a record that is already there or to delete or replace one that is not.

4

Data Structures for Database Processing

The file organization methods presented in Chapter 3 are inadequate for database processing. A DBMS must provide services far beyond the capabilities of sequential, indexed sequential, and direct file organizations. To provide these services, DBMS products create and maintain specialized data structures. These data structures will be discussed in this chapter.

We begin by discussing flat files and problems that can occur when these files need to be processed in different orders. This leads to a discussion of three data structures that will be used again and again: sequential lists, linked lists, and inverted lists (indexes). Next, we consider relationships that can exist among records. Three fundamental types of relationship are defined, and the representation of these relationships using linked and inverted lists is shown. Finally, the representation and processing of multiple keys are discussed.

This is an important chapter. The knowledge you gain from this chapter will help you to design databases, to understand database models, and to evaluate the advantages and disadvantages of different DBMS products. Choose another chapter to read lightly; this one you need to read carefully and understand completely.

FLAT FILES

A *flat file* is a file that has no repeating groups. Consequently, flat files are fixed in length. Figure 4-1a shows a flat file; Figure 4-1b shows a file that is not flat because of the Item repeating field. A flat file can be stored using sequential, indexed sequential, or direct file organizations.

Flat files have been used in commercial processing for many years. Flat files are a durable and simple technique for storing data. Any of the file organizations discussed in Chapter 3 can be used to store flat files.

ENROLLMENT Record

Student-number	Class-number	Semester

Sample Data

200	70	83S
100	30	82F
300	20	82F
200	30	83S
300	70	83S
100	20	83S

a. A Flat File

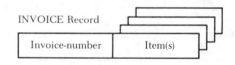

INVOICE Record

Invoice-number	Item(s)

Sample Data

1000	10	20	30	40
1010	50			
1020	10	20	30	
1030	50	90		

b. A Nonflat File

Figure 4-1   Examples of Flat and Nonflat Files

Processing flat files in multiple orders

Sometimes, however, users want to process a flat file in ways that are not readily supported by the file organizations in Chapter 3. Consider, for example, the ENROLLMENT records in Figure 4-1a. To produce student schedules, the records of this file must be processed in Student-number sequence. To produce class rosters, however, the records must be processed in Class-number sequence.

Clearly, these records can only be stored in one order, physically. They can be in order of Student-number or in order of Class-number, but not both at the same time. The traditional solution to the problem of producing both schedules and rosters is to sort the records in student order, process student schedules, sort the records in class order, and produce class rosters.

What happens, however, if both of these orders need to exist simultaneously? In this case, two copies of the ENROLLMENT file need to be created and sorted as shown in Figure 4-2. Since the data is listed in sequential order, this data structure is sometimes called a *sequential list*. Sequential lists may be stored using any of the three file organizations described in Chapter 3. Most commonly, they are stored using a sequential file organization.

Maintaining several orders by keeping multiple copies of the same sequential list is not usually effective. The duplicated sequential lists waste file space and create the potential for data integrity problems. Happily, there are other solutions. One method employs a data structure called *linked lists* and another uses *inverted lists*, or *indexes*. Before we discuss these structures, we need to make a digression to be more clear about record addressing.

Student-number	Class-number	Semester
100	30	82F
100	20	83S
200	70	83S
200	30	83S
300	20	82F
300	70	83S

a. Sorted by Student-number

Student-number	Class-number	Semester
300	20	82F
100	20	83S
100	30	82F
200	30	83S
200	70	83S
300	70	83S

b. Sorted by Class-number

Figure 4-2   ENROLLMENT Data Stored as Sequential Lists

A note on record addressing

Usually, the DBMS creates large physical records, or blocks, on its direct access files. These physical records are used as containers for logical records. There are typically many logical records per physical record. We will assume, realistically, that each physical record is addressed by its relative record number (RRN). Thus, a logical record might be assigned to physical record number 7 or 77 or 10,000. This relative record number is the logical record's physical address. If there is more than one logical record per physical record, the address will need to be expanded to specify where the logical record is located within the physical record. Thus the complete address for a logical record might be relative record 77, byte location 100. This means the record will begin in byte 100 of block 77.

To simplify illustrations in this text, we assume that there is only one logical record per physical record. Hence we need not be concerned with byte offsets within blocks. Every record begins in the first byte. This is unrealistic, but it simplifies the discussion to the essentials. Adding byte offsets to every record address would add little to your understanding of important issues.

Maintaining record order with linked lists

Linked lists can be used to keep records in logical order that are not necessarily in physical order. To create a linked list, a field is added to each record. This field is used to hold the address of the next record in the sequence. For example, in Figure 4-3, a linked list has been added to the ENROLLMENT records; this list maintains the records in Student-number order. Observe that the link for the last (alphabetically) student in the list is zero.

Relative Record Number	Student-number	Class-number	Semester	Link
1	200	70	83S	4
2	100	30	82F	6
3	300	20	82F	5
4	200	30	83S	3
5	300	70	83S	0
6	100	20	83S	1

Start of list = 2

Figure 4-3   ENROLLMENT Data Sorted by Student-number Using Linked Lists

Relative Record Number	Student-number	Class-number	Semester	Student Link	Class Link
1	200	70	83S	4	5
2	100	30	82F	6	1
3	300	20	82F	5	4
4	200	30	83S	3	2
5	300	70	83S	0	0
6	100	20	83S	1	3

Start of student list = 2
Start of class list = 6

Figure 4-4   ENROLLMENT Data Sorted Using Two Linked Lists

Figure 4-4 shows the ENROLLMENT records with two linked lists; one list maintains the Student-number order and the other list maintains the Class-number order. Two fields have been added to the records, one for each list.

When insertions and deletions are done, linked lists have great advantage over sequential lists. For example, to insert the ENROLLMENT record for student 200 and class 45, both of the lists in Figure 4-2 would need to be rewritten. (A gap would have to be created in both lists so that the new record could be inserted.) For the linked lists in Figure 4-4, however, the new record can be added at the end of the list; only two link fields need to be changed to place the new record in the correct sequences. These changes are shown in Figure 4-5.

Also, when a record is deleted, a gap would be created in the lists in Figures

Relative Record Number	Student-number	Class-number	Semester	Student Link	Class Link
1	200	70	83S	4	5
2	100	30	82F	6	7
3	300	20	82F	5	4
4	200	30	83S	7	2
5	300	70	83S	0	0
6	100	20	83S	1	3
7	200	45	83S	3	1

Start of student list = 2
Start of class list = 6

Figure 4-5   ENROLLMENT Data after Insertion of New Record (Sorted Using Two Linked Lists)

Relative Record Number	Student-number	Class-number	Semester	Student Link	Class Link
1	200	70	83S	7	5
2	100	30	82F	6	7
3	300	20	82F	5	2
4	200	30	83S	7	2
5	300	70	83S	0	0
6	100	20	83S	1	3
7	200	45	83S	3	1

Start of student list = 2
Start of class list = 6

Figure 4-6   ENROLLMENT Data after Deletion of Student 200, Class 30 (Sorted Using Two Linked Lists)

4-2 and 4-3. A record can be deleted from the linked list simply by changing pointer values. In Figure 4-6, the ENROLLMENT record for student 200, class 30 has been deleted. Even though the record still exists physically, since it has been removed from the lists, it has been deleted.

There are many linked list variations. We can make the list into a *circular list,* or *ring,* by changing the link of the last record from zero to make it point

Relative Record Number	Student-number	Class-number	Semester	Link
1	200	70	83S	4
2	100	30	82F	6
3	300	20	82F	5
4	200	30	83S	3
5	300	70	83S	2
6	100	20	83S	1

Start of list = 2

a. Circular Linked List

Relative Record Number	Student-number	Class-number	Semester	Ascending Link	Descending Link
1	200	70	83S	4	6
2	100	30	82F	6	0
3	300	20	82F	5	4
4	200	30	83S	3	1
5	300	70	83S	0	3
6	100	20	83S	1	2

Start of ascending list = 2
Start of descending list = 5

b. Two-way Linked List

Figure 4-7   ENROLLMENT Data Sorted by Student-number Using Circular and Two-way Linked Lists

to the first record in the list. Now we can reach every item on the list from any item on the list. Figure 4-7a shows a circular list for the Student-number order. Also, *a two-way linked list* has links for both directions. In Figure 4-7b, a two-way list has been created for ascending and descending student order.

Two-way lists have advantages over one-way lists. For one, they are easier to change since we can easily determine both the preceding and succeeding items in the list. Also, if we lose a pointer in a one-way list (due to a head crash or some other problem), we will be unable to reconstruct the list beyond the problem item. With a two-way list, however, we can reconstruct the entire list by processing the forward list down to the problem item and then processing the reverse list from the end up to the problem.

Records ordered using linked lists cannot be stored on a sequential file. Some type of direct access file organization is needed to be able to use the link values. Thus, either indexed sequential or direct file organizations are required for linked list processing. As mentioned in Chapter 3, DBMS nearly always use direct organization.

Maintaining record order with inverted lists

Record order can also be maintained using *inverted lists*, or as they are sometimes called, *indexes*. An inverted list is just a copy of the list which has been inverted (sorted) into the proper order and in which duplicated data has been replaced by links or pointers to the original list. A list of ENROLLMENT data is shown in Figure 4-8a; this list has been inverted on Student-number in Figure 4-8b, and the duplicated data in the inverted list has been replaced by links or pointers to the original file in Figure 4-8c.

Relative Record Number	Student-number	Class-number	Semester
1	200	70	83S
2	100	30	82F
3	300	20	82F
4	200	30	83S
5	300	70	83S
6	100	20	83S

a. ENROLLMENT Data

Student-number	Class-number	Semester
100	30	82F
100	20	83S
200	70	83S
200	30	83S
300	20	82F
300	70	83S

b. ENROLLMENT Data Inverted on Student-number

Student-number	Relative Record Number
100	2
100	6
200	1
200	4
300	3
300	5

c. Inverted List

Figure 4-8 Construction of an Inverted List

Student-number	Relative Record Number
100	2
100	6
200	1
200	4
300	3
300	5

Class-number	Relative Record Number
20	3
20	6
30	2
30	4
70	1
70	5

Figure 4-9   Two Inverted Lists for ENROLLMENT Data

The inverted list is simply an index on Student-numbers. Whereas the index of a book has topics and page numbers, the index in Figure 4-8c has Student-numbers and record numbers of those students' data. To process ENROLLMENT data sequentially, we just process the index sequentially, obtaining ENROLLMENT data by reading the records indicated in the links. Figure 4-9 shows two inverted lists for ENROLLMENT; one is for Student-number and the other is for Class-number. One list maintains the data in Student-number order and the other maintains the data in Class-number order.

To use an inverted list, the data to be ordered (here ENROLLMENT) must reside on an indexed sequential or direct file. The indexes, however, could reside on any type of file. In practice, almost all DBMS products keep both the data and the indexes on direct files. We will discuss the processing of inverted lists in greater detail when we discuss secondary keys.

Summary of data structures

Figure 4-10 summarizes techniques for maintaining ordered flat files. Three supporting data structures are possible. Sequential lists can be used, but data must be duplicated to maintain several orders. Both linked and inverted lists can be used without data duplication.

As shown in Figure 4-10, sequential lists can reside on any of the three types of file organizations discussed in Chapter 3. In practice, however, they are usually kept on sequential files. Additionally, while both linked and inverted lists can be stored using either indexed sequential or direct files, DBMS products almost always store them on files with direct organization.

OVERVIEW OF LOGICAL RECORD RELATIONSHIPS

If you ever design a database, you may need to specify the relationships that will exist among database records. As you talk with users, you will determine

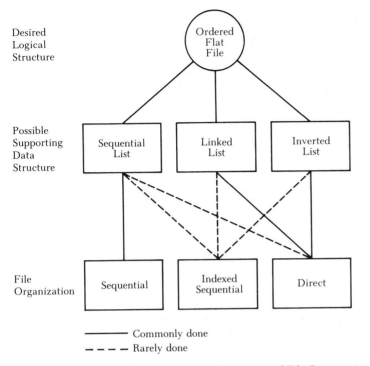

Figure 4-10   Summary of Supporting Data Structures and File Organization
for Ordered Flat Files

the requirements for their data. Most likely, there will be a large volume of data and a confusing array of record types. Specifying record relationships may become confusing. Your task will be simplified if you realize that there are three fundamental types of record relationships. These types are: tree (or hierarchy), simple network, and complex network. We will consider each of these types in turn.

Trees or hierarchies

A tree is a collection of records and one-to-many relationships among records. Figure 4-11 shows an example of a tree (sometimes also called a *hierarchy*). According to standard terminology, the records are called nodes, and the relationships between the records are called *branches*. The node at the top of the tree is called the *root* (what a metaphor—trees are normally shown upside down!). In Figure 4-11, node 1 is the root of the tree. Every node of a tree has a *parent*—the node immediately above it. Thus node 2 is the parent of node 5, node 4 is the parent of node 8, and so on. Trees are distinguished from other record relationships because *every node of a tree has exactly one parent* (except the root, which has no parent).

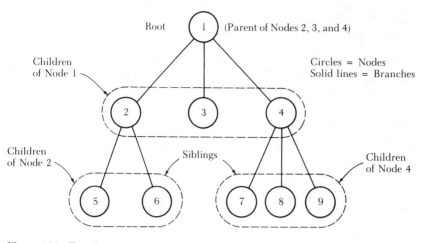

Figure 4-11   Tree Structure

The descendants of a node are called *children*. In general, there is no limitation on the number of children a node may have. Node 2 has two children—nodes 5 and 6; node 3 has no children; and node 4 has three children—nodes 7, 8, and 9. Nodes having the same parent are called *twins* or *siblings*.

To illustrate tree or hierarchical record relationships, consider an example involving faculty data. Suppose each faculty member has identifying data such as name and number. Additionally, each has job history data concerning previous jobs, and within each previous job, a salary history. Also, each faculty member has degree data and within each degree a listing of completed courses. Finally, suppose each has personal data such as spouse's name and names of children. These relationships are difficult to describe in words. They can, however, be easily represented by a tree; one occurrence of this tree is shown in Figure 4-12.

This tree is not a general description of the faculty data relationships. The tree shown indicates two job titles, two degrees, one and two salary records, and so forth. Figure 4-12 shows one occurrence, or one instance, of a faculty member's data. We want to portray the possibility of zero or more job titles, zero or more degrees, zero or more salary records, and so on. In other words, we want to portray a general form of the data.

One such general portrayal, attributed to Charles Bachman, is as follows: In a tree, a child can have only one parent. Consequently, the relationship from child to parent is always one-to-one. A parent can have many children, however, so the relationship from parent to child is one-to-many. We denote the relationship one-to-one by a single-headed arrow ($\rightarrow$) and the relationship one-to-many by a double-headed arrow ($\rightarrow\!\!\!\rightarrow$). Using this notation, a general description of faculty data is shown in Figure 4-13.

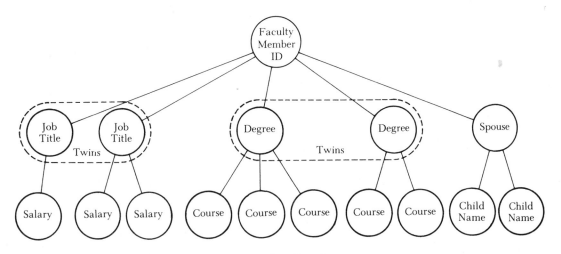

Figure 4-12   One Occurrence of a Faculty Member Database Record

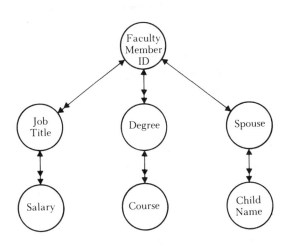

Figure 4-13   Schematic of Faculty Member Tree Structure

The double-headed arrow between faculty member ID and job title implies that there may be zero-to-many job titles. The single-headed arrow between ID and spouse implies there will be zero or one spouses. This raises an interesting point. In general, if a record does not exist, there can be no children of that record. Figure 4-13 implies that if there is no spouse, there can be no children. This is erroneous. A more accurate representation of the faculty mem-

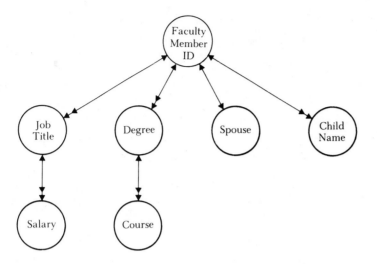

Figure 4-14 Schematic of Faculty Member Tree Structure (Revised)

ber data appears in Figure 4-14. Here, child names can exist even if a spouse node does not exist.

It is most important to distinguish between an *occurrence of a structure* and the *structure* itself. An occurrence is not a general structure; it is an example. Figure 4-12 is an example; Figure 4-13 is a structure. Throughout this book we will define structures and illustrate them with occurrences.

Simple networks

A simple network is also a collection of records and one-to-many relationships among records. For a simple network, however, a record may have more than one parent, as long as the parents are different types of records. For example,

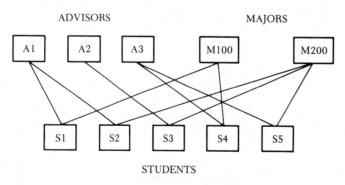

Figure 4-15 Occurrence of Simple Network

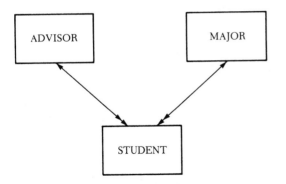

Figure 4-16   General Structure of a Simple Network

for the simple network in Figure 4-15, each STUDENT record has two parents. One of the parents is an ADVISOR record and the other is a MAJOR record. This would not be a simple network if the parents of STUDENT records were of the same type, say both ADVISOR records. Further, the data structure in Figure 4-15 is not a tree because STUDENT records have more than one parent.

Figure 4-16 shows the general structure of this simple network. Notice that all relationships are one-to-many, but that STUDENT has two parents. In this figure the parent records are on top and the children records are beneath the parents. This arrangement is convenient but inessential. You may see simple networks depicted with parents beside or below the children. You can identify simple networks in such arrangements by the fact that a single record type participates as a child in two (or more) one-to-many relationships.

Complex networks

A complex network is also a collection of records and relationships. The relationships, however, are many-to-many instead of one-to-many. To understand this, consider the complex network in Figure 4-17. Here, a student is enrolled in many classes (student A, for example, is enrolled in classes 1, 3, and 6). At the same time, a class is composed of many students (class 1 is composed of

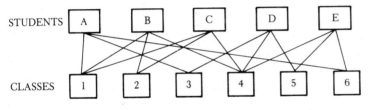

Figure 4-17   Occurrence of STUDENT/CLASS Complex Network

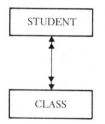

Figure 4-18 Schematic of STUDENT/CLASS
Complex Network

students A, B, and C). Thus the relationship between STUDENT and CLASS records is one-to-many in both directions, or put differently, many-to-many. The general structure of this relationship is shown in Figure 4-18.

With a many-to-many relationship, the parent/child terminology breaks down. It becomes arbitrary which record type is the parent and which is the child. Suppose we call STUDENT records the parents. Then we can say that CLASS records have many parents, and, unlike a simple network, the parents are of the same type. In Figure 4-17, for example, all of the parents of a CLASS record are STUDENT records.

Trees, simple networks, and complex networks are the fundamental record relationships. In the next three sections, we will discuss techniques for representing these three types of relationship.

PHYSICAL REPRESENTATIONS OF TREE RELATIONSHIPS

There are many ways of representing tree (hierarchical) record relationships. In this section we will describe and illustrate techniques using sequential, linked, and inverted lists. All of these techniques are used by commercial DBMS, although the linked list technique is by far the most common.

Sequential list representation of trees

To represent a tree in a sequential list, we just decompose the tree in some orderly fashion. One way, called *preorder traversal,* is to descend from the root as far as possible along the leftmost branches and list each node as it is encountered. This listing produces the list ABD for the tree in Figure 4-19. When the bottom is reached, we back up one level and descend the next branch as far as possible. When there are no more branches under the root, we stop. This results in the order ABD-EI-J-K-F-CG-H for the tree in Figure 4-19. Other methods for decomposing trees employ postorder and endorder traversal. See [56].

In practice, trees are seldom stored as sequential lists. Processing them sequentially is difficult at best since nodes cannot easily be added or deleted from a sequential listing. Usually some form of linked or indexed list is used instead.

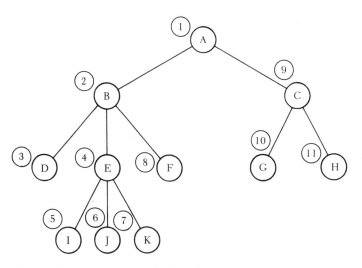

Figure 4-19   An Occurrence of a Tree Structure

Linked list representation of trees

Figure 4-20 shows a tree structure involving VENDOR records as parents, and INVOICE records as children. Figure 4-21 shows two occurrences of this structure. In Figure 4-22, all of the VENDOR and INVOICE records have been written to a direct access file. VENDOR AA is in relative record 1, and VENDOR BB is in relative record 2. The invoice records have been assigned to file records as illustrated. Note these records are not sorted, nor do they need to be.

Now, the problem is that we cannot tell from this file which invoices correspond to which vendors. To solve this problem, we will add a link field to every record in the file. In this field we will store addresses or *pointers* to other

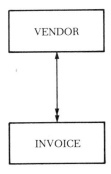

Figure 4-20   Sample Tree Relating VENDOR
and INVOICE Records

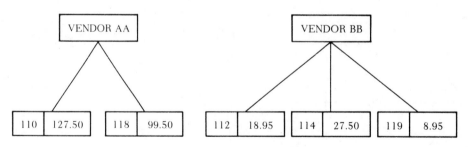

Figure 4-21   Two Occurrences of VENDOR-INVOICE Tree

Relative Record Number	Record Contents	
1	VENDOR AA	
2	VENDOR BB	
3	118	99.50
4	119	8.95
5	112	18.95
6	114	27.50
7	110	127.50

Relative Record Number	Record Contents		Link Field
1	VENDOR AA		7
2	VENDOR BB		5
3	118	99.50	0
4	119	8.95	0
5	112	18.95	6
6	114	27.50	4
7	110	127.50	3

Figure 4-22   File Representation of Trees in Figure 4-21

Figure 4-23   Tree Occurrences Represented by Linked Lists

records. We will make the record for **VENDOR AA** point to the first invoice belonging to AA. This is relative record number 7, which is INVOICE 110. Then, we will make relative record 7, in turn, point to AA's next child, which is INVOICE 118 at relative record 3. There are no more children for AA, so we insert a 0 in the link field of record 3. The zero is a signal that no more children exist for AA.

This technique is shown in Figure 4-23. If you examine the figure carefully, you will see that a similar technique has been used for **VENDOR BB**. This scheme is quite similar to the linked list used to order the flat file discussed earlier in this chapter.

The structure in Figure 4-23 will be much easier to modify than a sequential list of the tree. For example, suppose we add a new invoice, say number 111, to **VENDOR AA**. To do this, we just add the record to the file and insert it on the linked list. But, where should we put it? It could go first on the list, last, or somewhere in between. For this example, let's assume the children are to be kept in ascending order of invoice. In that case, INVOICE 111 should come between INVOICEs 110 and 118. We need to make INVOICE 110 point to

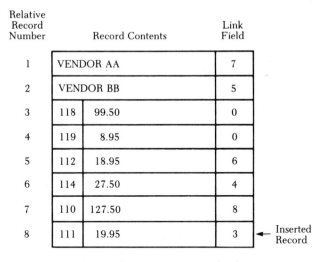

Relative Record Number	Record Contents		Link Field
1	VENDOR AA		7
2	VENDOR BB		5
3	118	99.50	0
4	119	8.95	0
5	112	18.95	6
6	114	27.50	4
7	110	127.50	8
8	111	19.95	3	← Inserted Record

Figure 4-24   Insertion of INVOICE 111 to File of Figure 4-23

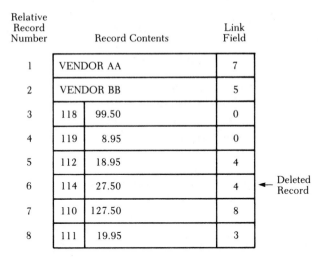

Relative Record Number	Record Contents		Link Field
1	VENDOR AA		7
2	VENDOR BB		5
3	118	99.50	0
4	119	8.95	0
5	112	18.95	4
6	114	27.50	4	← Deleted Record
7	110	127.50	8
8	111	19.95	3

Figure 4-25   Deletion of INVOICE 114 to File of Figure 4-24

INVOICE 111 (at record 8), and we need to make INVOICE 111, the new invoice, point to INVOICE 118 (at record 3). This modification is shown in Figure 4-24.

Similarly, deleting an invoice is easy. If INVOICE 114 is deleted, we just need to change the pointer in the invoice that is pointing at 114 (INVOICE 112 at record 5 in this case). We will give INVOICE 112 the pointer that INVOICE 114 had before deletion. In this way, record 112 will point directly to INVOICE 119. This change is shown for the data in Figure 4-25. Note that we created an unused record, or *garbage*, at record 6. Shortly we will see how to collect this garbage using another linked list.

Relative Record Number	Record Contents		Link Field	Reverse Link Field
1	VENDOR AA		7	3
2	VENDOR BB		5	4
3	118	99.50	1	8
4	119	8.95	2	6
5	112	18.95	6	2
6	114	27.50	4	5
7	110	127.50	8	1
8	111	19.95	3	7

Figure 4-26 Two-way Circular Linked List

Extensions to a one-way linked list The linked lists shown in Figures 4-23 through 4-25 can be extended in several ways. For one, we can make it into a circular linked list as discussed earlier. Also, we can add another set of link pointers to create a two-way list as shown in Figure 4-26.

In all the examples so far, there is no direct way to get back to the parent. For the circular or two-way lists, we can follow a list around until we get back to the parent. However, this sequence may be a long one. An alternative would be to add a parent pointer to every record on the list. Records with parent pointers are shown in Figure 4-27. Each record in this file has three different pointers: one forward, one reverse, and one parent.

In the examples given, the tree is a simple one, with a single one-to-many relationship. You may be wondering what we can do if the tree is more complex. Figure 4-28 presents a more complex tree. Here, we have VENDOR, INVOICE, INVOICE-ITEM, and PAYMENT records.

To represent this hierarchy with linked lists, we simply create a list for every one-to-many relationship. This technique is illustrated in Figure 4-29. Each arrow in this figure represents a link or pointer. The arrows mean that the address of the record being pointed to is stored in the record from which the arrow emerges.

Since the VENDOR is the parent of children in two one-to-many relationships (INVOICE and PAYMENT), it will have two sets of pointers (assuming a one-way list—there would be four pointers if the lists were two-way, and six if there were also parent pointers). INVOICE records participate in two one-to-many relationships. They are children in the relationship with VENDOR records, and they are parents in the relationship with INVOICE-ITEM records. Thus

Relative Record Number	Record Contents		Link Field	Reverse Link Field	Parent Link Field
1	VENDOR AA		7	3	
2	VENDOR BB		5	4	
3	118	99.50	1	8	1
4	119	8.95	2	6	2
5	112	18.95	6	2	2
6	114	27.50	4	5	2
7	110	127.50	8	1	1
8	111	19.95	3	7	1

Figure 4-27   Two-way Circular Linked List with Parent Pointers

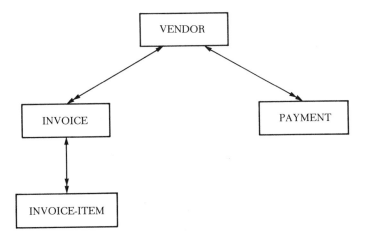

Figure 4-28   Tree with Three One-to-Many Relationships

INVOICE records will also have two sets of pointers. Finally, both INVOICE-ITEM and PAYMENT records will have a single set of pointers.

Figure 4-30 shows a direct access file containing the two occurrences shown in Figure 4-29. VENDOR records contain two pointers. The lefthand pointer contains the address of the first INVOICE child and the righthand pointer contains the address of the first PAYMENT child. INVOICE records also have two pointers. The lefthand pointer contains the address of the first ITEM child

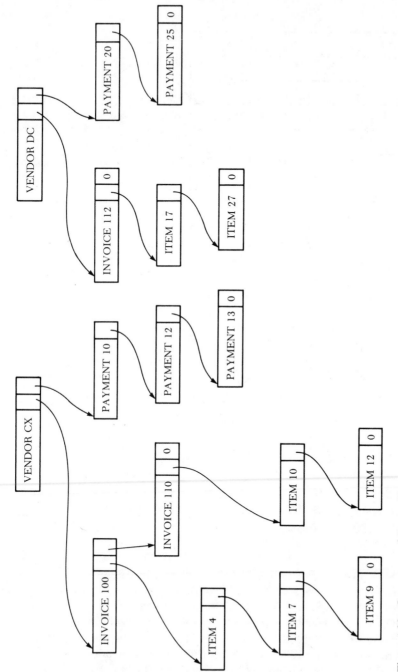

Figure 4-29 Occurrence of Tree in Figure 4-28

Relative Record Number	Record Contents	Link Fields	
1	VENDOR CX	4	5
2	VENDOR DC	6	15
3	PAYMENT 13		0
4	INVOICE 100	13	10
5	PAYMENT 10		7
6	INVOICE 112	12	0
7	PAYMENT 12		3
8	ITEM 7		17
9	ITEM 10		14
10	INVOICE 110	9	0
11	PAYMENT 25		0
12	ITEM 17		16
13	ITEM 4		8
14	ITEM 12		0
15	PAYMENT 20		11
16	ITEM 27		0
17	ITEM 9		0

Figure 4-30   Direct File Representation of Occurrences in Figure 4-29

and the righthand pointer contains the address of the next INVOICE sibling. PAYMENT and ITEM records use just one pointer. It contains the address of siblings. Study Figure 4-30 carefully to be certain you understand the role and meaning of each of the pointers.

Algorithms for processing a one-way linked list   So far we have illustrated techniques for creating and processing a linked list in an informal way. Now we will present algorithms for maintaining a one-way linked list.

Assume we have a tree with a single one-to-many relationship between vendors and invoices (Figure 4-20). Also, assume we have a direct file containing 15 records addressed by relative record number. We will place one VENDOR or one INVOICE record in each of these physical records. Finally, assume we

Relative Record Number	Record Contents	Link Field
1	VENDOR AA	0
2	VENDOR BB	0
3	Unused	4
4	Unused	5
5	Unused	6
6	Unused	7
7	Unused	8
8	Unused	9
9	Unused	10
10	Unused	11
11	Unused	12
12	Unused	13
13	Unused	14
14	Unused	0
15	Unused Record Pointer	3

Figure 4-31   File with Linked List of Unused Records

have two vendors, AA and BB, and these two vendors are assigned record locations 1 and 2. Initially, no invoices are assigned to the vendors. See Figure 4-31.

Before we assign invoices to vendors and build the linked lists, we need to have some way of identifying the file records that are unused. When we make an insertion, we need to know which file locations are available to hold the new record. One simple way to keep track of unused locations is to build an *unused chain,* or a linked list of unused records. To build an unused chain, we will reserve the last record in the file for a special purpose. The last record will be the head of a list of unused file locations. Its link will point to an unused record. Therefore, in Figure 4-31, record 15 points to record 3, the first unused record.

Record 3, in turn, points to record 4, another unused record, which points to record 5, which points to record 6, and so forth down to record 14. Record 14 has a 0 in its link field indicating that there are no more unused records. The order of the unused records has no meaning; we could have as easily started at record 14 and worked backwards, or collected the records in a random fashion.

Assume INVOICE 118 is to be assigned to VENDOR AA. An unused record must be taken off the unused chain, filled with data, and inserted on the used chain. Consequently, record 3 (the first unused record) is read into memory, and the pointer in record 15 (the unused header) is updated by setting it equal to the link field in record 3. This field contains 4, which is a pointer to the next unused record. Thus, record 15 now points to the current start of the unused list, record 4.

Next, record 3 is filled with INVOICE 118 and is inserted on the linked list for VENDOR AA. To do this, VENDOR AA's record is read, and since its pointer is 0, this means there are no invoices currently on the chain. Therefore, the pointer in VENDOR AA's record is set to 3 to point to the new INVOICE 118. Also, the pointer in INVOICE 118 is set to 0 to indicate it is the end of the list. The file appears as in Figure 4-32a.

Relative Record Number	Record Contents	Link Field
1	VENDOR AA	3
2	VENDOR BB	0
3	INVOICE 118	0
4	Unused	5
5	Unused	6
6	Unused	7
7	Unused	8
8	Unused	9
9	Unused	10
10	Unused	11
11	Unused	12
12	Unused	13
13	Unused	14
14	Unused	0
15	Unused Record Pointer	4

a. File with INVOICE 118 Inserted

Relative Record Number	Record Contents	Link Field
1	VENDOR AA	4
2	VENDOR BB	0
3	INVOICE 118	0
4	INVOICE 110	3
5	Unused	6
6	Unused	7
7	Unused	8
8	Unused	9
9	Unused	10
10	Unused	11
11	Unused	12
12	Unused	13
13	Unused	14
14	Unused	0
15	Unused Record Pointer	5

b. File with Two Invoices Inserted

Figure 4-32   File with Insertions and Deletions

Relative Record Number	Record Contents	Link Field
1	VENDOR AA	4
2	VENDOR BB	7
3	INVOICE 118	0
4	INVOICE 110	3
5	INVOICE 114	6
6	INVOICE 119	0
7	INVOICE 112	5
8	Unused	9
9	Unused	10
10	Unused	11
11	Unused	12
12	Unused	13
13	Unused	14
14	Unused	0
15	Unused Record Pointer	8

c. File after Five Insertions

Figure 4-32   (Cont'd.)

Now, assume invoice 110 is to be added to VENDOR AA's chain. Again, an unused record (record 4) is removed from the unused list, and the record is filled with INVOICE 110. To insert the new invoice on AA's chain, we start at AA, read the first invoice on the chain (record 3) and ask, Should the new invoice come before the invoice just read? In this case, it should. INVOICE 110 comes before INVOICE 118. Therefore, we move the pointer from VENDOR AA's record to INVOICE 110. Then we insert INVOICE 110's address into VENDOR AA's record. The result of this activity is shown in Figure 4-32b.

Figure 4-32c shows the file after INVOICEs 112, 114, and 119 have been inserted on VENDOR BB's chain. Note the unused pointer in record 15 has been updated. Can you tell from the appearance of this file the order in which the invoices were inserted?

Now consider a deletion. Suppose INVOICE 114 is to be deleted. In this case, the pointer in INVOICE 112 needs to be changed to skip over INVOICE

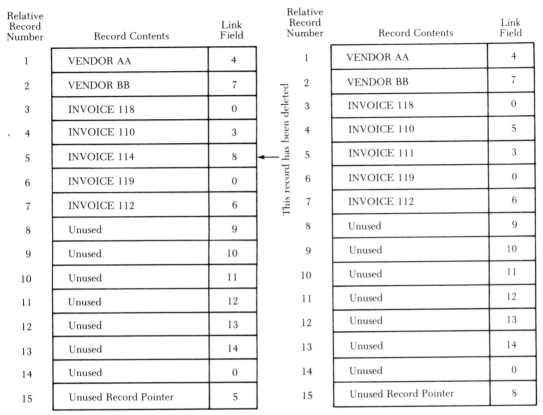

Relative Record Number	Record Contents	Link Field		Relative Record Number	Record Contents	Link Field
1	VENDOR AA	4		1	VENDOR AA	4
2	VENDOR BB	7		2	VENDOR BB	7
3	INVOICE 118	0		3	INVOICE 118	0
4	INVOICE 110	3		4	INVOICE 110	5
5	INVOICE 114	8	This record has been deleted	5	INVOICE 111	3
6	INVOICE 119	0		6	INVOICE 119	0
7	INVOICE 112	6		7	INVOICE 112	6
8	Unused	9		8	Unused	9
9	Unused	10		9	Unused	10
10	Unused	11		10	Unused	11
11	Unused	12		11	Unused	12
12	Unused	13		12	Unused	13
13	Unused	14		13	Unused	14
14	Unused	0		14	Unused	0
15	Unused Record Pointer	5		15	Unused Record Pointer	8

d. File after One Deletion

e. File after Next Insertion

Figure 4-32   (Cont'd.)

114. This change can be made by moving the pointer in INVOICE 114 to INVOICE 112. In this way, INVOICE 112 now points to INVOICE 119.

Once INVOICE 114 is deleted, its record (number 5) must be returned to the unused chain. Record 5 can be returned by moving the link field in record 15 to record 5. Then we set the link of record 15 equal to 5. See Figure 4-32d. In general, to place a record back on the unused chain, we move the pointer in record 15 to the link of the new unused record, and set the pointer in record 15 to the new unused record.

Suppose we now add INVOICE 111 to VENDOR AA. We will place 111 in the first unused record, which is now number 5. The file at this point is shown in Figure 4-32e.

An algorithm for processing this example appears in Figure 4-33. For the sake of simplicity, this algorithm assumes there will only be two vendors, AA and BB. A more realistic algorithm would allow for a variable number of vendors

```
        BEGIN VENDOR-INVOICE-LINK-PROCEDURE
             DO INITIALIZE
             DOWHILE OP-CODE NOT ="STOP"
                  IF OP-CODE = "I"
                       THEN DO INSERT
                       ELSE IF OP-CODE ="D"
                            THEN DO DELETE
                            ELSE WRITE "INVALID OP-CODE" ON PRINT FILE
                       END-IF
                  END-IF
                  READ OP-CODE, INVOICE-DATA, VENDOR-PARENT FROM DATA FILE
                  IF VENDOR-PARENT ="AA"
                       THEN P-REC = 1         /Record 1 is parent record./
                       ELSE P-REC = 2         /Assume, since parent not record 1,
                                               must be record 2./
                  END-IF
             END-DO
             CLOSE DATA, DIRECT, PRINT FILES
        END VENDOR-INVOICE-LINK-PROCEDURE
        *  *  *  *  *  *  *  *  *  *  *  *  *  *  *  *  *  *  *  *  *  *  *  *
        BEGIN INITIALIZE
             OPEN DATA, DIRECT, AND PRINT FILES
                  /Note:  B1 and B2 are buffers used to hold data for I/O to and from
                  DIRECT FILE.  Each buffer has a data field and a link field./
             READ VENDOR AA DATA INTO B1
             SET LINK(B1) = 0
             WRITE B1 TO DIRECT FILE RECORD 1
             READ VENDOR BB DATA INTO B1
             SET LINK(B1) = 0
             WRITE B1 TO DIRECT FILE RECORD 2
             DO FOR I = 3 TO 15
                  SET LINK(B1) = I + 1
                  WRITE B1 TO DIRECT FILE RECORD I
             END-DO
             SET LINK(B1) = 0
             WRITE B1 TO DIRECT FILE RECORD 14
             SET LINK(B1) = 3
             SET DATA (B1) = "UNUSED RECORD POINTER"
             WRITE B1 TO DIRECT FILE RECORD 15
                  /Note:  At this point, the file looks like Figure 4-31/
```

Figure 4-33 Algorithm for Processing the Linked List in Figure 4-32

```
          READ OP-CODE, INVOICE-DATA, VENDOR-PARENT FROM DATA FILE
          IF VENDOR-PARENT = "AA"
                THEN P-REC = 1          /Record 1 is parent record./
                ELSE P-REC = 2
          END-IF
     END INITIALIZE
*  *  *  *  *  *  *  *  *  *  *  *  *  *  *  *  *  *  *  *  *  *  *  *  *  *  *

BEGIN INSERT
     READ DIRECT FILE RECORD 15 INTO B1
     IF LINK(B1) = 0
          THEN WRITE "ERROR, NO ROOM IN FILE" ON PRINT FILE
          ELSE NEW-REC = LINK(B1)
                READ DIRECT FILE RECORD NEW-REC INTO B2
                LINK(B1) = LINK(B2)
                WRITE DIRECT FILE RECORD 15 FROM B1
                READ DIRECT FILE RECORD P-REC INTO B1
                /The vendor record is now in buffer B1./
                IF LINK(B1) NOT = 0
                     THEN DO INSERT-PROCESS
                     ELSE /Chain currently empty, insert first record./
                          LINK(B1) = NEW-REC
                          WRITE DIRECT FILE RECORD P-REC FROM B1
                          /This returns vendor record with correct pointer./
                          MOVE NEW INVOICE DATA TO B2
                          LINK(B2) = 0
                          WRITE DIRECT FILE RECORD NEW-REC FROM B2
                END-IF
     END-IF
END INSERT
*  *  *  *  *  *  *  *  *  *  *  *  *  *  *  *  *  *  *  *  *  *  *  *  *  *  *

BEGIN INSERT-PROCESS
     PRIOR = P-REC
     NEXT = LINK(B1)
     SUCCESS-FLAG = 0
     DOWHILE NEXT GREATER THAN 0 AND SUCCESS-FLAG = 0
          READ DIRECT FILE RECORD NEXT INTO B2
          IF NEW INVOICE-NUMBER IS LESS THAN INVOICE-NUMBER(B2)
                THEN /New record goes between PRIOR and NEXT./
```

Figure 4-33   (Cont'd.)

```
                              LINK(B1) = NEW-REC
                              WRITE DIRECT FILE RECORD PRIOR FROM B1
                              /Now fill and write NEW-REC.  NEXT goes to the link field./
                              MOVE NEW INVOICE DATA TO B1.
                              LINK(B1) = NEXT
                              WRITE DIRECT FILE RECORD NEW-REC FROM B1
                              SUCCESS-FLAG = 1
                       ELSE  /Move to next item on chain.  Save B2 data in B1./
                              MOVE DATA AND LINK IN B2 TO B1
                              PRIOR = NEXT
                              NEXT = LINK(B2)
                 END-IF
           END-DO
           IF SUCCESS-FLAG = 0
                 THEN /NEW-REC goes at end of chain./
                       LINK(B1) = NEW-REC
                       WRITE DIRECT FILE RECORD PRIOR FROM B1
                       MOVE NEW INVOICE DATA TO B1
                       LINK(B1) = 0
                       WRITE DIRECT FILE RECORD NEW-REC FROM B1
           END-IF
     END INSERT-PROCESS


     *  *  *  *  *  *  *  *  *  *  *  *  *  *  *  *  *  *  *  *  *  *  *  *  *


     BEGIN DELETE
           READ DIRECT FILE RECORD P-REC INTO B1
           IF LINK(B1) = 0
                 THEN WRITE "ERROR, NO RECORDS FOR THIS VENDOR" ON PRINT FILE
                 ELSE DO DELETE-PROCESS
           END-IF
     END DELETE
```

Figure 4-33   (Cont'd.)

```
BEGIN DELETE-PROCESS
      PRIOR = P-REC
      NEXT = LINK(B1)
      MATCH-FLAG = 0
      DO WHILE MATCH-FLAG = 0 AND NEXT NOT = 0
            READ DIRECT FILE RECORD NEXT INTO B2
            IF INVOICE-NUMBER = INVOICE-NUMBER(B2)
                  THEN MATCH-FLAG = 1
                  ELSE /Move down chain, save NEXT record's data./
                        PRIOR = NEXT
                        NEXT = LINK(B2)
                        MOVE DATA IN B2 TO B1
            END-IF
      END-DO
      IF MATCH-FLAG = 1
            THEN /NEXT is record to be deleted./
                        THEN /Delete first record./
                              LINK(B1) = 0      /This will be the link in the VENDOR
                                                record./
                  LINK(B1) = LINK(B2)
                  WRITE DIRECT FILE RECORD PRIOR FROM B1
                  END-IF
                  /Put NEXT into unused chain./
                  READ DIRECT FILE RECORD 15 INTO B1
                  LINK(B2) = LINK(B1)
                  LINK(B1) = NEXT
                  WRITE DIRECT FILE RECORD 15 FROM B1
                  WRITE DIRECT FILE RECORD NEXT FROM B2
            ELSE WRITE "RECORD NOT ON FILE" ON PRINT FILE
      END-IF
END DELETE-PROCESS
```

Figure 4-33   (Cont'd.)

and would provide for a way of locating vendors in the file. Inserting this logic into Figure 4-33 would make the algorithm unnecessarily complex for our purposes, so we do not insert it.

The control module calls the initialization procedure and then invokes the INSERT or DELETE procedure depending on the operation code. INITIAL-IZE opens files and creates the initial file in the form of Figure 4-31.

There are five valid situations that may arise when inserting a record:

a. The vendor has no invoices and the chain is empty. The new record will be the only one on the chain.
b. The new invoice will be the last on the chain.
c. The new invoice will be the first on the chain.
d. The new invoice will be in the middle of the chain.
e. There is no room in the file for the new invoice.

Using sample data, you should verify that the INSERT procedure will correctly process all five of these conditions.

Similarly, there are four valid situations that can occur when deleting a record:

a. The invoice is the only one on the chain.
b. The invoice to be deleted is the last one on the chain.
c. The invoice to be deleted is the first one on the chain.
d. The invoice to be deleted is in the middle of the chain.

Again, use sample data to verify that the DELETE procedure will correctly process all of these conditions.

Developing an algorithm for sequentially reading the invoice chain is relatively straightforward. It is left to the reader as an exercise.

Inverted list representation of trees

A tree structure can readily be represented using inverted lists. The technique involves storing each one-to-many relationship as an inverted list. These lists are then used to match parents and children.

Assume the tree in Figure 4-20 is stored on a direct file as shown in Figure 4-23. VENDOR AA (in relative record 1) has INVOICEs 110 (in relative record 7) and 118 (in relative record 3) as children. Thus relative record 1 is the parent of relative records 7 and 3. We can represent this fact with an inverted list as shown in Figure 4-34. This list simply associates the parent relative record number with the child relative record number.

If the tree has several one-to-many relationships (Figure 4-28), then several inverted lists will be required—one for each relationship. For the structure in Figure 4-28, three inverted lists will be required—one for the relationship between VENDOR and INVOICE records, one for the relationship between INVOICE and INVOICE-ITEM records, and one for the relationship between VENDOR and PAYMENT records.

Inverted list techniques will be discussed in greater detail in the secondary-key section of this chapter.

PARENT Record	CHILD Record
1	7
1	3
2	5
2	6
2	4

Figure 4-34   Inverted List Representation of VENDOR-
INVOICE Relationship

PHYSICAL REPRESENTATIONS OF SIMPLE NETWORKS

As with trees, simple networks can also be physically represented using sequential, linked, and inverted lists. To represent a simple network using sequential lists, the simple network would first be decomposed into trees and each tree would be represented with a sequential list as described in the last section. Although this application of sequential lists is possible, it is never done. Instead, linked or inverted lists are used. Consequently, this section focuses on linked and inverted list techniques.

Simple network decomposition

Consider the simple network in Figure 4-35. It is a simple network because SHIPMENT records have two parents—but of different types. Each SHIPMENT has a CUSTOMER parent and a TRUCK parent. The relationship from CUSTOMER to SHIPMENT is one-to-many because customers can have several shipments. The relationship from TRUCK to SHIPMENT is one-to-many because one truck can contain many shipments (assume shipments are small

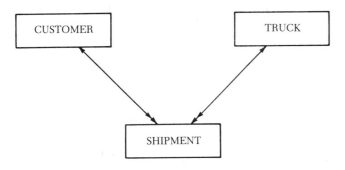

Figure 4-35   Simple Network Structure

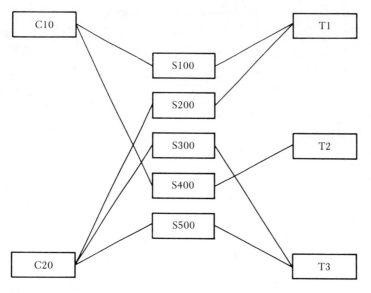

Figure 4-36 Occurrence of Simple Network in Figure 4-35

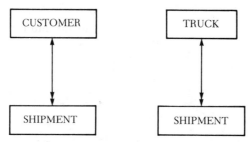

a. Tree Decomposition of Simple Network

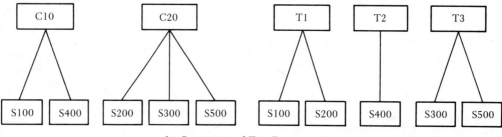

b. Occurrence of Tree Decomposition

Figure 4-37 Simple Network Decomposition

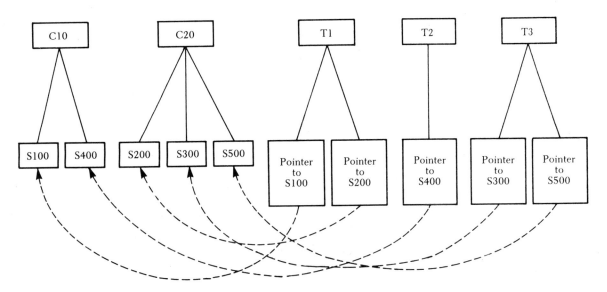

Figure 4-38   Tree Decomposition with Duplication Removed

enough to fit in one truck or less). An occurrence of this structure is shown in Figure 4-36.

One way to represent this simple network is to break it up into trees. We will have two trees: one between customers and shipments and one between trucks and shipments. Figure 4-37a shows the logical structure, and Figure 4-37b shows an occurrence using the data from Figure 4-36.

The disadvantage of decomposing this simple network into trees is that shipment data is duplicated. Each SHIPMENT occurs in two separate trees; one has a CUSTOMER parent and the other has a TRUCK parent. When we store this data on a file, the SHIPMENT data will appear twice.

To overcome this disadvantage, we need to eliminate the duplicated data. We can do this using pointers as follows:. We store the data once, and when there are other references to the data, instead of duplicating it, we insert a pointer to the record where the data actually exists. In Figure 4-38, all of the children of the TRUCK records are pointers to the real data. Figure 4-39 shows the occurrence in Figure 4-38 on a direct file. All of the TRUCK children are pointers to the real shipment data. Note that each pointer type record has two pointers. One pointer indicates where the real data will be found, and the other pointer shows which record is the next child of the TRUCK record.

This technique will work in the general case. Simple networks can always be decomposed into trees with duplication, and we can always eliminate the duplication with pointers. This strategy is used by a popular commercial database system called IMS. However, there is a more simple and straightforward technique.

Relative Record Number	Record Contents	Link Field
1	C10	6
2	C20	7
3	T1	11
4	T2	14
5	T3	13
6	S100	9
7	S200	8
8	S300	10
9	S400	0
10	S500	0
11	Pointer to S100 = 6	12
12	Pointer to S200 = 7	0
13	Pointer to S300 = 8	15
14	Pointer to S400 = 9	0
15	Pointer to S500 = 10	0

Figure 4-39 File Containing Tree Decomposition with Duplication Removed

Linked lists without decomposition

When we discussed using linked lists to represent trees, we discovered that we needed to create one set of pointers for each one-to-many relationship. We can use exactly the same technique for simple networks. Just represent each one-to-many relationship with a set of links.

Consider the structure of customers, trucks, and shipments in Figure 4-35. We can link CUSTOMER records to SHIPMENTs using one linked list, and TRUCK records to SHIPMENTs using another. Thus, CUSTOMER records will have one link field, SHIPMENT records will have two link fields (one for each parent), and TRUCK records will have one link field. This scheme is illustrated in Figure 4-40.

The structure in Figure 4-40 can be processed by a simple extension to the algorithm shown in Figure 4-33. We simply apply that algorithm to one linked list or another. This application is left as an exercise.

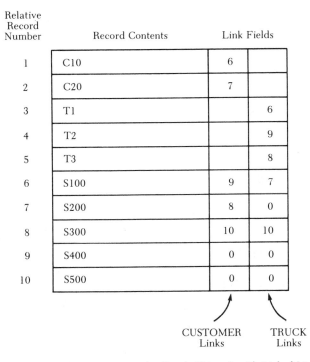

Relative Record Number | Record Contents | Link Fields

Relative Record Number	Record Contents	Link Fields	
1	C10	6	
2	C20	7	
3	T1		6
4	T2		9
5	T3		8
6	S100	9	7
7	S200	8	0
8	S300	10	10
9	S400	0	0
10	S500	0	0

CUSTOMER Links   TRUCK Links

Figure 4-40   Representation of a Simple Network with Linked Lists

Using linked lists in this manner is a simple way to represent one-to-many relationships. Wherever we find a one-to-many relationship, whether in a tree or in a simple network, we can represent it by a linked list. If we want, we can add reverse pointers and parent pointers as we did previously. Doing so would enable us to traverse the children in both directions and to find parents immediately. Linked lists are used in this manner by many DBMS products. Learning this linked list technique will help you understand those systems.

Inverted list representation

A simple network has two one-to-many relationships. Each relationship can be represented using indexed lists as described in the last section.

For example, consider the simple network of trucks, customers, and shipments in Figure 4-35. This network has one-to-many relationships between CUSTOMER and SHIPMENT records and between TRUCK and SHIPMENT records. We can use an inverted list to store each of these relationships. Figure 4-41 shows the two inverted lists needed to represent the example shown in Figure 4-36. Records are loaded in the same file positions as in Figure 4-40.

CUSTOMER Record	SHIPMENT Record
1	6
1	9
2	7
2	8
2	10

TRUCK Record	SHIPMENT Record
3	6
3	7
4	9
5	8
5	10

Figure 4-41   Inverted List Representation of Simple Network Relationships

If you compare Figure 4-40 with Figure 4-41, you can observe the essential difference between a linked list and an inverted list. With a linked list, pointers are stored with the data. Each record contains a pointer to the next location. With an inverted list, pointers are stored in separate indexes. The records themselves contain no pointers. Both techniques are used by commercial DBMS products.

REPRESENTATIONS OF COMPLEX NETWORKS

Complex networks can be physically represented in a variety of ways. They can be decomposed into trees or simple networks, and these simpler structures can then be represented using one of the techniques discussed in the previous two sections. Alternatively, they can be represented directly using inverted lists (linked lists are not used by any DBMS product to represent complex networks directly).

In practice, complex networks are nearly always decomposed into simpler structures. Therefore, we will consider only representations using decomposition.

Decomposition into trees

A complex network can be decomposed into trees in much the same manner as a simple network can be. Consider the complex network between students and classes. There is a one-to-many relationship in both directions. Students are enrolled in many classes, and each class is composed of many students.

An occurrence of this structure is presented in Figure 4-42a. The complex network has been decomposed into trees as shown in Figure 4-42b. Note, as with the decomposition of a simple network, the trees have duplicated some nodes. CLASSes C1, C3, and C5 occur three times, and CLASS C4 occurs twice. This duplication, however, can be eliminated in a manner identical to that used for the simple network decomposition. We simply replace all duplicated records with pointers to the single record that has the data.

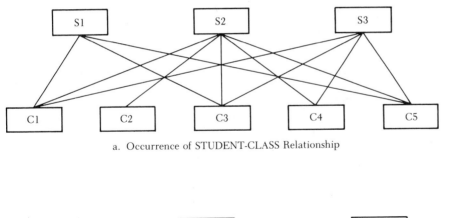

a. Occurrence of STUDENT-CLASS Relationship

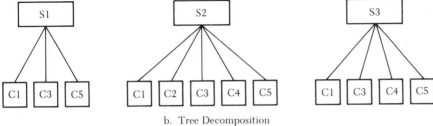

b. Tree Decomposition

Figure 4-42   Complex Network Decomposition

Again, this technique is used by the popular DBMS IMS. Other techniques are used by other database systems.

Decomposition into simple networks

A common representation of complex networks is to reduce them to simple networks, and then to represent the simple networks with linked or indexed lists as discussed in the previous section. Note, however, that a complex network involves a relationship between two records, whereas a simple network involves relationships among three records. Thus, to decompose a complex network into a simple one, we need to create a third record type.

The record that is created when a complex network is decomposed into a simple one is called an *intersection record*. This name implies that the record will represent the intersection, or coming together, of the two records. Consider the student-class complex network. To create an intersection record we take a unique key from the STUDENT record and concatenate it (stick an end of one to an end of the other) with a unique key for the CLASS record. Assume the names used for records in Figure 4-42a are unique. Then some of the intersection records created are: S1C1, S1C3, . . ., S3C4, S3C5. The general structure

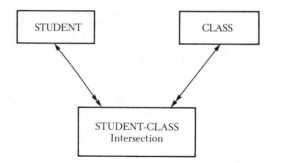

a. Complex Network to Simple Network Decomposition

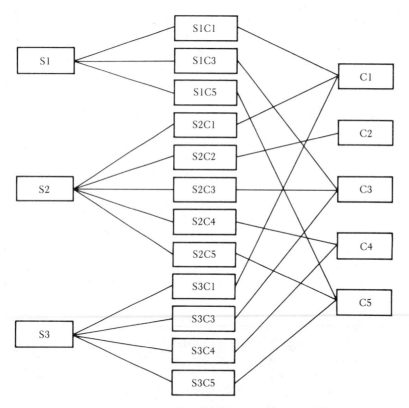

b. Simple Network Decomposition with Intersection Records

Figure 4-43   Transformation and Representation of Complex Network

of this decomposition is shown in Figure 4-43a. An instance is illustrated in Figure 4-43b.

Observe that the relationship from STUDENT to intersection record is one-to-many, and the relationship from CLASS to intersection record is also one-

Relative Record Number	Record Contents	Link Fields	
		STUDENT Links	CLASS Links
1	S1	9	
2	S2	12	
3	S3	17	
4	C1		9
5	C2		13
6	C3		10
7	C4		15
8	C5		11
9	S1C1	10	12
10	S1C3	11	14
11	S1C5	0	16
12	S2C1	13	17
13	S2C2	14	0
14	S2C3	15	18
15	S2C4	16	19
16	S2C5	0	20
17	S3C1	18	0
18	S3C3	19	0
19	S3C4	20	0
20	S3C5	0	0

Figure 4-44   File Containing the Network Occurrence in Figure 4-43

to-many. Thus we have created a simple network that can now be represented with the linked list or inverted list techniques shown previously. A file of this occurrence using this linked list technique is shown in Figure 4-44.

Quite often, intersection records have a meaning of their own. For the example here, the intersection of students and classes can be used to store grades.

Consider another example. Vendors and parts have a complex relationship. One vendor provides many parts, and a part can be provided by many vendors. The intersection record, which consists of a vendor name and a part number, represents a line-item on an order.

Summary of relationship representations

Figure 4-45 summarizes the representations of record relationships. Trees can be represented using sequential, linked, and inverted lists; the last two are most commonly used. A simple network can be decomposed into trees and then represented, or it can be represented directly using either linked or inverted lists. Finally, a complex network can be decomposed into a tree or simple network, or it can be represented directly using inverted lists.

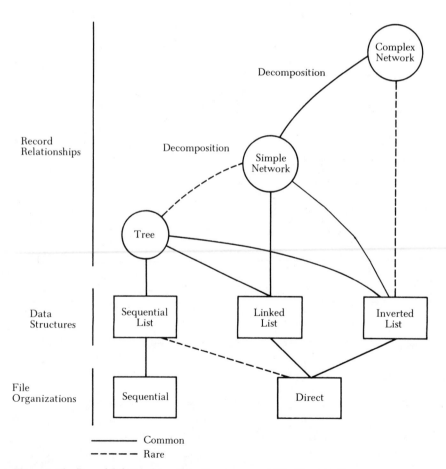

Figure 4-45   Record Relationships, Data Structures, and File Organizations

SECONDARY-KEY REPRESENTATIONS

In Chapter 1 we defined a key as a field used to identify a record. In Chapter 3 we saw how unique keys are used to allocate records to files. For indexed sequential files, records are maintained in key value order. For direct files, a hashing scheme is used to associate key values with physical file locations.

Sometimes, applications require that there be keys in addition to those keys we discussed in Chapter 3. Such additional keys are called *secondary keys*. *Unique secondary keys* identify one record for each key value. Social Security Number is an example. *Nonunique secondary keys* identify one or more records for each key value. Zip Code is an example of a nonunique key. In this section we will use the term *set* to refer to all records having the same value of a nonunique secondary key. For example, there is a set of records having Zip Code 98040.

In Chapter 3, keys were used to associate records with particular file locations. Clearly, only one key can be used in this way. We cannot use the values of two different keys to compute record locations. We cannot, for example, use a hashing scheme on Account-number to locate records and also use a hashing scheme on Account-name to locate the same records. Unless we are very lucky, the two keys will not hash to the same location. Thus only one key can be used to determine the physical location of records. We will call this key the *primary key*. Secondary keys can be used to identify records, but they must reference the physical locations as determined by the primary key.

Some DBMS products do not use key values to determine record locations at all. Instead, the DBMS assigns records to locations in accordance with available space and other considerations known only to the DBMS. For these systems, there are no primary keys. Every key is considered a secondary key and is processed using one of the techniques in this section.

Both linked and inverted lists are used to represent secondary keys. As you will see, linked lists are practical only for nonunique keys. Inverted lists, however, can be used for both unique and nonunique key representations. We will discuss the linked list representation first.

Linked list representation of secondary keys

Consider an example of CUSTOMER records as shown in Figure 4-46. The primary key is Account-number, and there is a secondary key on Credit-limit.

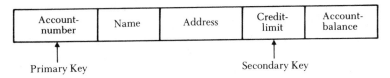

Figure 4-46   CUSTOMER Account Database Record

Relative Record Number	Link	Account-Number	Credit-Limit	Other Data
1	2	101	500	
2	7	301	500	
3	5	203	700	
4	6	004	1000	
5	10	204	700	
6	8	905	1000	
7	0	705	500	
8	9	207	1000	
9	11	309	1000	
10	0	409	700	
11	0	210	1000	

HEAD-500 = 1

HEAD-700 = 3

HEAD-1000 = 4

Figure 4-47   Credit-limit Key Using Linked List

Possible values for Credit-limit are 500, 700, or 1000. Thus there will be a set of records for the limit of 500, a set for 700, and a set for 1000.

To represent this key using linked lists, we will add a link field to the CUSTOMER records. Inside this link field, we will create a linked list for each set of records. Figure 4-47 shows a database of eleven customers; for brevity, only Account-number and Credit-limit are shown. A link field has been attached to the records. Assume one database record occupies one physical record on a direct file using relative record addressing.

The head of the $500 linked list is relative record 1. Record 1 links to record 2, which in turn links to record 7. Record 7 has a zero in the link position, indicating it is the end of the list. Consequently, the $500 credit limit set consists of records 1, 2, and 7. Similarly, the $700 set contains relative records 3, 5, and 10, and the $1000 set contains records 4, 6, 8, 9, and 11.

To answer a query like "How many accounts in the $1000 set have a balance in excess of $900?" the $1000 set linked list can be used. In this way, only records in the $1000 set need to be read from the file and examined. The advantage of this approach is not readily apparent in this small example. Suppose, however, there are 100,000 CUSTOMER records and only 100 of them are in the $1000 set. If there is no linked list, all 100,000 records must be sequentially examined. With the linked list, only the 100 records in the $1000 set need be examined. Using the linked list saves 99,900 reads.

When records are added to or deleted from this file, the linked list must be modified. Figure 4-48a shows this database after account 310 is added. Since

Relative Record Number	Link	Account-number	Credit-limit	Other Data
1	2	101	500	
2	7	301	500	
3	5	203	700	
4	6	004	1000	
5	10	204	700	
6	8	905	1000	
7	0	705	500	
8	9	207	1000	
9	11	309	1000	
10	12	409	700	
11	0	210	1000	
12	0	310	700	

HEAD-500 = 1
HEAD-700 = 3
HEAD-1000 = 4

a. Insertion of Account 310

Relative Record Number	Link	Account-number	Credit-limit	Other Data
1	2	101	500	
2	7	301	500	
3	5	203	700	
4	6	204	1000	
5	10	201	700	
6	9	905	1000	
7	0	705	500	
8				
9	11	309	1000	
10	12	409	700	
11	0	210	1000	
12	0	310	700	

HEAD-500 = 1
HEAD-700 = 3
HEAD-1000 = 4

b. Deletion of Account 207

Figure 4-48 Making Insertions and Deletions

account 310 has a Credit-limit of $700, it is added to the $700 chain. Figure 4-48b shows this database after account 207 is deleted. An unused record now exists. It can be added to an unused chain as illustrated previously.

Account-number is not needed in this example because physical addresses are used in the links. Of course, to satisfy a query such as "What is the balance of account 905?" the database system must convert Account-number to a physical address, perhaps using some hashing scheme. (What scheme seems to have been used here?)

A major disadvantage of using physical addresses as pointers is that a reorganization of the database may invalidate them. If, to improve efficiency, for example, records are moved to new locations, pointer values must be changed. This is not true if symbolic addresses are used. A final note about this example is that the records appear in an arbitrary order in the linked lists. In some applications, it may be desirable to order them alphabetically or by Account-number.

Disadvantages of linked lists for secondary-key representations   Linked lists are not an effective technique for every secondary-key application. In particular, if the records are processed nonsequentially in a set, linked lists are inefficient. For example, if it is often necessary to find the 10th or 120th or nth record in the $500 Credit-limit set in example 1, processing will be slow. Linked lists are inefficient for direct access.

Also, if the application requires that secondary keys be created or destroyed dynamically, the linked list approach is undesirable. Whenever a new key is created, a link field must be added to every record. This often requires reorganization of the database—a time-consuming and expensive process.

Finally, if the secondary keys are unique, each list has a length of 1 and a separate linked list exists for every record in the database. Since this situation is unworkable, linked lists cannot be used for unique keys.

For example, suppose the CUSTOMER records contain another unique field, say Social Security Number. If we attempt to represent this unique field using a linked list, every Social Security Number will be a separate linked list. Further, each linked list will have just one item on it. That item will be the single record having the indicated Social Security Number.

Inverted list representation of secondary key

A second technique for representing secondary keys uses an *inverted list,* which, as we have seen, is similar to the index of a book. One inverted list is established for each secondary key. The approach varies depending on whether key values are unique or nonunique.

Unique secondary keys   Suppose the CUSTOMER records in Figure 4-46 contain Social Security Number (SSN) as well as the fields shown. To provide

Relative Record Number	Account-number	Credit-limit	Social Security Number (SSN)
1	101	500	000-01-0001
2	301	500	000-01-0005
3	203	700	000-01-0009
4	004	1000	000-01-0003

Figure 4-49   Sample CUSTOMER Data (with SSN)

SSN	Relative Record Number
000-01-0001	1
000-01-0003	4
000-01-0005	2
000-01-0009	3

Figure 4-50   Inverted List for SSN Secondary Key

key access to the CUSTOMER records using SSN, we simply build an inverted list on the SSN field. Sample CUSTOMER data are shown in Figure 4-49, and a corresponding inverted list is illustrated in Figure 4-50. The inverted list shown uses relative record numbers as addresses. It would be possible to use Account-numbers instead, in which case the DBMS would locate the desired SSN in the inverted list, obtain the matching Account-number, and then hash to the record itself. The advantages and disadvantages of physical as compared to logical addresses are the same as discussed for linked lists in the last section.

If the inverted list is large, a lengthy search may be required to find the correct SSN. Techniques can be used to reduce the length of the search. One possibility is to employ a binary search on the inverted list; another is to hash into the inverted list as well as into the file.

Processing the inverted list with a binary search   A binary search can be employed if the inverted list entries are in sorted order. In this case, the list is usually kept in a buffer while the file is being processed (if the list is too large to fit, it is processed in sections). The desired SSN is compared to the middle value of the inverted list. If the middle value is greater than the desired SSN, then the SSN must be in the first (upper) half of the list. Consequently, the desired SSN is compared to the middle value of the upper half. If this middle

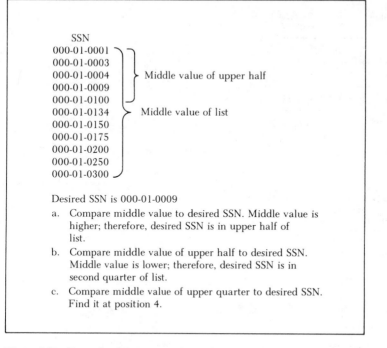

SSN
000-01-0001
000-01-0003
000-01-0004   Middle value of upper half
000-01-0009
000-01-0100
000-01-0134   Middle value of list
000-01-0150
000-01-0175
000-01-0200
000-01-0250
000-01-0300

Desired SSN is 000-01-0009

a. Compare middle value to desired SSN. Middle value is higher; therefore, desired SSN is in upper half of list.

b. Compare middle value of upper half to desired SSN. Middle value is lower; therefore, desired SSN is in second quarter of list.

c. Compare middle value of upper quarter to desired SSN. Find it at position 4.

Figure 4-51   Example of Binary Search on SSN Inverted List

value comes, say, before the desired SSN, then the desired SSN must be in the second quarter of the inverted list. The process of halving the remaining portion of the list is continued until the SSN is found. This process is illustrated in Figure 4-51. It has been shown that the number of entries to examine in a binary search approaches log $2N$, where N is the total number of entries. See references [36] and [57].

Processing the inverted list with hashing   Another method of reducing list search time is to use a hashing scheme on SSN to calculate the address of the appropriate entry in the inverted list. A technique such as the division/remainder method can be used to convert an SSN value to a position in the inverted list. Then, the DBMS can examine the calculated position to determine if the desired SSN is in that location. If not, the DBMS would examine the next location, and so on, as described previously.

Each inverted list record consists of two fields: one for the SSN and another for relative record number. In practice, such short list records are not stored in separate physical records. Instead, they are blocked. For example, 100 inverted list records may be blocked into one physical record. For the CUSTOMER file, this means inverted list entries for 100 customers would reside in one physical

Credit-limit	Account-number				
500	101	301	705		
700	203	204	409		
1000	004	905	207	309	210

Figure 4-52   Inverted List for Credit-limit Key of Figure 4-46

record. Up to 100 synonyms could be stored in the same physical record. Also, SSN can overflow into the next physical record if necessary.

If the list is not too large, it can be processed in main memory. For example, if there are only 500 customers, the list can be stored in an array. A hashing algorithm similar to the one presented in Chapter 3 can be used to generate addresses, but these addresses are interpreted as array subscripts rather than as a physical record number of a file.

Nonunique secondary keys   Inverted lists can be used to represent non-unique secondary keys in much the same way as unique keys. The only important difference is that the list entries are variable length. Figure 4-52 shows the Credit-limit inverted list for the CUSTOMER file.

In reality, the representation and processing of nonunique secondary keys are complex. Several different schemes are used by commercial DBMS products. One method that is typical uses a values table and an occurrence table.

Each values table entry consists of two fields. The first field has a key value. For the CUSTOMER Credit-limit key, example values are 500, 700, or 1000. The second field of the values table entry is a pointer into the occurrence table.

The occurrence table contains record addresses. Records having a common value in the secondary-key field appear together in the table. Figure 4-53 shows the values and occurrence tables for the Credit-limit key.

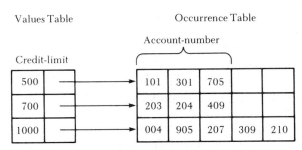

Figure 4-53   Values and Occurrence Tables for Credit-limit Key of Figure 4-46

To locate records having a given value of the secondary key, the values table is searched for the desired value. If the values table is loaded on a direct file, a binary search or hashing scheme may be employed. Once the given key value is located in the values table, the pointer is followed to the occurrence table to obtain the addresses of records having that key value. These addresses are used to obtain the desired records.

When a new record is inserted into the file, the DBMS must process each secondary-key field. For nonunique keys, it must ensure that the new record key value is in the values table; if so, it adds the new record address to the appropriate entry in the occurrence table. If not, it must insert new entries in the values and occurrence tables.

When a record is deleted, its address must be removed from the occurrence table. If no addresses remain in the occurrence table entry, the corresponding values table entry must also be deleted.

When the secondary-key field of a record is modified, the record address must be removed from one occurrence table entry and inserted in another. If the modification is a new value for the key, an entry must be added to the values table.

Inverted list secondary-key example   Consider the CUSTOMER file and suppose the CUSTOMER records are loaded on a direct file that is accessed using Account-number as the primary key. Also assume Credit-limit is the only secondary key, and its values and occurrence tables are allocated to a direct file using relative record addressing. This direct file contains fixed-length records having five fields each. (In common practice, the records would be larger, but we will assume they are small to save space in this book.)

The first record of the inverted list contains the first two entries of the values table plus an overflow pointer. This pointer links to the continuation of the values table. Figure 4-54a shows the inverted list corresponding to the data in Figure 4-54b. Note that record 4 holds the continuation of the values table. Each values table entry has two fields: the key value and a relative record number in the direct file pointing to the appropriate occurrence entry. Unused records are linked on an unused chain.

To understand how these files are processed, suppose the user wants to obtain all accounts having a credit limit of $500. The database system searches record 1 (the first record of the values table) for 500 and finds it in the second entry. The pointer value is 3, indicating that record 3 holds the account numbers of records having a $500 credit limit. The database system reads record 3 and finds that accounts 101, 301, and 705 have a $500 credit limit. These records are read from the direct file.

Now suppose the user wants all accounts having a $700 credit limit. The database system does not find 700 in record 1. Consequently, it follows the overflow pointer to record 4, where 700 is the first entry. Record 5 holds the occurrence table entry for 700, so it is read to obtain record IDs 203, 204, and 409.

Relative Record Number	Entries				Overflow	Unused
1	1000	2	500	3	4	7
2	004	207	210	309	6	
3	101	301	705	0	0	
4	700	5	0	0	0	
5	203	204	409	0	0	
6	905	0	0	0	0	
7	8					
8	9					
9	10					
10	0					

a. Direct File Containing Values and Occurrence Tables

Account-number	Credit-limit	Other Data
101	500	
301	500	
203	700	
004	1000	
204	700	
905	1000	
705	500	
207	1000	
409	700	
210	1000	
309	1000	

b. CUSTOMER Direct File

Figure 4-54   CUSTOMER Account Database

```
BEGIN INVERTED-FILE-LOAD
      DO INITIALIZE
      DO LOAD WHILE EOF-FLAG = 0
      DO TERMINATE
END INVERTED-FILE-LOAD


BEGIN INITIALIZE
      OPEN CUSTOMER DIRECT FILES        /Note:  Direct file will hold values and
                                        occurrence table entries./

      EOF-FLAG = 0
      READ ACCT, CL, and rest of account record; AT END SET EOF-FLAG = 1
END INITIALIZE


BEGIN LOAD
      INSERT ACCT RECORD ON CUSTOMER DIRECT FILE
      IF CL NOT IN VALUES TABLE
            THEN IF NO ROOM IN VALUES TABLE FOR ANOTHER ENTRY
                    THEN OBTAIN UNUSED RECORD
                          LINK UNUSED RECORD TO VALUES TABLE
                  END-IF
                  INSERT CL IN VALUES TABLE
                  OBTAIN UNUSED RECORD FOR NEW OCCURRENCE TABLE ENTRY
                  LINK UNUSED RECORD TO VALUE CL IN VALUES TABLE
            ELSE IF OCCURRENCE TABLE ENTRY FOR CL IS FULL
                    THEN OBTAIN UNUSED RECORD
                          LINK UNUSED RECORD TO CL'S OCCURRENCE TABLE LIST
                  END-IF
      END-IF
      INSERT ACCT INTO CL'S OCCURRENCE TABLE ENTRY
      READ ACCT, CL, and rest of account record; AT END SET EOF-FLAG = 1
END LOAD


BEGIN TERMINATE
      CLOSE CUSTOMER DIRECT FILES
END TERMINATE
```

Figure 4-55 Algorithm for Loading an Inverted File

If it is desired to obtain all accounts with a $1000 credit limit, the DBMS obtains the occurrence table entry from record 2. Accounts 004, 207, 210, and 309 appear. Also, the overflow pointer is nonzero, indicating a continuation of the entry. Record 6 is read to obtain account 905, the last account with a $1000 credit limit.

An algorithm to load a database having this format is shown in Figure 4-55. ACCT is the value of Account-number, and CL is a value for Credit-limit. To determine whether or not CL is in the values table, record 1 plus any values table overflow records must be searched.

If CL is not in the values table, it must be inserted. The values table entries are searched for an empty entry. If there are no empty entries, the system obtains an unused record and links it to the last values table record. Next, CL is inserted in the empty values table entry just found and an unused record is obtained for occurrences of records having the new CL value. The relative record number (RRN) of this record is inserted in the new values table entry. Finally, ACCT is inserted in the first field of the new occurrence table record.

If CL is already in the values table, the system must check for room in the appropriate occurrence table record for the new ACCT value. If there are no unused positions, a new occurrence table record is obtained and linked to the last occurrence table record for this key value. Then, ACCT is inserted in the occurrence table record. Figure 4-56 shows the files at various stages of loading.

Once the file is loaded, reading the records in a set is straightforward. If the records are to be processed sequentially in the order in which they appear in

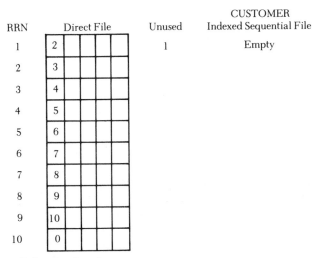

RRN	Direct File				Unused	CUSTOMER Indexed Sequential File
1	2				1	Empty
2	3					
3	4					
4	5					
5	6					
6	7					
7	8					
8	9					
9	10					
10	0					

a. Before Any Insertions

Figure 4-56   Stages of Database Loading

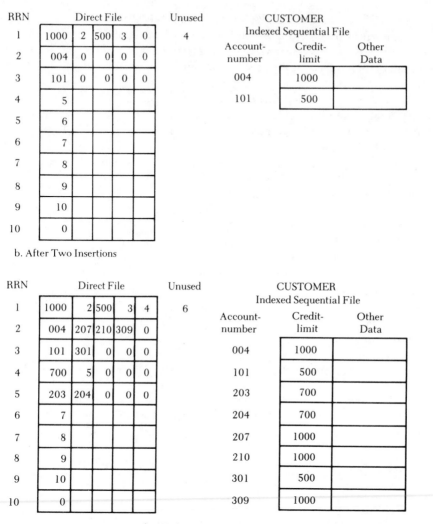

b. After Two Insertions

c. After Eight Insertions

Figure 4-56   (Cont'd.)

the set, all that needs to be done is to read the appropriate occurrence table entries and process the records in it. An algorithm for this process appears in Figure 4-57. Variable names are as follows:

CL = value of credit limit set to be processed
NV = record number of values table entry
NO = record number of occurrence table entry
BUF = five-word buffer
J = subscript of BUF
NI = account number in direct file

```
BEGIN PROCESS-CREDIT-LIMIT-SET (CL)
      /Note:  The value of CL is passed to this procedure./
      DO FIND-CL-IN-OT
      IF CL-OT = 0
            THEN DISPLAY "CREDIT-LIMIT NOT IN FILE" AND VALUE OF CL
            ELSE DO PROCESS-SET
      END-IF
END PROCESS-CREDIT-LIMIT-SET
* * * * * * * * * * * * * * * * * * * * * * * * * *
BEGIN FIND-CL-IN-OT
      CL-OT = 0
      NV = 1
      DOWHILE NV GREATER THAN 0
            READ RECORD NV FROM DIRECT FILE INTO ARRAY BUF
            /Search first and third entries for CL./
            DO FOR J = 1 TO 3 BY 2
                  IF CL = BUF(J)
                        THEN CL-OT = J + 1
                              GO TO END FIND-CL-IN-OT
                  END-IF
            END-DO
            NV = BUF(5)
      END-DO
END FIND-CL-IN-OT
* * * * * * * * * * * * * * * * * * * * * * * * * *
BEGIN PROCESS-SET
      DOWHILE CL-OT GREATER THAN 0
            READ RECORD CL-OT FROM DIRECT FILE INTO ARRAY BUF
            DO FOR J = 1 TO 4
                  NI = BUF(J)
                  IF NI GREATER THAN 0
                        THEN READ RECORD NI FROM DIRECT FILE
                              /Note:  A record having value CL has been read.
                              It should be processed (printed, or whatever)
                              here./
                  END-IF
            END-DO
            CL-OT = BUF(5)
      END-DO
END PROCESS-SET
```

Figure 4-57   Algorithm to Process Set with Credit-limit CL

If the user wants to process a particular record in a set, say the third one, the system just counts down the occurrence table entry to the desired record and then retrieves it from the direct file.

To delete a record from the file, the system must delete both the CUSTOMER record itself and the reference to the CUSTOMER record in the occurrence table entry. Algorithms for insertions and deletions to this file are left to the reader as an exercise.

The inverted list approach overcomes objections stated for the linked list approach. Direct processing of sets is possible. For example, the third record in a set can be processed without processing the first or second record. Also, it is possible to create or delete secondary keys dynamically. No change is necessary in the records themselves; the database system just creates additional values and occurrence tables. Finally, unique keys can be processed efficiently.

The disadvantages of the inverted list approach are that it requires more file space (the tables require more overhead than pointers) and that the DBMS programming task is more complex. Also, modifications are usually processed more slowly because I/O is required to access and maintain the values and occurrence tables.

SUMMARY

This chapter surveyed data structures used for database processing. A flat file has no repeating groups. Flat files can be ordered using sequential, linked, or inverted lists. A sequential list is a physical ordering of the records. A linked list imposes an order on the records via links or pointers. An inverted list orders records via an index of field values and pointers.

Sequential, linked, and inverted lists are fundamental data structures. They can be used to represent record relationships and secondary keys, as well as for ordering files.

There are three common forms of record relationships. Trees are structures in which each child record has at most one parent. Simple network structures allow records to have more than one parent, but the parent records must be of different types. For both trees and simple networks, all relationships are one-to-many. The third structure, the complex network, allows records to have multiple parents of the same type. Thus the relationship is one-to-many in both directions, or many-to-many.

Several common representations of each of these logical structures were discussed. Trees were represented by sequential, linked, and inverted lists. Simple networks were represented by decomposition to trees and by linked and inverted lists. An algorithm for linked list processing was discussed. Finally, the representation of complex networks by decomposition to trees and simple networks was illustrated.

In the last section, we considered data structures for secondary keys. The application of linked lists to nonunique secondary keys was shown. Additionally, inverted list data structures were applied to both unique and nonunique secondary keys.

This chapter concludes the fundamentals necessary for the study of database processing. In the next part, we consider the formalization of database definition and processing into database models.

Group I Questions

4.1 Define a flat file. Give an example of a file that is flat and another example of a file that is not flat.

4.2 Show how sequential lists can be used to maintain the file from question 4.1 in two different orders simultaneously.

4.3 Show how linked lists can be used to maintain the file from question 4.1 in two different orders simultaneously.

4.4 Show how inverted lists can be used to maintain the file from question 4.1 in two different orders simultaneously.

4.5 Explain why knowledge of the three types of record relationships is useful.

4.6 Explain the difference between a logical and a physical data structure.

4.7 Define a tree and give an example structure.

4.8 Give a specific occurrence of your structure in question 4.7.

4.9 Define a simple network and give an example structure.

4.10 Give a specific occurrence of your structure in question 4.9.

4.11 Define a complex network and give an example structure.

4.12 Give a specific occurrence of your structure in question 4.11.

4.13 Explain the difference between a one-to-many and a many-to-many relationship. Which logical data structures have one-to-many and which have many-to-many relationships?

4.14 Give occurrences of the following tree structures:

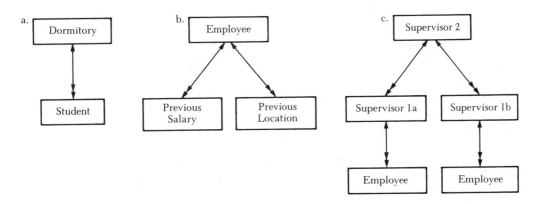

4.15 Show the preorder traversal of the following tree occurrence:

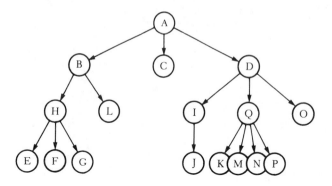

4.16 Sketch the appearance of the tree in Figure 4-24 after INVOICE 110 is deleted.

4.17 Sketch the appearance of the tree in Figure 4-24 after INVOICE 118 is deleted.

4.18 Sketch the appearance of the tree in Figure 4-24 after INVOICEs 108, 117, and 123 are added to VENDOR AA.

4.19 Modify your answer to question 4.18 for circular lists.

4.20 Modify your answer to question 4.19 to show forward and backward pointers.

4.21 Modify your answer to question 4.20 to show forward, backward, and parent pointers.

4.22 Use linked lists to physically represent the tree in question 4.15. Follow the format in Figure 4-30.

4.23 Add a third vendor to the occurrence shown in Figure 4-29. Supply several invoices, payments, and items for each parent record.

4.24 Modify Figure 4-30 to include your additional records from question 4.23.

4.25 Express the algorithm in Figure 4-33 in either structured flowchart, Nassi-Shneiderman, or Warnier-Orr format.

4.26 Develop an algorithm to read either VENDOR AA's or VENDOR BB's invoices for the file in Figure 4-32.

4.27 Sketch the general structure for a simple network involving books, authors, and publishers. Assume no books are coauthored or copublished.

4.28 Give an occurrence for the structure in question 4.27.

4.29 Decompose your example from question 4.27 into trees. Show both the general structure and your occurrence.

4.30 Sketch a file of the decomposition you used in question 4.29. Follow the format in Figure 4-39.

4.31 Repeat question 4.30, but eliminate duplication using linked lists as shown in Figure 4-40.

4.32 Sketch the relationship of actors to movies. Give the general structure and an occurrence.

4.33 Decompose your network from question 4.32 into trees. Show the general structure and an occurrence.

4.34 Decompose your network from question 4.32 into a simple network. Show the general structure and an occurrence.

4.35 What meaning might be given to the intersection record in question 4.34?

4.36 Sketch a file of records for your answer to question 4.34. Use Figure 4-44 as an example.

4.37 Explain the difference between primary and secondary keys.

4.38 Explain the difference between unique and nonunique keys.

4.39 Define the term *set*, as used in this chapter.

4.40 Give an example of a student record that has both unique and nonunique secondary keys. Show the record format and give an example of the records. Explain which records are in which sets.

4.41 For your example in question 4.40, show how linked lists can be used to represent the nonunique secondary key. Use Figure 4-47 as an example.

4.42 Attempt to use linked lists to represent the unique secondary key in your answer to question 4.40. What happens? Why is this approach infeasible?

4.43 Show an inverted list that represents the unique secondary key in your example from question 4.40.

4.44 Show an inverted list that represents the nonunique secondary key in your example from question 4.40. Use the format in Figure 4-56.

Group II Questions

4.45 Develop a schematic of a database for student administration. Show the record types and all relationships. If your schematic has any complex networks, decompose these into simple networks.

4.46 Develop an algorithm to process the example in Figure 4-32 with a two-way linked list.

4.47 Develop an algorithm to process the example in Figure 4-32 with two-way and parent pointers.

4.48 Develop an algorithm to process the tree in Figure 4-28.

4.49 Extend the algorithm in Figure 4-33 to allow a variable number of vendors. Assume vendor names will be unknown until execution time.

Option a: Put vendors on a file separate from invoices.

Option b: Hash vendors into the same file as invoices. Find a creative solution to collisions between VENDOR and INVOICE records.

4.50 Develop an algorithm to process the file format in Figure 4-39. Allow insertions and deletions to shipments. Assume any truck or customer having a shipment cannot be deleted (flag any such attempt as an error).

4.51 Same as question 4.50 but use the file format in Figure 4-40.

4.52 Develop algorithms to insert and delete records for the inverted list structure shown in Figure 4-54a.

Projects

Design, code, and test programs to implement the algorithms in the following figures and questions. Follow your instructor's documentation standards.

    A. Figure 4-33

    B. Figure 4-57

    C. Question 4.46

    D. Question 4.47

    E. Question 4.48

    F. Question 4.49

    G. Question 4.50

    H. Question 4.51

    I. Question 4.52

II
DATABASE
DESIGN

Part II of this book concerns the difficult process of database design. A database is the interface between people and machines. The nature of these components is utterly different. People are imprecise, intuitive, and their thinking is fuzzy. Machines are precise, predictable, and their processing is exact. The difficulty is to develop a database design which meets the needs of the people who will use it, and which is practical in terms of technology and hardware. Since the database is the bridge between humans on one side and hardware on the other, it must match the characteristics of each.

A database supports a community of users whose needs partly overlap, partly diverge, and partly conflict. Unfortunately, there is no algorithm for database design. Database design is both art and science. Dealing with people, understanding what they want today, predicting what they will want tomorrow, differentiating between individual needs and community needs, and making appropriate design tradeoffs are artistic tasks. There are principles and tools, but these must be used in conjunction with intuition and guided by experience.

Database design is a two-phased process. First, we examine the users' requirements and build a conceptual database structure that is a model of the organization. This phase of database design is often called *logical database design*. Once the logical design of the database is completed, this design is formulated in terms of a particular DBMS. Usually compromises must be made. For example, the DBMS may not be able to express relationships precisely as the users see them. The process of formulating the logical design in terms of DBMS facilities is called *physical database design*.

Part II considers both phases of database design. Chapter 5 introduces and surveys database design issues. Chapter 6 describes logical database design in general, and the semantic data model in particular. Chapters 7 and 8 discuss database design using the relational model; Chapter 7 presents concepts of the relational model, and Chapter 8 applies these concepts for the design of a small, sample database. Chapters 9 and 10 discuss database design using the CODA-SYL DBTG model. Chapter 9 presents concepts of this model, and Chapter 10 applies this model for the design of the same small database.

167

This part presents the fundamental design principles and tools, and when you finish it, you should be able to design simple databases for limited groups of people having clearly defined requirements. You will need to augment your knowledge with years of experience, however, before you will be prepared to design complex databases for large user communities.

5
Introduction to
Database Design

Sometime in the 1960s, in an unknown company, a manager asked the data processing staff what must have seemed a simple question: "The payroll system works well, and the production scheduling system is adequate, but isn't there a way you could integrate the two? I'd like to be able to assign labor costs to production projects."

This question and others like it opened the door for database processing. To data processing's surprise and to management's dismay, this door led down a path with many risks and pitfalls, to subjects of great uncertainty. The manager's question led to data integration, which led to data relationships, which led to the need for generalized models of data, which led to an attempt to understand how humans model data, which led to questions like, What is knowledge? What is meaning? How does one person's perception of knowledge differ from another's? How can we specify these differences? and so forth.

These questions are a long way from production management. The vice-president of operations hardly expected to ask a question that would raise these issues. Meanwhile, the products had to go out the door, and the board of directors and stockholders needed to be satisfied. So data processing learned to make compromises that avoid major pitfalls. These compromises necessitated predefining data structures, and to a certain extent, predefining the queries to be made of the database. In some cases, these compromises are crude and not satisfying, but they work. Perhaps in 50 years, there will be information systems that truly provide generalized ways of representing and processing data.

This chapter introduces the design of databases—a process of compromise. We begin by discussing databases as models, and then we describe processes for developing logical and physical database designs. Finally, we survey important design tools called *database models*.

DATABASES AS ENTERPRISE MODELS

What is a database? You may recall that it is a self-describing collection of integrated records. But, on a deeper level, what is it? Why have one? What good is a database? Let's be sure we understand the nature of databases before we try to design them.

Consider a flourishing business. Goods come and go. People come and go. Money comes and goes. Time passes. At some point, somebody (an owner, a tax agent, an employee, etc.) asks, "What is the state of the business?" We could answer this question by taking the person on a tour of the business, saying, "Here it is. See for yourself."

Chances are, this response wouldn't be helpful. Why? There's too much detail. Our questioner might say, "No, I meant, tell me how much money you have," or "How do sales compare to a year ago?" or "How many employees do you have?" Our questioner doesn't want to see the business directly; he or she wants a representation of the business.

To represent the business, we take measurements of business activity and record them. We gather names, count goods, count money, and so forth, and store the results. This stored data is a model of the business. However, it is incomplete. We cannot measure everything. If we did, we would be building another copy of the business. This duplication would not only be wasteful, but the second copy would be no more helpful to our questioner than the first. Instead, we select aspects of the business and measure them. During this selection we *aggregate* and *generalize*.

We aggregate data by combining it. For example, we may add all sales for a given day into a daily sales total. Or, we can determine the total due on an invoice by adding prices of individual items. Realize, however, that whenever we aggregate data, we lose something. For example, if we add all sales into a daily total, we lose the ability to report daytime vs evening sales or hourly sales. Thus when we aggregate, some questions become unanswerable.

We generalize when we ignore differences in objects and combine them into a single category. For example, a company may have wholesale, retail, and international sales. However, the distinction among types of sales may be unimportant. If so, we can generalize by grouping all three types of sales together. Just as with aggregation, however, we lose something. We are no longer able to report sales by type. Thus, when we generalize, still more questions become unanswerable.

Now consider the dilemma of the database designer. Databases exist to provide a representation of the condition of a company. The purpose of the representation is to answer questions. It is both undesirable and impossible to represent every aspect of the company. Therefore, we summarize data by aggregation and generalization. When we do this, however, some questions become unanswerable. The trick, for the database designer, *is to aggregate and gener-*

alize in such a way that the only questions that become unanswerable are questions that are never asked.

Although you must agree with this statement, you may find it unhelpful. Something like the securities advice to buy low and sell high. The point, during database design, is to realize the necessity and the cost of each aggregation or generalization. Make sure the right questions become unanswerable.

Sally Enterprises

To understand the need for summarization, consider the simplest possible business. Sally runs a lemonade stand (Figure 5-1). She makes lemonade out of lemons, sugar, and water in a pitcher which she displays on her stand. She sells lemonade for a fixed price per glass. When her supply runs low, Sally makes more. The amount she makes depends on her assessment of the weather, the time of day, and the number of customers she is likely to have.

When Sally runs out of lemons or sugar, she sends her friend Jeff to the store. Jeff isn't totally reliable and occasionally buys the wrong amounts or items. When Jeff buys accurately, Sally gives Jeff 5¢ for every glass she sells while he is gone. (She's sharing the profit she made by not leaving the stand.) Like many entrepreneurs, Sally sometimes wonders if it's worth it; she'd like to know how much money she actually makes.

Figure 5-1   Sally Enterprises

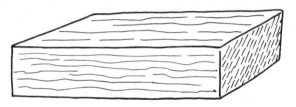

Figure 5-2 Highly Aggregated and Generalized Model of a Car

A model of Sally's business

Sally's simple business will illustrate the dilemmas we encounter when we try to design a database. First, we know we cannot represent everything, even for a lemonade business. We must decide to measure and store only some aspects of the business. These measurements will be a model of Sally's business. If we store many measurements, the model will be detailed; if we store only a few measurements, the model will be rough.

Suppose we decide to measure receipts, disbursements, and a count of the number of batches of lemonade produced. This model, having income, expense, and production units, is highly aggregated and generalized. Many questions are unanswerable. About all we can ask of this model is, How much money should be in the cash drawer? and, How many trips did Sally make to the kitchen? This model is akin to cutting a board 3 inches by 2 inches by 7 inches and calling the board a model of a car. (See Figure 5-2.)

We could refine our model and keep inventory records of raw materials (sugar and lemons). Also, when Sally sends Jeff to the store, we could account for his errors by keeping records of orders, shipments received, and cash disbursed. Furthermore, to pay Jeff we could mark records of sales that occurred while a purchase order was open. This model is more detailed, less aggregated, and less generalized. Many more questions can be answered. This model is like carving part of the wood out of the block to form the windshield.

We could add still more detail by including sales prediction data. We could maintain records of customers' purchases and buying habits, and relate those to the time of day and the weather. Also, we could improve production and inventory management by including Sally's recipes that describe how she makes batches of different sizes. More questions are answerable; our block of wood now has wheels.

Next, to help Sally determine how much money she earns, we could add records concerning fixed assets. Sally needs to depreciate her stand, chair, pitcher, and glasses. We could also add records of supplies used, like soap and cleaning brushes. Now we can answer questions posed by the Internal Revenue Service. We have wheels, a hood, and a trunk in our car model.

We can continue to remove aggregation and generalization indefinitely. Weather prediction could involve literally hundreds of records; we could refine sales projections by considering the day of the week, month, date, and economic factors such as growth in disposable income and inflation. We could depreciate fixed assets more accurately by adjusting for the percent of use in nonbusiness and business activity. Also, because some customers leave the glasses dirtier than others, we could build a cost accounting system to determine the amount of extra cleaning costs, and increase prices by this amount for messy customers. Etc., etc., etc.

Where should we stop this process? How much detail is enough? What is the appropriate amount of aggregation and generalization? How much of this data should be included in Sally's database? The answer is to the level that enables us to answer the questions that Sally wants to ask, within economic constraints.

Unfortunately, if we ask Sally what she wants, she is likely to respond, with a bit of frustration, "I want to know how much profit I am making." That's a typical response. Business people tend to describe their needs in a general, fuzzy way that makes sense to them. These descriptions are not helpful in the context of the designer's problems. We must pin Sally down. We should use the methods described in Chapter 2 to determine her requirements more specifically.

In addition to Sally's requirements, however, we must consider economic feasibility. Figure 5-3 shows Sally's operation after development of a very refined

Figure 5-3   Sally Enterprises Operation with Sophisticated Database Model

data model. Sally's system has predicted (quite accurately) that she can expect to sell no glasses of lemonade at the price she must charge to pay for her computer.

We will return to this issue in a subsequent section. For now, let's consider another aspect of database design.

Dynamics of Sally's database

Sally's business is active. People buy her lemonade, she makes new batches, she orders and receives raw materials, she invents new recipes, she pays Jeff, and so forth. As this activity occurs, Sally's model must be updated. Part of the job of the database designer is to decide how this updating will be done.

The designer may decide to create a transaction for every sale. Thus every time a glass of lemonade is purchased, Sally enters this fact on her CRT. Such purchase transactions cause the amount of lemonade in the pitcher to be decremented, and they increment the amount of money Sally should have in her cash drawer. Depending on Sally's requirements and the design of the system, this transaction may generate a message to Sally to make more lemonade when appropriate.

When Sally makes a new batch of lemonade, she could enter this as another transaction. The processing of this transaction causes the inventory of lemons and sugar to be decremented in accordance with the recipe she used (entered as part of the transaction). When inventory levels are decremented below a certain level, the system generates a message to Sally to order lemons or sugar.

Thus events occur in the world and are reported to the system as transactions. Transactions cause data to be modified, and they may also spawn other transactions. Whenever a transaction is processed, the model (database data) changes.

The designer must identify events that impact the database and decide how (or if) they will be modeled. Some, like the event of selling a glass of lemonade, will be represented by transactions. Other events may be ignored. For example, a fly lands in her lemonade pitcher and she removes it (along with 1/8 teaspoon of lemonade).

Events may also be aggregated. When Sally is busy, she may want to record several sales at once. Thus she may want to have a single transaction to record all sales that occurred during the busy period. The designer will have to find out from Sally what level of aggregation is appropriate. The decisions will be made on the basis of Sally's needs and costs.

Transactions can be less aggregated than the database data, but they cannot be more aggregated. For example, if Sally keeps records of sales by hour, she can have transactions that record sales every minute. She cannot, however, have a transaction that records daily sales; it would be impossible to correctly change the hourly sales data with such a transaction.

The possible transactions and the data the transactions would change are listed in Figure 5-4. Some of the transactions change data, some add new data,

Transaction	Data or Transaction Involved
SELL LEMONADE	Decrement lemonade in pitcher
	Increment money
	Possibly generate FILL PITCHER
	transaction
FILL PITCHER	Increment lemonade in pitcher
	Decrement lemons in inventory
	Decrement sugar in inventory
	Update production statistics
	Possibly generate BUY LEMONS or BUY
	SUGAR transactions
BUY LEMONS (or sugar)	Increment lemons (sugar) on order
	Decrement money
	Turn on incentive sales flag (for
	Jeff's payment)
RECEIVE LEMONS (or sugar)	Increment lemons (sugar) in inventory
	Decrement lemons (sugar) on order
	Possibly turn off incentive sales flag
	and add amount due Jeff to Accumulated
	Incentives
PAY JEFF	Decrement Accumulated Incentives

Figure 5-4 Possible Transactions for Sally Enterprises

some delete data, and some are simple queries. Note the variety of levels of aggregation and generalization.

Businesses have a way of surprising designers. We may define and correctly process all of the transactions in Figure 5-4, only to be surprised by an unknown event. Sally, in the noontime rush, drops the pitcher! We have no corresponding transaction.

Now watch what happens: Sally, an ambitious entrepreneur, responds quickly. She runs into the house, finds an old quart canning jar, and makes a new batch. She begins to sell lemonade. The system thinks she is still using the pitcher, which was almost empty. After three glasses, it issues a message to make a new batch, and decrements raw materials inventory. The supply of sugar was low, so the system generates a purchase order for more sugar and assumes that Jeff is on his way to the store. All sales are now marked as occurring while Jeff is at the store, and are therefore subject to Jeff's incentive. Actually, Jeff is asleep in a nearby hammock.

Sally continues to service her customers and, in the rush, ignores the messages that are being written on the CRT (she wouldn't know what to do about them even if she paid attention to them). Within an hour, the model of Sally's business that is contained in the database grossly disagrees with reality.

Luckily for Sally, she is probably not audited, and she probably does not have to justify her records to the Internal Revenue Service or other governmental agency. Also, her records are few enough that she can delete the entire database and start over the next day. Most database environments are not this forgiving.

We must plan on errors. For a large database it is simply impossible to prevent them. If, unlike Sally, we cannot start over after an error, we must design subsystems for database recovery. We will consider this issue in detail in Chapter 11.

Differences among user perceptions

Users of the database view data differently, and they assign data items different meanings. For example, both Sally and Jeff say they want to know *sales*. Sally, however, wants to know total sales, and Jeff wants to know sales on which he earns a commission. Sally defines *total revenue* as the number of glasses times the price per glass. Jeff defines total revenue as the number of glasses sold while he was on a supply run times 5. Sally measures *productivity* as her total revenue divided by the number of batches of lemonade. Jeff measures productivity as his total revenue divided by the number of purchase orders he has filled. Thus different users will have different meanings for terms, and different uses for the database data. These differences appear straightforward in Sally's business, but are less apparent for larger enterprises.

Additionally, as mentioned in Chapter 1, it may be desirable to restrict certain users' views of the data. Sally, for example, may allow Jeff to view inventory amounts and purchase orders, but she may not want him to see sales, customer, or production data.

Finally, there is a third, more serious kind of difference among users. At the end of one particularly busy day, Sally is asked a question by three different people: "How much sugar did you use?" However, this question has three different meanings. One of Sally's customers is actually asking, "Is the nausea I feel and the twitch in my left eyebrow due to a hyperglycemic fit caused by your syrupy lemonade, or is it something else?" Sally's older brother is actually asking (and stating), "Is there enough sugar left to make cookies for Back to School Night, tonight?—*and there better be!*" Sally's father is looking at the sugar all over the floor in the kitchen and asking, "How much sugar actually got into the lemonade?" In other words, he's asking how much wastage there was.

Database as a model of an enterprise

    Level of detail
        Cost of aggregation and generalization is unanswerable question
        Need to aggregate and generalize in light of requirements and
        financial resources

    Dynamics of database as model
        Enterprise changes, model must change
        Events occur, are represented by transactions
        Level of transaction important - transactions cannot be more
        aggregated or generalized than database data

    User views
        Different perception of data structure
        Different perception of data meaning
        Need for standardized meaning

Figure 5-5   Design Considerations for Databases as Models

These questions illustrate a problem for database design. Different users (and designers) will have different meanings and interpretations for data that is stored in the database. Questions that appear to be similar may in fact be different. However, the computer system is only able to respond to a single interpretation of a given question. Therefore, a query has to be standardized and compromised in terms of the system and data that is contained before it can be answered. The characteristics of databases as enterprise models are summarized in Figure 5-5.

LOGICAL DATABASE DESIGN

As stated, database design is an intuitive and artistic process. There is no algorithm for it. Typically, database design is an iterative process; during each iteration, the goal is to get closer to an acceptable design. Thus a design will be developed and then reviewed. Defects in the design will be identified, and the design will be redone. This process is repeated until the development team and users can find no major defects. (Unfortunately, this does not mean the design will work; it simply means no one can think of any reason why it won't.)

The database is the bridge between people and hardware. As mentioned earlier, the characteristics of both people and hardware need to be considered. Consequently, database design is divided into two phases: logical design, where

DESIGN

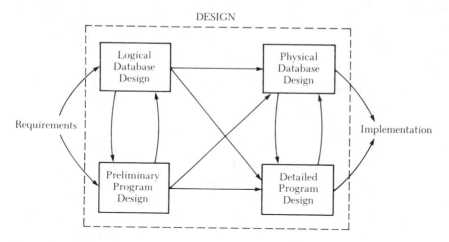

Figure 5-6   Database and Program Design Flow

the needs of people are specified, and physical design, where the logical design
is mapped into the constraints of particular program and hardware products.

Figure 5-6 illustrates the flow of work in a typical database design project.
User requirements are studied and a logical database design is developed. Con-
currently, the preliminary design of database processing programs is produced.
Next, the logical database and the preliminary program designs are used to
develop the physical database design and the detailed program specifications.
Finally, both of these are input to the implementation phase of the project.

Since this book is about database processing, we will focus primarily on the
design of the database. Realize, however, that this design does not occur in a
vacuum. Programs must be designed at the same time. In fact, the database
design cannot be evaluated until program specifications are developed, as we
will see.

We begin the discussion by considering the fuzzy process of logical database
design. To be certain of where we're going, we will first describe the outputs
of the process—what is supposed to be produced. Then, we will consider inputs
to logical database design—the ingredients we have to work with. Finally, we
will discuss a method or procedure for developing the logical database design.

Outputs of logical database design

A logical database design specifies the logical format of the database. The *records* to be maintained, their contents, and *relationships* among those records
are specified. Industry uses various terms for this design. It is sometimes called
the *schema*, the *conceptual schema*, or the *logical schema*. In this book, we will
use the term *logical schema* because it is the schema developed during logical
design.

Field	Description
CUSTOMER Record	
Customer-name	Alphabetic, 25 characters
Customer-address	Alphanumeric, 40 characters
Age	Numeric, 2 decimal digits
Parent-name	Alphabetic, 25 characters
ORDER Record	
Order-number	Numeric, 4 decimal digits
Customer-name	Alphabetic, 25 characters
Date	Format: YYMMDD
Time	Format: HH.MM
Number-of-glasses	Numeric, 2 decimal digits

Figure 5-7   Field Descriptions for CUSTOMER and ORDER Records

Logical database records   To specify logical records, the designer must determine the level of detail of the database model. If the model is highly aggregated and generalized, there will be few records. If the model is detailed, there will be many records. The database designer must examine the requirements to determine how coarse or how fine the database model should be. An example of this examination using data flow diagrams is presented later in this chapter.

The contents of these records are specified during logical design. Names of fields and their format must be determined. In Sally's case, the designer must specify how much data about customers, orders, and other records will be maintained. Also, the format of data items is specified. Figure 5-7 shows field descriptions for CUSTOMER and ORDER records.

As the requirements are evaluated and the design progresses, *constraints* on data items will be identified. These constraints are limitations on the values that database data can have. Three types of constraints are common. *Field constraints* limit the values that a given data item can have. They are sometimes called *edit constraints*. *Intrarecord constraints* limit values between fields within a given record. As an example, if the part color is blue, then the part number must end with a 1. *Interrecord constraints* limit values between fields in different records. For example, the part number must be unique (no other record can have this part number), or the department number in an employee record must match a department number in a department record (the employee's department must already be known in the database). Several constraints are shown in Figure 5-8.

Field Constraints:

Customer-name of CUSTOMER may not be null

Age of CUSTOMER must be from 1 to 80

MM in Date of ORDER must be from 1 to 12

Intrarecord Constraint:

IF MM in Date of ORDER is 1, 2, 3, 10, 11, or 12

    THEN HH in Time of ORDER must be from 12 to 17

    ELSE HH in Time of ORDER must be from 08 to 23

Interrecord Constraint:

Customer-name of ORDER must be a value of Customer-name of CUSTOMER

Figure 5-8   Examples of Constraints

Logical database record relationships   As stated several times already, the essence of database is the representation of record relationships. These relationships are specified during logical design. The designer studies the application environment, examines the requirements, and identifies necessary relationships.

Figure 5-9 shows possible relationships for several records in Sally's database. This figure is a data structure diagram like those discussed in Chapter 4. The arrows represent one-to-many relationships between database records. Data structure diagrams are not the only tool for expressing relationships. We will see other techniques when we discuss the semantic data model and the entity-relationship model. You may like these other techniques better.

To summarize, the output of logical database design is the specification of database records, their content, constraints, and relationships.

Inputs to logical database design

The inputs to logical database design are the system requirements and the project plan. Recall from Chapter 2 that requirements are determined by inter-

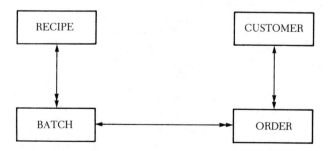

Figure 5-9   Data Structure Diagram of Sally Enterprises Database

views with users, and that they are approved by both users and management. The project plan describes the system environment, the development plan, and constraints and limitations on the system design.

If the methods described in Chapter 2 are followed, the requirements will be expressed in the form of data flow diagrams, policy statements, and the data dictionary. Having the requirements in this form will greatly facilitate the logical design process. Contents of the data dictionary can be transformed into the logical and user views. Policy statements can be used to develop the descriptions of logical database processing. The requirements can be used to verify the completeness of the logical design.

If the requirements are defined in narrative style, they will need to be converted to a format that facilitates logical database design. A data dictionary much like the one described in Chapter 2 will need to be developed, and concise statements of processing will need to be extracted from the requirements document. Thus the requirements will need to be transformed into a form similar to the one in Chapter 2. Since this is true, it is advisable to put the requirements into this format to begin with.

Procedures for logical database design

Many techniques have been defined for logical database design. Some techniques are completely intuitive and others involve specific procedures for processing the data dictionary. Others are between these extremes. The process described here is an amalgam of commonly accepted design tasks. See references [41], [45], [51], and [81]. The major steps in the logical design process are shown in Figure 5-10 and described below.

Identify data to be stored   First, the data dictionary is processed and data that is to be stored is identified and segregated. This step is necessary because the data dictionary will contain descriptions of reports, screens, and input documents that will not be part of the database.

Consolidate and clarify data names   The next step is to clarify the terms used for data. One task is to identify synonyms, to decide on standard names

1. Identify data to be stored
2. Consolidate and clarify data names
3. Develop the logical schema
4. Define processing
5. Review design

Figure 5-10   Stages of Logical Database Design

for synonyms, and to record aliases. *Synonyms* are two or more names for the same data item. They arise because of terminology differences within the company. What the marketing department calls SALES, the production department may call UNSCHEDULED-PRODUCTION, and the accounting department may call FUTURE-SALES. In this case, the development team will need to select a single, standard name for the data item in the logical schema of the database. Where possible, synonyms are eliminated. Where synonyms cannot be eliminated, they are recorded as alternate names, or *aliases*. Quite often synonyms cannot be eliminated because the users want to maintain their own terminology.

Identifying synonyms is not as easy as it sounds. There may be hundreds or thousands of data items in the logical schema. In this list there may be synonyms that sound completely different. Who would guess, for example, that SALES and UNSCHEDULED-PRODUCTION are the same data item?

Furthermore, even when potential synonyms are identified, it may not be easy to determine if the data names are truly synonymous. Suppose the marketing department records sales on the day in which they are submitted to production. However, suppose production will not record a sale if the item cannot be produced in the current quarter. This could mean that SALES and UNSCHEDULED-PRODUCTION are synonymous except for the last week of the quarter. Now, are they synonyms or aren't they? Are two separate data items needed in the database? Can the users be convinced to standardize on this data item? These questions exemplify realistic design issues.

Another task related to terminology is to ensure that data items having the same name are truly the same. If not, unique data item names will need to be developed (the original names may become aliases for the new, unique names). For example, consider the data item DATE. This can be the date of an order, the date of a shipment, the date of an employee termination, or some other date. The database designer must determine if all the uses of the DATE item are the same. If not, new and unique names will need to be determined.

Develop the logical schema   The third step in the design process is to develop the logical schema by defining records and relationships. Records are defined by determining the data items they will contain. Typically, assigning data items to records is straightforward and obvious for two-thirds to three-fourths of the record types. The design team examines the data flow diagrams and data dictionary, applies intuition to the business setting of the new system, and determines that certain records will need to exist.

For example, consider the data flow diagrams of Sally's business in Figure 5-11. Seven different files are shown in these DFDs. The designers of Sally's database might decide to create one database file for each of these seven. The contents of the records in these files will be determined from the data dictionary.

Once the obvious files have been identified, however, some interesting problems remain. First, some of these files may need to be combined. Should there be separate files for recipes and batch statistics? Do recipes need to be stored

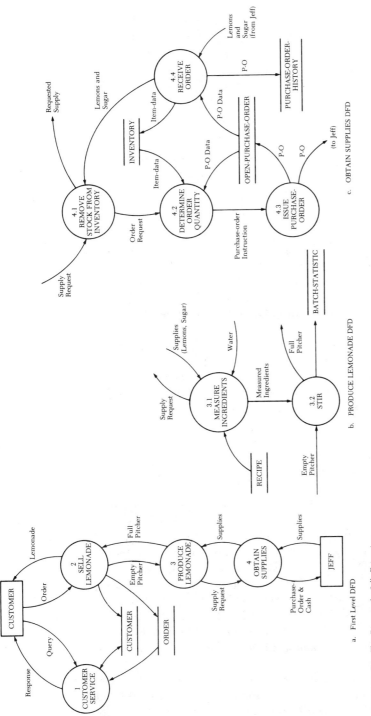

Figure 5-11 Data Flow Diagrams for Sally Enterprises

a. First Level DFD

b. PRODUCE LEMONADE DFD

c. OBTAIN SUPPLIES DFD

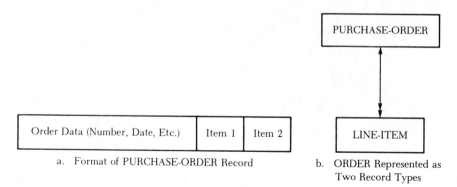

a. Format of PURCHASE-ORDER Record   b. ORDER Represented as Two Record Types

Figure 5-12 PURCHASE-ORDER Records

in the database? Would the design be effective if a recipe number were stored in the BATCH-STATISTIC record, and recipes stored manually? Similarly, can the OPEN-PURCHASE-ORDER and PURCHASE-ORDER-HISTORY files be combined? Can the PURCHASE-ORDER records have a flag indicating whether the order is open or not? The answer to these questions is maybe, depending on the requirements.

While some records may need to be combined, others may need to be separated. Figure 5-12a shows a PURCHASE-ORDER record. It has a header portion containing P-O Number, Date, and Vendor, and a variable portion that can contain up to two items. Figure 5-12b shows the same data stored as two separate record types. The PURCHASE-ORDER record has the header data, and the LINE-ITEM record has the items to be ordered.

Since lemonade consists only of lemons and sugar, it is tempting to say that the structure in Figure 5-12a is adequate. Sally will never order more than two items. However, databases have a way of existing longer than the designers anticipate, and Sally may expand her product line. What if next year she sells lemonade and cookies? Then she'll need to buy flour, shortening, eggs, oatmeal, and raisins. The PURCHASE-ORDER structure in Figure 5-12a will be inadequate. It will need to be expanded to allow for five or ten items, or a separate LINE-ITEM record will need to be defined. This simple dilemma characterizes the problems to be recognized and addressed during database design.

Figure 5-13 lists the records that were included in Sally's design. RECIPE and BATCH-STATISTIC records were not combined, but the OPEN-PURCHASE-ORDER and PURCHASE-ORDER-HISTORY records were. However, the structure of both of these records was modified to conform to Figure 5-12b. The designers thought the separated LINE-ITEM records would give Sally greater flexibility for the future.

A third problem regarding record definition concerns *implied* data. A data item is implied when it is needed to meet a requirement; but, because it is not visible to the user, it is not directly identified in the data dictionary. For exam-

```
CUSTOMER
ORDER
RECIPE
BATCH-STATISTIC
INVENTORY (Item-count)
PURCHASE-ORDER
LINE-ITEM
```

Figure 5-13   Records Included in Sally Enterprises Database

ple, Sally's recipes may call for sugar expressed in cups, but Jeff buys sugar in terms of pounds. Sally may want to send Jeff to the store to buy sugar for 10 pitchers. To produce the purchase order, Sally will need data to convert from volume to weight. This conversion data is not stated directly in the requirements, but is implied by them. Such data is difficult to ferret out of the requirements, but is essential for the database design.

The second step in developing the logical schema is to determine relationships among database records. At this point, we are not concerned about how the relationships will be represented by the database system. Instead, we want to model how the users see the relationships. We will probably have to adjust these relationships in the physical database design, but we do not want to constrain relationships to physical limitations yet. Doing so makes the logical schema far too complex, and may constrain our thinking so that we miss good design alternatives.

Generally, relationships are identified intuitively. The design team considers potential relationships among records that have been defined. Possible relationships for the records in Figure 5-13 are shown in Figure 5-14. Note all of these relationships are *binary;* the relationships exist between just two record types. However, a relationship may exist among three or four or more records. We will discuss this possibility in greater detail in the next chapter.

At this point, the design team must discriminate between theoretical and useful relationships. A theoretical relationship can exist logically, but may never be needed in practice. Examine the relationships in Figure 5-14. There is a many-to-many relationship between RECIPE and CUSTOMER. Is it needed? We can learn which customers have been served from a given recipe by traversing the BATCH and ORDER records (for each batch made by this recipe, find all orders; for each of these orders, list the customer). Similarly, we can learn which recipes a given customer has tasted by traversing the ORDER and BATCH records in the other direction. Thus, the RECIPE-to-CUSTOMER relationship may exist in theory, but be unneeded in fact. See if you can find other relationships in Figure 5-14 that may be unneeded.

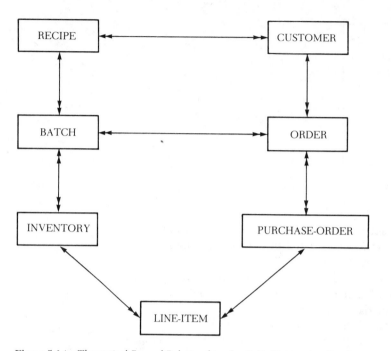

Figure 5-14 Theoretical Record Relationships for Sally Enterprises Database

In general, if there is any question regarding whether a relationship is useful or not, then the relationship should be included in the logical schema. The relationship can always be omitted later in physical design, whereas if the relationship were omitted during logical design, it would be difficult to add it later.

The determination of record types and relationships is an iterative process. While identifying relationships, the team may discover a reason for new record types; and while discussing record types, the team may identify a relationship. These two constructs are designed simultaneously. Only in a book is the process sequential and linear.

Recently techniques have been developed for obtaining record relationships directly by processing the data dictionary. Basically, these techniques operate by identifying one-to-many relationships in the data descriptions. The parent and child record types of each one-to-many relationship are recorded. If no record has more than one parent record type, then the database has a tree structure. If any record type has two or more parents, then a simple network structure exists. If a one-to-many relationship appears in both directions, then a complex relationship exists. See [35] and [63] for more information.

Define processing The next step in logical database design is to define the processing of the database. The requirements are examined to determine how the database should be manipulated to produce required results. The processing definitions can be developed in several ways. One method is to describe transactions and data to be modified, as was done in Figure 5-4.

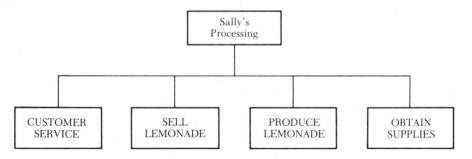

Figure 5-15   First-level Structure Chart for Sally Enterprises Programs

Another method for describing database processing is to develop structure charts of the programs that will access the database. One method for developing such processing descriptions is called *transform analysis*. This method has been extensively documented in [34], [35], and [65]. The output of transform analysis is a series of charts like those in Figure 5-15. The functions, inputs, and outputs of each programming module are defined. The impact on data and data relationships can be determined from these charts.

Purists would say that descriptions of the processing of the database are not appropriately part of database design. They would say that such descriptions are design issues for programs—not for databases. In a theoretical sense, such purists would be correct. However, logical descriptions of processing help the database designers identify design flaws.

For example, consider the first transaction in Figure 5-4: SELL LEMON-ADE. When this transaction is processed, the amount of lemonade in the pitcher is supposed to be decremented. Examine the records in Figure 5-13. Which one of these records contains the amount of lemonade in the pitcher? None of them. After all of this work, a basic data item like the amount of lemonade in the pitcher has been omitted. This fact is discovered by considering the requirements and transactions to be processed.

This omission forced a review of the logical schema. Of the records in Figure 5-11, the one most likely to hold the amount of lemonade in the pitcher is BATCH-STATISTIC. However, discussion of this fact revealed that this record is misnamed; for the data that it contains, it should actually be called PITCHER-STATISTIC, or just PITCHER. The format of this new record is shown in Figure 5-16.

Pitcher-number	Date	Time	Producer-name	Quantity-in-pitcher

Note: When a pitcher is empty, its quantity is zero, but the record remains in the database.

Figure 5-16   Format of PITCHER Record

The point of this discussion is that the concurrent design of programs and database will improve the database design. There is also evidence [52] that such concurrent design improves the quality of programs as well.

Design review   The final stage of logical database design is a review. The logical schema and user views are examined in light of the requirements and program descriptions. Every attempt is made to identify omissions, unworkable aspects, or other flaws in the design. Typically, a panel of independent data processing people is convened for this review. Documentation of the logical schema, user views, and program descriptions is examined by the panel, and oral presentations are evaluated.

To be effective, the design review must follow stringent guidelines. The purpose of the review is to *identify* flaws, not to *solve* them. Discussions on the various merits of solutions to problems should be avoided. Further, the atmosphere should be helpful, not judgmental. All panel members should realize the review is of the design, not of the personnel involved or of the management of the project. See [42] for more information concerning design reviews.

At the conclusion of the design review, the panel produces a list of problems discovered and a recommendation regarding the next step to be taken. The panel usually recommends that the project be continued while identified problems are fixed. Occasionally, however, the design panel may recommend that the database design be repeated. Very rarely, the panel may recommend that the project be discontinued.

If the project is large, the results of the logical database design review may be presented to management. If so, a request will be made for management approval for the next stage of the project—physical database design. Alternatively, for smaller projects, the design team proceeds to physical design without needing management approval.

PHYSICAL DATABASE DESIGN

The second stage of database design—physical design—is a stage of transformation. The logical schema is transformed into the particular data constructs that are available with the DBMS to be used. Whereas the logical design is DBMS-independent, the physical design is very much DBMS-dependent.

Detailed specifications of the database structure are produced. These specifications will be used during database implementation to write source statements that define the database structure to the DBMS. These statements will be compiled by the DBMS and the object form of the database structure will be stored within the database. See Figure 5-17.

Outputs of physical database design

Specific constructs vary widely from one DBMS to another. At this point, we cannot be very detailed. In general, two major specifications are produced.

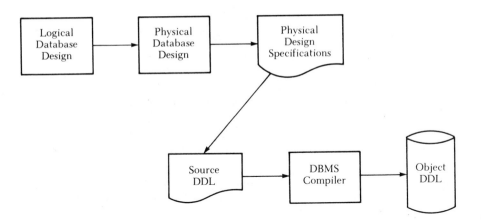

Figure 5-17   Role of Physical Design

First, the physical specification of the logical schema is defined. We will call this specification the *physical schema*. This schema is a transformation of the logical schema into the data modeling constructs available with the DBMS to be used. Second, user views are defined.

Physical schema   Figure 5-18a lists generic items that are defined in a physical schema design. The content of each record must be defined, and the name and format of each field of each record specified. Constraints from the logical database design are transformed into criteria for field descriptions (numeric, etc.). Keys of database records need to be identified, and overhead structures for supporting the keys defined. For example, the designer may specify that a particular key is to be supported by an inverted list.

Name of physical schema
Names of records
Format of records
Names of fields
Format of fields
Constraints
Names of keys
Supporting overhead data structures
Format of record relationships

Names of user view
Names (aliases) of records
Format of records
Names (aliases) of fields
Format of fields

a.   Contents of Physical Schema

b.   Contents of User Views

Figure 5-18   Results of Physical Database Design

Record relationships are also defined in the physical design. Limitations in the DBMS may necessitate that record relationships be changed from what the users wanted. A many-to-many relationship may need to be changed to a simple network, for example. We will see more examples of this in the following chapters.

User views   The second component of a physical database design is the user views. Since most users will need to view only a portion of the database, the logical design must specify which user groups will view which portions of the database. In Sally's case, there might be one user view for Sally and another for Jeff.

User views are generally a subset of the schema. Records or relationships may be omitted from a view; fields may be omitted or rearranged. Also, the names of records, fields, or relationships may be changed. This flexibility allows users to employ terminology that is familiar and useful to them. Figure 5-18b lists items to be defined for user views during physical design. We will discuss this topic further in Chapters 10, 12, and 13.

Inputs to physical database design

The inputs to the physical database design are the outputs of the logical database design, the system requirements, and the preliminary design of programs. These were discussed in the previous section.

Physical database design process

A physical database design is produced by transforming the logical design into a physical design. However, since the specific outputs vary from one DBMS to another, it is impossible to describe this process, other than very generally, without first discussing characteristics of the DBMS. Therefore, we will defer a discussion of the physical database design process until we have discussed specific DBMS features.

In particular, we will consider physical design for a relational DBMS (a type of DBMS to be defined in the next section) in Chapters 7 and 8, and physical design using a CODASYL DBTG DBMS in Chapters 9 and 10. Further, this parallel will be continued in the next part (Part IV). Implementation of a relational database will be discussed in Chapter 12, and implementation of a CODA-SYL DBTG database will be presented in Chapter 13. At this point, realize that physical database design follows logical design, but be patient and wait until we have developed more terminology before considering physical design.

DATABASE MODELS

A *database model* is a vocabulary for describing the structure and processing of a database. There are two reasons for studying database models. First, they

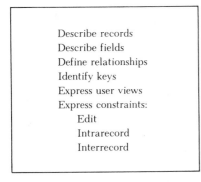

Describe records
Describe fields
Define relationships
Identify keys
Express user views
Express constraints:
    Edit
    Intrarecord
    Interrecord

Figure 5-19 Purposes of Data Definition
            Languages (DDL)

are an important database design tool. Database models can be used for both logical and physical database design—much as flowcharts or pseudocode are used for program design. Second, database models are used to categorize DBMS products. In this section, we will discuss the components of a database model and survey six important models.

Components of a database model

Database models have two major components. The *data definition language* (DDL) is a vocabulary for defining the structure of the database. The DDL must include terms for defining records, fields, keys, and relationships. In addition, the DDL should provide a facility for expressing a variety of user views. Ideally, the model will also provide a method for expressing database constraints. Figure 5-19 summarizes the purposes of data definition components in a database model.

Data manipulation language (DML) is the second component of a database model. The DML is a vocabulary for describing the processing of the database. Facilities are needed to retrieve and change database data. Two types of DML exist. *Procedural DML* is a language for describing actions to be performed on the database. Procedural DML obtains a desired result by specifying operations to be performed. For example, to find employees earning more than $50,000 per year, a procedural DML would require a series of statements like those in Figure 5-20a. In this example, the designer or user defines a method or process for obtaining the desired result.

For procedural DML, facilities are needed to define the data to be operated on and to express the actions to be taken. Both data items and relationships can be accessed or modified. Also, to ensure that the database can be accurately recovered in the case of failure, commands are needed to define *logical transactions* (atomic units of work—see Chapter 11), and to eliminate changes in case of a program-detected error.

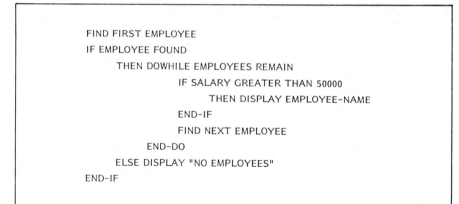

a. Procedural Processing

```
SELECT EMPLOYEE-NAME
FROM EMPLOYEE-FILE
WHERE SALARY GREATER THAN 50000
```

b. Nonprocedural Processing

Figure 5-20 Examples of Data Manipulation Language

Nonprocedural DML is a language for describing the data that is wanted without describing *how* to obtain it. For example, to find employees earning more than $50,000 per year, a nonprocedural DML would require statements like those in Figure 5-20b. In this example, the user simply states what is wanted, not how to get the result. The DBMS is given the job of determining how to get the result. Nonprocedural DML is descriptive, not prescriptive.

You will see more examples of these types of DML in later chapters. The SQL statements discussed in Chapter 7 are nonprocedural. The CODASYL DBTG statements discussed in Chapter 9 are procedural.

Survey of prominent database models

Figure 5-21 portrays six common and useful database models. The models are arranged on a continuum. Models on the left-hand side of this figure tend to be oriented to humans and human meaning, whereas those on the right-hand side are more oriented toward machines and machine specifications. The ANSI/X3/SPARC data model is in a class of its own, as will be explained.

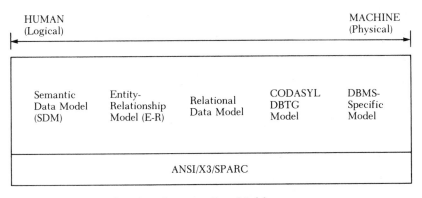

HUMAN
(Logical)

MACHINE
(Physical)

| Semantic Data Model (SDM) | Entity-Relationship Model (E-R) | Relational Data Model | CODASYL DBTG Model | DBMS-Specific Model |

ANSI/X3/SPARC

Figure 5-21   Relationship of Six Important Data Models

In this section, we will survey these models. Subsequent chapters will consider the data models (all but the ANSI model) in greater detail.

Before we turn to these models, you should realize that two categories of database model have been omitted from this section. These categories are the *hierarchical* and *network* data models. A model is hierarchical if its only data structure is a hierarchy (tree). With the hierarchical model, all networks must first be decomposed to trees before they can be represented. A model is network if its data structures are both trees and simple networks. Only complex networks need to be decomposed before they are represented.

These two models are omitted from this discussion because the distinction between them has become unimportant. The hierarchical data model has become too narrow and the network data model too broad. The only hierarchically based DBMS to survive has been IBM's product DL/I. Although seldom openly stated, the terms *hierarchical data model* and *DL/I* are synonymous. Additionally, many vastly different DBMS products are included in the network category. In fact, network DBMS products differ among each other as much or more than some network products differ from DL/I. Thus the adjectives *hierarchical* and *network* do little to characterize or discriminate between DBMS products, and we will not use these terms. A discussion of DL/I—as a DBMS product—appears in the Appendix.

Semantic data model   The first database model listed in Figure 5-21 is the semantic data model (SDM). The term *semantic* means meaning. The semantic data model provides a vocabulary for expressing the meaning as well as the structure of database data. As such, SDM is useful for logical database design and documentation. We will just touch on SDM in this survey; more details of the model are presented in Chapter 6.

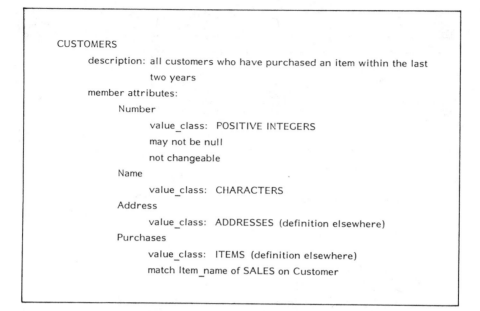

CUSTOMERS
    description: all customers who have purchased an item within the last
        two years
    member attributes:
        Number
            value_class: POSITIVE INTEGERS
            may not be null
            not changeable
        Name
            value_class: CHARACTERS
        Address
            value_class: ADDRESSES (definition elsewhere)
        Purchases
            value_class: ITEMS (definition elsewhere)
            match Item_name of SALES on Customer

Figure 5-22   Sample Record Definition with SDM

Figure 5-22 shows the SDM definition of a CUSTOMER record. We will consider SDM in detail in the next chapter. For now, simply note SDM's informal and meaning-oriented nature. First, an informal description of the record is provided and then each of the data items within the record is defined. Value_class is a special SDM term; the value_class identifies allowable values for data items. Constraints such as *may not be null* and *not changeable* can also be specified. The match statement in the Purchases data item defines a relationship with the SALES record (not shown). The essence of this statement is that a CUSTOMER record is related to a SALES record if the value of the data item Name (in CUSTOMER) is the same as the value of the data item Customer (in SALES). More will be said about the match statement in the next chapter.

No DBMS is based on SDM, and hence SDM cannot be used for physical database design. However, because of its semantic nature, SDM is recommended for logical database design. SDM can be used to describe what the users want to see. Later, once a DBMS has been selected, the SDM description will be transformed into the physical database constructs that are available. We will discuss SDM more fully in the next chapter.

The entity-relationship model   The entity-relationship model (E-R model) is primarily a logical database model, although it has some aspects of a physical model as well. *Entities* are representations of objects in the real world; examples are records of customers, invoices, salespeople, and so forth. Entities of similar

Figure 5-23   Entity-Relationship Diagram for CUSTOMER/SALESPERSON Relationship

structure are collected into *entity sets*. All **CUSTOMER** records form the customer entity set; all **SALESPERSON** records form the salesperson entity set.

A database contains data about entities and about relationships among entities. Figure 5-23 is an E-R diagram that shows the relationship of the customer and salesperson entity sets (a many-to-many relationship). Notice the relationship is named and represented in a diamond. This is typical E-R notation. Figure 5-24 presents data for the database in Figure 5-23. There are three tables of data. One has data about customer entities, one has data about salesperson

Customer-number	Customer-name	Other Data
10	A	
20	B	
30	C	
40	D	
50	E	

a.   CUSTOMER Data

Salesperson-number	Salesperson-name	Other Data
2000	Z	
2050	Y	
2100	X	

b.   SALESPERSON Data

Customer-number	Salesperson-number	Date of Call	Location of Call
10	2000	830104	Dallas
10	2100	830407	Houston
20	2050	830227	Boston
20	2050	830311	Chicago
20	2050	830429	Los Angeles
30	2000	830220	Atlanta

c.   Relationship Data

Figure 5-24   Three Tables of Data for the E-R Diagram in Figure 5-23

entities, and the third has data about the relationship. Notice the relationship has data of its own; in this case, the date and location of the most recent call.

The E-R model can be used for logical database design. Also, entity-relationship diagrams can be used to express a physical design for relational implementations. In this book, we will use the E-R model both ways. We will use many of the terms from the E-R model in Chapter 6 when we discuss logical design.

The relational model The relational database model is near the midpoint of the human/machine continuum in Figure 5-21 because it has both logical and physical characteristics. The relational model is logical in that data is represented in a format familiar to humans; the relational model is unconcerned with how the data is represented in computer files. On the other hand, the relational model is more physical than SDM or the E-R model. There are relational DBMS products. This means that databases designed according to the relational model need not be transformed into some other format before implementation. Thus the relational model can be used for both logical and physical database design.

A relation is simply a flat file. Figure 5-25 shows two relations, one for customers and the other for invoices. The rows of the relation are the file records. Rows are sometimes called *tuples* (rhymes with couples) of the relation. The fields of the relation are shown in the columns of Figure 5-25; they are sometimes called the *attributes* of the relation.

The significance of the relational model is not that data is arranged in relations. There is nothing spectacular about the data arrangement in Figure 5-25. Rather, the significance of the relational model is that relationships are considered to be implied by data values. For example, in Figure 5-25, a relationship is implied by the common attribute, Customer-number. Customer-number 10

Customer-number	Customer-name	Other Data
10	A	
20	B	
30	C	

a. CUSTOMER Relation

Invoice-number	Customer-number	Other Data
100	10	
120	30	
140	20	
160	20	
180	30	
200	10	
220	10	

b. INVOICE Relation

Figure 5-25 Sample Relations

Customer-number	Customer-name	Other Customer Data	Invoice-number	Customer-number	Other Invoice Data
10	A		100	10	
30	C		120	30	
20	B		140	20	
20	B		160	20	
30	C		180	30	
10	A		200	10	
10	A		220	10	

Figure 5-26   Join of CUSTOMER and INVOICE Relations

in the CUSTOMER relation is related to the three invoice records in the INVOICE relation having that same Customer-number. In fact, we can join these two relations together on a common value of Customer-number as shown in Figure 5-26. Note the joined records have equal values of Customer-number.

The principal advantage of carrying relationships in data is flexibility. Relationships need not be predefined. We can join CUSTOMER tuples with INVOICE tuples or CUSTOMER tuples with ACCOUNTS-RECEIVABLE tuples, or whatever, without having to predefine the relationships in the design.

More research has been done regarding the relational model than any other model. Much has been said regarding the best ways of structuring relations, and many different relational data manipulation languages have been defined. Some of these, such as SQL, are nonprocedural. Others, such as relational algebra, are procedural. Until recently, the problem with the relational model has been the lack of a commercially viable relational DBMS. However, there are now several relational DBMS products. We will discuss the relational model in greater detail in Chapters 7, 8, and 12.

CODASYL DBTG model   The CODASYL DBTG (Conference on Data System Languages, Database Task Group) data model was developed by the same group that formulated COBOL. It was developed during the late 1960s and is the oldest of the data models. The DBTG model is a physical database model. There are constructs for defining physical characteristics of data, for describing where data should be located, for instructing the DBMS regarding what data structures to use for implementing record relationships, and other similar physical characteristics.

A DBTG schema is the collection of all records and relationships. A subschema is a subset and possibly a reordering of records and relationships in the schema. DBTG record definitions are similar to those in a COBOL Data Division. Unlike the relational model, relationships become fixed when they are defined in the schema. The DBTG model provides a structure (the DBTG *set*) for expressing one-to-many relationships.

A procedural DML has been carefully and completely defined for this model. As you will see in Chapters 9 and 10, the DBTG DML is rich and somewhat confusing. There is no nonprocedural DML for the DBTG model.

Many DBMS products are based on the CODASYL DBTG model. However, because of its physical nature, the DBTG model is a long way from user requirements. Therefore, it is difficult to use for logical database design. Rather, the logical database design should be expressed with a model like SDM, and the logical design then transformed into a physical design using the DBTG model. We will consider the DBTG model in greater detail in Chapters 9, 10, and 12.

DBMS-specific models   There are over one hundred different commercial DBMS products. The DBMS are sometimes categorized in terms of their underlying data model. A DBMS is considered a relational system if it conforms, in essence, to the relational data model. Alternatively, a DBMS is considered to be a CODASYL system if it conforms, in essence, to the CODASYL DBTG data model. A third category of DBMS is *other*. If a DBMS does not conform to one of the above two data models, then it has its own, unique data model.

There are many systems that fall into the other category; some of them are exceedingly successful. They are not bad systems, they simply have a unique design. ADABAS, SYSTEM 2000, TOTAL, and IMAGE are names of successful DBMS that have their own data models. See the Appendix for descriptions of these DBMS.

When one of these products is to be used, the designer can develop the logical database design using a model like SDM. Then, the logical design is transformed into a physical design using the constructs of the available DBMS. There is so much variety among the other DBMS that it is difficult to make more specific comments.

ANSI/X3/SPARC data model   Look again at Figure 5-21. The ANSI/X3/SPARC (American National Standards Institute/Committee X3/Standards Planning and Requirements (Sub)-Committee) data model is shown at the bottom of this figure. Graphically, it seems to support the other data models, and in fact, it does support them. The X3 model is a model for *DBMS* design rather than for *database* design. We include it here for completeness and to show its relationship to the data models.

We have discussed the ANSI/X3/SPARC data model already, only you didn't know it. In Chapter 1, when we discussed the external, conceptual, and internal views, we were in fact discussing the X3 model. According to the X3 model, the global enterprise view of the data is defined in the conceptual schema. This schema can be defined using any data model; the X3 report does not specify a

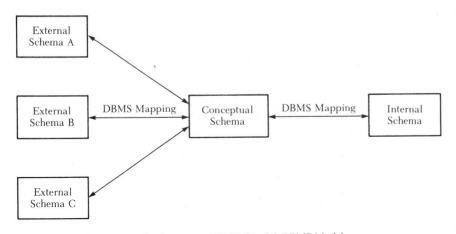

Figure 5-27   Three Types of Schema in ANSI/X3/SPARC DBMS Model

model to be used. Thus the conceptual schema could be expressed in terms of SDM, the relational model, the CODASYL model, or some other data model.

Users (either application programmers or query/update users) view the database via an external schema (see Figure 5-27). The external schema is a mapping of the conceptual schema. It can be expressed in terms of any data model, even a data model that differs from the one used for the conceptual view. Thus an external view might appear as a DBTG database to a user even though the conceptual schema was defined with the relational data model. Note in Figure 5-27 that a DBMS program must map the database from the conceptual view into the external view.

The third schema in the X3 model is the internal schema. This is the view of the database as seen from the vantage point of the processing computer. It includes the physical format of all data and overhead. The fact that a given key field is supported by an inverted list would be recorded in the internal schema. No model has been proposed for expressing internal schemas, either by the X3 Committee or by anyone else. The format of these schemas has been left to DBMS designers.

Since the X3 model is a model of a DBMS and not a model of databases, we will not consider it further in this text. The characteristics of the data models discussed in this section are listed in Figure 5-28.

APPLICATION OF DATABASE MODELS TO DATABASE DESIGN

Figure 5-29 shows the major steps involved in designing a database. This is a refinement of a portion of Figure 5-6, omitting program design tasks. Inputs to

Type	Characteristics	Application
Semantic Data Model	DDL language for storing meaning. High level DML. No DBMS based on this model.	Logical database design
Entity-Relation-ship Model	Entities and relationships modeled as data. E-R diagrams graphically show relation-ships. No DML.	Logical and physical database design
Relational Model	Data represented as tables. Relationships implied by data. Dynamic data relationships. Procedural and nonprocedural DML. A few DBMS based on this model.	Logical and physical database design
CODASYL DBTG Model	Oldest data model. Relationships must be predefined. Procedural DML. Extensive application in industry. Many DBMS based on this model.	Physical database design
DBMS-Specific Model	Models vary widely. DDL and DML closely conform to features of the DBMS.	Physical database design
ANSI/X3/ SPARC Data Model	DBMS model instead of database model. Three schema model. Can support a variety of different data models.	Design model for DBMS

Figure 5-28   Summary of Data Models

design are statements of data requirements from the specification data diction-ary. The output of design is a specification that can be used to implement the database using a commercial DBMS. The design that is produced depends very much on the DBMS to be employed. For this reason, Figure 5-29 shows two alternative design outputs. If we are going to use a DBMS based on the rela-tional model (the subject of Chapters 7, 8, and 12), we will produce a relational design. If we are going to use a DBMS based on the CODASYL DBTG model (the subject of Chapters 9, 10 and 13), we will produce a DBTG design.

The database design process is boxed in Figure 5-29. Within this box are two steps: logical (DBMS-independent) design and physical (DBMS-dependent) design. As shown, in this text we will express logical schemas, the output of logical design, using the semantic data model. This process will be considered in detail in Chapter 6.

After logical design, there is a branch, depending on the DBMS to be employed. If we are going to use a relational DBMS, then the output of physical design

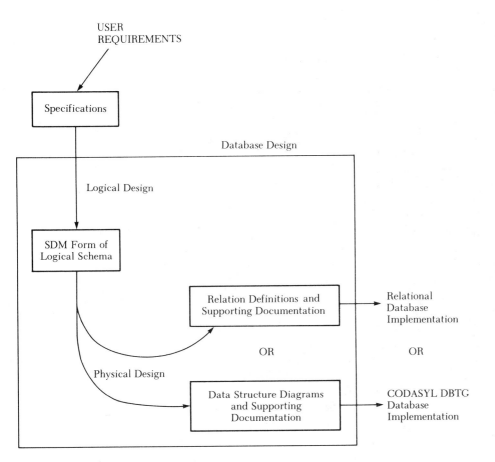

USER
REQUIREMENTS

Specifications

Database Design

Logical Design

SDM Form of
Logical Schema

Relation Definitions and
Supporting Documentation

Relational
Database
Implementation

OR

OR

Physical Design

Data Structure Diagrams
and Supporting
Documentation

CODASYL DBTG
Database
Implementation

Figure 5-29 Use of Models in Database Design

will be a relational design expressed as relation definitions and supporting documentation (perhaps E-R diagrams). This leg of the branch will be discussed in
Chapters 7 and 8.

If we are going to use a CODASYL DBMS, then the output of the physical
design will be a CODASYL design expressed as data structure diagrams and
supporting definitions. This leg of the branch is discussed in Chapters 9 and
10. This branch is necessary because of the vast conceptual differences between
the CODASYL and relational models.

If an organization employs a DBMS based on a model other than the CODA-
SYL or relational models, then they would follow whichever path is the better
path for the DBMS to be used. An appendix of this book describes commercial
DBMS and recommends one of these two directions. In either case, I believe
the SDM description is an appropriate first step.

SUMMARY

A database is a model of an enterprise. The designer of a database must determine the level of detail of the model and identify methods for keeping the model current as the organization changes. Also, users will have different perceptions of the database; the design of the database should accommodate these differences where possible.

There are two phases to database design. During logical design, the requirements specifications are examined to determine needed logical database structure. The objective is to specify the database as humans view it. The logical schema, the output of logical design, expresses database records and relationships. Physical design is the second phase. During this phase, the logical design is transformed to a physical design using data constructs of the DBMS to be used. Both the schema and user views are defined at this stage.

Database models provide tools for specifying database designs. Just as flowcharts, pseudocode, and other tools are used to specify program design, database models are used to specify database design. Important database models are the semantic data model, the entity-relationship model, the relational model, and the CODASYL DBTG model. The ANSI/X3/SPARC model is an important DBMS model. In addition, there are many commercially viable DBMS-unique models.

The database design process can be summarized as follows. Begin with the requirements definition. Express tentative logical database designs in terms of a logical database model. Review this design in light of requirements. Once the design is considered complete, convert the logical design to a physical design using the appropriate physical data model (the one that matches the DBMS to be used). Then implement the database using the features of the DBMS.

In this text we will use SDM to express logical database designs. Then, we will employ entity-relationship diagrams to express relational database designs. We will use data structure diagrams to express CODASYL DBTG designs. We will follow this process for the remainder of Part II. In the next chapter, we will discuss SDM and logical design in greater detail. Chapters 7 and 8 will be devoted to the relational database model, and Chapters 9 and 10 will be devoted to the CODASYL DBTG model.

Group I Questions

5.1   Explain why a database is a model of the enterprise in which it exists.

5.2   Define the terms *aggregate* and *generalize*. How do these terms pertain to database design?

5.3   What criteria should be used to determine the level of database detail?

5.4   What is an event? a transaction? How do these terms pertain to database processing?

5.5   Explain three ways that users of a database can differ with one another.

5.6   What are the two phases of database design? What is the objective of each phase?

5.7   Define the term *logical schema*.

5.8   Describe the outputs of logical database design.

5.9   Describe the inputs to logical database design.

5.10 List the major activities of logical database design.

5.11 What considerations need to be made when developing the logical schema?

5.12 Explain why the definition of the processing of the database is considered part of database design.

5.13 Describe guidelines for database design review meetings.

5.14 Define the outputs of physical database design.

5.15 Define the term *database model*.

5.16 What is the purpose of DDL? What characteristics of the database are described with DDL?

5.17 What is the purpose of DML? Name and explain two types of DML.

5.18 Describe two characteristics of the semantic data model. What is the purpose of this model?

5.19 Describe two characteristics of the entity-relationship model. What is the purpose of this model?

5.20 Describe two characteristics of the relational data model. What is the purpose of this model?

5.21 Describe two characteristics of the CODASYL DBTG model. What is the purpose of this model?

5.22 Explain the term *DBMS-specific data model*.

5.23 What is the ANSI/X3/SPARC model? How does it differ from the other models discussed in this chapter?

5.24 Explain the process of database design and describe the application of SDM, E-R diagrams, data structure diagrams, the relational model, and the CODASYL DBTG model.

Group II Questions

5.25 Suppose Sally decides to keep records of cash received and disbursed.

   a. Change the DFD in Figure 5-11 to show cash flows and necessary files.

  b. Modify the DSD of theoretical relationships in Figure 5-14 to include any new files.

  c. What transactions will be needed to maintain the new data?

5.26 Review the records for Sally Enterprises in Figure 5-13. Specify a set of records for this application that is less generalized than the records in Figure 5-13. Specify a set of records for this application that is less aggregated.

5.27 Explain how a database designer could determine which of the theoretical relationships in Figure 5-14 must be expressed in the database. For each of the binary record relationships, specify requirements that would necessitate expressing the relationship in the database. Make whatever assumptions are necessary for the relationships to be required.

Projects

A. Locate a business in your area that is using a DBMS. Interview the development personnel to determine how the database was designed. Which, if any, of the models in this chapter were used to develop the design? Is the design an effective one? How would the company change the design? How would the company proceed with database design in the future?

B. Consider the problem of scheduling students into classes:

  1. Construct a set of data flow diagrams for this problem. If you need data, interview someone in your administration.

  2. Using your data flow diagrams, build the records and relationships for a logical schema of this problem. Express your schema using data structure diagrams.

  3. Describe events that will change this model. Define transactions for these events and list the data that will be modified by them.

C. Locate a small business in your community that is not using database technology. Interview the employees and owner, if possible, and repeat the activities in project B. Also, determine user groups, and define the records contained in appropriate user views.

6

Logical

Database Design

Logical design is the process of transforming the system specifications into a human-oriented database design. The term *human-oriented* means a design that has meaning to people rather than to computer systems. After the logical design has been specified and reviewed, the designers transform it into a physical design for implementation using a specific DBMS.

In this chapter we first discuss primitives, or logical design structures. Then we will present essential features of the semantic data model (SDM), a language for expressing logical designs. Finally, we will illustrate the logical design process for the design of a database for Sally Enterprises.

Much of the terminology of this chapter originated with the entity-relationship model published by Peter Chen in 1976 [18]. Although this book directly uses only part of the E-R model (the E-R diagrams), you should realize that much of the conceptual foundation for this chapter and much of the foundation for SDM will be found in the entity-relationship model.

This chapter introduces discrepancies in punctuation as mentioned in the Preface. Specifically, multiple-word names will be connected with underscores rather than hyphens. Underscores are the standard in industry for SDM and the relational model. There is no significance in this difference, but it is standard and you may as well become accustomed to it. We will continue to use the hyphen in the discussion of the CODASYL DBTG model as well as all nonrelational DBMS products.

LOGICAL DESIGN PRIMITIVES

A logical database design is a representation of reality. It is a model of aspects of some activity that are of interest to sponsors (users and management) of the database. As mentioned in the last chapter, such models represent selected portions of reality; the models are developed by aggregation and generalization. Since the database represents a subset of reality, some questions about reality become unanswerable. The goal when developing a database design is to make only uninteresting questions unanswerable. Unfortunately, this goal is seldom attained completely.

Primitives in the real world

Before we begin to design files and relationships and the like, we need to describe, as best we can, the foundations of data modeling. We need to answer questions like: Where do we begin? What is it that we are trying to represent? With what aspects of reality are we to be concerned? We have to be careful when answering these questions, however, because we can fall into endless epistemological (the philosophy of knowledge) debate. Very interesting conversations can take place in this realm, but they don't help to get the products out the door.

To make progress, therefore, we need to establish a starting point. We will begin with a set of fundamental structures or primitives. We will choose to believe that these primitives exist because they make sense to us. We can nod our heads in agreement that we understand the meaning of these primitives. Whether they really exist, or whether they are creations of the human mind, we do not know. To get the products out the door, it doesn't matter.

The first primitive is the *object*. The real world has objects; they are phenomena that can be represented by nouns. A person, place, thing, event, and instruction are all objects. Sally is an object. A sale is an object. A recipe is an object.

Objects are grouped into *object classes*, another primitive. This is done by generalization. Objects are lumped together on the basis of similarities; differences in objects are ignored. PEOPLE is an example of an object class. People have similarities that differentiate them from trees, from marshmallows, from sales orders, etc. People also have differences, such as height, weight, age, and so forth, but these are ignored when forming a class of people.

Objects have *properties*. A property is a characteristic of an object. A person's name and height are properties. The date of a sale is a property and so is the number of a part. Properties are either inherent or, for the purposes of the database, considered to be inherent in objects.

The collection of all possible instances of a property is called a *property value set*. Such sets are unusual and a bit philosophical. The property value set for person height (in inches) is the collection of all heights for all possible people objects. It is *not* a collection of integers from, say, 0 to 100. These numbers are representations of heights, not the heights themselves. Rather, the property set is a collection of concepts or ideas which we call *heights*. The integer 72 is a representation of the property 72 inches tall, but it is not that property. The essence of the thing called *height* is what is in the property value set. Figure 6-1 summarizes the primitives we are defining.

A *fact* is an assertion that, for a given object, a particular property has a particular element from the property value set. Thus the statement that the

Primitive	Definition and Examples
Object	Phenomena that can be represented by nouns. An employee, an order, an invoice.
Object Classes	A group of objects formed by generalization. EMPLOYEES, ORDERS, INVOICES.
Properties	Characteristics of objects. Age, Date, Invoice_number.
Property Value Set	The collection of values that a given property may have. All ages of all people in 1983.
Fact	The intersection of a given object with a given property value set. Employee 12345 is 27 years old.
Association	A connection of objects of the same or different classes. Employee 12335 placed Order ABC.

Figure 6-1 Primitives in the Real World

height of Ben Parks is 72 inches is a fact. The statement that sales invoice number 10032 is dated March 3, 1982, is a fact. Note in Figure 6-2 that a fact is the intersection of a given object with a given property value set.

Objects can be related to one another. These relations are called *associations*. Associations can exist between objects of the same class or of different classes. The association *Parent* exists between objects of the same class—between people and other people. The association *Purchase* exists between two different classes—between people and sales invoices. Also, an object can have an asso-

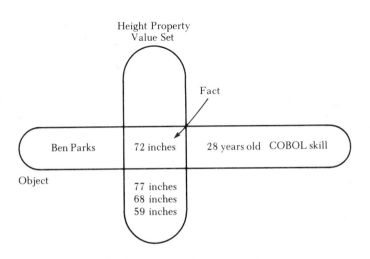

Figure 6-2 Example of a Fact as an Intersection of an Object with a Property Value Set

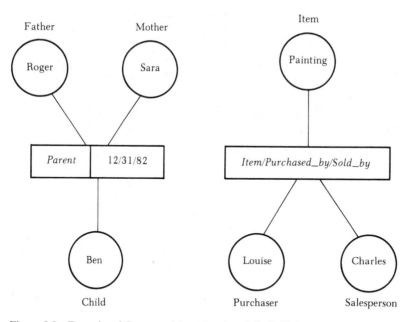

Figure 6-3   Examples of *Parent* and *Item/Purchased_by/Sold_by* Associations

ciation to itself. The association *Best_friend* exists among people, and some people are their own *Best-friend*.

Associations can exist among two or three or more objects. The association *Siblings* exists among potentially many brothers and sisters. The association *Item/Purchased_by/Sold_by* is an association of objects of three different types: an item, a customer, and a salesperson. Figure 6-3 shows an instance of the *Parent* association and of the *Item/Purchased_by/Sold_by* association.

Associations may have properties just as objects have properties. The *Parent* association may have a property such as date of last meal together or degree of harmony or something else. The property corresponds to the association, however, and not to any single one of the objects. Thus child's weight is not a property of the *Parent* association. Rather, it is a property of the Child object.

Primitives in the conceptual world

When we model an aspect of reality, we make a representation of it. When we write Ben Parks' name on a piece of paper, we are making a representation of Ben Parks. We are not putting Ben Parks himself on the paper. Similarly, when we design or process a database, we are not working with real world primitives like objects and properties. We are working with representations of these primitives. A 72-inch person can be inserted into a chair or a bed, but not into a database.

Real World Primitive	Conceptual Primitive
Object	Entity
Object Class	Entity Class
Property	Attribute
Property Value Set	Domain
Fact	Value
Association	Relationship

Figure 6-4   Equivalencies between Real World and Conceptual Primitives

Database experts have defined a conceptual primitive for each of the real world primitives defined in the last section. See Figure 6-4. An *entity* is a conceptual representation of an object. An entity can be a line on a report, a circle on a map, a record in a computer, a blue flag, or some other representation.

Although entities are like records in a computer file, during logical database design we do not restrict an entity to record format. As a representation of an object, an entity is unrestricted by the constraints of computers. You will see entities in the next section that cannot be represented by a computer, but they are useful for the development of computer models. During physical database design, entities will be transformed into computer records, but not until then.

Entities can be grouped into *entity classes*. An entity class is a representation of an object class. Thus an entity class consists of all the entities that represent the objects of an object class. If there is an object class called PEOPLE, then there can be an entity class called PEOPLE. If there is an object class called SALES_INVOICE, then there can be an entity class called SALES_INVOICE.

Entities have *attributes* that are representations of properties of objects. Attributes characterize and describe entities. Examples of attributes are Height, Name, and Sales_date. Note that attributes and properties are not the same. A property is a characteristic of an object, whereas an attribute is a representation of that characteristic. The property *72 inches tall* is represented by the attribute *72*. Again, properties exist as some aspect of an object in reality; attributes are *representations* of properties.

As shown in Figure 6-4, the conceptual primitive that represents property value sets is called a *domain*. A domain is the collection of all values that an attribute can have. The domain of Heights (in inches) is the integers from 0 to 100. The domain of Names is a collection of character strings of some appropriate length, and so forth.

In everyday thinking, we often confuse properties and attributes. We think of the number 72 as being someone's height; but actually 72 is a *representation* for the amount of space between that person's toes and the top of his or her head. When designing or processing databases, this distinction is important.

All items recorded in a database are attributes; they are not properties. In the accounts receivable data, the number 104,567 *represents* a stack of money, but it is not that stack.

You may be asking, So what? The importance of this distinction is that properties change as the business evolves, but attributes do not change, unless someone causes them to. Unfortunately, there is no automatic tie between properties and attributes such that whenever the property changes, the attribute changes as well. For example, the property *Age* automatically changes on an employee's birthday, but the attribute Age, stored in a database, will not automatically change on that date. The designer of the system must create a program or procedure to update Age. In general, the database designer must construct the system so that when properties change, attributes will be updated within an acceptable period of time.

To continue with conceptual primitives, a *value* is the representation of a fact. It is the intersection of a given entity with a given domain. The statement "The date of the sales invoice entity numbered 10032 is March 3, 1982" is a value.

A *relationship* is the conceptual representation of an association. Similar to associations, relationships can exist among entities in the same class or in different classes. An entity can have a relationship to itself. Entities have a *role* in the relationship. The role defines the function served by the entity in the relationship. Consider the *Parent* relationships shown in Figure 6-5. One entity has the role Mother, one has the role Father, and a third has the role Child.

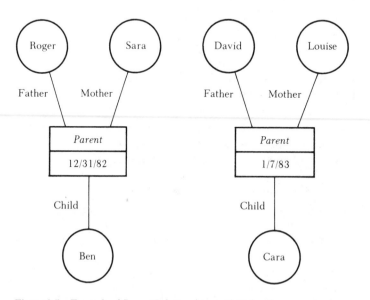

Figure 6-5   Example of *Parent* Relationships with Roles Shown

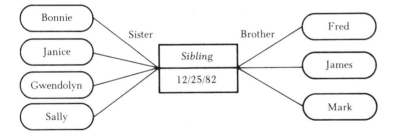

Figure 6-6   Example of *Sibling* Relationship with Roles

Figure 6-6 shows the *Sibling* relationship. Here, some of the entities have the role Brother and others have the role Sister.

A relationship can have attributes, just as associations can have properties. In Figure 6-5, the attribute Date_of_last_meal (12/31/82 and 1/7/83) represents the day on which the three people represented by the entities last shared a meal. In Figure 6-6, the relationship has the attribute Date_of_last_reunion (12/25/82).

You should review Figure 6-4 carefully. Be certain you understand each of the terms in both the real and the conceptual worlds. The terms defined in this section will be used throughout the remainder of this book. Understanding them is important.

THE SEMANTIC DATA MODEL

The semantic data model (SDM) was developed by Hammer and McLeod and first published in 1981 [44]. We will use it as a tool for expressing a logical schema design. Although an SDM DML has been defined, we will not consider it in this book. Rather, we will discuss those aspects of SDM useful for defining database structure. We will not discuss all features of SDM. Refer to [35] or [44] for a more complete discussion.

The chief advantage of SDM is that it provides a facility for expressing meaning about the data in the database. During logical database design, we need such a facility to avoid confusion and to document learnings, design decisions, and constraints. SDM provides better facilities for such documentation than other data models.

For example, suppose we learn that the entity class CUSTOMER_INVOICE has a very particular meaning. It may be that this entity is created only for sales to large, national customers for commissionable sales in excess of $10,000. Since we would never guess this constraint from the name CUSTOMER_INVOICE, we need to document this fact in the logical schema. Without such documentation, both programming and processing errors are likely. As you will see, SDM has a facility for documenting this as well as other types of meaning.

Another advantage of SDM is that it allows data to be described in context. Users see data from different perspectives. For example, to the sales force, an order belongs to a given customer. To the production department, however, an order belongs to a particular production run. Thus users see the same data, but they see it differently; they see it relative to their field of operation. SDM allows relative data definition.

A third advantage of SDM is that constraints on database data can be defined. For example, if a given item is not changeable, SDM allows this fact to be stated. Also, if an attribute must conform to a particular format (part numbers start with 1, for example), these considerations can readily be defined. With other data models, such constraints are not part of the schema description and are documented separately, if at all. In practice, the constraints are inserted into application programs, which hides them to an extent that they are practically inaccessible.

SDM is like pseudocode, but instead of describing the structure of programs as pseudocode does, SDM describes the structure of data. Like pseudocode, SDM has certain structures and rules, and within those structures and rules the designer has a good deal of latitude and flexibility.

Defining entity classes

Entities are organized into classes. Each SDM entity class may have a name, a description, members (the entities), and two kinds of attributes. Figure 6-7 shows the basic format of an SDM entity class description. We have not yet described all of these terms; the definitions will be given as the discussion of SDM progresses.

Figure 6-8 shows a sample SDM logical schema for Sally Enterprises. This logical schema includes records for recipes, batches (pitchers), customers, and orders. The purchase-order, line-item, and inventory-item records in Figures 5-7 and 5-9 have been omitted in order to shorten the logical schema description. For now, assume the database includes only these four record types. We will discuss Figure 6-8 over the next ten pages or so, so do not be put off by its size. (Note, however, that this schema is for a lemonade stand; imagine the schema for a manufacturing plant or similar enterprise.)

In Figure 6-8, entity class names are printed in capital letters. Also, SDM terms are shown in small letters followed by a colon. Thus the terms *description:* and *member attributes:* are SDM terminology and not the designer's.

PITCHERS is the first class defined. The class is named, and then an informal description of the class is provided. The description, which is optional, defines the purpose and content of the class. Special remarks are also written here. Next, the member attributes are defined. These are attributes of the entities

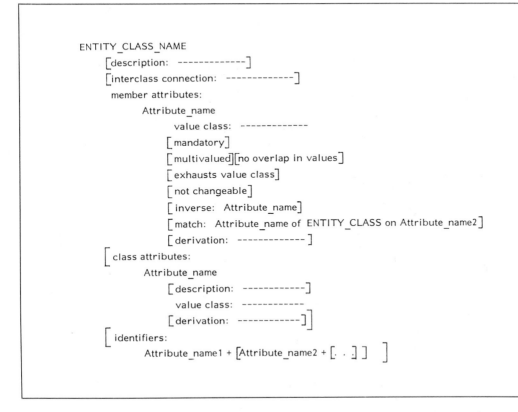

ENTITY_CLASS_NAME
    [description: ------------]
    [interclass connection: ------------]
    member attributes:
        Attribute_name
           value class: ------------
        [mandatory]
        [multivalued][no overlap in values]
        [exhausts value class]
        [not changeable]
        [inverse: Attribute_name]
        [match: Attribute_name of ENTITY_CLASS on Attribute_name2]
        [derivation: ------------]
  [class attributes:
        Attribute_name
           [description: -----------]
           value class: ------------
           [derivation: -----------]]
  [identifiers:
      Attribute_name1 + [Attribute_name2 + [. . .]]]

Figure 6-7   Format of SDM Entity Class Descriptions

in this class. For PITCHERS, the member attributes are Number, Date, and Recipe_used. Note that in SDM, attribute names are printed with initial letters capitalized. The structure of members in the PITCHERS entity class is shown in Figure 6-9.

For now, skip over the definition of the member attributes and find the term, *class attributes:*. These attributes, which are optional, belong to the class as a whole and not to any particular member. Thus Total_produced is a class attribute; it contains the sum of the amounts of all PITCHERs. Active_pitcher and Amount_left are also class attributes. Active_pitcher contains the number of the batch that is currently being sold. Amount_left describes the amount of lemonade in the active pitcher. (Active_pitcher and Amount_left are class attributes because only one pitcher in the class can be active and only one pitcher can have any lemonade remaining.) Sample data for a PITCHERS class is shown in Figure 6-10.

PITCHERS
      description: the number, date of preparation and recipe used for a pitcher of lemonade. Amount left in the pitcher is stored here.
      member attributes:
          Number
              value class: PITCHER_NUMBERS
              mandatory
              not changeable
          Date
              value class: DATES
          Recipe_used
              value class: RECIPES
              inverse: Where_used
      class attributes:
          Total_produced
              description: This attribute contains the sum of the lemonade of all pitchers produced by Sally. It is updated by application program.
              value class: QUARTS
          Active_pitcher
              description: the number of the pitcher (batch) that is currently in use
              value class: PITCHER_NUMBERS
              derivation: maximum pitcher number in this class
          Amount_left
              description: the amount of lemonade remaining in the active pitcher
              value class: QUARTS
    identifiers:
          Number

RECIPES
      description: all formulae used for the preparation of lemonade
      member attributes:
          Name
              value class: RECIPE_NAMES
          Amount_of_sugar
              description: amount specified in cups
              value class: CUPS

Figure 6-8   Sally's Logical Schema Number 1

Amount_of_lemons

    description: amount specified in whole medium California lemons

    value class: LEMON_COUNT

Amount_of_water

    description: amount of water in quarts

    value class: QUARTS

Where_used

    description: the pitchers made with this recipe

    value class: PITCHERS

    inverse: Recipe_used

    multivalued

    exhausts value class

identifiers:

    Name

CUSTOMERS

    description: all people who have purchased lemonade

    member attributes:

        First_name

            value class: PEOPLE_NAMES

            not changeable

        Last_name

            value class: PEOPLE_NAMES

            not changeable

        Date_of_birth

            value class: DATES

            not changeable (unfortunately)

        Family_members

            description: people in this customer's family

            value class: CUSTOMERS

            derivation: all CUSTOMERS with identical last names

            multivalued

        Past_amounts_purchased

            description: amounts this customer has purchased

            value class: CUPS

            match: Amount of ORDERS on Customer

            multivalued

            exhausts value class

        Total_amount

            description: the total amount of lemonade purchased

Figure 6-8   (cont'd.)

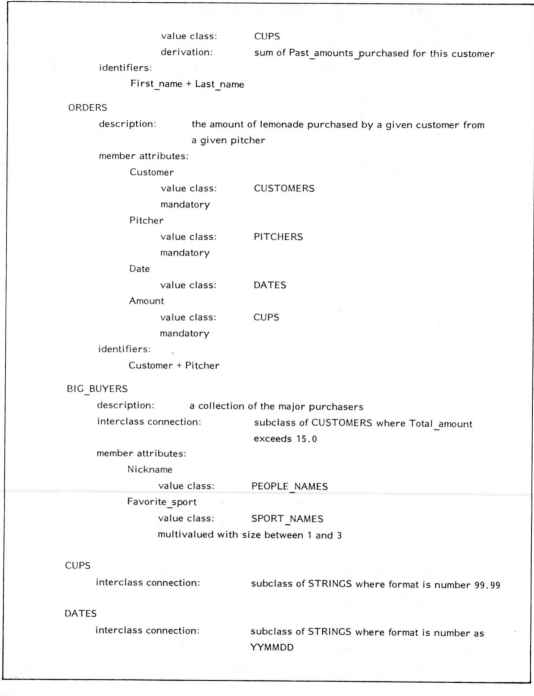

value class: CUPS

derivation: sum of Past_amounts_purchased for this customer

identifiers:

First_name + Last_name

ORDERS

description: the amount of lemonade purchased by a given customer from a given pitcher

member attributes:

Customer

value class: CUSTOMERS

mandatory

Pitcher

value class: PITCHERS

mandatory

Date

value class: DATES

Amount

value class: CUPS

mandatory

identifiers:

Customer + Pitcher

BIG_BUYERS

description: a collection of the major purchasers

interclass connection: subclass of CUSTOMERS where Total_amount exceeds 15.0

member attributes:

Nickname

value class: PEOPLE_NAMES

Favorite_sport

value class: SPORT_NAMES

multivalued with size between 1 and 3

CUPS

interclass connection: subclass of STRINGS where format is number 99.99

DATES

interclass connection: subclass of STRINGS where format is number as YYMMDD

Figure 6-8   (cont'd.)

LEMON_COUNT
    interclass connection: subclass of STRINGS where format is positive
                                     integer less than 10

PEOPLE_NAMES
    interclass connection: subclass of STRINGS where length is less than 20
                                     characters where specified

PITCHER_NUMBERS
    interclass connection: subclass of STRINGS where format is positive
                                     integer less than 500

QUARTS
    interclass connection: subclass of STRINGS where format is number 9.99

RECIPE_NAMES
    interclass connection: subclass of STRINGS where length is less than 10
                                     characters where specified

SPORT_NAMES
    description: sports that Sally can knowledgeably discuss
    interclass connection: subclass of STRINGS where value is 'SOCCER',
                                     'FOOTBALL', 'TENNIS', 'BASKETBALL', or
                                     'SKIING'

Figure 6-8   (Cont'd.)

Base entity classes   An SDM class can either be *base* or *nonbase*. If base, then the class exists independently of all other classes. If nonbase, then the class is derived from other classes. In Figure 6-8, the class CUSTOMERS is a base class. It exists independently of other classes. Data for this class originates outside of the database. The class BIG_BUYERS, however, is a nonbase class. It is a subset of the CUSTOMERS class, and hence is derived from this class.

Number	Date	Recipe_used

Figure 6-9   Structure of PITCHERS Entity Class from Figure 6-8

Number	Date	Recipe_used
102	820704	RECIPE B
101	820703	RECIPE A
100	820703	RECIPE A

Total_produced	Active_pitcher	Amount_left
47	102	2

Figure 6-10   Sample Data for PITCHERS Entity Class

Base classes can have *identifiers*. These are attributes that uniquely identify members. For example, the Number attribute uniquely identifies members of PITCHERS. For CUSTOMERS, the concatenation of First_name and Last_name uniquely identifies CUSTOMERS members.

Nonbase entity classes   Nonbase classes are constructed from subsets of other classes, or as aggregations of other classes. For our purposes, we will only consider subsets. See [44] for aggregations.

Every nonbase class has an entry, *interclass connection:*, that describes how the class is to be constructed. For subsets, the interclass connection names another class, and specifies which members of that class are to be included in the new class. For example, in Figure 6-8, BIG_BUYERS is defined as a subclass of CUSTOMERS where Total_amount (a member attribute of CUSTOMERS) exceeds 15.0. Figure 6-11 shows the relationship of CUSTOMERS and BIG_BUYERS entity classes.

The designer has a good deal of latitude in describing the members to be included in a subset. Hammer and McLeod [44] show three ways; actually, any

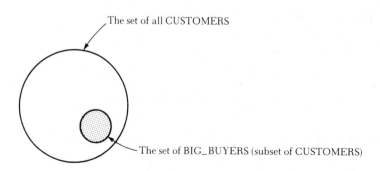

The set of all CUSTOMERS

The set of BIG_BUYERS (subset of CUSTOMERS)

Figure 6-11   Relationship of CUSTOMERS and BIG_BUYERS Entity Classes

Descriptor	Status	Remarks
Name	Mandatory	Initial capital letter
Description	Optional	Remarks about attribute
Value class	Mandatory	The domain of the attribute (another SDM value class)

Descriptor Characteristics	Default Value
Single or multivalued	Single
Value optional or mandatory	Optional
Changeable or not changeable	Changeable
Exhaustive or nonexhaustive	Nonexhaustive
Overlapping or nonoverlapping	Overlapping

Figure 6-12   Summary of Attribute Descriptors

nonambiguous statement that identifies members should be allowed. The point is to provide the database designer with a facility for defining entity classes that are subsets of other entity classes.

Defining attributes

Each entity, or member, of a class has a set of attributes. These attributes represent the properties of objects. In SDM, each attribute has a name, an optional description, a value class, and a set of optional characteristics. These are summarized in Figure 6-12.

As stated, attribute names are printed with initial capitals. They must be unique within the class where they are defined. Also, they must be unique within all classes that are derived from their class of definition. Thus, in Figure 6-8, within CUSTOMERS there can be only one attribute named First_name. Also, within BIG_BUYERS, a class derived from CUSTOMERS, there can be no supplemental attribute named First_name. All of the attributes of CUSTOMERS are inherited by BIG_BUYERS; if BIG_BUYERS had an additional attribute named First_name, there would be ambiguity in attribute names.

Attribute value classes   As stated, each attribute must have a *value class*. Value class is another term for domain. In SDM, value classes are defined as entity classes. For example, in Figure 6-8 the value class of the attribute Number in PITCHERS is PITCHER_NUMBERS. This value class (domain) is defined subsequently in Figure 6-8 as another entity class. The definition of the entity class PITCHER_NUMBERS is near the end of Figure 6-8.

Thus the definition of every attribute references another value class. This could become an infinite regression; each class references another class, which references another, and on and on. However, this regression is stopped in SDM by the existence of a special class called *STRINGS*. STRINGS is a default entity class; it needs no definition. STRINGS contains any character string that the designer wants. Thus, in Figure 6-8, the class PITCHER_NUMBERS is a subclass of STRINGS such that the allowed values are decimal numbers between 1 and 499. The last eight class definitions in Figure 6-8 are all subclasses of STRINGS. Note the variety of definitions. Again, like pseudocode, SDM provides the designer with considerable latitude within its structure. Any non-ambiguous definition of a string is allowed.

There are two major advantages of defining attribute domains as entity classes. First, the format and constraints on data items are clearly specified. In Figure 6-8 there is no question regarding the valid format of any value.

Second, allowing attributes to be members of entity classes permits a very natural, human-oriented way of expressing relationships. In Figure 6-8, examine the attribute Recipe_used in PITCHERS. The value class (domain) of this attribute is the entity RECIPES. Thus this attribute is actually *another entity*. To the user of PITCHERS, it appears as if the RECIPE for the pitcher is part of the pitcher entity. See Figure 6-13.

In reality, the logical schema defines PITCHERS and RECIPES as separate entity classes. However, RECIPES is made to look like part of PITCHERS. From the standpoint of the production department (the PITCHERS users), this definition will make great sense.

We will explain more about defining relationships in the next section. For now, try to become comfortable with the somewhat strange (but ever so useful) idea that an attribute can either be a subset of STRINGS (a mundane data definition akin to COBOL's PICTURE clause), or it can be another entity.

Additional attribute characteristics   In addition to name and value class, an attribute definition can, optionally, include a description and any of a set of characteristics. Attributes can be *single* or *multivalued* (like a repeating field); they can be *mandatory*, meaning that a null value is never to be accepted; attributes can be *not changeable*, meaning that, except to correct errors, the

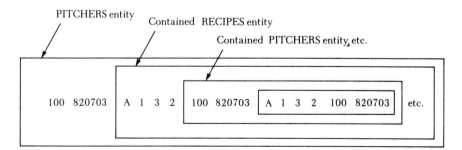

Figure 6-13   SDM Entities Nested within Other Entities

value of the attribute must remain the same. If multivalued, constraints can be placed on the number of repetitions allowed.

Additionally, an attribute can be *exhaustive,* meaning that every member of the value class must be used. For example, in Figure 6-8 the attribute Where_ used in RECIPES exhausts its value class, which is PITCHERS. This means that every member of PITCHERS must belong to some member of RECIPES. Intuitively, this makes sense. A batch of lemonade in a pitcher must have had some recipe. Having this constraint ensures that no user can enter a mystery batch into the database.

Finally, multivalued attributes can be specified as *nonoverlapping.* This means that a member of the value class can be used *at most* once (it need not be used at all). In Figure 6-8, if we wanted a recipe to be used just once (we do not, but if we did), then the description of the attribute Where_used would include the characteristic *no overlap in values.* Since this attribute is also exhaustive, each recipe would have to be used, and it would be used just once.

Defining relationships

SDM provides three facilities for defining relationships. All three facilities use the SDM characteristic that entities can be contained within entities.

Defining relationships with inverses   The *inverse* facility causes two entities to be contained within each other. Physically, this is impossible, so this idea may seem a bit strange. It's a bit like looking into two opposing mirrors; perhaps you have done this at the hairdresser's. Each mirror is reflected in the other and there is a seemingly infinite number of reflections. See Figure 6-14.

Figure 6-14   Mirror Images Contained within Mirror Images

In Figure 6-8 the entity classes PITCHERS and RECIPES are inverses of each other. This is specified by a pair of inverse phrases. In PITCHERS, the attribute Recipe_used has the value class RECIPES and the inverse attribute Where_used. In RECIPES, the attribute Where_used has the value class PITCHERS and the inverse attribute Recipe_used. Inverses are always specified by such pairs. Notice, too, that Where_used is a multivalued attribute. An instance of this inverse structure is shown in Figure 6-15. Recipe A was used for pitchers 100, 101, and 103, and recipe B was used for pitchers 102 and 104.

Observe the infinite regression. Pitcher 100 contains recipe A; however, recipe A contains pitcher 100. Further, this contained pitcher 100 contains the same copy of recipe A. And on and on, in a loop.

For our purposes, we will ignore the infinite regression. After the first level, all the regressions are duplications of data and hence unimportant. The learning to be taken from Figures 6-14 and 6-15 is the graphical portrayal of the interdependencies of data (and interdependencies of business departments). For design purposes, it suffices to say that recipes contain the pitchers that have been produced from them, and pitchers contain the recipe that was used in their production.

Unless you have practical business experience, you will probably not appreciate the strength and appropriateness of this definition. However, to people in production, recipes *are* contained within pitchers. That is how production people view the world. They believe, with all their hearts, that recipes are a portion of the object pitcher. They will consider any other view of the data as artificial and inadequate.

At the same time, in marketing analysis, pitchers *are* contained within recipes. Marketing analysis people want to evaluate the popularity of a given recipe.

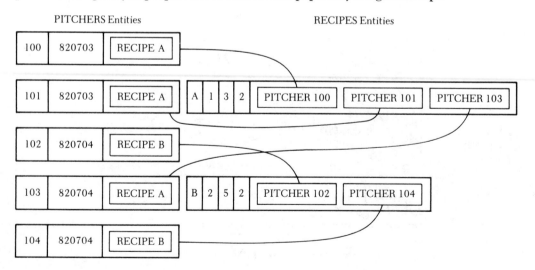

Figure 6-15   Sample Data for PITCHERS and RECIPES Entity Classes

To do this, their view of reality has recipe objects containing pitcher objects. They, too, will consider any other view of the data as artificial and inadequate.

Thus the beauty of SDM is that users can have it both ways. They can see data as they want to see data, even if these ways are seemingly contradictory. In actuality, these views do not conflict at all. They are simply different views of the same thing. It just depends on which of the hairdresser's mirrors you look into first. When we study physical database design, we will find ways to physically store the data that will allow the DBMS to provide both logical views.

Defining relationships with matching   The second SDM facility for representing relationships is *matching*. With matching, a member of one entity class is matched with a member of another entity class. Then, the value of an attribute in one of the members is moved to the other. For example, in Figure 6-8 Past_amounts_purchased of CUSTOMERS is defined with the phrase: *match Amount of ORDERS on Customer*. This means that a member of CUSTOMERS is to be matched with a member of ORDERS and that the Amount attribute in ORDERS is to be moved to the Past_amounts_purchased attribute in CUS-TOMERS. The words *on Customer* define how the members in the two classes must match. In this example, the member in the CUSTOMERS class must match the value in Customer of ORDERS.

ORDERS Entities

Customer		Pitcher	Date	Amount
Ben	Parks	P100	820703	2
Linda	Veld	P100	820703	3
Ben	Parks	P101	820703	3
Linda	Veld	P101	820703	5
Linda	Veld	P102	820704	6

CUSTOMERS Entities

First_name	Last_name	Other Data
Ben	Parks	· · ·
Linda	Veld	· · ·

a.   Example Data for CUSTOMERS and ORDERS Entities

First_name	Last_name	Other Data	Past_amounts_purchased			Total_amount
Ben	Parks	· · ·	2	3		5
Linda	Veld	· · ·	3	5	6	14

b.   Example of Past_amounts_purchased from Matching

Figure 6-16   Matching Members of Entity Classes

Consider the instance shown in Figure 6-16a. The member Ben Parks of CUSTOMERS matches two members in ORDERS. More precisely, the CUSTOMERS member, Ben Parks, resides in the Customer attribute of two members of ORDERS. Keep in mind that the entire member resides in the Customer attribute as indicated by the enclosed rectangles in the Customer attribute. Additionally, the member Linda Veld matches three members in ORDERS.

According to the match phrase in Figure 6-8, attribute Past_amounts_purchased of CUSTOMERS is to be matched with attribute Amount of ORDERS on Customers. This means the attribute, Amount, will be copied from ORDERS members to matching CUSTOMERS members. In Figure 6-16b, the amounts 2 and 3 have been copied to Ben Parks' data; these amounts have been placed in the attribute Past_amounts_purchased. Also, the amounts 3, 5, and 6 have been copied to Past_amounts_purchased in Linda Veld's data.

Even though this definition of Past_amounts_purchased is cumbersome, observe how convenient the definition will be to the user. The amounts purchased will appear to be part of the CUSTOMERS data, even though they are taken from the Amount attribute of ORDERS.

Defining relationships with derivations   SDM provides a derivation capability for attributes. Hammer and McLeod specify rules on derivations. For our purposes, any nonambiguous statement about how to derive an attribute is appropriate. For example, the attribute Total_amount of CUSTOMERS is derived from Past_amounts_purchased by summation as specified.

Derivation can be used to specify relationships among members in the same entity class. This has been done using the attribute Family_members in CUSTOMERS. The value class of this attribute is CUSTOMERS; this indicates that CUSTOMERS entities will contain CUSTOMERS entities within themselves. That may seem strange, but remember, this is a logical view only. We are not attempting to describe a physical structure.

The CUSTOMERS that are to be contained within a CUSTOMERS member are specified by the derivation term. All CUSTOMERS members with the same last name are to be contained. Thus every Parks CUSTOMERS member will contain all other Parks CUSTOMERS members. This type of derivation is a very convenient way of specifying relationships within an entity class.

The logical form of four entity classes defined in Figure 6-8 is shown in Figure 6-17. The users of each of these records will have a view of the data that seems natural to them. The records appear to be logically integrated, even though they are defined separately in the logical schema.

These three techniques for expressing relationships using SDM are subtle, almost covert. Some people believe that relationships should be expressed more explicitly. This can be done within the framework of SDM by using some of the constructs from the entity-relationhip model. We consider this alternative in the next section.

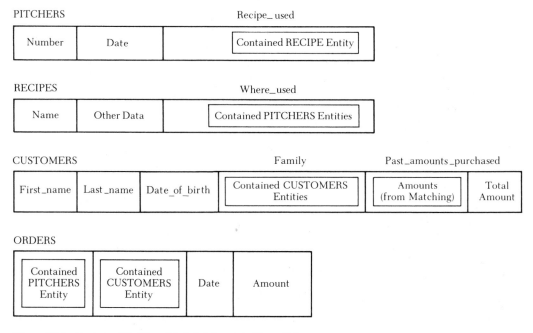

Figure 6-17   Contained Entities of Sally's Schema in Figure 6-8

THE ENTITY-RELATIONSHIP MODEL

As its name implies, the E-R model is explicit about relationships. Unlike SDM, in the E-R model both entities and relationships are considered to be different constructs. Entities are grouped into *entity sets,* and relationships are grouped into *relationship sets.*

When we used SDM in Figure 6-8, we defined entity classes for CUSTOMERS, PITCHERS, and ORDERS. For the E-R model, however, only CUSTOMERS and PITCHERS would be considered entity sets. Since ORDERS represents the relationship of CUSTOMERS to PITCHERS, it would be considered a relationship set and not an entity set (the terms *entity class* in SDM and *entity set* in E-R are synonymous).

In a relationship set, each of the entities being related has a *role.* The role is the purpose or function that the entity serves in the relationship. Figure 6-18 depicts the ORDERS relationship set and shows roles. Roles are usually denoted this way for E-R relationship sets.

Note in Figure 6-18 that both CUSTOMERS and PITCHERS *entities* are represented in the relationship. Thus, E-R, like SDM, allows entities to be included within entities. However, for E-R, only relationship entities can include other entities.

Entity Set Name	PITCHERS	CUSTOMERS		
Role	Supply	Buyer		
Relationship Data			Date	Amount
	100	Ben Parks	820704	3
	100	Linda Veld	820704	4
	101	Ben Parks	820704	2
	101	Fred Parks	820704	1
	101	Jane Veld	820704	7

Figure 6-18   Example of the ORDERS Relationship Set (E-R Model)

Entity-relationship diagram

An *entity-relationship diagram* is a graphical portrayal of entities and their relationships. It is similar to the data structure diagrams shown in Chapter 4, but it supports the representation of more general relationships.

Figure 6-19 is an E-R diagram for a logical schema equivalent to Figure 6-8. Entity sets are shown in rectangles and relationship sets are shown in diamonds. The RECIPE_USED relationship is one-to-many from RECIPES to PITCH-

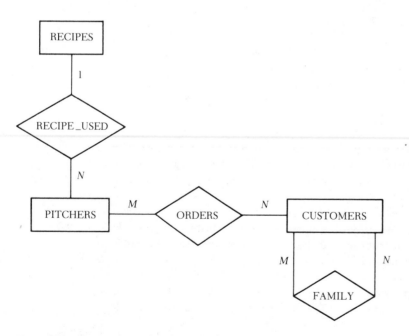

Figure 6-19   Entity-Relationship Diagram of Schema in Figure 6-8

ERS. This is depicted by the 1 and N on the lines connecting the entity sets to RECIPE_USED. The ORDERS relationship is many-to-many. A pitcher has many customers, and a customer may order from different pitchers. This relationship is depicted by the M and N on the lines from the entity sets to ORDERS. (The letters M and N simply signify that there may be many (N) ORDERS for a given PITCHER and many ORDERS (M) for a given CUSTOMER and that the number of ORDERS corresponding to each may be different.) Finally, the relationship FAMILY is many-to-many from CUSTOMERS back to CUSTOMERS.

If you compare Figure 6-8 to Figure 6-19, you will see that relationships are much more explicit in the E-R model. The RECIPE_USED relationship is hidden in the SDM description. It is defined by the paired inverse clauses in RECIPES and PITCHERS. ORDERS is explicitly shown in the SDM logical schema, but it is called an entity class and not a relationship. The FAMILY relationship is also hidden in the SDM description. It is a derivation of the Last_name attribute of CUSTOMERS.

Comparison of record definitions using SDM and E-R models

There are both advantages and disadvantages to E-R's explicit definition of relationships. One disadvantage is inconvenience. With SDM, we could define the relationships in context—whatever seemed easiest. It was convenient to define FAMILY as a derivation on Last_name, so we did it. We could have defined the family relationship using a separate entity class (see question 6.24), but that would have been awkward. Also, we did not need to store any data about the family as a unit. Had we needed to store family religious preference, or some similar family-oriented attribute, then we would have been forced to define FAMILY as a separate entity class, similar to ORDERS.

Further, Recipe_used could have been defined as a separate entity class. This has been done in Figure 6-20. Note that RECIPE_USED has two attri-

RECIPE_USED

Recipe_name	Pitcher_number
A	100
A	101
B	102
A	103
B	104

Figure 6-20   Use of Entity Class to Explicitly Define the Recipe/Pitcher Relationship

butes, Recipe_name and Pitcher_number. It was easier to use SDM's inverse facility. Defining an entity class for a relationship that has no data seems wasteful and unnecessary, at least from the user's perspective.

Finally, ORDERS was defined as a separate entity class. We did this because we wanted to maintain the date and amount of each order. If we did not want this data, the ORDERS relationship could have been specified using the inverse facility.

Thus the disadvantage of E-R's explicit record definition is that it forces us to define a relationship, even if the relationship has no data. This will seem to be unnecessary to the user.

On the other hand, this disadvantage becomes an advantage during physical database design. We will need to explicitly define each relationship to the DBMS because there is (yet) no DBMS that can process an SDM logical schema. We must produce an E-R diagram like the one in Figure 6-19 (or its equivalent) before we can prepare the physical database design.

So, both models have an important role. One possibility is to use SDM for the initial logical design; SDM can be used to transform requirements into the first cut at the database design. Then, the database designer can transform the SDM description into an E-R diagram. Using E-R diagrams like this will be especially helpful when a relational DBMS is used.

LOGICAL DESIGN ILLUSTRATED

To gain more familiarity with SDM concepts, we will now illustrate the evolution of the logical schema design for Sally Enterprises. You have seen the first cut design of Sally's database in Figure 6-8. This first cut has deficiencies, as you will see. We will describe how these deficiencies were remedied by Sally's development staff.

At each design iteration, be certain you understand the changes that have been made and the rationale behind them. The final iteration of this design will be input to Chapters 8 and 10. In turn, the physical design produced in those chapters will be input to Chapters 12 and 13. Therefore, it is important for you to understand all of the statements in Sally's logical design.

The evolution of Sally's database design

Figure 6-21 summarizes the process we have followed in developing an SDM description of the database. We identified objects and properties in Chapter 5 and the first part of this chapter; we defined entity classes in this chapter; and we have described the relationships. The rule regarding relationship definition follows from the discussion comparing SDM and the E-R model. We now come to the point of evaluating the design.

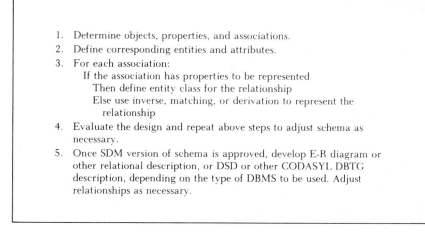

1. Determine objects, properties, and associations.
2. Define corresponding entities and attributes.
3. For each association:
   If the association has properties to be represented
     Then define entity class for the relationship
     Else use inverse, matching, or derivation to represent the
       relationship
4. Evaluate the design and repeat above steps to adjust schema as
   necessary.
5. Once SDM version of schema is approved, develop E-R diagram or
   other relational description, or DSD or other CODASYL DBTG
   description, depending on the type of DBMS to be used. Adjust
   relationships as necessary.

Figure 6-21   Summary of Logical Design Steps

In practice such a design evaluation would involve professional computer people as well as involved and concerned users. The development team would probably present sketches of relationships like those in Figure 6-17, and perhaps teach the users the meaning of the logical schema in Figure 6-8. The review panel would then deliberate on the appropriateness of the design.

Sally's design evaluation

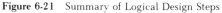

Sally, who was the principal reviewer, had three objections to the design shown in Figure 6-8. First, she believed that with this description, a customer could only order one glass from a given pitcher. "Otherwise," she said, "Customer + Pitcher would not be a unique identifier." "Doesn't this mean," she asked, "that there will be only one entity for a given customer and pitcher?"

Much to the dismay of the designers, Sally was right. (As you can see, Sally is sharp. She has to be for the purposes of this chapter.) They started to respond with solutions, but Sally cut them off. "I want to present all of my objections, then you figure out how to fix them, and let me know." (Had Sally read reference [42]?)

Sally stated her second objection. "Sometimes," she said, "I fill an order from two pitchers. If someone orders the giant 3-cup lemonade and I don't have that much left in the pitcher, I pour what I have, then make another batch, and finish filling their glass from the second batch."

Finally, Sally was concerned that the schema in Figure 6-8 would not allow the marketing analysis department to assess the efficacy of her recipes. "I want to know how much lemonade I'm selling from each recipe, and how many reorders I get for each recipe. That doesn't appear possible." Sally correctly perceived that although there is a relationship from RECIPES to PITCHERS (because of the inverse attributes Where_used and Recipe_used), there is no relationship from PITCHERS to ORDERS (neither inverse nor matching attributes exist between PITCHERS and ORDERS).

"Fix these up," she said, "and let me know when you've got a solution."

Sally's logical design number 2   After the design review, the analysts licked their wounds and repeated the steps in Figure 6-21 for each of Sally's objections. Considering Sally's first objection, the analysts' response was: "Well, when someone orders another glass from the same pitcher, we could just add the amount to the order data that already exists. The order entity would then contain the total amount consumed by a given customer from a given pitcher."

"That's an ugly patch," said one analyst. "Sally would never agree to that. When someone reorders, that's a reorder, and the marketing analysis people need to know it. A single order for 5 cups is completely different from 5 orders for 1 cup."

This led to a discussion about whether ORDERS needed a unique identifier. The answer was no. An entity class doesn't necessarily have to have a unique identifier. However, during the discussion, the team realized that marketing analysis needed to know the time of the order. When reorders occurred, they wanted to know how much time had expired between them. Thus time needed to be added to the ORDERS entity class. Then, the concatenation, Customer + Pitcher + Time, would yield a unique key, anyway.

After discussion on Sally's second objection, the analysts decided to let Pitcher be a multivalued attribute. But, since no order could be for an amount greater than the size of the pitcher, no order could have more than two pitchers. Hence Pitcher was defined as multivalued between 1 and 2.

Finally, to overcome Sally's third objection, the analysts added a Where_sold attribute to PITCHERS, and made this attribute an inverse of the attribute Pitcher of ORDERS. Figure 6-22 shows the next version of ORDERS along with the new version of PITCHERS. Note also in this figure that the Where_sold attribute is multivalued.

Sally's logical design number 3   After these changes had been made and discussed, the development team met again with Sally for a review. Sally had a question. "Would it impact what you're doing," she asked, "if I added a salesperson? I've been so busy lately, that I just can't handle all of the customers. However, to keep overhead down, I would only pay commissions. This means I would need to know who is making which sales."

The team informed Sally that such a change would definitely impact their work. At the logical design stage, however, the impact would be minimal—certainly nothing like the impact that would be caused if she made this change during implementation. The team asked Sally to cancel the meeting and allow them to develop a third version of her schema.

PITCHERS
    description: the date and time of preparation and recipe used for a
                           pitcher of lemonade. Amount left in the pitcher is stored
                           here.
        member attributes:
            Number
                value class: PITCHER_NUMBERS
                may not be null
                not changeable
            Date
                value class: DATES
            Recipe_used
                value class: RECIPES
                inverse: Where_used
            Where_sold
                value class: ORDERS
                inverse: Pitcher
                multivalued
        class attributes:
            Total_produced
                description: This attribute contains the sum of the lemonade
                                    of all pitchers produced by Sally. It is updated
                                    by application program.
                value class: QUARTS
            Active_pitcher
                description: the number of the pitcher (batch) that is
                                    currently in use
                value class: PITCHER_NUMBERS
                derivation: maximum pitcher number in this class
            Amount_left
                description: the amount of lemonade remaining in the active
                                    pitcher
                value class: QUARTS
        identifiers:
            Number

ORDERS
    description: the amount of lemonade purchased by a given customer from a
                           given pitcher
        member attributes:
            Customer
                value class: CUSTOMERS
                mandatory

Figure 6-22   Changes to Figure 6-8 for Sally's Logical Schema Number 2

```
              Pitcher
                    value class:          PITCHERS
                    mandatory
                    multivalued with size between 1 and 2
                    inverse:              Where_sold
              Date
                    value class:          DATES
              Time
                    value class:          TIMES
              Amount
                    value class:          CUPS
                    mandatory
          identifiers:
              Customer + Pitcher + Time


     TIMES
          description:        the time of day; 24 hour clock
          interclass connection:          subclass of STRINGS where value is HH.MM; HH is
                                          integer between 0 and 23, and MM is integer
                                          between 0 and 59
```

Figure 6-22   (cont'd.)

The third version is shown in Figure 6-23. A new entity class, SALESPEO-PLE, has been added, and a Salesperson attribute inserted in the ORDERS entity class. Also, Name of SALESPEOPLE and Salesperson of ORDERS have been made inverses. The contained records of this schema are shown in Figure 6-24.

In their next meeting, Sally could find no objection to the logical schema in Figure 6-23. Therefore, the team proceeded to the next step of database design.

The iteration shown in this example is typical of the database design process. As the team indicated to Sally, changing the design at this stage is so much easier and cheaper than changing it after physical design or during implementation. Thus, when users can foresee that something will not work at this point, that observation should be considered a success. Much work has been saved. As the carpenters say, we want to measure twice and cut once. SDM provides a tool for measuring twice.

If the team expects to implement the database with a relational DBMS, then an E-R diagram or other relational description is prepared. If a CODASYL DBTG system will be used, then a DSD or other CODASYL DBTG description is developed. We will consider each of these alternatives in Chapters 8 and 10.

RECIPES
    description: all formulae used for the preparation of lemonade
    member attributes:
        Name
                value class: RECIPE_NAMES
        Amount_of_sugar
                description: amount specified in cups
                value class: CUPS
        Amount_of_lemons
                description: amount specified in whole medium California lemons
                value class: LEMON_COUNT
        Amount_of_water
                description: amount of water in quarts
                value class: QUARTS
        Where_used
                description: the pitchers made with this recipe
                value class: PITCHERS
                inverse: Recipe_used
                multivalued
                exhausts value class
    identifiers:
        Name

PITCHERS
    description: the date and time of preparation and recipe used for a
                        pitcher of lemonade. Amount left in the pitcher is stored
                        here.
    member attributes:
        Number
                value class: PITCHER_NUMBERS
                may not be null
                not changeable
        Date
                value class: DATES

        Recipe_used
                value class: RECIPES
                inverse: Where_used

Figure 6-23   Sally's Logical Schema Number 3

Where_sold
    value class: ORDERS
    inverse: Pitcher
    multivalued
class attributes:
    Total_produced
        description: This attribute contains the sum of the lemonade of all pitchers produced by Sally. It is updated by application program.
        value class: QUARTS
    Active_pitcher
        description: the number of the pitcher (batch) that is currently in use
        value class: PITCHER_NUMBERS
        derivation: maximum pitcher number in this class
    Amount_left
        description: the amount of lemonade remaining in the active pitcher
        value class: QUARTS
identifiers:
    Number

CUSTOMERS
    description: all people who have purchased lemonade
    member attributes:
        First_name
            value class: PEOPLE_NAMES
            not changeable
        Last_name
            value class: PEOPLE_NAMES
            not changeable

        Family_members
            description: people in this customer's family
            value class: CUSTOMERS
            derivation: all customers with identical last names
            multivalued
        Past_amounts_purchased
            description: amounts this customer has purchased
            value class: CUPS

Figure 6-23 (Cont'd.)

match: Amount of ORDERS on Customer

multivalued

Total_amount

description: the total amount of lemonade purchased

value class: CUPS

derivation: sum of Past_amounts_purchased for this customer

identifiers:

First_name + Last_name

ORDERS

description: the amount of lemonade purchased by a given customer from a
                   given pitcher from a given salesperson

member attributes:

Customer

value class: CUSTOMERS

mandatory

Pitcher

value class: PITCHERS

mandatory

multivalued with size between 1 and 2

inverse: Where_sold

Salesperson

value class: SALESPEOPLE

mandatory

Date

value class: DATES

Time

value class: TIMES

Amount

value class: CUPS

mandatory

identifiers:

Customer + Pitcher + Time

SALESPEOPLE

description: the names of Sally's salespeople

member attributes:

Name

Figure 6-23   (cont'd.)

description: a unique name. Sally calls some of her
                 salespeople by first name, some by last name,
                 some by both, and some by nickname. Whatever
                 she uses is stored here.

value class: PEOPLE_NAMES
mandatory

Past_amounts_sold
    description: amounts sold by this person
    value class: CUPS
    match: Amount of ORDERS on Salesperson
    multivalued

identifiers:
    Name

BIG_BUYERS
    description: a collection of the major purchasers
    interclass connection: subclass of CUSTOMERS where Total_amount exceeds
                   15.0
    member attributes:
        Nickname
            value class: PEOPLE_NAMES
        Favorite_sport
            value class: SPORT_NAMES
        multivalued with size between 1 and 3

CUPS
    interclass connection: subclass of STRINGS where format is number 99.99

DATES
    interclass connection: subclass of STRINGS where format is number as
                   YYMMDD

LEMON_COUNT
    interclass connection: subclass of STRINGS where format is positive
                   integer less than 10

PEOPLE_NAMES
    interclass connection: subclass of STRINGS where length is less than 20
                   characters where specified

Figure 6-23   (cont'd.)

PITCHER_NUMBERS
      interclass connection: subclass of STRINGS where format is positive integer less than 500

QUARTS
      interclass connection: subclass of STRINGS where format is number 9.99

RECIPE_NAMES
      interclass connection: subclass of STRINGS where length is less than 10 characters where specified

SPORT_NAMES
      description: sports that Sally can knowledgeably discuss
      interclass connection: subclass of STRINGS where value is 'SOCCER', 'FOOTBALL', 'TENNIS', 'BASKETBALL', or 'SKIING'

TIMES
      description: the time of day; 24 hour clock
      interclass connection: subclass of STRINGS where value is HH.MM; HH is integer between 0 and 23, and MM is integer between 0 and 59

Figure 6-23   (cont'd.)

SUMMARY

We believe that certain knowledge primitives exist in the real world. These are objects, object classes, properties, property value sets, facts, and associations. Corresponding to each of these real world primitives is a conceptual primitive used for defining a database. These primitives are (in the same order) entities, entity classes, attributes, domains, values, and relationships. We cannot know whether these primitives exist in the real world or whether they are creations of our minds. To get the products out the door, it does not matter.

The semantic data model is a language for expressing a logical database design. This model allows more meaning to be stored in the definition than other data models. Also, it enables relationships to be defined so that data appears to users in a natural manner. Relationships are presented in a relative manner.

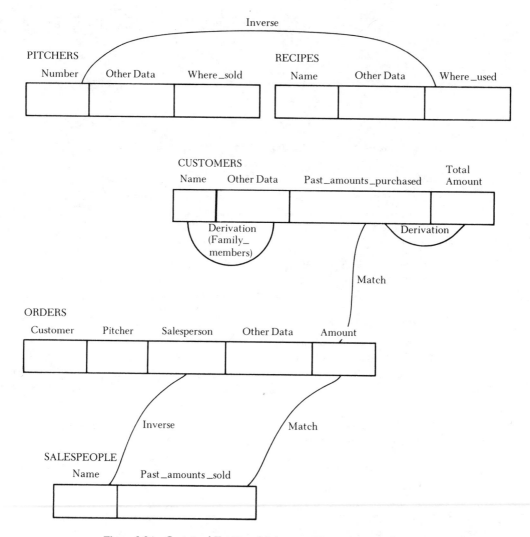

Figure 6-24 Contained Entities of Schema in Figures 6-23 and 6-8

Objects are represented by entities in SDM. Each entity set consists of entities or members which in turn have attributes. The domain of each attribute is another entity class. Such domains are either subsets of the special class, STRINGS, or they are other entity classes defined in the database. Consequently, attributes can have entities as values.

Relationships in SDM can be defined using inverse attributes, matching, or derivation. Alternatively, the E-R concept of a relationship set can be added to SDM concepts. In this case, relationships are defined as separate entity classes.

A logical schema is usually developed in an iterative manner. The schema is defined, reviewed, and changed. The process repeats until no one can find substantial problems with the schema. At this point, the logical schema is transformed into a physical design. Such transformations are the subjects of the next four chapters.

Group I Questions

6.1 What role do primitives have in data modeling?

6.2 Define the terms *object, object class, property, property value set, fact,* and *association*.

6.3 Consider the property *Age*. Define its property value set.

6.4 Explain the difference between the set of positive integers from 1 to, say, 85 and the property value set for height.

6.5 Define the terms *entity, entity class, attribute, domain, value, relationship,* and *role*.

6.6 Explain the importance of the distinction between property value sets and domains.

6.7 Describe three advantages of the semantic data model.

6.8 Compare SDM to pseudocode. How are they alike? How are they different?

6.9 For an SDM entity class, explain the difference between a class attribute and a member attribute.

6.10 Describe the difference between a base class and a nonbase class.

6.11 How is the term *interclass connection* used in SDM?

6.12 Define the term *value class*.

6.13 Explain the use of the default entity class, STRINGS.

6.14 Explain the usefulness of allowing value classes to be entity classes.

6.15 Define the terms *multivalued, mandatory, not changeable, exhaustive,* and *no overlap in values*.

6.16 Construct an SDM description for an entity class called STUDENTS. The members of this class have four attributes: Student_number, Name, Age, and Major. Student_number ranges between 10000 and 49599, and the other attributes have the obvious formats. Provide all needed entity class descriptions.

6.17 Explain the use of inverses in Figure 6-8 for the relationship between PITCHERS and RECIPES. Why is Where_used a multivalued attribute?

6.18 Define an entity class called MAJORS. The members of this class have the attributes Name, Department_chairperson, and Number_of_majors.

Provide all needed entity class descriptions. Connect the MAJORS entity class to the STUDENTS entity class in question 6.16. Use inverses.

6.19 Why will defining relationships with inverses appeal to users?

6.20 Explain the use of matching between ORDERS and SALESPEOPLE in Figure 6-23. Which amounts will be contained in SALESPEOPLE?

6.21 Construct an SDM description for the entity class GRADES. Attributes are Class_number, Student_number, and Grade. Modify the student definition from your answer to question 6.16 to include a Grade attribute. Use matching to fill this field with grade values from the GRADES entity class just defined.

6.22 Discuss how the SDM derivation facility can be used to define relationships. In the SALESPEOPLE entity class in Figure 6-23, how could derivation be used to relate all salespeople in a given region. (*Hint:* This requires defining two new attributes, Region and Colleagues.)

6.23 Explain the statement that the E-R model is more explicit about relationships than SDM. What are the disadvantages of this explicitness? What are the advantages of this explicitness?

6.24 Explicitly define the family relationship implied in Figure 6-8 by constructing a separate entity class, FAMILY. Assume the data in this class is Date_of_last_reunion.

6.25 Explain why Sally was right when she said that a customer can order only once for a given pitcher for the schema in Figure 6-8.

6.26 In Figure 6-23, why is Pitcher defined to be multivalued with values between 1 and 2? What is the significance of the 2?

6.27 Why was it undesirable to sum a customer's repeat orders from the same pitcher into one record?

Group II Questions

6.28 In Chapter 5 we considered seven record types for Sally's logical schema. Only four of those types were defined in Figure 6-8; we omitted purchase-order, line-item, and (inventory) item records. Augment Figure 6-8 by defining SDM entity classes for these three records. Define relationships that you believe are appropriate. Express these relationships as entity classes, inverses, or matching, depending on which you believe is best. Explain your choice.

6.29 Develop a logical schema for class scheduling. The logical schema should contain data about classes, students, enrollments, grades, and professors. Ensure that your schema contains sufficient information to answer the following questions:

a. Which classes are full?
b. How many seats are available in all sections of Sociology 403?
c. What is the prerequisite of Sociology 403?
d. How many sections of Chemistry 101 are being offered?
e. Which classes are taught by Professor Hart?
f. Which students are in a class taught by Professor Hart?
g. Which classes is Nicole Emily taking?
h. How many students have dropped a class? (count all students in all drops)
i. List grades for Nicole Emily.

7

The Relational Model

As stated in Chapter 5, the relational model of data is midway on the continuum of data models. It falls between a logical model like SDM, and a more physical model like the CODASYL DBTG. In this text, we will use the relational model to express designs of databases to be processed by relational DBMS products.

The relational model was first proposed by Dr. E. F. Codd in a seminal paper in 1970 [28]. Since then, this model has been the focus of extensive intellectual activity. An important series of theoretical papers have been written concerning the most appropriate way to express relations. At the same time, other papers have been written describing different techniques and languages for manipulating relational data.

Although the relational model has many desirable characteristics, until recently it was only of theoretic interest because no commercially viable relational DBMS was available. However, the early 1980s saw the announcement of several important relational DBMS products. SQL/DS (vended by IBM) and ORACLE (vended by Relational Software Incorporated) are two examples. Since these announcements, the relational model has come to be of greater practical significance.

We will approach the relational model in an informal and largely intuitive manner. Our objective is to understand relational concepts from a practitioner's standpoint and to apply these concepts to database design. Readers interested in greater precision and rigor should see Date [33], Ullman [75], and the excellent series of papers that have appeared in the ACM (Association for Computing Machinery) *Transactions on Database Systems* [18].

The first section of this chapter presents relational data definition concepts. It defines the essential terminology and shows how relationships are represented using the relational model. The remaining two sections discuss relational data manipulation. First, a survey of four types of relational DML (data manipulation language) is presented, and then relational algebra is discussed. Finally,

SQL (the language used by both SQL/DS and ORACLE) is described in detail. The concepts presented in this chapter will be used in Chapter 8 for the design of a relational schema for Sally Enterprises.

RELATIONAL DATA DEFINITION

The relational model represents data in the simple form of tables. Other than some strange-sounding terminology, you may wonder what the balleyhoo is all about. As you will see, the importance of this model lies in the way that relationships are represented. First we will present data definition terminology, and then we will discuss relationships.

Terminology

A *relation* is simply a two-dimensional table that has several properties. First, the entries in the table are single-valued; neither repeating groups nor arrays are allowed. Using the terminology of Chapter 4, relations are *flat files*. Second, the entries in any column are all of the same kind. For example, one column may contain employee numbers, and another ages. Further, each column has a unique name and the order of the columns is immaterial. Columns of a relation are referred to as *attributes*. Finally, no two rows in the table are identical and the order of the rows is insignificant. Figure 7-1 portrays a relation.

Each row of the relation is known as a *tuple*. If the relation has n columns, then each row is referred to as an *n-tuple*. Also, a relation that has n columns or n attributes is said to be of *degree n*. The relation in Figure 7-1 is of degree 4, and each row is a 4-tuple.

Each attribute has a domain, which is the set of values that the attribute can have. For example, the domain of the Sex attribute in Figure 7-1 is the two

	Col. 1	Col. 2		
	Name	Age	Sex	Employee_number
Row 1	ANDERSON	21	F	010110
Row 2	DECKER	22	M	010100
.	GLOVER	22	M	101000
.	JACKSON	21	F	201100
.	MOORE	19	M	111100
.	NAKATA	20	F	111101
	SMITH	19	M	111111

Figure 7-1   EMPLOYEE Relation

Name	Position	Spouse_name	Age	Spouse_age	Department
SMITH	PROFESSOR		42		10
JONES	ASST. PROF.	JANE	41	39	20
PARKS	ASSOC. PROF.	MARY	29	28	10
ADAMS	PROFESSOR	FRED	35	41	10
BOLDER	ASST. PROF.	FRED	37	28	20

Figure 7-2 FACULTY Relation

value, M and F. The domain of the Age attribute is all positive integers less than, say, 100.

A relation of degree n has n domains, not all of which need be unique. For example, the relation in Figure 7-2 has age and age of spouse attributes. The domains of the two attributes are the same, integers from 1 to 100. To differentiate between attributes that have the same domain, each is given a unique *attribute name*. The attribute names for the relation in Figure 7-2 are Name, Position, Spouse_name, Age, Spouse_age, and Department.

Figures 7-1 and 7-2 are *examples*, or *occurrences*. The generalized format, EMPLOYEE (Name, Age, Sex, Employee_number), is called the *relation structure*, and is what most people mean when they use the term *relation*. If we add constraints on allowable data values to the relation structure, we then have a *relational schema* [39].

Keys

We want to be able to identify each tuple in a relation by values of its attributes. Clearly, one way to identify a tuple is to list a value for every attribute. For example, the value JONES, ASST. PROF., JANE, 41, 39, 20 constitutes a unique identifier. It will be unique because duplicate tuples are not allowed.

If possible, however, we want a key with fewer attributes. The designer of the relation in Figure 7-2 may know that names will always be unique. If so, the attribute Name, by itself, is a key. If names will not necessarily be unique, then the key must be a combination of Name and other attributes, perhaps Name and Department. This approach assumes that two people named SMITH, for example, will never teach in the same department. If this assumption is unrealistic, then some other combination of attributes would need to be selected as the key.

When we pick attributes as a key, we are saying that for all instances of the relation, over all time, the attributes will have unique values. Expressed equivalently, when we define a key, we add a uniqueness constraint on the key attribute to the relational schema.

To understand the importance of this concept, examine Figure 7-2. In this example, Age is unique. Most likely, however, Age will not be unique for all instances of this structure over all time. In this case, Age should not be considered a key.

Remember, a database is a model of the real world. To determine if an attribute will be unique, the designer must look at reality and decide if uniqueness for that attribute is realistic. If so, it is realistic for the model. This idea is sometimes expressed by saying that the designer must examine the semantics (the meaning) of the data—not just the data values.

In some cases, a relational schemata will have more than one attribute or combination of attributes that are unique. For the relation in Figure 7-1, attributes Name and Employee_number may both be unique. If so, they are both called *candidate keys*. In the design of the database, one of them will be chosen as the *primary key*.

"Big deal!" you may be saying. Fancy words for familiar concepts. Why don't we just call this structure a *table* instead of a relational schemata; call the columns *fields* instead of attributes; call the rows *records* instead of tuples? The answer is, we could, and will, in Chapter 12 (SQL/DS uses the common terms). Meanwhile, welcome to the reality of a developing field. The relational model originated in relational mathematics. The specialized terminology came from that discipline, and the terms are still with us. Perhaps in ten or fifteen years these strange terms will disappear. For now, however, you need to be familiar with both sets of terminology.

Correspondence to SDM terminology

Relational data definition terms correspond closely to SDM terminology. A *relation* corresponds to an SDM *entity set*. The *tuples* of a relation correspond to the *members* of an SDM entity set. Relational *attributes* correspond to SDM *attributes*. A relational *domain* corresponds to a *STRINGS value class*. (The relational model will not allow a tuple to be contained within another tuple as SDM does.)

Expressing relationships with the relational model

You may be skeptical of all these definitions. You may be asking, "What's so special about defining data in this way?" The answer lies in the way that the relational model represents relationships.

Recall in Chapter 4 that we used linked and inverted lists to represent relationships of trees, simple networks, and complex networks. Using lists in that way was effective in that the relationships were stored. However, such representations have an undesirable property: the relationships are hidden from the user. The user cannot directly examine a linked list to learn, for example, which employees work in Department 10. Instead, the user must ask the DBMS, and quite often, the asking is cumbersome.

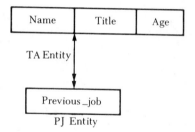

Figure 7-3 Tree Representation of Faculty Data Record

With the relational model, relationships are carried in the data. The fact that employee 12345 works in Department 10 is stored in the Department attribute of the EMPLOYEE relation. If the user wants to combine the employee data with the department data, the relational model provides facilities to do so, as you will see.

To understand how relationships are carried in the data, consider each of the three fundamental types of relationship.

Tree or hierarchical relationships   Figure 7-3 illustrates a two-level tree of faculty data. In this figure, TA (Title and Age) entities contain faculty names, titles, and ages. PJ (Previous_job) entities contain faculty names and the titles of previous jobs.

This tree can be modeled by constructing two relations as in Figure 7-4. Relation TA contains the Name, Title, and Age attributes, and relation PJ contains the Name and Previous_job attributes. Name is the primary key of the TA relation, and Name and Previous_job together are the primary key of the PJ relation. Both attributes are required since neither is unique by itself. Note that person B has no entry in the PJ relation.

Name	Title	Age
A	PROFESSOR	42
B	ASST. PROF.	35
C	ASSOC. PROF.	37
D	PROFESSOR	47

Name	Previous_job
A	ASSOC. PROF.
A	ASST. PROF.
A	INSTRUCTOR
C	ASST. PROF.
C	INSTRUCTOR
D	ASSOC. PROF.
D	ASST. PROF.

a. Title and Age (TA) Relation

b. Previous_job (PJ) Relation

Figure 7-4   Relational Representation of Figure 7-3

Where is the relationship? In the data values. For example, we know the first professor tuple in TA (professor A) is connected to the first three tuples in PJ because there is a match in Names. Similarly, the third tuple in relation TA is connected to the fourth and fifth tuples in PJ, again because of a match in Names. This is a natural and convenient way to construct a relationship.

With the relational model, users are allowed to access and combine data using data values. They need not be aware of any underlying data structures such as linked or inverted lists, or other specialized structures. These structures may, in fact, exist, but users do not need them to accomplish their data management objectives. As you will see in Chapter 9, other data models are not so convenient.

Consider an extension to this example. Suppose we want to maintain faculty salary histories for each previous job. There will be many salaries for each. We can store these salaries by adding another entity, say JS (Job_salary). The structure of the data is shown in Figure 7-5.

This structure can be represented by the three relations as shown in Figure 7-6. Here we have the TA and PJ relations from Figure 7-4 plus the JS relation. The primary keys of TA and PJ are the same as before, and the primary key of JS is the combination of Name, Previous_job, and Start_date.

To avoid later confusion, we need to be careful with terminology here. Figures 7-6 and 7-8 depict examples, or occurrences, of relation structures. The relation structures themselves are definitions of data formats, not particular data values. The relation structures for Figure 7-6 are:

TA (<u>Name</u>, Title, Age)
PJ (<u>Name</u>, <u>Previous_job</u>)
JS (<u>Name</u>, <u>Previous_job</u>, <u>Start_date</u>, Salary, End_date)

Customary relational notation is to underline the attributes that form the primary key.

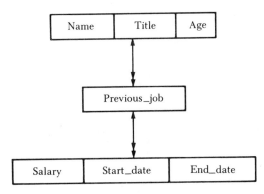

Figure 7-5   Faculty Data Tree Representation

Name	Title	Age
A	PROFESSOR	42
B	ASST. PROF.	35
C	ASSOC. PROF.	37
D	PROFESSOR	47

TA Relation

Name	Previous_job
A	ASSOC. PROF.
A	ASST. PROF.
A	INSTRUCTOR
C	ASST. PROF.
C	INSTRUCTOR
D	ASSOC. PROF.
D	ASST. PROF.

PJ Relation

Name	Previous_job	Start_date	Salary	End_date
A	ASSOC. PROF.	SEP 83	28000	
A	ASSOC. PROF.	SEP 82	27000	SEP 83
A	ASST. PROF.	SEP 81	26000	SEP 82
A	ASST. PROF.	SEP 80	24000	SEP 81
A	INSTRUCTOR	SEP 79	22000	SEP 80
C	ASST. PROF.	SEP 83	28500	
C	ASST. PROF.	SEP 82	28000	SEP 83
C	INSTRUCTOR	SEP 81	24000	SEP 82
D	ASSOC. PROF.	SEP 83	28000	
D	ASST. PROF.	SEP 82	27500	SEP 83
D	ASST. PROF.	SEP 81	27000	SEP 82
D	ASST. PROF.	SEP 80	25000	SEP 81

JS Relation

Figure 7-6 Relational Representation of Figure 7-5

In addition to these relation structures, we can also specify a *relational schema*. To do so, we would add definitions of constraints on data values. Two examples of necessary constraints for this schema are:

1. The values of Name in PJ must be a subset of the values of Name in TA, and

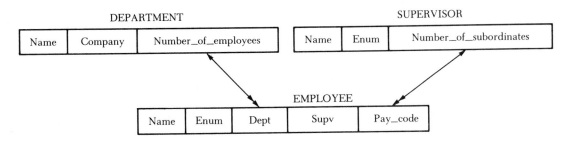

Figure 7-7 Department/Supervisor/Employee Schema

2. The values of Name and Previous_job in JS must be a subset of Name and Previous_job in PJ.

Without these constraints, we could have previous jobs or job salaries that do not correspond to a faculty tuple. More examples of constraints will be shown in Chapter 8.

Simple network relationships   Consider the department/supervisor/employee relationship shown in Figure 7-7. DEPARTMENT entities have Name, Company, and Number_of_employees attributes; SUPERVISOR entities have Name, Employee_number, and Number_of_subordinates attributes; and EMPLOYEE entities have Name, Employee_number, Department, Supervisor, and Pay_code attributes. The DEPARTMENT-to-EMPLOYEE and SUPERVISOR-to-EMPLOYEE relationships are both one-to-many. Consequently, this is an example of a simple network.

The following relation structure will represent this network:

DEPARTMENT (<u>Name</u>, Company, Num_emp)
SUPERVISOR (<u>Name</u>, Enum, Num_emp)
EMPLOYEE (Name, <u>Enum</u>, Dept, Supv, Pay_code)

Observe that the attribute name, *Name*, occurs three times. Since this is the case, when we wish to refer to a particular Name attribute, we must qualify it with its relation name. Thus we refer to DEPARTMENT.Name, SUPERVISOR.Name, or EMPLOYEE.Name. Note we cannot duplicate an attribute name within a relation; if we did, we would have no way of specifying which attribute we mean.

Examples for these relational schemata are shown in Figure 7-8. Again, observe there are no special constructs to represent the relationships. Instead, relationships can be determined by pairing equal values of attributes. For example, to respond to the query, "How many people work in the same department as employee NAKATA?" we need to determine the department in which NAKATA works. To do this, we first find the EMPLOYEE tuple for NAKATA; it contains the name of NAKATA's department (ACCOUNTING). Next, find the

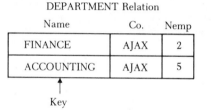

DEPARTMENT Relation

Name	Co.	Nemp
FINANCE	AJAX	2
ACCOUNTING	AJAX	5

↑
Key

SUPERVISOR Relation

Name	Enum	Nsub
BAMMER	0100	2
RATTLEMARKER	1001	1
ZARTER	1000	1

↑
Key

EMPLOYEE Relation

Name	Enum	Dept	Supv	Pcode
ANDERSON	0210	ACCOUNTING	ZARTER	10
GLOVER	2000	FINANCE	RATTLEMARKER	05
JACKSON	2001	ACCOUNTING	BAMMER	30
NAKATA	2101	ACCOUNTING	BAMMER	30

↑
Key

Figure 7-8   Example of Relational Representation of Figure 7-7

ACCOUNTING tuple in the DEPARTMENT relation. Finally, we obtain Number_of_employees from this tuple. Throughout this process, we use only attribute values to establish relationships among tuples.

When an attribute in one relation is a key of another relation, the attribute is called a *foreign key*. The term means that the attribute is a key, but in a foreign relation. Thus, in Figure 7-7, attributes Dept and Supv of EMPLOYEE are foreign keys. To construct the relationships, we will match Dept with values of DEPARTMENT.Name, and Supv with values of SUPERVISOR.Name.

Foreign keys are important when defining constraints across relations. For example, the database designer may want to specify that no DEPARTMENT tuple can be deleted if its Name is a value of a foreign key. We will see more of this in Chapter 8.

Complex network relationships   The relational model representation of a complex relationship is similar. Figure 7-9a shows the complex relationship of students to classes. An entity-relationship diagram of this relationship is shown in Figure 7-9b. A straightforward way of representing this structure is to define three relations: one for students, one for classes, and one for the relationship between students and classes. This last relation is an intersection record as we discussed in Chapter 4.

The structure of these relations is shown in Figure 7-10a, and an example is shown in Figure 7-10b. To determine the names of students in a given class, say AP150, we access the STUDENT_CLASS relation looking for the value AP150. When we find such a value, we obtain the corresponding student num-

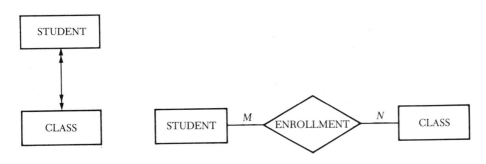

a. Student/Class Schema   b. Entity-Relationship Diagram of Student/Class Relationship

Figure 7-9 Complex Network Relationship of Students to Classes

STUDENT (Snum, Sname, Major)
CLASS (Cname, Time, Room)
STUDENT_CLASS (Snum, Cname)

a. Relations for Representing Student/Class Schema

Snum	Sname	Major
0110	ANDERSON	ACCOUNTING
1000	GLOVER	ANTHROPOLOGY

STUDENT Relation

Cname	Time	Room
BA482	MW 3	C-150
BD445	TR 2	C-213
BA491	TR 3	C-141
AP150	MWF 9	D-412

CLASS Relation

Snum	Cname
0110	BA482
0110	BD445
0110	BA491
1000	AP150
1000	BD445

STUDENT_CLASS Relation

b. Example Data

Figure 7-10 STUDENT, CLASS, and STUDENT_CLASS Relations

ber, and use it to access the student data. For the data in Figure 7-10, student 1000 is enrolled in AP150. We use this student number to determine the name of the student, which is GLOVER.

Again, be aware that we are using only data values to represent and process relationships among tuples. The advantage of this is that users can access the data using terms and values that are familiar to them.

RELATIONAL DATA MANIPULATION

In the previous examples, we described the processing of relations in a general and intuitive manner. This is fine for learning purposes, but to process relations with a computer, we need a clear, unambiguous language for expressing what we want to do. Four different strategies for relational data manipulation have been proposed (so far).

Categories of relational DML

Relational algebra, one of the strategies, defines operators that work on relations (akin to the operators $+$, $-$, etc., in high school algebra). Relations can be manipulated using these operators to achieve a desired result. Relational algebra is hard to use, partly because it is procedural. That is, when using relational algebra we must know not only *what* we want, but also *how* to get it. Although relational algebra is seldom used in industry, the underlying concepts are important; you need to understand how relations can be broken up and recombined. Consequently we will discuss relational algebra later in this section.

Relational calculus is a second strategy for manipulating relations. Relational calculus is nonprocedural; it is a language for expressing what we want without expressing how to get it. Do you remember integration in calculus? Remember the variable of integration? It is a variable that ranges over an interval to be integrated. Well, relational calculus has a similar variable. For *tuple relational calculus*, the variable ranges over the tuples of a relation. For *domain relational calculus*, the variable ranges over the values of a domain.

Unless you are going to become a designer of relational database systems, or a theoretician of relational technology, you will probably get along very well in this world without knowledge of relational calculus. Therefore, it will not be discussed in this text. See Ullman [75] if you want to know more.

Database experts realized that although relational calculus is hard to understand and use, its nonprocedural property is exceedingly desirable. Therefore, these people looked for other nonprocedural techniques. This led to the last two categories of relational DML.

Transform-oriented languages are a class of nonprocedural languages that use relations to transform input data into desired outputs. These languages provide

```
Relational Algebra
Relational Calculus
Transform Languages (SEQUEL)
Graphic Systems (Query-by-Example)
```

Figure 7-11   Four Categories of Relational DML

easy-to-use structures for expressing what is desired in terms of what is known. SQUARE [12], SEQUEL [16], and SEQUEL's offspring, SQL [47] are all transform-oriented languages. As stated at the beginning of this chapter, since SQL is the basis of at least two commercial relational DBMS products, we will discuss it at some length.

The fourth category of relational DML is *graphic*. Systems based on this technology provide the user with a picture of the structure of a relation. The user fills in an example of what he or she wants, and the system responds with actual data in that format. Query-by-Example (QBE) is an example. QBE is important and interesting, but we will not discuss it here. See [82] for more information. The four categories of relational DML are summarized in Figure 7-11.

Example schema

Examples will be needed to discuss and illustrate relational algebra and SQL. To save time and ease the discussion, the example schema shown in Figure 7-12 will be used throughout. There are six relations having attributes and keys as shown. Observe that the attribute Name is used in several relations. When we want to refer to a specific attribute, we will qualify it with its relation name.

The format of the AGES and the CLASS_SIZES domains is the same, yet the domains are different. Even though two domains have the same values, they are not the same, semantically, if they do not represent the same entities. The integer 21 in AGES represents 21 years; the same integer 21 in CLASS_SIZES represents a number of people in a class. Thus the value 21 represents entirely different entities.

In the following discussion, character values will be shown in single quotes. Characters not in quotes represent names. Thus, 'ROOM' differs from ROOM. 'ROOM' is a value, whereas ROOM is, say, a domain name. Concerning numeric data, numbers not in quotes refer to numeric quantities. Numbers in quotes refer to character strings. Thus, 123 is a number, '123' is a string of the characters '1', '2', and '3'.

1. JUNIOR (<u>Snum</u>, Name, Major)
2. HONOR_STUDENT (<u>Number</u>, Name, Interest)
3. STUDENT (<u>SID</u>, Name, Major, Grade_level, Age)
4. CLASS (<u>Name</u>, Time, Room)
5. ENROLLMENT (<u>Student_number, Class_name</u>, Position_number)
6. FACULTY (<u>FID</u>, Name, Department)

a. Relation Definitions

	Attribute	Domain
1.	Snum	PEOPLE_IDENTIFIERS
	Name (of JUNIOR)	PEOPLE_NAMES
	Major	SUBJECT_NAMES
2.	Number	PEOPLE_IDENTIFIERS
	Name (of HONOR_STUDENT)	PEOPLE_NAMES
	Interest	SUBJECT_NAMES
3.	SID	PEOPLE_IDENTIFIERS
	Name (of STUDENT)	PEOPLE_NAMES
	Major	SUBJECT_NAMES
	Grade_level	CLASSES
	Age	AGES
4.	Name (of CLASS)	CLASS_NAMES
	Time	CLASS_TIMES
	Room	ROOMS
5.	Student_number	PEOPLE_IDENTIFIERS
	Class_name	CLASS_NAMES
	Position_number	CLASS_SIZES
6.	FID	PEOPLE_IDENTIFIERS
	Name (of FACULTY)	PEOPLE_NAMES
	Department	SUBJECT_NAMES

b. Attribute Domains

Figure 7-12   Relation and Domain Definitions for DML Examples

Domain Name	Format	
PEOPLE_IDENTIFIERS	Decimal (3)	
PEOPLE_NAMES	Char (8)	(unrealistic, but handy for these examples)
SUBJECT_NAMES	Char (10)	
CLASSES	One of [FR, SO, JR, SN, GR]	
AGES	Decimal from 0 to 100	
CLASS_NAMES	Char (5)	
CLASS_TIMES	Char (5)	format: DDDHH, where D is one of [M, T, W, R, F, – or blank] and HH is decimal between 1 and 12
ROOMS	Char (5)	format: BBRRR, where BB is a building code and RRR is a room number
CLASS_SIZES	Decimal from 0 to 100	

c. Domain Definitions

Figure 7-12   (Cont'd.)

Relational algebra

Although conceptually similar, relational algebra is a far cry from the algebra you learned in high school. In high school algebra, variables represented numbers, and operations like $+$, $-$, $\times$, and $/$ operated on numeric quantities. For *relational* algebra, however, the variables are relations, and the operations manipulate relations to form new relations. For example, the operation $+$ (or union) combines the tuples of one relation with the tuples of another relation. The result is a third relation.

Although we have not stated it previously, relations are sets. The tuples of a relation can be considered elements of a set. Therefore, operations that can be performed on sets can also be performed on relations. We will first show four such set operators, and then discuss operators that are peculiar to relational algebra.

Union   The *union* of two relations is formed by combining the tuples from one relation with those of a second relation to produce a third. Duplicate tuples are eliminated. For this operation to make sense, the relations must be *union compatible*. This means that each relation must have the same number of attributes, and the attributes in corresponding columns must come from the same domain. If, for example, the third attribute of one relation comes from the

Snum	Name	Major
123	JONES	HISTORY
158	PARKS	MATH
271	SMITH	HISTORY

a. Example JUNIOR Relation

Number	Name	Interest
105	ANDERSON	MANAGEMENT
123	JONES	HISTORY

b. Example HONOR_STUDENT Relation

Snum or Number	Name	Major or Interest
123	JONES	HISTORY
158	PARKS	MATH
271	SMITH	HISTORY
105	ANDERSON	MANAGEMENT

c. Union of JUNIOR and HONOR_STUDENT Relations

Figure 7-13   JUNIOR and HONOR_STUDENT Relations and Their Union

AGES domain, then the third attribute of the second relation must also come from the AGES domain.

In Figure 7-12 the JUNIOR and the HONOR_STUDENT relations are union compatible. They both have three attributes, and corresponding attributes come from the same domain. SID (Student ID) and Snum have the domain PEOPLE_IDENTIFIERS; Name and Name have the domain PEOPLE_NAMES; and Major and Interest have the domain SUBJECT_NAMES.

The relations JUNIOR and CLASS both have three attributes, but they are *union incompatible*. The three attributes do not have the same domain.

Figure 7-13 shows the union of two instances of the JUNIOR and HONOR_STUDENT relations. Note that the tuple, [123, JONES, HISTORY], which occurs in both relations, is not duplicated in the union.

Difference   The *difference* of two relations is a third relation containing tuples which occur in the first relation but not in the second. The relations must be union compatible. The difference of JUNIOR and HONOR_STUDENT is shown in Figure 7-14. As with arithmetic, the order of the subtraction matters. A − B is not the same as B − A.

Snum	Name	Major
158	PARKS	MATH
271	SMITH	HISTORY

Figure 7-14   JUNIOR Minus HONOR_STUDENT Relations

Snum or Number	Name	Major or Interest
123	JONES	HISTORY

Figure 7-15   Intersection of JUNIOR and HONOR_STUDENT Relations

Intersection   The *intersection* of two relations is a third relation containing common tuples. Again, the relations must be union compatible. In Figure 7-15 the intersection of JUNIOR and HONOR_STUDENT is the single tuple, [123, JONES, HISTORY]. This is the sole tuple that occurs in both JUNIOR and HONOR_STUDENT.

Product   The *product* of two relations (sometimes called the *Cartesian product*) is the concatenation of every tuple of one relation with every tuple of a second relation. The product of relation A (having *m* tuples) and relation B (having *n* tuples) has *m* times *n* tuples. The product is denoted A × B or A TIMES B. In Figure 7-16, relation STUDENT has four tuples and relation

SID	Name	Major	Grade_level	Age
123	JONES	HISTORY	JR	21
158	PARKS	MATH	GR	26
105	ANDERSON	MANAGEMENT	SN	27
271	SMITH	HISTORY	JR	19

a.   STUDENT Relation

Student_number	Class_name	Position_number
123	H350	1
105	BA490	3
123	BA490	7

b.   ENROLLMENT Relation

Figure 7-16   Examples of STUDENT and ENROLLMENT Relations

SID	Name	Major	Glev	Age	Snum	Cname	Pnum
123	JONES	HISTORY	JR	21	123	H350	1
123	JONES	HISTORY	JR	21	105	BA490	3
123	JONES	HISTORY	JR	21	123	BA490	7
158	PARKS	MATH	GR	26	123	H350	1
158	PARKS	MATH	GR	26	105	BA490	3
158	PARKS	MATH	GR	26	123	BA490	7
105	ANDERSON	MANAGEMENT	SN	27	123	H350	1
105	ANDERSON	MANAGEMENT	SN	27	105	BA490	3
105	ANDERSON	MANAGEMENT	SN	27	123	BA490	7
271	SMITH	HISTORY	JR	19	123	H350	1
271	SMITH	HISTORY	JR	19	105	BA490	3
271	SMITH	HISTORY	JR	19	123	BA490	7

Figure 7-17 Product of STUDENT and ENROLLMENT Relations in Figure 7-16

ENROLLMENT has three. STUDENT TIMES ENROLLMENT will therefore have 12 tuples. These tuples are shown in Figure 7-17.

Projection *Projection* is an operation that selects specified attributes from a relation. The result of the projection is a new relation having the selected attributes. In other words, projection picks columns out of a relation. For example, consider the STUDENT relation data in Figure 7-16. The projection of STUDENT on Name and Major attributes, denoted with brackets as STUDENT[Name, Major], is shown in Figure 7-18a. The projection of STUDENT on Major and Grade_level, denoted STUDENT[Major, Grade_level], appears in Figure 7-18b.

Name	Major
JONES	HISTORY
PARKS	MATH
ANDERSON	MANAGEMENT
SMITH	HISTORY

a. STUDENT[Name, Major]

Major	Grade_level
HISTORY	JR
MATH	GR
MANAGEMENT	SN

b. STUDENT[Major, Grade_level]

Figure 7-18 Projection of STUDENT Relations

SID	Name	Major	Glev	Age
158	PARKS	MATH	GR	26

a. STUDENT WHERE Major = 'MATH'

SID	Name	Major	Glev	Age
123	JONES	HISTORY	JR	21
271	SMITH	HISTORY	JR	19

b. STUDENT WHERE Age < 25

Figure 7-19 Examples of Relational Selection Operation

Note that although STUDENT has four tuples to begin with, the projection STUDENT[Major, Grade_level] has only three. A tuple was eliminated because, after the projection was done, the tuple [HISTORY, JR] occurred twice. Since the result of projection is a relation, and since relations cannot contain duplicate tuples, the redundant tuple is eliminated.

Projection can also be used to change the order of attributes in a relation. For example, the projection STUDENT[Age, Grade_level, Major, SID] reverses the order of STUDENT attributes (see Figure 7-12 for the original order). This feature can sometimes be used to make two relations union compatible.

Selection   Whereas the projection operator takes a vertical subset (columns) of a relation, the *selection* operator takes a horizontal subset (rows). Projection identifies *attributes* to be included in the new relation; selection identifies *tuples* to be included in the new relation. Selection is denoted by specifying the relation name, followed by the keyword WHERE, followed by a condition involving attributes. Figure 7-19a shows the selection of the relation STUDENTS WHERE Major = 'MATH'. Figure 7-19b shows the selection of STUDENTS WHERE Age < 25.

Join   The *join* operation is a combination of the product, selection, and (possibly) projection operations. The join of two relations, say A and B, operates as follows: First, form the product of A times B. Then, do a selection to eliminate some tuples (the criteria for the selection are specified as part of the join). Then, (optionally) remove duplicate attributes with projection.

Consider the STUDENT and ENROLLMENT relations shown in Figure 7-16. Suppose we want to know the position number of each student in the class. To obtain this, we need to join STUDENT tuples with matching (on SID) ENROLLMENT tuples. We denote such a join as STUDENT JOIN (SID = Student_number) ENROLLMENT. The meaning of this expression is "Join a STUDENT tuple to an ENROLLMENT tuple if SID of STUDENT equals Student_number of ENROLLMENT."

SID	Name	Major	Glev	Age	Snum	Cname	Pnum
123	JONES	HISTORY	JR	21	123	H350	1
123	JONES	HISTORY	JR	21	123	BA490	7
105	ANDERSON	MANAGEMENT	SN	27	105	BA490	3

a.   Equijoin

SID	Name	Major	Glev	Age	Cname	Pnum
123	JONES	HISTORY	JR	21	H350	1
123	JONES	HISTORY	JR	21	BA490	7
105	ANDERSON	MANAGEMENT	SN	27	BA490	3

b.   Natural Join

Figure 7-20   Examples of Joining STUDENT and ENROLLMENT Relations

To form this join, we first take the product of STUDENT and ENROLL-MENT. This operation was shown in Figure 7-17. Now, we SELECT those tuples from the product where SID of STUDENT equals Student_number of ENROLLMENT. This operation leads to the relation in Figure 7-20a. Observe that two attributes are identical: SID and Student_number. One of these two is unnecessary, so we eliminate one of them (Student_number) with projection. The result is the join in Figure 7-20b.

The join in Figure 7-20a is called the *equijoin;* the one in Figure 7-20b is called the *natural join*. Normally, unless otherwise specified, when people say join, they mean the natural join.

In reality, forming the product of two large relations may be time-consuming. Consequently, other, more efficient, methods have been devised for joining two relations. The output of these other methods is identical to the output described here.

It is possible to join on conditions other than equality; for example, STU-DENT JOIN (SID not = Student_number) ENROLLMENT, or STUDENT JOIN (SID < FID) FACULTY. The latter join would result in tuples where student numbers are less than faculty numbers. Such a join may have meaning if, say, PEOPLE_IDENTIFIERS are assigned in chronological order. Such a join would portray pairs of students and teachers such that the student had been at the institution longer than the teacher.

There is one important limit on the conditions of a join, however. The attributes in the condition must arise from a common domain. Thus, STUDENT JOIN (Age = Class_size) ENROLLMENT is *illegal*. Even though the values of Age and Class_size are compatible, they do not arise from the same domain. Semantically, this type of a join makes no sense. (Unhappily, some relational DBMS products will permit such a join. They should be ashamed!)

Type	Format	Example
Set operations	+, −, intersection, product	STUDENT[Name]—JUNIOR[Name]
Selection	SELECT relation WHERE condition	SELECT CLASS WHERE Name = 'A'
Projection	relation[list of attributes]	STUDENT[Name, Major, Age]
Join	relation1 JOIN (condition) relation2	STUDENT JOIN (SID = Student_number) ENROLLMENT

Figure 7-21   Summary of Relational Algebra Operations

Expressing queries in relational algebra

Figure 7-21 summarizes the basic relational operations discussed. Set operations include +, −, intersection, and product. Selection picks specific tuples (rows) from a relation in accordance with conditions on attribute values. Projection picks specific attributes (columns) from a relation by attribute name. Finally, join concatenates the tuples of two relations in accordance with a condition on values of attributes.

We will now illustrate how relational operators can be used to express queries. We will use relations STUDENT, ENROLLMENT, and CLASS from Figure 7-12; sample data is shown in Figure 7-22. The purpose of this demonstration is to illustrate the manipulation of relations. Although you will probably never use relational algebra in a commercial environment, these examples will help you understand how relations can be processed.

a. What are the names of all students?

STUDENT[Name]

This is simply the projection of the Name attribute of the STUDENT relation. The result is:

JONES
PARKS
BAKER
GLASS
RUSSELL
RYE

SID	Name	Major	Grade_level	Age
100	JONES	HISTORY	GR	21
150	PARKS	ACCOUNTING	SO	19
200	BAKER	MATH	GR	50
250	GLASS	HISTORY	SN	50
300	BAKER	ACCOUNTING	SN	41
350	RUSSELL	MATH	JR	20
400	RYE	ACCOUNTING	FR	18
450	JONES	HISTORY	SN	24

a. STUDENT Relation

Student_number	Class_name	Position_number
100	BD445	1
150	BA200	1
200	BD445	2
200	CS250	1
300	CS150	1
400	BA200	2
400	BF410	1
400	CS250	2
450	BA200	3

b. ENROLLMENT Relation

Name	Time	Room
BA200	M-F9	SC110
BD445	MWF3	SC213
BF410	MWF8	SC213
CS150	MWF3	EA304
CS250	MWF12	EB210

c. CLASS Relation

Figure 7-22 Example Data for Relations Defined in Figure 7-12

Observe that duplicate names have been omitted. The names JONES and BAKER actually occur twice in the relation STUDENT, but have been omitted because the result of a projection is a relation, and relations may not have duplicate tuples.

b. What are the student numbers of all students enrolled in a class?

ENROLLMENT[Student_number]

This is similar to query *a*, but the projection occurs on the relation ENROLL-MENT. The result is:

100
150
200
300
400
450

Again, duplicate tuples have been omitted.

c. What are the student numbers of all students not enrolled in a class?

STUDENT[SID] − ENROLLMENT[Student_number]

This expression takes the difference of the projection of two relations. STU-DENT[SID] has the student numbers of all students. ENROLL-MENT[Student_number] has the student numbers of all students enrolled in a class. The difference is the students not enrolled in a class. The result is:

250
350

d. What are the numbers of students enrolled in the class 'BD445'?

ENROLLMENT WHERE Class_name = 'BD445' [Student_number]

This expression selects the appropriate tuples and then projects them onto the attribute Student_number. The result is:

100
200

e. What are the names of the students enrolled in class 'BD445'?

STUDENT JOIN (SID = Student_number) ENROLLMENT WHERE Class_
name = 'BD445' [STUDENT.Name]

To answer this query, data from both STUDENT and ENROLLMENT are needed. Specifically, student names must come from STUDENT, whereas the condition, "enrolled in BD445," must be checked in ENROLLMENT. Since both relations are needed, they must be joined. After STUDENT and ENROLLMENT have been joined, the select is applied, followed by a projection on student names. The result is:

As stated previously, when two or more relations are considered, attribute names can become ambiguous. Therefore, for clarity, the relation name may be prefixed to the attribute name. Thus, in the above example, the projection is on [STUDENT.Name]. This prefix was added only for clarity in this example, since all the attribute names are different. When attribute names are identical (a join involving STUDENT and CLASS will yield two attributes, both called Name), the prefix is required. Consider the following:

f. What are the names and meeting times of PARKS' classes?

To answer this query, we must bring together data in all three relations. We need STUDENT data to find PARKS' student number, we need ENROLL-MENT data to learn which classes PARKS is in, and we need CLASS data to determine class meeting times. One way to respond to this query is as follows:

STUDENT WHERE Name = 'PARKS' JOIN (SID = Student_number) ENROLLMENT JOIN (Class_name = Name) CLASS [CLASS.Name, Time]

This expression first selects PARKS' tuple and joins it to matching ENROLL-MENT tuples. Then, the result is joined to matching CLASS tuples. Finally, the projection is taken to print classes and times. The result is:

BA200	M-F9

We must specify CLASS.Name; simply specifying Name is ambiguous because both STUDENT and CLASS have an attribute called Name.

There are other, equivalent ways of responding to this query. One is:

STUDENT JOIN (SID = Student_number) ENROLLMENT JOIN (Class_
name = Name) CLASS WHERE STUDENT.Name = 'PARKS' [CLASS.Name, Time]

This expression differs from the first one because the select on PARKS is not done until after all of the joins have been performed. Assuming a computer performs the operations as stated, this latter expression will be much slower than the former one. Many more tuples will be joined.

Such differences are an important disadvantage of relational algebra. To the user, two equivalent queries should take the same time (and hence cost the same). Imagine the frustration if one form of a query costs 17¢ and another costs $4,356. To the unwary and unsophisticated user, the cost algorithm will appear capricious. To eliminate this situation, relational algebra expressions need to be optimized before they are processed. See [55] for more information.

RELATIONAL DML—SQL

SQL is a transform-oriented relational language. As such, SQL provides language to transform inputs into desired outputs via relations. If you work with relational DBMS products, you will likely use SQL (or a related version). Consequently, we will discuss this language at some length.

SQL was developed in the mid-1970s under the name SEQUEL. A forerunner of SEQUEL, called *SQUARE* [12], has the same capability of SEQUEL, but uses mathematical notation, including subscripts. Because of this, SQUARE was hard for the layperson to learn and also difficult to use on a computer terminal. Consequently, SQL has seen far more attention.

A version of SEQUEL was developed at the IBM San Jose research facilities and tested with college students. Some aspects of the original SEQUEL were found confusing, and SEQUEL was revised. In November 1976, specifications for SEQUEL 2 were published [16]. The DBMS, ORACLE, is based on SEQUEL 2. In 1980 more, minor revisions were made to SEQUEL, and it was renamed SQL. (The name SEQUEL had already been used for an unrelated hardware product. A new name was selected to avoid confusion and other problems.) At the same time, IBM announced a DBMS product called *SQL/DS*.

This section discusses the core of these languages (akin to the core of COBOL). We will refer to these core concepts as SQL. When you encounter a version of SQL, however, be aware that there may be minor differences.

SQL can be run as a query/update language by itself, or SQL commands can be embedded in application programs. The query/update version was designed to be used by both technical and nontechnical people. In this section, we assume that the commands are part of a query/update language. Application programming considerations are discussed in Chapter 9.

Also, SQL includes commands for data definition, data manipulation, and data control. This section discusses only the DML portions of SQL. We assume relations have already been defined. Specific DDL, DML, and control language will be presented for the product SQL/DS in Chapter 12.

Querying a single relation

First, we consider SQL facilities for manipulating a single relation. To follow custom, all SQL commands will be shown in capital letters. This convention will require us to specify attributes in all capital letters, instead of just initial capitals as in SDM. Although less clear than the convention we have been using, it will bring the discussion in line with others. Also, at times, SQL expressions will be indented. This is shown for clarity; in SQL, the position of expressions is arbitrary. Finally, to provide reference numbers for text discussion, each SQL example will be numbered. These numbers are not part of SQL; they are inserted for discussion purposes.

SQL projections To form a projection with SQL, we list the attributes we want to see in a special format. To illustrate, the projection STUDENT[SID, Name, Major] is created by specifying:

1) SELECT   SID, NAME, MAJOR
   FROM   STUDENT

The keywords SELECT and FROM are always required. The attributes to be obtained are listed after SELECT. The relation to be used is listed after FROM. The result of this projection for the data in Figure 7-22 is:

100	JONES	HISTORY
150	PARKS	ACCOUNTING
200	BAKER	MATH
250	GLASS	HISTORY
300	BAKER	ACCOUNTING
350	RUSSELL	MATH
400	RYE	ACCOUNTING
450	JONES	HISTORY

Do not confuse the keyword SELECT with the relational algebra operator *selection*. SELECT is part of an SQL expression; *selection* is the operation of obtaining tuples from a relation. Consider another example,

2) SELECT   MAJOR
   FROM   STUDENT

The result of this operation is the following:

HISTORY
ACCOUNTING
MATH
HISTORY
ACCOUNTING
MATH
ACCOUNTING
HISTORY

As you can see, duplicate tuples remain. SQL does not follow the relational model convention that duplicate tuples will be eliminated. This decision was made because such removal can be expensive and in many cases is not desired. If we want duplicate tuples to be removed, then the qualifier UNIQUE must be specified as follows:

```
3) SELECT   UNIQUE MAJOR
   FROM     STUDENT
```

The result of this operation is:

HISTORY
ACCOUNTING
MATH

SQL selections   The relational algebra selection operator is specified in SQL form as follows:

```
4) SELECT   SID, NAME, MAJOR, GRADE_LEVEL, AGE
   FROM     STUDENT
   WHERE    MAJOR = 'MATH'
```

The SELECT expression specifies the names of all attributes of the relation. FROM specifies the relation to be used, and the new expression, WHERE, provides the conditions for the selection. The format SELECT—FROM—WHERE is the fundamental structure of SQL commands.

The following is an equivalent form of query example 4.

4a) SELECT   *
    FROM   STUDENT
    WHERE   MAJOR = 'MATH'

The * means that all attributes of the relation are to be obtained. The result of either of these operations is:

200	BAKER	MATH	GR	50
350	RUSSELL	MATH	JR	20

We can combine selection and projection as follows:

5) SELECT   NAME, AGE
   FROM   STUDENT
   WHERE   MAJOR = 'MATH'

The result is:

BAKER	50
RUSSELL	20

Several conditions can be expressed in the WHERE clause. For example, the expression,

6) SELECT   NAME, AGE
   FROM   STUDENT
   WHERE   MAJOR = 'MATH'
      AND   AGE > 21

obtains the following:

BAKER	50

The conditions in WHERE clauses can refer to a set of values. To do this, the keyword IN or NOT IN is used. Consider:

7) SELECT   NAME
   FROM   STUDENT
   WHERE   MAJOR IN ['MATH', 'ACCOUNTING']

This expression means, "Present the names of students who have either a math or an accounting major." The result is:

PARKS
BAKER
BAKER
RUSSELL
RYE

The expression,

8) SELECT   NAME
   FROM   STUDENT
   WHERE   MAJOR NOT IN ['MATH', 'ACCOUNTING']

will cause the names of students other than math or accounting majors to be presented. The result is:

JONES
GLASS
JONES

The expression MAJOR IN means that the value of the Major attribute can equal *any* of the listed majors. The expression MAJOR NOT IN means the value must be different from *all* of the listed majors.

SQL built-in functions   SQL provides five built-in functions to facilitate query processing. They are: COUNT, SUM, AVG, MAX, and MIN. COUNT and SUM sound similar but are different. COUNT computes the number of tuples in a relation; SUM totals numeric attributes. AVG, MAX, and MIN also operate on numeric attributes. AVG computes the average value; MAX and MIN obtain the maximum and minimum values of an attribute in a relation.

The query expression,

9) SELECT   COUNT(*)
   FROM   STUDENT

counts the number of STUDENT tuples and displays this total in a relation having a single tuple and single attribute as follows:

With the exception of GROUP BY (considered below), built-in functions cannot be intermixed with attribute names in the SELECT statement. Thus, SELECT NAME, COUNT(*) is not allowed.

Consider the expressions:

10) SELECT   COUNT(MAJOR)
     FROM   STUDENT

11) SELECT   COUNT(UNIQUE MAJOR)
     FROM   STUDENT

Expression 10 counts all majors, including duplicates. Expression 11 counts only unique majors. The results are:

10) | 8 |

11) | 3 |

The special functions can be used to request a result, as in the above examples. Also, in some versions of SQL, built-in functions can be used as part of a WHERE clause. Consider:

12) SELECT   SID, NAME
     FROM   STUDENT
     WHERE   AGE > AVG(AGE)

The result (the average age is 30.38) is:

200	BAKER
250	GLASS
300	BAKER

Built-in functions can appear in both SELECT and WHERE clauses:

13) SELECT   COUNT(*)
     FROM   STUDENT
     WHERE   AGE = MAX(AGE)

This operation produces the number of students having the maximum age. The result is:

| 2 |

since two tuples have the age 50. (MAX obtains the maximum of the ages in the data; this is not the maximum possible age in the AGE domain, which is 100.)

Built-in functions and grouping   To increase the utility of built-in functions, they can be applied to groups of tuples within a relation. Such groups are formed by collecting tuples together (logically, not physically) that have the same value of a specified attribute. For example, students can be grouped by major. This means one group will be formed for each value of MAJOR. For the data in Figure 7-22, there will be a group of HISTORY majors, a group of ACCOUNT-ING majors, and a group of MATH majors. These groups are similar to what we called *sets* (imposed by nonunique keys) as discussed in Chapter 4.

The SQL keyword GROUP BY instructs the DBMS to group tuples together that have the same value of an attribute. Consider:

```
14) SELECT     MAJOR, COUNT(*)
    FROM       STUDENT
    GROUP BY   MAJOR
```

The result of this expression is:

HISTORY	3
ACCOUNTING	3
MATH	2

The tuples of the STUDENT relation have been logically grouped by the value of MAJOR. Then, the COUNT function sums the number of tuples in each group. The result is a relation having two attributes, the major name and the count. Thus, for subgroups, both attributes and built-in functions can be specified in the SELECT command.

In some cases, we do not want to consider all of the groups. For example, we might form groups of students having the same major and then wish to consider only those groups that have more than two students. In this case, we use the SQL HAVING clause to identify the subset of groups we want to consider.

Suppose we want to know the major and average age of students of all those majors having more than two students. The following SQL statements will obtain this result:

```
15) SELECT     MAJOR, AVG(AGE)
    FROM       STUDENT
    GROUP BY   MAJOR
    HAVING     COUNT(*) > 2
```

Here, groups of students having the same major are formed. Then, groups having more than two students are selected. (Other groups are ignored.) The major and the average age of these selected groups are produced. The result is:

HISTORY	31.67
ACCOUNTING	26

For even greater generality, WHERE clauses can be added as well. Consider the following:

```
16) SELECT      MAJOR, AVG(AGE)
    FROM        STUDENT
    WHERE       GRADE_LEVEL = 'SN'
    GROUP BY    MAJOR
    HAVING      COUNT(*) > 1
```

The result of this operation will be different depending on whether the WHERE condition is applied before or after the HAVING condition. To eliminate ambiguity, the SQL convention is that WHERE clauses are applied first. Thus, in the above operation, senior students are selected. Then groups are formed, then the groups are selected by the HAVING condition, and then the result is presented. In this case, the result is:

HISTORY	37

Querying multiple relations

In this section we extend the discussion of SQL to include operations on two or more relations. The STUDENT, CLASS, and ENROLLMENT data in Figure 7-22 will be used to illustrate SQL features.

Retrieval using subquery   Suppose we need to know the names of students enrolled in the class BD445. If we know that only students 100 and 200 are enrolled in this class, then the following will produce the correct names:

```
17) SELECT   NAME
    FROM     STUDENT
    WHERE    SID IN [100,200]
```

Usually, we will not know the SIDs of students in a class. We do have a facility, however, for determining those SIDs. Consider the operation:

18) SELECT   STUDENT_NUMBER
    FROM   ENROLLMENT
    WHERE   CLASS_NAME = 'BD445'

The result of this operation is:

100
200

These are the student numbers we need. Now, combining expressions 17 and 18, we obtain the following:

19) SELECT   NAME
    FROM   STUDENT
    WHERE   SID IN
          SELECT   STUDENT_NUMBER
          FROM   ENROLLMENT
          WHERE   CLASS_NAME = 'BD445'

It may be easier for you to understand these statements if you work from the bottom and read up. The last three statements obtain the student numbers for people enrolled in BD445. The first three statements produce the names for the two students selected. The result of this query is:

JONES
BAKER

This strategy can be very useful. Realize, however, that for this operation to be semantically correct, SID and STUDENT_NUMBER must arise from the same domain.

This strategy can be applied to three or even more relations. For example, suppose we want to know the names of the students enrolled in classes on Monday, Wednesday, and Friday at 3 o'clock (denoted MWF3 in our data). First, we need the names of classes that meet at that time:

20) SELECT   CLASS.NAME
    FROM   CLASS
    WHERE   TIME = 'MWF3'

(Since we will be dealing with three different relations, we will qualify attribute names with relation names to avoid confusion and ambiguity.) Now, what are the identifying numbers of students in these classes? We can specify:

21) SELECT   ENROLLMENT.STUDENT_NUMBER
    FROM   ENROLLMENT
    WHERE   ENROLLMENT.CLASS_NAME IN
             SELECT   CLASS.NAME
             FROM   CLASS
             WHERE   TIME = 'MWF3'

This yields:

which are the numbers of the students in class MWF3. Now, to obtain the names of those students, we specify:

22) SELECT   STUDENT.NAME
    FROM   STUDENT
    WHERE   STUDENT.SID IN
             SELECT   ENROLLMENT.STUDENT_NUMBER
             FROM   ENROLLMENT
             WHERE   ENROLLMENT.CLASS_NAME IN
                      SELECT   CLASS.NAME
                      FROM   CLASS
                      WHERE   CLASS.TIME = 'MWF3'

The result is:

JONES
BAKER
BAKER

This strategy works well as long as the desired result (the answer) comes from a single relation. If, however, the result comes from two or more relations, we have a problem. For example, suppose we want to know the names of students and the names of their classes. Say we need SID, student name, and class name. In this case, the results come from two different relations (STUDENT and ENROLLMENT) and the subquery strategy will not work. We need to be able to join the relations together.

Joining with SQL   To produce the names of every student's classes, we need to join the STUDENT relation with the ENROLLMENT relation. The following statements will do this:

23) SELECT   STUDENT.SID, STUDENT.NAME, ENROLLMENT.CLASS_
                 NAME
      FROM   STUDENT, ENROLLMENT
      WHERE   STUDENT.SID = ENROLLMENT.STUDENT_NUMBER

Recall that a join is the combination of a product operation, followed by a selection, followed (usually) by a projection. In expression 23, the FROM statement expresses the product of STUDENT and ENROLLMENT. Then, the WHERE statement expresses the selection. The meaning is, "Select from the product of STUDENT and ENROLLMENT those tuples in which SID of STUDENT equals STUDENT_NUMBER of ENROLLMENT." Finally, after the selection, the projection of student number, name, and class name is taken. The result is:

100	JONES	BD445
150	PARKS	BA200
200	BAKER	BD445
200	BAKER	CS250
300	BAKER	CS150
400	RYE	BA200
400	RYE	BF410
400	RYE	CS250
450	JONES	BA200

The WHERE clause can contain qualifiers in addition to those needed for the join. For example:

24) SELECT   STUDENT.SID, ENROLLMENT.CLASS_NAME
      FROM   STUDENT, ENROLLMENT
      WHERE   STUDENT.SID = ENROLLMENT.STUDENT_NUMBER
      AND   STUDENT.NAME = 'RYE'
      AND   ENROLLMENT.POSITION_NUMBER = 1

This operation will list the student number and class name of all students named RYE who were first to enroll in a class. The result is:

400	BF410

When data is needed from more than two relations, we can follow a similar strategy. In the following example, three relations are joined:

25) SELECT   STUDENT.SID, CLASS.NAME, CLASS.TIME, ENROLL-
      MENT.POSITION_NUMBER
 FROM   STUDENT, ENROLLMENT, CLASS
 WHERE   STUDENT.SID = ENROLLMENT.STUDENT_NUMBER
    AND ENROLLMENT.CLASS_NAME = CLASS.NAME
    AND STUDENT.NAME = 'BAKER'

The result of this operation is:

200	BD445	MWF3	2
200	CS250	MWF12	1
300	CS150	MWF3	1

Comparison of SQL subquery and join Join can be used as an alternate way of expressing subqueries. For example, in expression 19, we used a subquery to determine the students enrolled in the class BD445. We can also use a join to express this query as follows:

26) SELECT   STUDENT.NAME
 FROM   STUDENT, ENROLLMENT, CLASS
 WHERE   STUDENT.SID = ENROLLMENT.STUDENT_NUMBER
    AND ENROLLMENT.CLASS_NAME = 'BD445'

Similarly, the query, "What are the names of the students in class MWF at 3?" can be expressed as:

27) SELECT   STUDENT.NAME
 FROM   STUDENT, ENROLLMENT, CLASS
 WHERE   STUDENT.SID = ENROLLMENT.STUDENT_NUMBER
    AND ENROLLMENT.CLASS_NAME = CLASS.NAME
    AND CLASS.TIME = 'MWF3'

Although join expressions can substitute for subquery expressions, the converse is not true. Subqueries cannot always be substituted for joins. When using a join, the displayed attributes can come from any of the joined relations; when using a subquery, the displayed attributes can come from only the relation named in the FROM expression in the first SELECT.

For example, suppose we want to know the names of classes taken by undergraduates. We can express this as a subquery:

28) SELECT   UNIQUE CLASS_NAME
 FROM   ENROLLMENT
 WHERE   STUDENT_NUMBER IN
    SELECT   SID
    FROM   STUDENT
    WHERE   GRADE_LEVEL NOT = 'GR'

or as a join:

29) SELECT   UNIQUE ENROLLMENT.CLASS_NAME
    FROM   ENROLLMENT, STUDENT
    WHERE   ENROLLMENT.STUDENT_NUMBER = STUDENT.SID
            AND STUDENT.GRADE_LEVEL NOT = 'GR'

However, if we want to know both the names of the classes and the grade levels of the undergraduate students, then we must use a join. A subquery will not suffice because the desired results arise from two different relations. The names of the classes are stored in ENROLLMENT, and the names of the students are stored in STUDENT. The following will obtain the correct answer:

30) SELECT   UNIQUE ENROLLMENT.CLASS_NAME, STUDENT.
              GRADE_LEVEL
    FROM   ENROLLMENT, STUDENT
    WHERE   ENROLLMENT.STUDENT_NUMBER = STUDENT.SID
          AND STUDENT.GRADE_LEVEL NOT = 'GR'

The result will be:

BA200	SO
CS150	SN
BA200	FR
BF410	FR
CS250	FR
BA200	SN

EXISTS and NOT EXISTS   EXISTS and NOT EXISTS are logical operators; their value is either true or false depending on the presence or absence of tuples that fit qualifying conditions. For example, suppose we want to know the student numbers of students enrolled in more than one class.

31) SELECT   UNIQUE STUDENT_NUMBER
    FROM   ENROLLMENT A
    WHERE   EXISTS
            SELECT *
            FROM ENROLLMENT B
            WHERE   A.STUDENT_NUMBER = B.STUDENT_
                             NUMBER
                 AND A.CLASS_NAME NOT = B.CLASS_
                             NAME

In this example, the query and the subquery both refer to the ENROLL-MENT relation. To prevent ambiguity, these two uses of ENROLLMENT have been assigned a different name. In the first FROM statement, ENROLLMENT is assigned a temporary (and arbitrary) name, A. Then, in the second FROM statement, it is assigned another temporary name, B.

The meaning of the subquery expression is this: Find two tuples in ENROLL-MENT having the same student number but different class names. (This means the student is taking more than one class.) If two such tuples exist, then the logical value of EXISTS is true. In this case, present the student number in the answer. Otherwise, the logical value of the EXISTS is false; do not present that STUDENT_NUMBER in the answer.

Another way of viewing this query is to imagine two separate and identical copies of the ENROLLMENT relation. Call one copy relation A and the other copy relation B. We will compare each tuple in A with each tuple in B. First, consider the first tuple in A and the first tuple in B. In this case, since the two tuples are identical, both the STUDENT_NUMBERs and the CLASS_NAMEs will be the same. Do not display the STUDENT_NUMBER.

Now, consider the first tuple in A and the second tuple in B. If the STU-DENT_NUMBERs are the same and the CLASS_NAMEs are different, then display the STUDENT_NUMBER. In this case, we are comparing the first tuple of ENROLLMENT with the second tuple of ENROLLMENT. For the data in Figure 7-22, neither the STUDENT_NUMBERs nor the CLASS_NAMEs are the same.

We continue comparing the first tuple of A with each tuple of B. If the conditions are ever met, we print the student number. When all of the tuples in B have been examined, we move to the second tuple of A. It is compared to all of the tuples in B (actually, if we are considering the nth tuple in A, then only tuples greater than n need be considered in B).

The result of this query is:

200
400

To illustrate the application of NOT EXISTS, suppose we want to know the names of students taking all classes. Another way of expressing this query is to say we want the names of students such that there are no classes that the student did not take. The following expresses that statement. This query has three parts. In the bottom part, we try to find classes the student did not take. The middle part determines if any classes were found that the student did not take. If not, then the student is taking all classes, and the student's name is displayed.

```
32) SELECT   STUDENT.NAME
    FROM     STUDENT
    WHERE    NOT EXISTS
             SELECT *
             FROM     ENROLLMENT
             WHERE    NOT EXISTS
                      SELECT   *
                      FROM     CLASS
                      WHERE    CLASS.NAME = ENROLLMENT.
                      CLASS_NAME
                  AND ENROLLMENT.STUDENT_NUMBER =
                      STUDENT.SID
```

This query may be difficult to understand. If you have trouble with it, use the data in Figure 7-22 and follow the query instructions. The answer, for that data, is that no student is taking all classes. You might try to change the data so that a student does take all classes. Another approach for understanding this query is to attempt to solve it by not using NOT EXISTS. The problems you encounter will help you understand why NOT EXISTS is necessary.

A final example combines many SQL concepts and illustrates the power of this language. Suppose we want to know the names of graduate students taking classes only with other graduate students.

```
33) SELECT   A.NAME
    FROM     STUDENT A
    WHERE    STUDENT.GRADE_LEVEL = 'GR'
         AND NOT EXISTS
             SELECT   *
             FROM     ENROLLMENT B
             WHERE    STUDENT.SID = B.STUDENT_NUMBER
                  AND B.CLASS_NAME IN
                      SELECT   C.CLASS_NAME
                      FROM     ENROLLMENT C
                      WHERE    B.CLASS_NAME = C.CLASS_NAME
                           AND C.STUDENT_NUMBER IN
                               SELECT   D.SID
                               FROM     FROM STUDENT D
                               WHERE    C.STUDENT_NUMBER = D.SID
                                    AND D.GRADE_LEVEL NOT = 'GR'
```

The meaning of this query is: "Present the names of students where there is no tuple in ENROLLMENT that matches the student with a class which is one of the classes that are matched with students who have a grade level other than graduate." The result of this query is:

$$\boxed{\text{JONES}}$$

The last three queries are complicated. Do not assume from this that SQL is complicated. Actually, compared to the alternatives, SQL is simple; these last three queries are difficult because we are solving queries that are, logically, quite complex. For most day-to-day problems, SQL queries are quite simple and straightforward.

Changing data

SQL has provisions for changing data in relations by inserting new tuples, deleting tuples, and modifying values in existing tuples. SQL also has facilities for changing data structure. However, we will not consider changing data structure until we study SQL/DS in Chapter 12.

Inserting data   Tuples can be inserted into a relation one at a time or in groups. To insert a single tuple, we state:

34) INSERT   INTO ENROLLMENT
             [400, 'BD445', 44]

If we do not know all of this data, say we do not know Position_number, we could say:

35) INSERT   INTO ENROLLMENT (STUDENT_NUMBER, CLASS_NAME)
             [400, 'BD445']

Position_number could then be added later. Note that this causes the value of Position_number to be null. We defer a discussion of the processing of null values to Chapter 12.

We can also copy tuples en masse from one relation to another. For example, suppose we want to fill the JUNIOR relation that was defined in Figure 7-12.

36) INSERT   INTO JUNIOR
             SELECT   SID, NAME, MAJOR
             FROM   STUDENT
             WHERE   GRADE_LEVEL = 'JR'

This example, and all of the techniques for identifying data developed in the previous two sections, can be used to identify tuples to be moved. This feature provides quite powerful capabilities.

Deleting data As with insertion, tuples can be deleted one at a time or in groups. The following example will delete the tuple for student number 100:

37) DELETE   STUDENT
            WHERE STUDENT.SID = 100

Note that if student 100 is enrolled in classes, this deletion will cause an integrity problem. The ENROLLMENT tuples having STUDENT_NUMBER 100 will have no corresponding STUDENT tuple. We will address such integrity problems in Chapter 8.

Groups of tuples can be deleted as shown in the following two examples.

38) DELETE   ENROLLMENT
            WHERE ENROLLMENT.STUDENT_NUMBER IN
                      SELECT   STUDENT.SID
                      FROM   STUDENT
                      WHERE   STUDENT.MAJOR = 'ACCOUNTING'

39) DELETE   STUDENT
            WHERE STUDENT.MAJOR = 'ACCOUNTING'

The order of these two operations is important. If the order were reversed, none of the ENROLLMENT tuples would be deleted because the matching STUDENT tuples would have already been deleted.

Modifying data Tuples can also be modified one at a time or in groups. The keyword SET is used to change an attribute value. After SET, the name of the attribute to be changed is specified and then the new value or way of computing the new value. Consider two examples:

40) UPDATE   ENROLLMENT
    SET   POSITION_NUMBER = 44
    WHERE   STUDENT_NUMBER = 400

41) UPDATE   ENROLLMENT
    SET   POSITION_NUMBER = MAX (POSITION_NUMBER) + 1
    WHERE   STUDENT_NUMBER = 400

In operation 41, the value of the attribute will be calculated using the MAX built-in function.

To illustrate mass updates, suppose the name of a course has been changed from BD445 to BD564. In this case, to prevent integrity problems, both the ENROLLMENT and the CLASS relations need to be changed.

```
42) UPDATE   ENROLLMENT
    SET      CLASS_NAME = 'BD564'
    WHERE    CLASS_NAME = 'BD445'
    UPDATE   CLASS
    SET      CLASS_NAME = 'BD564'
    WHERE    CLASS_NAME = 'BD445'
```

SUMMARY

The relational model represents and processes data in the form of tables called *relations*. The columns of the tables are called *attributes*, and the rows are called *tuples*. The values of attributes arise from domains. The degree of a relation is the number of attributes it possesses.

With the relational model, relationships are contained in data values. Two tuples can have a relationship if they have two attributes that arise from the same domain. Trees and simple and complex networks are readily represented.

There are four categories of relational DML: relational algebra, relational calculus, transform-oriented languages, and graphic systems. Relational algebra consists of a group of relational operators that can be used to manipulate relations to obtain a desired result. Relational algebra is procedural. The transform-oriented languages provide a nonprocedural capability to use relations to transform given data into wanted results. SQL is an example.

SQL constructs are simple. The SELECT, FROM, and WHERE clauses are flexible and can be used in different ways to obtain many results. Even though the constructs are simple, SQL is an exceedingly powerful language. The return for time invested to learn SQL is great.

Some aspects of SQL may seem confusing (such as NOT EXISTS); these are actually very sophisticated concepts. SQL would be quite powerful with just the basic, simple facilities. In fact, most run-of-the-mill, day-to-day query requests can be expressed with only a knowledge of SELECT, FROM, and WHERE operators.

This chapter provides an introduction to the relational model. In the next chapter, the concepts presented here will be used to design relational databases.

Group I Questions

7.1   Define the following terms: *relation, attribute, tuple, degree,* and *domain*.

7.2   Explain the difference between a relational schemata and a relation.

7.3   Define *key* and *candidate key*.

7.4   Give an example of a hierarchical relationship among two relations. Show the DSD (like Figure 7-3), the relational schemata, and example data.

7.5   Give an example of a hierarchical relationship among three or more relations. Show the DSD, the relational schemata, and example data.

7.6   Give an example of a simple network relationship. Show the DSD, the relational schemata, and example data.

7.7   Give an example of a complex network relationship. Show the DSD, the relational schemata, and example data.

7.8   Explain, in a few words, how relationships are represented using the relational model.

7.9   Name and briefly explain four categories of relational DML.

7.10 How does relational algebra differ from high school algebra?

7.11 Define *union compatible*. Give an example of two relations that are union-compatible, and two that are union incompatible.

Questions 7.12 through 7.14 refer to the following two relations:

COMPANY (Name, Number_employees, Sales)
MANUFACTURERS (Name, People, Revenue)

7.12 Give an example of a union of these two relations.

7.13 Give an example of a difference of these two relations.

7.14 Give an example of an intersection of these two relations.

Questions 7.15 through 7.23 refer to the following three relations:

SALESPERSON (Name, Age, Salary)
ORDER (Number, Cust_name, Salesperson_name, Amount)
CUSTOMER (Name, City, Industry_type)

7.15 Develop sample data for each of these relations. For your data, give an example of the product of SALESPERSON and ORDER.

7.16 For your data, show an example of

SALESPERSON[Name, Salary]
SALESPERSON[Age, Salary]

Under what conditions will SALESPERSON[Age, Salary] have fewer tuples than SALESPERSON?

7.17 For your data, show an example of a select on SALESPERSON [Name], on SALESPERSON [Age], on both SALESPERSON [Name and Age].

7.18 For your data, shown an example of an equijoin and a natural join of SALESPERSON and ORDER where Name of SALESPERSON equals Salesperson name of ORDER.

7.19 Show relational algebra expressions for:

   a. The names of all salespeople

   b. The names of all salespeople having an ORDER tuple

    c. The names of salespeople not having an ORDER tuple

    d. The names of salespeople having an order with **ABERNATHY CONSTRUCTION**

    e. The ages of salespeople having an order with **ABERNATHY CONSTRUCTION**

    f. The city of all CUSTOMERs having an order with salesperson JONES.

7.20 Show SQL expressions for the following queries:

    a. The ages and salaries of all salespeople

    b. The ages and salaries of all salespeople (duplicates omitted)

    c. The names of all salespeople less than 30 years old

    d. The names of all salespeople having an order with **ABERNATHY CONSTRUCTION**

    e. The names of all salespeople not having an order with **ABERNATHY CONSTRUCTION**

7.21 Show SQL expressions for the following queries:

    a. The number of orders

    b. The number of different customers having an order

    c. The number of salespeople older than the average

    d. The name of the oldest salesperson

    e. The number of orders for each salesperson

    f. The average size of orders for each salesperson

    g. The average size of orders for each salesperson, considering only orders having an amount exceeding 500

7.22 Show SQL expressions for the following queries:

    a. The age of salespeople having an order with **ABERNATHY CONSTRUCTION** (use subquery)

    b. The age of salespeople having an order with **ABERNATHY CONSTRUCTION** (use join)

    c. The age of salespeople having an order with a customer in **MEMPHIS** (use subquery)

    d. The age of salespeople having an order with a customer in **MEMPHIS** (use join)

    e. The industry type and ages of salespeople of all orders for companies in **MEMPHIS**

    f. The names of salespeople having two or more orders

    g. The names and ages of salespeople having two or more orders

    h. The names and ages of salespeople having an order with all customers

7.23 Show SQL expressions for the following update operations:

    a. Insert a new tuple into CUSTOMER.

    b. Insert a new name and age into SALESPERSON; assume salary is undetermined.

    c. Insert tuples into the relation HIGH ACHIEVER (Name, Age) where, to be included, a salesperson must have a salary of at least 100,000.

    d. Delete customer ABERNATHY CONSTRUCTION.

    e. Delete all orders for ABERNATHY CONSTRUCTION.

    f. Change the salary of salesperson JONES to 45,000.

    g. Give all salespeople a 10-percent pay increase.

    h. Assume salesperson JONES changes name to PARKS. Make appropriate changes.

Group II Questions

7.24 Suppose you have the task of explaining to management why relational database processing is important. Prepare a three-page report to management that discusses the significance of relational database processing. Present the major findings in this report to your class.

7.25 Obtain information on relational calculus [33] and [75]. Show how the example queries 1 through 33 would be processed using relational calculus.

7.26 Obtain information on SQUARE [12]. Compare and contrast SQUARE with SQL.

7.27 Obtain information on the DBMS product QBE [82]. Show how queries 1 through 33 would be processed using QBE.

7.28 Obtain information on the DBMS product INGRES [72]. Show how queries 1 through 33 would be processed using INGRES.

7.29 Use relational algebra to express queries 1 through 33.

7.30 Consider the problem of computing joins. Express an algorithm for joining two relations assuming that the relations must be processed sequentially (no linked or inverted lists). Express a second join algorithm assuming that the attributes involved are supported by inverted lists.

7.31 Obtain information about the product IDM 500 [14]. How does this product's DML differ from SQL? How does it differ from INGRES? What are the strengths of IDM 500? The weaknesses?

7.32 If possible, obtain a copy of the micro DBMS dBASE II. Store the data in Figure 7-22 using this product. Process the queries 1 through 33 using this DBMS.

8
Relational
Database Design

This chapter concerns the design of relational databases. It has three major sections. The first section discusses theory of relational normal forms. We will study this theory because it will help us to structure and evaluate relations. In the second section, relational theory is applied to the problem of relational database design. This discussion leads to criteria for designing and evaluating relational databases. Finally, the last section of this chapter considers the design of a relational database for Sally Enterprises. The logical design developed with SDM in Chapter 6 will be transformed into a design of a relational database.

RELATIONAL NORMAL FORMS

Not all relational database designs are equal. Some are better than others. Obviously, a design that meets the users' needs is better than one that does not, but there are other criteria as well. With some relations, changing data can have unexpected consequences. These consequences, called *modification anomalies*, are undesirable. As you will see, anomalies can be eliminated by changing the database design. Usually relations without modification anomalies are preferred. Some relations are independent, others are interdependent. Generally, but not always, the less interdependency, the better. This section defines terms and discusses these issues in light of relational database theory.

Modification Anomalies

Consider the ACTIVITY relation in Figure 8-1. It has the attributes SID (student identifier), Activity, and Fee. The meaning of a tuple is that the student engages in the named activity for the specified fee.

Suppose that the fee for an activity depends only on the activity; the activity costs the same for all students. For the data in Figure 8-1, if we delete the tuple for student 100, we will lose not only the fact that student 100 is a skier, but

ACTIVITY (SID, Activity, Fee)
Key: SID
Example Data

SID	Activity	Fee
100	SKIING	200
150	SWIMMING	50
175	SQUASH	50
200	SWIMMING	50

Figure 8-1   The ACTIVITY Relation

also the fact that skiing costs $200. This is called a *deletion anomaly;* we are losing more information than we want to. We lose facts about two entities with one deletion. This characteristic is considered undesirable because it is usually unintended.

Also, suppose we want to enter the fact that SCUBA costs $175. We cannot enter this data into the ACTIVITY relation until a student enrolls in SCUBA. This restriction seems silly. Why should we have to wait until someone takes the activity before we can record its price? This situation is called an *insertion anomaly.* We gain facts about two entities with one insertion; or, stated negatively, we cannot insert a fact about one entity until we have an additional fact about another entity.

These anomalies can be eliminated by creating two new relations via projection. We take ACTIVITY[SID, Activity] to form a new relation called *STU_ACT*, and ACTIVITY[Activity, Fee] to form a new relation called *ACT_COST*. (Recall that square brackets indicate a projection.) Figure 8-2 shows the new relations.

If we delete student 100 from STU_ACT, we do not lose the fact that SKIING

STU_ACT (SID, Activity)
Key: SID

SID	Activity
100	SKIING
150	SWIMMING
175	SQUASH
200	SWIMMING

ACT_COST (Activity, Fee)
Key: Activity

Activity	Fee
SKIING	200
SWIMMING	50
SQUASH	50

Figure 8-2   Division of ACTIVITY via Projection

costs $200. Further, we can add SCUBA and its fee before anyone enrolls. Thus the deletion and insertion anomalies have been eliminated.

The elimination of the anomalies may, however, have a disadvantage as well. Student 250 wants to enroll in RACKETBALL. We can store this tuple in STU_ACT, but should we? Should a student be allowed to enroll in an activity that is not in the relation ACT_COST? Such an enrollment would have been disallowed in the schema in Figure 8-1.

Observe from this that when a relation is divided by projection, we (may) lose anomalies, but we (may) gain interrelation constraints. In this case, the constraint might be: No activity is allowed in STU_ACT that is not already in ACT_COST. We will have more to say about interrelation constraints later in this chapter.

Classes of modification anomalies

There are many different types of modification anomalies. In the 1970s relational theorists chipped away at these types. Someone would find an anomaly, classify it, and think of a way to prevent it. This process generated improved criteria for designing relations. These criteria are called *normal forms*.

Codd, in his 1970 paper [28] defined first, second, and third normal forms (1NF, 2NF, 3NF). Later, Boyce-Codd normal form (BCNF) was postulated, and then fourth and fifth normal forms were defined. As you can see in Figure 8-3, each of these normal forms contains the other. A relation in fifth normal form is automatically in 1, 2, 3, BC, and 4 normal forms.

These normal forms were helpful, but they had a serious limitation. No theorist was able to guarantee that any of these forms would eliminate all anomalies; each form would eliminate just certain anomalies. This situation changed, however, in 1981 when R. Fagin defined a new normal form called *domain/key normal form* (DK/NF). In a landmark paper [39], Fagin showed that a relation in domain/key normal form is free of all modification anomalies, regardless of their type.

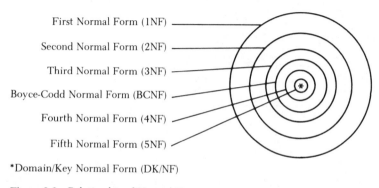

First Normal Form (1NF)

Second Normal Form (2NF)

Third Normal Form (3NF)

Boyce-Codd Normal Form (BCNF)

Fourth Normal Form (4NF)

Fifth Normal Form (5NF)

*Domain/Key Normal Form (DK/NF)

Figure 8-3   Relationship of Normal Forms

Until DK/NF was identified, it was necessary for relational database designers to continue looking for more and more anomalies, and more and more normal forms. Fagin's proof, however, greatly simplified the situation. If we can put a relation in DK/NF, then we are guaranteed it will have no anomalies, period. The trick is to find ways to put relations in DK/NF. Unfortunately, we do not even know if all relations can be put into DK/NF.

The next section surveys normal forms. You should strive to gain an intuitive understanding of 1, 2, 3, BC, 4, and 5 normal forms. Because of its importance, you should strive to completely understand DK/NF. If you can put relational designs in DK/NF, then you are guaranteed there will be no modification anomalies. Thus DK/NF will become a design goal.

First, second, third, and Boyce-Codd normal forms

First normal form is the starting point; all relations are in first normal form. Relations in first normal form have modification anomalies. As mentioned, we can eliminate some of these anomalies by putting the relation in second normal form. We can eliminate even more when the relation is put in third normal form, and even more with Boyce-Codd normal form. Second, third, and Boyce-Codd normal forms all address anomalies caused by inappropriate *functional dependencies*. Therefore, before we can discuss these forms we must define functional dependency and two other terms as well.

Functional dependencies, determinants, and keys　A functional dependency is a relationship between attributes. Attribute Y is said to be functionally dependent on attribute X if the value of X determines the value of Y. Another way of saying this is that if we know the value of X, we can determine the value of Y. For example, suppose we rent an apartment for $500 per month. If we know how many months we have lived in the apartment (M), then we know how much rent we have paid ($500 times M). In this case, Total_rent_paid is functionally dependent on Months_in_residence.

This functional dependency occurs because there is an equation relating months to dollars paid. Functional dependencies can exist that do not involve equations. They may simply involve established facts. Suppose you know that everyone living in a given dorm pays the same rent. People living in dorm A pay $400; people living in dorm B pay $500; and people living in dorm C pay $400. In this case, you can say that Rent is functionally dependent on Dorm_name. This is denoted Dorm_name → Rent (read as, "Dorm_name determines Rent").

Consider another example, Activity → Fee. This dependency means that the value of Activity determines the value of Fee. This functional dependency holds for the ACTIVITY relation of Figure 8-1.

An attribute is a *determinant* if it occurs on the left-hand side of a functional dependency. In the examples so far, both Dorm_name and Activity are determinants.

Many students mistakenly believe that the values of a determinant must be unique. For example, they believe that if Activity → Fee, then the relation can have only one value of Activity. Do not make this mistake. Determinants may or may not be unique. The Activity determinant in Figure 8-1 is not unique because the value SWIMMING occurs twice in this relation. However, since Activity → Fee, then wherever the value SWIMMING occurs, we are guaranteed that the value of Fee will be the same. In this example, SWIMMING costs $50 in both tuples two and four.

Additionally, the dependency Activity → Fee does not imply that Fee values need be unique, either. Both SWIMMING and SQUASH can cost $50 without violating Activity → Fee.

Functional dependencies can involve groups of attributes. It might be that the combination (SID, Activity) determines Fee. This means that the value of Fee depends on the name of the activity and the student who is participating. This situation would occur if fees were different for undergraduates and graduates, or if they were different for students who live on campus, or for some other reason.

One (or more) attributes can determine (→) several attributes. For example, considering campus addresses, we might have SID → (Bldg, Room). However, if this is true, then SID → Bldg and SID → Room.

In general, if $X → (Y, Z)$, then $X → Y$ and $X → Z$. But, if $(X, Y) → Z$, then it is not necessarily true that $X → Z$ or $Y → Z$.

A key of a relation comprises one or more attributes that functionally determine, or identify, a tuple. For the relation ACTIVITY, assume that students are allowed to have just one activity. (As an aside, how would you know this? This fact must originate in the requirements; the educational institution might allow students to engage in only one recognized activity. This constraint would be expressed via SDM in the logical design.) If a student may have just one activity, then SID is a key of this relation. A given value of SID determines a particular tuple.

Suppose students can have more than one activity. This situation is represented by the relation ACTIVITIES, shown in Figure 8-4. For this relation, SID does not determine a unique tuple, and hence SID is not a key. Student 100, for example, has two activities. In fact, for ACTIVITIES, no single attribute is a key.

The key of ACTIVITIES must be a combination of attributes. In this case, the key is the combination (SID, Activity). This means that a value of SID together with a value of Activity will determine a unique tuple.

Now you need to make a very important distinction. The value of a key must be unique, but the value of a determinant may or may not be unique. Consider the attribute SID. In relation ACTIVITY, SID is a determinant and *also* a key. In relation ACTIVITIES, Activity is a determinant but *not* a key. Consequently, in ACTIVITY there will be one and only one occurrence of a given SID value. 100, for example, occurs once. In ACTIVITIES, on the other hand, there can be many instances of a given SID. 100 can occur as many times as student 100 enrolls in activities.

ACTIVITIES (SID, Activity, Fee)
Key: (SID, Activity)

SID	Activity	Fee
100	SKIING	200
100	GOLF	65
150	SWIMMING	50
175	SQUASH	50
175	SWIMMING	50
200	SWIMMING	50
200	GOLF	65

Figure 8-4   Relation with a Two-Attribute Key

Why must keys be unique? A key functionally determines the entire tuple. If the value of the key were duplicated, then the entire tuple would be duplicated. But this is not allowed. By the definition of relation, tuples must be unique. Thus, when we say an attribute is a key, we know that it will be unique. (The relational model requires tuples to be unique. Some applications of this model, such as the language SQL, do allow duplicate tuples. We will consider this fact further in Chapter 12.)

Modification anomalies regarding functional dependencies

The ACTIVITIES relation in Figure 8-4 has modification anomalies. If we delete the tuple for student 175, we lose the fact that SQUASH costs $50. Also, we cannot enter an activity until a student enrolls.

The problem with this relation is that it has a dependency involving only part of the key. The key is the combination (SID, Activity), but the relation contains a dependency, Activity → Fee. The determinant of this dependency is only part of the key. The modification anomalies could be eliminated if the nonkey attribute, *Fee*, were dependent on all of the key, not just part of it. This leads to a definition of second normal form: A relation is in second normal form if all nonkey attributes are dependent on *all* of the key.

ACTIVITIES can be decomposed via projection to form two relations in second normal form. The relations to be formed are ACTIVITIES[SID, Activity], and ACTIVITIES[Activity, Fee].

Unfortunately, relations in second normal form also have anomalies. Consider the HOUSING relation in Figure 8-5a. The key is SID, and the functional dependencies are SID → Building and Building → Fee. This means that a student lives in only one building and that for each building there is only one fee. Everyone living in Randolph Hall, for example, pays $1200 per quarter.

HOUSING (SID, Building, Fee)
Key: SID
Functional
dependencies: Building → Fee
                SID → Building → Fee

SID	Building	Fee
100	RANDOLPH	1200
150	INGERSOLL	1100
200	RANDOLPH	1200
250	PITKIN	1100
300	RANDOLPH	1200

a. Relation with Transitive Dependency

STU_HOUSING (SID, Building)   BLDG_FEE (Building, Fee)
Key: SID   Key: Building

SID	Building
100	RANDOLPH
150	INGERSOLL
200	RANDOLPH
250	PITKIN
300	RANDOLPH

Building	Fee
RANDOLPH	1200
INGERSOLL	1100
PITKIN	1100

b. Relations Eliminating the Transitive Dependency

Figure 8-5 Elimination of Transitive Dependency

Since SID determines Building and since Building determines Fee, then, indirectly, SID → Fee. Thus this relation is in second normal form (both Fee and Building are determined by SID). But, it has anomalies.

What happens if we delete the second tuple in the HOUSING relation? We lose not only the fact that student 150 lives in Ingersoll Hall, we also lose the fact that it costs $1100 to live there. This is a deletion anomaly. Further, how can we record the fact that the Fee for Baransy Hall is $1500? We can't until a student decides to move in. This is an insertion anomaly.

So, second normal form is not enough. To eliminate these anomalies, the transitive dependencies must be eliminated. This leads to a definition of third normal form: A relation is in third normal form if it is in second normal form and if it has no transitive dependencies.

The HOUSING relation can be divided by projection into two relations in third normal form. The relations STU_HOUSING (SID, Building) and BLDG_FEE (Building, Fee) in Figure 8-5b are examples.

The ACTIVITY relation shown in Figure 8-1 is another example of a relation having transitive dependencies. In ACTIVITY, SID determines Activity and Activity determines Fee. Therefore, ACTIVITY is not in third normal form. To eliminate anomalies, the relations STU_ACT (SID, Activity) and ACT_COST (Activity, Fee) should be used.

Unfortunately, even relations in third normal form can have anomalies. Consider the ADVISOR relation in Figure 8-6a. Students have majors and are advised by faculty personnel. Fname is the unique name of a faculty person.

ADVISOR (SID, Major, Fname)

Key (primary):   (SID, Major)
Key (candidate):   (SID, Fname)

Functional
dependencies: Fname → Major

SID	Major	Fname
100	MATH	CAUCHY
150	PSYCHOLOGY	JUNG
200	MATH	RIEMANN
250	MATH	CAUCHY
300	PSYCHOLOGY	PERLS

a.   Relation in Third Normal Form but Not in BC Normal Form

STU_ADV (SID, Fname)
Key: SID

ADV_SUBJ (Fname, Subject)
Key: Fname

SID	Fname
100	CAUCHY
150	JUNG
200	RIEMANN
250	CAUCHY
300	PERLS

Fname	Subject
CAUCHY	MATH
JUNG	PSYCHOLOGY
RIEMANN	MATH
PERLS	PSYCHOLOGY

b.   Relations in Boyce-Codd Normal Form

Figure 8-6   Boyce-Codd Normal Form

Since students can have several majors and hence several advisors, SID is not a sufficient key. Either the combination (SID, Major) or the combination (SID, Fname) is required. When two or more attributes or attribute collections can be key, they are called *candidate keys*. When one of the candidates is selected to be the key, it is called the *primary key*.

For ADVISOR, we assume that a faculty member can advise in only one major, but there are several advisors in each major. Thus the functional dependency Fname → Major holds, but not the reverse.

ADVISOR is in first normal form by definition. Since it has no no-key attributes, it is also in second normal form. Further, it is in third normal form because it has no transitive dependencies. In spite of all this, however, it has modification anomalies.

Suppose student 300 drops out of school. If we delete student 300's tuple, we lose the fact that PERLS advises in PSYCHOLOGY. This is a deletion anomaly. Similarly, how can we store the fact that KEYNES advises in ECONOMICS? We can't until a student majors in economics. This is an insertion anomaly.

Situations like this lead to the definition of Boyce-Codd normal form (BCNF). A relation is in BCNF if every determinant is a candidate key. As with the other examples, ADVISOR can be decomposed with projection into relations having no anomalies. For example, the relations STU_ADV (SID, Fname) and ADV_SUBJ (Fname, Subject) in Figure 8-6b have no anomalies.

Since relations in BCNF have no anomalies regarding functional dependencies, this seemed to put the issue of modification anomalies at rest. However, it was soon discovered that anomalies can arise from situations other than functional dependencies.

STUDENT (SID, Major, Activity)
Key: (SID, Major, Activity)

Multivalued
dependencies: SID→→ Major
                SID→→ Activity

SID	Major	Activity
100	MUSIC	SWIMMING
100	ACCOUNTING	SWIMMING
100	MUSIC	TENNIS
100	ACCOUNTING	TENNIS
150	MATH	JOGGING

Figure 8-7   Relation with Multivalued Dependencies

Anomalies from multivalued dependencies

Consider the STUDENT relation in Figure 8-7. It shows the relationship of students, majors, and activities. Suppose that students can enroll in several different majors and several different activities. Since this is so, the only key is the combination of attributes (SID, Major, Activity). Student 100 majors in MUSIC and ACCOUNTING. She also participates in SWIMMING and TENNIS. Student 150 majors only in MATH and participates in JOGGING.

What is the relationship between SID and Major? It is not a functional dependency, because students have several different majors. There is some sort of relationship, however. To see why, suppose that student 100 decides to enroll in SKIING, and so we add the tuple [100, MUSIC, SKIING] to the relation as shown in Figure 8-8a. As the modified relation stands, it seems to imply that

STUDENT (SID, Major, Activity)
Key: (SID, Major, Activity)

SID	Major	Activity
100	MUSIC	SKIING
100	MUSIC	SWIMMING
100	ACCOUNTING	SWIMMING
100	MUSIC	TENNIS
100	ACCOUNTING	TENNIS
150	MATH	JOGGING

a. Insertion of a Single Tuple

SID	Major	Activity
100	MUSIC	SKIING
100	ACCOUNTING	SKIING
100	MUSIC	SWIMMING
100	ACCOUNTING	SWIMMING
100	MUSIC	TENNIS
100	ACCOUNTING	TENNIS
150	MATH	JOGGING

b. Insertion of Two Tuples

Figure 8-8 STUDENT Relations with Insertion Anomalies

student 100 skis as a MUSIC major but does not ski as an ACCOUNTING major. This implication is illogical. To make the relation semantically correct, we must also add the tuple [100, ACCOUNTING, SKIING]. This has been done in Figure 8-8b, where each value of Major is now matched with each value of Activity.

The relationship between SID and Major is a *multivalued dependency*. SID determines not a single value, but instead, several values. Thus, in Figure 8-8b the SID 100 determines a set of majors [MUSIC, ACCOUNTING] and a set of activities [SWIMMING, TENNIS, SKIING]. The SID 150 determines a set of majors [MATH] and a set of activities [JOGGING].

This relation is all key and thus must be in BCNF; however, it has deficiencies. If student 100 adds another major, we must search out her activities, and add one tuple for each of them. In this case, three tuples would be added. This is ridiculous. Why should we insert three tuples just to add a new major? However, if we do not add these tuples, the semantics of the relation are misleading. A student does not lose two activities because she has added a new major.

Furthermore, suppose student 100 develops tennis elbow and drops out of tennis. In this case, two tuples must be deleted—one for each major. But, what do majors have to do with tennis elbow?

The solution to this problem is to break this relation using projection. The relations STU_MAJOR (SID, Major) and STU_ACT (SID, Activity) do not have anomalies. With these projections we can add majors or activities in a straightforward fashion. See Figure 8-9.

Actually, as you will see, the term *multivalued dependency* is misleading. A better term would be *multivalued, independent attributes*. To see why, consider the definition of multivalued dependency: In a relation having at least three attributes, a multivalued dependency exists between two attributes, say A and B, if the value of B depends only on the value of A, regardless of the values of other attributes in the relation. By this definition, a multivalued dependency can only exist in a relation having three or more attributes.

STU_MAJOR (SID, Major)
Key: (SID, Major)

STU_ACT (SID, Activity)
Key: (SID, Activity)

SID	Major
100	MUSIC
100	ACCOUNTING
150	MATH

SID	Activity
100	SKIING
100	SWIMMING
100	TENNIS
150	JOGGING

Figure 8-9 Elimination of Multivalued Dependency by Projection

Consider the relation R(A,B,C). The multivalued dependency A $\twoheadrightarrow$ B (read A multidetermines B) exists if the value of B depends only on the value of A and is independent of C. For the STUDENT relation in Figure 8-7, SID $\twoheadrightarrow$ Major because Major depends only on the value of SID and not on the value of Activity. Also, SID $\twoheadrightarrow$ Activity because the value of Activity depends only on the value of SID and not on the value of Major.

Multivalued dependencies always occur in pairs. In R, if A $\twoheadrightarrow$ B, then A $\twoheadrightarrow$ C. This must be so because if B is unrelated to C, then C must also be unrelated to B.

The reason that STUDENT in Figure 8-7 has anomalies is *not* just because it has independent attributes, and *not* just because it has attributes having multiple values; rather, STUDENT has anomalies because it has both independent attributes *and* they have multiple values. Thus the term *multivalued, independent attributes* would be more accurate.

Viewed another way, Majors and Activities are unrelated; having a particular major implies nothing about activities. Since majors and activities are unrelated, whenever we add a new Major, we must add a tuple for every value of Activity. Otherwise, there will *appear* to be a relationship between a major and an activity. For example, in the above situation, student 100 appeared to enjoy SKIING as a MUSIC major, but not to enjoy SKIING as an ACCOUNTING major. (Actually, ask any CPA during tax season, and he or she will say this is good training.)

The independence among attributes is not a problem if the attributes have a single value. For example, in the relation STUDENT (SID, Shoe_size, Marital_status), Shoe_size and Marital_status are independent. However, since both of these attributes have only a single value, anomalies cannot occur. In Figure 8-10, we can delete any of the tuples with no problem. Also, we can add to

STUDENT (SID, Shoe_size, Marital_status)
Key: SID
Functional
dependencies: SID $\rightarrow$ Shoe_size
               SID $\rightarrow$ Marital_status

Multivalued
dependencies: SID $\twoheadrightarrow$ Shoe_size | Marital_status

SID	Shoe_size	Marital_status
100	8	M
150	10	S
200	5	S
250	12	S

Figure 8-10   Relation in Fourth Normal Form

STUDENT the tuple [300, 5, M] and not need to make any other insertions.

This observation leads to the definition of fourth normal form. A relation is in *fourth normal form* if it is in BCNF and has no multivalued dependencies, or if it is in BCNF and all multivalued dependencies are also functional dependencies. This definition means that if a relation has multivalued dependencies and is in fourth normal form, then the multivalued dependencies have a single value. In other words, if A $\twoheadrightarrow$ B, then, to be in fourth normal form, A $\rightarrow$ B. This is confusing terminology. A better expression would be to say that all independent attributes have a single value.

The relation in Figure 8-7 is not in fourth normal form because it has the multivalued dependencies SID $\twoheadrightarrow$ Major and SID $\twoheadrightarrow$ Activity, *and* because Major and Activity have more than one value. Thus there are no functional dependencies between SID and Major or SID and Activity.

In Figure 8-9, since the relations have only two attributes, they can have no multivalued dependencies. Therefore, they are in fourth normal form because they are in BCNF (every determinant is part of the key) and because they have no multivalued dependencies.

In Figure 8-10, the relation has two multivalued dependencies, SID $\twoheadrightarrow$ Shoe_size and SID $\twoheadrightarrow$ Marital_status. However, since SID is the key of the relation, then SID $\rightarrow$ Shoe_size and SID $\rightarrow$ Marital_status. Thus both of the multidependencies are also functional dependencies.

As a final note, when a relation has multivalued dependencies, the easiest way to eliminate anomalies is to divide the relation into several with projection. The division should be done such that each independent attribute is in a relation of its own.

Anomalies from join dependencies

A join dependency is an assertion that a relation can be constructed by the join of its projections. For example, consider the relation STUDENT (SID, Major, Grade_level). Two projections of this relation are STUDENT[SID, Major] and STUDENT[SID, Grade_level]. A join dependency involving these projections is: * ((SID, Major), (SID, Grade_level)).

This dependency is a constraint indicating that, for all values of the attributes, it must be possible to reconstruct STUDENT from these two projections. In this simple case, it is easy to verify that this constraint will hold. For more complex cases, however, the situation is more obscure.

Join dependencies are strange phenomena. Unlike functional and multivalued dependencies, they have no ready, intuitive meaning. Further, Fagin [39] has shown that the satisfaction of join constraints interacts with the size of the domains of attributes in an unusual way. Specifically, for a relation having n attributes, to have no anomalies with regard to join dependencies, the size of the domain of each *prime attribute* (an attribute that is part of the key) must be greater than or equal to $C(n, [n/2])$. (This means the combinations of n things taken $n/2$ at a time. If n is odd, the fraction is truncated.)

We will not consider join dependencies in this text except to make two remarks. First, a relation is considered to be in fifth normal form (meaning anomalies with regard to join dependencies are eliminated) if all join constraints are logically implied by keys, and if the size of the prime attributes meets the constraints in the last paragraph. Second, it seems likely that more work will be done in this area. At the moment, join dependencies seem a bit mysterious; we do not know what the consequences of join dependencies are, nor even if there are any practical consequences. See Ullman [75] and Date [33] for more information.

Domain/key normal form

In 1981, R. Fagin published an important paper [39] in which he defined domain/key normal form (DK/NF). In this paper he showed that a relation in DK/NF will have no insertion or deletion anomalies. He also showed that a relation having no insertion or deletion anomalies must be in DK/NF. This finding establishes a bound on the definition of normal forms. No higher normal form will be needed, at least for the purpose of eliminating modification anomalies. (This does not mean that creative work is completed in this subject; rather, DK/NF establishes an upper bound on normal forms. Which relations can be put into DK/NF and how this is to be done are still very much open questions.)

Even more importantly, DK/NF involves only the concepts of key and domain. These concepts are fundamental and close to the heart of database practitioners. They are readily supported by DBMS products. In a sense, Fagin's work formalized and justified what many practitioners believed intuitively, but were unable to express precisely.

In concept, DK/NF is quite simple. A relation is in DK/NF if every constraint on the relation is a logical consequence of the definition of keys and domains. *Constraint* in this definition is a broad term. Fagin defines a constraint as any rule on static values of attributes that is precise enough that we can evaluate whether or not it is true. Thus edit rules, intra- and inter-relation constraints, functional dependencies, multivalued dependencies, and join dependencies are all examples of constraints. Fagin expressly excludes constraints having to do with *changes* in data values. For example, the rule "Salesperson salary in the current period can never be less than salary in the prior period," is excluded from Fagin's definition of constraint. Except for such constraints on changes in data values, Fagin's definition of constraint is very broad.

DK/NF means that if we can find a way to define keys and domains such that all constraints will be satisfied when the key and domain definitions are satisfied, then modification anomalies are impossible. Again, stated differently, if a relation is in DK/NF, then by enforcing domain definitions via editing, and by requiring key attributes to be unique, we can guarantee there will be no modification anomalies.

Unfortunately, there is no known way to convert a relation to DK/NF automatically, nor is it even known which relations can be converted to DK/NF. In

```
STUDENT (SID, Grade_level, Building, Fee)

Key: SID

Constraints:        Building → Fee
                    SID must not begin with digit 1
```

Figure 8-11 DK/NF Example 1

spite of this, DK/NF can be exceedingly useful for practical database design.

DK/NF is a design objective. We wish to define our relations such that constraints are logical consequences of domains and keys. For many designs, this objective can be accomplished. Where it cannot be accomplished, the constraints must be built into application programs that process the database. We will see more of this later in this chapter. First, however, we will illustrate DK/NF with three examples.

DK/NF example 1 Consider the STUDENT relation in Figure 8-11. It contains SID, student grade level, the building in which the student lives, and the student's fee for living in that building. The key of the relation is SID. Assume we know, from the specification of requirements, that there are two constraints: Building → Fee and SIDs must not begin with 1.

Now, without worrying about whether this relation is in 1, 2, 3, BCNF, 4, or 5 normal forms, we can be certain, by Fagin's theorem, there will be no modification anomalies if we can find a way to express these constraints as logical consequences of domain and key definitions. Happily, for this example, it will be easy.

To enforce the constraint that student numbers not begin with 1, we simply define the domain for student numbers to incorporate this constraint. This definition causes the first constraint to be a logical consequence of domain definitions.

Next, we need to make the functional dependency Building → Fee a logical consequence of keys. If Building were a key attribute, then Building → Fee would be a logical consequence of a key. Therefore, the question becomes, "How can Building become a key?" It cannot be a key in STUDENT because more than one student lives in the same building. It could be a key of its own relation, however. Thus we define the relation BLDG_FEE (Building, Fee) with Building as a key. Given this relation, Fee can be removed from STUDENT. Figure 8-12 presents this alternative design.

This is the same result we obtained when converting a relation from 2NF to 3NF. However, in this case it was simpler. We did not need to know that we

```
Domain Definitions

    SID         IN    CDDD, where C is decimal digit not = 1; D = decimal
                      digit
    Grade_level IN    { 'FR', 'SO', 'JR', 'SN', 'GR' }
    Building    IN    CHAR (4)
    Fee         IN    DEC (4)


Relations and Key Definitions

    STUDENT (SID, Grade_level, Building)
    Key: SID

    BLDG_FEE (Building, Fee)
    Key: Building
```

Figure 8-12 Domain/Key Definition of Example 1

were eliminating a transitive dependency. Nor do we need to remember the definitions of other normal forms. We simply need to creatively search for relations such that all constraints are logically implied by domain and key definitions.

DK/NF example 2 The next example, in Figure 8-13, is a bit more complicated. The relation PROFESSOR concerns professors, the classes they teach,

```
    PROFESSOR (FID, Fname, Class, SID, Sname)
    Key: (FID, Class, SID)
    Constraints:    FID → Fname
                    Fname → FID
                    FID →→ Class | SID
                    Fname →→ Class | SID
                    SID → FID
                    SID → Fname
                    SID → Sname
                    FID must start with 1; SID must not start with 1
```

Figure 8-13 DK/NF Example 2

and the students they advise. FID and Fname are both unique. Either FID or Fname multidetermines Class and advisee (SID). SID determines Sname, but Sname does not necessarily determine SID. SID determines the FID or Fname of his or her advising professor. The attributes (FID, Class, SID) are the key of the relation. Note the constraints on FID and SID.

Figure 8-14 shows a transformation of this relation into DK/NF (not the only transformation, and we do not know if it is the best one. "What is best?" and "How do we know if this is best?" are research questions.) The transformation has three relations. The first, FACULTY, shows the relationship of FID and Fname. FID is the key, and Fname is an alternate key. This terminology means both attributes are unique in the relation. Because both are keys, the functional dependencies FID → Fname and Fname → FID are logical consequences of keys.

The multivalued dependencies have been eliminated by placing the class data and the student data in different relations. The correspondence of faculty and classes is shown in the relation PREPARATION (Fname, Class).

Domain Definitions

FID	IN	CDDD, C = 1; D = decimal digit
Fname	IN	CHAR (30)
Class	IN	CHAR (10)
SID	IN	CDDD, C is decimal digit, not = 1;
		D = decimal digit
Sname	IN	CHAR (30)

Relation and Key Definitions

FACULTY (FID, Fname)
Key (primary):   FID
Key (candidate):   Fname

PREPARATION (Fname, Class)
Key: Fname

ADVISOR (SID, Sname, Fname)
Key: SID

Figure 8-14   Domain/Key Definition of Example 2

```
ADVISING (FID, Fname, Grad_faculty_status, SID, Sname)

Key: SID

Constraints:      FID → Fname
                  Fname → FID
                  FID or Fname → Grad_faculty_status
                  Only graduate faculty can advise graduate students
                  FID begins with 1
                  SID must not begin with 1
                  SID of graduate students begins with 9
```

Figure 8-15   DK/NF Example 3

The ADVISOR relationship has SID, Sname, and Fname attributes with SID as key. This relation makes the functional dependencies SID → Sname and SID → Fname the logical consequence of keys. Thus Figure 8-14 expresses all of the constraints of Figure 8-13 as a logical consequence of domain and key definitions. It is therefore in DK/NF.

DK/NF example 3   The next example shows a situation which was not considered by any of the other normal forms, but which occurs frequently in practice. In Figure 8-15, ADVISING has FID, Fname, Grad_faculty_status, SID, and Sname attributes. The domains are shown in Figure 8-16. Grad_faculty_status can have only one of two values. It is zero if the faculty person is not on the graduate faculty, and one if the person is a member of the graduate faculty.

The key of the relation is SID since there is only one tuple per student. The functional dependencies are as shown, and observe that the relation is not in DK/NF since several dependencies are not implied by SID. The last constraint is unlike others we have seen: only members of the graduate faculty can advise graduate students.

This relation has been transformed into three relations in Figure 8-16. These three relations are all in DK/NF. FACULTY has two keys, and Grad_faculty_status is dependent on both of them. Thus its constraints are logical consequences of keys. The remaining two relations have been formed as follows: All graduate students and their advisors have been placed in relation GRAD_STU, while all undergraduates and their advisors have been placed in relation U_GRAD_STU. Note the domains on SID have been defined to ensure that only the correct students are in the relations. The key of both of these relations is SID, and all

Domain Definitions

FID	IN	CDDD, where C = 1; D = decimal digit
Fname	IN	CHAR(30)
Grad_faculty_status	IN	{ 0,1 }
SID	IN	CDDD, where C not = 1; C = 9 if graduate student; D = decimal digit
Sname	IN	CHAR(30)

Additional Domain Definitions

GRAD_STU.Fname	IN	SELECT	FACULTY.Fname
		FROM	FACULTY
		WHERE	GRAD_FACULTY_STATUS = 1

Relations and Key Definitions

FACULTY (FID, Fname, Grad_faculty_status)
Key: FID or Fname

GRAD_STU (SID, Sname, Fname)
Key: SID

U_GRAD_STU (SID, Sname, Fname)
Key: SID

Figure 8-16 Domain/Key Definition of Example 3

functional dependencies have SID as a determinant, so these relations are in DK/NF.

"Wait a minute," you may be saying. "What about the faculty?" What happened to the constraint that graduate students can only be advised by members of the graduate faculty? The answer is, we define the domain of GRAD_STU.Fname to include only faculty having Grad_faculty_status = 1. With this domain definition, these relations are in DK/NF.

We can formalize the domain definition of GRAD_STU.Fname using SQL terminology:

```
GRAD_STU.FNAME IN
SELECT      FACULTY.FNAME
FROM        FACULTY
WHERE       FACULTY.GRAD_FACULTY_STATUS = 1
```

Since there is no limitation on undergraduate advising, all faculty members can exist in U_GRAD_STU. Thus we need not define a similar constraint for U_GRAD_STU.

As long as we define the domain of Fname using the above criteria, then the relations are in DK/NF. However, we have not seen constraints such as this before; are they valid? Can such an expression exist in the definition of a domain?

We are approaching the limit of development in database technology, and our tools are beginning to weaken. Here is the difficulty: So far, we have discussed the evaluation of relations as independent entities. Until this last example, we were able to eliminate anomalies from relations by considering each relation by itself. In this last example, however, we cannot eliminate anomalies unless we constrain Fname via FACULTY as described.

This is an example of an *interrelation constraint*. The legitimacy of the value of an attribute depends on a data condition in another relation.

Here is another way of stating the difficulty: Anomalies and normal forms have been defined to evaluate single relations. However, as we design *schemas* of relations, we will discover interrelation constraints. No tools have yet been developed to help us evaluate these constraints. We need a DK/NF or equivalent for schemas of relations, as well as for relations by themselves. As yet, there is no such form.

To summarize, we can say that the relations in Figure 8-16 are in DK/NF if we add the interrelation constraint in the domain definition of Fname. Thus there will be no modification anomalies. However, little is yet known about the consequences of such interrelation constraints; we do not know if there is some other undesirable characteristic lurking among the domains. In light of this possibility, we will consider these constraints in more detail.

Before continuing, you may wish to review the definitions of various normal forms. Figure 8-17 summarizes the seven forms discussed.

Form	Defining Characteristic
1NF	Any relation
2NF	All no-key attributes are dependent on all of the keys.
3NF	There are no transitive dependencies.
BCNF	Every determinant is a candidate key.
4NF	Every multivalued dependency is a functional dependency.
5NF	Join dependencies are satisfied.
DK/NF	All constraints on relations are logical consequences of domains and keys.

Figure 8-17   Summary of Normal Forms

Interrelation constraints

The problem of interrelation constraints has been with us since the start of the chapter, but we have ignored it. Every time we have used projection to split a relation, however, we have created an interrelation constraint.

Figure 8-1 presents the relation ACTIVITY (SID, Activity, Fee). We saw that this relation had modification anomalies, and we eliminated these anomalies by splitting the relation into STU_ACT (SID, Activity) and ACT_COST (Activity, Fee). When we did this, we created the possibility of an interrelation constraint, because two relations share the attribute Activity.

We can determine if there is an interrelation constraint by considering the following question: If a value of Activity exists in one of the relations, must it exist in the other? Specifically, if a value, say POLO, exists in ACT_COST, must it exist in STU_ACT? Also, if a value exists in STU_ACT, must it exist in ACT_COST?

The answer to these questions lies in the semantics of the database. These semantics arise in turn from the definition of requirements. What do the users want? What is consistent with their needs? Suppose the users' response is the following: Activities can exist in ACT_COST that do not exist in STU_ACT. This means an activity has been defined, its cost has been determined, and no student has yet enrolled. However, an activity may *not* exist in STU_ACT if it is not in ACT_COST. A student may not enroll in an activity if that activity has not been defined or priced.

This response defines an interrelation constraint. It says that the values of Activity in STU_ACT must be a subset of the values of Activity in ACT_COST. Or, put in terms of projection,

STU_ACT [Activity] SUBSET OF ACT_COST [Activity]

Or, written using set terminology,

STU_ACT [Activity] $\subseteq$ ACT_COST [Activity]

This means that the set of Activity values from STU_ACT must be contained in, or equal to, the set of Activity values from ACT_COST.

Unfortunately, interrelation constraints have been the poor stepchild of database technology. They have received little attention from either theorists or practitioners. Often they are ignored until program design; or even worse, until program testing; or worse yet, until an error occurs in user processing. No DBMS product, as yet, allows interrelation constraints to be defined, nor does any DBMS automatically enforce them. Instead, application programmers must insert them into application code, and query/update users must simply be careful about what they do. This is an unfortunate situation and one that will likely be rectified in the future.

We will include a description of the interrelation constraints as part of the physical database design. Chapter 12 will show how such constraints are represented using an existing relational DBMS product.

RELATIONAL DATABASE DESIGN CRITERIA

This section presents several different criteria for producing an effective relational database design. As discussed in Chapter 5, database design is as much an art as a science. These criteria reflect this situation. We cannot state that any given rule should be followed in all circumstances. Sometimes the rules conflict, and much depends on what the users will do. Unfortunately, user behavior is often unpredictable. Examples in this section will illustrate these problems.

Elimination of modification anomalies

The first criterion is the elimination of modification anomalies. As we have seen, if relations can be put into DK/NF, then no modification anomalies can occur. Thus DK/NF becomes a design objective, and relations that are in DK/NF are usually preferred.

Not all relations, however, can be put into DK/NF. This occurs when there are constraints that cannot be expressed as logical consequences of keys and domains. An example described by Fagin [39] is a relation having the following constraint: The relation must never have fewer than three tuples. There is no way to express this constraint in terms of domains and keys. Thus it has a modification anomaly. In fact, this strange relation has a deletion anomaly but no insertion anomaly. (We cannot delete any tuple where there are just three tuples remaining; we can, however, add a tuple at any time.)

When relations cannot be transformed into DK/NF, the constraint that cannot be expressed in terms of domains and keys must be inserted into application programs. This is undesirable because the constraint is hidden. For this simple example, it is hard to imagine any great difficulty occurring, but if there were many such constraints, and if they were more complex, the situation would be more serious.

Relation independence

A second relational database design goal is relation *independence*. Two relations are independent if modifications can be made to one without regard for the other. In general, the greater the independence, the better. However, independence is not always achievable. For example, interrelation constraints are a form of relation dependence. To eliminate this dependence, the relations can be joined together. The joined relation, however, may have modification anomalies.

Here we see the conflict in design goals. To eliminate modification anomalies, we split relations; but in so doing, we create interrelation dependencies. In this case we have to choose the least of the evils, based on the requirements of the application.

STU_ACT (SID, Activity)
Key: SID

STU_FEE (SID, Fee)
Key: SID

SID	Activity
100	SKIING
150	SWIMMING
175	SQUASH
200	SWIMMING

SID	Fee
100	200
150	50
175	50
200	50

Figure 8-18   Undesirable Projection of ACTIVITY in Figure 8-1

The interrelation constraints we have observed so far are *inclusion constraints*. They specify that a value of an attribute in one relation must also exist in another relation. There are worse dependencies, however.

For example, consider the ACTIVITY relation in Figure 8-1, with SID, Activity, and Fee attributes. To eliminate modification anomalies, we split this relation in STU_ACT (SID, Activity) and ACT_COST (Activity, Fee) in Figure 8-2. Another split is possible. Suppose we divide ACTIVITY into STU_ACT and STU_FEE as shown in Figure 8-18. This is a legitimate split in that we can reconstruct the original relation using join. Now, is this a desirable schema?

We know ACTIVITY has the following dependencies: SID → Activity, Activity → Fee, and SID → Fee (transitively, via Activity). The design in Figure 8-18 shows the first and third of these dependencies, but not the second. To observe the second dependency, we must first join the relations together.

Even worse, since Activity determines Fee, whenever we change the value of Activity we must change the value of Fee. A change to STU_ACT necessitates a change to STU_FEE. Further, suppose the cost of SWIMMING increases. To record this change, we must use STU_ACT to find which students are enrolled in SWIMMING, and then, for the appropriate SIDs, change the fee in STU_FEE. This is a cumbersome prospect.

The problem is that we have split a functional dependency across relations. Since Activity and Fee do not occur in the same relation, this dependency is not directly expressed. In conclusion, where possible, we want to avoid splitting dependencies across relations.

A note on nonloss projections   There is still another way of splitting the ACTIVITY relation. It is the projections STU_FEE (SID, Fee) and ACT_FEE (Activity, Fee). However, this split is completely undesirable because it generates false data. The join of these projections creates fictitious tuples. Figure 8-19 shows the join of these projections. If you compare it to Figure 8-1 you will see that new tuples have been created.

STU_FEE (SID, Fee)   ACT_FEE (Activity, Fee)
Key: SID   Key: Activity

SID	Fee
100	200
150	50
175	50
200	50

Activity	Fee
SKIING	200
SWIMMING	50
SQUASH	50

STU_FEE JOIN (STU_FEE.Fee = ACT_FEE.Fee) ACT_FEE

100	200	SKIING
150	50	SWIMMING
150	50	SQUASH
175	50	SWIMMING
175	50	SQUASH
200	50	SWIMMING
200	50	SQUASH

Figure 8-19   Example of Loss Projection

Projections that generate false data upon joining are called *loss projections* (yes, loss projections—such terminology!). Projections that do not cause false data to be generated on rejoining are called *nonloss projections*.

Why is data generated in a loss projection? The projections in Figure 8-19 do not capture the essence of the functional dependencies. These projections represent the functional dependencies Activity → Fee and SID → Fee. But, since several activities can cost the same amount, when we join on Fee, we get too much.

Obviously, loss projections cannot be allowed in a database design. We can add this to our list of relational database design objectives. Also, from now on we will consider only nonloss projections. If you are interested in this topic, or in the origin of this cumbersome terminology, see [38], [33], or [75].

Ease of use

A third criterion for a relational design is ease of use. As far as possible, we strive to structure the relations so that they are familiar and seem natural to

---

SHIPMENT (Invoice_number, Customer, Street, City, State, Zip)
Key: Invoice_number

Constraints: Zip → City
                    Zip → State

Figure 8-20   SHIPMENT Relation (Not in DK/NF)

users. Sometimes this goal conflicts with the elimination of anomalies or with independence.

For example, consider the relation SHIPMENT in Figure 8-20. The key is Invoice_number. Is this relation in DK/NF? To answer this question, we must determine the functional dependencies. At first, we might think Customer determines shipping address; but if a customer has several such addresses, this would be untrue. However, note that Zip → City and Zip → State.* These are functional dependencies that are not logically implied by the key. Hence SHIPMENT is not in DK/NF, and this relation has modification anomalies.

To achieve DK/NF, we must split this relation. One possibility is shown in Figure 8-21. Cities and states have been removed from SHIPMENT, and the ZIP_CODE relation has been created.

Is the design in Figure 8-21 preferred to the design in Figure 8-20? The answer depends on the application, but most likely Figure 8-20 is preferred, even though it has modification anomalies. There are two reasons. First, eliminating city and state from SHIPMENT creates problems for users. Who can remember the correspondences of Zip Codes and cities and states? Second, even though SHIPMENT has anomalies, they are unlikely to be a problem. Zip Codes almost never change. Therefore, the design in Figure 8-20 would likely be chosen over the one in Figure 8-21, in spite of the modification anomalies.

This choice would not be true for all applications, however. Consider order entry. One way to increase order entry throughput is to decrease the number of keystrokes. Clearly, fewer strokes will be required to enter data for SHIPMENT_1 than for SHIPMENT. Why, after all, should the company reenter the City, State, and Zip Code relationship, hour after hour, day after day, on every order? Also, if the order entry clerks need to see City and State, then

---

*In a few geographic areas, Zip does not determine city. If the organization owning the database ships into those areas, this assumption is inappropriate. For the purposes of discussion, assume these functional dependencies hold.

```
        SHIPMENT-1 (Invoice_number, Customer, Street, Zip)
        Key: Invoice_number


        ZIP_CODE (Zip, City, State)
        Key: Zip
```

Figure 8-21   Domain/Key Definition of SHIPMENT Example

order entry application programs can access relation ZIP_CODE and display the City and State to them.

Conflict in design criteria

The design criteria discussed in this section (elimination of modification anomalies, creation of relation independence, and ease of use) can conflict. When they do, the designer must assess priorities and make the best possible compromise in light of requirements. There is no single rule of priority. In some applications, ease of use is most important, while in others, the elimination of anomalies is the most important. Fortunately, in many cases, these decisions only concern how data is to be *stored*. User views can be constructed so that users *see* a joined relation, for example, when two separate relations are actually stored. Sometimes, however, the conflict is not so readily resolved. In this case, the project team must make the best decision they can and check it out with the users.

A RELATIONAL DESIGN FOR SALLY ENTERPRISES

The remainder of this chapter illustrates physical database designs for Sally Enterprises. In this section, we will present a physical design for schema 3, developed in Chapter 6. Also, we will consider changes to this design to conform to a new requirement that Sally identifies.

Before proceeding, we need to be clear about what we are going to produce. Specifically, what is a relational database design? What are its components?

Components of a relational database design

A relational database design has three major components as listed in Figure 8-22. First, the design specifies relations, attributes of relations, and keys. Candidate keys may also be specified.

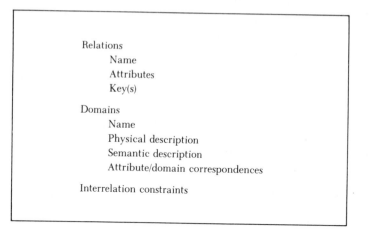

Relations
     Name
     Attributes
     Key(s)

Domains
     Name
     Physical description
     Semantic description
     Attribute/domain correspondences

Interrelation constraints

Figure 8-22   Components of a Relational Database Design

Second, a relational database design specifies domains and attribute/domain correspondences. Domains are defined both physically and semantically. Recall that even if two domains have the same physical appearance, say CHAR(30), they are not the same domain if they do not have the same meaning. Even if Part_names and Child_games are defined as CHAR(30), they do not have the same domain.

Finally, the design of a relational database should specify interrelation constraints. These constraints can be stated in terms of the projection operator and set operators $<$, $\leq$, $=$, $>$, and $\geq$.

These three components are the minimal ones. The design can be augmented with whatever additional documentation seems helpful. For example, relations and their potential relationships can be graphically portrayed using entity-relationship diagrams.

Review of Sally Enterprises' logical design

Figure 8-23 synopsizes the logical design of Sally's schema 3. Six relations were defined having the attributes and keys as shown. Be certain you understand the notes. Recall that with SDM a tuple can be contained within another tuple. Thus the Where_used attribute of RECIPE is actually a PITCHER tuple. Also, observe that Where_used is a multivalued attribute (like a repeating field).

The PITCHER relation also has contained tuples; they are ORDER and RECIPE tuples. Furthermore, PITCHER has three class attributes. Considering SALESPERSON, its tuples contain the Amount attribute of ORDER tuples. Hence SALESPERSON contains part of another relation's tuples as a repeating field.

CUSTOMER has several unique characteristics. First, the Family_members

RECIPE (Name, Sugar, Lemon, Water, Where_used)

    Key: Name

    Note: Where_used is a contained PITCHER tuple; multivalued

PITCHER (Number, Date, Recipe_used, Where_sold)

    Key: Number

    Notes: 1.   Where_sold is a contained ORDER tuple; multivalued

              2.   Current_pitcher and Amount_left are class attributes

SALESPERSON (Name, Past_amount_sold)

    Key: Name

    Note: Past_amount_sold is contained attribute Amount of ORDER;
                  multivalued

CUSTOMER (F_name, L_name, Family, Past_amount_purchased, Total_amount)

    Key: (F_name, L_name)

    Notes: 1.   Family is a contained CUSTOMER tuple having the same
                     L_name; multivalued

              2.   Past_amount_purchased is contained attribute Amount of
                     ORDER; multivalued

              3.   Total_amount is SUM (Past_amount_purchased)

ORDER (Customer, Pitcher, Salesperson, Date, Time, Amount)

    Key: (Customer, Pitcher, Time)

    Notes: 1.   Customer is combination of F_name, L_name

              2.   Pitcher is multivalued between 1 and 2; used for orders
                     filled from two pitchers

BIG_BUYER (attributes of CUSTOMER, Nickname, Sport)

    Key: F_name, L_name

    Note: Sport is multivalued between 1 and 3

Figure 8-23 Summary of Logical Design for Sally Enterprises Schema 3

attribute contains other CUSTOMER tuples as a repeating field. Further, the Past_amounts_purchased attribute is a repeating field having the Amount attribute of ORDER. Total_amount is the sum of the amount fields.

ORDER tuples do not contain other tuples. There is, however, one repeating field. Since an order can be filled from two pitchers, Pitcher can have two values.

Finally, BIG_BUYER is an extension of CUSTOMER records. It contains Nick-names and up to three Favorite_sport for frequent customers.

Eliminating contained tuples and repeating attributes

The logical design in Figure 8-23 cannot be a physical design of a relational database for two reasons. First, most of these relations have multivalued attributes. Such attributes are not allowed in a relation, as defined in Chapter 7. Somehow, we must transform the relations so that each attribute has only one value per tuple. Second, the logical design in Figure 8-23 allows tuples to be contained in other tuples. As mentioned in Chapter 6, although we can envision this possibility in our minds, it cannot be done physically. Physically, either A contains B, or B contains A, or neither is true. The relations have to be redefined to eliminate this physical impossibility.

To see how to eliminate these problems, consider the relations RECIPE and PITCHER. Where_used of RECIPE is actually a collection of tuples representing pitchers made from the RECIPE. Thus, if PITCHERs 101, 104, and 107 were produced using RECIPE A, then they will be contained in RECIPE A's Where_used attribute. See Figure 8-24.

Storing contained tuples as joined relations   One way to represent this situation physically is to store the join of the RECIPE and PITCHER relations. Such a join is shown in Figure 8-25. (For the moment, to simplify the discussion, we will ignore the attribute Where_sold of PITCHER.). Since this is an equi-join, RECIPE.Name and PITCHER.Recipe_used are equal. We can eliminate one of these as shown in Figure 8-26. RECIPE tuples have been physically concatenated to the appropriate PITCHER tuples.

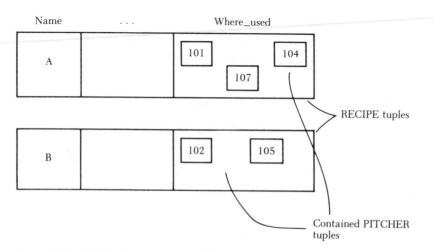

Figure 8-24   RECIPE Tuples that Logically Contain PITCHER Tuples

REC_PITCH (Name, Sugar, Lemon, Water, Number, Date, Recipe_used)
Key: Number

Name	Sugar	Lemon	Water	Number	Date	Recipe_used
A	2	4	3	101	830731	A
A	2	4	3	104	830801	A
A	2	4	3	107	830804	A
B	3	3	2	102	830802	B
B	3	3	2	105	830803	B

Figure 8-25   Equijoin of RECIPE and PITCHER Relations

REC_PITCH (Name, Sugar, Lemon, Water, Number, Date)
Key: Number

Name	Sugar	Lemon	Water	Number	Date
A	2	4	3	101	830731
A	2	4	3	104	830801
A	2	4	3	107	830804
B	3	3	2	102	830802
B	3	3	2	105	830803

Figure 8-26   Natural Join of RECIPE and PITCHER Tuples

Do we want to store RECIPE and PITCHER data this way? It certainly is feasible, but is it desirable? Recalling our design criteria, we observe that this relation is not in DK/NF. The key of this relation is Number, and there are dependencies that are not logical consequences of this key. For example, Name → Sugar and Name → Lemons. Since this relation is not in DK/NF, it will have modification anomalies. Also, this relation seems inappropriate because there is much duplicated data. Thus this joined relation appears to be an inappropriate choice for the physical design.

Contained tuples constructed by DML joins   The preceding join indicates a direction to an effective solution. Remember, the reason for having the Where_ used attribute of RECIPE is to maintain the relationship of recipes and pitchers. How can we store this relationship in the data? We can store the name of the recipe used in the Recipe_used attribute of PITCHER. Then, using this attri-

RECIPE (Name, Lemon, Sugar, Water)
Key: Name

PITCHER (Number, Date, Recipe_used)
Key: Number

Name	Lemon	Sugar	Water
A	2	4	3
B	3	3	2

Number	Date	Recipe_used
101	830731	A
104	830801	A
107	830804	A
102	830802	B
105	820803	B

Figure 8-27   RECIPE and PITCHER Relations to be Stored

bute, we can join the relations RECIPE and PITCHER whenever we want. The result will be combined RECIPE and PITCHER tuples. Thus we do not have to store the join; we can build it whenever a user needs it.

Assume we store the relations RECIPE (Name, Sugar, Lemon, Water) and PITCHER (Number, Date, Recipe_used). See Figure 8-27. We have omitted Where_used from RECIPE, but we can construct the relationship it represents dynamically using a join. Where_used, then, will be *constructed* and not *stored*.

To illustrate, suppose we want to know the numbers and dates of all pitchers made according to any recipe having exactly three lemons. This query necessitates bringing together data from both RECIPE and PITCHER relations. We can do this with a join as follows (SQL language):

```
SELECT      PITCHER.NUMBER, PITCHER.DATE
FROM        PITCHER, RECIPE
WHERE       PITCHER.RECIPE_USED = RECIPE.NAME
    AND    RECIPE.LEMON = 3
```

Thus, even though we have not stored the attribute Where_used of RECIPE, we can construct it when we need it by using a join. The result of this query for the data in Figure 8-27 is:

102	830802
105	830803

Strategy for representing contained tuples

The strategy just described can be employed for many of the contained tuples in the logical schema of Figure 8-23. Specifically, it can be used to represent all contained tuples of a one-to-many relationship. For the logical schema in Figure 8-23, it can be used for the relationship between RECIPE and PITCHER as just described; it can also be used for the relationship between PITCHER and ORDER, SALESPERSON and ORDER, and CUSTOMER and ORDER.

In general, the stragegy for eliminating contained tuples in such relationships is this: First, replace the contained tuple in the child relation with the key of the parent tuple. Second, discard the repeating child tuple in the parent tuple. Finally, to obtain occurrences of the relationship, join the relations on the key of the parent tuple.

To illustrate, consider the relationship between RECIPE and PITCHER. This relationship is one-to-many with RECIPE as parent and PITCHER as child. We first replace the Recipe_used attribute of PITCHER with the key of RECIPE. This key is the Name of the RECIPE. Next, we discard the Where_used attribute of RECIPE. Finally, we join RECIPE and PITCHER on Name when we want to generate occurrences of the relationship. The result is the relations shown in Figure 8-27. This process is summarized in Figure 8-28.

This strategy will not work for many-to-many relationships. To represent such relationships in the general case, we must construct an intersection relation, e.g., GRADES for the relationship between STUDENT and CLASS. In special cases, however, we can work around this general solution as will be shown for the relationship between PITCHER and ORDER.

Furthermore, when using this strategy, we must consider interrelation constraints. For this example, can a PITCHER tuple have a value of Recipe_used that is not in RECIPE? It seems unlikely since every PITCHER must have a recipe. Thus the value of Recipe_used in PITCHER must equal the name of some tuple in RECIPE. Expressed another way,

PITCHER[Recipe_used] SUBSET OF RECIPE[Name]

Now, consider the reverse condition. Must every recipe be used? If so, then RECIPE Names must be a subset of Recipe_used in PITCHER. This seems less likely, and we will assume that recipes can exist that are unused. Perhaps the

---

1. In child, replace contained parent tuple with key attribute of parent.

2. In parent, discard attribute containing repeating child tuple.

3. To obtain occurrences of the relationship, form join on key of parent attribute.

Figure 8-28 Summary of Strategy for Representing One-to-Many Relationships

tuple represents a bad recipe, but Sally doesn't want to delete it lest she forget it and try it again. However they are developed, interrelation constraints must be documented as part of the database design.

A relational design for Sally Enterprises schema 3

The process just described can be used to transform the logical schema in Figure 8-23 into a relational schema. The resulting design is shown in the next three figures. Figure 8-29 shows the relations and attributes, Figure 8-30 shows inter-relation constraints, and Figure 8-31 shows the domains and attribute/domain correspondences.

All contained tuples have been replaced using the strategy described above. The Where_used attribute of RECIPE has been deleted and an interrelation constraint added. Similarly, Where_sold of PITCHER has been eliminated, and the following constraint added:

RECIPE (Name, Sugar, Lemon, Water)
    Key: Name

PITCHER (Number, Date, Recipe_used)
    Key: Number

SALESPERSON (Name)
    Key: Name

CUSTOMER: (F_name, L_name)
    Key: (F_name, L_name)

ORDER (Cust_f_name, Cust_l_name, Pitcher, Salesperson, Date, Time, Amount)
    Key: Cust_f_name, Cust_l_name, Pitcher, Time)

NICKNAME (Cust_f_name, Cust_l_name, Nickname)
    Key: (Cust_f_name, Cust_l_name)

CUST_SPORT (Cust_f_name, Cust_l_name, Favorite_sport)
    Key: Cust_f_name, Cust_l_name, Favorite_sport)

CLASS_ATTRIBUTE (Relation_name, Attribute_name, Value)
    Key: (Relation_name, Attribute_name)

Figure 8-29 Relations of Sally Enterprises Schema 3

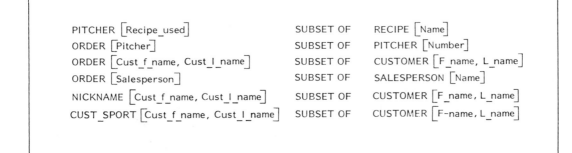

Figure 8-30   Interrelation Constraints for Sally Enterprises Schema 3

ORDER[Pitcher] SUBSET OF PITCHER[Number]

The class attributes of PITCHER present a problem. We have no ready structure in which to store these attributes. To solve this problem, we create a special relation called CLASS_ATTRIBUTE, having the attributes Class_name, Attribute_name, and Value. For this application, CLASS_ATTRIBUTE will have three tuples as follows:

PITCHER	Total_produced	vvv
PITCHER	Active_pitcher	vvv
PITCHER	Amount_left	vvv

where vvv is an appropriately defined value.

SALESPERSON and CUSTOMER have also been transformed to eliminate contained tuples. For both relations, the contained tuples represented one-to-many relationships with ORDER. Consequently, Past_amounts_sold has been deleted from SALESPERSON and Past_amounts_purchased has been deleted from CUSTOMER. Both of these relationships can be constructed by join when needed. This operation necessitates the definition of the third through fifth interrelation constraints in Figure 8-30.

The CUSTOMER and SALESPERSON relations contain only names. Since these names are duplicated in ORDER, you may be asking why have these relations at all? In fact, they could be deleted. However, if Sally Enterprises needs a list of customers or salespeople, regardless of whether they have an order on file, then CUSTOMER and SALESPERSON will be needed. Consequently, we will leave CUSTOMER and SALESPERSON in the design.

Since Past_amounts_purchased is to be extracted from a join, CUSTOMER.Total_amount must also be extracted. The following SQL expression will build Total_amount for Mary Jones:

Domain Name	Format and meaning
CUPS	numeric 99.99; measurement of sugar
DATES	numeric YYMMDD
LEMON_COUNT	positive integer less than 10
F_NAMES	CHAR(10); first names of people
L_NAMES	CHAR(20); last names of customers
S_NAMES	CHAR(20); names (first last, whatever) of SALESPEOPLE
N_NAMES	CHAR(20); nicknames of customers
PITCHER_NUMBERS	positive integer less than 500
QUARTS	numeric 9.99; measurement of water and finished lemonade
RECIPE_NAMES	CHAR(10)
SPORT_NAMES	value is 'SOCCER', 'FOOTBALL', 'TENNIS', 'BASKETBALL', or 'SKIING'
TIMES	HH.MM; HH is integer between 0 and 23, and MM is integer between 0 and 59; the time of day, 24 hour clock.

a. Domains

Figure 8-31   Domains and Attribute/Domain Correspondences for Schema 3

```
SELECT      SUM (Amount)
FROM        ORDER
WHERE       F_name = 'Mary'
    AND     L_name = 'Jones'
```

The Family-members attribute of CUSTOMER is also a contained tuple. In fact, CUSTOMER tuples contain other CUSTOMER tuples in this attribute. Because the contained tuples are of the same type, no interrelation constraint need be defined. We just join on last name. For example, the following SQL expression determines the total purchases of families having a member whose first name is John.

```
SELECT      CUSTOMER.L_name, SUM(ORDER.Amount)
FROM        CUSTOMER, ORDER
WHERE       CUSTOMER.F_name = 'JOHN'
    AND     CUSTOMER.L_name = ORDER.L_name
```

Attribute	Domain
RECIPE.Name	RECIPE_NAMES
RECIPE.Sugar	CUPS
RECIPE.Lemon	LEMON_COUNT
RECIPE.Water	QUARTS
PITCHER.Number	PITCHER_NUMBERS
PITCHER.Date	DATES
PITCHER.Recipe_used	RECIPE_NAMES
SALESPERSON.Name	S_NAMES
CUSTOMER.F_name	F_NAMES
CUSTOMER.L_name	L_NAMES
ORDER.Cust_f_name	F_NAMES
ORDER.Cust_l_name	L_NAMES
ORDER.Pitcher	PITCHER_NUMBERS
ORDER.Salesperson	S_NAMES
ORDER.Date	DATES
ORDER.Time	TIMES
ORDER.Amount	QUARTS
NICKNAME.Cust_f_name	F_NAMES
NICKNAME.Cust_l_name	L_NAMES
NICKNAME.Nickname	N_NAMES
CUST_SPORT, Cust_f_name	F_NAMES
CUST_SPORT, Cust_l_name	L_NAMES
CUST_SPORT, Favorite_sport	SPORT_NAMES

b.   Attribute/Domain Correspondences

Figure 8-31   (Cont'd.)

The qualifying customer last name is selected so that if a family has two members with the first name John, this can be identified. An alternative way of expressing this query is to join ORDER to itself.

The relationship between PITCHER and ORDER poses a special problem since it is a many-to-many relationship. As with any many-to-many relationship, we would transform it into a simple network by defining an intersection relation. Then both of the one-to-many relationships in the simple network could be represented using the strategy summarized in Figure 8-28.

This approach would be overkill for this example, however. We know from the requirements that there will never be more than two PITCHER tuples corresponding to a single ORDER. In most cases, in fact, there will be just one. Constructing an intersection record seems heavy-handed.

Another possibility is to define two attributes, say Pitcher and Extra_pitcher in ORDER. Extra_pitcher would be null unless the order were completed from a second pitcher. The definition of two such attributes would make some SQL operations awkward, however.

A third possibility is to define Pitcher as single-valued, and to represent orders that are filled from two pitchers with two tuples. This makes SQL processing straightforward. In this case, the key of the relation is (F_name, L_name, Pitcher, Time). An order filled from two pitchers can be identified by locating two tuples with the same name and time. For the design in Figure 8-29, we will use this third strategy.

BIG_BUYER is an extension of the CUSTOMER tuples. These tuples have all the attributes of CUSTOMER, plus they have Nickname and Favorite_sport. An obvious way to represent this relation is,

BIG BUYER (F_name, L_name, Nickname, Favorite_sport)

with a key of F_name, L_name, and Favorite_sport. This relation, however, is not in DK/NF. Can you see what the problem is? There is a multivalued dependency that is not also a functional dependency (or, equivalently, that is not implied by the key). Suppose Stan Ashley, nicknamed DOC, engages in BASKETBALL, SKIING, and GOLF. If Stan changes his nickname to BUBBLES, then three tuples must be changed (one for each of the sports). This is the problem with multivalued dependencies. Changing the value of one attribute necessitates redundant updates.

Consequently, BIG_BUYER is not defined in the design in Figure 8-29. Instead, the projection of BIG_BUYER is defined. NICKNAME is the projection of the first three attributes of BIG_BUYER, and CUST_SPORT is the projection of the names and Favorite_sport. These two relations are in DK/NF.

Is this a good design? Considering the criteria previously defined, it appears to be. The relations in the schema in Figures 8-29 through 8-31 are in DK/NF. Consequently, there will be no insertion or deletion anomalies. Also, all of the interrelation constraints are inclusion constraints. No functional dependencies have been split across relations. Finally, the relations seem natural; Sally and her employees should be able to relate to this schema. (This, however, is a dangerous assumption. Only Sally and her employees can say for sure. They should be asked.)

A change to the design of the Sally Enterprises database

While the project team developed the design for Sally's database, Sally encountered a problem. Some of her younger salespeople were insensitive to the needs of her older customers. One day Sally visited the design team and announced a change in her policy. "From now on," she said, "I'm not letting the younger salespeople sell to the older customers." After some questioning, the team determined that Sally wanted to implement the following constraint (which we label C):

C: Only old salespeople (11 or older) can sell to old customers (17 or older)

Constraint C is a constraint on combinations of customers and salespeople. The combination of a customer and a salesperson is expressed in ORDER tuples. (In other words, ORDER tuples have both Customer and Salesperson attributes.) Thus, constraint C really defines conditions on ORDER tuples.

Figure 8-32 illustrates this situation. OFY are orders for young customers and OFO are orders for old ones. OFO orders must have the name of an old customer together with the name of an old salesperson. OFY orders must have the name of a young customer, but they can have the name of any salesperson.

In order to determine the age of people, we need to add age variables to the CUSTOMER and SALESPERSON relations. Although we could add the attribute Age, this is not advised, because ages change. Further, ages stored in different years are incompatible; the age of a customer inserted in the database in 1982 is not directly comparable to the age of a customer inserted in the

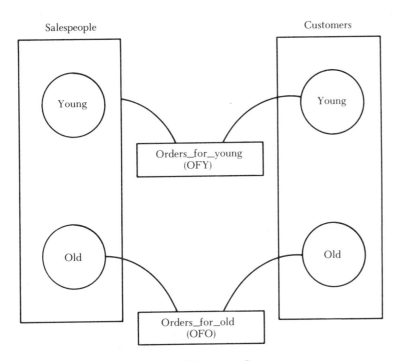

Figure 8-32   Graphical Portrayal of Constraint C

CUSTOMER (F_name, L_name, DOB)
SALESPERSON (Name, DOB)
OFO (Cust_f_name, Cust_l_name, Pitcher, Salesperson, Date, Time, Amount)
OFY (Cust_f_name, Cust_l_name, Pitcher, Salesperson, Date, Time, Amount)

a. Relations

OFO [Cust_f_name, Cust_l_name]   SUBSET OF   CUSTOMER [F_name, L_Name]
                                 AND   CUSTOMER.DOB indicate
                                             customer is 17 or older

OFO [Salesperson]   SUBSET OF   SALESPERSON [Name]
                                 AND   SALESPERSON.DOB indicate
                                             salesperson is 11 or older

OFY [Cust_f_name, Cust_l_name]   SUBSET OF   CUSTOMER [F_name, L_name]
                                 AND   CUSTOMER.DOB indicate
                                             customer is under 17

OFY [Salesperson]   SUBSET OF   SALESPERSON [Name]

b. Interrelation Constraints

Figure 8-33   Logical Implications of Constraint C

database in 1984. Therefore, instead of storing ages directly, we will store date of birth (in attribute DOB).

Constraint C is expressed more precisely in Figure 8-33. This figure shows the adjusted CUSTOMER and SALESPERSON relations, and the two new relations, OFO and OFY. The interrelation constraints among these four relations are shown.

Figure 8-33 shows that constraint C can be expressed in terms of domains and keys, and is thus in DK/NF. It has, therefore, no modification anomalies. However, this is another situation (like the one for graduate students and faculty) where the domain constraint involves a different relation. Since there is no ready way to express such a constraint with existing DBMS products, we must put this constraint, in one form or another, into application programs.

---

1. Use schema 3 (Figures 8-29, 8-30, 8-31) and put constraint C in application programs.

2. Define relations OFO and OFY and add to schema 3. Put interrelation constraints in application programs.

3. Define relations OFO, OFY, Y_CUSTOMER, O_CUSTOMER, O_SALESPERSON. Define domains to ensure that only valid joins and attribute comparisons can occur.

4. Remove constraint C from the database. Use SQL to interrogate database to identify violations of policy.

Figure 8-34   Alternatives for Expressing Constraint C

DESIGN ALTERNATIVES

Figure 8-34 lists four alternatives for implementing constraint C. For alternative 1, we simply use schema 3, with DOB added to CUSTOMER and SALESPERSON, and enforce constraint C in application programs. Thus the application program that inserts ORDER tuples would check to make sure that constraint C is followed. If not, this application program would generate an error message and ignore the update request.

Since alternative 1 makes no changes to the schema structure, the constraint is nearly invisible to the user. Not until an error message is generated is this constraint known. Also, the user who queries this database will not be aware of this constraint unless he or she observes it in the data. Further, if a user employs SQL to update the database, it will be possible to violate this constraint. Thus alternative 1 has serious disadvantages.

In alternative 2 the relations OFO and OFY are defined. Only orders for old people are inserted into OFO and only orders for young people are inserted into OFY. However, since the DBMS does not enforce the contraints as defined in Figure 8-33, it will still be incumbent on the application program to ensure that the correct orders are inserted into the correct relation.

Alternative 2 does have an advantage over alternative 1. The user of the schema will observe two different order relations. It will be apparent to the user that, for some reason, orders are being differentiated on the basis of age. The reason for the differentiation, however, will not be clear. Also, the SQL user will still have an opportunity to violate the constraint.

In alternative 3 we define OFO, OFY, Y_CUSTOMER, O_CUSTOMER, and O_SALESPERSON. The relations, constraints, and domains are as shown in Figure 8-35. Notice we have a new class of constraint: *intrarelation*, or *tuple constraints*. These constraints do not refer to other relations. Instead, they are

O_CUSTOMER (F_name, L_name, DOB)
Y_CUSTOMER (F_name, L_name, DOB)
SALESPERSON (Name, DOB)
O_SALESPERSON (Name, DOB)
OFO (Cust_f_name, Cust_l_name, Salesperson, Date, Time, Amount)
OFY (Cust_f_name, Cust_l_name, Salesperson, Date, Time, Amount)

a. Relations

OFO [Cust_f_name]	SUBSET OF	O_CUSTOMER [Cust_f_name]
OFO [Cust_l_name]	SUBSET OF	O_CUSTOMER [Cust_l_name]
OFO [Salesperson]	SUBSET OF	O_SALESPERSON [Name]
YFO [Cust_f_name]	SUBSET OF	Y_CUSTOMER [Cust_f_name]
YFO [Cust_l_name]	SUBSET OF	Y_CUSTOMER [Cust_l_name]
YFO [Salesperson]	SUBSET OF	SALESPERSON [Name]
O_SALESPERSON Name	SUBSET OF	SALESPERSON [Name]
	AND	O_SALESPERSON.DOB indicate that salesperson is 11 or older

b. Interrelation Constraints

Y_CUSTOMER.DOB indicate that customer is younger than 17
O_CUSTOMER.DOB indicate that customer is 17 or older

c. Intrarelation Constraints

Figure 8-35 Relations, Constraints, and Domains Defined for Alternative 3

constraints within a relation. For example, a tuple cannot be inserted into Y_CUSTOMER unless the DOB of the tuple implies that the person is less than 17 years old.

The major difference in alternative 3, however, is the way that domains are defined. Names for O_CUSTOMER and OFO arise from the same domain, and

Domain Name	Format and Meaning
OLD_SALESPERSON_NAMES	CHAR(20); names of old salespeople
SALESPERSON_NAMES	CHAR(20); names of all salespeople
OLD_CUST_F_NAMES	CHAR(10); first names of old customers
OLD_CUST_L_NAMES	CHAR(20); last names of old customers
YOUNG_CUST_F_NAMES	CHAR(10); first names of young customers
YOUNG_CUST_L_NAMES	CHAR(20); last names of young customers

d. Domain Definitions

Attribute	Domain
O_CUSTOMER.F_name	OLD_CUST_F_NAMES
O_CUSTOMER.L_name	OLD_CUST_L_NAMES
OFO.Cust_f_name	OLD_CUST_F_NAMES
OFO.Cust_l_name	OLD_CUST_L_NAMES
Y_CUSTOMER.F_name	YOUNG_CUST_F_NAMES
Y_CUSTOMER.L_name	YOUNG_CUST_L_NAMES
OFY.Cust_f_name	YOUNG_CUST_F_NAMES
OFY.Cust_l_name	YOUNG_CUST_L_NAMES
OLD_SALESPERSON.Name	OLD_SALESPERSON_NAMES
OFO.Salesperson	OLD_SALESPERSON_NAMES
SALESPERSON.Name	SALESPERSON.NAMES
OFY.Salesperson	SALESPERSON.NAMES
CUST_SPORT.Cust_f_name	F_NAMES
CUST_SPORT.Cust_l_name	L_NAMES
CUST_SPORT.Favorite_sport	SPORT_NAMES

e. Attribute/Domain Correspondences

Figure 8-35   (Cont'd.)

this domain is different from the domain of Y_CUSTOMER and OFY. This difference is important because by enforcing domain consistency, we will enforce constraint C.

In other words, if the DBMS will enforce domain consistency and only allow attributes to be compared or joined if they are from the same domain, then it will be impossible for the query/update user to violate constraint C. If someone tries to put an old customer into OFY, the DBMS will observe that the domain of the old customer is not compatible with the customer name domain of OFY. It will then prohibit this update.

Alternative 3, therefore, is the only alternative that does not require that constraint C be put into application programs, and it is the only one that provides protection for the SQL user. Now, unfortunately, for the small print: current DBMS products do not enforce domain consistency. However, they could. And hopefully, they will soon.

For products that exist today, however, the essential difference between alternatives 1, 2, and 3 is that constraint C becomes more visible (because it is embedded into schema structure) in 3 than in 2, and more visible in 2 than in 1. This simply means that users are less likely to make mistakes in 3 than in 2, and in 2 than in 1.

Alternative 4 is the alternative you will probably find least desirable, but it is probably the most realistic. Essentially, alternative 4 says: Constraint C does not belong in the database.

Does Sally really want the computer system to prohibit a sale? Suppose some aggressive 5-year-old salesperson makes a sale to a 70-year-old grandfather. Even if this is a violation of Sally Enterprises' policy, should the computer deny the old gentleman his lemonade? (and Sally the revenue? and the 5-year-old the commission?)

If a development team were to consider alternative 4, they might return to Sally with that question. Sally might say something like, "No, I really don't want to prevent such sales, but I want to know who's doing it, so I can control the practice."

If so, then constraint C does not belong in the database. Rather, schema 3 should be used, and SQL employed after the fact to determine which salespeople are violating the policy. Then, Sally can take whatever corrective action she wants, without having lost any sales. Also, users of the computer system will be far less hostile. (Imagine how the aggressive salesperson feels when, having convinced the customer, the computer disallows the sale. Very frustrating!)

Again, we see the artistic side of database design. Remember this example. Quite often requirements are difficult to incorporate into the design because they are misstated. Do not be forced into awkward designs until you have clearly challenged both the design and the statement of requirements.

SUMMARY

Not all relational schema are equal. Some suffer modification anomalies, some have unacceptable dependencies among relations, and some are poorly suited to users.

A variety of normal forms have been defined. Relations in these forms avoid modification anomalies of one sort or another. Domain/key relations are an upper bound on normal forms because a relation in domain/key normal form has no modification anomalies. Unfortunately, not all relations can be put into DK/NF, nor is it even known which kinds cannot be put into this normal form. Thus DK/NF is a relational design objective.

There are several forms of interrelation constraints. Inclusion constraints specify that a value of an attribute in one relation must be the value of an attribute in another relation. Domain inclusion constraints specify that values for an attribute must be a subset of the values of an attribute in another relation. Finally, if a functional dependency is split across relations, a dependency inter-relation constraint is created. Such dependency constraints are undesirable and are to be avoided as far as possible.

Criteria for assessing the quality of relational designs are reduction or elimination of modification anomalies, minimization of interrelation constraints, and ease of use.

A relational design has three components. First, it contains descriptions of relations, attributes, and keys. Second, it defines domains and attribute/domain correspondences; and third, it specifies interrelation constraints. An example relational design is illustrated in Figures 8-29, 8-30, and 8-31. Finally, four alternative designs were considered for incorporating constraint C into a database for Sally Enterprises.

Group I Questions

8.1 What is a deletion anomaly? Give an example.

8.2 What is an insertion anomaly? Give an example.

8.3 Explain the relationship of 1, 2, 3, BC, 4, 5, and DK normal forms.

8.4 Define *functional dependency*. Give an example of two attributes having a functional dependency. Give an example of two attributes that do not have a functional dependency.

8.5 If SID functionally determines Activity, does this mean that only one value of SID can exist in the relation? Why or why not?

8.6 Define *determinant*.

8.7 Give an example of a relation having a functional dependency in which the determinant has two or more attributes.

8.8 Define a *key*.

8.9 If SID is a key of a relation, is it a determinant? Can there be more than one occurrence of a given value of SID in the relation?

8.10 Define *second normal form*. Give an example of a relation in 1NF but not in 2NF. Transform the relation into relations in 2NF.

8.11 Define *third normal form*. Give an example of a relation in 2NF but not in 3NF. Transform the relation into relations in 3NF.

8.12 Define *BCNF*. Give an example of a relation in 3NF but not in BCNF. Transform the relation into relations in BCNF.

8.13 Define a *multivalued dependency*. Give an example.

8.14 Why must multivalued dependencies exist in pairs?

8.15 Why might the term *multivalued, independent attribute* be a better term than *multidependency*?

8.16 Define *fourth normal form*. Give an example of a relation in BCNF that is not in 4NF. Transform the relation into 4NF.

8.17 Describe join dependencies. Are they important for practical database design?

8.18 Define *domain/key normal form*. Why is it important?

8.19 Transform the following relation into DK/NF. Make appropriate assumptions about functional dependencies and domains. State your assumptions.

HARDWARE (Manufacturer, Model, Memory_size, Site_number, City, State, Zip)

8.20 Transform the following relation into DK/NF. Make appropriate assumptions about functional dependencies and domains. State your assumptions.

INVOICE (Number, Customer_name, Customer_number, Customer_address, Item_number, Item_price, Item_quantity, Salesperson_number, Tax_district_of_sale, Tax, Total_due)

8.21 Same as 8.20, except add attribute Customer_tax_status (0 if nonexempt, 1 if exempt). Also, add the constraint: There will be no tax if Customer_tax_status = 1.

8.22 Give an example of an inclusion constraint. Describe a situation in which a functional dependency is split across two relations. Why is this latter interrelation dependency more serious than an inclusion constraint?

8.23 Describe three criteria for evaluating a database design.

8.24 Define a *nonloss projection*. Give a projection that is nonloss and one that is not nonloss.

Group II Questions

8.25 Answer question 6.28 at the end of Chapter 6. Develop a relational database design for your answer. Express relations, attributes, domains, attribute/domain correspondences, and constraints. Specifically show how you represented each of the contained tuples of your SDM design.

8.26 Answer question 6.29 at the end of Chapter 6. Develop a relational database design for your answer. Define relations, attributes, domains, attribute/domain correspondences, and constraints. Specifically, show how you represented each of the contained tuples of your SDM design.

9
The CODASYL Model

This chapter introduces the second major model that can be used for physical database design—the CODASYL DBTG model. The concepts and facilities of the model are discussed here. Application of this model to the physical database design process is discussed in Chapter 10.

CODASYL (Conference on Data Systems Languages) is the group that developed the standards for COBOL. The benefit of that effort has been immense; in fact, the popularity and effectiveness of COBOL is due, in large measure, to the presence of COBOL language standards. Unfortunately, the benefits of the CODASYL database standardization activity have been less dramatic.

Several reasons account for the lukewarm response that the CODASYL model has received. First, as you will see, this model is complex and incohesive. A statement in a schema definition can combine with a seemingly unrelated operation in an application program to produce spurious results. Designers and programmers must learn more concepts and be more careful than with the relational model. Second, the CODASYL model has a decidedly COBOL flavor to it. This similarity has been an issue in organizations where COBOL is not the language of choice. Further, the development of the CODASYL database model has been heavily politicized; it appears that decisions have not always been made on technical merit. Reading the number and variety of options, formats, etc., on CODASYL database commands is reminiscent of the statement that a zebra is a horse designed by committee! Finally, although most of the core concepts of the model are defined and agreed upon, there are many not-agreed-on variants of the core concepts. These variants create confusion and lead to a dilemma for us.

HISTORY OF CODASYL DATABASE ACTIVITY

To understand this dilemma, consider Figure 9-1, which portrays a history of the CODASYL database activities. The late 1960s saw the successful commercial use of a few DBMS products. Of those, the most influential was IDS, developed

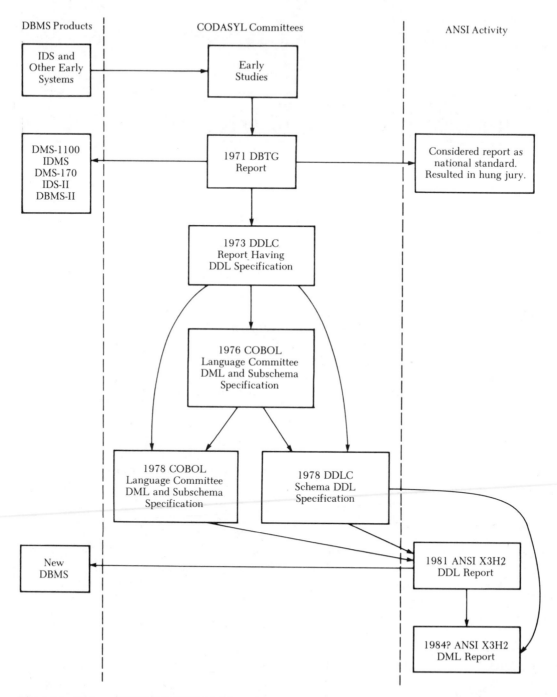

Figure 9-1   History of CODASYL DBTG Model Development

by a team of people headed by Charles Bachman, then with General Electric. IDS and other early systems were studied by a special group (the Database Task Group, or DBTG) within CODASYL in the late 1960s. The result of this study was the first database standard specification, called the CODASYL DBTG 1971 Report. This report (and all subsequent DBTG models) was heavily influenced by IDS.

In 1972 the DBTG became a permanent part of CODASYL and changed its name to Data Description Language Committee (DDLC). The name change is significant. At that point, the DDL and DML were separated; the CODASYL DDLC left DML specifications to another committee. You know by now that the DDL and the DML need to be tailored to fit one another, and that the two should be designed hand in hand. That is not, however, what happened. In 1976 the CODASYL COBOL Language Committee revised the 1971 DBTG report and developed specifications for the subschema and DML facilities in COBOL. This group accepted, by and large, the 1973 DDLC report, except that some names were changed. (The 1971 and 1973 specifications called for an inappropriate use of fifteen or so COBOL reserved words.) Then, in 1978, reports from each of these groups were published. The DDLC published an updated version of the schema DDL facilities, and the COBOL Language Committee published updated subschema DDL and DML facilities. These reports use different terminology, but otherwise are comparable. no Standards.

The CODASYL effort created subsidiary effects along the way. ANSI (the American National Standards Institute) considered the 1971 DBTG model for establishment as a national standard. The consideration resulted in a hung jury; it was neither accepted nor rejected. However, most vendors saw the possibility of a standard and developed DBMS products that conformed or at least could arguably conform to the 1971 standard. The products were implemented and sold even though the 1971 report did not become a national standard.

In 1978 the CODASYL DDLC DDL was sent to ANSI for consideration again as a national standard. (Since the DML was very COBOL oriented, it was not sent to ANSI for standards consideration.) The ANSI X3H2 committee, which received the DDLC DDL, found parts of it objectionable and changed it. Essentially, this committee eliminated all constructs in the DDL that referred to physical data formats. The X3H2 committee believed the DDL should only have logical constructs.

In 1981, X3H2 published a draft of its proposed DDL standard. A vote on this standard failed (the vote was 10-8 in favor, but two-thirds majority was required), principally because there is no DML corresponding to the X3H2 DDL. As of early 1982, the ANSI X3H2 committee was working on a standard for a DML to match its DDL, and the plan is to take another vote after that development.

The dilemma for us is this: Which CODASYL database model shall we discuss? We can choose the 1971 model, on which most of the "CODASYL" DBMS products are based. Or, we could discuss the 1978 model, which was the last time a consistent CODASYL DDL and DML were defined. Or, we could discuss the 1981 DDL proposal, and adjust the 1978 DML to correct for changes in the 1981 DDL.

The last alternative is most promising. The 1981 DDL reflects recent thinking in nonrelational data definition and is therefore worth learning. The changes made since 1978 do not appear to require revolutionary changes in DML. Hence we can discuss the 1978 DML and make adjustments as needed. This is the course of action we shall follow.

Although only the 1971 specification was called the *DBTG model*, that name has stuck. Most people use the term *CODASYL DBTG* to refer to one, any, or all of the versions in Figure 9-1. We will follow that custom and keep the name *CODASYL DBTG Model*. When we need to be specific about a particular version, the name *DBTG* will be qualified with a date. Thus the 1981 DBTG model refers to the 1971 DBTG DDL that was revised in 1973 and 1978 by the CODASYL DDLC Committee and then revised again in 1981 by the ANSI X3H2 Committee. Perhaps we should call it the *CODASYL DBTG/DDLC/ANSI X3H2 Model!*

OVERVIEW OF CHAPTER

The plan for this chapter is as follows. We will focus on the general architecture and concepts of the CODASYL models. Where specifics are necessary, they will be taken from the 1981 DDL and the 1978 DML models. Where there is a discrepancy in terminology between DDLC and the COBOL Language Committee, we will follow the Language Committee's terms. This will reduce confusion by avoiding double meanings for COBOL-reserved words. Also, we will omit discussion of many specialized features of the DBTG model. In particular, features that appear vulnerable to change or deletion will be omitted. Finally, you are forewarned that these models are evolving; if you are reading this book after 1984, change is likely to have occurred.

ARCHITECTURE OF A CODASYL DBTG DBMS

The architecture of a DBMS based on the CODASYL model is evolving toward the ANSI/X3/SPARC model. Whereas at one time the CODASYL model allowed only two types of schemas (schema and subschema), it now allows for three (schema, subschema, and data structure description). This is shown in Figure 9-2. Users interact with the database via an application program. One or more users can execute a single program (if concurrently, the programs must be reentrant). Each user has a data area called a *user working area* (UWA). This area contains database data for a particular user. The execution of a program in behalf of one of the users is called a *run-unit*. In Figure 9-2 there are three run-units for Application Program A.

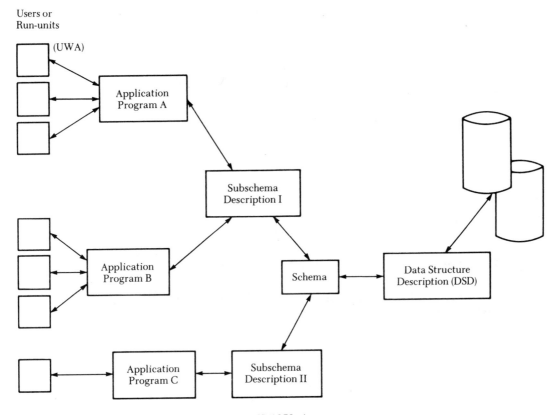

Figure 9-2   Architecture of a CODASYL DBTG DBMS (1978+)

Application programs view the database through a *subschema*. Programs may share subschemas, or they each may have their own subschema. As normally envisioned,* subschemas are subsets of schemas. A schema may have records, fields, and relationships that are not exposed in a given subschema. Also, subschemas can rename records, fields, and relationships, and they may reorder fields within records. The format of a data-item may differ in a subschema and in the schema (numeric character to decimal, say).

The *schema* is the complete, logical view of the database. Every record, field, and relationship must be defined in the schema. Note the difference between the DBTG model and the relational model. Here, relationships *must be* predefined.

---

*In the 1978 and 1981 models, subschemas are allowed to have records that are constructed from schema records. A customer credit record, for example, might be constructed by concatenating a customer address record with that customer's accounts receivable record. In the subschema, this would appear as one logical record.

Physical constructs are avoided in the schema description because they are not part of the complete logical view. They do not belong in the schema. For example, record keys are not defined in the schema. Any field can be used by a program to identify a record or records. If a field is frequently used for identification, a key structure, say an inverted file, should be constructed. This construct, however, is not coded into the schema. Thus the schema contains only the description of the data, and it need be changed only when the data definition changes—not when processing modes, program requirements, or direct access hardware change. Another way of saying this is that eliminating physical constructs reduces the number of pathological connections in the database architecture.

The *data structure description* (DSD) is the CODASYL equivalent of an internal schema. The DSD maps the schema records, fields, and relationships to physical storage. In 1978 the CODASYL DBA WG (Database Administration Working Group) published a standard for the DSD language. This standard specifies terminology for mapping schema records to physical records, pages (a block of physical records), and areas (a group of pages). Also, this flexible standard gives DBMS designers the options of using inverted files or linked lists, and direct or indirect addressing for representing relationships. We will not discuss the data structure description further in this text. See [24] if you want further information.

CODASYL DATA DEFINITION

This section describes the basic constructs for defining data using the CODASYL model. Database designers use these constructs to define the structure of the schema. First, we will discuss data definition primitives, and then we will show how those primitives are used to represent record relationships.

In the balance of this chapter, we will ease our way into the morass of technical details by presenting only the essence of DBTG DDL and DML specifications. To keep the complexity level down, we will omit some required details in the DDL and DML examples. The intent of this chapter is to give you the big, conceptual picture of the DBTG model. Chapter 10 will then add the necessary technical details to the big picture and thus provide an accurate description of the DBTG model.

Data definition primitives

The three fundamental building blocks of DBTG data definition are data-items, records, and sets.

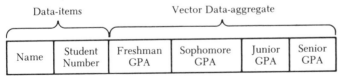

a. Record Composed of Data-items

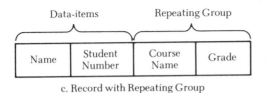

b. Record Composed of Data-items and a Vector Data-aggregate

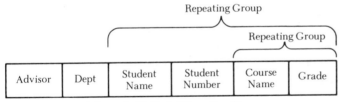

c. Record with Repeating Group

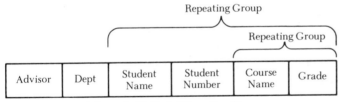

d. Record with Nested Repeating Group

Figure 9-3   DBTG Records

or Column

Data-items   A *data-item* is a field; it corresponds to *attribute* in SDM. Data-items have names and formats. Examples of data-items are Name, Address, Major, etc. Although data-items arise out of domains just as attributes do, the DBTG model does not pay any attention to this. Domains are simply not considered.

Records   A *record* is a collection of data-items. It corresponds to an SDM entity class. Figure 9-3 shows several DBTG record examples. The DBTG model allows vectors, which are repetitions of a data-item (like GPA in Figure 9-3b), and it allows repeating groups, such as duplications of the data-items Course Name and Grade in Figure 9-3c. Although repeating groups are allowed,

Row or Tuple of relational DB.

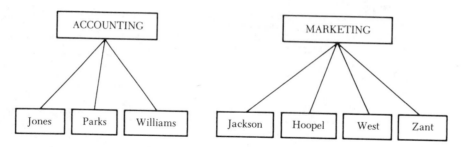

Figure 9-4 Two Occurrences of the DEPT-FAC Set

they are unnecessary and generally not recommended. (Repeating groups can usually be better represented by one-to-many relationships as discussed in the next section.)

Sets A *set* is a one-to-many relationship between records. Sets have *owners* and *members*. The owner of a set is the parent. In Figure 9-4 the ACCOUNTING department is the owner of a set, and the MARKETING department is the owner of another set. Members of a set are the children of the one-to-many relationship. In Figure 9-4, JONES, PARKS, and WILLIAMS are the members of the set owned by ACCOUNTING.

Figure 9-4 shows two occurrences of a general structure. These occurrences represent instances of a one-to-many relationship between DEPARTMENT and FACULTY records. Figure 9-5 is a generalized representation of this relationship. It is customary to call the general structure, as shown in Figure 9-5, the *set*, and examples of that structure, as shown in Figure 9-4, *instances* or *occurrences* of the set.

To define a set, we specify a set name and identify the type of record that will be the owner and the type (or types) of records that will be the members.

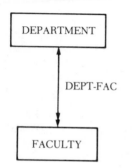

Figure 9-5 General Form of DEPT-FAC Set

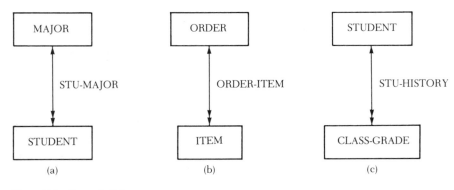

Figure 9-6   Example Sets

For example, the set STU-MAJOR has MAJOR owner records and STUDENT member records. The set ORDER-ITEM has ORDER owner records and ITEM member records. The set STU-HISTORY has STUDENT owner records and CLASS-GRADE member records. These sets are shown in Figure 9-6.

Set (c) in Figure 9-6 is an equivalent way of representing the repeating group record in Figure 9-3c. In Figure 9-6c, there are two record types—one for the student and one for classes the student has taken—and a set. In Figure 9-3c, there is one record type with a repeating group. Using terminology from the relational model, the structure in Figure 9-3c is unnormalized. Since it is not a flat file, it is not in first normal form. However, the structure in Figure 9-6 is normalized. Both STUDENT and CLASS-GRADE records are flat files. In general, normalized records are preferred; they are easier to understand and process. Because of this, some people believe that repeating groups should never be used, and that the repeating group facility should be removed from the DBTG model.

The DBTG model has specific rules regarding set definition. First, a set can have only one type of record as owner. However, one or more record types can be members. Figure 9-7a shows the set ACTIVITY; the owner record is CLUB, and the member records are PROFESSOR and STUDENT. Figure 9-7b shows two instances of this set. Both PROFESSOR and STUDENT records are members of the SKIING and BOWLING clubs.

According to the DBTG model, a member record can only belong to one instance of a set. Stated another way, a record may not have two parents in the same set. This means, in Figure 9-7, that Professor Guynes can only have the SKIING parent record. He may not have BOWLING as well. Furthermore, Professor Pipkin can only have the BOWLING record as parent. She may not have SKIING as well. If faculty members want to belong to more than one club, then a set cannot be used to represent this relationship. We will see how to represent such a relationship in the next section.

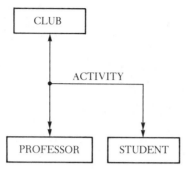

a. Set with Two Member Record Types

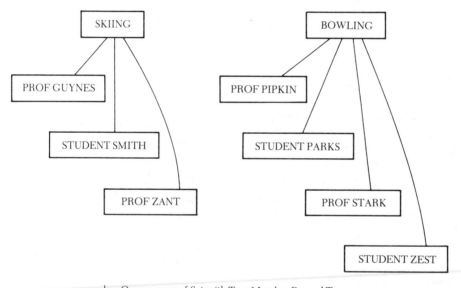

b. Occurrences of Set with Two Member Record Types

Figure 9-7 Set with Two Member Record Types and Example Occurrences

Although a record cannot have two owners in the same set, a record may have two owners if they are in different sets. For example, a professor may have one ACTIVITY owner and one JOB-TITLE owner. Figure 9-8 extends Figure 9-7 to allow this possibility. Dr. Guynes, for example, has both SKIING and FULL PROFESSOR records as parents.

The restrictions on set membership just described mean that a set can readily be used to represent trees and simple networks. However, complex networks cannot be represented by sets. We will amplify these statements in the next section.

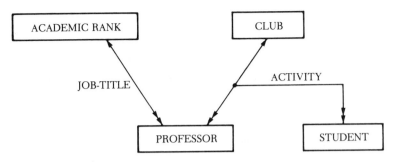

a. Record Belonging to Two Different Sets

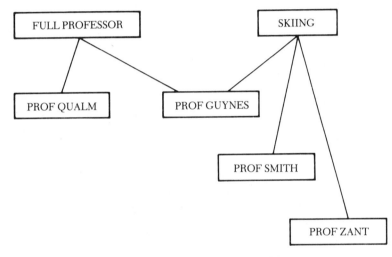

b. Instance of Set Structure in (a)

Figure 9-8   Example of Two-Owner Record in Different Sets

Until 1981 the CODASYL model included a fourth type of data definition construct called an *area* (the term used by the DDLC) or *realm* (the term for the same construct used by the COBOL Language Committee). A realm was a collection of records and sets that could be allocated to a physical entity such as a file, disk pack, or whatever. All DBTG reports were indefinite about how records or sets were to get into realms. The decision regarding the use of realms was left to DBMS product designers.

In 1981 this construct was deleted by the ANSI X3H2 committee because it was considered a physical construct and therefore inappropriate for a schema or subschema description. Consequently, we will not consider realms any further in discussion of the CODASYL DBTG model. It will occur, however, when we discuss a CODASYL DBMS in Chapter 13. That's because present CODA-SYL DBMS products are based on the 1971 model.

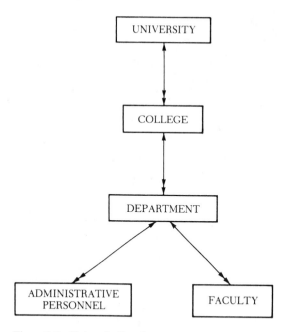

Figure 9-9   University Tree Structure

CODASYL DBTG representation of record relationships

This section describes how the DBTG model can be used to represent trees and simple networks, and how complex networks can be transformed and then represented. Finally, the special cases of loops, cycles, and intrarecord relationships will be described.

Trees   A tree is represented by sets in a straightforward manner. Consider the example in Figure 9-9. Five record types are connected by four relationships. Since each relationship is a one-to-many relationship, each can be represented by a DBTG set. Thus there is a university/college set, a college/department set, a department/administrative personnel set, and a department/faculty set.

If there are two universities in the database, there are two occurrences of the university/college set. One is owned by University A, and the other is owned by University B. If there are 14 colleges in A and 12 in B, then there are 14 members in A's occurrence of the university/college set type and 12 members in B's occurrence of that set type. This means there are 26 college records, and consequently, 26 college/department sets.

As shown in Figure 9-10, each UNIVERSITY, COLLEGE, and DEPARTMENT record owns a set, and each COLLEGE, DEPARTMENT, ADMINISTRATIVE PERSONNEL, and FACULTY record is a member of a set. The children of the DEPARTMENT record can be represented in either of two

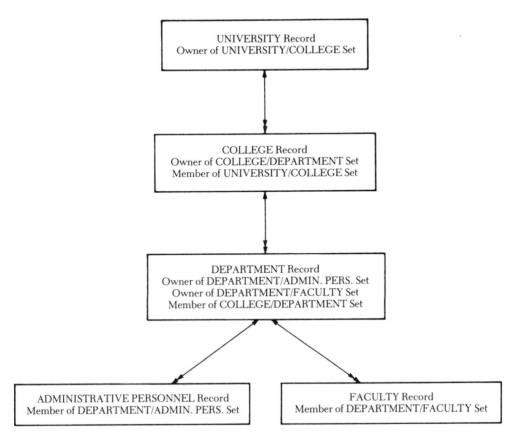

UNIVERSITY Record
Owner of UNIVERSITY/COLLEGE Set

COLLEGE Record
Owner of COLLEGE/DEPARTMENT Set
Member of UNIVERSITY/COLLEGE Set

DEPARTMENT Record
Owner of DEPARTMENT/ADMIN. PERS. Set
Owner of DEPARTMENT/FACULTY Set
Member of COLLEGE/DEPARTMENT Set

ADMINISTRATIVE PERSONNEL Record
Member of DEPARTMENT/ADMIN. PERS. Set

FACULTY Record
Member of DEPARTMENT/FACULTY Set

Figure 9-10   Set Representation of Tree in Figure 9-9

ways. First, as shown in Figure 9-10, a separate set could be defined for each type of employee. Administrative personnel would belong to one set and faculty to another. Alternatively, a single set could be defined, and that set would have both types of records as its members. This design is similar to Figure 9-7a. The choice between these two must be made in light of requirements. Will it ever be necessary to process the relationships of one type of personnel without the other? If so, then two sets should be defined. (Again you see the need for knowing requirements before database design.)

In general, then, to represent a tree with the DBTG model, we just replace each one-to-many relationship with a set. If a parent has more than one type of child record, either one or several sets may be defined.

Simple networks   A simple network can also be represented by sets in a straightforward manner. Since simple networks have only one-to-many relationships, we can again replace each relationship by a set. This means that

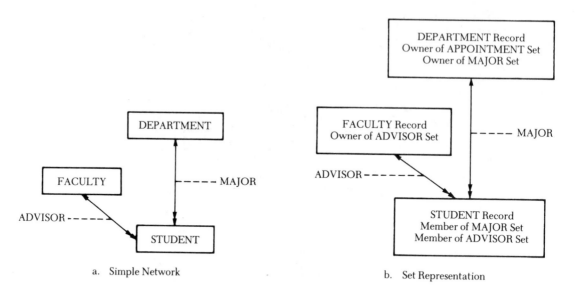

Figure 9-11 Set Representation of Simple Network

records having more than one parent are members of more than one set occurrence. However, since the relationship is simple, these parents will be different types of records. In Figure 9-11a, the STUDENT record has two parent record types, so in the DBTG model representation in Figure 9-11b, the STUDENT record is a member of two different sets.

The wording is important. The STUDENT record is a member of two occurrences of *different sets*. It is not a member of two set occurrences of the same set. The latter situation is prohibited by the DBTG model.

Complex networks A complex network cannot be directly represented using the DBTG model. Recall in Figure 9-7, a professor could only belong to one club. If he or she wanted to join a second club, that would have meant that the professor would have been a member of two set occurrences of the same type. Figure 9-12 shows another complex network; this one is between department and faculty records. The relationship is many-to-many because a professor can teach in one or more departments and a department can have several professors.

Suppose we try to model this relationship with a set (appointment) between DEPARTMENT and FACULTY records. This is shown in Figure 9-12b. In this case, Jones, Smith, and Sharp would appear in the appointment set owned by the Music department, and Bull and Jones would appear in the appointment set owned by the Veterinary Medicine department. Since Jones has a joint appointment, she must appear in two sets of the same type. This situation is prohibited.

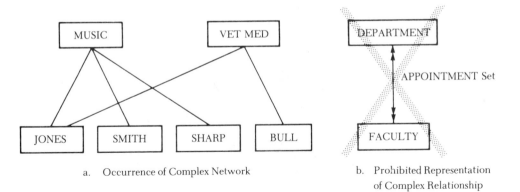

a.   Occurrence of Complex Network

b.   Prohibited Representation
     of Complex Relationship

Figure 9-12   Example of Prohibited Relationship in DBTG

There is a way around the problem. Since the DBTG model cannot represent complex relationships, we first reduce every complex relationship in the network to two simple ones. We do this by defining a new record type and letting records of this type hold data about the intersection of two records. For example, an intersection record for the network in Figure 9-12a could contain the salary that a department pays a faculty member, or the amount of time the faculty member spends teaching in that department. Figure 9-13 shows how the complex DEPARTMENT/FACULTY relationship is reduced to simple relationships by the addition of the DEPARTMENT/FACULTY INTERSECTION record.

Once we have the complex relationship reduced, we just model each simple relationship by a set type. Figure 9-14 shows an occurrence of the structure in Figure 9-13. The intersection records contain salary data as suggested above.

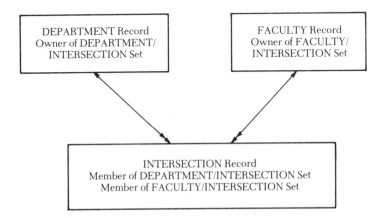

Figure 9-13   Reduction of Complex Network in Figure 9-12b to a Simple Network

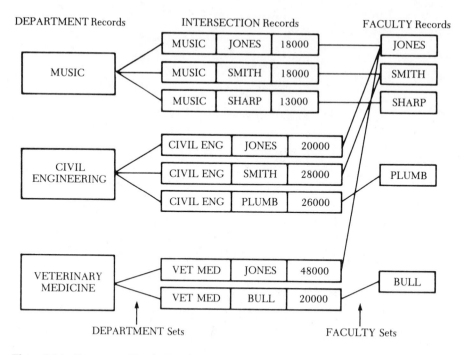

Figure 9-14   Department/Faculty Database Occurrence

Jones, a versatile professor, has appointments in the Music, Civil Engineering, and Veterinary Medicine departments. Her colleague, Smith, has appointments in the Music and Civil Engineering departments. Sharp, Plumb, and Bull have appointments in the Music, Civil Engineering, and Veterinary Medicine departments, respectively. There is one intersection record occurrence for each appointment, and every intersection record occurrence is a member of a department set and of a faculty set. To determine the total salary paid to one faculty member, the database system refers to all intersection records in the faculty set owned by that faculty member. To determine the total salary expense of a department, the system refers to all intersection records in the department set owned by that department. Jones, for example, earns a total of $48,000 (versatility pays) and the Civil Engineering department spends $74,000 on faculty salaries.

Another example of the reduction of a complex network to a simple one is shown in Figure 9-15. Here the student/class relationship is complex: one student can be a member of several classes, and one class consists of many students. The complex relationship is reduced to a simple one by the addition of the STUDENT/CLASS/GRADE record. Here the intersection of STUDENT and CLASS is STUDENT/GRADE.

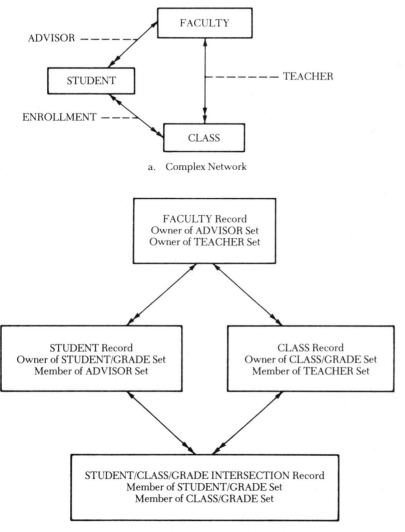

a.   Complex Network

b.   DBTG Reduction to Simple Network

Figure 9-15   Reduction of Student/Class Relationship through INTERSECTION Record

Cycles and intrarecord relationships   A *cycle* is a sequence of record types
such that there is a path from one record type through other record types back
to the original record type. For example, suppose students can have a major in
more than one department. The cycle structure in Figure 9-16 is formed. Start-

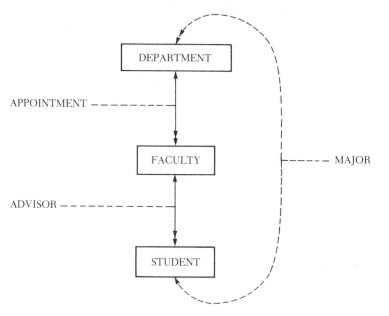

Figure 9-16   A Cycle

ing from a department, say Music, we can obtain a **FACULTY** record, say Jones. If Jones teaches Smith, we can retrieve Smith's record from the **ADVISOR** set. If Smith is majoring in computer science and mathematics, we can retrieve the records of those departments—thus we find ourselves back to the record type with which we started. Note that we are not necessarily back to the Music record.

The DBTG model does not prohibit cycles. They are easily represented with the set construct and do not violate any of the DBTG set concepts. The DBTG left it to implementers of the model to decide whether or not cycles were permitted in their DBMS products.

Intrarecord relationships are relationships among records of the same type. Figure 9-17a shows seven employee records. Suppose these employees are divided into two project teams as follows: Jones, Williams, Zadorojny, and Kwan work on a team headed by Kwan, and the remaining employees work on a team headed by Ortega. These teams can be represented by two one-to-many relationships as shown in Figure 9-17b. The logical structure of this relationship appears in Figure 9-17c. Since the record has a relationship to itself, this structure is called a *loop*.

Should loops be allowed? In DBTG terms, can a single record type be defined as both the owner and the member of a single set? For the example in Figure 9-17, can **EMPLOYEE** be defined as both the owner record type and the member record type of **PROJECT-TEAM**? Further, can the same record be both a

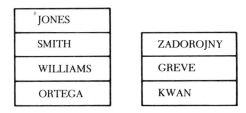

a.   EMPLOYEE Records

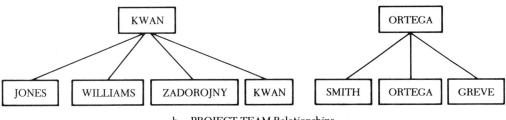

b.   PROJECT-TEAM Relationships

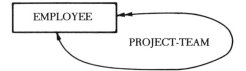

c.   Set Representation of PROJECT-TEAM Relationship

Figure 9-17   Intrarecord Relationships

member and an owner? In Figure 9-17b, both Kwan and Ortega are owners and members. Should this be allowed?

The original specification of the DBTG model prohibited such relationships. In 1978, however, this limitation was removed. The DBTG model as it stands today will allow a record to be defined as both an owner and a member. Thus loops are allowed. However, since a record must still be a member of only one set occurrence, no employee can work on two teams.

Figure 9-17b shows project leaders as members of their own teams. A single record is both an owner and a member of the same set. As stated, this duality is allowed. However, depending on requirements, we may choose to represent teams differently. Another possibility is shown in Figure 9-18a. Leaders are not on their own teams. In this case, a record may be an owner of one set occurrence and a member in another set occurrence. This situation would occur if one project leader is a member of another team. For example, suppose Kwan works

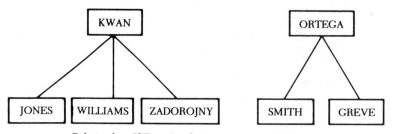

a. Relationships If Team Leaders Are Not Considered on Team

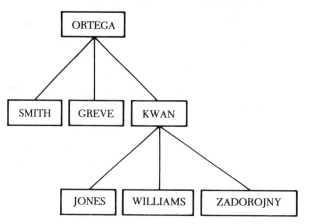

b. A Record in Two Set Occurrences—One as Member and One as Owner

Figure 9-18   Owner and Member Record Relationships

for Ortega as shown in Figure 9-18b. This means that Kwan is a member of Ortega's occurrence of the PROJECT-TEAM set, and an owner of her own occurrence of the PROJECT-TEAM set. This, too, has been allowed since the 1978 standard was published.

What happens if employees are assigned to two or more teams? The result is a complex *intra*record relationship. The situation is analogous to a complex *inter*record relationship. (STUDENTs to CLASSes, for example.) We create an intersection record that represents the intersection of a given employee with a given team leader. Figure 9-19 shows possible team assignments for the data in Figure 9-17. The entries in the table are the percent of time that a given employee works for a given team.

In Figure 9-20a, we have created one intersection record for each employee-team assignment. The intersection record contains the name of the employee, the name of the team leader, and the percent of time. Each employee owns a set of ASSIGNMENTS. Smith, for example, owns a set having the second and third intersection records. Similarly, each team leader owns a set of TEAM-MEMBERS. This situation is identical to that in Figure 9-14, except that the owners of the sets are all EMPLOYEE records. (In Figure 9-14, one set of owners was FACULTY records and the other set was DEPARTMENT records.)

	KWAN	ORTEGA
JONES	100	0
SMITH	50	50
WILLIAMS	20	80
ZADOROJNY	70	30
GREVE	100	0

Figure 9-19   Team Assignments Assuming Employees Belong to Two Projects

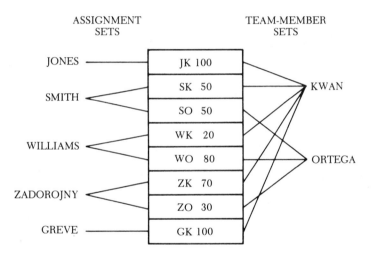

a.   Intersection Records for Multiple Team Assignments

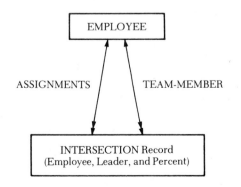

b.   Set Structure Having Single Record with Intersection

Figure 9-20   Intersection Record Relationships

The logical structure of these relationships is shown in Figure 9-20b. This is actually a simple network, except that instead of having two record types for owners, we have just one. Figure 9-21 summarizes characteristics of DBTG sets.

CODASYL DBTG DATA MANIPULATION LANGUAGE

In this section we will present the essence of the DBTG DML. First, we will define a simplified form of a DBTG schema and subschema. This example will be used to illustrate DBTG DML commands. Next, DML processing of a single record will be demonstrated. Finally, we will discuss DML processing of several records using sets.

Example schema and subschema

The example to be used for illustrating DBTG DML is the same example used to illustrate SQL in Chapter 7 (Figure 7-12). A data structure diagram of the

---

- — A set is a collection of records.
- — There are an arbitrary number of sets in the database.
- — Each set has one owner record type and one or more member record types.
- — Each owner record occurrence defines a set occurrence.
- — There are an arbitrary number of member record occurrences in one set occurrence.
- — A record may be a member of more than one set.
- — A record may not be a member of two occurrences of the same set.
- — A record may be a member and an owner of the same set.

Figure 9-21   Summary of Set Characteristics

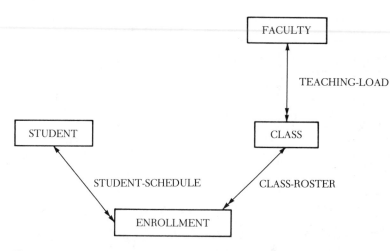

Figure 9-22   Data Structure Diagram of Example Schema

schema of this example is shown in Figure 9-22. There are four record types and three set types.

Figure 9-23 shows a simplified (some essential details are omitted) DBTG schema definition of Figure 9-22. Each record is named, and the contained

```
          SCHEMA NAME IS UNIVERSITY.

          RECORD NAME IS FACULTY.
                FID;                    TYPE IS DECIMAL 3.
                NAME;                   TYPE IS CHAR 30.
                DEPARTMENT;             TYPE IS CHAR 10.

          RECORD NAME IS STUDENT.
                SID;                    TYPE IS DECIMAL 3.
                NAME;                   TYPE IS CHAR 30.
                MAJOR;                  TYPE IS CHAR 10.
                GRADE-LEVEL;            TYPE IS CHAR 2.
                AGE;                    TYPE IS DECIMAL 2.

          RECORD NAME IS CLASS.
                NAME;                   TYPE IS CHAR 5.
                TIME;                   TYPE IS CHAR 5.
                ROOM;                   TYPE IS CHAR 5.

          RECORD NAME IS ENROLLMENT.
                STUDENT-NUMBER;    TYPE IS DECIMAL 3.
                CLASS-NAME;        TYPE IS CHAR 5.
                GRADE;             TYPE IS CHAR 2.

          SET NAME IS TEACHING-LOAD.
                OWNER IS FACULTY.
                MEMBER IS CLASS.

          SET NAME IS STUDENT-SCHEDULE.
                OWNER IS STUDENT.
                MEMBER IS ENROLLMENT.

          SET NAME IS CLASS-ROSTER.
                OWNER IS CLASS.
                MEMBER IS ENROLLMENT.
```

Figure 9-23 Partial DBTG Schema for Database in Figure 9-22

data-items and their formats are defined. Data-item format is defined physically and not semantically. There is no meaning attached to formats; we don't know from a DBTG schema definition if two data-items having a CHAR 5 format are comparable or not. For example, TIME and ROOM of CLASS appear to be comparable. In actuality, they are not. See the domain definitions in Figure 7-12 to recall why.

The schema in Figure 9-23 names each set and also names the owner and member record types. In this example, every set has just one member record type. The set descriptions in Figure 9-23 are incomplete; by the end of Chapter 10, we will have covered sufficient material to be able to present a complete set description. You will see complete descriptions in Chapter 13 as well.

Figure 9-24 shows a simplified subschema for the schema in Figure 9-23. The name of the subschema (declared in the SS statement) is SCHEDULING, and it has just three of the four records in the schema. FACULTY has been omitted. Also, only two sets are defined in set definition statements (SD). The TEACH-ING-LOAD set does not appear in the SCHEDULING subschema. All of the records and data-items have the same names and formats as the schema. As you will see in Chapter 10, names and formats can change.

```
TITLE DIVISION.
SS SCHEDULING WITHIN UNIVERSITY.
STRUCTURE DIVISION.
01      STUDENT.
        05      SID.
        05      NAME.
        05      MAJOR.
        05      GRADE-LEVEL.
        05      AGE.
01      CLASS.
        05      NAME.
        05      TIME.
        05      ROOM.
01      ENROLLMENT.
        05      STUDENT-NUMBER.
        05      CLASS-NAME.
        05      GRADE.
SD      STUDENT-SCHEDULE.
SD      CLASS-ROSTER.
```

Figure 9-24   Simplified Subschema for Schema in Figure 9-23

There is one difference between this example and the one in Figure 7-12. Position_number in ENROLLMENT has been changed to GRADE. It requires too much verbiage and space to show how to maintain Position_number using the DBTG model. It can be done, but it's not educationally worth the time and space. See question 9.24. The DBTG model does not have built-in functions.

With the exception of GRADE, the data in Figure 7-22 will be used for this chapter. It is duplicated for convenience in Figure 9-25.

SID	Name	Major	Grade-level	Age
100	JONES	HISTORY	GR	21
150	PARKS	ACGOUNTING	SO	19
200	BAKER	MATH	GR	50
250	GLASS	HISTORY	SN	50
300	BAKER	ACCOUNTING	SN	41
350	RUSSELL	MATH	JR	20
400	RYE	ACCOUNTING	FR	18
450	JONES	HISTORY	SN	24

a. STUDENT Records

Student-number	Class-name	Grade
100	BD445	
150	BA200	
200	BD445	
200	CS250	
300	CS150	
400	BA200	
400	BF410	
400	CS250	
450	BA200	

b. ENROLLMENT Records

Name	Time	Room
BA200	M-F9	SC110
BD445	MWF3	SC213
BF410	MWF8	SC213
CS150	MWF3	EA304
CS250	MWF12	EB210

c. CLASS Records

Figure 9-25   Example Data for STUDENT, ENROLLMENT, and CLASS Relations

DBTG DML—general concepts

Most DBTG DML operations are executed in two phases. First, a FIND command is issued to identify a record to be acted upon. The FIND command does not read or otherwise manipulate the indicated record. Rather, it identifies a record. Once a record has been identified, a second DML command is issued to perform an operation. Typical patterns are FIND, GET; or FIND, MODIFY; or FIND, ERASE. The only DML command that does not follow this pattern is STORE. Since this command inserts a new record into the database, there is nothing to be found before it is executed.

As stated, every DBTG run-unit (a particular user connected to a particular program) has a user working area (UWA). The records in the subschema are stored in the UWA. For our example, the UWA has three records with the data-items listed in Figure 9-24 (data-item format is shown in Figure 9-23). The UWA contains other data as well. In particular, it contains *currency indicators* and *special registers*.

Currency indicators   Currency indicators are placemarkers. When the programmer issues a FIND command, a record is found, and its place is marked in a special variable called a *currency indicator*. Subsequently, when a GET, MODIFY, ERASE, or other command is issued, the DBMS references the currency indicator to determine which record to act upon. Also, currency indicators are used as reference points for sequentially oriented commands like FIND NEXT or FIND PRIOR as discussed below.

There are several currency indicators. Every record type and set type in the subschema has its own currency indicator. These indicators identify the most recently processed record of a type or in a set. Also, the run-unit itself has a currency indicator that marks the most recently processed record of any type. For the subschema in Figure 9-24, there are currency indicators for STUDENT, for CLASS, for ENROLLMENT, for STUDENT-SCHEDULE, and for CLASS-

Currency Indicator	Value*
Current of run-unit	Null
Current of STUDENT	Null
Current of CLASS	Null
Current of ENROLLMENT	Null
Current of STUDENT-SCHEDULE	Null
Current of CLASS-ROSTER	Null

*These are initial values.

Figure 9-26   Currency Indicators for Subschema SCHEDULING

ROSTER. Initially, all of these currency indicators are null, indicating that no record has been accessed. As records are processed, however, the currency indicators will be updated.

The currency indicators can be envisioned as variables in a table. Figure 9-26 lists the currency indicators for the SCHEDULING subschema. The first indicator is current of run-unit (the most recently processed record of any type). The other indicators refer to record and set types as shown.

The FIND command sets these indicators. For example, when a FIND command is executed to find the student with SID = 150, the current of run-unit, current of STUDENT, and current of STUDENT-SCHEDULE would all be set to point to the record for Student 150. (See Figure 9-27a.) If a FIND command were then issued to locate the ENROLLMENT record for Student 200 and Class BD445, then the current of run-unit, current of ENROLLMENT, current of STUDENT-SCHEDULE, and current of CLASS-ROSTER would be set to point to the ENROLLMENT record having 200, BD445. The modified

Currency Indicator	Value
Current of run-unit	STUDENT 150
Current of STUDENT	STUDENT 150
Current of CLASS	Null
Current of ENROLLMENT	Null
Current of STUDENT-SCHEDULE	STUDENT 150
Current of CLASS-ROSTER	Null

   a.   Currency Indicators after FIND of STUDENT 150

Currency Indicator	Value
Current of run-unit	ENROLLMENT 200, BD445
Current of STUDENT	STUDENT 150
Current of CLASS	Null
Current of ENROLLMENT	ENROLLMENT 200, BD445
Current of STUDENT-SCHEDULE	ENROLLMENT 200, BD445
Current of CLASS-ROSTER	ENROLLMENT 200, BD445

   b.   Current Indicators after FIND of STUDENT 150 and
          Subsequent FIND of ENROLLMENT 200, BD445

Figure 9-27   Currency Indicators for FIND Commands

indicators are shown in Figure 9-27b. The current of STUDENT would be unaffected by this second FIND command.

Special registers   Values for special registers are also kept in the UWA. The DBMS places return codes in a register called *DB-STATUS*. (The term *register* may be misleading. This is a data-item in the UWA, not a machine register.) After a DML call, if DB-STATUS is zero, the command has been executed without problem. If not, then an error code is placed in DB-STATUS. Perhaps the most common use of this register is to signal end of data.

Other special registers are DB-SET-NAME, DB-DATA-NAME, and DB-RECORD-NAME. The first two of these registers are set only when an error occurs. The DBMS places the name of the record and of the data-item it was processing at the time of the error in these registers. DB-RECORD-NAME is set when an error occurs, and also whenever a FIND or STORE command has been executed. This data is useful when the application program is finding records in a set that has more than one record type as members.

DBTG DML—single record processing

The following examples show how FIND is used in conjunction with other commands to process the database. As in Chapter 7, these examples will be numbered for easy reference. The numbers are not part of the DBTG commands, however. Also, this chapter will show commands in pseudocode form. Chapter 13 shows exact language commands for the CODASYL product IDMS. For now, think of the DML commands as new COBOL (or other language) instructions.

Suppose we want to read the STUDENT record for Student 100. The following commands will do this:

1) MOVE 100 TO SID IN STUDENT
   FIND ANY STUDENT USING SID
   GET STUDENT

The FIND command sets the current of run-unit, current of STUDENT, and current of STUDENT-SCHEDULE to point to Student 100's record. Then the GET command brings the record into the STUDENT record description in the UWA. GET always operates on the current of run-unit record.

Suppose we want to read all of the history majors' student records.

2) MOVE 'HISTORY' TO MAJOR IN STUDENT
   FIND ANY STUDENT USING MAJOR
   DOWHILE DB-STATUS = 0
           GET STUDENT
           (process student record)
           FIND DUPLICATE STUDENT USING MAJOR
   END-DO

DB-STATUS is used here to stop the loop. This code assumes that DB-STA-TUS will be set only when there are no more history majors. A more sophisticated algorithm would examine the value of DB-STATUS to ensure that no other error occurred. We will consider that level of detail when we discuss DBTG implementation in Chapter 13.

The first FIND specified that ANY record could be found. The next FIND specified DUPLICATE. This keyword means the desired record must have the same value of MAJOR that the current of STUDENT record has.

To illustrate the elimination of records, suppose we want to delete the records of all seniors (it's graduation day).

```
3) MOVE 'SN' TO GRADE-LEVEL IN STUDENT
   FIND FOR UPDATE ANY STUDENT USING GRADE-LEVEL
   DOWHILE DB-STATUS = 0
           ERASE STUDENT
           FIND FOR UPDATE DUPLICATE STUDENT USING GRADE-
           LEVEL
   END-DO
```

The logic is similar to that for the GET. The ERASE command is used instead of GET, however. Also, the words FOR UPDATE are added to the FIND command. These keywords inform the DBMS that an update is to occur. The DBMS will lock the record for the run-unit. The technology involved in processing concurrent updates will be discussed in Chapter 11. For now just accept that FOR UPDATE is required when finding for operations other than GET.

To illustrate modification of records, suppose Student 150 changes his or her major to mathematics:

```
4) MOVE 150 TO SID IN STUDENT
   FIND FOR UPDATE ANY STUDENT USING SID
   GET STUDENT
   IF DB-STATUS = 0
           THEN MOVE 'MATH' TO MAJOR IN STUDENT
                   MODIFY MAJOR
           ELSE do error processing
   END-IF
```

In this case, the MODIFY statement is stating that only the MAJOR data-item has been changed. If no data-item name is listed, the DBMS assumes that the entire record (or this subschema's view of it) has been changed.

To create a new record, we build it in the UWA and then execute a STORE command. The following inserts a STUDENT record into the database:

5) MOVE 275 TO SID IN STUDENT
   MOVE 'ABERNATHY' TO NAME IN STUDENT
   MOVE 'HISTORY' TO MAJOR IN STUDENT
   MOVE 'FR' TO GRADE-LEVEL IN STUDENT
   MOVE 18 TO AGE IN STUDENT
   STORE STUDENT

After the STORE command, the program should examine DB-STATUS to determine if the command executed successfully. Actually, DB-STATUS should be examined after every DBMS command. In these examples, and in the following, we will sometimes omit this examination and subsequent error processing. This omission simplifies the discussion. Remember, however, that actual application programs would need to examine DB-STATUS after every DBMS operation and do appropriate error processing. The 1978 DBTG COBOL Language Committee Specification provides a list of standard DBTG error messages.

Set processing with CONNECT, DISCONNECT, and RECONNECT

The DBTG provides a group of commands to put records into set occurrences, to take records from set occurrences, and to move records around within set occurrences. The allowable commands depend on the definition of set membership, which involves two concepts. First, how do members get into set occurrences, and second, once in, how can members get out (if at all)?

Set insertion status Although we did not show it in Figure 9-23, when a set is defined in the schema, it is given an *insertion status*. This status can be either AUTOMATIC or MANUAL. If AUTOMATIC, then whenever a member record is created, the DBMS automatically inserts the record into the set. If the insertion status is MANUAL, then a member record is not put into a set occurrence until the application program executes a CONNECT command.

Set retention status Additionally, when a set is defined in the schema, it is given a *retention status*. This status can be FIXED, MANDATORY, or OPTIONAL. If FIXED, then once a record is connected to a set occurrence, it must remain in that set occurrence. It can never be connected to another set occurrence. It must be deleted from the database and recreated before its set membership can change.

If the retention status is MANDATORY, then once a record is connected to a set occurrence, it must always belong to a set occurrence; however, the occurrence need not be the initial one. Thus MANDATORY sets require that once a record is put into a set occurrence, it must stay in some occurrence of the set. The RECONNECT command is used to move a member record from one occurrence to another.

	FIXED	MANDATORY	OPTIONAL
AUTO-MATIC	DBMS puts record in set at time of creation. Once in, it cannot be taken out.	DBMS puts record in set at time of creation. Can be moved to another occurrence with RECONNECT.	DBMS puts record in set at time of creation. Can be disconnected, reconnected, or connected.
MANUAL	Application program puts record into set. Once in, it cannot be taken out.	Application program puts record into set. Can be moved to another occurrence with RECONNECT.	Application program puts record into set. Can be disconnected, reconnected, or connected.

Figure 9-28   Meaning of Set Insertion and Set Retention Status

Finally, if the retention status is OPTIONAL, then member records can be disconnected, connected, or reconnected without restriction. Figure 9-28 describes how the insertion and retention status definitions work together.

Processing MANUAL-OPTIONAL sets   Figure 9-29 shows part of a schema definition for the STUDENT-CLASS and CLASS-ROSTER sets. Insertion and retention status have been added. As shown, both STUDENT-SCHEDULE and CLASS-ROSTER are MANUAL, OPTIONAL. Assume this is the case for the next several examples.

```
SET NAME IS STUDENT-SCHEDULE.
     OWNER IS STUDENT.
     MEMBER IS ENROLLMENT;
          INSERTION IS MANUAL
          RETENTION IS OPTIONAL.
SET NAME IS CLASS-ROSTER.
     OWNER IS CLASS.
     MEMBER IS ENROLLMENT;
          INSERTION IS MANUAL
          RETENTION IS OPTIONAL.
```

Figure 9-29   Portion of Schema Definition: Insertion and Retention Status for STUDENT-SCHEDULE and CLASS-ROSTER Sets

Suppose Student 150 decides to enroll in Class BD445. In this case, we need to create an ENROLLMENT record and connect it to the STUDENT-SCHED-ULE and CLASS-ROSTER sets. The following will accomplish these tasks:

```
6)  MOVE 150 TO STUDENT-NUMBER IN ENROLLMENT
    MOVE 'BD445' TO CLASS-NAME IN ENROLLMENT
    MOVE 'NG' TO GRADE IN ENROLLMENT
    STORE ENROLLMENT
    MOVE 150 TO SID IN STUDENT
    FIND ANY STUDENT USING SID
    CONNECT ENROLLMENT TO STUDENT-SCHEDULE
    MOVE 'BD445' TO NAME IN CLASS
    FIND ANY CLASS USING NAME
    CONNECT ENROLLMENT TO CLASS-ROSTER
```

The first four statements create the new ENROLLMENT record and insert it into the database. At that point, the new record is current of run-unit, current of ENROLLMENT, and current of STUDENT-SCHEDULE and CLASS-ROS-TER. The CONNECT command will connect the current of the named record (in the above cases this is ENROLLMENT) into the current occurrence of the set. Thus, before we can issue the CONNECT command, we have to issue a FIND to establish the correct current of set.

In the above example, the new ENROLLMENT record should be connected to the STUDENT-SCHEDULE occurrence owned by Student 150, and it should be connected to the CLASS-ROSTER occurrence owned by Class BD445. Thus, after the STORE command, 150 is moved to SID, and Student 150's record is established as the current of STUDENT-SCHEDULE. The CONNECT command then puts the new ENROLLMENT record into this occurrence of the STUDENT-SCHEDULE set. The processing is similar for the connection into the CLASS-ROSTER set.

To illustrate the use of the RECONNECT command, suppose that Class CS150 is canceled and all of the students in that class are assigned to CS250. Assume that for recordkeeping purposes, the ENROLLMENT records are not to be changed; they are just to be moved to the set owned by CS250.

```
7)  MOVE 'CS250' TO NAME OF CLASS
    FIND ANY CLASS USING NAME
    MOVE 'CS150' TO CLASS-NAME OF ENROLLMENT
    FIND ANY ENROLLMENT USING CLASS-NAME
    DOWHILE DB-STATUS = 0
            RECONNECT ENROLLMENT TO CLASS-ROSTER
            FIND DUPLICATE ENROLLMENT USING CLASS-NAME
    END-DO
```

RECONNECT works by disconnecting the current of the named record (here current of ENROLLMENT) from its present occurrence of the named set (here CLASS-NAME) and connecting it into the current occurrence of the named set. In this case, the first two statements make the current of CLASS-ROSTER be the set owned by CS250. Then, the first ENROLLMENT record for Class CS150 is located. It is reconnected by taking it out of whatever set occurrence it is presently in and connecting it into the set occurrence owned by CS250. Then, the next CS150 class is found, reconnected, etc., until no more CS150 classes can be found.

To illustrate the DISCONNECT command, suppose Student 200 drops the Class BD445. Again, for recordkeeping purposes, we do not want to erase the ENROLLMENT record from the database, but we do want to take it out of the CLASS-ROSTER set.

8) MOVE 200 TO STUDENT-NUMBER OF ENROLLMENT
   FIND ANY ENROLLMENT USING STUDENT-NUMBER
   DISCONNECT ENROLLMENT FROM CLASS-ROSTER

Processing other MANUAL sets If the insertion status is MANUAL and the retention status is FIXED, then both the DISCONNECT and the RECON-NECT commands are invalid. Once the record is connected, it must stay in its set occurrence.

If the insertion status is MANUAL and the retention status is MANDATORY, then DISCONNECT is invalid, but RECONNECT can be used. Once the record is connected, it must stay in some set occurrence. RECONNECT can be used to move it.

Processing AUTOMATIC sets When the set insertion status is AUTOMATIC, then the DBMS connects records into the set when they are created. This means that an appropriate record must be current of set before the new record is created. Suppose that both STUDENT-SCHEDULE and CLASS-ROSTER are defined to be AUTOMATIC sets. Then, before an ENROLLMENT record is created, the appropriate records must be made current of these sets.

Suppose that Student 150 decides to enroll in BD445. When the new ENROLLMENT record is created, we want the DBMS to connect it into the STUDENT-SCHEDULE set owned by STUDENT 150 and the CLASS-ROS-TER set owned by BD445. This can be accomplished as follows:

9) MOVE 150 TO SID IN STUDENT
   FIND ANY STUDENT USING SID
   MOVE 'BD445' TO NAME IN CLASS
   FIND ANY CLASS USING NAME
   MOVE 150 TO STUDENT-NUMBER OF ENROLLMENT
   MOVE 'BD445' TO CLASS-NAME OF ENROLLMENT
   MOVE 'NG' TO GRADE OF ENROLLMENT
   STORE ENROLLMENT

The first two statements make STUDENT 150 the current of STUDENT-SCHEDULE. The next two make Class 'BD445' the current of CLASS-ROSTER. The next three statements create the new ENROLLMENT record, and finally, the record is stored. At the time of the STORE, the DBMS will insert the record into the appropriate sets.

If a set with AUTOMATIC insertion status has OPTIONAL retention status, then, after the DBMS connects the record, the application program can RECONNECT it and DISCONNECT it. Also, if the record is disconnected, it can later be connected by the application program.

If a set with AUTOMATIC insertion status has MANDATORY retention status, then, after the DBMS connects the record, the application program can RECONNECT it into another set occurrence. The record can never be disconnected, and consequently, there will never be a need for the record to be connected.

If a set with AUTOMATIC insertion status has FIXED retention status, then, after the DBMS connects the record, neither DISCONNECT nor RECONNECT is valid. Further, there will never be a need for CONNECT.

The impact of set membership on ERASE commands

If a record owns a set occurrence, then special considerations apply when the record is deleted. The application program can request that all children (and children of children) be erased when the record is erased, or it can be more selective.

Suppose we want to delete a class and all of the ENROLLMENT records belonging to that class. We may do this because the class is canceled and we want to eliminate all evidence that anyone ever enrolled.

10) MOVE 'BD445' TO NAME OF CLASS
     FIND FOR UPDATE ANY CLASS USING NAME
     ERASE ALL CLASS

The keyword ALL in the above ERASE command directs the DBMS to erase all ENROLLMENT records belonging to this set.

If ALL is not specified in the ERASE command, then the result depends on the retention status of owned sets. If, for example, we execute an ERASE CLASS command, the result depends on the retention status defined for the set CLASS-ROSTER. If the retention status is MANDATORY, and if the record to be erased owns members, then the DBMS will refuse to process the ERASE. It does this because the members must belong to some set (MANDATORY retention), and the DBMS does not know what set occurrence to put them into.

If the retention status is FIXED, then the ERASE will be successful, and any owned ENROLLMENT records will be deleted by the DBMS. If the retention status is OPTIONAL, then the ERASE will be successful, and any owned ENROLLMENT records will be disconnected from the CLASS-ROSTER set. The disconnected ENROLLMENT records will remain in the database, however.

Using sets for record retrieval

Once records have been inserted in sets, set membership can be used to retrieve records by relationship. For example, suppose that ENROLLMENT records have been assigned to CLASS-ROSTER sets and that grades have been recorded in the Grade data-item of ENROLLMENT. The following statements will produce a listing of class numbers and grades for Class BA200:

```
11)  MOVE 'BA200' TO NAME IN CLASS
     FIND ANY CLASS USING NAME
     FIND FIRST ENROLLMENT WITHIN CLASS-ROSTER
     DOWHILE DB-STATUS = 0
          GET ENROLLMENT
          (process ENROLLMENT to print Student-number and Grade)
          FIND NEXT ENROLLMENT WITHIN CLASS-ROSTER
     END-DO
```

The first FIND statement establishes BA200 as the current of CLASS-ROSTER. The second FIND establishes the first ENROLLMENT record in the set owned by BA200 as the current of run-unit. The GET then retrieves that ENROLLMENT record.

The third FIND establishes the next ENROLLMENT record in BA200's set as the current of run-unit. This sets up the GET in the next iteration through the loop. The DBTG model provides a FIND LAST and FIND PRIOR capability as well.

Suppose we want more than the student's number and grade. Say we want the student's name and major as well. In this case, once we have the ENROLLMENT record, we want to go back to its STUDENT parent. This can be done as follows:

```
12)  MOVE 'BA200' TO NAME IN CLASS
     FIND ANY CLASS USING NAME
     FIND FIRST ENROLLMENT WITHIN CLASS-ROSTER
     DOWHILE DB-STATUS = 0
          GET ENROLLMENT
          (save Grade in working-storage)
          FIND OWNER WITHIN STUDENT-SCHEDULE
          GET STUDENT
          (process STUDENT record)
          FIND NEXT ENROLLMENT WITHIN CLASS-ROSTER
     END-DO
```

The FIND OWNER statement establishes the owner of the ENROLLMENT record as current of run-unit. The next GET retrieves the STUDENT record.

SUMMARY

The CODASYL DBTG model has evolved considerably since it was introduced in 1971. The CODASYL DDLC, the COBOL Language Committee, and the ANSI X3H2 Committee have all modified the form of the CODASYL DBTG model. As a consequence, there are many varieties and flavors of the DBTG model. In spite of this variation, there is a core of DBTG concepts. This core, as interpreted in the 1981 model, is discussed in this textbook.

A DBMS based on the DBTG model provides three views of data (similar to the ANSI/X3/SPARC data model). Users are connected to application programs that view the database through subschemas. Subschemas are subsets of the schema, which is the complete, logical view of the database. The schema is mapped to physical storage by the data structure description. In this text, we consider only the subschema and schema descriptions.

The fundamental data definition structures are data-items, records, and sets. Data-item is synonymous with attribute and with field. A record is a logical collection of data-items. A set is a one-to-many relationship among records. Sets have one owner record type and one or more member record types. An owner record defines an instance or occurrence of a set. A record can be a member of several set occurrences, as long as they are different types of sets. Also, according to the 1981 model, a record may be an owner and a member of the same set. In fact, an owner can own itself. A record may not, however, be a member of two occurrences of the same set type.

Trees and simple networks are readily represented by sets. Each one-to-many relationship is just replaced by a set. Complex networks cannot be directly represented by sets because a record cannot be a member of two occurrences of the same set. Instead, complex networks must be reduced to simple networks by defining intersection records.

Most DBTG DML operations are executed in two phases. Records are identified by a FIND command, and subsequently processed. Once a FIND has been executed, GET, MODIFY, ERASE, CONNECT, RECONNECT, or DISCONNECT commands can be issued. The STORE command does not follow this pattern because, before the STORE is executed, there is no record to be found.

The DBTG DML relies on currency indicators to mark records that have been found or processed. Current-of-run-unit, current-of-record, and current-of-set indicators are maintained. Also, several status registers are also maintained.

Assumptions and restrictions can be defined for set processing. For example, the insertion status of a set can be defined to be AUTOMATIC. If so, the DBMS will attempt to connect records automatically when they are created. Also, retention status can be defined as FIXED, MANDATORY, or OPTIONAL. This status determines which DML set processing commands will be allowed.

This chapter has surveyed the essence of the DBTG model. In the next chapter, we will illustrate these concepts by presenting DBTG schema and subschema designs for Sally Enterprises.

Group I Questions

9.1   Explain the significant events in the development of the CODASYL DBTG model that occurred in 1971, 1973, 1978, and 1981.

9.2   What was the significance of the proposal to make the 1971 DBTG model a national standard?

9.3   Explain the relationship of user, run-unit, application program, subschema, schema, data structure definition, database, and DBMS.

9.4   Define *data-item*. How are data-items related to domains? How are domains defined using the DBTG model?

9.5   Define *record* (in the sense of the DBTG).

9.6   Define the following terms and explain their purpose: *set, owner, member, set occurrence*.

9.7   Give an example of a set structure. Sketch two occurrences of this set.

9.8   Consider the following tree: School districts have schools, and schools have pupils (one record type) and teachers (another record type). Teachers, in turn, have past assignments. Show a DBTG representation of this tree. Describe two occurrences.

9.9   Consider the following simple network: Fathers have children and teachers teach children. Show a DBTG representation of this simple network. Describe two occurrences.

9.10 Consider the following complex network: Children have many hobbies, and a hobby is held by many children. Show a DBTG representation of the complex network. Describe two occurrences.

9.11 Give an example of a cycle. Sketch an occurrence. Show a DBTG representation of this cycle.

9.12 Give an example of a loop. Sketch an occurrence. Show a DBTG representation of this loop.

9.13 Describe a valid situation in which a record is an owner and a member of the set occurrence. Describe a valid situation in which a record is an owner of one occurrence and a member of another occurrence (both occurrences in the same set type).

9.14 List the DBTG currency indicators and describe situations in which each would be used.

9.15 List the DBTG status registers and indicate the role of each.

9.16 Explain the two-phased nature of the DBTG model.

For questions 9.17 through 9.22, provide pseudocode similar to that in the chapter. Refer to the following schema:

SALESPERSON with data-items NAME, AGE, SALARY
ORDER with data-items NUMBER, CUST-NAME, SALESPERSON-NAME, AMOUNT
CUSTOMER with data-items NAME, CITY, INDUSTRY-TYPE
SET SALE with owner SALESPERSON and member ORDER
SET PURCHASE with owner CUSTOMER and member ORDER

9.17 Retrieve:

    a. Customer with name ABC CONSTRUCTION

    b. Order with number 12345

    c. All orders for customer ABC CONSTRUCTION

9.18 Delete all orders for salesperson PARKS.

9.19 Change the industry type of ABC Construction to type 'J' (assume INDUSTRY-TYPE is a character data-item).

9.20 Store a new SALESPERSON record, name is CURTIS, age is 39, salary is 65,000.

9.21 Change the name of customer ABC Construction to SoftSystems. Make changes to ORDER records as well, assuming the retention status of PUR-CHASE is:

    a. OPTIONAL

    b. MANDATORY

    c. FIXED

9.22 Assume that both SALE and PURCHASE are MANUAL, OPTIONAL sets.

    a. Create an ORDER record and place it in the correct set occurrences of PURCHASE and SALE.

    b. Change the name of customer in an ORDER record and RECONNECT it to the correct occurrence (assume the record is already in an occurrence).

    c. Remove all ORDERs for customer JONES from sets to which they belong.

Group II Questions

9.23 Obtain references [22], [23], [24], and [25]. Summarize the changes in the DBTG model over the last ten years. Do you think the model has been improved or damaged by its development? Why or why not? Should the 1981 standard become a national standard? Why or why not?

9.24 Suppose that, instead of Grade, Position-number (denoted Position_number in Chapter 7) is kept in ENROLLMENT records. Assume that Position-numbers are assigned by adding 1 to the highest Position-number of all students already enrolled in the class. Show pseudocode to add a new ENROLLMENT record to any class. Compute and store the correct Position-number.

9.25 Compare and contrast the DBTG model with the relational model. Which model is easier to understand? Which do you think would be easier to use? For what applications would the DBTG model be preferred to the relational model? For what applications would the relational model be preferred to the DBTG model? Which, if either, of these models do you think should become a national standard?

Project

A. Locate a company in your community that uses a CODASYL DBTG DBMS. Interview personnel and determine how schemas and subschemas are designed. If possible, obtain a copy of a schema, subschema, and application program. Compare these to the concepts defined in this chapter.

10
Physical Design Using the
CODASYL DBTG Model

In this chapter we will apply the concepts of Chapter 9 to the design of a DBTG database for Sally Enterprises. This chapter has four sections. The first presents techniques for transforming SDM designs into DBTG designs. The second applies these techniques to the design of a schema for Sally Enterprises, and the third section presents two subschemas for this schema. Finally, the processing of these subschemas is discussed in the last section.

You will observe in this chapter the conflict in punctuation rules of various database models. When we refer to an item in the context of SDM, we will use an underscore (e.g., Where_used). When we refer to an item in the context of the DBTG model, we will use a hyphen and all capital letters (e.g., WHERE-USED). Do not let this difference confuse you; it has no signficance. This situation is unfortunate but currently unavoidable.

TRANSFORMING SDM DESIGNS TO CODASYL DBTG DESIGNS

To illustrate the design of DBTG databases, we will use the SDM design of Sally Enterprises Schema 3. For convenience, Figure 10-1 summarizes this logical design using SDM punctuation. This schema is probably familiar by now; it was developed in Chapter 6 and used for the relational model in Chapter 8 (Figure 8-22).

To represent an SDM design using the DBTG model, we need to transform each entity class, its attributes, and its relationships (expressed via inverse, matching, and derivation) to DBTG data-items, records, and sets.

The DBTG representation of SDM base classes is straightforward. Each base class simply becomes a DBTG record. Further, all attributes having a value class that is a subset of STRINGS are easily represented. We just define a DBTG data-item for all such attributes. Nonbase classes and attributes that are contained entities are not as simple.

370

RECIPE (Name, Sugar, Lemon, Water, Where_used)
> Key: Name
> Note: Where_used is a contained PITCHER tuple; multivalued

PITCHER (Number, Date, Recipe_used, Where_sold)
> Key: Number
> Notes: 1.   Where_sold is a contained ORDER tuple; multivalued
> 2.   Current_pitcher and Amount_left are class attributes

SALESPERSON (Name, Past_amounts_sold)
> Key: Name
> Note: Past_amounts_sold is contained attribute Amount of ORDER;
> multivalued

CUSTOMER (F_name, L_name, Family_member, Past_amount_purchased, Total_amount)
> Key: (F_name, L_name)
> Notes: 1.   Family is a contained CUSTOMER tuple having the same
> L_name; multivalued.
> 2.   Past_amounts_purchased is a contained attribute Amount of
> ORDER; multivalued
> 3.   Total_amount is SUM (Past_amounts_purchased)

ORDER (Customer, Pitcher, Salesperson, Date, Time, Amount)
> Key: (Customer, Pitcher, Time)
> Notes: 1.   Customer is a combination of F_name, L_name
> 2.   Pitcher is multivalued between 1 and 2; used for orders
> filled from two pitchers

BIG_BUYER (attributes of CUSTOMER, Nickname, FAVORITE_sport)
> Key: (F_name, L_name)
> Note: FAVORITE_sport is multivalued between 1 and 3

Figure 10-1   Summary of Logical Design (in SDM) for Sally Enterprises Schema 3

Representation of nonbase classes

As we have defined them, nonbase classes are subsets of base classes. They can be treated in one of two ways. First, we can do nothing about them. When the application program needs a BIG_BUYER, for example, it can simply search the database for qualifying records.

A second approach recognizes that for any subset, the relationship from the name of the subset to the members of the subset is one-to-many. Since this is true, every subset can be represented by a DBTG set. Using this approach for the BIG_BUYER example, a CLASSIFICATION record type would be defined;

it would have two records: BIG-BUYER and OTHER. Then a set, say CUS-TOMER-CLASS, would be defined with CLASSIFICATION as owner and CUSTOMER as members. All CUSTOMER records that qualify as big_buyers would be connected into the CUSTOMER-CLASS owned by BIG-BUYER. All other CUSTOMER records would be connected to the occurrence owned by OTHER. All subsets can be represented similarly. See Figure 10-2.

Representation of contained entity attributes

Each attribute that contains another entity as its value represents a relationship. For example, in Figure 10-1 the attribute Where_used of RECIPE is a PITCHER entity. It defines a relationship between RECIPE and PITCHER.

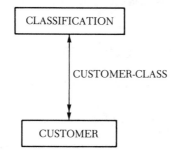

a. Set Representation of SDM Subset BIG_BUYER

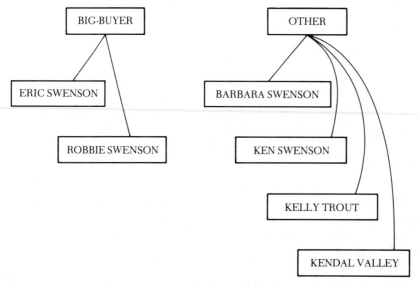

b. Occurrence

Figure 10-2 DBTG Set Representation of SDM Subset

Such contained entities are valid for presenting logical relationships, but they are impossible for physical representations. Two entities cannot be physically inside each other. In Chapter 8 we eliminated such contained tuples by representing them as joins of relations. In this chapter we will describe how to eliminate such contained entities by representing them with DBTG sets. Recall that relationships are defined in SDM with inverse, match, and derived attributes.

To illustrate the representation of inverse attributes, consider the RECIPE and PITCHER entities. Each recipe logically contains the pitchers that were made from it, and each pitcher logically contains the recipe that was used. Since we cannot physically put two entities inside of each other, we must look for another form of this arrangement. Observe that RECIPE and PITCHER tuples have a one-to-many relationship since many pitchers are made from the same recipe. See Figure 10-3a. Therefore, we can eliminate the containing attributes and replace them with a one-to-many relationship. Now, in the last chapter we

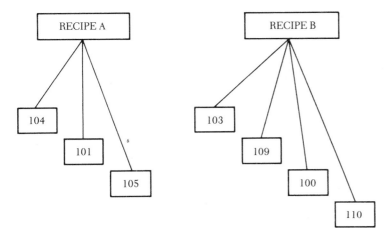

a.   One-to-Many Relationships Implied by RECIPE/PITCHER Relationship

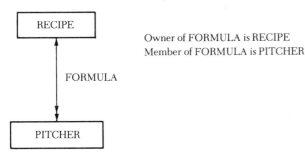

Owner of FORMULA is RECIPE
Member of FORMULA is PITCHER

b.   DBTG Set Representation of RECIPE/PITCHER Relationship

Figure 10-3   Use of DBTG Sets to Represent SDM Contained Entities

discussed how to represent one-to-many relationships with DBTG sets. We just replace each one-to-many relationship with a set. Figure 10-3b shows the DBTG representation of the relationship between RECIPE and PITCHER.

A similar process can be followed for the contained entities between SALES-PERSON and ORDER. One salesperson generates many orders, but an order is generated by only one salesperson. Thus the attributes containing entities can be removed and replaced by one-to-many relationships. These relationships can, in turn, be represented by DBTG sets.

Both the RECIPE/PITCHER and the SALESPERSON/ORDER relationships are defined by SDM *inverse attributes*. The representation of *match attributes* is less convenient. Consider the match attribute Past_amounts_purchased in CUSTOMER. Past_amounts_purchased consists of just part of the ORDER entity; it is the attribute, Amount. Since Past_amounts_purchased is multivalued, it represents a one-to-many relationship (from CUSTOMER to ORDER). Therefore, to associate Amount of ORDER with CUSTOMER, we define a DBTG set between CUSTOMER and ORDER. To obtain Amount, however, the application programs must access this set and extract Amount from all ORDERs that belong to the CUSTOMER. This process would yield all values of Amount. Total_amount could then be computed from these values.

Thus DBTG sets can be used to represent match attributes as well as inverse attributes. The process of obtaining the matching values, however, must be done by application program. The DBTG model has no facility to allow matching attributes to be computed automatically.

The third SDM form of relationship results from *derivations*. Consider Figure 10-1, where the CUSTOMER entities have a relationship to other entities with the same last name. The key to representing this relationship with the DBTG model is to realize that the relationship from last name to family member is one-to-many. Thus we can represent a family by creating a new record, called *FAMILY-NAME*, and connecting it via a set (FAMILY) to CUSTOMER records. (We are making the assumption that all family members have the same last name. This is obviously incorrect, and you have an opportunity to fix this error in project A at the end of this chapter.)

So far all relationships have been one-to-many. What happens, however, when relationships are many-to-many? Consider the entities between PITCHER and ORDER. They do not represent a one-to-many relationship. Instead, they represent a two-to-many relationship, since, according to note 2 under PITCHER in Figure 10-1, two pitchers can be related to one order.

There are two possibilities for representing this relationship with the DBTG model. We could use a strategy like the one used for the relational model in Chapter 8. When an order is filled from two pitchers, we simply create two records in the ORDER file. Each one is owned by a different pitcher.

A second strategy is to recognize this two-to-many relationship as a special case of a complex relationship. Therefore, we can represent this relationship using the same strategy as is used for complex relationships in general: transform the complex network into a simple network by creating an intersection record.

Then, represent the one-to-many relationships in the simple network with DBTG sets.

For Sally Enterprises, few orders will be filled from two pitchers. Therefore, the second strategy would be wasteful. For most orders, the relationship from the order to the intersection record would be one-to-one. Hence we will follow the first strategy; orders filled from two pitchers will have two ORDER records. If Sally's users find this undesirable, we can mark the two records in a special way and combine them when producing reports.

The last relationship in Figure 10-1 that needs to be represented concerns BIG_BUYERs. First, we must decide how the CUSTOMER classification will be represented. As stated, the classification can be ignored, and qualifying records found by searching, or the classification can be represented by a set. In this case, there is only one subset: BIG-BUYER. All other records are OTHER. Since there is only a binary categorization, a set seems wasteful. Thus we will construct no special structure for BIG BUYERs, but will find them by sequential search when necessary.

Sally wants to store the nickname and up to three favorite sports for BIG-BUYERs, however. To meet this need, we will create space in every CUS-TOMER record for a nickname to be stored. Sally can fill this space only for large purchasers, if she wants. Then, we will create a separate FAVORITE-SPORT record type. Each BIG BUYER can own a set of up to three of these records.

Figure 10-4 presents a data structure diagram of the schema design for Sally

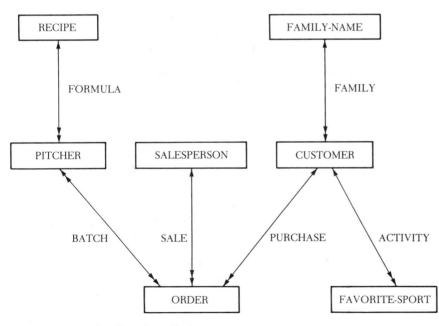

Figure 10-4   DSD of Schema for Sally Enterprises

```
FIRST
LAST
NEXT
PRIOR
SYSTEM DEFAULT
SORTED
```

Figure 10-5   DBTG Set Member Ordering Options

Enterprises. As discussed, there are seven record types and six sets. The names of the records and sets are shown in Figure 10-4.

More DBTG set concepts

In the last chapter, we discussed the major concepts of DBTG sets. Several details were omitted, however. Since we will need these details for the DBTG schema descriptions, we discuss them now.

Member record ordering   Examine the set occurrences in Figure 10-3. Recipe A owns PITCHERs 104, 101, and 105. As shown, these members appear to be in random order. The DBTG model allows the database designer, however, to define a particular order for set members. As shown in Figure 10-5, several options are allowed.

If the set order is FIRST, then when new records are connected to a set occurrence, they will be placed (logically, not physically) in the first position. Thus the set members will occur in reverse chronological order. If the set order is LAST, then new records will be placed in the last position. Set members will be in chronological order.

If the order is NEXT, then new members will be connected in the next position after the position of current of set member. In Figure 10-3, if the order of the FORMULA set is NEXT, and if PITCHER 101 is the current of FORMULA, then a new record would be connected between 101 and 105. If the order is PRIOR, and if PITCHER 101 is the current record, then a new record would be connected between 104 and 101. If the current were the owner, and the order were NEXT (PRIOR), then a new record would be placed in the front (back) of the set.

If set order is defined as SYSTEM DEFAULT, then the designer is stating that the order is immaterial to the application. The DBMS can determine the order. Finally, set members can be SORTED on the value of a data-item they

Set Name	Member Record Type	Order of Member Records
FORMULA	PITCHER	Chronological
BATCH	L-ORDER	Reverse chronological
SALE	L-ORDER	Sorted by Customer-name
PURCHASE	L-ORDER	Sorted by Salesperson
FAMILY	CUSTOMER	Arbitrary
ACTIVITY	FAVORITE-SPORT	Prior

Figure 10-6 Order of Set Member Records

contain. If so, then the name of the data-item is identified in a separate KEY clause as will be shown.

The design team for Sally Enterprises decided on the member orders shown in Figure 10-6. These decisions were made on the basis of the most frequent processing requirements.

Set interrecord constraints The DBTG model allows constraints between owner and member records to be defined in the schema. These constraints can exist only when owner and member records have data-items sharing a common domain. (The term *domain* is not a DBTG term, but it ought to be.) Interrecord constraints for the set records of Sally Enterprises are listed in Figure 10-7. As you will see, these constraints are described in two ways using the DBTG model.

There is debate among database experts regarding the desirability of creating sets with such constraints. When the constraints are enforced, the sets become

Set Name	Constraint between Owners and Members
FORMULA	R-NAME in RECIPE = RECIPE-USED in PITCHER
BATCH	P-NUMBER in PITCHER = PITCHER-NUMBER in L-ORDER
SALE	S-NAME in SALESPERSON = SALESPERSON in L-ORDER
PURCHASE	F-NAME and L-NAME in CUSTOMER = CUST = F-NAME and CUST = L-NAME in L-ORDER
FAMILY	FAM = NAME in FAMILY-NAME = L-NAME in CUSTOMER
ACTIVITY	None

Figure 10-7 Interrecord Constraints

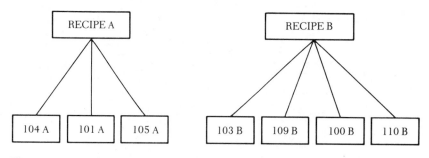

Figure 10-8 Match between R-NAME in RECIPE and RECIPE-USED in PITCHER

redundant. For example, consider Figure 10-8. Two set occurrences of FOR-MULA are shown—one for RECIPE A and the other for RECIPE B. Given the constraint, R-NAME in RECIPE = RECIPE-USED in PITCHER, the set memberships are redundant. Enforcing the constraints is the same as connecting records into sets.

There are two views of this situation. According to one view, such sets are *inessential* and should be avoided. Either the constraint should be expressed and the set not defined, or the set defined and the duplicative data-item (here RECIPE-USED) in the member omitted.

The other view is that this situation is entirely appropriate. The sets exist to facilitate DML FIND processing. At the same time, the duplicative data-items exist so that data will not be buried in overhead structures (this occurs when the fact that PITCHER 104 was based on RECIPE A is not stored as part of PITCHER 104, but rather is deduced from the fact that PITCHER 104 is in the set owned by RECIPE A). This position holds that facts should be recorded in data-items, not in set overhead.

You can decide for yourself. I favor the latter position. Sets *would be* inessential if the DBTG DML conveniently allowed an equivalent of the relational join. There is no such equivalent, however, and the logic of join operations must be coded into application programs. Consequently, inessential sets are only inessential for DDL purposes; they are essential for DML purposes. Also, I agree that little good is served by burying data in overhead.

System sets When records are stored in the database, they are placed in no particular logical or physical order. Rather, the DBMS places records wherever it wants. Sometimes, however, the logic of application programs necessitates that records be processed sequentially in some order. For example, a payroll program may require that EMPLOYEE records be retrieved in Employee-number order.

To support this type of processing, the DBTG model allows records to be logically ordered. This ordering is done by defining a *system set*. A system set is a special set that has only one occurrence—the occurrence owned by the

Set Name	Insertion Status	Retention Status
FORMULA	AUTOMATIC	FIXED
BATCH	AUTOMATIC	FIXED
SALE	AUTOMATIC	MANDATORY
PURCHASE	MANUAL	FIXED
FAMILY	MANUAL	OPTIONAL
ACTIVITY	MANUAL	MANDATORY

Note: MANUAL on PURCHASE because CUSTOMER may not exist at time of sale.

Figure 10-9   Summary of Set Insertion and Retention Status

DBMS. To provide sequential processing, the set is defined as an ordered set based on one or more fields. Thus, if RECIPE records are to be processed sequentially in order of R-NAME, a system set having RECIPE records as members and order of R-NAME would be created. The set-oriented FIND command can then be used to process records in order. We will illustrate this capability in the next section.

Set insertion and retention status for Sally Enterprises   We discussed the concept of insertion and retention status in the last chapter. Insertion status indicates whether the DBMS or the application program inserts records. Retention status determines how, if at all, records can be removed from sets. Figure 10-9 lists the insertion and retention status of sets decided upon by the project team at Sally Enterprises.

DBTG schema for Sally Enterprises

This section presents a schema description for Sally Enterprises. The general format for a 1981 DBTG schema description is shown in Figure 10-10. We will follow this general form and use the syntax that is current as of late 1982. We will not pay attention to syntactic details, however, because they are evolving. Since this is a model, such details are not too important, in any case. Strive to understand the concepts.

Figure 10-11 shows a schema description for Sally Enterprises. This schema describes records, data-items, and sets. According to the 1981 standard, no punctuation is required because keywords indicate the boundaries of phrases and expressions.

The word *ORDER* is a reserved keyword. Consequently, we must rename the ORDER record. In Figure 10-11 and subsequent figures, ORDER is called *L-ORDER* (for lemonade order).

SCHEMA NAME IS _____

RECORD NAME IS _____

    Optional DUPLICATES clauses

    DATA-ITEM clauses

(Repetitions of RECORD descriptions)

SET NAME IS _____

    OWNER clause

    ORDER clause

    MEMBER clause

    INSERTION/RETENTION clause

    Optional KEY clause

    Optional CHECK clause

    Optional SELECTION clause

(Repetitions of SET descriptions. . .)

Figure 10-10   General Format of DBTG Schema Description

Record definitions   The record definitions are largely self-explanatory. The DUPLICATES statement is used to identify unique data-items. The presence of this statement does not imply that the data-item will be a key (it did in earlier versions of DBTG model).

Be sure you understand the implications when there are two or more DUPLI-CATES statements. For example, in CUSTOMER, duplicates are not allowed for the combination F-NAME, L-NAME, and they are not allowed for NICK-NAME. This means that a first name may be duplicated and a last name may be duplicated, but the combination of a first name and a last name may not. Further, the second DUPLICATES statement means that no NICKNAME may be repeated. Contrast this situation with the situation if only one DUPLICATES statement is coded. Be certain you understand the meaning of a phrase such as DUPLICATES ARE NOT ALLOWED FOR F-NAME, L-NAME, NICKNAME.

Two digits are sometimes listed after the type, FIXED. To understand this, consider the definition of SUGAR in the RECIPE record. SUGAR is type FIXED 4 2. This means that sugar data-items have four decimal places, with two places to the right of the FIXED decimal point. Thus the format of sugar is 99.99 (but the decimal point is assumed—it will not physically appear in the data). When only one digit is coded after FIXED, then the decimal point is assumed to be on the far right. Thus the format of FIXED 3 is 999.

For consistency, all data-item formats correspond to the domain definitions used in Chapter 8. See Figure 8-29.

```
SCHEMA NAME IS LEMONADE-SALES
      RECORD NAME IS RECIPE
           DUPLICATES ARE NOT ALLOWED FOR R-NAME
           R-NAME                TYPE IS    CHARACTER  10
           SUGAR                 TYPE IS    FIXED           4    2
           LEMON                 TYPE IS    FIXED           1
                                 CHECK IS   NOT EQUAL       0
           WATER                 TYPE IS    FIXED           3    2

      RECORD NAME IS PITCHER
           DUPLICATES ARE NOT ALLOWED FOR P-NUMBER
           P-NUMBER              TYPE IS    FIXED           3
                                 CHECK IS   LESS THAN     500
           DATE                  TYPE IS    FIXED           6
           RECIPE-USED           TYPE IS    CHARACTER  10

      RECORD NAME IS SALESPERSON
           DUPLICATES ARE NOT ALLOWED FOR S-NAME
           S-NAME                TYPE IS    CHARACTER  20

      RECORD NAME IS CUSTOMER
           DUPLICATES ARE NOT ALLOWED FOR F-NAME, L-NAME
           DUPLICATES ARE NOT ALLOWED FOR NICKNAME
           F-NAME                TYPE IS    CHARACTER  10
           L-NAME                TYPE IS    CHARACTER  20
           NICKNAME              TYPE IS    CHARACTER  20

      RECORD NAME IS L-ORDER
           CUST-F-NAME           TYPE IS    CHARACTER  10
           CUST-L-NAME           TYPE IS    CHARACTER  20
           PITCHER-NUMBER        TYPE IS    FIXED           3
                                 CHECK IS   LESS THAN     500
           SALESPERSON           TYPE IS    CHARACTER  20
           DATE                  TYPE IS    FIXED           6
           TIME                  TYPE IS    FIXED           4    2
           AMOUNT                TYPE IS    FIXED           3    2

      RECORD NAME IS FAMILY-NAME
           DUPLICATES ARE NOT ALLOWED FOR FAM-NAME
           FAM-NAME              TYPE IS    CHARACTER  20

      RECORD NAME IS FAVORITE-SPORT
           DUPLICATES ARE NOT ALLOWED FOR FS-F-NAME, FS-L-NAME, SPORT-NAME
           FS-F-NAME             TYPE IS    CHARACTER  10
           FS-L-NAME             TYPE IS    CHARACTER  20
           SPORT-NAME            TYPE IS    CHARACTER  10

      SET NAME IS FORMULA
           OWNER IS RECIPE
           ORDER IS LAST
           MEMBER IS PITCHER
           INSERTION IS AUTOMATIC, RETENTION IS FIXED
           CHECK IS R-NAME IN RECIPE = RECIPE-USED IN PITCHER
           SET SELECTION IS BY VALUE OF R-NAME
```

Figure 10-11   DBTG Schema Description for Sally Enterprises Logical Schema 3

```
        SET NAME IS BATCH
             OWNER IS PITCHER
             ORDER IS FIRST
             MEMBER IS L-ORDER
             INSERTION IS AUTOMATIC; RETENTION IS FIXED
             SET SELECTION IS STRUCTURAL PITCHER-NUMBER = P-NUMBER

        SET NAME IS SALE
             OWNER IS SALESPERSON
             ORDER IS SORTED BY DEFINED KEYS
             MEMBER IS L-ORDER
             INSERTION IS AUTOMATIC; RETENTION IS MANDATORY
             KEY IS ASCENDING CUST-L-NAME, CUST-F-NAME
             SET SELECTION IS STRUCTURAL SALESPERSON = S-NAME

        SET NAME IS PURCHASE
             OWNER IS CUSTOMER
             ORDER IS SORTED BY DEFINED KEYS
             MEMBER IS L-ORDER
             INSERTION IS MANUAL; RETENTION IS FIXED
             KEY IS ASCENDING SALESPERSON
             SET SELECTION IS STRUCTURAL      CUST-F-NAME = F-NAME
                                      AND     CUST-L-NAME = L-NAME

        SET NAME IS FAMILY
             OWNER IS FAMILY-NAME
             ORDER IS SYSTEM DEFAULT
             MEMBER IS CUSTOMER
             INSERTION IS MANUAL; RETENTION IS OPTIONAL
             CHECK IS L-NAME IN CUSTOMER = FAM-NAME IN FAMILY-NAME

        SET NAME IS ACTIVITY
             OWNER IS CUSTOMER
             ORDER IS PRIOR
             MEMBER IS FAVORITE-SPORT
             INSERTION IS MANUAL; RETENTION IS MANDATORY
             SET SELECTION IS BY VALUE OF F-NAME, L-NAME

        SET NAME IS RECIPE-SEQUENCE
             OWNER IS SYSTEM
             ORDER IS SORTED BY DEFINED KEYS
             MEMBER IS RECIPE
             INSERTION IS AUTOMATIC; RETENTION IS FIXED
             KEY IS ASCENDING R-NAME

    END SCHEMA
```

Figure 10-11 (Cont'd.)

Set definitions According to the 1981 report, set definitions must appear after the set's owner and member records have been defined. For convenience here, all sets have been defined together at the end of Figure 10-11. Consider the definition of FORMULA. The owner of this set is RECIPE, the order is LAST, and the member is PITCHER. (Phrases must occur in the order shown.) As stated, "ORDER IS LAST" means that when new members are connected into the set, they will be placed last. Hence the records will appear in chronological order in the set.

The fourth statement in the FORMULA definition describes member record insertion and retention status. Next, a CHECK statement defines a constraint between owner and member records. The CHECK statement means that the DBMS is not to CONNECT a member to an owner unless the value of R-NAME in RECIPE (the owner) matches the value of RECIPE-USED in PITCHER (the member). If an application program attempts to make a connection that violates this constraint, an error condition will occur.

The SET SELECTION statement defines a default selection for CONNECT and FIND (via set) commands. According to Figure 10-11, the set selection for FORMULA is BY VALUE OF R-NAME. This means that when a CONNECT or FIND (via set) is issued, the DBMS is to use the current value of R-NAME to identify an owner. For example, suppose at some point in processing, the value of R-NAME is 'A', and at that point a CONNECT RECORD PITCHER TO SET FORMULA is issued. In this case, the current record of PITCHER will be connected into the set occurrence owned by RECIPE 'A'. However, because of the CHECK clause, the connection will be successful only if the value of RECIPE-USED in the current of PITCHER is also 'A'.

Actually, in the case of FORMULA, the CONNECT instruction will be issued automatically by the DBMS when a PITCHER record is created. This step occurs because the insertion status of FORMULA is AUTOMATIC. Further, since the retention status is FIXED, PITCHER records cannot be disconnected. Thus the only connection that will ever occur is done by the DBMS during PITCHER record creation.

Observe the interaction of set insertion and retention status, of CHECK statements, and of SET SELECTION statements. The three operate together to constrain, sometimes severely, the operations allowed on the set. Opponents of the DBTG model dislike this interaction. They say it is too mysterious; if the application programmer does not recall substantial detail, seemingly magical results can occur.

Consider the definition of the set BATCH. Since the order of BATCH is FIRST, the records will be kept in reverse chronological order (the design team wanted the most recent order first in the set because the most recent order is the one most frequently requested). BATCH has no CHECK clause, as such, but the SET SELECTION statement incorporates the essence of a CHECK. The set selection for BATCH is STRUCTURAL PITCHER-NUMBER = P-NUMBER. This statement means that when a CONNECT is issued, the DBMS is to find a PITCHER record having, as its value of P-NUMBER, the current value of PITCHER-NUMBER. For example, suppose the current of L-ORDER has a value of 104 for PITCHER-NUMBER. When a CONNECT RECORD L-ORDER TO BATCH is issued, the DBMS will search for a PITCHER having

104 as its value of P-NUMBER. If one is found, the current of L-ORDER will be connected into the set. Otherwise, the CONNECT fails.

As with FORMULA, the application program will never issue a CONNECT on BATCH. The reason is that the insertion status of BATCH is AUTOMATIC, and the retention status is FIXED. Instead, when the L-ORDER record is created, the DBMS will make the CONNECT. If the CONNECT fails, the L-ORDER record cannot be stored in the database.

For STRUCTURAL SET SELECTION to work, the field value in the owner must have unique values. In the case of BATCH, P-NUMBER in PITCHER must be unique. If P-NUMBER were not unique, then the DBMS would not know which PITCHER record to use as owner. Hence, when an owner field is defined in a STRUCTURAL SET SELECTION statement, the field must have been declared in a DUPLICATES NOT ALLOWED statement in the record definition.

The SALE set is similar to BATCH and FORMULA except that the order of the set is SORTED. Here, ORDER IS SORTED BY DEFINED KEYS. This statement means that the DBMS is to place records in sets so as to preserve an order defined in the KEY clause that follows. (Other types of member sorting are defined in the 1981 report, but we will not discuss them.) The KEY clause specifies that the order is to be ascending, and it lists two data-items. The order of the data-items is significant. The leftmost data-item is the major sort key, the rightmost data-item is the minor key. In this example, L-ORDER records are to be organized in the set so that members are sorted by last name, and then by first name. Figure 10-12 shows two occurrences of this set.

The PURCHASE set is similar to other sets. The unique aspect of this set is that two fields are defined for SET SELECTION. This simply means there must be a match on both fields for the record to be successfully connected. Also, since the insertion status of this set is MANUAL, if records are to be inserted into PURCHASE, the application program must issue the CONNECT.

The FAMILY set has order of SYSTEM DEFAULT. This means that the order of members in this set is immaterial to the applications. The DBMS can put members into sets in whatever order it wants. The ACTIVITY set has SET SELECTION BY VALUE OF two data-items. When a CONNECT is issued, the DBMS will look for a CUSTOMER record matching the current value of both F-NAME and L-NAME.

DBTG SUBSCHEMA DESCRIPTIONS

As stated in Chapter 9, and shown in Figure 9-2, application programs in the DBTG model do not access the database schema directly. Instead, they view the database via subschemas. These subschemas are basically subsets of the schema.

Unfortunately, there is currently no accepted DBTG standard regarding sub-schema descriptions. The 1981 ANSI schema language (which we have been

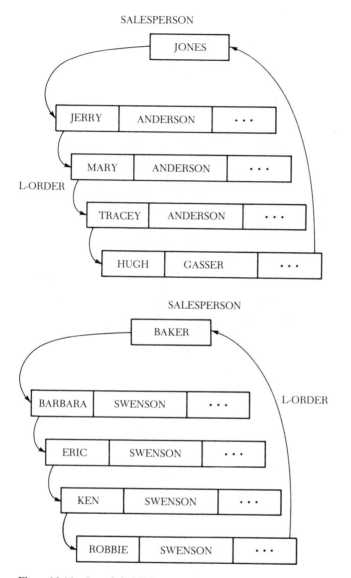

SALESPERSON

JONES

JERRY | ANDERSON | . . .

MARY | ANDERSON | . . .

L-ORDER

TRACEY | ANDERSON | . . .

HUGH | GASSER | . . .

SALESPERSON

BAKER

BARBARA | SWENSON | . . .   L-ORDER

ERIC | SWENSON | . . .

KEN | SWENSON | . . .

ROBBIE | SWENSON | . . .

Figure 10-12   Sorted SALE Set (KEY IS ASCENDING CUST-L-NAME, CUST-F-NAME)

using) is incompatible with the 1978 COBOL Language Committee subschema language. In light of this situation, we will adjust the 1978 standard to the conventions of the 1981 standard as best as possible. Even so, you will note incompatibilities. For example, sentences in the subschema language are terminated by periods. In the schema language, they are not. Also, if you know COBOL, you will see a definite COBOL resemblance to the subschema language.

Subschemas for Sally Enterprises

The three major purposes of a subschema are to rename database components, to restrict the view of the database, and to reorder data-items as desired. We will illustrate these purposes with two subschemas: PRODUCTION and FAMILY-MEMBER.

PRODUCTION subschema   Several items have been renamed in this subschema. The record PITCHER has been renamed PRODUCTION-UNIT; the set BATCH has been renamed SALES-BY-UNIT, and the data-item PITCHER-NUMBER (in L-ORDER) has been renamed BATCH-ID. Usually, aliases are defined like this because users have different names for common database entities.

Concerning restricting the view of the database, a subschema can omit records, data-items, or sets that are defined in the schema. As shown in Figure 10-13, the PRODUCTION subschema contains only RECIPE, PRODUCTION-UNIT (alias PITCHER), and L-ORDER records. The other schema records have been omitted because the application programs that access PRODUCTION have no need to see them.

Also, only FORMULA and SALES-BY-UNIT (alias BATCH) sets are included in this subschema. Sets that involve records that are omitted in this subschema must also be omitted. Although this subschema does include both of the sets that involve RECIPE, PRODUCTION-UNIT (alias PITCHER), and L-ORDER records, this was not mandatory. Either or both of these sets could be omitted

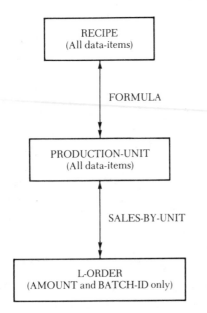

Figure 10-13   Format of PRODUCTION Subschema

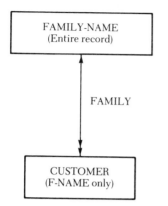

Figure 10-14 Format of FAMILY-MEMBER Subschema

as well. Further, only part of L-ORDER records are defined in this subschema. The BATCH-ID (alias PITCHER-NUMBER) and AMOUNT data-items are included; the remaining data-items exist, but are not visible to the application programs that access this subschema.

Finally, the format of the L-ORDER record has been modified by reordering the data-items. In the schema, PITCHER-NUMBER comes before AMOUNT; in the PRODUCTION subschema, BATCH-ID (alias PITCHER-NUMBER) comes after AMOUNT. In general, the format of any subschema record can be reorganized in this way.

FAMILY-MEMBER subschema   Figure 10-14 depicts a second subschema, FAMILY-MEMBER. This subschema contains only two records and one set. Furthermore, only the F-NAME data-item of CUSTOMER is present in this subschema. No aliases have been defined in FAMILY-MEMBER, and the order of data-items in records is unchanged.

Subschema definitions

The general format of a subschema definition is shown in Figure 10-15. Each subschema description has three divisions. The TITLE DIVISION contains the name of the subschema, the MAPPING DIVISION contains alias descriptions, and the STRUCTURE DIVISION indicates which items in the schema are to be present in the subschema.

Figure 10-16 presents a subschema description for PRODUCTION. The three aliases described above are defined in the ALIAS SECTION. In the STRUC-TURE DIVISION, both RECIPE and PRODUCTION-UNIT (the new name for PITCHER) records have the keyword ALL. This keyword means that all data-items are to be present in the subschema in the order in which they are defined in the schema.

```
TITLE DIVISION.
(subschema name)
MAPPING DIVISION.
ALIAS SECTION.
(alternate names for records or sets)
STRUCTURE DIVISION.
RECORD SECTION.
(records and data-items to appear in the subschema)
SET SECTION.
(sets to appear in the subschema)
```

Figure 10-15   Format of Subschema, 1978 Specification

```
TITLE DIVISION.
SS    PRODUCTION WITHIN LEMONADE-SALES.
MAPPING DIVISION.
ALIAS SECTION.
AD    RECORD PITCHER IS PRODUCTION-UNIT.
AD    SET BATCH IS SALES-BY-UNIT.
AD    PITCHER-NUMBER IS BATCH-ID.
STRUCTURE DIVISION.
RECORD SECTION.
01    RECIPE ALL.
01    PRODUCTION-UNIT ALL.
01    L-ORDER.
      05    AMOUNT    PIC 9V99.
      05    BATCH-ID  PIC 999.
SET SECTION.
SD    FORMULA.
SD    SALES-BY-UNIT.
```

Figure 10-16   PRODUCTION Subschema Description

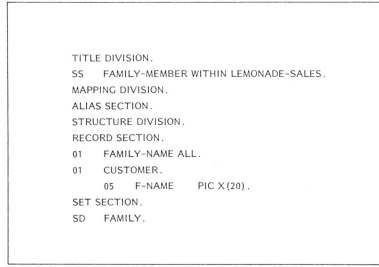

```
        TITLE DIVISION.
        SS    FAMILY-MEMBER WITHIN LEMONADE-SALES.
        MAPPING DIVISION.
        ALIAS SECTION.
        STRUCTURE DIVISION.
        RECORD SECTION.
        01    FAMILY-NAME ALL.
        01    CUSTOMER.
              05    F-NAME    PIC X(20).
        SET SECTION.
        SD    FAMILY.
```

Figure 10-17   FAMILY-MEMBER Subschema Description

The subschema description (or a version of it) will be placed in the application program's DATA DIVISION (or equivalent). When this occurs, the entry, REC-IPE ALL, will be replaced by the complete record description. This description will have a valid COBOL (or other language equivalent) structure including appropriate PICTURE clauses (data format definitions).

The FAMILY-MEMBER subschema description is presented in Figure 10-17. Entries are similar to those for PRODUCTION.

Processing the Subschemas

Application programs can process the LEMONADE-SALES schema via either of the two subschemas that have been defined: PRODUCTION or FAMILY-MEMBER. In this section we will illustrate the logic of several data manipulation operations. First, however, you need to understand how data definitions have restricted DML operation.

Restrictions on DML processing

The definitions of the LEMONADE-SALES schema and the PRODUCTION and FAMILY-MEMBER subschemas have placed restrictions on which DML operations will be allowed. Some of these restrictions are obvious and some others are quite surprising. The table in Figure 10-18a shows restrictions on DML command by record type. Consider each record in turn.

Record Name

	RECIPE	PITCHER (Alias PRODUCTION-UNIT)	L-ORDER
STORE	OK	OK, if RECIPE exists that matches RECIPE-USED value	No; some data-items invisible
ERASE	OK, but can cause PITCHER and L-ORDER to be erased	OK, but can cause L-ORDER records to be erased	OK; will cause disconnection from invisible sets
MODIFY	OK, except can't change R-NAME	OK, except can't change P-NUMBER or RECIPE-USED	Yes, AMOUNT No, BATCH-ID

a. Restrictions on PRODUCTION Record Processing

Set Name

	FORMULA	SALES-BY-UNIT
CONNECT	No	No
RECONNECT	No	No
DISCONNECT	No	No

b. Restrictions on PRODUCTION Set Processing

Figure 10-18 PRODUCTION Processing Restrictions

Restrictions on RECIPE processing RECIPE records can be stored in the database without restriction. They can also be erased, but doing so will cause any PITCHER (alias PRODUCTION-UNIT) records that belong to the erased RECIPE record to be erased as well. For example, if PITCHERs 101 and 104 belong to the set owned by RECIPE A, and if RECIPE A is erased, then PITCHERs 101 and 104 will also be erased. This effect occurs because the RETENTION status of FORMULA is fixed. By convention, when the owner of a FIXED set is erased, the members are erased as well.

These implied deletions will cascade downward. When a PITCHER record is erased, all of the L-ORDER records that it owns will be also be erased. (Again, this occurs because L-ORDER records are FIXED members of the

BATCH set owned by PITCHER records.) As an additional complication, when L-ORDER records are erased, they will be deleted from SALE and PUR-CHASE sets as well. Since these sets are not present in the PRODUCTION subschema, the application programmer may not even know these deletions are occurring.

(Thus the ramifications of erasing a RECIPE record are great. Such surprising activity can make developing and testing application programs a nightmare. Criticism of the DBTG model on this issue may well be justified.)

RECIPE records can be modified, but with one restriction. The R-NAME field cannot be changed. The reason for this is that R-NAME is part of a CHECK statement in the definition of the FORMULA set. If R-NAME is changed, the CHECK will be violated, and whatever PITCHER records are owned must be disconnected. However, the retention status of FORMULA is FIXED. Thus members cannot be disconnected. As a consequence, if the application program attempts to change R-NAME, the DBMS will generate an error message.

Restrictions on PRODUCT-UNIT (alias PITCHER) processing
Considering restrictions on the processing of PITCHER (alias PRODUC-TION-UNIT) records, there is a limitation on STORE operations. A new PITCHER can only be stored if the appropriate RECIPE set owner exists. For example, to store a new PITCHER with a value of 'B' for RECIPE-USED, a RECIPE with an R-NAME of B must already exist. The reason for this is that the insertion status of FORMULA is AUTOMATIC. When the PITCHER is stored, the DBMS will attempt to connect the pitcher to the RECIPE parent. For a CHECK condition in FORMULA to be acceptable, the RECIPE record must already exist.

PRODUCTION-UNIT records can be erased from the database. However, doing so will cause the erasure of owned L-ORDER records. Such derived erasures may have undesirable consequences in other subschemas as described previously.

Only the DATE data-item of PITCHER records can be modified. Neither P-NUMBER nor RECIPE-USED can be changed. RECIPE-USED cannot be changed because it is part of a CHECK condition on set FORMULA, and the retention status of FORMULA is FIXED. P-NUMBER cannot be changed because it is part of a structural SET OCCURRENCE statement for set BATCH (alias SALES-BY-UNIT). If P-NUMBER is changed, then the STRUCTURAL statement will be violated. This means the L-ORDER members must be dis-connected. That action cannot be done, however, because the retention status of L-ORDER is FIXED.

Restrictions on L-ORDER processing
The restrictions on L-ORDER rec-ords are slightly different, since L-ORDER does not own any sets. First, L-ORDER records cannot be stored by users of PRODUCTION because not all of the record is visible. The names of customers and salespeople, as well as the

date and time of the order, are invisible. The absence of SALESPERSON is the most critical, because SALESPERSON is part of a STRUCTURAL SET SELECTION in the set SALE. Further, the insertion status of SALE is AUTO-MATIC. This means that if the user of PRODUCTION were to attempt to STORE L-ORDER, the DBMS would attempt to connect the new record into the SALE set. However, the value of SALESPERSON would be undetermined because SALESPERSON is excluded from the subschema. (The 1981 DBTG report includes the concept of *default values;* such values are supplied by the DBMS for situations like this. The precise processing of these values is unclear.)

L-ORDER records can be erased without causing the erasure of other records because L-ORDER owns no sets. However, if an L-ORDER record is erased, it will be removed from sets that are not visible in PRODUCTION, namely, SALE and PURCHASE. This may have undesirable consequences on users of other subschemas.

The AMOUNT data-item in L-ORDER can be changed. BATCH-ID (alias PITCHER-NUMBER) cannot be changed. It is part of a STRUCTURAL SET SELECTION of the set SALES-BY-UNIT, and L-ORDER records are FIXED members of this set. Changing BATCH-ID will cause the DBMS to attempt a DISCONNECT, and the DISCONNECT would fail because of the FIXED status.

Restrictions on PRODUCTION set processing The PRODUCTION sub-schema has two sets: FORMULA and SALES-BY-UNIT (alias BATCH). Both of the sets have AUTOMATIC insertion with FIXED retention. Hence neither CONNECT nor DISCONNECT is valid. CONNECT is not needed because the DBMS will insert records into sets when they are created. DISCONNECT is not allowed because of the FIXED retention.

Restrictions on FAMILY-MEMBER record and set processing Restrictions on the processing of FAMILY-MEMBER subschema are shown in Figure 10-19. FAMILY-NAME records can be stored without restriction. They can also be erased, and the erasure will not cause any other records to be deleted. This is because FAMILY-NAME owns only the set FAMILY, which is MANUAL, OPTIONAL. If a FAMILY-NAME record owns a FAMILY set occurrence when FAMILY-NAME is erased, then the members will just be disconnected, they will not be deleted.

The FAMILY-NAME record has just one data-item, FAM-NAME. This data-item can be changed, but doing so will cause CUSTOMER records to be dis-connected from the FAMILY set. The disconnection occurs because FAM-NAME is part of a CHECK in the FAMILY definition. Changing FAM-NAME will cause existing members in FAMILY to be invalid. Since they are OPTIONAL members, they will be removed from the set.

Record Name

	FAMILY-NAME	CUSTOMER
STORE	OK	No; data-items invisible
ERASE	OK; may cause disconnection in FAMILY set	No; it causes disconnection of invisible L-ORDER records
MODIFY	OK; change in FAM-NAME may cause disconnection in FAMILY set	No

a. Restrictions on FAMILY-MEMBER Record Processing

Set Name

	FAMILY
CONNECT	Yes
RECONNECT	Yes
DISCONNECT	Yes

b. Restrictions on FAMILY-MEMBER Set Processing

Figure 10-19 FAMILY-MEMBER Processing Restrictions

CUSTOMER records cannot be stored by users of FAMILY-MEMBER because only the F-NAME portion of this record is visible. CUSTOMER records that own any L-ORDER records (not visible in this subschema, but still possible) cannot be erased. Such deletion will be prohibited because L-ORDER records are MANDATORY members of the SALE set. If CUSTOMERs are erased, then the DBMS will not know where to put the orphan L-ORDERs that are created. They must be put into some set, since their retention status is MANDATORY. Because of this confusion, the DBMS will simply prevent the erasure of CUSTOMER records.

CUSTOMER records may not be modified. Only one data-item is visible, F-NAME. A change to this data-item will cause the STRUCTURAL SET SELEC-

TION of PURCHASE to be violated. Since members of PURCHASE are FIXED, they cannot be disconnected. Hence the DBMS will prohibit changes to F-NAME.

FAMILY-MEMBER contains one set, FAMILY. Members of this set are MANUAL, OPTIONAL. Thus the user of FAMILY-MEMBER must CONNECT CUSTOMERs into FAMILY sets. Once there, both DISCONNECT and RECONNECT are valid.

Example transactions

Figures 10-20 and 10-21 show the logic for sample transactions against the PRODUCTION subschema. The algorithm in Figure 10-20 shows the creation of RECIPE and PRODUCTION-UNIT (alias PITCHER) records. After the PRODUCTION-UNIT is created, the DBMS will CONNECT it into the FORMULA set owned by Recipe CC. This occurs because the insertion status of FORMULA is AUTOMATIC, because the SET SELECTION IS BY VALUE OF R-NAME, and because the current value of R-NAME is 'CC.'

The algorithm in Figure 10-21 finds the name of the recipe having the greatest

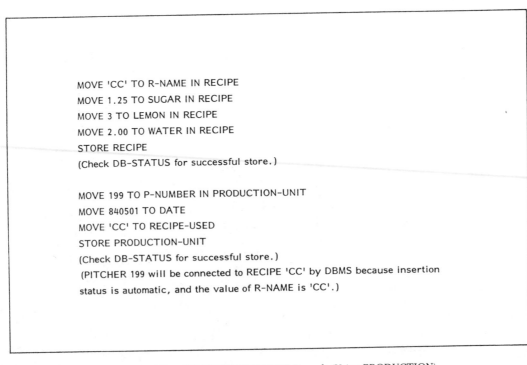

```
MOVE 'CC' TO R-NAME IN RECIPE
MOVE 1.25 TO SUGAR IN RECIPE
MOVE 3 TO LEMON IN RECIPE
MOVE 2.00 TO WATER IN RECIPE
STORE RECIPE
(Check DB-STATUS for successful store.)


MOVE 199 TO P-NUMBER IN PRODUCTION-UNIT
MOVE 840501 TO DATE
MOVE 'CC' TO RECIPE-USED
STORE PRODUCTION-UNIT
(Check DB-STATUS for successful store.)
(PITCHER 199 will be connected to RECIPE 'CC' by DBMS because insertion
status is automatic, and the value of R-NAME is 'CC'.)
```

Figure 10-20 Creation of RECIPE and PRODUCTION-UNIT Records (Using PRODUCTION)

```
MOST-POPULAR-RECIPE = '   '
GREATEST-SALES = 0
FIND ANY RECIPE
GET RECIPE
DOWHILE DB-STATUS = 0
      FIND FIRST PRODUCTION-UNIT WITHIN FORMULA
      DOWHILE DB-STATUS = 0
            TOTAL-SALES = 0
            FIND FIRST L-ORDER WITHIN SALES-BY-UNIT
            DOWHILE DB-STATUS = 0
                  GET L-ORDER
                  TOTAL-SALES = TOTAL-SALES + AMOUNT
                  FIND NEXT L-ORDER WITHIN SALES-BY-UNIT
            END-DO
            FIND NEXT PRODUCTION-UNIT WITHIN FORMULA
      END-DO
      IF TOTAL-SALES GREATER THAN GREATEST-SALES
            THEN GREATEST-SALES = TOTAL-SALES
                  MOST-POPULAR-RECIPE = R-NAME
      END-IF
      FIND NEXT RECIPE
END-DO
```

Figure 10-21   Algorithm to Find Most-Popular-Recipe

total sales. Recipes are accessed sequentially in DBMS-determined order. (If we wanted the recipes in order of R-NAME, we would need to use the system set, RECIPE-SEQUENCE. To do this, the PRODUCTION subschema would need to be changed to include the RECIPE-SEQUENCE set.) Once a RECIPE record is retrieved, then all children (PRODUCTION-UNIT) and children of children (L-ORDER) are accessed. Amounts are totaled and the RECIPE with the greatest sales is identified. Since no data in PRODUCTION-UNIT is needed, the program need not perform a GET on this record. However, the FIND is needed to access the L-ORDER records that belong to the RECIPE. This algorithm assumes that the only reason DB-STATUS is nonzero is end-of-data within set. Actually, other errors might occur; the algorithm should be extended to allow for these possibilities.

SUMMARY

The conversion of an SDM logical design to a DBTG physical design is straight-forward. All SDM base classes become DBTG records. Nonbase classes can be ignored, or they can be represented by subset records and sets. All SDM attributes having value classes that are subsets of STRINGS become DBTG data-items. Other attributes represent relationships. In one way or another, every such relationship must be converted to a one-to-many relationship. Each of these relationships is then represented by a DBTG set.

Set members can be ordered. A variety of orders are allowed, including sorting by data-item values. Constraints can also be defined between set member and owner record data-items. Finally, system sets, which have only one occurrence that is owned by the DBMS, can be defined to allow sequential processing of records.

A DBTG schema consists of definitions of records, data-items, and sets. Sub-schemas define aliases and identify records, data-items, and sets that will be visible to the application program using the subschema. The definitions of insertion and retention status, CHECK clauses, and STRUCTURAL SET OCCUR-RENCEs limit allowable DML commands. Also, these definitions can interact to cause strange and surprising actions such as the erasure or disconnection of records that are not visible in the subschema.

Group I Questions

10.1 Explain how SDM base classes are represented using the DBTG data model.

10.2 Explain two ways that SDM nonbase classes are represented using the DBTG model.

10.3 How are SDM STRINGS attributes represented in the DBTG model?

10.4 How can inverse attributes representing a one-to-many relationship be defined using the DBTG model?

10.5 How can match attributes representing a one-to-many relationship be defined using the DBTG model?

10.6 How can derived attributes representing a one-to-many relationship be defined using the DBTG model?

10.7 How can many-to-many relationships be represented using the DBTG model?

10.8 Explain the following types of DBTG set ordering:

   a. FIRST

     b. LAST

     c. NEXT

     d. PRIOR

     e. SYSTEM DEFAULT

     f. SORTED BY DEFINED KEYS

10.9   What is an essential set?

10.10 What is an inessential set?

10.11 Do you believe inessential sets are appropriate?

10.12 What is a system set? How many occurrences does a system set have? What is the purpose of a system set?

     Note: Questions 10.13 through 10.17 are related. You should read all of the questions before you answer any of them.

10.13 Define a DBTG schema for the example used in questions 9.17 through 9.22. Make assumptions regarding set insertion and retention status, ordering, CHECK, and SELECTION. Justify your assumptions.

10.14 Define a subschema for the schema in question 10.13. Assume the subschema has CUSTOMER and ORDER records.

10.15 For your answers to questions 10.13 and 10.14, explain the validity and consequences of STORE, ERASE, MODIFY, CONNECT, and DISCONNECT commands.

10.16 Present an algorithm to create a new customer and enter an order into your subschema from question 10.14.

10.17 Present an algorithm to list all orders of all customers for the subschema in question 10.14. Put your customers in alphabetical order by customer name.

Group II Questions

10.18 Answer question 6.28 if you have not already done so. Convert your answer to a DBTG schema. Present the schema description and a subschema that could be used for purchasing items for inventory. Develop an algorithm to add a purchase order and line-items, and another algorithm to list inventory levels.

10.19 Answer question 6.29 if you have not already done so. Convert your answer to a DBTG schema. Present a schema and subschema description that could be used to schedule students into classes. Develop an algorithm to add students and classes, and to print both student schedules and class rosters.

Project

A. Sally objects to the design in Figure 10-11. She says that not all family-members have the same last name. Change the design in Figure 10-11 to fix this error. Also, change the FAMILY-MEMBER subschema as well. Justify your change to explain why it is better than other alternatives.

III
DATABASE
IMPLEMENTATION

The next four chapters concern database implementation. In these chapters we will discuss how DBMS products are used to create, query, and process databases. We will also consider database administration.

Chapter 11 surveys DBMS functions. Such functions include not only storing, retrieving, and updating data, but also concurrent processing control, failure recovery, security, and other tasks.

In Chapter 12 we consider the implementation of a relational database. There are currently many relational DBMS; we will briefly survey these systems, and then discuss and illustrate the use of one important relational DBMS called *SQL/DS*. Next, in Chapter 13, we consider the implementation of a DBTG database. As with relational systems, there are many DBTG DBMS products. Again, we will briefly survey these systems, and then discuss and illustrate the use of one important DBTG DBMS product, IDMS.

Finally, Chapter 14 describes database administration. The major functions of the database administrator are defined, and the organizational placement of the DBA is discussed.

11

Functions of a Database Management System

So far we have discussed database management systems as if the only service they provide is to store, retrieve, and update data. Actually, in an operational environment, the DBMS provides other functions as well. In this chapter, we will first survey major DBMS functions and then discuss three of these functions in detail: control of concurrent processing, failure recovery, and security.

SURVEY OF DBMS FUNCTIONS

Figure 11-1 lists nine major DBMS functions [27]. DBMS products vary in the degree to which they provide these functions. Currently, no commercial DBMS provides all nine functions entirely satisfactorily. These functions are necessary and important, however, and this situation should change as DBMS products evolve and as new products are developed.

The first two functions have been discussed in previous chapters. Clearly, the DBMS must *store, retrieve,* and *update* data. In addition, the DBMS should *provide integrity services* to enforce constraints on the data. As mentioned in the design chapters, such constraints can be interrelation (interrecord), intra-relation (intrarecord), and domain (data-item). Currently, only limited constraint checking is provided by commercial DBMS. Development concerning DBMS support for database integrity is underway, however, and features to enforce database constraints are likely in the future. The specifics are currently under debate by database experts.

The management of large, complex databases is difficult. Maintaining a database with dozens of records and hundreds of data-items—particularly a database that is processed by hundreds of application programs—can be time-consuming. Changes can be risky. Questions like "Which programs are affected by a switch to nine-digit Zip Codes?" or "Which records contain Student ID?" are frequent.

1. Store, retrieve, and update data
2. Provide integrity services to enforce database constraints
3. Provide a user-accessible catalog of data descriptions
4. Control concurrent processing
5. Support logical transactions
6. Recover from failure
7. Provide security facilities
8. Interface with communications control programs
9. Provide utility services

Figure 11-1   Functions of a DBMS

Since databases are self-describing, much of the data needed to answer these questions is stored within the database. However, unless special provisions are taken in the design of the DBMS, this data may not be readily accessed by humans. Therefore, the third capability in Figure 11-1 is to provide a *user-accessible catalog* of data descriptions. The usefulness of the catalog is greater if it contains not only data descriptions but also data about the relationship between programs and data, e.g., which programs access which data, and what they do with it.

A database is a shared resource, and users will want to access it simultaneously. For example, two airline passengers may call, at the same time, to reserve a seat on the same flight. When this occurs, the DBMS must provide facilities to ensure that the reservation requests do not interfere with one another. The result of the concurrent processing of two requests should be the same as it would be if the two requests were processed separately in serial fashion. To meet this goal, the DBMS must provide controls over concurrent operations. We will have more to say about this subject in the next section.

Quite often, users want to perform a series of actions on the database such that either all of the actions are completed successfully or the database is left unchanged. A series of activities processed this way is said to be *atomic*. For example, the processing of a new order may require an atomic series of activities. First, CUSTOMER and SALESPERSON records are modified, and then a new ORDER record is inserted in the database. See Figure 11-2. To maintain correct data, either all of these actions should be done, or the database should be left unchanged. Consider the confusion that would result if the CUSTOMER and SALESPERSON records were changed, but the ORDER record was not successfully inserted. (This situation could occur because of insufficient file space, for example.)

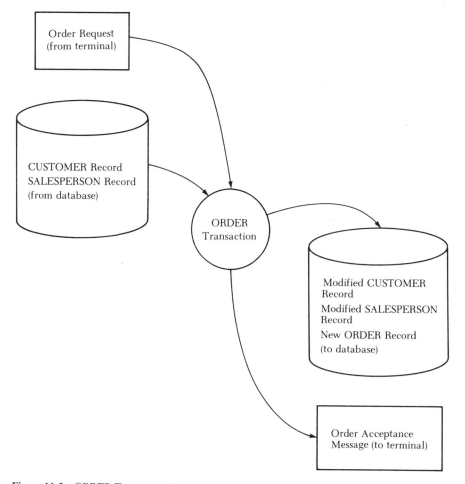

Figure 11-2   ORDER Transaction Inputs and Outputs

A *logical transaction* (or, more simply, transaction) is a sequence of activities performed atomically. Transactions transform input data into changes in the database, and they produce messages that can be displayed on terminals, written to reports, or input to other transactions. Figure 11-3 shows the general format of a transaction.

Usually, transactions include several, or even many, actions on the database. Unfortunately, the DBMS product cannot know which groups of actions are logically related. Thus the DBMS must provide facilities for the application programmer to define transaction boundaries.

Transactions that are processed successfully, in their entirety, are said to have *completed*. If the transaction fails at any point, it has *aborted*. All database

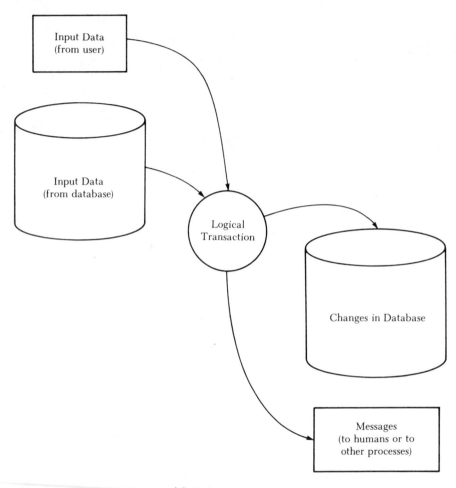

Figure 11-3   Transaction Inputs and Outputs

changes made by completed transactions must be visible to subsequent transactions, and no change made by an aborted transaction must be visible. Database changes made by a transaction in process are said to be *uncommitted*. Once the transaction completes successfully, changes are said to be *committed*.

Considering the next function in Figure 11-1, the DBMS must be able to *recover from failure*. Put another way, the database must be durable. Once a change is committed to the database, the DBMS must provide facilities to ensure that it survives machine failures, disk head crashes, berserk programs, and unenlightened users.

Databases are valuable resources. As discussed in Chapter 5, a database is a model of the current condition of an organization. A DBMS provides powerful

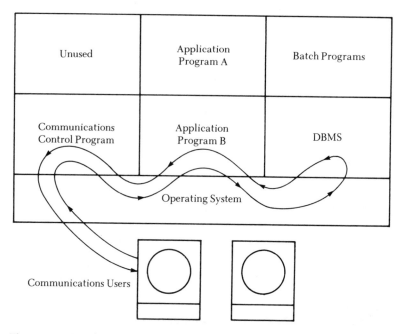

Figure 11-4   Interface between DBMS and CCP

capabilities for accessing this model. Unfortunately, the DBMS improves the efficiency and effectiveness of the unauthorized and perhaps criminal user just as much as it improves the efficiency and effectiveness of authorized users. If the database is divulged to improper or unauthorized people, considerable loss can occur. To reduce the likelihood of such loss, the DBMS must provide *security facilities* by which users can be defined and identified and authorizations enforced.

In addition to these functions, the DBMS must *interface with a communications processing subsystem*. Figure 11-4 shows a typical database processing environment. Batch applications communicate directly with the DBMS, but users at terminals do not. Instead, terminal users interact with a communications control program (CCP; examples are CICS, IDMS-DC, IERCOMM, or TASKMASTER), which controls the flow of transactions to application programs which then call upon the DBMS. Since the CCP may also control concurrent processing and provide recovery services, the interface and protocol between the DBMS and the CCP must be carefully defined.

Finally, the DBMS must provide *utility programs* to facilitate database maintenance. Human activity is usually iterative. Seldom do we get things right the first time. Since this is true, the database may need to be unloaded, reloaded, recreated, and so forth. People may not follow established procedures, and it may be necessary to determine if one copy of a database (or a portion of a database) is identical to another. Also, there may be a need to make mass insertions or deletions of data in or out of the database. DBMS utility programs facilitate these activities.

The nine capabilities in Figure 11-1 can be used as decision criteria. Although no current system provides all of these functions in an entirely satisfactory way, many DBMS products provide most of these functions. A system that does not provide—in one form or another—most of them is not truly a DBMS. When you read about products that are called DBMS by their vendors, consider these nine functions. You may find that the vendor has stretched reality in calling the product a DBMS. File manager is sometimes a more accurate term.

RESPONSIBILITY FOR FUNCTIONS

Although most database experts would agree that the nine functions in Figure 11-1 are required, they would not necessarily agree regarding how some of these functions should be performed. Some people believe that these functions should be provided by the DBMS automatically. Others believe that some of them should be performed by application programs or by users.

Figure 11-5 shows a responsibility continuum. To understand this, consider, as an example, the definition of logical transaction. We could place the responsibility for defining the start and end of a logical transaction entirely with the user. This situation corresponds to the rightmost point in Figure 11-5. In this case, an order entry clerk, for example, would have the responsibility for sending a Start Transaction message to the DBMS and, after an order has been entered, an End Transaction. This alternative is flexible, but unreliable. People can forget, they can be poorly trained, and they often make mistakes.

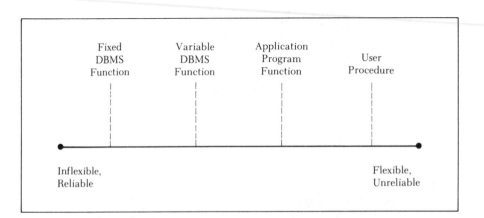

Figure 11-5 Continuum of Responsibilities

Alternatively, at the other end of the continuum, the vendor could construct the DBMS so that it has a fixed definition of when transactions start and end. For example, the DBMS could be programmed to start a transaction whenever a user issues the first DBMS command, and end a transaction whenever that user signs off of the system. This alternative is inflexible but reliable. The DBMS will not forget.

There are alternatives between these two extremes. The definition of transactions could be specified by the development team when the DBMS is installed. In this case, the DBMS will have a fixed definition of transactions, but that definition will be provided by the development team not by the vendor. The definition is specified via parameters input to the DBMS. A fourth alternative is to leave the definition of logical transactions to the application program. In this case, programs issue Start Transaction and End Transaction messages to the DBMS.

Alternatives on the righthand side of the continuum in Figure 11-5 tend to be flexible but unreliable. Alternatives on the lefthand side tent to be inflexible but reliable.

Which of these alternatives is best? None is best for all circumstances. For applications that involve public safety, such as air traffic control or nuclear technology, high reliability is critical. For the example discussed, coding the definition of logical transaction into the DBMS may be the best alternative. On the other hand, in a small office with two terminals, concurrent processing may never occur. Perhaps only one user will be signed-on to a database application at a time. In this case, there is no need to define transactions at all. User definition of transactions may be workable because transactions need never be defined.

Thus, as with other database alternatives we have discussed, the decision depends on requirements. The responsibility for many of the functions may lie with the DBMS, with application programs, with users, or with other entities, depending on the services required by the users of the database.

We have assumed that the developers have a choice regarding responsibility for definition of transactions (or other functions). Realize that with some DBMS products, there may be no choice. A DBMS may not support the definition of logical transactions at all. Or, it may *require* application programs to define such transactions. If this is the case, then the developers should bear this limitation in mind when selecting the DBMS.

When you evaluate DBMS products, remember Figure 11-5. A vendor may state that its product supports logical transactions, but it may turn out that such transactions place a large burden on the application program. Or, it may turn out that the DBMS is programmed to support only one type of logical transaction. When evaluating such features, you should ask, "Who is responsible for what?" and "What choices exist?"

In the next three sections we will discuss control of concurrent processing, recovery, and security. At the end of each of these sections we will consider the responsibility continuum in Figure 11-5.

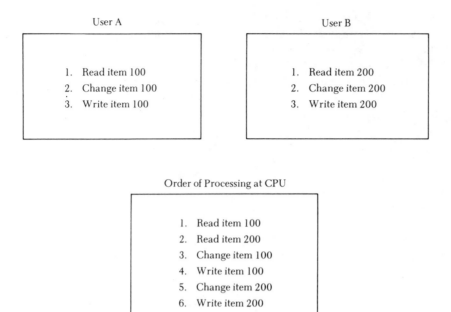

Figure 11-6 Example of Concurrent Processing of Two Users' Tasks

CONCURRENT PROCESSING CONTROL

Concurrent processing occurs when two transactions are interleaved. Concurrent processing is different from simultaneous processing. Figure 11-6 shows two concurrent transactions. User A's transaction reads item 100, changes it, and rewrites the item in the database. User B's transaction takes the same actions, but on item 200. The CPU processes user A until it encounters an I/O wait. Then it shifts to user B. It processes user B until an I/O wait and then shifts back to A. Thus the processing is interleaved, or concurrent. Processing is not simultaneous because no two actions take place at the same time. Users A and B can make their requests simultaneously, and they may believe their processing has been simultaneous, but they believe this only because processing has been fast relative to A and B's perceptive abilities.

Simultaneous processing can occur, but it requires two CPUs and two copies of the DBMS. If user A and user B have their own CPUs and DBMS copies, then processing can be simultaneous. For example, two students operating on different microcomputers, each with a DBMS, can process simultaneously.

When databases are distributed on two or more computer systems, simultaneous updating becomes a possibility (and a headache). The control over updates in distributed databases is a complex subject and beyond the scope of

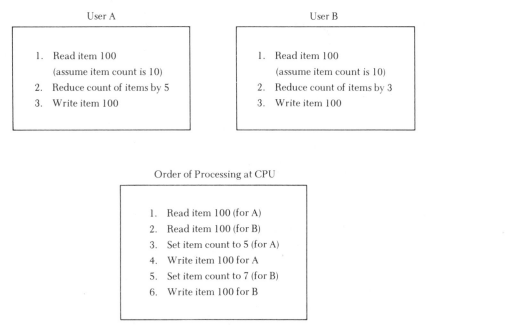

User A

1. Read item 100
    (assume item count is 10)
2. Reduce count of items by 5
3. Write item 100

User B

1. Read item 100
    (assume item count is 10)
2. Reduce count of items by 3
3. Write item 100

Order of Processing at CPU

1. Read item 100 (for A)
2. Read item 100 (for B)
3. Set item count to 5 (for A)
4. Write item 100 for A
5. Set item count to 7 (for B)
6. Write item 100 for B

Note: The change and write in steps 3 and 4 are lost.

Figure 11-7   Concurrent Update Problem

this text. If you are interested in update control in distributed database systems, see [7]. From now on, we will only be concerned with the concurrent processing of a database on a single computer.

The concurrent update problem

The concurrent processing illustrated in Figure 11-6 poses no problems because the users are processing different data. However, suppose that both users want to process item 100. Let's say, for example, that user A wants to order 5 items 100 and user B wants to order 3 items 100.

Figure 11-7 shows the problem that can develop. User A reads the item 100 record into its user work area. According to the record, there are 10 items 100 in inventory. Then user B reads the item 100 record into its user work area. Again, according to the record there are 10 in inventory. Now user A takes 5, decrements the count of items in its user work area to 5, and rewrites the record for item 100. Then, user B takes 3, decrements the count in its user work area to 7, and rewrites the item 100 record. The database now shows that there are 7 items 100 in inventory. To review: we started with 10 in inventory, user A took 5, user B took 3, and the database shows that 7 are in inventory. Is this the new math?

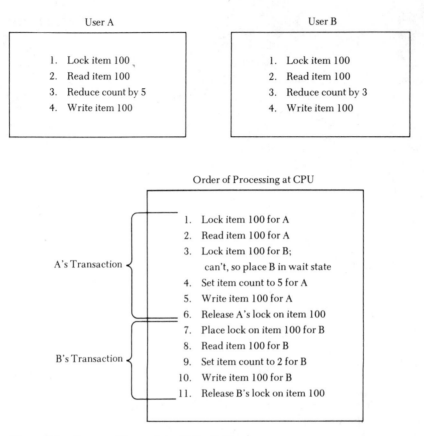

Figure 11-8   Concurrent Processing with Explicit Locks

Both users obtained current data from the database. However, when user B read the record, user A already had a separate copy that it was about to update. A remedy for this problem is to prevent applications from having two copies of the same record when the record is about to be changed. We consider this remedy next.

Resource locking

To prevent the concurrent update problem, data that is retrieved for the purpose of update must not be shared among users. (In this sense, the term *user* refers to the user of the DBMS, not necessarily the system user. Thus user can be either a person sitting at a terminal using the DBMS query/update facility, or an application program that calls upon the DBMS for service.) To stop such sharing, the DBMS can place locks on data that is in the process of update. Figure 11-8 shows the order of processing using a lock command. User B is

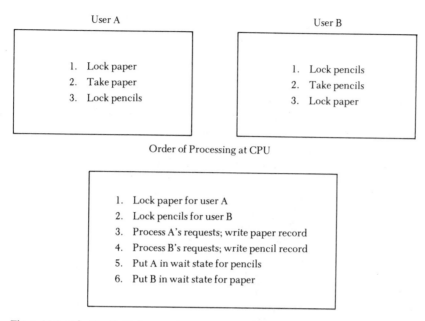

User A

1. Lock paper
2. Take paper
3. Lock pencils

User B

1. Lock pencils
2. Take pencils
3. Lock paper

Order of Processing at CPU

1. Lock paper for user A
2. Lock pencils for user B
3. Process A's requests; write paper record
4. Process B's requests; write pencil record
5. Put A in wait state for pencils
6. Put B in wait state for paper

Figure 11-9 The Deadly Embrace

placed in the wait state until user A is finished with the record. Using this strategy, user B can only read the item 100 record after user A has completed the modification. In this case, the item count stored in the database will be 2, as it should be. (We started with 10, A took 5, and B took 3, leaving 2.)

The deadly embrace

Consider two users who want to acquire items from inventory. Suppose user A wants to order some paper, and if user A gets the paper, she wants to order some pencils. Further, suppose that user B wants to order some pencils, and if he gets some pencils, he wants to order some paper. The order of processing could be as shown in Figure 11-9.

What has happened? Users A and B are locked in the *deadly embrace*. They are each waiting on a resource which the other person has locked. If A and B are the only users on the system, things are likely to get boring around the CPU.

There are three common ways of solving this situation. The first two ways prevent the embrace, the third breaks the embrace once it occurs. One way to prevent the deadly embrace is to allow users to have only one lock in process at a time. Users must lock all the records they want at once. For the example in Figure 11-9, users A and B must both lock paper and pencils at the start. It may turn out that one or both of these people do not modify both records; but they must lock both, if there is a chance they will modify both. Using this strategy, if a user determines that another lock is needed, the user must first release the lock it has, and then relock the old items plus the new ones. This strategy may be difficult to implement if a transaction is halfway processed and partly updated data must be unlocked. For this and other reasons, this strategy has met with only limited success.

A second way of eliminating the deadly embrace is to lock all items in a predetermined order. For example, the convention might be established to lock inventory items in ascending order of item number, or in alphabetical order of item name. Assume the latter. For the situation in Figure 11-9, paper must be locked before pencils (*pa* comes before *pe*). Since this is true, user B can never be granted a lock on a resource that user A already holds. Unfortunately, users may not request items in the correct order, and this strategy is impractical in many other situations.

The third strategy is to allow the deadly embrace to occur, to detect it, and, when detected, to break it. Unfortunately, there is only one way to break the deadly embrace (are you ready?): kill one of the transactions. Once the situation in Figure 11-9 has occurred, one of the two transactions must be destroyed. The transaction for either user A or user B can be eliminated. Suppose user B is eliminated. Then, the lock on pencils will be released and user A can proceed.

When the transaction for user B is destroyed, all changes that B has made to the database must be removed. Otherwise, when B is restarted, some updates will be made a second time. Also, it is possible that the transaction for B will never be restarted (the customer gives up). In that case as well, the changes from the partial transaction must be removed. It is possible to remove partial transactions; we will discuss the technique in the next section of this chapter. For now, realize that of the three techniques for dealing with the deadly embrace, the third strategy seems to have had the most success.

Dimensions of resource locking

A wide variety of resource-locking strategies is used by DBMS products. This variety can be classified according to four dimensions as listed in Figure 11-10.

Lock level   The first dimension concerns the *level* of the lock, or as it is sometimes called, the *lock granularity*. At the highest level, a lock can be placed on the entire database. This strategy is used by DBMS products that invoke the lock for a short time during the processing of a single database request. At the lowest level, locks can be placed on a single data-item. In between these extremes, locks can be placed on records, on files, and on major sections of the database.

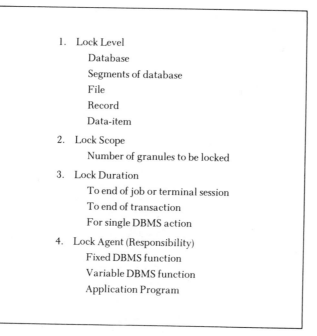

1. Lock Level
   - Database
   - Segments of database
   - File
   - Record
   - Data-item

2. Lock Scope
   - Number of granules to be locked

3. Lock Duration
   - To end of job or terminal session
   - To end of transaction
   - For single DBMS action

4. Lock Agent (Responsibility)
   - Fixed DBMS function
   - Variable DBMS function
   - Application Program

Figure 11-10   Dimensions of Resource Locking

There are tradeoffs among these alternatives. A lock of the entire database is simple for the DBMS to administer. However, throughput may be slow because there will be many conflicts among transactions. On the other hand, locks of small granularity will be complex to administer but such locks will cause few conflicts. Throughput will tend to be faster (if the overhead of processing the locks does not consume the time savings of reduced conflicts). As always, the choice among alternatives (when the DBMS allows a choice) depends on requirements.

Lock scope   Scope is the second lock dimension. How broad should the lock be? Or stated differently, How many grains should be locked at a time? If locking occurs at the record level, how many records should be locked? All records? An entire file? A single record?

Tradeoffs here are similar to those for lock level. If many grains are locked, the lock will be easier to administer, but conflicts will be frequent. If a few grains are locked, then administration will be more complex, but there will be fewer conflicts.

Lock duration   The duration of a lock is the length of time the lock is held. At the maximum, the lock can be held for the length of an entire job or terminal session. At the minimum, the lock can be held for a single database request (a READ command, for example). Short locks will be easy to administer (there will tend to be fewer outstanding at any time) and will cause fewer conflicts. Long locks will be harder to administer and will cause more conflicts. Since these tradeoffs appear to favor short locks, you may wonder, Why have long locks at all?

In most situations, the duration of a lock must be related to the definition of a transaction. Generally, locks are held from the time they are invoked until the transaction either completes successfully or aborts. This policy is followed to keep other transactions from accessing data before it is committed. If locks are too short, say the length of a single database request, then logical transactions will be infeasible. Even if locks can encompass several DBMS requests, they may not be long enough to meet the requirements for a complex logical transaction.

Thus you see the conflict among goals. We may want high throughput (generally provided by short locks), and, at the same time, we may want logical transactions of a dozen or more DBMS commands (generally requiring long locks). Again, the choice depends on tradeoffs among requirements and on the facilities that the DBMS provides.

Lock agent (responsibility)   The fourth lock dimension concerns the continuum of responsibility presented in Figure 11-5. Who is responsible for placing the lock? If application programs or even users are required to place locks, then the lock is called an *explicit lock*. The DBTG command FIND FOR UPDATE discussed in Chapter 9 is an example of an explicit lock. If the DBMS product places a lock, then the lock is called an *implicit lock*.

As you would expect from the discussion of Figure 11-5, explicit locks are more flexible but less reliable (the application programmer may err and forget to place the lock). Implicit locks are more reliable but less flexible. Again, the choice (if the DBMS product allows a choice) depends on requirements.

As an aside, users can never be relied upon to explicitly place locks. The typical accounts receivable clerk, for example, cannot be depended upon to lock data before modifying it. Users generally do not understand the rationale for locks; they will forget, and the consequences of not locking are severe (and consequent errors will be blamed on the computer).

This situation poses a problem for DBMS query/update programs. The query/update facility will have to place the lock for the user without knowledge of the boundaries of underlying logical transactions. In these cases, the DBMS must place the lock from the context of processing. For example, when a user signs on to the system, if he or she requests update permission for a file (or relation), the DBMS must assume that all reads of that file (or relation) must be for the purpose of update. In this case, locks will always be placed. Note that locks may exist for some period of time if users do much reading without updating (this could happen if the user wants to primarily prepare reports, with an occasional update).

This unfortunate situation is unavoidable. In Chapter 12, you will see how such processing is done for ISQL, the query/update processor for the product SQL/DS.

DATABASE RECOVERY

Systems fail. Computers stop unexpectedly, disk heads crash, operators drop disks, programs have bugs, people input incorrect data, and procedures are ignored. Unfortunately (or perhaps fortunately), when systems fail, business does not stop. Customers continue to deposit and withdraw money, they continue to order products, and the assembly line continues to produce goods. Therefore, system failures must be repaired and recovered from as soon as possible. Furthermore, business demands that jobs which were in processing when the failure occurred be recovered in such a way that their outputs are identical to what would have been produced had there been no interruption in service. In other words, failures should be transparent in their effect on data.

Performing recovery is exceedingly difficult. It is impossible to simply fix the problem and resume program processing where it was interrupted. Even if no data is lost during a failure (which assumes that all types of memory are non-volatile—an unrealistic assumption), the timing and scheduling of computer processing is too complex to be accurately recreated. Enormous amounts of overhead data and processing would be required for the operating system to be able to restart processing precisely where it was interrupted. It is simply not possible to roll back the clock and put all the electrons in the same configuration they were in at the time of the failure.

Recovery via reprocessing

Since processing cannot be resumed precisely at a point, the next best alternative is to go back to a known point and reprocess the workload. The simplest form of this type of recovery is to periodically make copies of the database (called *database saves*) and to keep a record of all transactions that have been processed since the save. Then, when failure occurs, restore the database from the save and reprocess all transactions.

Unfortunately, this simple strategy is often infeasible. First, reprocessing transactions takes the same amount of time as processing them in the first place. This means that 24 hours will be required to recover 24 hours of processing. If the computer is heavily scheduled, the system may never catch up. Second, when transactions are processed concurrently, it is impossible to guarantee that they will be reprocessed in exactly the same order as they were originally processed. Slight variations, such as an operator mounting a tape more slowly, may cause one transaction to get ahead of another. Whereas customer A got the last widget from inventory during the original processing, customer B may get the last widget during reprocessing. For these reasons, reprocessing is not usually a viable form of recovery.

Recovery via rollback/rollforward

A second approach is to save the results of transactions, and when failure occurs, to recover by removing changes (called *rollback*) and then reapplying changes (called *rollforward*). The particulars of this process depend on the cause of the failure, as you will see. In general, however, this mode of recovery has four steps:

1. Recreate (or not destroy) the outputs of all completed transactions.
2. Abort all transactions in process at the time of the failure.
3. Remove database changes generated by aborted transactions.
4. Restart aborted transactions

This strategy will accurately recover the database. However, what about humans who have received messages from transactions that are subsequently aborted? What happens if a human receives an order confirmation from an ORDER transaction, and that transaction is subsequently aborted? Suppose further that by the time the transaction is rescheduled, its input data has changed. If so, the ORDER transaction may generate different outputs. In this case, the customer may receive both an order confirmation and an order rejection for the same order!

Some transaction outputs, called *real outputs* by Gray [43], cannot be undone. A change to the database is never a real output because database changes can always be undone. Real outputs are messages like order confirmations or inputs to other transactions. Because they cannot be undone, real outputs should not be produced until the transaction completes. Gray recommends keeping a log of real outputs. When the transaction completes, the actions on the log are done and the real outputs become visible. To ensure correct processing, if a failure occurs when the real outputs are being produced, each output could be numbered and a log kept of the real outputs that have been generated. See [43] for more information.

Transaction logging

To be able to undo or redo database changes, a log must be kept of transaction results. The log contains a record of data changes in chronological order. Figure

Application Programs

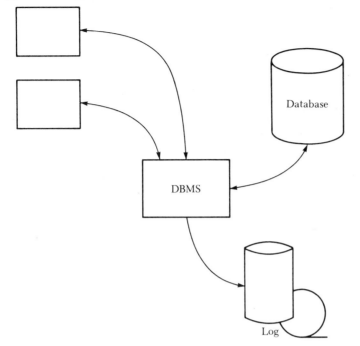

Figure 11-11   DBMS with Log Facility

11-11 shows the relationships of application programs, the DBMS, the database, and the log.

The log is shown as residing on either disk or tape. For several reasons, the modern approach is to place the log on disk. Disk storage per unit can be cheaper, disks are larger, disk processing is faster, and the log can be processed in random order. Also, processing logs on disks does not require any operator intervention; and, if the log does not occupy all of the disk, the unused portion can be used for other purposes. Unused tape capacity cannot be so used. One objection to putting the log on disk is that disks are more vulnerable to destruction by head crashes and the like. If this is a concern, however, two copies of the log can be kept on separate disks.

When a failure occurs, the log is used to both undo and redo transactions, as shown in Figure 11-12. To undo a transaction, the log must contain a copy of every database record (or block) before it was changed. Such records are called *before images*. A transaction is undone by applying before images of all of its changes to the database.

To redo a transaction, the log must contain a copy of every database record (or block) after it was changed. These records are called *after images*. A trans-

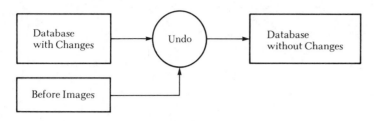

a.   Removing Database Changes

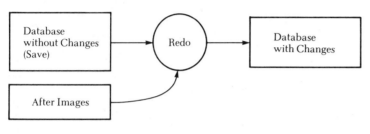

b.   Repeating Database Changes

Figure 11-12   Undo and Redo Transaction Procedures

action is redone by applying after images of all of its changes to the database. Possible data-items of a transaction log are shown in Figure 11-13a. For this example log, each transaction has a unique name for identification purposes. Further, all images for a given transaction are linked together with two-way linked lists. The recovery subsystem can use these links to rapidly locate all records for a particular transaction. Figure 11-13b shows an example of the linking of log records. Other data-items in the log are the time of the action, the type of operation (MODIFY, INSERT, etc.), the object acted upon such as record type and identifier, and finally, the old and new values.

In Figure 11-13, the objects of the log are individual database records. In reality, the object would more likely be the block of data in which the record resides. The block would probably contain several additional records. Also, when data is changed, the change may necessitate changes to overhead structure. A change in a key field, for example, may force a change in an inverted list. Changes to such structure must also be recorded in the log.

Write-ahead log

Should the log records be written before or after changes have been made to the database? Suppose the database is changed first and then the log is written. In this case, if a failure occurs after the database has been changed but before the log has been written, there will be changes in the database that are not recorded in the log. In Figure 11-14, changes made by the transaction in prog-

Transaction ID	Type of Operation
Reverse Pointer	Object
Forward Pointer	Old Value
Time	New Value

a. Possible Data-items of a Log Record

Relative
Record
Number

1	OT1	0	2	11:42	START			
2	OT1	1	4	11:43	MODIFY	CUST 100	(old value)	(new value)
3	OT2	0	8	11:46	START			
4	OT1	2	5	11:47	MODIFY	SP AA	(old value)	(new value)
5	OT1	4	7	11:47	INSERT	ORDER 11		(value)
6	CT1	0	9	11:48	START			
7	OT1	5	0	11:49	COMMIT			
8	OT2	3	0	11:50	COMMIT			
9	CT1	6	10	11:51	MODIFY	SP BB	(old value)	(new value)
10	CT1	9	0	11:51	COMMIT			

b. Log Instance for Three Transactions

Figure 11-13   Transaction Log

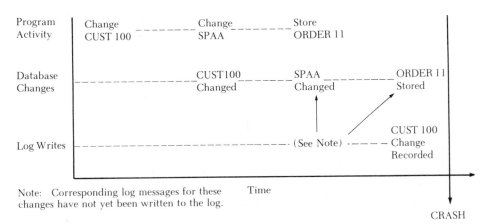

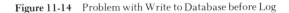

Note: Corresponding log messages for these
changes have not yet been written to the log.

Figure 11-14   Problem with Write to Database before Log

ress need to be backed out of the database; but, unfortunately, the record of those changes never made it to the log. Thus the changes cannot be removed, and this strategy is therefore unworkable.

On the other hand, if the log is written first and then changes are made to the database, when a failure does occur after the log has been written but before the database has been changed, all activity will be known. In this case, the recovery processor may attempt to undo changes that have not yet occurred. This anomaly will be harmless, however, because the recovery processor will only be placing before images in the database. Records will be replaced by copies of themselves. This situation will be wasteful but not harmful.

Rollback/rollforward examples

Given a log with both before and after images, the undo and redo actions are straightforward (to describe, anyway). To undo the transaction in Figure 11-15, the recovery processor simply replaces each changed block with its before image. When all before images have been restored, the transaction is undone.

To redo a transaction, the recovery manager starts with the version of the database at the time the transaction started, and applies all after images. This action assumes that an earlier version of the database is available from a database save.

There are four typical situations necessitating the need for recovery. They are:

I. Transaction failure
II. Database destruction
III. System failure
IV. Erroneous transaction

Recovery from these situations will be illustrated with the following example:

Assume that three users are processing two types of transactions. ORDER transactions (OT) read order data, a CUSTOMER record, and a SALESPER-SON record. They produce modified CUSTOMER and SALESPERSON records, a new ORDER record, and an Order Confirmation message. COMMIS-SION transactions (CT) compute the commission to be paid to a given salesperson. They input commission data and a SALESPERSON record. They produce a modified SALESPERSON record and a Check (in several copies). Figure 11-16 shows a processing history for the three users. We assume that all data is locked before it is modified.

Transaction failure (type I)   Suppose that transaction OT4 in Figure 11-16a fails. Possible reasons for the failure include terminal hardware failure, user error, bad data, or transaction OT4 might be in a deadly embrace with transaction OT3. Whatever the reason, to recover the database the changes made

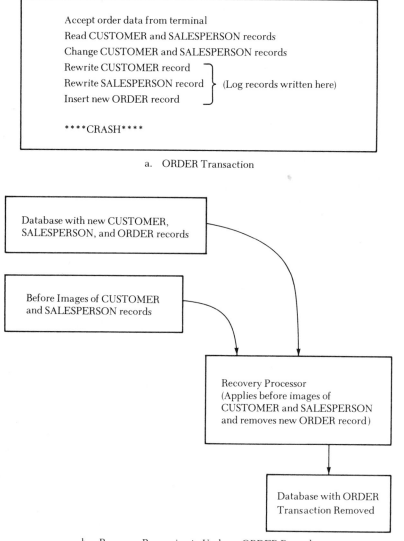

Accept order data from terminal
Read CUSTOMER and SALESPERSON records
Change CUSTOMER and SALESPERSON records
Rewrite CUSTOMER record ⎤
Rewrite SALESPERSON record ⎬ (Log records written here)
Insert new ORDER record ⎦

****CRASH****

a. ORDER Transaction

Database with new CUSTOMER,
SALESPERSON, and ORDER records

Before Images of CUSTOMER
and SALESPERSON records

Recovery Processor
(Applies before images of
CUSTOMER and SALESPERSON
and removes new ORDER record)

Database with ORDER
Transaction Removed

b. Recovery Processing to Undo an ORDER Record

Figure 11-15 Example of Recovery Strategy

by OT4 must be removed. The recovery processor recovers by applying all of
the before images in the log for transaction OT4.

Perhaps now you can see more clearly the necessity of locks. If transaction
OT3 were allowed to modify the same data as OT4, when the recovery manager
undoes OT4's data, the copy of the data used by OT3 may be made invalid. This

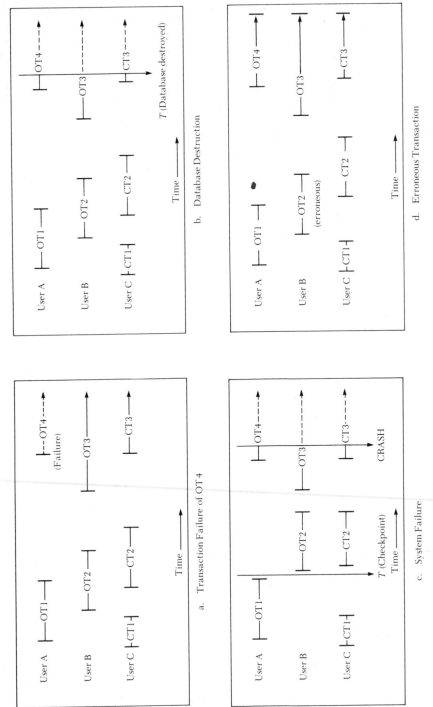

Figure 11-16 Example Processing History of ORDER and COMMISSION Transactions

situation also indicates why it is desirable for the lock to endure until the transaction completes.

We are assuming, so far, that locks are obtained only when records are read for the purpose of update. We may need locks even when records are read without intent to update. Suppose that OT3 reads a record (not for the purpose of update) that has been changed by OT4. Further suppose that OT3 does not lock this record and that OT4 fails and its change to the record is backed out. In this case, OT3 is reading, and utilizing, data that has been undone. This possibility is real, and if the logic of the OT transaction is such that this situation is intolerable, then locks will have to be obtained before reading, regardless of whether the data is to be modified.

Consider another example involving the CT transaction. Suppose that CT3 reads the same SALESPERSON record that OT4 reads. If, as we have assumed so far, CT transactions modify the SALESPERSON record, then CT3 will issue a lock on the SALESPERSON record. Since OT4 has already locked the record, CT3 will wait. After OT4 has failed and the recovery manager has undone OT4's changes, then CT3 will obtain the lock on the record and correctly compute the salesperson's commission, not including order OT4.

Now change this example and suppose that CT transactions do not modify SALESPERSON records. In this case, since CT3 is just reading the SALESPERSON records, it need not issue a lock. If not, then CT3 could read the SALESPERSON record after OT4 has modified it but before OT4 has failed. CT3 will compute a commission assuming the order in OT4 was actually consummated. After OT4 fails, the SALESPERSON record will be undone, and the commission check generated by CT3 will be incorrect.

To summarize this situation, a transaction that is going to read a record for the purpose of update must first lock the record. Otherwise, the transaction may read uncommitted data and unintentionally redo what the recovery manager has undone. Furthermore, if the logic of the transaction is such that it must never read uncommitted data, then it will have to lock the data even if it does not intend to update it.

Database destruction (type II) Figure 11-16b shows the same scenario of users and transactions as in Figure 11-16a. However, assume that at time *T*, the disk head crashes and destroys the database. To regenerate the database, the recovery processor must restore that database from a prior database save and reapply data changes of all completed transactions. Transactions in process will need to be restarted. Be aware that if there is no prior save, then there is no way of recovering the database.

For the situation in Figure 11-16b, the recovery manager will apply the after images of all completed transactions. After images of transactions OT1, CT1, OT2, and CT2 will be applied. Transactions OT3, OT4, and CT3 will need to be restarted. Sometimes, recovery subsystems in commercial DBMS will automatically restart aborted transactions. Other DBMS products will not. Instead, they assume that aborted transactions will be resubmitted by users.

System failure (type III)   Suppose the system crashes, but in such a way that the database is undamaged. Further assume that all transactions in process at the time of the crash are lost. See Figure 11-16c.

To recover the database, all changes that were made by uncompleted transactions need to be undone. The recovery processor does this by applying before images of these transactions. For the situation in Figure 11-16c, the before images of transactions OT3, OT4, and CT3 must be applied.

This procedure, however, is not sufficient to ensure that the database is correct. For reasons explained previously, records are written to the log before they are written to the database. Suppose that the after images and the Commit message for transaction CT3 have been written to the log but not written to the database. The write commands to change the database may have been in process when the system crashed. For the situation in Figure 11-16c, the only way to be certain that all changes have been made to the database is to reapply *all* after images of all changes to the database since the last save. If there have been many intervening transactions, this may be a time-consuming process.

DBMS products provide a facility called *checkpoint* for this situation. The uncertainty just described occurs because it is not known if all changes written to the log have also been written to the database. We do not know if the log and the database are synchronized. A checkpoint command provides a point of synchronization. To perform a checkpoint, the DBMS refuses to accept any new requests, it finishes processing outstanding requests, and it empties its buffers. The DBMS then waits until the operating system notifies it that all outstanding write requests to the database and to the log are complete. At this point, the log and the database are synchronized. A checkpoint record is then written to the log. When the database is recovered, after images need only be applied for transactions that started after the checkpoint. In Figure 11-16c, if a checkpoint has been taken at time *T*, then only transactions OT2 and CT2 need to be redone.

Checkpoints may be inexpensive operations, and often it is feasible to take three or four checkpoints per hour (or more). In this way, no more than fifteen or twenty minutes of processing will need to be recovered.

Erroneous transaction (type IV)   Suppose that transaction OT2 in Figure 11-16d is erroneous. Perhaps the data is bad, or the operator made an error, or for some other reason OT2 should never have occurred. Is it possible to undo OT2 after it has completed? Considering the real outputs, the answer is no. A message cannot be realistically retrieved. It is going to be delivered (or it already has been delivered). All that can be done regarding real outputs is to execute compensating transactions. A letter of change, or advisement, or an apology are examples.

Considering database changes, transaction OT2 may possibly be undone. If no transaction since OT2 has used (read or changed) any of the blocks that were modified by OT2, then clearly OT2's before images can be reapplied to the database. However, how do we know? In order to know whether a transaction has used any of OT2's changes, reads must be recorded on the log. For almost all situations, this is prohibitively expensive. With most DBMS, then, the answer is that a committed transaction cannot be undone. Instead, compensating transactions are executed to correct for the inappropriate activity.

If reads are recorded in the log, then it is possible to undo OT2 even if other transactions have used OT2's data. The recovery processor simply undoes all changes made by transactions that have used OT2's data, or data from another transaction that is undone. Clearly, this procedure could cascade into a large number of transactions to be undone and rescheduled. In theory, however, if reads are recorded on the log, it is possible to undo such transactions.

RECOVERY RESPONSIBILITIES

The recovery strategies described above involve three tasks. The workload must be divided into transactions; records must be locked; and a procedure involving rollback/rollforward must be invoked to accomplish the recovery.

Within this general structure, there are many different ways of performing recovery. These alternatives vary according to who performs the three tasks. Consider again the responsibility continuum in Figure 11-5. One recovery alternative corresponds to the leftmost, or Fixed DBMS Function, point. For this alternative, the DBMS is programmed to divide workload into transactions, to lock records automatically, and to invoke rollback/rollforward procedures to recover from failures of types I, II, and III. (The DBMS cannot automatically recover from failures of type IV since it must be informed as to which transactions are erroneous.)

For this situation, the DBMS would need to define transactions grossly since it would not know application logic. A transaction might be defined as all activity between the first DBMS request and the end of job. Further, the DBMS might decide to lock all retrieved records since it would not know ahead of time which retrieved records will be changed. Finally, the DBMS could recover from failures of types I and III by rolling back changes of uncompleted transactions and rescheduling them. The DBMS could recover from failures of type II by keeping records of database saves (it could be programmed to request the saves itself) and sending a message to the operator to mount the save tape when needed during recovery. This alternative is totally automated, reliable, inflexible, and probably slow.

Another, slightly more flexible alternative also involves automated recovery by the DBMS. For this second alternative, however, the parameters of recovery are set by the database development team during installation. Thus the team would instruct the DBMS how to identify and delineate transactions of particular types. The DBMS could be informed, for example, that program OE134 generates ORDER transactions and that such transactions begin with a READ of a CUSTOMER record and end with a WRITE of an ORDER record. In this way, the DBMS would be able to generate smaller transactions and throughput would likely be greater. The team could also inform the DBMS under what conditions to invoke record locking.

A third possible alternative is far less automated. For this alternative, application programs denote transaction boundaries with Start and End Transaction messages. Application programs also lock records when necessary. Finally, recovery procedures are manual. The operations staff instructs the DBMS how to proceed with recovery, mounting save tapes when necessary from operations records.

This third alternative is manual, flexible, possibly efficient, and unreliable. Application programmers can make errors such as defining transactions inappropriately or locking records incorrectly. The operations staff can also make mistakes when following procedures.

Again you can see the tradeoffs among alternatives, and again, a decision among alternatives must be made in light of requirements. The DBMS should be selected with requirements for recovery in mind. Additionally, where the DBMS allows choices among recovery strategies, the selections should be made in light of requirements.

DATABASE SECURITY

Companies that develop databases are vulnerable. A database contains a representation of the present, much of the history, and some of the future of the company that it models. At the same time, much time and effort have been invested in the design of DBMS to make them easy to use for both programmers and end-users. Hence a database is a valuable resource that is easily accessed and changed. The valuable resource, and thus the company that owns it, is vulnerable to intentional abuse or unintentional error. Recognizing this need, most vendors of DBMS have incorporated security features into their products.

Physical security

Physical security is concerned with protecting the physical resources used for processing the database. Protection of computer hardware, file media, backup data, systems and applications software, documentation, and the like are the concerns of physical security. What happens after flood, fire, or earthquake? Additionally, this topic includes control over the physical access to the system. Who can enter facilities having terminals or other equipment? Who is authorized to use them? At what times? These are questions within the purview of physical security. Although these questions are important, they represent issues broader than just database processing, and we will not consider them in this text.

A model of database security

Of the users and programmers who are authorized to have physical access to the database system, not all have equal authority. Some users and programmers

Subject	Object	Action	Constraint
PGM OE104J	ORDER Record	Insert	Amount less than $500,000
Sally Smith	ORDER Record	Read	None
Payroll Dept	EMPLOYEE Record	Read	Hourly workers
Payroll Dept	EMPLOYEE Record	Modify	Hourly workers
Payroll Dept	EMPLOYEE Record	Insert	Hourly workers
Payroll Supv	EMPLOYEE Record	Delete	Hourly workers
Payroll Supv	Read Permission of EMPLOYEE Records	Grant	To payroll personnel

Figure 11-17   Sample of Authorization Rules

have more rights than others. Generally speaking, good security means that people have access to the data they need to accomplish their job function, and no more. Since job functions vary, data access authorizations vary as well.

In *Database Security and Integrity*, Fernandez, Summers, and Wood develop a model of database security. Their model is essentially a table of processing permissions or *authorization rules*. As shown in Figure 11-17, the table has four columns representing subjects, objects, actions, and constraints. A row in this table indicates that the named subject has permission to take the indicated action on the listed object, subject to the stated constraints. Thus row 1 indicates that the program OE104J is authorized to insert records as long as the amount of the order is less than $500,000.

Although no DBMS provides security in the form of this model, the model is an effective framework for understanding security capabilities. When evaluating a DBMS, the security features of the system can be put into this form. They can then be compared against security requirements. We will discuss the capabilities of SQL/DS and IDMS in terms of this model in the next two chapters. Before we do that, however, we will discuss this model in greater detail.

Subjects   A subject is any identifiable entity that can process the database. Examples of subjects are particular people (Sally Smith), groups of people (everyone in the payroll department), people operating in particular roles (Sally Smith executing deposit transactions), application programs, and remote computers.

An age-old problem is to determine whether or not a subject who claims to be a particular subject is in fact that subject. People have been identified by fingerprints, retinal images, physical dimensions, pictures, letters of identity, and specialized knowledge (passwords, personal data, and the like). Computer equipment is identified by hardware configuration (say, the line connected to port 4), and by the presence or absence of specialized signals. Programs are usually identified by name, position in memory, or specialized protocol.

Although any of these techniques could conceivably be used to identify a human subject in a database application, the most frequently used are name, account number, and password. The entity desiring access to the object provides his/her/its name, account number, or password. Where it is known that only certain entities are authorized access through certain hardware, this constraint can be checked. In practice, this type of verification is rare. Most often, the DBMS looks up the name of the entity and other data in a table, and if the name is found, the subject is assumed to be who or what it claims to be.

Objects The second attribute of the security table in Figure 11-17 is object. Objects are the entities to be protected by security. Examples of objects (using relational terminology) are databases, relations, attributes, tuples, views, the DBMS, programs, transactions, knowledge of status (existence or nonexistence of an entity), and the like.

The term *granularity* is often used to refer to the size of security objects in the same sense it was used to refer to the size of locks. A security system that allows access to the database as a unit has large granularity. A security system that allows access to a particular attribute of a particular tuple has small granularity.

Small-granularity security systems allow close control over data. Users can truly be limited to the data they need to perform their jobs. On the other hand, the smaller the granularity, the larger the overhead of administering the security system. If the DBMS must check authorization every time a user accesses, say, every attribute of every tuple, then processing will be slow and expensive. In addition, overhead for the user will be high. If every tuple has its own password, then users will have to know, remember, and administer hundreds of passwords.

Thus deciding the granularity of a security system involves making a tradeoff between closely tailored security and processing efficiency As security increases, efficiency (human and machine) decreases.

Actions The *action* attribute identifies what the subject can do to the object. Possibilities include reading, inserting, deleting, modifying, creating, destroying, and granting. Inserting and creating sound similar, but they differ as follows: inserting means adding data to an existing structure; creating means building the structure. Thus a subject can insert a *tuple* or create (the structure of) a *relation*. Similarly, deleting means removing data, and destroying means eliminating data and structure.

In a DBTG system, creating and destroying involve changing the fixed structure of the schema and subschemas and recompiling them (and perhaps application programs). In a relational system, creating and destroying can, in many cases, be done during processing. We will see how this is done with SQL/DS in the next chapter.

The *grant* action means to bestow a permission on another subject. For example, a person may have authority to grant access authority to another person. In Figure 11-17, the last row of the table specifies that the payroll supervisor has authority to grant payroll personnel permission to read EMPLOYEE records.

Constraints Constraints specify limitations on permissions concerning subject, object, action. Several examples of constraints are shown in Figure 11-17. For example, the payroll department can only operate on EMPLOYEE records for hourly workers. Supervisory and executive payroll data may not be processed by these people.

Security in DBMS products

No commercial DBMS provides as general a security capability as that shown in Figure 11-17. Instead, a subset of this capability is provided from the standpoint of one or more of the attributes. For example, some systems provide subject-oriented security, some provide object-oriented security, and some provide a combination of other facilities.

Subject-oriented security With subject-oriented security, subjects are defined to the DBMS, and each subject is allocated permissions. The tables in Figure 11-18 are an example of permissions that have been assigned to two users. In this case, the subjects are transactions. All ORDER transactions (type OT) are

Objects

		CUSTOMER Records	SALESPERSON Records	ORDER Records
	Read	Y	Y	Y
	Insert	N	N	Y
Actions	Modify	Y	Y	Y
	Delete	N	N	N

a.   Authorizations for ORDER Transactions

Objects

		CUSTOMER Records	SALESPERSON Records	ORDER Records
	Read	N	Y	Y
	Insert	N	N	N
Actions	Modify	N	Y	N
	Delete	N	N	N

b.   Authorizations for COMMISSION Transactions

Figure 11-18   Subject-oriented Security Examples

authorized to read CUSTOMER, SALESPERSON, and ORDER records. Further, OT transactions may insert only ORDER records, and they may modify all three types of records. OT transactions are not authorized to delete any data, nor can they grant any rights to other subjects.

CT transactions may not access CUSTOMER records at all. They may, however, read SALESPERSON and ORDER records and they may modify SALESPERSON data. No other activity is authorized.

Subject-oriented security is provided in one of two ways. First, a table like those in Figure 11-18 can be defined for each subject in the database. This approach is used by several commercial DBMS products.

A second technique for implementing subject-oriented security is via views and subschemas. If an object is not included in a view, then the subject cannot access it (with the exception of those bizarre cases in the DBTG model involving FIXED membership of invisible members). Therefore, objects over which the subject has no authority at all are just omitted from the subschema or view. If the object appears in a view but the actions on the object are restricted, then these restrictions need to be part of the subschema definition. This, in fact, is part of the subschema definition of most DBTG database systems.

Object-oriented security Another approach to security defines authorizations from the standpoint of objects. In this case, each object has an authorization matrix. The matrix shows what actions can be taken by various subjects on that object. Most often, the subjects are defined by passwords. For example, in Figure 11-19, subjects who can provide the password SESAME can read, insert, modify, and delete SALESPERSON records. People who supply the password ABALONE can read SALESPERSON records but take no other action.

Combination of subject- and object-oriented security Some DBMS provide both subject- and object-oriented security. In this case, both subjects and objects have authorization matrices. The matrices for subjects may exist in the form of subschema definitions or views. The matrices for objects probably are defined in terms of passwords.

SALESPERSON Record Object

		Subjects Who Know Password SESAME	Subjects Who Know Password ABALONE
	Read	Y	Y
	Insert	Y	N
Actions	Modify	Y	N
	Delete	Y	N

Figure 11-19 Object-oriented Security Example

Constraints via user exits   Constraints on authorization rules are not generally supported by DBMS products. However, some DBMS have an indirect way of enforcing constraints. These DBMS will exit to (call) user written routines during processing of DML statements. To achieve this capability, the database designer will specify, during schema definition, the name of a routine to be called whenever a given action is performed on a given object. The routine can then provide the logic appropriate for the constraint.

For example, suppose no order in excess of $50,000 is to be accepted after 3:00 pm on a Friday or day before a holiday. Instead, such orders are to be referred to a supervisor. In this case, the designer would specify in the schema that whenever an ORDER record is created, a special user routine, say OECHK, is to be called. This routine will determine if the above conditions are in effect. If so, the routine will disallow the insert and send a message to a supervisor.

User exists provide a great deal of flexibility. They can be utilized to supplement capabilities or compensate for deficiencies in DBMS functionality. Their advantage is flexibility; their disadvantage is that the using organization must develop and test user exit routines.

Responsibility for security

Security responsibilities can also be viewed from the standpoint of the responsibility continuum in Figure 11-5. The DBMS can be programmed to provide security measures fixed by the vendor. As an example, the DBMS might be constructed to allow the user of any subschema to have complete, unlimited access to all entities visible in that subschema and to have no access to any other entity. Further, the DBMS could be programmed to allow user access to all of the data description catalog, to part of it, or to none of it. Again, the advantage of fixed DBMS responsibilities is reliability. The disadvantage is inflexibility.

An alternative in the middle of the responsibility continuum is to allow the project team to specify security restrictions to the DBMS at installation (or later). A subject-oriented security table could be input to the DBMS and the DBMS could enforce security. An alternative toward the manual side of the responsibility continuum would be for the DBMS to provide no security at all. Instead, application programs would be programmed to view only certain portions of the database, and access to such programs would be strictly controlled using manual procedures. Again, the tradeoffs in responsibility concern reliability and flexibility.

Security responsibilities differ in one regard from responsibilities for controlling concurrent processing and for recovery. An effective security alternative entails responsibilities for all of the components on the continuum in Figure 11-5. Good security would not result from assigning security responsibility only to the DBMS or only to application programs. Such an alternative would not provide effective checks and balances among system components.

Rather, an effective security alternative places responsibility for security on all of the entities in Figure 11-5. Some security measures should be fixed by the vendor (security over DBMS internal data, for example). Some security provisions should be input to the DBMS by the development team for later enforcement by the DBMS. Additionally, some security should be provided by and enforced by application programs. Finally, additional security measures need to be provided by user procedures and controls. Thus good security involves a balance of responsibilities among system components.

The administration of a security program is part of the database administration function. We defer discussion of this function until Chapter 14.

SUMMARY

Although the principal function of the DBMS is to store, retrieve, and modify data, the DBMS provides other important functions as well. We identified nine of them in this chapter. Although database experts agree on these functions, there is debate about which system components bear responsibility for some of them.

A continuum of responsibility exists among the DBMS, application programs, and users. On one end of the continuum, functions fixed in DBMS programming are reliable but inflexible. On the other end of the continuum, functions provided by users are unreliable but flexible. Alternatives on this continuum need to be evaluated in light of requirements.

The DBMS must provide a facility to control concurrent processing. Transactions must not interfere with one another; they must generate the same results whether they are run concurrently or serially. This constraint necessitates some form of resource locking. Unfortunately, locking introduces the possibility of the deadly embrace. This problem, although rare, must be resolved. Of the three resolution methods discussed in this text, killing a transaction and undoing its updates appears to be best. Dimensions of resource locking include lock level, lock scope, lock duration, and lock agent.

The database must be durable. It must survive all threats to its existence including machine crashes, program bugs, media failures, and user errors. Recovery can be done using a combination of locking, transaction logging, and database saves. These resources are used to undo database changes that must be removed and to redo database changes that are lost. Four basic situations call for recovery: transaction failure, database destruction, system failure, and erroneous transaction. The responsibility for recovery can lie primarily with the DBMS, primarily with people, or at some point in between. The best alternative depends on the requirements and the capability of the DBMS.

The database is a valuable resource that can be easily and efficiently processed. Database technology improves the productivity of both authorized and unauthorized users. Therefore, access to the database must be controlled; the DBMS must provide an authorization mechanism for security. In this chapter, a model of security having four-part authorization rules was discussed. These rules define what a particular subject can do to a particular object, and under what conditions. Although no DBMS provides security in precisely this format, this framework can be used to understand and evaluate security that is provided. An effective security system places responsibility for security on the DBMS, on application programs, and on user procedures and controls.

Group I Questions

11.1 List and describe the nine capabilities for a DBMS described in this chapter.

11.2 Explain the term *atomic series of activities*. How does this pertain to database processing?

11.3 Define *logical transaction*.

11.4 Explain the difference between committed and uncommitted changes.

11.5 Why are utility programs needed for database processing?

11.6 Considering the responsibility continuum in Figure 11-5, discuss tradeoffs between functions provided by fixed programming in the DBMS and functions that are provided by people following manual procedures. Use the definition of logical transaction as an example function in your discussion.

11.7 Explain the difference between concurrent processing and simultaneous processing.

11.8 Describe the concurrent processing of two transactions that does not cause the concurrent update problem (other than the example in this text).

11.9 Describe the concurrent processing of two transactions that does cause the concurrent update problem (other than the example in this text).

11.10 Explain the difference between explicit and implicit locks.

11.11 Describe a situation that results in the deadly embrace.

11.12 Describe two ways of preventing the deadly embrace. What are the disadvantages of these techniques?

11.13 Describe a way of resolving the deadly embrace once it occurs. What is the disadvantage of this technique?

11.14 Define the following terms: *lock level, lock scope, lock duration, lock responsibility*, and *granularity*.

11.15 Explain the tradeoffs between programming the DBMS to provide locks in a fixed fashion and allowing application programs to invoke locks. What are the advantages and disadvantages of each alternative?

11.16 Explain how the database can be recovered by reprocessing. Why is this technique not usually feasible? Are there any special situations in which this strategy is effective?

11.17 Define the terms *rollback* and *rollforward*.

11.18 Explain the four basic steps for recovering a database via rollback/rollforward.

11.19 Why does the modern approach place the transaction log on direct access devices?

11.20 Define the terms *before image* and *after image*. Give an example.

11.21 How are before images used to undo a transaction? How are after images used to redo a transaction?

11.22 Define *real output*. Give an example.

11.23 List typical contents of a transaction log. Why are transaction entries linked together?

11.24 Explain why log records must be written before database changes are made. Give an example of a problem if this is not done.

11.25 List and describe the four categories of failure discussed in this chapter.

11.26 Explain how to recover the database when a transaction fails.

11.27 Explain how to recover the database when it is destroyed.

11.28 Explain what to do if the database is destroyed and there is no database save available.

11.29 Explain how to recover the database when the system crashes but the database is undamaged.

11.30 Define *checkpoint*. How are checkpoints used for recovery?

11.31 Explain how, and under what conditions, the effects of a transaction may be successfully removed from processing.

11.32 Discuss recovery strategies in terms of the responsibility continuum in Figure 11-5. What are the advantages and disadvantages of programming the DBMS to perform automated recovery? What are the advantages and disadvantages of manually directed recovery?

11.33 Explain the Fernandez, Summers, and Wood security model. In terms of this model, define *subject*, *object*, *action*, and *constraint*.

11.34 Explain how a DBMS implements subject-oriented security.

11.35 Explain how a DBMS implements object-oriented security.

11.36 Explain the use of user exits for security.

Group II Questions

11.37 Describe general conditions under which it would be permissible to allow concurrent update without locking. Describe conditions under which it would be permissible to allow concurrent reading while another task is updating. Describe conditions under which no concurrent activity should be allowed while update is underway.

11.38 A few DBMS products lock at the database level. To enable concurrent processing, such locks are held only for the length of a single database request. Describe the advantages and disadvantages of this level of locking. Describe how a DBMS with database level locking could perform recovery from failures of types I, II, and III.

11.39 How would you decide the optimum level of locking granularity? Make assumptions regarding the cost (in terms of time) of invoking and releasing locks, the frequency of data conflicts (for various levels of granularity), and the duration of data conflicts. Under what conditions do large granularity locks make sense? Under what conditions do small granularity locks make sense?

11.40 Assume you are designing a query/update facility. Your program must define logical transactions in behalf of users. Describe three alternative methods for accomplishing this task.

Projects

A. Obtain literature on three commercial DBMS products, not including SQL/DS or IDMS. Evaluate these DBMS in terms of the nine capabilities described in this chapter. How would you decide which of these DBMS to purchase?

B. Select a commercial DBMS other than SQL/DS or IDMS. How does this DBMS control concurrent processing? Are locks explicit or implicit? What is the granularity of lock? How does the DBMS do recovery? Is there a transaction log? If so, what is recorded on it? Compare the recovery strategy of your DBMS with those described in this chapter. What are the security features of this DBMS? Discuss this system's security in terms of the Fernandez, Summers, and Wood model. Do you think this is a complete DBMS product?

C. Interview personnel of a company that uses database processing in a communications environment. How does this company control concurrent processing? Examine application programs and query/update facilities. How frequently does failure occur? Which types of failure occur most often? How long is their system typically down? What is the longest that company personnel can remember the system being down? What happened? What security does this company have? Have they ever had a security problem? If so, what happened? What do data processing personnel and users think about the security system they have? Characterize this company's concurrency control, recovery, and security techniques in terms of the responsibility continuum of Figure 11-5.

12
Relational Database Implementation

This chapter describes and illustrates the implementation of a database system using a relational DBMS. We begin by defining a relational DBMS, and then we consider one specific relational DBMS called *SQL/DS*. The general facilities of this system are defined, and then the DDL and DML commands are presented. Next, concurrent processing, recovery, and security features are discussed. Finally, an example database for Sally Enterprises is defined and processed with actual SQL/DS statements.

In Chapter 7 we defined a relation as having attributes and tuples. This is standard terminology in relational theory. In this chapter, we will switch to terminology that is more commonly used in practice. The new terminology, which is easier for nonspecialists to understand, substitutes the terms *table* for relation, *row* for tuple, and *column* for attribute.

RELATIONAL DATABASE MANAGEMENT SYSTEMS

The last chapter defined nine functions of a full-capability DBMS. Ideally, for a product to be a relational DBMS, it would be a full-capability DBMS, plus it would model and process data as relations. In practice, no relational DBMS product currently provides all nine functions. There are systems, however, that have almost all of them. Thus we will consider a relational DBMS to be a system that has most of the nine functions of a full-capability DBMS and which also models and processes data as relations. In the future there will undoubtedly be truly full-capability DBMS which are also relational.

Relational characteristics

What characteristics must a DBMS have to be considered a relational product? In his Turing lecture, E. F. Codd [27] defined a relational DBMS as one in which data is defined in tables and processed by SELECT, PROJECT, and unrestricted

JOIN operations, or their equivalent. Codd called a system having these characteristics *minimally relational*. He defined other, more comprehensive capabilities for more advanced relational products.

The term *table* refers to what Chapter 7 called a *relation in first normal form*. Essentially the table has rows and columns. Each entry in the table is simple; there are no repeating fields. Also, data in each column of the table is assumed to arise from the same domain. Finally, the order of the rows and the columns is immaterial. Rows are identified by contents (the value of SID, for example), and columns are identified by name.

SELECT, PROJECT, and JOIN were also defined in Chapter 7. To review, the SELECT obtains rows of the table according to criteria on row contents. PROJECT obtains columns of a table by column name. Finally, JOIN brings two relations together based on the relationship between two (or more) columns having the same domain. For example, we might join the table STUDENT to the table ENROLLMENT such that STUDENT.SID = ENROLL-MENT.Student_Number. For the *natural join*, one of the two duplicated columns is eliminated. You will need these concepts in this chapter, so review Chapter 7 if you have forgotten them.

Some DBMS products specify that only certain columns can be used as JOIN criteria. For example, a DBMS may require the columns used as JOIN criteria to be indexed. This implies the undesirable situation of restricting user activity because of physical data representation. To the nonspecialist user, this restriction appears arbitrary. In fact, there is no logical reason for this restriction; it exists only to improve performance. To eliminate this situation, Codd specifies that a minimally relational system must have *unrestricted joins*. This means that any column can be used as criteria for the join.

Commercial relational DBMS

There are currently many commercial DBMS products that claim to be relational. Some are more relational in name than in actuality. The criteria in the previous section can be used to assess whether or not a product is truly a relational product. Specifically, the DBMS should model data as tables, and it should support SELECT, PROJECT, and unrestricted JOIN operations. A system that supports restricted JOIN operations falls in a gray area. Some people would call the system a *relational* system in spite of this limitation. Others, such as Codd, would call it a *tabular* system. You should expect to encounter both definitions.

Relational DBMS can be divided into three groups. One group is based on the data language SQL, one on the data language QUEL, and one group contains systems falling into neither of these categories.

Three major SQL-based DBMS products are SQL/DS, System R, and ORACLE. SQL/DS will be discussed in greater detail in this chapter. System R is a research system developed by IBM for the study of relational technology.

System R has been used in a prototype mode by several major industrial concerns. SQL/DS is a commercial version of System R.

ORACLE is vended by Relational Software Incorporated (RSI). Originally, ORACLE was developed for operation on Digital Equipment Corporation PDP minicomputers. Since its origination, ORACLE has been converted to operate on IBM mainframes as well. ORACLE's user interface is based on SEQUEL II, an earlier version of SQL. According to RSI, ORACLE will soon be compatible with the current version of SQL.

QUEL (QUEry Language) is a data language like SQL. (Just as COBOL and PL/I are alternative programming languages, SQL and QUEL are alternative data languages.) QUEL is based on tuple relational calculus (see Chapter 7). QUEL is nonprocedural and allows the user to process data without concern for physical data structures. See reference [72].

The database product INGRES, vended by Relational Technology, Inc., is based on QUEL. INGRES, which was originally developed at the University of California/Berkeley, operates on Digital Equipment PDP hardware and runs under the UNIX operating system. IDM 500, the database machine developed and sold by Britton-Lee, Inc., is also based on QUEL.

There are many other relational DBMS. Figure 12-1 lists some of the major systems as of late 1982. There is even a microcomputer relational product: dBASE II, which is vended by Ashton-Tate. dBASE II operates on CP/M-based micros. dBASE II is an example of a relational (or tabular) DBMS that restricts join operations. The join columns must be indexed.

Relational products are in development in many companies. If you are reading

SQL-Based Systems
    SQL/DS, IBM
    ORACLE, Relational Software, Inc.
    System R, IBM

QUEL-Based Systems
    INGRES, Relational Technology, Inc.
    IDM 500, Britton-Lee, Inc.

Other Relational Systems
    MRDS/LINUS, Honeywell
    NOMAD, National Computer Sharing Services
    ENCOMPASS, Tandem Computers
    RIM, Boeing Computer Services
    dBASE II, Ashton-Tate

Figure 12-1   Relational DBMS Products and Vendors

this book more than a year after its publication, many more relational products likely exist. Developments are likely for both large mainframe and small micro-computer applications.

The balance of this chapter concerns the DBMS product SQL/DS. This system was chosen because, except for the processing of constraints, it is a full-capability relational DBMS. It is also available on popular hardware (currently IBM 4300 systems). Additionally, SQL/DS is based on SQL, and it is likely that SQL or a language close to it will become a *de facto* standard for relational systems. Therefore, assuming you only have time to study one relational product, an SQL product would appear to be the best choice.

Do not construe this chapter's discussion of SQL/DS to imply that SQL/DS is the only relational DBMS, or even the best one. Many of the products in Figure 12-1 are excellent. Doubtless more will be announced in the near future. You should read the balance of this chapter not as an endorsement for any given product, but as an example of one of many effective products.

NULL VALUES

Before we can proceed with the discussion of relational database implementation, we need to discuss a real-world problem. This problem concerns NULL values.

Sometimes when a row is inserted into the database, one or more of the values of a column are unavailable. In this case, the column is assigned a special value called *NULL*. This means either that the value of the column is unknown or that the value is inapplicable.

For example, consider Figure 12-2 which shows data for the relation EMPLOYEE (Number, Name, Family_insur_co, Age). The value of Family_insur_co for employee Kant is NULL. This means either that the name of employee Kant's family insurance company is unknown or that Kant has no family and a value for his family insurance company is inappropriate.

Number	Name	Family_insur_co	Age
100	JONES	A	36
200	FRANKLIN	D	50
300	PARKS	D	21
400	FRANKLIN	H	24
500	KANT	NULL	35

Figure 12-2   EMPLOYEE Relation with NULL Value

NULL values and keys

NULL values create several problems. One such problem occurs if NULL values are allowed in keys. Suppose, for example, that Number is a key of the EMPLOYEE table and assume that NULL values are permitted for Number. Using the data in Figure 12-2, what happens if we issue the following SQL commands to SQL/DS:

```
UPDATE     EMPLOYEE SET NUMBER = NULL
WHERE      NAME = 'FRANKLIN'
```

After this command is executed, we will be unable to distinguish between two rows. One of the employees is 50 and has insurance with company D. The other employee is 24 and has insurance with company H. We do not know, however, which is which. To which objects in the real world do these rows refer? Because of the possibility of such ambiguity, NULL values are normally not allowed for keys.

Null values in the evaluation of conditions

NULLs admit other problems as well. Ambiguity can occur when conditions (sometimes called *predicates*) are evaluated in the processing of SQL expressions. Consider the following SELECT:

```
SELECT     NAME
FROM       EMPLOYEE
WHERE      AGE > 30 AND FAMILY_INSUR_CO = 'D'
```

For the data in Figure 12-2, does Kant's data satisfy this condition or not? Kant may have insurance with company D, he or she may have insurance with another company, he or she may not have family insurance, or he or she may not have a family. When this condition is evaluated, it is neither true nor false. It is unknown.

NULL values in the evaluation of an AND expression will cause the condition to be considered not true. In the above case, Kant's row would not be displayed.

What about the evaluation of OR conditions? What happens in the following case:

```
SELECT     NAME
FROM       EMPLOYEE
WHERE      AGE > 30 OR FAMILY_INSUR_CO = 'D'
```

In the evaluation of this expression, Kant's NULL value for Family_insur_co will cause the insurance company condition to be unknown. However, since Kant is older than 30, and since the conditions are connected with OR, his or her record will be displayed.

The evaluation of conditions involving NULL values is summarized in Figure 12-3. SQL/DS will only select rows in which the result of the evaluation is true. Rows will not be selected if the evaluation is either false or unknown.

AND	T	NULL	F
T	T	?	F
NULL	?	?	F
F	F	F	F

a. Three-Valued Predicate Logic
for AND Operation

OR	T	NULL	F
T	T	T	T
NULL	T	?	?
F	T	?	F

b. Three-Valued Predicate Logic
for OR Operation

NOT	
T	F
NULL	?
F	T

c. Three-Valued Predicate Logic
for NOT Operation

Figure 12-3   Predicate Evaluation of NULL Values

Null values and joins

A third problem concerning NULLs occurs when tables are joined. Consider
the INSURANCE relation in Figure 12-4a. What will occur when the following
expression is executed:

```
SELECT      NAME, COST
FROM        EMPLOYEE, INSURANCE
WHERE       EMPLOYEE.FAMILY_INSUR_CO = INSURANCE.NAME
```

Should Kant be included in this join or not? Kant could have insurance with
none, one, or several of these companies.

For the join as we have defined it, the NULL value will not match any value
of INSURANCE NAME. Thus the result will be:

JONES	100
FRANKLIN	150
PARKS	150
FRANKLIN	75

In practice, this result may be undesirable. The insurance clerk in the Personnel office may only see data through a view based on this join. To that clerk,

Number	Name	Cost
10	A	100
20	D	150
30	H	75
40	NULL	80
50	NULL	100

Number	Name	Cost
10	A	100
20	D	150
30	H	75

a. Without NULL Values   b. With NULL Values

Figure 12-4   Example Data for INSURANCE Relation

employee Kant will not exist. Kant may in fact have a family and family insurance, but because a NULL value was entered, the clerk will never know that.
Kant may miss an important insurance notice because of this situation. This
problem will have to be solved with office procedures. The computer system
will not solve it.

Now consider what happens if there are NULL values in the NAME column
of INSURANCE. Figure 12-4b shows this possibility. The result of the previous
SELECT will be the following:

JONES	100
FRANKLIN	150
PARKS	150
FRANKLIN	75
KANT	80
KANT	100

In this case, Kant's paycheck may be reduced by the amount of two insurance
policies. Imagine Kant's response if he or she does not even have a family!

To eliminate this situation, NULL values would need to be excluded from
the join. The following expression will perform such an exclusion:

```
SELECT      NAME, COST
FROM        EMPLOYEE, INSURANCE
WHERE       EMPLOYEE.FAMILY_INSUR_CO = INSURANCE. NAME.
    AND     EMPLOYEE.FAMILY_INSUR_CO IS NOT NULL
```

To summarize, NULL values are a problem. Generally, we will not allow
NULLs in key columns. Further, the three-valued logic summarized in Figure
12-3 will be used to evaluate predicates when NULL values are encountered.
Finally, NULL values can generate surprising results when tables are joined,

especially when users only see data after it has been joined. Implementers of relational databases need to be aware of these problems and to create manual procedures to control their impact. We now consider the implementation of a relational database using SQL/DS.

SQL/DS OVERVIEW

SQL/DS (Structured Query Language/Data Store) is vended by IBM to medium and large computer users. The first deliveries of SQL/DS occurred in April 1982. SQL/DS grew out of several years of research in relational DBMS products. System R, a research database system, is one of the predecessors of SQL/DS. Many of the publications about System R, such as references [3], [5], [9], and [43], also pertain to SQL/DS.

SQL/DS has eight of the nine capabilities defined for a full-capability DBMS in Chapter 11. It does store, retrieve, and update data, and it does provide a user-accessible catalog of data description. In addition, SQL/DS has facilities to control the processing of concurrent activities, and users can define atomic transactions. Also, SQL/DS has a complete recovery system as discussed in Chapter 11; there are facilities for limiting and authorizing activities; and SQL/DS does interface with at least one (CICS) communications control program. Finally, facilities are provided for database maintenance.

The omission from the list of functions in Chapter 11 is a lack of integrity services to enforce database constraints. The only such service provided by SQL/DS is that columns can be required to have unique values. Otherwise, there are no services for tuple, intratable, or intertable constraints. This limitation is particularly important for subset constraints. For example, the application program must ensure that the value of Pitcher for a new ORDER is a valid Number of PITCHER.

Another important limitation of SQL/DS is that the concept of domains is unsupported. A join may be done using any columns having the same physical format, regardless of the meaning of the columns. Thus apples and oranges may be joined if they happen to have the same format.

Before proceeding with the detailed discussion of SQL/DS, we will first summarize how SQL/DS is accessed and introduce its data and physical storage structures.

Two modes of access

SQL/DS can be used either interactively from a terminal or via application programs. The interactive processor, ISQL, processes SQL commands to perform query and update activities. No application programming is required when using ISQL. For this type of access, users must be connected to a communications control program such as CICS or equivalent.

A second form of access is via application programs. In this mode, SQL/DS commands are embedded in standard programming text like COBOL, PL/I, or assembler language. These embedded commands are nearly identical to the commands that are issued to ISQL. This means that application programmers need learn only one data language; the single data language can be used from application programs or interactively with ISQL. Users claim the near identity between ISQL statements and embedded SQL/DS statements helps them to develop application programs. Programmers can develop database commands interactively, verify them for correctness using ISQL, and then include those commands in application programs.

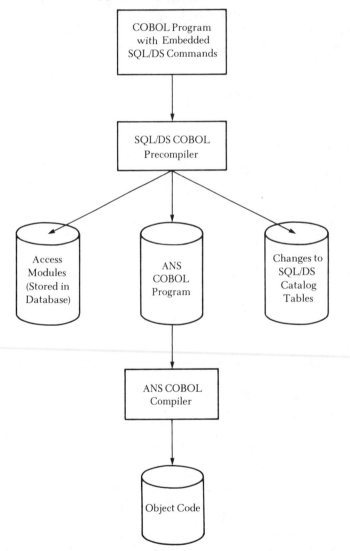

Figure 12-5   Role of SQL/DS Precompiler

Figure 12-5 shows the processing of embedded SQL/DS statements. Programs containing SQL/DS commands are input to a precompiler that examines the statements for correctness and builds small SQL/DS *access modules* that will perform the desired database service. These modules are stored in the database. At the same time, program instructions are inserted into the application program to call the stored access modules when needed. The precompiler generates these instructions in standard COBOL, PL/I, or assembler. As shown in Figure 12-5, the output of the precompiler is then input to a standard language compiler for compilation in normal fashion. An example of inputs and outputs of the precompiler is illustrated in Figure 12-6.

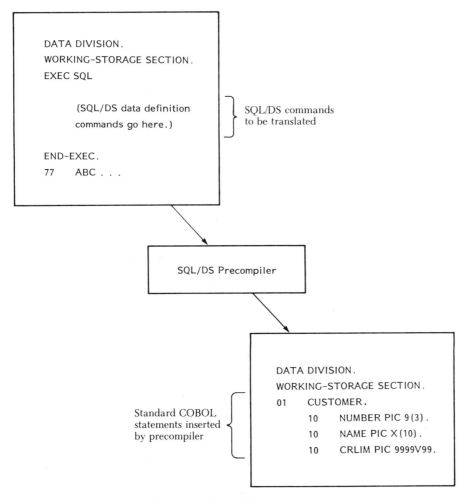

Figure 12-6   Sample Inputs and Outputs of SQL/DS Precompiler

Data structures

The fundamental SQL/DS data structures—at least the data structures visible to users of SQL/DS are *tables* and *indexes*. (The data structures used internally by SQL/DS are not publicly available and are beyond the scope of this discussion, anyway.)

Tables   As stated, a table is a relation in (at least) first normal form. Tables are processed using SQL, the data language discussed in Chapter 7. No physical constructs such as relative record numbers, linked or inverted lists, physical addresses, etc., are used when processing a table. Rows are identified by the value of their contents, not by their position in the table.

All ISQL operations and many application program operations are performed table-at-a-time. Users need not construct logic to read the first row, process the row, read the next row, process the next row, etc. Instead, SQL/DS is expected to provide such logic in behalf of the user. For example, the following SQL statement will add 5000 to all employees in the ACCOUNTING department:

UPDATE   EMPLOYEE SET SALARY = SALARY + 5000
WHERE   DEPARTMENT = 'ACCOUNTING'

The unit of operation in this expression is a table, not a row of a table. Table-at-a-time logic greatly simplifies applications logic.

Row-at-a-time processing does occur in one situation. In application programs, cursors can be defined on SELECT statements. The cursors point to individual rows of tables. Cursor processing will be illustrated in subsequent sections.

SQL/DS stores system data in its own SQL/DS tables. The format of tables, the names and format of columns, the definition of authorities, names of access modules, and the like are stored in system tables. Figure 12-7 lists several SQL/DS system tables.

User tables can be created and dropped dynamically (by users who are authorized to create and destroy tables, that is). There is no fixed schema to be changed and recompiled. Also, a column may be dynamically added to an existing table.

Table	Contents
SYSCATALOG	Description of each table and view
SYSCOLUMNS	Description of each column of every table
SYSINDEXS	Description of each index
SYSUSERAUTH	User IDs, passwords, and authority levels

Figure 12-7   Example SQL/DS System Tables

Index		Name	Table Number	CRLIM
119		ABC INC	487	3000.00
219		ABERBOTH	858	7000.00
307		ZIPPDYDO	307	9999.99
487		MACCAN	219	5500.00
529		CAPITAL	529	7500.00
858		QUICKPRINT	119	3400.50
902		PIKES PL	902	8700.00

Figure 12-8   Index Example

A *view* is a virtual table that is constructed from other tables. Views may be subsets of tables, or they may be combinations of tables. In addition, a view may contain *virtual data*. This is data that is not stored, but rather is computed from stored data at the time of retrieval.

Indexes   A second SQL/DS data structure is the *index*. Indexes (what we called *inverted lists* in Chapter 4) are created to improve performance. An example of an index is shown in Figure 12-8.

Finding rows by data value is, in most cases, substantially faster using an index than it is when sequentially searching. This means both SELECTION and JOIN operations can be faster if data in the identifying columns is indexed. On the other hand, indexes take space, and extra processing is required when data is changed. Therefore, not every column should be indexed.

If indexes are available, the precompiler uses them when building access modules. As you will see, however, indexes can be created and destroyed dynamically. This means that stored access modules will be invalidated when an index is deleted. For example, an access module using the index on, say, SID of STUDE will be invalid if someone destroys the SID index.

To adjust for such changes, SQL/DS stores, in its own tables, the names of indexes used by every access module. When an index is destroyed, access modules that use it are marked invalid. The next time such an access module is called by a program, SQL/DS will automatically recompile it (from the original SQL/DS statements, which are also stored in the database). The compiler will build the most efficient access module using indexes that are now available. Thus, when indexes are destroyed, no programmer needs to change programs.

Unfortunately, when indexes are added, SQL/DS does not automatically recompile access modules to use the new index. For existing application programs to take advantage of the new index, the programs must be re-precompiled.

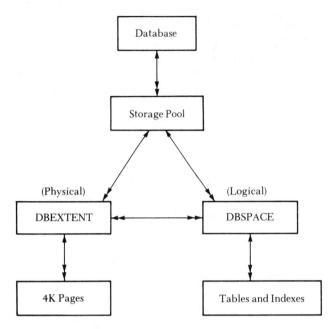

Figure 12-9 Relationship of SQL/DS Storage Structures

Physical storage

Figure 12-9 presents a data structure diagram of the SQL/DS storage entities. The database is composed of one or more *storage pools*. Physically, a storage pool is composed of one or more *DBEXTENTs*. Each DBEXTENT is a group of 4096-byte *pages* (blocks) on a direct access device. In Figure 12-10, the billing database is composed of two storage pools. Storage pool 1 contains two DBEXTENTs and storage pool 2 contains one DBEXTENT. DBEXTENT1 and DBEXTENT2 have 384 and 256 pages, respectively. DBEXTENT3 has 1024 pages.

From a logical standpoint, each SQL/DS storage pool is divided into one or more *DBSPACEs* (Figure 12-9). Each DBSPACE contains one or more tables plus supporting indexes. A DBSPACE may have more than one table, but a table may not span more than one DBSPACE. Tables must be completely contained within a single DBSPACE.

There are three types of DBSPACE: *public, private,* and *internal*. Concurrent processing facilities differ between public and private DBSPACEs. Public DBSPACEs contain tables that can be readily shared by several users concurrently. If data in a public DBSPACE is locked when a user needs it, the user is put into the wait state until the data is available. Private DBSPACEs contain tables that are usually not shared. If data in a private DBSPACE is locked when a user needs it, the user is not put into the wait state; instead, an error code is returned. Internal DBSPACEs are temporary spaces used by SQL/DS as workspaces.

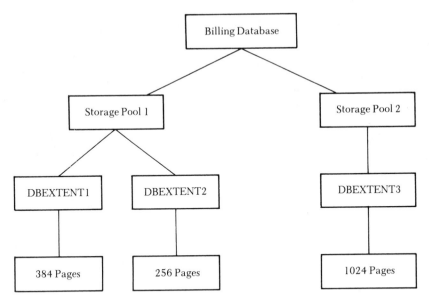

Figure 12-10   Example of Physical Storage Structures

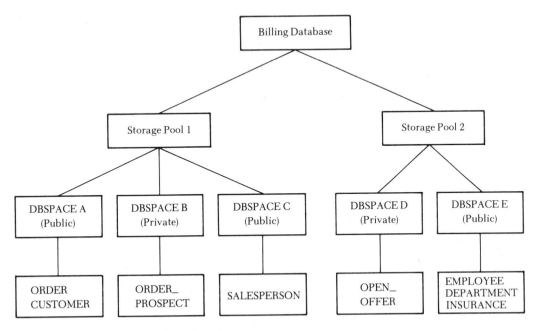

Figure 12-11   Example of Logical Database Structures

Figure 12-11 shows five DBSPACEs, three in storage pool 1 and two in storage pool 2. DBSPACEs A, C, and E are public. DBSPACEs B and D are private. Tables contained in each DBSPACE are also listed.

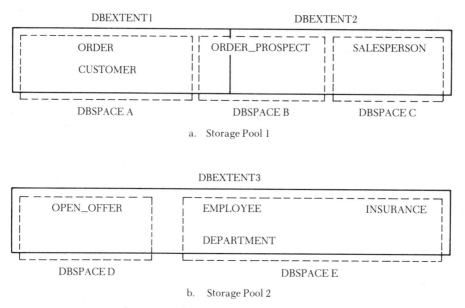

Figure 12-12 Example Relationship of DBEXTENTs, DBSPACEs, and Tables

The relationship between **DBEXTENTs** and **DBSPACEs** is many-to-many. One **DBEXTENT** may contain many **DBSPACEs**, and one **DBSPACE** may be composed of many **DBEXTENTs**. A possible mapping of **DBEXTENTs** and **DBSPACEs** for the example is illustrated in Figure 12-12.

```
CREATE TABLE CUSTOMER
        (CNAME          CHAR(10) NOT NULL,
        NUMBER          DECIMAL(3) NOT NULL,
        CRLIM           DECIMAL(6,2))

CREATE TABLE ORDER
        (ONUM           DECIMAL(5) NOT NULL,
        CNUM            DECIMAL(3) NOT NULL,
        SPNUM           SMALLINT NOT NULL,
        DATE            DECIMAL(6),
        AMOUNT          DECIMAL(6,2))
```

Figure 12-13 Example SQL/DS Table Creation Commands

SQL/DS DATA DEFINITION

The commands to create and change data definitions are simple and straight-forward. These commands can be executed directly from a terminal or embedded in an application program. The only restriction on the use of these commands is that the subject (person or program) issuing the command must be authorized to do so.

Tables

A table is created using the CREATE TABLE command. The name of the table is specified along with the name and format of each column. Figure 12-13 shows the creation of CUSTOMER and ORDER tables. SQL/DS supports the definition of four types of numeric data and three types of character data as shown in Figure 12-14. The corresponding COBOL definitions are also shown in Figure 12-14. Observe the notation DECIMAL(6,2) means six decimal digits with two of them to the right of a decimal point.

Several column definitions in Figure 12-13 contain the keywords NOT NULL. SQL/DS will not allow a row to be created with any of these columns equal to NULL. Further, no UPDATE command will be processed that attempts to set these columns equal to NULL.

Tables can be readily dropped. The commands,

DROP TABLE CUSTOMER
DROP TABLE ORDER

SQL/DS Type	Description	COBOL Equivalent
INTEGER	31-bit signed integer.	S9(9) COMPUTATIONAL
SMALLINT	15-bit signed integer.	S9(4) COMPUTATIONAL
DECIMAL(m,n)	Packed decimal of m digits, n to the right of the decimal.	S9(k)V9(n) COMPUTATIONAL-3 where $k = m - n$
FLOAT	64-bit floating point number.	COMPUTATIONAL-2
CHAR (n)	Fixed length character string of n characters.	$X(n)$
VARCHAR (n)	Variable-length character string. Only the actual length is stored. n must be less than 255.	See reference [46]
LONG VARCHAR	Variable-length character string up to 32767 bytes long.	See reference [46]

Figure 12-14 Data Types Supported by SQL/DS

will eliminate the structure and any data that has been stored in the CUS-TOMER and ORDER tables.

A new column may be added to an existing table with the ALTER TABLE command. The name of the new column and its format are specified as follows:

ALTER TABLE ORDER ADD TAX DECIMAL(4,2)

After this command is executed, the ORDER table includes a new column called *TAX*.

Views

A view is a virtual table that is constructed from other tables. Views can differ from their underlying tables in several ways. First, a view can change the name or the order of columns. Also, a view can be a selection or a projection of a table. Further, a view may be the join of two or more tables. Finally, a view may contain virtual columns.

Views are defined by naming the view, listing its columns, and then providing an SQL SELECT statement to identify the view contents. In Figure 12-15a, the view CUSTCR is defined by reordering, renaming, and projecting on two columns of CUSTOMER. Figure 12-15b shows a view defined by selection, and Figure 12-15c shows a view defined by join. This view simply concatenates CNAME with order numbers and amounts. Finally, Figure 12-15d shows a view containing a virtual column. TOTALAMT is computed on retrieval by adding AMOUNT and TAX together.

Views can be dropped by the commands,

DROP VIEW CUSTCR
DROP VIEW BIGRISKS

and so forth. When a view is dropped, the underlying relations are not modified. Only the view definition is eliminated.

A column may not be added to a view. A new view must be defined to include any new columns. If the needed column exists in a base table, the new definition can include that column. If the new column does not yet exist, then, unless it is a virtual column, it must first be added to a base table. Then, the new column can be added to the view.

Indexes

To improve performance, indexes can be created on one or more columns. However, an index may not be defined on a column of a view.

For the CUSTOMER table defined in Figure 12-13, we can create an index on NUMBER with the command,

CREATE INDEX CNINDEX
    ON CUSTOMER
    (NUMBER)

```
CREATE VIEW CUSTCR
      (CNUM, LIMIT)
      AS SELECT NUMBER, CRLIM
      FROM CUSTOMER
```

a.   View as PROJECTION

```
CREATE VIEW BIGRISKS
      (NAME, RISK)
      AS SELECT CNAME, CRLIM
      FROM CUSTOMER
      WHERE CRLIM > 5000.00
```

b.   View as PROJECTION and SELECTION

```
CREATE VIEW CUSTORDER
      (CNAME, ONUM, AMOUNT)
      AS SELECT CNAME, ONUM, AMOUNT
      FROM CUSTOMER, ORDER
      WHERE NUMBER = CNUM
```

c.   View as JOIN

```
CREATE VIEW T_ORDER
      (ONUM, DATE, TOTALAMT)
      AS SELECT ONUM, DATE, (AMOUNT + TAX)
      FROM ORDER
```

d.   View with Virtual Column

Figure 12-15   Example SQL/DS View Definitions

When the WHERE clauses of SELECT statements involve two or more columns, an index can be created on those columns. For example, suppose the following query command is often needed:

```
SELECT    ONUM, DATE, AMOUNT, TAX
FROM      ORDER
WHERE     CNUM = xxx
   AND    SPNUM = xxxx
```

(TAX was created by the ALTER command as shown previously.) For this query, performance can be improved by defining an index on the combination of CNUM and SPNUM. The following command will do this:

```
CREATE INDEX CSINDEX
     ON ORDER
     (CNUM, SPNUM)
```

Indexes, or inverted lists as we have called them, take file space. They also must be updated when data is inserted, modified, or deleted. Updating the index takes processing time. Because of these costs, indexes should be destroyed if they become unnecessary or obsolete (perhaps because processing needs change). The following command destroys the CSINDEX index:

```
DROP INDEX CSINDEX
```

SQL/DS DATA MANIPULATION

There are some differences between SQL/DS statements for the interactive user and for the application programmer. The differences occur because of differences in environments. The interactive user is concerned with displaying the results he or she wants on a screen; the application programmer is concerned with placing the columns from a row of a table into his or her program variables. We discuss these issues in this section.

Interactive data manipulation

Interactive SQL/DS, or ISQL, supports all of the SQL commands described in Chapter 7. The full range of SELECT commands as discussed in that chapter is supported by SQL/DS. This includes ORDER, GROUP BY, and the built-in functions.

Update commands The function of update commands is the same as described in Chapter 7. However, the format is slightly different. The following two examples illustrate ISQL formats:

```
INSERT INTO CUSTOMER
     VALUES ('QUICKPRINT', 876, 3500.00)
```

INSERT INTO ORDER
   VALUES (33448, 876, 9500, 840302, 178.50, 17.85)

To modify data contents, the column name and new value are specified as shown in the following two examples:

```
UPDATE      CUSTOMER SET CRLIM = 5000.00
WHERE       CNAME = 'QUICKPRINT'

UPDATE      ORDER SET AMOUNT = 155.00, TAX = 15.50
WHERE       CNUM = 876
     AND    SPNUM = 9500
```

Finally, deleting a row can be accomplished by the command,

```
DELETE FROM CUSTOMER
    WHERE CNAME = 'QUICKPRINT'
```

Recall that SQL/DS provides no intertable constraint checking. Therefore, it is possible to create errors by deleting rows that refer to other tables. In the above example, CUSTOMER QUICKPRINT may have a row in the ORDER table. If so, the data about QUICKPRINT has been removed. A join of ORDER and CUSTOMER will not reveal the QUICKPRINT ORDER. The order will appear not to exist. With SQL/DS, the responsibility for checking intertable constraints lies with the user.

Updating views   There are restrictions on updating views. First, no modification, of any type, can be done on a view constructed by a JOIN of two or more tables. Data changes must be made to the base tables, instead. Second, no virtual column may be updated. Thus the column TOTALAMT of T_ORDER in Figure 12-15d cannot be changed. Also, insertion is prohibited on a view that contains virtual columns. Deletion of a row in a view with virtual columns is allowed so long as the virtual column is not computed using built-in functions.

Additional ISQL features   ISQL provides commands for users to control the formatting of screen layouts and to write reports. These features do not concern database technology, and they pertain only to one specific software product. Therefore, they will not be discussed here.

Additionally, the ISQL user can save ISQL commands that are used repetitively. This stored routine can then be accessed as if it were a program. Such stored routines can be written to accept variable data as well.

Using SQL/DS from application programs

SQL/DS can be accessed from COBOL, PL/I, and assembler programs. Examples in this textbook will be shown in COBOL. Reference [46] has example programs in PL/I and assembler.

As shown in Figure 12-5, all application programs that access SQL/DS must be processed by the SQL/DS precompiler. In order for the precompiler to recognize the statements intended for it, all SQL/DS commands are embedded in keywords. Specifically, every SQL/DS statement is preceded by the keywords EXEC SQL and succeeded by the keyword END-EXEC. Further, unless the SQL/DS command occurs in a COBOL IF statement, the keyword END-EXEC is followed by a period. Thus the general form of an SQL/DS statement embedded in COBOL is:

EXEC SQL   command   END-EXEC.

Only one command can be included within the EXEC SQL . . . END-EXEC. framework. Multiple commands require multiple EXEC SQL statements.

SQL/DS statements are included in either the DATA DIVISION or the PROCEDURE DIVISION. As you would expect, definitions of data-items appear in the DATA DIVISION, and commands for action appear in the PROCEDURE DIVISION.

SQL/DS statements in the DATA DIVISION

Two types of statements are embedded in the DATA DIVISION. The first describes data-items that will be used to pass *database* data between the application program and SQL/DS. The second type describes *system* data that will be shared between the application program and SQL/DS.

Definition of database data   Figure 12-16 shows part of a COBOL program to process the CUSTOMER table defined in Figure 12-13. The DATA DIVISION includes data-item definitions for all three columns of CUSTOMER: CNAME, NUMBER, and CRLIM (new names have been assigned: NAME for CNAME, CUST-NUM for NUMBER, and LIMIT for CRLIM).

Observe that data definition using ISQL differs from data definition using COBOL. For the ISQL definition in Figure 12-13, CNAME is defined as CHAR(10). For the COBOL definition in Figure 12-16, NAME is defined as PICTURE X(10). Similarly, CRLIM is defined as DECIMAL(6,2) using ISQL in Figure 12-13. LIMIT is defined as PICTURE S9(4)V9(2) COMPUTATIONAL-3 using COBOL in Figure 12-16. The correspondence of ISQL and COBOL data definitions is shown in Figure 12-14.

So that the SQL/DS precompiler can identify those data-items that SQL/DS and the application program will share, a convention is established. All data-items to be shared with SQL/DS are grouped together in the DATA DIVISION. (We will show these statements in WORKING-STORAGE. They could be elsewhere in the DATA DIVISION as well. See [46].) Further, this group data-items will be preceded by the SQL/DS message BEGIN DECLARE SECTION, and terminated with the SQL/DS message END DECLARE SECTION. In Figure 12-16, the definition of CUST is contained within these messages.

```
        DATA DIVISION.
        WORKING-STORAGE SECTION.
        EXEC SQL   BEGIN DECLARE SECTION      END-EXEC.
        01     CUST.
              05     NAME        PICTURE X(10).
              05     CUST-NUM  PICTURE S9(3) COMPUTATIONAL-3.
              05     LIMIT       PICTURE S9(4)V9(2) COMPUTATIONAL-3.
        EXEC SQL   END DECLARE SECTION        END-EXEC.


        EXEC SQL   INCLUDE SQLCA              END-EXEC.


        PROCEDURE DIVISION.


              MOVE 123 TO CUST-NUM.
              EXEC SQL   SELECT CNAME, CRLIM
              INTO : NAME, : LIMIT
              FROM CUSTOMER
              WHERE NUMBER = : CUST-NUM      END-EXEC.
```

Figure 12-16   Example COBOL Statements to Read Data into COBOL Variables

Definition of system data   The DECLARE section is used to define data-items that will be used to pass *database* data to or from SQL/DS. In addition, the program and SQL/DS also need to share *system* data. For example, after every SQL/DS statement is executed, SQL/DS sets a return code that indicates whether or not an error occurred. Both SQL/DS and the application program need to be able to access this return code.

System data is the same for every SQL/DS application. Therefore, the application need not define the format of system data; it must simply include the system data definition. This is done with the SQL/DS message INCLUDE SQLCA. When the SQL/DS precompiler processes this INCLUDE statement, it will insert the data definitions in Figure 12-17a into the application program.

Figure 12-17b does not define all of these data-items. Understanding all of them would add little to your knowledge of general concepts. You will need, however, to understand how SQLCODE is used.

```
   01   SQLCA.
        05    SQLCAID              PICTURE X(8).
        05    SQLCABC              PICTURE S9(9) COMPUTATIONAL.
        05    SQLCODE              PICTURE S9(9) COMPUTATIONAL.
        05    SQLERRM
              49    SQLERRML       PICTURE S9(4) COMPUTATIONAL.
              49    SQLERRMC       PICTURE X(70).
        05    SQLERRP              PICTURE X(8).
        05    SQLERRD              OCCURS 6 TIMES
                                   PICTURE S9(9) COMPUTATIONAL.
        05    SQLWARN.
              10    SQLWARN0       PICTURE X(1).
              10    SQLWARN1       PICTURE X(1).
              10    SQLWARN2       PICTURE X(1).
              10    SQLWARN3       PICTURE X(1).
              10    SQLWARN4       PICTURE X(1).
              10    SQLWARN5       PICTURE X(1).
              10    SQLWARN6       PICTURE X(1).
              10    SQLWARN7       PICTURE X(1).
        05    SQLEXT               PICTURE X(8).
```

a.   COBOL Description of SQLCA

Data-item	Content
SQLCODE	Return code. Set by SQL/DS after each command. Zero indicates successful operation. Positive value indicates normal condition (such as end of data). Negative value indicates abnormal error.
SQLERRM	Error message. Set when SQLCODE is less than 0.
SQLERRP	Name of SQL/DS routine detecting error. Set when SQLCODE is less than 0.
SQLERRD	SQL/DS system status.
SQLWARN	Warning flags. Set for conditions such as data-item truncation (receiving data-item too small), null values encountered when processing SUM, AVG, MIN, or MAX, recovery from deadlock and so forth.

b.   Content of Selected SQLCA Data-items

Figure 12-17   SQL/DS Communications Area

SQLCODE is set by SQL/DS after every SQL/DS command is executed. If the command is executed in normal fashion, SQLCODE is set to zero. If an unusual but normal condition occurs, SQLCODE is set to a positive value. For example, end of data is indicated by the value 100. If an abnormal unexpected condition occurs, SQLCODE is set to a negative value. An example of such a condition is insufficient file space. This error is indicated by a negative value of SQLCODE.

PROCEDURE DIVISION statements

SQL/DS statements placed in the PROCEDURE DIVISION cause SQL/DS to do something. In Figure 12-16, for example, a SELECT statement has been placed in the PROCEDURE DIVISION. This statement will cause the name and credit limit of CUSTOMER 123 to be placed in the data-items NAME and LIMIT. With one exception, the format of the SELECT statement is the same as defined for ISQL and in Chapter 7. The exception is that the INTO statement is added to inform SQL/DS where to place the values it obtains. Otherwise, the SELECT is coded as normal SQL.

The SQL/DS precompiler has a problem, however. From syntax, it cannot tell the difference between a column name (CNAME or CRLIM) and a data-item (NAME and LIMIT). In fact, the situation could occur in which a name, say NUMBER, is used as a column name and as a data-item, but for different columns. Because of this problem, SQL/DS requires that data-item names be specially marked with a preceding colon. Thus, within SQL/DS statements in the PROCEDURE DIVISION, every data-item name must be preceded by a colon.

Processing multiple-row queries   COBOL is a record-at-a-time language. The structure of COBOL is oriented to obtaining a single record, processing it, obtaining the next record, and so forth. SQL/DS, on the other hand, is oriented toward table-at-a-time processing. SQL/DS obtains tables. Thus there is an incompatibility of processing styles between SQL/DS and COBOL (and most other languages as well). To use COBOL, we must constrain SQL/DS to record-at-a-time processing. We do this with cursors.

A cursor is a placemarker defined to operate on a SELECT statement. In Figure 12-18, for example, the cursor CURRENT is defined to operate over the SELECT statement:

```
SELECT      CNAME
FROM        CUSTOMER
WHERE       CRLIM > 5000.00
```

In subsequent statements, the program uses CURRENT to sequentially process the table. As you can see from Figure 12-18, the logic is the same as the sequential processing logic you have already learned. The cursor is opened, the first row is fetched, and then a loop is executed to process the rest of the table. Processing stops when SQLCODE is returned with the value 100, indicating end of data. We ignore error processing for now.

The format of the FETCH command is:

```
FETCH       cursor-name       INTO       data-item(s)
```

The data-items in the FETCH statement must match the column names identified in the SELECT statement where the cursor is defined.

```
          PROCEDURE DIVISION.
                   .
                   .
                   .
              MOVE 5000.00 TO MAX.
              EXEC SQL    DECLARE CURRENT CURSOR FOR
                          SELECT CNAME
                          FROM CUSTOMER
                          WHERE CRLIM > : MAX           END-EXEC.
                   .
                   .
                   .
              EXEC SQL    OPEN CURRENT END-EXEC.
              EXEC SQL    FETCH CURRENT INTO : NAME  END-EXEC.
              PERFORM PROCESS-FETCH UNTIL SQLCODE NOT = 0.
              EXEC SQL    CLOSE CURRENT              END-EXEC.
                   .
                   .
                   .
          PROCESS-FETCH.
              (process NAME)
              EXEC SQL    FETCH CURRENT INTO : NAME  END-EXEC.
```

Figure 12-18   Use of Cursor to Sequentially Process a Table

As an aside, note how the cursors and iteration logic needed for application programs complicate processing. In previous ISQL examples, neither cursors nor iteration were needed. This simplification is one reason that ISQL not only makes processing easier, but it reduces the likelihood of error.

This section has presented a general overview of programming techniques with SQL/DS. More details will be shown in the example in the last section of this chapter.

SQL/DS CONCURRENT PROCESSING AND RECOVERY

SQL/DS provides facilities to control concurrent processing and to recover the database in the event of failure. These include locking, logical unit of work (transaction), and recovery facilities. We consider each in turn.

SQL/DS locking

In SQL/DS, whenever a user reads data, a *share lock* is placed on that data. Whenever a user changes the data, an *exclusive lock* is placed on that data. The size (level) of the lock and the processing of requests to read or update the data depend on the type of DBSPACE in which the data is located, and on the types of locks already in place (if any).

For public DBSPACEs, three levels of lock are available. Locks can be placed on the entire DBSPACE, or on the pages in which data is contained, or on the individual row being processed. As stated in Chapter 11, large locks (DBSPACE level) are cheaper to administer, but conflicts are more frequent. Small locks (row level) are more expensive to administer, but conflicts are less frequent. The size of locks is determined when the DBSPACE is created.

Figure 12-19a shows processing that occurs for data located in a public DBSPACE. When a user attempts to read data, if the data is unlocked, or if only share locks are in place, then the read is allowed. However, if an exclusive lock is in place, then the user is put into a queue and waits until the data is available. When a user attempts to change data in a public DBSPACE, the user will wait if either a share or an exclusive lock is in place.

Private DBSPACEs can only be locked at the DBSPACE level. Processing for data in private DBSPACEs is shown in Figure 12-19b. If a user attempts to read data in a DBSPACE that is locked exclusively, then the read is disallowed

	No Lock	Share Lock in Place	Exclusive Lock in Place
Read	Process	Process	Queue/wait
Change	Process	Queue/wait	Queue/wait

(Lock size determined by creator of DBSPACE.)

a. Tables in Public DBSPACEs

	No Lock	Share Lock in Place	Exclusive Lock in Place
Read	Process	Process	Error code
Change	Process	Error code	Error code

(Lock size is entire DBSPACE.)

b. Tables in Private DBSPACEs

Figure 12-19 Lock Processing for Tables in Public and Private DBSPACEs

and an error code is returned. The user is not put into the wait state. Also, if a user attempts to change data in a DBSPACE having either a share or an exclusive lock, then the change is disallowed and an error code is returned. Thus there is no waiting for data that resides in a private DBSPACE. As with a busy telephone, the user must try again later.

SQL/DS can detect the deadly embrace. When it occurs, the user who has done the least amount of processing is terminated and uncommitted changes are backed out.

SQL/DS logical units of work

For SQL/DS all database activity is grouped into transactions called *logical units of work* (LUW). The definition of LUWs differs between application programs and ISQL.

LUWs for application programs   For an application program, when the first database service is requested, SQL/DS initiates an LUW. Later, when the program completes a logical sequence of activity, say a complete order has been created, the program issues a COMMIT WORK command. At this point, the LUW is concluded, all changes to the database are committed, and a new LUW is initiated. If no COMMIT WORK command is ever issued, then the entire program is considered to be an LUW. In this latter case, if the program is processing data needed by others, lengthy delays will result.

Additionally, a program can terminate an LUW without committing database changes. For example, after making changes to CUSTOMER and SALESPERSON tables, a program may determine that the order it is creating is invalid. If so, it would issue a ROLLBACK WORK command. SQL/DS will then back out all changes since the last COMMIT WORK command (or since sign-on if no COMMIT WORK command has been issued).

LUWs for ISQL   ISQL, by default, considers each command to be an LUW. Thus SELECT commands, UPDATE commands, DELETE commands are each, in themselves, an LUW. ISQL issues a COMMIT WORK command after each. For many situations this practice is unacceptable. Just as with application programs, an ISQL user may need to process a transaction atomically. The user may want to read data and make several updates, and have either all of the commands executed successfully, or none of them.

To support this need, SQL/DS allows users to execute the AUTOCOMMIT OFF command. In this case, ISQL will not issue COMMIT WORK commands; it will expect the ISQL user to issue them instead. When AUTOCOMMIT is turned off, the ISQL user processes LUWs just like an application program. Changes can be committed when desired, and they can be removed with the ROLLBACK WORK command. Also, once AUTOCOMMIT is turned off, if the user issues no COMMIT WORK commands, then data resources will be locked until the user signs off; this may result in extensive delays for others.

SQL/DS recovery   SQL/DS recovery is very similar to the recovery process discussed in Chapter 11. Before and after images of all database changes are recorded on a log. Changes are written to the log before they are written to the database. SQL/DS periodically checkpoints itself. When checkpoints occur, all changes residing in system buffers are written to the database, and a checkpoint record is written to the log. At the time of a checkpoint, the log and the database are synchronized.

Unsuccessful LUW termination   When an LUW is terminated unsuccessfully, all of its changes are removed from the database. The removal is accomplished by applying all before images created by that LUW. Since an exclusive lock must be obtained before data can be changed, applying before images will not remove changes made by other LUWs, nor will it impact the data that other LUWs have read.

System crashes   SQL/DS can automatically recover from system crashes. After a crash, when the system again becomes operational, the SQL/DS recovery processor applies all before images that have been created since the last checkpoint. This action makes the database consistent as of that checkpoint. Then, the after images of all committed LUWs are applied. This procedure ensures that all committed changes endure the crash. LUWs that were in processing at the time of the crash must be restarted.

Database damage   In the case of a disk or other media failure in which the database is damaged, the database must be recreated. To do this, the SQL/DS using organization must periodically save the database. The save is usually stored on tape. To recover after disk failure, the operations personnel run a utility program to restore the database from the save tape and apply after images of all LUWs that committed subsequent to the save. This action ensures that all committed changes are restored to the database. LUWs that were in processing at the time of the failure must be restarted.

SQL/DS allows database saves (called *archives*) to be taken concurrently with processing. Activity on the database need not stop while the archive is being made. However, while the archive is in progress, no checkpoints can be taken. SQL/DS will automatically start an archive if the log file approaches overflow, although allowing this action is not always recommended. The archive may begin at an undesirable time, say the busiest period of the day, or when the console is unattended.

SQL/DS SECURITY

SQL/DS provides a wide range of authorization facilities. Some of these facilities concern access to SQL/DS, and some concern access to data. We will discuss each of these types of authorization using the Fernandez, Summers, and Wood model discussed in Chapter 11.

Authority by subject classification

To access SQL/DS, the user signs on with an ID and password. SQL/DS uses this data to place the user into one of three categories. *CONNECT users* are authorized to sign on to SQL/DS and to use its facilities to process existing tables, views, and indexes. The CONNECT user may not add new tables, views, or indexes. See Figure 12-20. *RESOURCE users* have the same authorities as CONNECT users plus they may create new tables, indexes, and views.

DBA users have unlimited use of SQL/DS facilities. Essentially, DBA users are exempt from SQL/DS security. DBA users can read and change their own data and anyone else's data as well. DBA users can also GRANT and REVOKE all privileges to other users, including revoking DBA privileges from another DBA.

Authority by object classification

In addition to the three categories of users, SQL/DS authorities are also attached to specific objects. As shown in Figure 12-21, the creator of a table can SELECT, INSERT, DELETE, UPDATE, ALTER, CREATE an index, and DROP the table. Further, the creator of a view can SELECT, INSERT, DELETE, and UPDATE that view (subject to the restrictions concerning joined views and virtual columns).

The creator of either a table or a view can GRANT authorities to other SQL/DS users. Examples of the GRANT command are:

GRANT SELECT ON CUSTOMER TO PARKS
GRANT SELECT, UPDATE, INSERT ON ORDER TO ABERNATHY
GRANT SELECT ON CUSTOMER TO DOLAN WITH GRANT OPTION

The last example not only gives Dolan permission to SELECT from the CUSTOMER table, she also has authority to grant SELECT authority to other SQL/DS users. The only option that cannot be granted to another user is DROP.

Subject	Object	Action	Constraint
CONNECT User	Tables Indexes Views	SELECT CHANGE	After receiving permissions via GRANT.
RESOURCE User	Tables Indexes Views	The above CREATE DROP	Drop only tables created by self.
DBA	All	All	Must be at least one DBA.

Figure 12-20   Authorities of Three Classes of SQL/DS Subjects

Subject	Object	Action	Constraint
Creator of Table	Table	SELECT INSERT DELETE UPDATE ALTER INDEX DROP GRANT REVOKE	Except cannot grant DROP authority.
Creator of View	View	SELECT INSERT DELETE UPDATE DROP GRANT REVOKE	INSERT, DELETE, and UPDATE are subject to constraints for view processing. Except DROP.
Grantee	Table or View	As granted	Can grant if given GRANT option.

Figure 12-21   Authorities for Tables and Views

Only the creator and users having DBA authority may drop a table or view. Finally, authorities can be taken away using the REVOKE command.

Since CONNECT users may not create tables, indexes, or views, the only way they can access data is to be granted access to it by another user. Thus the activity of CONNECT users can be carefully controlled.

SQL/DS security examples

The combination of SQL/DS security features and the flexible method of defining views results in a highly specific and useful authorization system. To illustrate this system, suppose there are two users, A and B. A has created the CUSTOMER and ORDER tables shown in Figure 12-13. B is a CONNECT user that is to process these tables.

Unless A (or a DBA) grants permission to B, B will be unable to access this data. Thus the data is initially protected. Suppose that A wants B to be able to read the CUSTOMER table. In this case, A would issue the command

GRANT SELECT ON CUSTOMER TO B

as previously discussed. Suppose, however, that A wants B to view only CNAME and NUMBER. In this case, the above GRANT command would not be issued. Instead, user A would create a view of CUSTOMER having CNAME and NUMBER columns, and grant user B permission to view that table. The following commands would accomplish this action:

```
CREATE VIEW CNAMENUM
    (CNAME, NUMBER)
    AS
    SELECT CNAME, NUMBER FROM CUSTOMER
GRANT SELECT ON CNAMENUM TO B
```

After these commands have been issued, B would be able to read customer names and numbers, but would not be able to read customer credit limits. If A so desires, these capabilities can be made even more restrictive. Suppose that A wants B to be able to read only the names and numbers of customers with credit limits less than $3000. In this case, the commands

```
CREATE VIEW CNAMENUM
    (CNAME, NUMBER)
    AS
    SELECT CNAME, NUMBER
    FROM CUSTOMER
    WHERE CRLIM < 3000.00
GRANT SELECT ON CNAMENUM TO B
```

will achieve the desired result. Even more possibilities occur with views constructed from joins and with views having virtual data. To illustrate these, we will turn to the example of Sally Enterprises.

RELATIONAL IMPLEMENTATION USING SQL/DS

In this section we will discuss SQL/DS commands to create and process the database designed for Sally Enterprises in Chapter 8. First, we create the database using ISQL commands. Then, several queries and updates will be illustrated using ISQL. Finally, an application program will be presented that processes the same queries and updates. The application program will also insert a new order to the database and check intertable constraints.

Creating the database structure

ISQL commands to create the database structure presented in Figures 8-29 through 8-31 are shown in Figure 12-22. As you can see, these commands are

```
CREATE    TABLE      RECIPE
          (NAME            CHAR(10) NOT NULL,
          SUGAR            DECIMAL(4,2),
          LEMON            SMALLINT,
          WATER            DECIMAL(3,2))

CREATE    TABLE      PITCHER
          (NUMBER          SMALLINT NOT NULL,
          DATE             DECIMAL(6),
          RECIPE_USED      CHAR(10))

CREATE    TABLE      SALESPERSON
          (NAME            CHAR(20) NOT NULL)

CREATE    TABLE      CUSTOMER
          (F_NAME          CHAR(10) NOT NULL,
          L_NAME           CHAR(20) NOT NULL)

CREATE    TABLE      ORDER
          (CUST_F_NAME     CHAR(10) NOT NULL,
          CUST_L_NAME      CHAR(20) NOT NULL,
          PITCHER          SMALLINT,
          SALESPERSON      CHAR(20),
          DATE             DECIMAL(6),
          TIME             DECIMAL(4,2) NOT NULL,
          AMOUNT           DECIMAL(3,2))

CREATE    TABLE      NICKNAME
          (CUST_F_NAME     CHAR(10) NOT NULL,
          CUST_L_NAME      CHAR(20) NOT NULL,
          NICKNAME         CHAR(20) NOT NULL)

CREATE    VIEW       RECIPE_UTILIZATION
          (RECIPE, DATE, TIME, AMOUNT)
          AS    SELECT    RECIPE_USED, DATE, TIME, AMOUNT
                FROM      PITCHER, ORDER
                WHERE     PITCHER.NUMBER = ORDER.PITCHER
```

Figure 12-22   ISQL Statements to Create Tables and a View for Sally Enterprises' Database

very straightforward. Since we determined the domain of each column in Chapter 8, we know the format of each column of each table in the new database. Now, we simply specify that format using ISQL facilities.

The last CREATE statement in Figure 12-22 builds a view. This view is based on the join of PITCHER and ORDER tables. We will use it to determine the amount sold for each recipe type. Since this view is constructed from a join, we cannot perform any update operations on it. SQL/DS will permit only SELECT operations on RECIPE_UTILIZATION.

In addition to the commands in Figure 12-22, storage pools, DBEXTENTs, and DBSPACEs must also be defined. Since the particulars of the process require a knowledge of IBM job control language, and since these particulars relate only to the product SQL/DS, we will omit them from this discussion. For an actual implementation, however, the project team would need to provide these details.

ISQL examples

Figure 12-23 shows three sample queries of the database for Sally Enterprises. The first presents the name of the recipe using the maximum amount of sugar.

```
1.   Display recipe using the most sugar:

     SELECT     NAME, MAX (SUGAR)
     FROM       RECIPE


2.   Display names of all recipes using exactly 2 lemons:

     SELECT     NAME
     FROM       RECIPE
     WHERE      LEMON = 2


3.   Display all recipes and total amounts sold for each:

     SELECT     RECIPE, SUM (AMOUNT)
     FROM       RECIPE_UTILIZATION
     GROUP BY   RECIPE
     ORDER BY   RECIPE
```

Figure 12-23   ISQL Statements for Sample Queries

The second query displays the names of recipes that use exactly two lemons. The third query example uses the RECIPE_UTILIZATION view. The rows of this join will be grouped by common values of RECIPE name. Then, the sum of AMOUNT for each group will be calculated and displayed.

Figure 12-24 presents ISQL statements to update and delete rows from the database. In Figure 12-24a, all rows having the last name 'JONES' will have their last name set to 'PARKS'. To keep the database consistent, this change must be made to the CUSTOMER, ORDER, and NICKNAME tables. If the change were made to only one of these tables, the correspondence of customer names would be lost.

In the example in Figure 12-24b, all NICKNAME rows for 'BRAD JONES' are being deleted. If the update in Figure 12-24b is processed after the update in Figure 12-24a, there will be no such rows. All the JONESs will have been changed to PARKSs. Imagine the confusion that might result if one user sub-

```
UPDATE      CUSTOMER
SET         L_NAME = 'PARKS'
WHERE       L_NAME = 'JONES'


UPDATE      ORDER
SET         CUST_L_NAME = 'PARKS'
WHERE       CUST_L_NAME = 'JONES'


UPDATE      NICKNAME
SET         CUST_L_NAME = 'PARKS'
WHERE       CUST_L_NAME = 'JONES'
```

a. Change Family Name from JONES to PARKS

```
DELETE      FROM NICKNAME
WHERE       CUST_F_NAME = 'BRAD'
    AND     CUST_L_NAME = 'JONES'
```

b. Delete All Nicknames for CUSTOMER BRAD JONES

Figure 12-24 ISQL Statements for Sample Updates

mitted change *a* and another user submitted change *b,* and the two users were unaware of each other. Also, these two changes illustrate the importance of locking. Great confusion could result if these two updates were processed concurrently.

Application program example

Figure 12-25 presents a COBOL application program that performs the queries in Figure 12-23 and the updates in Figure 12-24. Also, this application program inserts a new ORDER row into the database, after ensuring that the new data will not violate subset intertable constraints.

Figure 12-25 shows all the commands necessary for this program to interface with SQL/DS. It does not show the structures and commands necessary to communicate with a user at a terminal. Since such commands and structures depend on the communications control program in use and have little to do with database processing, we will not discuss them. Instead, we assume that the input data structure ORDER-DATA is filled by application code that is not shown. Also, all nondatabase output will be displayed. This program does not produce reports.

In this section, we will discuss program SQL-EXAMPLE in sequential order of the listing. We begin with the DATA DIVISION.

Data Division   As discussed previously, all data-items that will send data to or receive data from SQL/DS must be defined in the DECLARE section. The formats of these data-items must correspond to the formats of the columns to which they will refer. For example, R-NAME will be used to receive NAME of RECIPE. Since NAME of RECIPE is CHAR(10), R-NAME is declared PIC-TURE X(10). The correspondence of SQL/DS data definitions and COBOL PICTURE statements is shown in Figure 12-14.

For this example, the values of USER-ID and USER-PW (password) are hard-coded into the program. Such hard-coding is unrealistic; usually the user-ID and password would be obtained from the user at a terminal. Also, observe that SQLCA is to be included in this program. This option will allow the variable SQLCODE to be checked after database operations.

Procedure Division   The first paragraph in the PROCEDURE DIVISION simply performs paragraphs to initialize processing, to satisfy the queries, to make modifications, and to terminate processing. We consider each of these paragraphs in turn.

```
            IDENTIFICATION DIVISION.
            PROGRAM-ID.  SQL-EXAMPLE.
            ENVIRONMENT DIVISION.
            CONFIGURATION SECTION.
            SPECIAL-NAMES.
                  (Special names go here.)
            INPUT-OUTPUT SECTION.
            FILE-CONTROL.
                  SELECT      (SELECT statements for nondatabase files go here.)
            DATA DIVISION.
            FILE SECTION.
            FD    (FDs for nondatabase files go here.)
            WORKING-STORAGE SECTION.
      *
      *     DECLARE VARIABLES FOR USE WITH SQL/DS.
      *
            EXEC SQL   BEGIN DECLARE SECTION   END-EXEC.
      77    R-NAME                 PICTURE X(10).
      77    R-SUGAR                PICTURE S9(4)V9(2) COMPUTATIONAL-3.
      77    P-NUMBER               PICTURE S9(4) COMPUTATIONAL.
      77    SP-NAME                PICTURE X(20).
      77    C-FNAME                PICTURE X(10).
      77    C-LNAME                PICTURE X(20).
      77    O-FNAME                PICTURE X(10).
      77    O-LNAME                PICTURE X(20).
      77    O-PNUM                 PICTURE S9(4) COMPUTATIONAL.
      77    O-SALESPERSON          PICTURE X(20).
      77    O-DATE                 PICTURE S9(6) COMPUTATIONAL.
      77    O-TIME                 PICTURE S9(4)V9(2) COMPUTATIONAL-3.
      77    O-AMOUNT               PICTURE S9(3)V9(2) COMPUTATIONAL-3.
      77    USER-ID                PICTURE X(8) VALUE 'EXAMP-ID'.
      77    USER-PW                PICTURE X(8) VALUE 'EXAMP-PW'.
      77    SUM-AMT                PICTURE S9(6)V9(2) COMPUTATIONAL-3.
      *
            EXEC SQL   END DECLARE SECTION   END-EXEC.
      *
      *       NOW ASK SQL/DS PRECOMPILER TO ADD DEFINITIONS FOR
      *       COMMUNICATIONS AREA.
      *
            EXEC SQL   INCLUDE SQLCA   END-EXEC.
      *
      *     NONDATABASE VARIABLES
      *

      01    ORDER-DATA.
            05    CUST-FNAME-IN  PICTURE X(10).
            05    CUST-LNAME-IN  PICTURE X(20).
            05    PITCHER-IN     PICTURE S9(4) COMPUTATIONAL.
            05    SALESPERSON-IN PICTURE X(20).
            05    DATE-IN        PICTURE S9(6) COMPUTATIONAL-3.
            05    TIME-IN        PICTURE S9(4)V9(2) COMPUTATIONAL-3.
            05    AMOUNT-IN      PICTURE S9(3)V9(2) COMPUTATIONAL-3.

      77    SUGAR-OUT            PICTURE ZZ.99.
      77    SUM-OUT             PICTURE ZZZZ.99.
      77    ERROR-CODE           PICTURE -------999.

      (Other nondatabase working-storage definitions go here.)
```

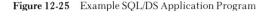

Figure 12-25   Example SQL/DS Application Program

```
                PROCEDURE DIVISION.
                    PERFORM    INIT.
                    PERFORM    QUERY1.
                    PERFORM    QUERY2.
                    PERFORM    QUERY3.
                    PERFORM    NAME-CHANGE.
                    PERFORM    NICKNAME-DELETE.
                    PERFORM    ADD-ORDER THRU ADD-ORDER-EXIT.
                    PERFORM    TERM.
                    STOP RUN.
            *
             INIT.
            *
            *       INFORM SQL/DS TO PROCESS ERRORS IN PARAGRAPH ERR, AND TO IGNORE
            *       WARNINGS.  THEN CONNECT TO SQL/DS WITH ID AND PASSWORD.
            *
                    EXEC SQL    WHENEVER  SQLERROR GO TO ERR    END-EXEC.
                    EXEC SQL    WHENEVER  SQLWARNING CONTINUE END-EXEC.
                    EXEC SQL    CONNECT   : USER-ID IDENTIFIED BY : USER-PW END-EXEC.
            *
            *       NONDATABASE INITIALIZATION
            *
             (Place OPEN and other nondatabase initialization statements here.)
```

```
             QUERY1.
            *
            *       FIND THE RECIPE USING THE MOST SUGAR.
            *

                    EXEC SQL
                            SELECT NAME, MAX (SUGAR)
                            INTO : R-NAME, : R-SUGAR
                            FROM RECIPE
                    END-EXEC.
            *
            *
            *       R-NAME AND R-SUGAR CAN NOW BE USED AS TYPICAL COBOL VARIABLES.
            *
                    MOVE R-SUGAR TO SUGAR-OUT.
                    DISPLAY 'RECIPE WITH MAXIMUM SUGAR IS: ', R-NAME.
                    DISPLAY 'MAXIMUM AMOUNT OF SUGAR IS: ', SUGAR-OUT.
```

```
             QUERY2.
            *
            *       DISPLAY ALL RECIPE NAMES USING EXACTLY 2 LEMONS.
            *
                    EXEC SQL
                            DECLARE    C1 CURSOR FOR
                            SELECT     NAME
                            FROM       RECIPE
                            WHERE      LEMON = 2
                    END-EXEC.
                    EXEC SQL    OPEN      C1                        END-EXEC.
                    EXEC SQL    FETCH     C1    INTO : R-NAME       END-EXEC.
                        PERFORM    DISPLAY-Q2 UNTIL SQLCODE = 100.
                    EXEC SQL    CLOSE     C1                        END-EXEC.

             DISPLAY-Q2.
                    DISPLAY 'RECIPE ', R-NAME, ' USES 2 LEMONS.',
                    EXEC SQL    FETCH    C1    INTO : R-NAME        END-EXEC.
            *
```

Figure 12-25   (Cont'd.)

```
    QUERY3.
*
*       DISPLAY RECIPE NAMES AND TOTAL AMOUNTS SOLD FOR EACH
*       IN SORTED ORDER BY RECIPE NAME.
*
        EXEC SQL
                    DECLARE    C1 CURSOR FOR
                    SELECT     RECIPE, SUM (AMOUNT)
                    FROM       RECIPE_UTILIZATION
                    GROUP BY   RECIPE
                    ORDER BY   RECIPE
        END-EXEC.
        EXEC SQL    OPEN       C1                            END-EXEC.
        EXEC SQL
                    FETCH      C1
                    INTO       : R-NAME, : SUM-AMT
        END-EXEC.
                    PERFORM    DISPLAY-Q3 UNTIL SQLCODE = 100 .
        EXEC SQL    CLOSE      C1                            END-EXEC.
*
    DISPLAY-Q3.
        MOVE SUM-AMT TO SUM-OUT.
        DISPLAY 'RECIPE ', R-NAME, ' SOLD ', SUM-OUT.
        EXEC SQL
                    FETCH      C1
                    INTO       : R-NAME, : SUM-AMT
        END-EXEC.
```

```
    NAME-CHANGE.
*
*       CHANGE THE FAMILY NAME 'JONES' TO 'PARKS'
*       FIRST CHANGE CUSTOMER TABLE, THEN ORDER AND NICKNAME TABLES.
*
        EXEC SQL
                    UPDATE     CUSTOMER
                    SET        L_NAME = 'PARKS'
                    WHERE      L_NAME = 'JONES'
        END-EXEC.
        EXEC SQL
                    UPDATE     ORDER
                    SET        CUST_L_NAME = 'PARKS'
                    WHERE      CUST_L_NAME = 'JONES'
        END-EXEC.
        EXEC SQL
                    UPDATE     NICKNAME
                    SET        CUST_L_NAME = 'PARKS'
                    WHERE      CUST_L_NAME = 'JONES'
        END-EXEC.
*
*       IN GENERAL CAN SET USING A VARIABLE AS WELL. EXAMPLE:
*                   SET        L_NAME = : NEW-NAME.
*       WHERE NEW-NAME OBTAINS A VALUE FROM A READ OR OTHER STATEMENT.
*
```

Figure 12-25   (Cont'd.)

```
    NICKNAME-DELETE.
*
*        DELETE ALL NICKNAMES FOR 'BRAD JONES'.
*
         EXEC SQL
                    DELETE FROM    NICKNAME
                    WHERE          CUST_F_NAME = 'BRAD'
                         AND       CUST_L_NAME = 'JONES'
         END-EXEC.
*
```

```
    ADD-ORDER.
*
*        ADD A ROW TO THE ORDER TABLE.  DO NOT ALLOW INSERTION UNLESS
*        MATCHING SALESPERSON AND PITCHER ROWS EXIST.  IF CORRESPONDING
*        CUSTOMER ROW DOES NOT EXIST, THEN CREATE THE CUSTOMER.  ORDER-DATA
*        HAS ALREADY BEEN FILLED BY ANOTHER PARAGRAPH.
*
         Code to fill ORDER-DATA goes here.
*
         EXEC SQL WHENEVER NOT FOUND GO TO ERR     END-EXEC.
*
*        SEE IF CORRESPONDING PITCHER AND SALESPERSON ROWS EXIST.
*
         MOVE PITCHER-IN TO P-NUMBER.
         MOVE SALESPERSON-IN TO SP-NAME.
         EXEC SQL
                    SELECT    NUMBER
                    INTO      :P-NUMBER
                    FROM      PITCHER
                    WHERE     NUMBER = :P-NUMBER
         END-EXEC.
         EXEC SQL
                    SELECT    NAME
                    INTO      :SP-NAME
                    FROM      SALESPERSON
                    WHERE     NAME = :SP-NAME
         END-EXEC.
*
*        IF CORRESPONDING ROWS DO NOT EXIST, RUN WILL HAVE STOPPED IN
*        ERR PARAGRAPH.  OTHERWISE, PROCESSING CONTINUES.
*        NOW ADD CUSTOMER ROW, IF NECESSARY.
*
```

Figure 12-25   (Cont'd.)

```
            EXEC SQL WHENEVER NOT FOUND GO TO ADD-CUST END-EXEC.
            MOVE CUST-FNAME-IN TO C-FNAME.
            MOVE CUST-LNAME-IN TO C-LNAME.
            EXEC SQL
                        SELECT      F_NAME
                        INTO        : C_FNAME
                        FROM        CUSTOMER
                        WHERE       F_NAME = : C-FNAME
                             AND    L_NAME = : C-LNAME
            END-EXEC.
            GO TO ADD-ORDER-EXIT.
*
*       ADD-CUST IS EXECUTED ONLY IF THE CUSTOMER ROW DID NOT EXIST.
*
    ADD-CUST.
            EXEC SQL
                        INSERT INTO     CUSTOMER (F_NAME, L_NAME)
                        VALUES                   (: C-FNAME, : C-LNAME)
            END-EXEC.
*
    ADD-ORDER-EXIT.
*
*       CONSTRAINTS HAVE BEEN MET, NOW INSERT NEW ROW IN ORDER TABLE.
*
            MOVE CUST-FNAME-IN TO O-FNAME.
            MOVE CUST-LNAME-IN TO O-LNAME.
            MOVE PITCHER-IN TO O-PNUM.
            MOVE SALESPERSON-IN TO O-SALESPERSON.
            MOVE DATE-IN TO O-DATE.
            MOVE TIME-IN TO O-TIME.
            MOVE AMOUNT-IN TO O-AMOUNT.
*
            EXEC SQL
                        INSERT INTO     ORDER
                                        (CUST_F_NAME, CUST_L_NAME, PITCHER,
                                        SALESPERSON, DATE, TIME, AMOUNT)
                        VALUES          (: O-FNAME, : O-LNAME, : O-PNUM,
                                        : O-SALESPERSON, : O-DATE, : O-TIME,
                                        : O-AMOUNT)
            END-EXEC.
```

```
*
    TERM.
            EXEC SQL    COMMIT WORK     END-EXEC.
            (CLOSE and other nondatabase statements go here.)
*
    ERR.
*
*       THIS ROUTINE IS EXECUTED IF SQL/DS FINDS AN ERROR.
*
            MOVE SQLCODE TO ERR-CODE.
            DISPLAY 'ERROR DETECTED BY SQL/DS.'.
            DISPLAY 'SQLCODE : ', ERR-CODE.
            DISPLAY 'SQLERRM : ', SQLERRMC.
            DISPLAY 'SQL ROUTINE DETECTING ERROR : ', SQLERRP.
*
*       TURN OFF ERROR PROCESSING TO AVOID RECURSION.
*
            EXEC SQL    WHENEVER SQLERROR CONTINUE     END-EXEC.
            EXEC SQL    ROLLBACK WORK                  END-EXEC.
            STOP RUN.
```

Figure 12-25 (Cont'd.)

INIT Paragraph

Three SQL/DS statements are issued in paragraph INIT. The WHENEVER statements inform SQL/DS what to do when error or warning conditions occur. SQL/DS is to transfer control to paragraph ERR when an error is detected, but it is to do nothing when it detects a warning condition.

The general format of WHENEVER is:

WHENEVER condition   action

Condition can be either SQLERROR, SQLWARNING, or NOT FOUND. The action can be either CONTINUE, GO TO paragraph-name, or STOP RUN. You will see how WHENEVER statements can be used to advantage in the ADD-ORDER paragraph.

The third SQL/DS statement in INIT is a CONNECT statement. When this statement is executed, communication will be established between SQL/DS and this program. All necessary locks will be obtained, and a logical unit of work will be initiated.

QUERY1 Paragraph

This paragraph performs the same query function as was performed in ISQL in the first example of Figure 12-23. Observe that R-SUGAR must be moved to SUGAR-OUT because the format of R-SUGAR cannot be displayed.

QUERY2 Paragraph

The second query may result in more than one row. Therefore, to display all qualifying rows, the application program must define and process a cursor variable. The cursor is opened and the table resulting from the SELECT is processed using typical sequential file processing methodology.

QUERY3 Paragraph

QUERY3 and its related paragraph DISPLAY-Q3 process the view RECIPE_ UTILIZATION and display the name of each recipe and the total amount sold of that recipe type. Observe that views are processed in the same way that base tables are processed.

NAME-CHANGE Paragraph

This paragraph issues SQL statements to change the last name JONES to PARKS in the tables CUSTOMER, ORDER, and NICKNAME. These statements are identical to the ISQL statements having the same function.

NICKNAME-DELETE Paragraph

This paragraph issues SQL statements to delete all NICKNAME rows for 'BRAD JONES'. Again, observe that this statement is identical to the ISQL statement that performed the same function.

ADD-ORDER Paragraph

ADD-ORDER and its related paragraphs ADD-CUST and ADD-ORDER-EXIT insert a new order into the database. This paragraph assumes that the record ORDER-DATA has already been filled by another routine (not shown).

Since SQL/DS has no facilities for enforcing intertable constraints, the application program must enforce them. Three intertable constraints pertain to ORDER. First, ORDER.SALESPERSON must be a subset of SALESPERSON.NAME. Therefore, before ADD-ORDER inserts the new order data, it must ensure that the new value of ORDER.SALESPERSON already exists in the SALESPERSON table. Second, ORDER.PITCHER must be a subset of PITCHER.NUMBER. Thus ADD-ORDER must ensure that the new value of ORDER.PITCHER is already present in the PITCHER table. Third, the new values of customer first and last names are supposed to be a subset of the names in the CUSTOMER table.

For this program, we will assume that if the constraint relating to salespeople or the constraint relating to pitchers is not met, then the program would terminate abnormally. For customers, however, we will assume that if the customer names are not already present in the CUSTOMER table, the program would accept the order anyway, and add the names to the CUSTOMER table.

Assumptions such as these arise from requirements. In this case, Sally does not want to lose an order just because someone has never purchased from her before. On the other hand, she does not want to accept orders from bogus salespeople, nor does she want to accept orders filled from pitchers that do not exist. Again, you see the importance of determining requirements.

In a more realistic case, the application program would not terminate abnormally if salesperson or pitcher constraints are not met. Instead, the program would probably display an error message on the terminal. Most likely, the constraint has been violated because of a keying error.

To implement these rules, ADD-ORDER uses the SQL/DS WHENEVER facility. The statement WHENEVER NOT FOUND GO TO ERR will cause SQL/DS to execute the error routine if data cannot be found. Then, to find out if the PITCHER and SALESPERSON data exists, the application program asks SQL/DS to read the appropriate rows. If the data exists, the program continues. If the data does not exist, then ERR will be executed.

After the SELECT statements for PITCHER and SALESPERSON have been processed, another WHENEVER statement is executed. WHENEVER NOT FOUND GO TO ADD-CUST will cause SQL/DS to transfer to the ADD-CUST paragraph if the customer data does not exist. ADD-CUST will add the new customer data. If the customer data is found, then SQL/DS will not execute ADD-CUST and control will go to paragraph ADD-ORDER-EXIT.

ADD-ORDER-EXIT moves the new customer data into the data-items known to SQL/DS (because they were defined in the DECLARE section) and then executes the insert command.

TERM and ERR Paragraphs

The remaining two paragraphs of this program concern termination. If the program has executed successfully, the control paragraph will perform paragraph TERM. This paragraph terminates the logical unit of work by issuing the COMMIT WORK command.

If the program generated or otherwise encountered errors, SQL/DS will have transferred control to the ERR paragraph. This paragraph displays data from SQLCA, executes a ROLLBACK WORK command, and stops.

A note on transaction processing

This program does not exemplify transaction processing. A transaction processing program would accept a command code as input, and then perform an action (query, name change, nickname delete, or add order) depending on the command code. In this case, the logical unit of work would be terminated at the end of the processing of each update command (there would be no need to COMMIT after a query request). Thus COMMIT WORK would be done after each transaction instead of at the end of the program. See Project A at the end of this chapter.

SUMMARY

For the benefit of nonspecialists, some relational terminology is changed when discussing relational implementation. Specifically, the terms *table, column,* and *row* are substituted for relation, attribute, and tuple, respectively. A relational DBMS models data as tables and processes them using SELECT, PROJECT, and JOIN. Many experts would say that a DBMS must allow unrestricted joins to be considered a relational DBMS. Others would not make this stipulation.

There are three main types of relational DBMS. Some are based on SQL, some are based on QUEL, and some are based on other data languages. Several DBMS systems are listed in Figure 12-1.

Null values are a problem for relational implementation. A null value either means that the data value is unknown, or it means that the value is inapplicable. Nulls present problems when they are values for key columns, when predicates are evaluated, and when relations are joined.

SQL/DS is a relational DBMS having eight of the nine characteristics defined in Chapter 11 for a full-capability DBMS. SQL/DS does not support integrity services for enforcing database constraints. SQL/DS can be accessed from either a query facility or from application programs. SQL/DS language is nearly identical for either mode.

SQL/DS supports tables, views, and indexes. A database is composed of storage pools. Each storage pool is composed, physically, of DBEXTENTs, which are groups of 4096-byte pages. Storage pools are composed, logically, of DBSPACEs. A DBSPACE, in turn, contains tables and indexes. SQL/DS supports public, private, and internal DBSPACEs.

CREATE and DROP commands can be used to build and destroy tables, indexes, and views. The full range of SQL commands presented in Chapter 7 can be processed by SQL/DS. Update commands are essentially the same as well (there are minor differences in format).

Application programs contain SQL/DS commands which are translated by an SQL/DS precompiler. SQL/DS is table oriented, and most programming languages are row-at-a-time oriented. To resolve this incompatibility, a program can declare a cursor. The cursor is used to process rows within a SELECT statement.

SQL/DS supports share and exclusive locks. The action of these two locks differs between public and private DBSPACEs. The SQL/DS term for transaction is *logical unit of work* (LUW). Once an LUW is committed, it is durable; it will survive system and media crashes. LUWs can be aborted using the ROLLBACK WORK command. SQL/DS can recover from unsuccessful LUW termination, from system crashes, and from damage to the database (assuming a database save is available). Security features are available to control access to SQL/DS, and to control actions that users may perfrom on tables and indexes. Users may be given the authority to grant authorities to other users. Three types of SQL/DS users are CONNECT, RESOURCE, and DBA.

This chapter concluded with SQL/DS statements required to implement the database for Sally Enterprises designed in Chapter 8. Both ISQL and application program statements were illustrated.

Group I Questions

12.1   Define the terms *table, column,* and *row* as they pertain to relational processing.

12.2   What are the criteria for determining if a DBMS is a relational DBMS?

12.3   Define the term *unrestricted join*.

12.4   Name three categories of relational DBMS products.

12.5   What is a NULL value? Give two possible meanings.

12.6   Describe the problem that results if NULL values are allowed for key columns.

12.7   Why are NULL values a problem for predicate evaluation? Explain the meaning of the truth tables in Figure 12-3.

12.8   Describe two ways in which NULL values can be a problem when two relations are joined.

12.9   Is SQL/DS a full-capability DBMS? What, if any, characteristics does it lack?

12.10 Describe two modes of SQL/DS access.

12.11 Explain the role of the SQL/DS precompiler. Why is it needed?

12.12 What is an *access module*? What is the advantage of storing access modules in the database?

12.13 Define the term *virtual data*. How is virtual data used?

12.14 What is the purpose of an index? How are indexes used by the precompiler? How does SQL/DS treat access modules when an index is deleted?

12.15 Explain the relationship of database, storage pool, DBEXTENT, DBSPACE, table, index, and page.

12.16 Name and describe three types of DBSPACE.

12.17 Show SQL/DS statements that create a table, an index, and a view. Assume the table has customer name, address, and number data. Build an index on customer number. Assume the view presents unique customer names.

12.18 Show SQL/DS statements that drop the table, index, and view defined in question 12.17.

12.19 Explain the role of cursors in SQL/DS processing.

12.20 How can an application program detect errors that occur when an SQL/DS statement is executed?

12.21 Explain the difference between share and exclusive locks. How does the processing of these locks differ between public and private DBSPACEs?

12.22 Define the term *logical unit of work*.

12.23 Explain how SQL/DS can recover from:

    a. Unsuccessful LUW termination

    b. System crash

    c. Database damage

12.24 Explain the difference between CONNECT, RESOURCE, and DBA users.

12.25 Explain the role of the GRANT command. How can GRANT authority be given to another user?

Group II Questions

12.26 Locate a company that is using SQL/DS. Determine how long they have had the system, why they chose it, and how well they like it. Have the productivity improvements promised been received? Does the company use ISQL or application programs? Do any users do their own programming (using ISQL)? What is the design of their database? If possible, obtain a copy of an application program. Explain the meaning and purpose of SQL/DS statements. Compare the copy of the program before precompilation with the copy afterward. How does this company do locking? How does the company do recovery? Have they ever had recovery problems? Has performance ever been a problem? If so, what did the company do? Explain whether you believe SQL/DS has been an effective system for that company.

12.27 Locate a company having a relational DBMS other than SQL/DS. Answer the questions in 12.26 for this DBMS.

Project

A. Modify the application program in Figure 12-25 to be a transaction processing program. Assume the program receives a command code and other data as input. The value of the command code determines the function to be performed as well as the other data that is to be input. Command codes, functions, and input data are as follows:

Code	Command	Additional Input Data
1	Perform QUERY1	None
2	Perform QUERY2	None
3	Perform QUERY3	None
4	Perform NAME-CHANGE	Old name, new name
5	Perform NICKNAME-DELETE	Last name of CUSTOMER whose nickname is to be deleted
6	Perform ADD-ORDER	ORDER-DATA
7	Stop run	None

Assume that the program does not cease execution when an error occurs. Rather, error data is displayed, work is rolled back, and the user has an opportunity to enter a new command.

13

CODASYL DBTG
Database
Implementation

This chapter presents database implementation using a DBMS based on the CODASYL DBTG model. We will first describe what constitutes a DBTG DBMS, and then illustrate DBTG implementation using IDMS, a product vended by the Cullinane Corporation.

WHAT IS A DBTG DBMS?

Unfortunately, describing a DBTG DBMS is more difficult than describing a relational system. Confusion occurs because there have been many versions of the DBTG model since the model's inception in 1971. Some of these versions are substantially different, and two DBMS that conform to two different versions of the DBTG model may vary considerably.

For purposes of this text, we will say a DBMS conforms to the DBTG model if it has the following five characteristics. First, the database structure is defined in a single specification called the *schema*, and user views of the database are defined in subsets of the schema called *subschemas*. Second, the entities described in the database are represented by *records*. Properties of entities are represented by *data-items*. Third, relationships are defined using DBTG *sets*. Thus every relationship must be put into the form of a one-to-many relationship and each such relationship is represented by a set.

Fourth, a DBTG DBMS supports the concept of *record currency*. Records identified by key value, or sequential position, or set membership become current of some class (record, set, etc.). Finally, to be a DBTG system, a DBMS must provide the commands of FIND, GET, STORE, MODIFY, ERASE, CONNECT, and DISCONNECT (or their equivalent). These characteristics are summarized in Figure 13-1.

1. Schema/subschema data are defined.
2. Entities are represented by records, and properties by data-items.
3. Relationships are represented by DBTG sets.
4. DML processing uses record currency.
5. FIND, GET, STORE, MODIFY, ERASE, CONNECT, and DISCONNECT commands (or equivalent) are provided.

Figure 13-1   Five Characteristics That Define a DBTG DBMS

DBTG DBMS products

As mentioned in Chapter 9, it appeared in the early 1970s that the DBTG model would become a national standard. Because of this possibility, many of the major hardware vendors initiated development of DBTG systems. The result today is that most (but not all) DBTG DBMS are provided by hardware vendors. Figure 13-2 lists vendors and DBTG DBMS products.

The grandfather of all of these systems is Honeywell's IDS. Actually, IDS preceded the development of the DBTG model; many DBTG concepts originated in IDS. IDS was developed at General Electric, and acquired by Honeywell when Honeywell bought General Electric's computer products division.

This text has insufficient space to discuss each of these DBMS in detail. Furthermore, since all of these systems are based on the DBTG model, a brief survey would not add to your learning. Since you know the DBTG model, you know the essence of the facilities of each of these systems. Therefore, as in Chapter 12, we will select one of these systems and study it in detail.

Vendor	DBMS Product
Burroughs	DMS II
CDC	DMS-170
Cullinane	IDMS
DEC	DBMS 10, DBMS 11
Honeywell	IDS II
International Database Systems	SEED
Univac	DMS-1100

Figure 13-2   DBTG Database Management Systems

Comparison of relational and DBTG DBMS products

Successful DBTG systems, like other successful, nonrelational DBMS, provide heads-down, let's-get-the-job-done type of service. DBMS in this category lack the flexibility of relational systems, but they make up for it in being able to process larger amounts of data more quickly. Systems like this excel at standardized, repetitive applications such as online teller processing, or large-scale order entry, and the like. They may not be elegant, but they can do large amounts of work, and do it well.

Thus we have the following situation: Relational systems are easy to use, applications can be quick to develop, but processing of very large amounts of data can be unacceptably slow. On the other hand, DBTG (and other successful nonrelational systems) are more difficult to use, but large amounts of work can be quickly and efficiently accomplished.

This generalization is true in 1983, but development efforts are underway in both camps to eliminate it. Vendors of relational systems are striving to improve performance, whereas vendors of nonrelational systems are attempting to make their systems easier to use. One way they are doing this is to give the nonrelational systems a relational face. An example of this is IDMS's Logical Record Facility discussed later in this chapter. For now, you should be aware of this generalization, and as your career develops, watch to see it disappear (as it ultimately will).

The balance of this chapter considers one particular DBTG DBMS called *IDMS* (Integrated Data Management System). This product was chosen to illustrate DBTG implementation because it is a near-full-capability DBMS with good design and proven performance. Also, IDMS has been a viable DBMS product since the early 1970s, and is currently the most widely used DBTG DBMS. Therefore, by the law of averages, if you use a DBTG DBMS, you are likely to use IDMS.

IDMS OVERVIEW

IDMS is vended by the Cullinane Corporation to medium and large IBM and compatible computer installations. IDMS was originally developed at Goodrich Tire Company for its own internal use, and was acquired by Cullinane in 1971. Since then, Cullinane has substantially improved IDMS, while successfully installing it in more than 1000 companies.

IDMS provides eight and a half of the nine characteristics defined in Chapter 11 for a full-capability DBMS. It *stores, retrieves,* and *updates data;* it has an exceptionally good *user-accessible catalog* of data description; and it provides facilities for *control over concurrent processing.* Further, IDMS provides several different ways of defining and supporting *transactions;* it provides *recovery* capabilities defined in Chapter 11; and several different types and levels of *authorization* are available. Finally, IDMS interfaces with several major *communications control programs*, and a host of utilities are available for database maintenance.

IDMS provides only limited integrity services for enforcing constraints. Key values can be defined to be unique, and IDMS will enforce this definition. Also, IDMS will ensure that mandatory set members always belong to a set.

Beyond these features, there is no general facility for defining and enforcing constraints. However, the database designer can specify in the schema that IDMS is to exit to a user written routine (called a *user exit* or *database procedure*) whenever a particular DML command is executed. The database procedure may then check to determine if the command will violate a constraint. If execution of the command will violate a constraint, the routine can cause IDMS to disallow the request.

Unfortunately, database procedures have an important limitation. They cannot use IDMS commands. Thus a database procedure may not read another database record, nor check its existence. Consequently, only intrarecord constraints can be checked. Data-items may be edited, for example, or a constraint between two data-items in the same record can be checked, but data-items in different records may not be compared if such a comparison requires the database procedure to issue an IDMS command.

Before proceeding with detailed descriptions of IDMS, we will first discuss how an IDMS database is defined and accessed, and how data is physically stored.

IDMS database definition and access

Defining an IDMS database and preparing application programs is a five-step process as illustrated in Figure 13-3. First, the Interactive Data Dictionary (IDD) is used to define data-items and records. Unlike file processing, data-items are not defined as part of a record. Instead, they are defined in their own right. Records are then constructed by naming the data-items to be grouped into the record.

For example, a database designer might define the data-item SID as PIC 999. Later, when defining STUDENT and ENROLLMENT records, the designer would indicate to the IDD that SID is to be contained in both records. IDD would insert the format of SID into the STUDENT and ENROLLMENT records. Thus IDD guarantees that data-items will have a consistent definition in all records in which they occur.

Once data-items and records are defined, the next step is to define and compile the schema. The schema contains the complete view of the database including names of all records, data-items, and sets, as well as other descriptions as discussed later in this chapter. The third step is to compile the Device Media Control Language (DMCL) description. This description defines physical characteristics of the media used to store the database. It includes definitions of

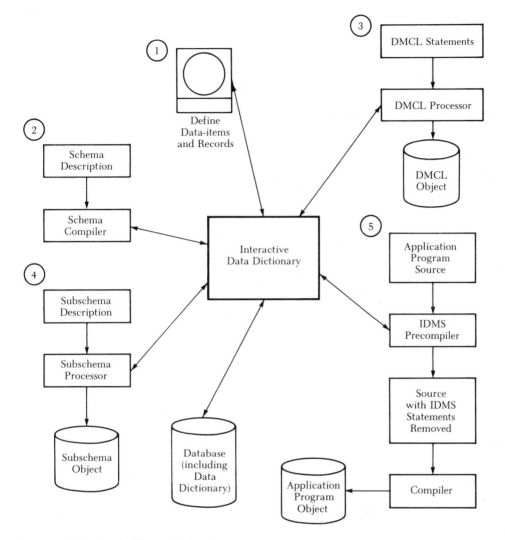

Figure 13-3   Using the IDMS Data Directory

block and buffer sizes, a definition of the file(s) used for journaling, and other physical file definitions. The result of the DMCL compilation is data for the operating system when the database files are opened. There may be one or more DMCL descriptions for each schema.

In step 4 of this process, the subschema descriptions are compiled. For IDMS, a subschema must be a subset of the schema; records, data-items, and sets can be omitted. Also, data-items can be reordered. There may be many subschemas for each schema.

The last step is to compile application programs. As with SQL/DS, programs using IDMS contain embedded DML statements that are not valid COBOL. These statements, such as FIND or STORE, are translated by the precompiler into valid COBOL call statements. At the same time, the precompiler places data in the data dictionary concerning which programs do what to which data. This data is most useful for database maintenance. IDMS includes COBOL, PL/I, FORTRAN, and assembler precompilers.

IDMS query languages IDMS has two separate query facilities. *Online English* is a query and report writing system that processes an IDMS database, as shown in Figure 13-4a. This system can be used to retrieve definitional data from the data dictionary as well as operational data from the database.

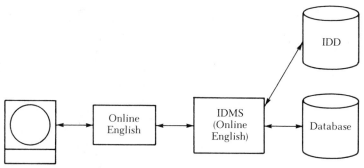

Query User

a. Access via Online Query Processor

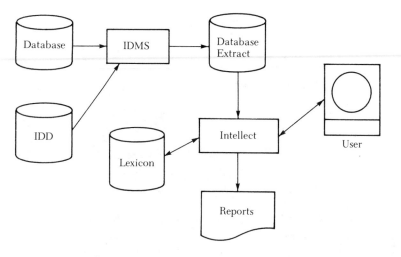

b. Access via Intellect Processor

Figure 13-4 IDMS Query Facilities

Intellect is an easy-to-use query system that processes a database extract, as shown in Figure 13-4b. Intellect was developed from research in artificial intelligence, and it allows users to formulate questions in terminology familiar to them. At installation time, definitions of common user terms are stored in the Intellect lexicon (dictionary). Subsequently, if a user employs a term that Intellect cannot understand, it learns the meaning of the term from the user and adds it to the lexicon. Thus Intellect terminology becomes more and more familiar to the user. As shown in Figure 13-4, Intellect cannot process the database directly. Rather, Intellect processes an extract of the database. This will be a disadvantage if the requirements necessitate user access to up-to-the-minute data. Also, unlike SQL/DS, different languages are used for Online English, Intellect, and application program DML.

Physical storage

Figure 13-5 shows IDMS storage structures. Each database is composed, logically, of one or more areas. Each area, in turn, contains one or more record types. In Figure 13-6, the EXAMPLE database is composed of two areas, AREA-A and AREA-B. AREA-A contains SALESPERSON, ORDER, and CUSTOMER records; and AREA-B contains EMPLOYEE, DEPARTMENT, and INSURANCE records.

Areas can be envisioned as partitions of the database. IDMS allows backup and recovery on an area basis. Thus the entire database need not be saved or restored at once. This feature can result in large time savings for large databases.

Physically, each IDMS database is composed of one or more direct access files. The relationship between areas and files is many-to-many. A file may hold

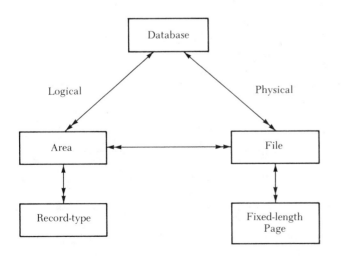

Figure 13-5 IDMS Storage Structures

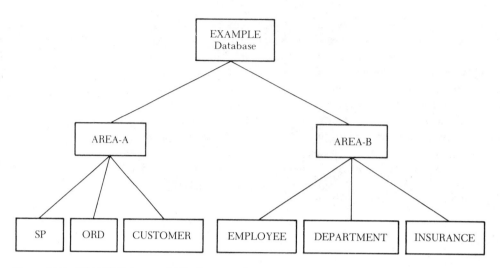

Figure 13-6   EXAMPLE Area and File Correspondence

one or more areas or parts of areas. Furthermore, each area may reside on one or more files or parts of files. The particular correspondence of areas and files is determined by the database designer and specified in the schema description, as you will see. Figure 13-7 shows one possible correspondence of files and areas for the billing database.

Page structure   Each file has fixed-length blocks, called *pages*. File pages contain logical records and unused space. The structure of a page is shown in Figure 13-8. Pages have header and footer sections that contain system data. Additionally, there is a line index for each logical record in the page (the first one is next to the footer, and so on, moving backwards). The line index has the record ID, the location of the record in the page, the total length of the record, and the length of the record's pointer portion. The database key (**DBKEY**) is the number of the page containing the record, concatenated with the record's line index number (counting backwards from the footer) in the page. If the page in Figure 13-8 is numbered 2008, the DBKEY value for logical record C is 2008/3.

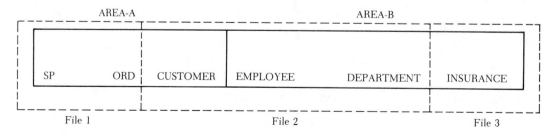

Figure 13-7   Area, Record, and File Correspondence

Header	Logical Record A	
Logical Record B		Logical Record C
Logical Record D		
Unused Space		
		D
C	B	A	Footer

Figure 13-8   Structure of an IDMS Page

When a record is erased, remaining records are moved up to collect the unused space in the middle of the page. Line indexes are updated to indicate the new locations. The line index of the erased record is not removed, because, unless it is the last index, doing so would change the database key of one or more of the remaining records. The index is marked as unused and may be reused during a STORE. Consequently, DBKEY values do not change.

IDMS has space management pages that contain the amount and location of unused space. These pages are scattered throughout the database files. When a STORE is done, IDMS calculates a page location for the record. If that page is full, IDMS consults a space management page for unused space near the desired page. The record is stored at a nearby available page, and a pointer is set up from the full page to the new page.

Set representation   Linked lists (called *chains*) are used to represent set relationships. For each set, a forward pointer field is added to owner and member records. Optionally, there may be reverse pointers for the set, and owner pointers as well. Figure 13-9 shows pointers for the simple network of CUST, SP, and ORD records. The set between CUST and ORD records has forward, backward, and owner pointers. The set between SP and ORD records has only forward pointers. See Chapter 4 for more details about such linked list processing.

An IDMS pointer is a DBKEY value. For example, if salesperson A's DBKEY is 2008 (the record is located in page 2008, and pointed to by index position 1), then the pointer to A's record would be 2008/1.

IDMS DATA DEFINITION FACILITIES

IDMS is based, primarily, on the 1971 DBTG model. Consequently, there are significant differences between it and the 1981 model discussed in Chapters 9

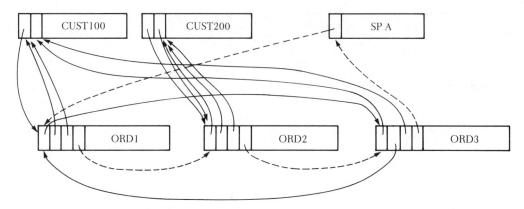

Figure 13-9   Linked Lists Used to Represent DBTG Sets

and 10. We will discuss these differences and then describe the contents of schema, DMCL, and subschema descriptions.

DDL differences from the 1981 DBTG model

The first major difference is that IDMS supports the concept of *areas*. As mentioned, an area is a group of one or more record types. Areas are mapped, in the schema, to particular locations on physical files. In the 1981 specification, the ANSI X3H2 Committee decided to eliminate all physical constructs from schema and subschema descriptions. Since areas correspond to physical locations, they were removed from the model.

Record differences   There are two important differences between IDMS and the 1981 model concerning records. First, when records are defined, they must be assigned to areas. Specifically, the schema definition of a record must include the phrase,

WITHIN AREA (area-name)

Second, a location mode must be defined for each record. This mode defines a way of allocating the record to storage and of finding it later. Three options are available. First, the location mode can be CALC (for calculation); this means a data-item of the record will be hashed to a page number. If the page is full, the record will overflow to another page. The second location mode option is VIA (a set). With this option, the record will be stored physically close to a set owner of the record. Obviously, if the record belongs to more than one set, it can only be stored close to one of its owners. In this sense, *close to* means on the same page, if possible.

The third location mode option is DIRECT. With this mode, the user suggests to IDMS the page on which the record is to be stored. IDMS will place the record on that page, or as close to it as possible. This option allows application programs to have great control over physical location of data. Most people feel

1. Areas supported

2. Record definitions:
   Assigned to areas
   Location mode required:
       CALC
       VIA
       DIRECT

3. Some set constructs not supported:
   No CHECK
   No SET SELECTION
   No FIXED Members

Figure 13-10   Differences between IDMS DDL and 1981 DBTG DDL

such control is just about enough rope for the application programmer to hang himself or herself. DIRECT location mode is seldom recommended; only sophisticated users with requirements for high performance are likely to use it satisfactorily. Figure 13-10 summarizes the differences in record definitions.

Figure 13-11 presents a typical IDMS record description. The record is named (ORD) and given a unique number (101). Then its location mode is described.

```
RECORD NAME IS ORD.
RECORD ID IS 101.
LOCATION MODE IS CALC           USING ORD-NUM
                                DUPLICATES NOT ALLOWED.
WITHIN AREA-A.
      05    ORD-NUM             PIC 9999.
      05    SP-NUM              PIC 999.
      05    SP-NAME             PIC X(15).
      05    ORD-DATE            PIC 9(6).
      05    CUST-NUM            PIC 999.
      .
      .
      .
      etc. for remaining data-item definitions.
```

Figure 13-11   Sample IDMS Schema Record Definition

For this example, ORD-NUM will be used to hash to the record's location. All occurrences of the record are to be stored in AREA-A. Finally, the data-items in the record are defined using COBOL-like notation.

Sets   IDMS does not support three of the set features described in Chapter 9. First, there is no CHECK facility. IDMS will not ensure that specified data conditions exist among member and owner data-items. Second, there is no SET SELECTION clause. Third, there is no FIXED retention status. Only MANDATORY and OPTIONAL retention status are allowed.

In addition to these omissions, IDMS requires several additions to the 1981 set specification. Figure 13-12 illustrates these additions. First, the phrase MODE IS CHAINED is always required. It means the set is to be represented using linked lists. LINKED TO PRIOR is an optional phrase. It means that IDMS is to add reverse pointers as well. Additionally, the designer must specify the position of the pointers (called *DBKEY POSITION*) for the owner and members of each set. For the SALES set in Figure 13-12, the forward pointer in the owner (SP) is to be in the third position and the reverse pointer in the fourth position (the first and second positions are used for another set). For the member record (ORD), the forward pointer is in the first position and the reverse pointer is in the second position. An example of this structure is shown in Figure 13-13. Other entries in the set description correspond to the discussion in Chapter 9.

Subschema difference   The major difference between the 1981 DBTG model and IDMS subschemas concerns aliases. IDMS will not allow record, set, or

```
SET NAME IS SALES.
ORDER IS SORTED.
MODE IS CHAINED,              LINKED TO PRIOR.
OWNER IS SP                   NEXT DBKEY POSITION IS 3
                             PRIOR DBKEY POSITION IS 4.

MEMBER IS ORD                 NEXT DBKEY POSITION IS 1
                             PRIOR DBKEY POSITION IS 2
                             MANDATORY AUTOMATIC
                             ASCENDING KEY IS ORD-DATE
                                 DUPLICATES ALLOWED.
```

Figure 13-12   Sample IDMS Schema Set Definition

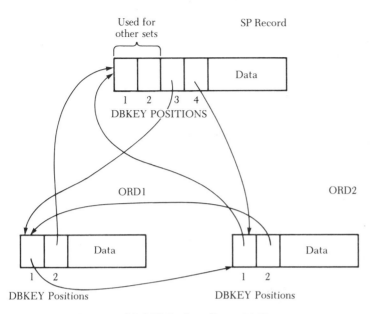

Figure 13-13 Instance of SALES Set from Figure 13-12

data-item names to be changed between the schema and the subschema. All names used in the subschema must have been defined in the schema.

Schema definition

Figure 13-14 shows the structure of an IDMS schema description. There are five major sections. The first section defines the name of the schema and records optional comments. The second section defines files. For the example in Figure 13-14, three files are defined. The names DB1 through DB3 are names of files in the external job control language (DDNAMEs). The operating system will recognize these names and be able to associate them with physical devices.

The third section of the schema defines areas. In Figure 13-14, two areas are defined. AREA-A is 500 pages long. The first 400 of these pages reside on FILE1 on relative blocks 101 through 500 of that file. The remaining 100 pages reside on FILE2 on relative blocks numbered 101 through 200 of that file.

AREA-B resides on FILE2 and FILE3. The first 500 pages of AREA-B reside on FILE2 on relative blocks 401 through 900. The remaining 500 pages reside on FILE3 on relative blocks 1501 through 2000. (Unallocated pages on the files are used for other purposes or reserved for future expansion.)

The fourth section of the schema contains record descriptions, and the fifth portion contains set descriptions. We have already discussed these entries. A complete schema is presented and discussed in the last section of this chapter.

```
SCHEMA DESCRIPTION.
SCHEMA NAME IS EXAMPLE.
FILE DESCRIPTION.
FILE NAME IS FILE1 ASSIGN TO DB1.
FILE NAME IS FILE2 ASSIGN TO DB2.
FILE NAME IS FILE3 ASSIGN TO DB3.
AREA DESCRIPTION.
AREA NAME IS AREA-A
       RANGE IS    1 THRU 500
       WITHIN FILE1 FROM 101 THRU 500;
       WITHIN FILE2 FROM 101 THRU 200.
AREA NAME IS AREA-B
       RANGE IS    1 THRU 1000
       WITHIN FILE2 FROM 401 THRU 900;
       WITHIN FILE3 FROM 1501 THRU 2000.
RECORD DESCRIPTION.


       (Record descriptions like those in Figure 13-11 go here.)


SET DESCRIPTION.


       (Set descriptions like those in Figure 13-12 go here.)
```

Figure 13-14   IDMS Schema for EXAMPLE Database

DMCL description

The Device Media Control Language describes file page sizes and the journal file. It has four sections as shown in Figure 13-15. The first section is the Device-Media Description which names both the DMCL module and the schema to which it corresponds. The second section defines buffers (areas of main memory used to transfer data to and from the files). The third part of the DMCL description names areas and associates them with buffers. The area descriptions need not be repeated; the DMCL compiler will copy them from the schema.

The last section of the DMCL description names the journal files and specifies the type of device on which the journals reside. If the journals will reside on direct access devices (which is recommended), then two of them are normally used. Also, in this case, an archive for the journal files is defined. This archive is a file on a tape device to which the journals will be copied when they become full.

```
DEVICE-MEDIA DESCRIPTION.
DEVICE-MEDIA NAME IS EX-DMCL OF EXAMPLE.
BUFFER SECTION.
        BUFFER NAME IS BUFFPOOL
        PAGE CONTAINS 3156 CHARACTERS
        BUFFER CONTAINS 7 PAGES.
AREA SECTION.
        COPY AREA-A
                BUFFER IS BUFFPOOL.
        COPY AREA-B
                BUFFER IS BUFFPOOL.
JOURNAL SECTION.
        (A description of journal files, devices, and the journal archive go
        here.  Details are beyond the scope of this discussion.)
```

Figure 13-15   Sample IDMS DMCL Module

Subschema descriptions

An IDMS subschema description has two divisions: IDENTIFICATION and DATA. As shown in Figure 13-16, the IDENTIFICATION DIVISION specifies

```
SUBSCHEMA IDENTIFICATION DIVISION.
SUBSCHEMA NAME IS EX-SUB OF EXAMPLE.
DEVICE-MEDIA NAME IS EX-DMCL.
SUBSCHEMA DATA DIVISION.
AREA SECTION.
        COPY AREA-A AREA.
RECORD SECTION.
        COPY RECORD SP.
        01    ORD.
              05    ORD-NUM.
              05    ORD-DATE.
              05    SP-NUM.
SET SECTION.
        COPY SET SALES.
```

Figure 13-16   Sample IDMS Subschema Description

the name of the subschema, the name of the schema on which it is based, and the name of the associated DMCL module.

The DATA DIVISION has three sections, one for areas, one for records, and one for sets. The AREA SECTION copies areas that have been defined in the schema and DMCL. In Figure 13-16, only AREA-A is to be included in the EX-SUB subschema. The RECORD SECTION describes records to be contained in the subschema. Since only records SP, ORD, and CUSTOMER (see Figure 13-6) are included in AREA-A, only they can be included in the subschema. If the designer wanted, say, EMPLOYEE records in the subschema, then AREA-B would have to be included as well.

Two options are available for defining records. First, they can be copied from the schema. In Figure 13-16, record SP is copied in its entirety.

Alternatively, a subset of the data-items in a record can be included. In this case, the portion to be included must be defined. As mentioned previously, all names in the subschema description must correspond to names in the schema description. In Figure 13-16, the data-items ORD-NUM, ORD-DATE, and SP-NUM of ORD are included.

The last section of the DATA DIVISION of the subschema is the SET SECTION. Here, sets are copied from the schema. For a set to be present in the subschema, both its owner and member record types must also be present.

A note on processing of sets

Recall in Chapter 10 that certain bizarre results could occur when records were stored, erased, or modified, if those records owned or belonged to sets that were not present in the subschema. Since IDMS does not support CHECK and SET SELECTION facilities, some of these bizarre conditions cannot occur.

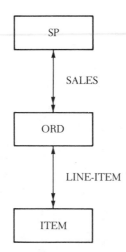

Figure 13-17 Example of Owned and Derived Sets for Record SP

Specifically, modification of data-items will not cause records to be moved to other set occurrences.

STORE and ERASE can create difficulties, however. In order for IDMS to process a STORE command, all sets in which the record participates as an AUTOMATIC member must be present in the subschema. For the sets in Figure 13-17, if ORD is an AUTOMATIC member of SALES, and if SALES is owned by SP, then both SP and SALES must exist in all subschemas in which ORD is stored. If not, IDMS will disallow the STORE commands.

Additionally, if the location mode of a record is via a set, then both the set and the set owner must be present in all subschemas in which the member is stored. For example, if the location mode of ORD is VIA SALES, then both SALES and SP must be present in a subschema if ORD records are to be stored.

To erase a record, all owned sets and members of those sets (children) must be in the subschema. Further, all sets owned by children, and members of those sets (grandchildren), and so forth, all the way to the bottom of the schema, must also appear in the subschema. For the example in Figure 13-17, for IDMS to accept an ERASE SP command, sets SALES and LINE-ITEM must be present as well as records ORD and ITEM. If not, the erase command will be disallowed. The rules for processing of STORE and ERASE commands are summarized in Figure 13-18.

IDMS DATA MANIPULATION FACILITIES

Basically, IDMS provides the same DML facilities as were discussed in Chapters 9 and 10. The format of some commands, however, is different, and several additional options are available because IDMS supports areas. We consider data retrieval commands first, and then update commands.

STORE:
    If the record is an automatic member of a set,
        then the set and its owner record type must be in the subschema.
    If the location mode of the record is via,
        then the set and its owner record type must be in the subschema.

ERASE:
    All sets owned by the record to be erased and all of its derived sets
    must be in the subschema.
    All members of all owned and derived sets must be in the subschema.

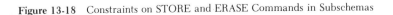

Figure 13-18 Constraints on STORE and ERASE Commands in Subschemas

Retrieval commands

IDMS DML commands function in the same two-phase mode as described for the DBTG commands in Chapter 9. First, a record is found; this establishes the found record as current of run-unit. Then, an action is taken with regard to the current record.

For example, to retrieve a record, it is first found and then a GET command is issued. Since the pair FIND/GET is frequently used, IDMS combines these two into a single new command called *OBTAIN*. OBTAIN is a FIND with an automatic GET, and it has the same parameters as FIND. Therefore, in the following discussion, all the options and parameters defined for FIND are also available for OBTAIN.

IDMS supports six formats of the FIND (and OBTAIN) command, as shown in Figure 13-19. The first format causes a record which is current of its record type, or current of a set, or current of an area to become current of the run-unit. The second form of FIND is used to identify a record by its position in a set or an area. For example, the command,

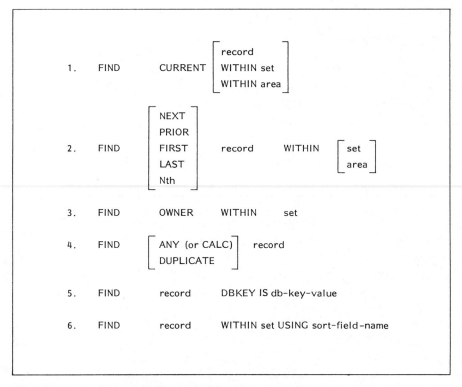

Figure 13-19   Six Formats of FIND (and OBTAIN) Recognized by IDMS

FIND FIRST ORD WITHIN AREA-A.

will identify the first order record in AREA-A. Since IDMS requires every record of a given type to reside in the same area, all records of a type can be processed sequentially using this form of FIND. However, the order of these records will be determined by the system; they will be in no particular logical order.

(As an aside, IDMS does not support system sets. Instead, when there is a need to process records in one or more sequential orders, IDMS provides a special feature called the *Sequential Processing Facility* (SPF). This facility substitutes for system sets as defined in Chapter 10; further discussion of SPF is beyond the scope of this text. See reference [31].)

The third form of FIND identifies records by ownership. Consider the set SALES with owner SP and members ORD. If an ORD record is current of run-unit, then the command,

FIND OWNER WITHIN SALES.

will establish the owner of the ORD record as the current of run-unit.

The fourth version of the FIND command identifies records based on a CALC field. To use this form of FIND, the location mode of the record must be CALC. The application program sets the value of the CALC field and then issues the FIND. For example, if the location mode of ORD is CALC USING ORD-NUM, then the following commands will identify an ORD record:

MOVE 123 TO ORD-NUM
FIND ANY ORD.

and then,

FIND DUPLICATE ORD.

The second FIND command is valid only if the schema description for ORD records includes the phrase DUPLICATES ARE ALLOWED in the location mode declaration.

The fifth mode of FIND can only be used if the application program knows a record's DBKEY. Suppose that the DBKEY for a record is stored in the variable REC-KEY. If so, the following FIND can be used:

FIND ORD DBKEY IS REC-KEY.

This type of FIND can be used whether the record's location mode is DIRECT or not. DBKEY values can be obtained from IDMS in a variety of ways. Again, using such keys, however, is generally not good practice.

The last form of FIND can be used for records belonging to sorted sets. Assume the set SALES is ordered by the data-item ORD-DATE. Then,

MOVE 841225 TO ORD-DATE.
FIND ORD WITHIN SALES USING ORD-DATE.

will find the first ORD record in the SALES set having an ORD-DATE equal to 841225.

As mentioned, all these formats are also valid for OBTAIN. For example,

MOVE 841225 TO ORD-DATE
OBTAIN ORD WITHIN SALES USING ORD-DATE

will retrieve (FIND and GET) the first qualifying ORD record.

Update commands

The IDMS update commands are nearly identical to the DBTG update commands described in Chapter 9. Examples are shown in Figure 13-20. To STORE a record, the data-items of the record are first filled, and then the STORE command is executed. If the new record is an automatic member of any sets, then currency indicators of those sets need to be established before the STORE is issued. For example, in Figure 13-20, a SALES set occurrence is established before the STORE ORD is issued.

The MODIFY command changes the values of data-items. The recommended way of changing data-items is to first fill the data-items with an OBTAIN command. Then, data-item values to be modified are changed, and the MODIFY is issued. If the CALC data-item is changed, IDMS may move the record in the database. In this case, the record's DBKEY value may change.

```
1.    Fill ORD data-items
      Establish SALES set occurrence.
      STORE ORD.

2.    OBTAIN ORD (using any of six forms)
      Change data-items.
      MODIFY ORD.

3.    ERASE ORD.
      ERASE ORD PERMANENT MEMBERS.
      ERASE ORD SELECTIVE MEMBERS.
      ERASE ORD ALL MEMBERS.
```

Figure 13-20 Examples of IDMS Update Commands

The IDMS ERASE command has four options. ERASE ORD deletes the current of run-unit record (which must be an ORD record). However, if that record owns any sets, the ERASE command is ignored. The ERASE PERMANENT command deletes the identified record and all mandatory set members that are connected to it. Optional set members are disconnected. ERASE SELECTIVE commands delete the identified record and all mandatory set members connected to it. Optional members are also deleted if they do not belong to an occurrence of another set. Finally, the ERASE ALL command deletes the indicated record and all records that are connected to it, whether they are mandatory or optional.

IDMS CONNECT and DISCONNECT commands operate exactly as described in Chapter 9.

IDMS CONCURRENT PROCESSING AND RECOVERY

IDMS provides complete facilities for control of concurrent processing and for recovery. These facilities include several different forms of locking and several ways of declaring transactions. The IDMS recovery mechanism is similar to, but slightly different from, recovery techniques discussed so far. We consider each of these in turn.

IDMS locking facilities

IDMS locking can be done at two levels of granularity. A lock can be placed on an entire *area*, or locks can be placed on individual *records*. Area locks are placed when the area is first opened; record locks are placed when records are used, or at the discretion of the application program.

Area locks   Before an application program can access data, the area that contains the data must be opened. This is done by issuing a READY command. READY informs IDMS that the application program will be accessing data in the area, and whether the access will be retrieval only, or update as well. Additionally, depending on parameters in the READY command, locks will be placed on the area. When an application has completed processing an area, it issues a FINISH command. When this command is issued, all locks are released.

When the READY command is issued, the program must inform IDMS of its processing intent. An area can be opened for RETRIEVAL, meaning the application program will only issue FIND/GET/OBTAIN commands. Alternatively, an area can be opened for UPDATE, in which case all IDMS commands may be issued.

Further, when an area is readied, the application program may ask for a PROTECTED lock, an EXCLUSIVE lock, or no lock at all. A PROTECTED lock prevents other run-units from making concurrent updates of data in the area. An EXCLUSIVE lock prevents other run-units from concurrently accessing the area in any way. NO LOCK would be requested if the application was processing the database in the single user mode, or if record locks were going to be used instead of area locks. Examples of valid READY commands are:

READY AREA-A RETRIEVAL.   (no lock, retrieval only)
READY AREA-A PROTECTED RETRIEVAL.   (PROTECTED lock,
                                      retrieval only)
READY AREA-A EXCLUSIVE UPDATE.   (EXCLUSIVE lock,
                                      retrieval and update)

The different combinations of locks and processing intents are defined in Figure 13-21a. The consequences of issuing PROTECTED and EXCLUSIVE locks are presented in Figure 13-21b.

Lock Request

PROCESSING INTENT		NONE	PROTECTED	EXCLUSIVE
	RETRIEVAL	No area lock. Read only.	No concurrent update. Read only.	No concurrent access. Read only.
	UPDATE	No area lock. Update allowed	No concurrent update. Update allowed.	No concurrent access. Update allowed.

a. READY Command Options

Lock Status at Time of Request

	NONE	PROTECTED	EXCLUSIVE
RETRIEVAL/ PROTECTED	Process	Process	Wait
UPDATE/ PROTECTED	Process	Wait	Wait
RETRIEVAL/ EXCLUSIVE	Process	Wait	Wait
UPDATE/ EXCLUSIVE	Process	Wait	Wait

b. Process of READY Commands

Figure 13-21   READY Command Definitions

Normally, an area will contain many records and much data. Also, an application program may keep an area for an extended period. If so, considerable waiting may result from area level locking. Under these conditions, record locking may be more appropriate.

Record locks If an area is readied with no lock, then IDMS will provide record level locking. Two types of record locks, analogous to the two types of area locks, are available. A *shared lock* prevents concurrent update of the record, but will allow concurrent retrieval. An *exclusive lock* prevents concurrent access of any kind. Futhermore, record locks can be placed *implicitly* by IDMS, or *explicitly* by the application program.

If, when IDMS is installed, the implicit lock feature is selected, then IDMS will place locks automatically on records in unlocked areas. A shared lock will be placed on the current of run-unit, current of each record type, current of each set, and current of each area. Shared locks are released when currency indicators change. An exclusive lock will be placed on all modified records (STORE, MODIFY, ERASE, CONNECT, DISCONNECT). The exclusive lock will be held until a FINISH, COMMIT, or ROLLBACK command is issued (see next section).

Explicit locks are set by application programs in two ways. First, a lock may be obtained by issuing either a FIND or OBTAIN command with an embedded lock request. The keyword KEEP is a signal to IDMS to obtain a lock. For example,

FIND KEEP FIRST ORD WITHIN AREA-A.
FIND KEEP EXCLUSIVE FIRST ORD WITHIN AREA-A.

The first example places a shared lock on the found record, and the second example places an exclusive lock on that record. A second way to obtain a lock on a record is to use the KEEP command. This command places a lock on a current record. For example,

KEEP CURRENT ORD.
KEEP CURRENT WITHIN AREA-A.
KEEP EXCLUSIVE CURRENT WITHIN SALES.

The first two examples place shared locks. The first locks current of ORD record type, and the second locks current of an area. The third example obtains an exclusive lock on the current of the SALES set.

All explicitly acquired locks are held until a FINISH, COMMIT, or ROLL-BACK command is issued.

IDMS checkpoints

The term *checkpoint* has a different meaning for IDMS than it does for SQL/DS. An IDMS checkpoint is equivalent to what we called a *transaction* in

Chapter 11 and what SQL/DS calls a *logical unit of work*. A checkpoint is a complete, atomic, durable set of actions that is performed by a single run-unit.

A checkpoint is initiated when the READY command is issued. A checkpoint is terminated when a FINISH, COMMIT, or ROLLBACK command is issued.

FINISH not only terminates the checkpoint, it also releases all locks and closes all areas from further processing. All currency indicators are set to null. The format of a finish command is

FINISH.

The COMMIT command terminates the current checkpoint and initiates a new one. Once a COMMIT command has been successfully completed, all changes made to the database become permanent. They will endure system crashes.

IDMS COMMIT processing differs from SQL/DS COMMIT processing. When an IDMS COMMIT is executed, all changes made to the database are written to the log, and system buffers containing these changes are written to the database. After the operating system informs IDMS that both of these actions have been completed, a checkpoint message is then written to the log. The run-unit then resumes processing. Thus, at a COMMIT point, the recovery system is guaranteed that the database and the log are synchronized.

COMMIT has two formats as follows:

COMMIT.
COMMIT ALL.

The first command commits all changes to the database and releases all locks except those on current records. Currency indicators are unchanged. The second format commits all changes to the database and releases all locks, including those on current records. The currency indicators are set to null.

The ROLLBACK command aborts a checkpoint. If the journal file is kept on a disk device, all changes made in the current checkpoint are automatically removed from the database. If the log is on tape, then changes are flagged as invalid, but they remain in the database until a utility program processes the log.

There are two forms of ROLLBACK:

ROLLBACK.
ROLLBACK CONTINUE.

A run-unit issuing the first command will abort the current checkpoint and also be terminated. This command is equivalent to abort with FINISH. The second format rolls back the current checkpoint, but allows processing to continue.

IDMS recovery

IDMS has two modes of recovery. One is used when the journal is maintained on tape, and another when the journal is on disk. We will assume in this discussion that the journal is on disk.

Recovery techniques using a disk journal are very similar to those discussed previously. The IDMS journal file records the start and end of checkpoints, and the before and after images of all changes to the database. The journal is used to recover from failures. The next three sections discuss recovery from unsuccessful checkpoints, system crashes, and database damage.

Unsuccessful checkpoint termination   A run-unit can abort by executing a ROLLBACK command, by unexpectedly terminating, or by *timing out*. This last term needs explanation. Whenever a run-unit goes into the wait state, IDMS monitors the time it has been waiting. If wait time exceeds a predetermined amount (set at installation), then the run-unit is automatically aborted. Time-out might occur when a run-unit waits too long for another run-unit to release a lock, or it might occur because of the deadly embrace. Whatever the reason, a run-unit waiting too long will be aborted.

When a run-unit aborts, the before images of all changes in the current checkpoint are reapplied to the database. Assuming that implicit locks are in use, rollback will cause no problem to another run-unit, since all records changed by the run-unit have been exclusively locked. If explicit locks are used, there will be no problem if the locks have been used correctly. (If programmers do locking, they better do it right.)

System crashes   When the system crashes, recovery is straightforward (at least to describe). The before images of all changes made by open checkpoints are applied to the database. Checkpoints in process then need to be restarted. This means that programs should be written to be restartable at any checkpoint.

Recovery in this circumstance is more simple for IDMS than it is for SQL/ DS. IDMS recovery knows that the journal and the database are synchronized at each checkpoint. Thus every after image of a committed checkpoint is in the database. There is no need to search the log for a synchronization point. (Observe the conflict in terminology!)

Database damage   When the database is damaged, it must be recovered from a previous database save. The saved copy (normally on tape) is restored to the database files, and all after images of completed checkpoints are applied to the database. Checkpoints in process at the time of the crash must be restarted.

IDMS provides flexibility in that the entire database can be saved (and recovered), or areas within the database can be saved (or recovered). Note, however, that saving and recovering portions of the database generates considerable complexity for the operations staff. Still, for large databases (hopefully having able and well-trained support personnel), this feature has great benefits.

IDMS SECURITY

IDMS provides several security features. All of these features are optional, however, and the database designer must decide which of them to use, and how they should be used. We will consider subject-oriented security, and again use the Fernandez, Summers, and Wood security model. IDMS security features are summarized in Figure 13-22.

User authorization

IDMS provides no security to restrict people from using application programs; such authorization is left to the application program itself. For example, a table of users and their authorization to use programs could be stored in the database, and each application program could check this table before interacting with a user.

Subject	Object	Action	Constraint
User	Programs	Any	Determined by programs.
Programs	Subschema	Use	Can be controlled with program registration facility.
Subschema	Area	RETRIEVAL UPDATE PROTECTED	YES or NO YES or NO YES or NO
Subschema	Records	FIND(OBTAIN) GET STORE ERASE MODIFY CONNECT DISCONNECT KEEP	YES or NO YES or NO YES or NO YES or NO YES or NO YES or NO YES or NO YES or NO
Subschema	Sets	CONNECT DISCONNECT FIND KEEP	YES or NO YES or NO YES or NO YES or NO
Any	Any	Any except IDMS command.	Use database procedure.

Figure 13-22   Security Provided by IDMS

Program authorization

In general, any program can access any subschema. If an application programmer knows the name of a subschema and can determine its contents, then that person can write a program to use the subschema.

If this freedom is considered undesirable, then the database designer can invoke an optional IDMS feature called *Program Registration*. When this feature is used, no application program can access a subschema (and hence the database) unless the name of the application program has been registered in the data directory. Furthermore, the name(s) of the subschema(s) that it can access is also registered so that a registered application program may only access the authorized subschemas. Clearly, for this facility to be effective, the program register must be protected from unauthorized use.

Subschema authorization

When subschemas are defined, authorities can be defined regarding which actions can be taken with regard to which entities in the database. Authorities can be defined for areas, records, and sets.

Area security   When an area is copied into the subschema, the designer of the subschema can optionally state which types of READY commands the user of the subschema can issue. As shown in Figure 13-22, the user of the subschema can have permission to ready the area for retrieval or update in either the PROTECTED, EXCLUSIVE, or NO LOCK modes. This permission is either YES or NO. It is not conditioned on the user of the subschema being able to supply a password or other data.

Record security   When a record is copied or defined in the subschema, the designer has the option of specifying which record-oriented DML commands the user of the subschema can issue. All of the commands listed in Figure 13-22 are possibilities. Again, the permission is an unconditional YES or NO.

Set security   When a set is copied into the subschema, the designer has the option of specifying which set-oriented DML commands can be issued by the user of the subschema. FIND and KEEP refer to options of the FIND command that use set membership, e.g., FIND . . . WITHIN (a set).

Authorization by database procedure

IDMS will exit to a database procedure while processing any DML command, and the database designer has the option of implementing security measures in these procedures. The procedure could conduct a conversation with the user, ask for passwords, or request other identifying data. The only restriction is that no IDMS command may be issued from the procedure. Thus security data, if any, would need to be stored in other files.

IDMS EXAMPLE

The following section presents a portion of an IDMS implementation for Sally Enterprises. First, an IDMS schema and subschema based on the DBTG database design in Chapter 10 will be presented. Then, COBOL application program code will be discussed for the queries and update actions presented for SQL/DS in Chapter 12.

IDMS Schema for Sally Enterprises Database

Figure 13-23 summarizes an IDMS implementation of the Sally Enterprises database design developed in Chapter 10. The seven record types and six sets are the same as described in Figure 10-11. The content of two records, however, has been slightly changed in Figure 13-23. Specifically, RECIPE-USED has been deleted from PITCHER, and PITCHER has been deleted from L-ORDER.

RECIPE-USED is a copy of R-NAME in RECIPE. Therefore we do not lose any data by deleting it. Its deletion, however, does change the nature of the FORMULA set. FORMULA becomes an *information-bearing set*. The fact that a given PITCHER was produced using a given RECIPE is no longer stored in data. Rather, that fact is now recorded by the PITCHER's presence in a particular FORMULA set. When we need to obtain all PITCHERs produced from a given RECIPE, we must use the FORMULA set.

Similar remarks pertain to the deletion of PITCHER from L-ORDER. BATCH has become an information-bearing set. We will only be able to determine which orders were filled from a given pitcher by accessing the BATCH set.

Observe that none of the other four sets is information bearing. For example, since SNAME is contained in L-ORDER, we can obtain all L-ORDERs for a salesperson Smith by searching L-ORDER records for the value SMITH. Although we can also use the SALE set to find these records, we are not *required* to use this set.

The IDMS database was defined in this way so that you can observe the processing differences between information-bearing and non-information-bearing sets. The advantage of information-bearing sets is that fewer data-items need be changed. You will see this when we change the family name JONES to PARKS. On the other hand, the advantage of non-information-bearing sets is that data is more readily available. For example, we can obtain L-ORDER records and immediately determine the SALESPERSON who placed the order. We need not access the set to determine this name.

Data dictionary entries As shown in Figure 13-3, the first step in building an IDMS database is to store the description of data-items and records in the IDMS data dictionary. The vendor provides an online Data Dictionary Processor for this purpose. Figure 13-24 shows inputs to this processor for the Sally Enterprises database. As shown, all of the elements (data-items) are defined first using ADD ELEMENT commands. Then, records are defined by listing

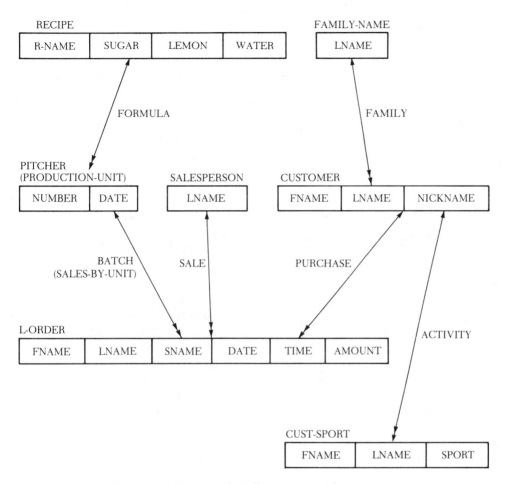

Figure 13-23   Records, Sets, and Data-items for Sally Enterprises Schema

the elements they are to contain. For example, RECIPE is to contain record elements R-NAME, SUGAR, LEMON, and WATER. Each of these elements was defined previously using **ADD ELEMENT** commands.

Some of the elements will be used in more than one record. For example, DATE will appear in both the PITCHER and the L-ORDER records. To give each of these occurrences a unique name, a record prefix can be added. For example, the prefix "P-" is defined for PITCHER records and will be added to the names of each data-item in the record. Thus the data-items in PITCHER will be named P-NUMBER and P-DATE. Prefixes are defined for all records except RECIPE; RECIPE data-items occur in only the RECIPE record type.

IDMS differs from the DBTG model in the way it processes alternate names. Aliases can be defined in the data dictionary but not in a subschema. Once a

```
ADD ELEMENT R-NAME
     PICTURE X(10).
ADD ELEMENT LNAME
     PICTURE X(20).
ADD ELEMENT SNAME
     PICTURE X(20).
ADD ELEMENT NICKNAME
     PICTURE X(20).
ADD ELEMENT FNAME
     PICTURE X(10).
ADD ELEMENT SUGAR
     PICTURE 99V99.
ADD ELEMENT LEMON
     PICTURE 9.
ADD ELEMENT WATER
     PICTURE 9V99.
ADD ELEMENT NUMBER
     PICTURE 9(3).
ADD ELEMENT DATE
     PICTURE 9(6).
ADD ELEMENT TIME
     PICTURE 99V99.
ADD ELEMENT AMOUNT
     PICTURE 9V99.
ADD ELEMENT SPORT
     PICTURE X(10).

  ADD RECORD RECIPE.
       RECORD ELEMENT R-NAME.
       RECORD ELEMENT SUGAR.
       RECORD ELEMENT LEMON.
       RECORD ELEMENT WATER.
```

```
ADD RECORD PITCHER.
     RECORD NAME SYNONYM PRODUCTION-UNIT.
     PREFIX IS P-.
          RECORD ELEMENT NUMBER.
          RECORD ELEMENT DATE.
ADD RECORD SALESPERSON.
     PREFIX IS S-.
          RECORD ELEMENT LNAME.
ADD RECORD CUSTOMER.
     PREFIX IS C-.
          RECORD ELEMENT FNAME.
          RECORD ELEMENT LNAME.
          RECORD ELEMENT NICKNAME.
ADD RECORD L-ORDER.
     PREFIX IS O-.
          RECORD ELEMENT FNAME.
          RECORD ELEMENT LNAME.
          RECORD ELEMENT SNAME.
          RECORD ELEMENT DATE.
          RECORD ELEMENT TIME.
          RECORD ELEMENT AMOUNT.
ADD RECORD FAMILY-NAME.
     PREFIX IS FAM-.
          RECORD ELEMENT LNAME.
ADD RECORD CUST-SPORT.
     PREFIX IS CS-.
          RECORD ELEMENT FNAME.
          RECORD ELEMENT LNAME.
          RECORD ELEMENT SPORT.
```

Figure 13-24 Element and Record Data Dictionary Definitions

name is used in a schema, that same name must be used in all subschemas based on that schema. For example, in Figure 13-24, the record name PITCHER is defined as having a synonym PRODUCTION-UNIT. When we define a schema, we can use either of these names. Say we decide on PRODUCTION-UNIT. Once we use PRODUCTION-UNIT in the schema, we must continue to use that name in all subschemas. We cannot use the name PITCHER in any sub-schema. If we construct a second schema, however, we can again use either PITCHER or PRODUCTION-UNIT.

Schema definition   Figure 13-25 presents an IDMS schema definition for the database shown in Figure 13-23. The structure of this description corresponds to Figure 13-14. There are five sections: name, file, area, record, and set.

The name of this schema is LEMONADE. The version number is used to facilitate maintenance to the schema structure. The database is to be stored on one physical file (LEMFILE) having the device characteristics of an IBM 3350 disk. Further, the database will have just one area (LEM-REGION); this area will consist of 500 pages, and these will be stored on blocks 1 through 500 of the physical file. This is a simple arrangement. As noted previously, several physical files and several areas could be defined having a many-to-many relationship.

The seven records shown in Figure 13-23 are defined in this schema. RECIPE is defined first. Its name, ID, location mode, and area are specified. The record ID is a unique three-digit number. IDs start with 100 since numbers less than 100 are reserved for IDMS. The location mode of RECIPE is CALC using R-NAME. This means RECIPE records can be found by hashing on R-NAME. Since RECIPE was defined in the dictionary, we only need to copy its definition here. Thus the statement COPY RECIPE RECORD VERSION 01 will cause the data-item descriptions to be inserted.

The remaining six record types are defined similarly. The name PRODUC-TION-UNIT is used instead of RECIPE. Also, note that the record prefix has been added to PRODUCTION-UNIT data-items. Both NUMBER and DATE are listed in the schema as P-NUMBER and P-DATE. The IDMS dictionary processor supplied these prefixes to the schema compiler. This feature is par-ticularly useful for data-item names like FNAME and LNAME. Wherever LNAME appears, it has been prefixed. Thus the schema has S-LNAME (in SALESPERSON), O-LNAME (in L-ORDER), FAM-LNAME (in FAMILY-NAME), C-LNAME (in CUSTOMER), and CS-LNAME (in CUST-SPORT).

Two types of location mode are used. Records RECIPE, PRODUCTION-UNIT, SALESPERSON, and FAMILY-NAME can be accessed by CALC data-items. Records L-ORDER, CUSTOMER, and CUST-SPORT can be accessed VIA sets. This means records of these three types will be stored physically close to their set owners. It also means that these records cannot be located by content. They must be found via the set or sequentially within area (LEM-REGION). If there is a frequent need for access via a data-item, this design could have performance problems. Again, decisions regarding location modes must be made on the basis of requirements.

```
SCHEMA DESCRIPTION.
SCHEMA NAME IS LEMONADE VERSION 01.

FILE DESCRIPTION.
FILE NAME IS LEMFILE
        ASSIGN TO LEMFILE                      DEVICE TYPE 3350.
FILE NAME IS JOURNAL
        ASSIGN TO SYSJRNL.

AREA DESCRIPTION.
AREA NAME IS LEM-REGION
        RANGE IS 0001 THRU 0500                WITHIN FILE LEMFILE
                                               FROM 1 THRU 500.

RECORD DESCRIPTION.
RECORD NAME IS RECIPE.
RECORD ID IS 101.
LOCATION MODE IS CALC                          USING R-NAME
                                               DUPLICATES NOT ALLOWED.
WITHIN LEM-REGION.
COPY RECIPE RECORD VERSION 01.
02      R-NAME
        USAGE IS DISPLAY
        PICTURE IS X(10).
02      SUGAR
        USAGE IS DISPLAY
        PICTURE IS 99V99.
02      LEMON
        USAGE IS DISPLAY
        PICTURE IS 9.
02      WATER
        USAGE IS DISPLAY
        PICTURE IS 9V99.

RECORD NAME IS PRODUCTION-UNIT.
RECORD ID IS 102.
LOCATION MODE IS CALC                          USING P-NUMBER
                                               DUPLICATES NOT ALLOWED.
WITHIN LEM-REGION.
COPY PRODUCTION-UNIT RECORD VERSION 01.
02      P-NUMBER
        USAGE IS DISPLAY
        PICTURE IS 9(3).
```

Figure 13-25 Sally Enterprises Schema DDL Listing

Set definitions are shown in Figure 13-25. Observe the order of members and the descriptions of chains. FORMULA is sorted chronologically. The first records connected to the set will occur first. BATCH is sorted in reverse chronological order. The most recently connected records will occur first. SALE is

```
         RECORD NAME IS CUSTOMER.
         RECORD ID IS 106.
         LOCATION MODE IS VIA            FAMILY SET.
         WITHIN LEM-REGION.
         COPY CUSTOMER RECORD VERSION 01.
         02    C-FNAME
               USAGE IS DISPLAY
               PICTURE IS X(10).
         02    C-LNAME
               USAGE IS DISPLAY
               PICTURE IS X(20).
         02    C-NICKNAME
               USAGE IS DISPLAY
               PICTURE IS X(20).

         RECORD NAME IS CUST-SPORT.
         RECORD ID IS 107.
         LOCATION MODE IS VIA            ACTIVITY SET.
         WITHIN LEM-REGION.
         COPY CUST-SPORT RECORD VERSION 01.
         02    CS-FNAME
               USAGE IS DISPLAY
               PICTURE IS X(10).
         02    CS-LNAME
               USAGE IS DISPLAY
               PICTURE IS X(20).
         02    CS-SPORT
               USAGE IS DISPLAY
               PICTURE IS X(10).


         SET DESCRIPTION.

         SET NAME IS FORMULA.
         ORDER IS LAST.
         MODE IS CHAIN                   LINKED TO PRIOR.
         OWNER IS RECIPE                 NEXT DBKEY POSITION IS 1
                                         PRIOR DBKEY POSITION IS 2.
         MEMBER IS PRODUCTION-UNIT       NEXT DBKEY POSITION IS 1
               LINKED TO OWNER           OWNER DBKEY POSITION IS 2
                                         PRIOR DBKEY POSITION IS 3
               MANDATORY AUTOMATIC.

         SET NAME IS BATCH.
         ORDER IS FIRST.
         MODE IS CHAIN.
         OWNER IS PRODUCTION-UNIT        NEXT DBKEY POSITION IS 4.
         MEMBER IS L-ORDER               NEXT DBKEY POSITION IS 1
               LINKED TO OWNER           OWNER DBKEY POSITION IS 2
               MANDATORY AUTOMATIC.
```

Figure 13-25   (Cont'd.)

ordered alphabetically by value of O-LNAME. DUPLICATES LAST means that when records have duplicate values of O-LNAME, they will be placed in chronological order. Other set orders are as shown in Figure 13-25.

Members in the FORMULA set have forward, reverse, and owner pointers.

```
02      P-DATE
        USAGE IS DISPLAY
        PICTURE IS 9(6).

RECORD NAME IS SALESPERSON.
RECORD ID IS 103.
LOCATION MODE IS CALC                    USING S-LNAME
                                         DUPLICATES NOT ALLOWED.
WITHIN LEM-REGION.
COPY SALESPERSON RECORD VERSION 01.
02      S-LNAME
        USAGE IS DISPLAY
        PICTURE IS X(20).

RECORD NAME IS L-ORDER.
RECORD ID IS 104.
LOCATION MODE IS VIA                     BATCH SET.
WITHIN LEM-REGION.
COPY L-ORDER RECORD VERSION 01.
02      O-FNAME
        USAGE IS DISPLAY
        PICTURE IS X(10).
02      O-LNAME
        USAGE IS DISPLAY
        PICTURE IS X(20).
02      O-SNAME
        USAGE IS DISPLAY
        PICTURE IS X(20).
02      O-DATE
        USAGE IS DISPLAY
        PICTURE IS 9(6).
02      O-TIME
        USAGE IS DISPLAY
        PICTURE IS 99V99.
02      O-AMOUNT
        USAGE IS DISPLAY
        PICTURE IS 9V99.

RECORD NAME IS FAMILY-NAME.
RECORD ID IS 105.
LOCATION MODE IS CALC                    USING FAM-LNAME
                                         DUPLICATES NOT ALLOWED.
WITHIN LEM-REGION.
COPY FAMILY-NAME RECORD VERSION 01.
02      FAM-LNAME
        USAGE IS DISPLAY
        PICTURE IS X(20).
```

Figure 13-25   (Cont'd.)

The forward pointer is placed in **DBKEY** position 1, the owner pointer in position 2, and the reverse pointer in position 3. Sets **BATCH, SALE, FAMILY,** and **PURCHASE** have forward and owner pointers, while set **ACTIVITY** has forward, owner, and reverse pointers. As with location mode, decisions regarding which records have which pointers depend on processing requirements.

```
SET NAME IS SALE.
ORDER IS SORTED.
MODE IS CHAIN.
OWNER IS SALESPERSON                NEXT DBKEY POSITION IS 1.
MEMBER IS L-ORDER                   NEXT DBKEY POSITION IS 3
      LINKED TO OWNER               OWNER DBKEY POSITION IS 4
      MANDATORY AUTOMATIC.
      ASCENDING KEY IS O-LNAME
         DUPLICATES LAST.

SET NAME IS FAMILY.
ORDER IS NEXT.
MODE IS CHAIN.
OWNER IS FAMILY-NAME                NEXT DBKEY POSITION IS 1.
MEMBER IS CUSTOMER                  NEXT DBKEY POSITION IS 1
      LINKED TO OWNER              OWNER DBKEY POSITION IS 2
      MANDATORY AUTOMATIC.

SET NAME IS PURCHASE.
ORDER IS SORTED.
MODE IS CHAIN.
OWNER IS CUSTOMER                   NEXT DBKEY POSITION IS 3.
MEMBER IS L-ORDER                   NEXT DBKEY POSITION IS 5
      LINKED TO OWNER              OWNER DBKEY POSITION IS 6
      MANDATORY MANUAL
      ASCENDING KEY IS O-SNAME
         DUPLICATES LAST.


SET NAME IS ACTIVITY.
ORDER IS PRIOR.
MODE IS CHAIN                       LINKED TO PRIOR.
OWNER IS CUSTOMER                   NEXT DBKEY POSITION IS 4
                                   PRIOR DBKEY POSITION IS 5.
MEMBER IS CUST-SPORT               NEXT DBKEY POSITION IS 1
                                   PRIOR DBKEY POSITION IS 2
      LINKED TO OWNER             OWNER DBKEY POSITION IS 3
      OPTIONAL MANUAL.
```

Figure 13-25 (Cont'd.)

DMCL definition

Figure 13-26 shows the IDMS DMCL description for this schema. This description defines the buffer length for input and output of LEM-REGION area pages. Since the journal file was defined in the schema description, it need not be defined again here. This DMCL is simple because the Sally Enterprises database has just one area and one file. More complication would result if there were several files and areas.

```
DEVICE-MEDIA DESCRIPTION.

DEVICE-MEDIA NAME IS LEMDMCL
        OF SCHEMA NAME LEMONADE VERSION 01.

BUFFER SECTION.
        BUFFER NAME LEMBUFF
        PAGE CONTAINS 4628 CHARACTERS
        BUFFER CONTAINS 10 PAGES.

AREA SECTION.
        COPY LEM-REGION AREA
              FROM SCHEMA NAME LEMONADE VERSION 01.
```

Figure 13-26   IDMS DMCL Description

Subschema definition

The ideal subschema contains no data beyond that needed to satisfy the requirements of its users. To define a subschema, therefore, we need to be clear about the processing to be done. Figure 13-27a summarizes the query and update operations that were illustrated for SQL/DS in Chapter 12. We will use these same operations to illustrate IDMS in this chapter. Figure 13-27b lists the records and data-items necessary to satisfy these operations.

How many subschemas do we need? If we wish to perform all of these operations from a single subschema, then that subschema must contain all records and sets in the schema. Such a subschema provides no authorization protection and would probably be undesirable. If we wish maximum protection, we could define a different subschema for each operation. We would need just five subschemas, however, since Queries 1 and 2 use the same data.

To make this decision in practice we would consult Sally's requirements. We would balance the needs of users against the need for security and arrive at a definition of subschemas. Many of these decisions would already have been made in design, but some decisions might have to wait until the schema design is complete.

For our purposes, we will define four subschemas. The first subschema will be used for the three query commands. It will contain RECIPE, PRODUC-TION-UNIT, and L-ORDER records as well as the FORMULA and BATCH sets. The remaining subschemas will be developed for the modification operations. We will construct a separate subschema for the update, one for the delete, and another for the insert operations. The contents of these subschemas will correspond to the data needs described in Figure 13-27b.

Query 1:   Display name of RECIPE with most sugar

Query 2:   Display names of RECIPEs with 2 lemons

Query 3:   Display names of all RECIPEs and total amounts sold of each

Update: Change family name of JONES to PARKS

Delete: Remove nickname and sport names for 'BRAD JONES'

Insert: Add new L-ORDER record if PITCHER and SALESPERSON records
            exist. Insert new CUSTOMER and FAMILY-NAME records, if
            necessary.

a.   Sample Queries for Sally Enterprises Database

	Action	Records Needed	Sets Needed
Query 1:	Display RECIPE with most sugar	RECIPE	None
Query 2:	Display RECIPEs with 2 lemons	RECIPE	None
Query 3:	Display RECIPEs and amounts sold	RECIPE PRODUCTION-UNIT L-ORDER	FORMULA BATCH
Update:	Change CUSTOMER last name from JONES to PARKS	FAMILY-NAME CUSTOMER L-ORDER CUST-SPORT	FAMILY PURCHASE ACTIVITY
Delete:	Delete nickname and sports for 'BRAD JONES'	FAMILY-NAME CUST-SPORT CUSTOMER	FAMILY ACTIVITY
Insert:	Add L-ORDER if PITCHER and SALESPERSON records exist. Insert CUSTOMER and FAMILY-NAME records if not already present.	PRODUCTION-UNIT SALESPERSON CUSTOMER FAMILY-NAME L-ORDER	BATCH SALE PURCHASE FAMILY

b.   Record and Set Types Needed for Example Activities

Figure 13-27   Queries and Needed Data for Sally Enterprises Example

```
         ADD SUBSCHEMA·NAME IS LEMQUERY
              OF SCHEMA NAME LEMONADE
              DMCL IS LEMDMCL.
         ADD AREA NAME IS LEM-REGION
              DEFAULT USAGE IS RETRIEVAL.
         ADD RECORD NAME RECIPE
              ELEMENTS ARE ALL.
         ADD RECORD NAME PRODUCTION-UNIT
              ELEMENTS ARE ALL.
         ADD RECORD NAME L-ORDER
              ELEMENTS ARE ALL.
         ADD RECORD NAME CUSTOMER
              ELEMENTS ARE ALL.


         ADD SET NAME FORMULA.
         ADD SET NAME BATCH.
         ADD SET NAME PURCHASE.


         ADD LOGICAL RECORD IS PITCHERS-ORDERED
              ELEMENTS ARE RECIPE, PRODUCTION-UNIT, L-ORDER.


         ADD LOGICAL PATH OBTAIN PITCHERS-ORDERED
              SELECT FOR FIELDNAME  EQ R-NAME
                   OBTAIN RECIPE WHERE CALCKEY IS R-NAME OF REQUEST
                   OBTAIN EACH PRODUCTION-UNIT WITHIN FORMULA
                   OBTAIN EACH L-ORDER WITHIN BATCH.
```

Figure 13-28   LEMQUERY Subschema Definition

Figure 13-28 shows an IDMS subschema description for the query sub-schema. The name of the subschema is LEMQUERY. It contains records and sets as shown.

LEMQUERY contains an IDMS *logical record*. Logical records are records that do not exist physically, but are constructed by IDMS on demand. They are similar to SQL/DS views based on joins. For this example, logical record PITCHERS-ORDERED consists of the concatenation of RECIPE, PRODUC-TION-UNIT, and L-ORDER records.

The component records in a logical record are concatenated based on instructions in a logical path definition. This definition must also be defined in the subschema. Here, logical path OBTAIN PITCHERS-ORDERED is defined. When this path is used, it will take R-NAME as input (that is the meaning of the phrase R-NAME OF REQUEST). Further, it will build logical record PITCHERS-ORDERED by executing the three OBTAIN commands shown. These commands will be executed automatically. To the user, the record PITCHERS-ORDERED will appear to exist in the database. You will see how such records are used when the code to process Query 3 is discussed.

IDMS application program examples

This section will illustrate the interface between IDMS and application programs. A nearly complete COBOL program that processes query requests will be illustrated and discussed. Then, portions of programs that do update, delete, and insert operations will be shown. Before studying these programs, however, you need to understand the program code that is inserted into application programs by the IDMS precompiler.

Code inserted by the IDMS precompiler   Like SQL/DS, the IDMS precompiler will insert code to facilitate communication between the application program and IDMS. Figure 13-29a shows code that is inserted into a COBOL program's WORKING-STORAGE SECTION. (Similar code would be inserted into programs written in other languages.) After an IDMS command is executed, the application program can access this data. ERROR-STATUS will contain a zero if the command was executed successfully.

For purposes of this illustration, you need to know that IDMS will set ERROR-STATUS to 307 when it reaches the end of a set or area. This value will occur after execution of sequentially oriented commands like OBTAIN NEXT WITHIN LEM-REGION. Further, IDMS will set ERROR-STATUS to 326 if it cannot find a record. This value occurs after execution of commands like OBTAIN CALC RECIPE.

We will not use the other fields shown in Figure 13-29a. For your information, DBKEY will be set to the DBKEY of the current record, and RECORD-NAME and AREA-NAME will be set to the names of the current record type and area. The other fields are set after an error occurs. See [32] for more information about this data.

Figure 13-29b shows code that will be inserted into the PROCEDURE DIVISION when the programmer issues the command COPY IDMS SUBSCHEMA-BINDS. The purpose of this code is to connect (bind) application program data areas to IDMS. When the BIND commands are executed, IDMS will determine the addresses of the records in the application program. In this way, IDMS will know where to put/take data-item values.

```
01      SUBSCHEMA-CTRL.
        03      PROGRAM-NAME            PICTURE X(8).
        03      ERROR-STATUS            PICTURE X(4).
        03      DBKEY                   PICTURE S9(9) COMPUTATIONAL
                                        SYNCHRONIZED.
        03      RECORD-NAME             PICTURE X(16).
        03      AREA-NAME               PICTURE X(16).
        03      ERROR-SET               PICTURE X(16).
        03      ERROR-RECORD            PICTURE X(16).
        03      ERROR-AREA              PICTURE X(16).

        other data
```

a. Portion of Code Inserted into WORKING-STORAGE SECTION

```
MOVE 'EX-PROGRAM' TO PROGRAM-NAME
BIND RUN-UNIT.
BIND RECIPE.
BIND PRODUCTION-UNIT.
BIND L-ORDER.
BIND CUSTOMER.
BIND PITCHERS-ORDERED.
```

b. Code Inserted by Copy IDMS SUBSCHEMA-BINDS

```
IDMS-STATUS     SECTION.
        IF ERROR-STATUS = 0 GO TO ISABEX.
        PERFORM IDMS-ABORT.
        DISPLAY [error messages on console].
        DISPLAY [key data-items on console].
        ROLLBACK.
        CALL 'ABORT'.
ISABEX. EXIT.
```

c. Code Inserted by Copy IDMS IDMS-STATUS

Figure 13-29 COBOL Code Inserted by IDMS Precompiler

The code presented in Figure 13-29c will be inserted when the application program issues the COPY IDMS IDMS-STATUS command. This code will examine ERROR-STATUS. If it is zero, it will return with no action. If ERROR-STATUS is nonzero, various error messages will be issued, a user-written error routine (IDMS-ABORT) will be called, changes will be rolled back, and IDMS will cause the job to abort.

We will call IDMS-STATUS after each IDMS command. However, when the command might generate normal error messages like end of data, we will first check to determine if that error has occurred. If so, we will not call IDMS-STATUS. Doing so would cause a fatal error.

ENVIRONMENT DIVISION   Figure 13-30 presents EX-PROGRAM, an example program that performs the three query operations defined in Figure 13-27. The first IDMS statements occur in the ENVIRONMENT DIVISION. Here the programmer codes messages in the IDMS-CONTROL SECTION that describe whether the program is operating in the communications environment, and if so, which communications control programs and interface protocols are being used. In this example, the PROTOCOL is defined as MODE IS BATCH-AUTOSTATUS. This simply means the program is to be run by itself without a communications control program. This assumption is made to simplify the example.

DATA DIVISION   The precompiler will insert control and subschema data definitions in the DATA DIVISION. The precompiler searches for the SCHEMA SECTION identifier, and determines the names of the subschema and schema from this section. It then adds SUBSCHEMA-CTRL (Figure 13-29a) and subschema record descriptions at the end of the WORKING-STORAGE SECTION.

For the LEMQUERY subschema, record descriptions will be inserted for RECIPE, PRODUCTION-UNIT, and L-ORDER records. Since all of these records are included in LEMQUERY, the record descriptions will be identical to those in the schema (Figure 13-25). The application program can therefore refer to data-item names such as R-NAME and P-NUMBER as if it had declared them in WORKING-STORAGE itself.

The SUBSCHEMA-CTRL data structure will also be inserted into working storage. This allows the program to refer to control data such as ERROR-STATUS.

PROCEDURE DIVISION main paragraph   The first paragraph of the PROCEDURE DIVISION controls the flow of the program. First, record structures are bound to IDMS by code that is inserted via the statement COPY IDMS SUBSCHEMA-BINDS. Then, the area is opened with a READY statement. Since this program only queries the database, the usage-mode is declared retrieval. Next, three query paragraphs are performed, a FINISH command is issued to close the database, and the run is stopped.

```
        IDENTIFICATION DIVISION.
        PROGRAM-ID.  EX-PROGRAM.

        ENVIRONMENT DIVISION.
        INPUT-OUTPUT SECTION.
        FILE-CONTROL.
             SELECT [nondatabase file selects go here]
        IDMS-CONTROL SECTION.
        PROTOCOL.                          MODE IS BATCH-AUTOSTATUS.

        DATA DIVISION.
        SCHEMA SECTION.
        DB LEMQUERY WITHIN LEMONADE.
        FILE SECTION.
        COPY IDMS FILE.
        [nondatabase file descriptions go here]
        WORKING-STORAGE SECTION.
   *
   *              NONDATABASE WORKING-STORAGE DESCRIPTIONS
   *
        77    MAX-SUGAR              PICTURE 99V99.
        77    MAX-SUGAR-OUT          PICTURE 99.99.
        77    MAX-R-NAME             PICTURE X(10).
        77    TOTAL-AMOUNT           PICTURE 9(4)V99.
        77    TOTAL-AMOUNT-OUT       PICTURE 9(4).99.
   *
   *              DATABASE SUBSCHEMA DESCRIPTION
   *
        IDMS precompiler will insert record descriptions from the subschema
        here.
        IDMS precompiler will insert SUBSCHEMA-CTRL here.


   PROCEDURE DIVISION.
        COPY IDMS SUBSCHEMA-BINDS.
        READY USAGE-MODE IS RETRIEVAL.
        PERFORM IDMS-STATUS.
        PERFORM QUERY1.
        PERFORM QUERY2.
        PERFORM QUERY3.
        FINISH.
        STOP RUN.
   *
   QUERY1.
        MOVE 0 TO MAX-SUGAR.
        MOVE SPACES TO MAX-R-NAME.
        OBTAIN FIRST RECIPE WITHIN LEM-REGION.
        PERFORM Q1-SEARCH UNTIL ERROR-STATUS NOT = 0.
        IF ERROR-STATUS NOT = 307
             PERFORM IDMS-STATUS.
        MOVE MAX-SUGAR TO MAX-SUGAR-OUT.
        DISPLAY 'RECIPE : ', MAX-R-NAME, ' HAS THE MOST SUGAR.  SUGAR = ',
             MAX-SUGAR-OUT.
```

Figure 13-30 Sample Program for Query Operations

```
        Q1-SEARCH.
            IF SUGAR GREATER THAN MAX-SUGAR
                MOVE SUGAR TO MAX-SUGAR
                MOVE R-NAME TO MAX-R-NAME.
            OBTAIN NEXT RECIPE WITHIN LEM-REGION.
  *
    QUERY2.
            OBTAIN FIRST RECIPE WITHIN LEM-REGION.
            PERFORM Q2-SEARCH UNTIL ERROR-STATUS NOT = 0.
            IF ERROR-STATUS NOT = 307
                PERFORM IDMS-STATUS.
            DISPLAY 'END OF QUERY2'.
    Q2-SEARCH.
            IF LEMON = 2 DISPLAY R-NAME, ' HAS 2 LEMONS.'.
            OBTAIN NEXT RECIPE WITHIN LEM-REGION.
  *
    QUERY3.
            OBTAIN FIRST RECIPE WITHIN LEM-REGION.
            PERFORM Q3-PROCESS-RECIPE UNTIL ERROR STATUS NOT = 0.
            IF ERROR-STATUS NOT = 307
                PERFORM IDMS-STATUS.
    Q3-PROCESS-RECIPE.
            MOVE 0 TO TOTAL-AMOUNT.
            OBTAIN FIRST PITCHERS-ORDERED WITHIN LEM-REGION.
            PERFORM Q3-PROCESS-ORDERS UNTIL ERROR STATUS NOT = 0.
            IF ERROR-STATUS NOT = 307
                PERFORM IDMS-STATUS.
            MOVE TOTAL-AMOUNT TO TOTAL-AMOUNT-OUT.
            DISPLAY 'RECIPE :', R-NAME, ' SOLD ', TOTAL-AMOUNT-OUT.
            OBTAIN NEXT RECIPE WITHIN LEM-REGION.
    Q3-PROCESS-ORDERS.
            ADD AMOUNT TO TOTAL-AMOUNT.
            OBTAIN NEXT PITCHERS-ORDERED WITHIN LEM-REGION.
  *
  *          ERROR PROCESSING SECTION.
  *
    COPY IDMS IDMS-STATUS.
  *
  *          THE IDMS PRECOMPILER WILL INSERT PARAGRAPH IDMS-STATUS HERE.
  *          IF A NON-ZERO ERROR IS DETECTED, IDMS WILL STOP THE PROGRAM.
  *          JUST BEFORE STOPPING, HOWEVER, IDMS-ABORT WILL CALL ROUTINE
  *          IDMS-ABORT.  THIS GIVES THE PROGRAM ONE LAST GASP.
  *
    IDMS-ABORT.
            DISPLAY 'ABORT-USER EXIT CALLED.'.
    IDMS-ABORT-EXIT.
            EXIT.
```

Figure 13-30   (Cont'd.)

Observe that after the READY command is issued, the program performs IDMS-STATUS. This paragraph, which was shown in Figure 13-29c, will be copied into the program by the precompiler at the COPY IDMS IDMS-STATUS statement at the end of the PROCEDURE DIVISION. IDMS-STATUS will return control if no error occurred during the READY statement. If an error did occur, IDMS-STATUS will display error data and terminate.

Query1 processing   QUERY1 and Q1-SEARCH paragraphs determine the name of the recipe having the most sugar. In case of a tie, it prints the first recipe encountered.

QUERY1 obtains the first RECIPE record in LEM-REGION. Then it performs Q1-SEARCH, until the IDMS sets ERROR-STATUS to a nonzero value. Two situations can cause a nonzero value. If ERROR-STATUS is 307, then the last RECIPE record in LEM-REGION has been encountered. This is an expected occurrence, and the program does not call IDMS-STATUS for error processing and termination. The program displays results instead. If ERROR-STATUS is any value other than 307, then the error was unexpected and IDMS-STATUS is called. IDMS-STATUS will display data and terminate the run.

Q1-SEARCH processes the RECIPE record that has been obtained and obtains the next RECIPE record. This paragraph is performed until either the end of the area is reached or an error occurs.

Be aware that records are stored in an area in whatever order is convenient to IDMS. Therefore, first and next have no particular logical significance. If a particular logical order were needed, the program would need to use the IDMS Sequential Processing Facility [31].

Query2 processing   QUERY2 and Q2-SEARCH paragraphs display the names of RECIPEs having exactly two lemons. The logic is very similar to QUERY1. Q2-SEARCH is performed until ERROR-STATUS is not zero. The value is processed as described for QUERY1.

There was considerable difference in processing between QUERY1 and QUERY2 for SQL/DS. For that DBMS product, QUERY2 required the application program to declare a cursor, whereas QUERY1 did not. For IDMS, the essence of a cursor was required for both queries, so they appear very similar.

Query3 processing   QUERY3, Q3-PROCESS-RECIPE, and Q3-PROCESS-ORDERS paragraphs list each RECIPE name and the total amount that recipe sold. This list will be in no particular order. If a sorted list were needed, then the list would need to be written to a table or file and sorted via COBOL sort facilities. Or, the IDMS Sequential Processing Facility could be used.

These paragraphs use the IDMS logical record PITCHERS-ORDERED. This record is composed of the three records RECIPE, PRODUCTION-UNIT, and L-ORDER. When an OBTAIN is issued for PITCHERS-ORDERED, IDMS will fill these three records in accordance with instructions in the logical path defined in the subschema (Figure 13-28). In this case, IDMS will find a REC-IPE, the first PRODUCTION-UNIT record owned by that RECIPE, and the first L-ORDER record owned by the PRODUCTION-UNIT record. When the next OBTAIN is issued, IDMS will find the next L-ORDER record belonging to the same PRODUCTION-UNIT and RECIPE records. As OBTAINs are issued, IDMS will find all L-ORDER records until the end of the set owned by the current PRODUCTION-UNIT. Then, it will obtain the next PRODUC-TION-UNIT record and process all L-ORDER members owned by it.

For example, suppose Recipe A owns PRODUCTION-UNIT records 100 and 101. Further, suppose there are two orders for unit 100 and three orders for unit 101. Five OBTAIN commands will need to be issued to retrieve all of this data. IDMS will present the logical records in the following order:

RECIPE Record	PRODUCTION-UNIT Record	L-ORDER Record
A	100	First A/100 order
A	100	Second A/100 order
A	101	First A/101 order
A	101	Second A/101 order
A	101	Third A/101 order

If there are no more PRODUCTION-UNIT records for this RECIPE, then the application program will display results and process the next RECIPE.

Paragraph QUERY3 obtains R-NAME values by reading RECIPE records. It finds the first RECIPE within area LEM-REGION, processes this recipe, and then finds and processes all subsequent recipes. Each time an OBTAIN PITCHERS-ORDERED statement is processed, it takes the current value of R-NAME as input. Then it performs the three OBTAINs defined in the logical path.

Query3 could be accomplished without using the logical path. The application program would need to perform all of the OBTAINs and process the end-of-set conditions correctly. Logical paths do not provide any new capability; they simply do processing in behalf of the programmer and make applications programming easier.

Update examples We will not show complete programs for the update examples. Instead, the relevant portions of the PROCEDURE DIVISION code will be illustrated. These examples assume subschemas that correspond to the data requirements in Figure 13-27b. For example, UPDATE-EXAMPLE assumes a subschema containing FAMILY-NAME, CUSTOMER, L-ORDER, and CUST-SPORT records. It also assumes FAMILY, PURCHASE, and ACTIVITY sets.

Additionally, since update activity is involved, these programs assume that the area has been readied for update and that whatever locking needs to be done has been done. Since the programs do not issue OBTAIN FOR UPDATE commands, they assume that areas have been readied for EXCLUSIVE or PRO-TECTED UPDATE, or that the installer of IDMS has declared that IDMS is to issue implicit locks.

Name change example COBOL code to change the names of customers having the last name of JONES to PARKS is shown in Figure 13-31. Last name

```
        UPDATE-EXAMPLE.
            MOVE 'JONES' TO FAM-LNAME.
            OBTAIN CALC FAMILY-NAME.
            IF ERROR-STATUS = 326
                DISPLAY 'JONES FAMILY NOT PRESENT IN DATABASE'
                GO TO UPDATE-EXAMPLE-EXIT
            ELSE PERFORM IDMS-STATUS.
            MOVE 'PARKS' TO FAM-LNAME.
            MODIFY FAMILY-NAME.
            PERFORM IDMS-STATUS.
            OBTAIN FIRST CUSTOMER WITHIN FAMILY.
            PERFORM UPDATE-RECS UNTIL ERROR-STATUS NOT = 0.
            IF ERROR-STATUS NOT = 307
                PERFORM IDMS-STATUS.
        UPDATE-EXAMPLE-EXIT.
            EXIT.
    *
    *            NOW CHANGE CUSTOMER AND CUST-SPORT RECORDS
    *
        UPDATE-RECS.
            MOVE 'PARKS' TO C-LNAME.
            MODIFY CUSTOMER.
            PERFORM IDMS-STATUS.
            OBTAIN FIRST L-ORDER WITHIN PURCHASE.
            PERFORM UPDATE-L-ORDER UNTIL ERROR-STATUS NOT = 0.
            IF ERROR-STATUS NOT = 307
                PERFORM IDMS-STATUS.
            OBTAIN FIRST CUST-SPORT WITHIN ACTIVITY.
            PERFORM UPDATE-SPORT UNTIL ERROR-STATUS NOT = 0.
            IF ERROR-STATUS NOT = 307
                PERFORM IDMS-STATUS.
            OBTAIN NEXT CUSTOMER WITHIN FAMILY.
    *
        UPDATE-L-ORDER.
            MOVE 'PARKS' TO O-LNAME.
            MODIFY L-ORDER.
            PERFORM IDMS-STATUS.
            OBTAIN NEXT L-ORDER WITHIN PURCHASE.
    *
        UPDATE-SPORT.
            MOVE 'PARKS' TO CS-LNAME.
            MODIFY CUST-SPORT.
            PERFORM IDMS-STATUS.
            OBTAIN NEXT CUST-SPORT WITHIN PURCHASE.
```

Figure 13-31 Example COBOL Code to Change Family Name 'JONES' to 'PARKS'

occurs in FAMILY-NAME, CUSTOMER, L-ORDER, and CUST-SPORT records, so all of these need to be changed.

The general strategy of the code in Figure 13-31 is to find the appropriate FAMILY-NAME record using OBTAIN CALC, and then to obtain instances of the last name JONES using the FAMILY, PURCHASE, and ACTIVITY sets. In all cases, the name is changed by obtaining the old record and value, moving the name 'PARKS' to the data-item containing last name, and then issuing the MODIFY command. Observe that IDMS-STATUS is called after each IDMS command. An ERROR-STATUS value of 326 means a record cannot be found.

Deletion example   Figure 13-32 shows example code to remove the nickname for customer BRAD JONES and to delete all of his CUST-SPORT records. Since

```
DELETE-EXAMPLE.
      MOVE 'JONES' TO FAM-LNAME.
      OBTAIN CALC FAMILY-NAME.
      IF ERROR-STATUS = 326
            DISPLAY 'JONES FAMILY NOT IN DATABASE'
            GO TO DELETE-EXAMPLE-EXIT
      ELSE PERFORM IDMS-STATUS.
      OBTAIN FIRST CUSTOMER WITHIN FAMILY.
      PERFORM SEARCH-CUST UNTIL
                            C-FNAME = 'BRAD'
                  OR    ERROR-STATUS NOT = 0.
      IF ERROR-STATUS = 0
            PERFORM DELETE-NN-SPORTS
      ELSE IF ERROR-STATUS = 307
              DISPLAY 'BRAD JONES DATA NOT IN DATABASE'
            ELSE PERFORM IDMS-STATUS.
DELETE-EXAMPLE-EXIT.
      EXIT.
*
*            FIND BRAD JONES RECORD, IF IT EXISTS
*
  SEARCH-CUST.
      OBTAIN NEXT CUSTOMER WITHIN FAMILY.
*
*            NOW ELIMINATE NICKNAME AND OWNED CUST-SPORTS
*
  DELETE-NN-SPORTS.
      MOVE SPACES TO C-NICKNAME.
      MODIFY CUSTOMER.
      OBTAIN FIRST CUST-SPORT WITHIN ACTIVITY.
      PERFORM ERASE-CUST-SPORT UNTIL ERROR-STATUS NOT = 0.
      IF ERROR-STATUS NOT = 307
            PERFORM IDMS-STATUS.
  ERASE-CUST-SPORT.
      ERASE CUST-SPORT.
      PERFORM IDMS-STATUS.
      OBTAIN NEXT CUST-SPORT WITHIN ACTIVITY.
```

Figure 13-32 COBOL Code to Change Special Status of 'BRAD JONES'

the location mode of CUSTOMER is via the FAMILY set, the program cannot obtain the BRAD JONES CUSTOMER record directly on name. Instead, it must sequentially search the JONES FAMILY set to find the BRAD JONES CUSTOMER record. If the record is found, paragraph DELETE-NN-SPORTS is performed. Otherwise, an error message is displayed.

DELETE-NN-SPORTS moves spaces to BRAD JONES NICKNAME and modifies the record. Then it erases all CUST-SPORT records owned by BRAD JONES.

Insertion example Figure 13-33 presents code to insert a new L-ORDER record. Following the same interrecord constraints used in Chapter 12, the record will not be inserted if the appropriate PRODUCTION-UNIT and SALESPERSON records do not exist. Furthermore, if the CUSTOMER record does not exist, then it is to be added. Also, for this schema, if a CUSTOMER record is added, then a FAMILY-NAME record may need to be added as well.

The program in Figure 13-33b assumes that data for the new L-ORDER record has already been read into record structure DATA-IN. Data-item names and formats are shown in Figure 13-33a.

Since the location mode of both PRODUCTION-UNIT and SALESPERSON is CALC, the program can easily check to see if these records exist. OBTAIN CALC commands are issued for both PRODUCTION-UNIT and SALESPERSON records. If both of these records exist, then paragraph ADD-ORDER is performed.

ADD-ORDER checks for the customer record by attempting to obtain the FAMILY-NAME record for the LNAME of the new order. If such a record does not exist, the program stores a new FAMILY-NAME record. Then, the FAMILY set is used in an attempt to find the appropriate CUSTOMER record. If the record is not found, the program adds a new CUSTOMER record.

Paragraph STORE-ORDER moves the new order data to L-ORDER data-items and then issues the STORE command. Finally, the new L-ORDER record

```
01    DATA-IN.
      05    P-NUMBER-IN           PICTURE 9(3).
      05    SP-NAME-IN            PICTURE X(20).
      05    CUST-FNAME-IN         PICTURE X(10).
      05    CUST-LNAME-IN         PICTURE X(20).
      05    DATE-IN               PICTURE 9(6).
      05    TIME-IN               PICTURE 99V99.
      05    AMOUNT-IN             PICTURE 9V99.
```

a. WORKING-STORAGE Code

Figure 13-33 COBOL Code to Insert a New Order

```
        INSERT-EXAMPLE.
            MOVE P-NUMBER-IN TO P-NUMBER.
            OBTAIN CALC PRODUCTION-UNIT.
            IF ERROR-STATUS = 326
                DISPLAY 'PITCHER NOT IN DATABASE'
                GO TO INSERT-EXAMPLE-EXIT.
            PERFORM IDMS-STATUS.
            MOVE SP-NAME-IN TO S-LNAME.
            OBTAIN CALC SALESPERSON.
            IF ERROR-STATUS = 326
                DISPLAY 'SALESPERSON NOT IN DATABASE'
                GO TO INSERT-EXAMPLE-EXIT.
            PERFORM IDMS-STATUS.
            PERFORM ADD-ORDER.
        INSERT-EXAMPLE-EXIT.
            EXIT.
*
        ADD-ORDER.
            MOVE CUST-LNAME-IN TO FAM-LNAME.
            OBTAIN CALC FAMILY-NAME.
            IF ERROR-STATUS = 326
                STORE FAMILY-NAME .
            PERFORM IDMS-STATUS.
            MOVE 'NO' TO CUST-EXIST.
            OBTAIN FIRST CUSTOMER WITHIN FAMILY.
            PERFORM CHECK-ADD-CUST UNTIL
                                    CUST-EXIST = 'YES'
            PERFORM IDMS-STATUS.
            PERFORM STORE-ORDER.
*
        CHECK-ADD-CUST.
            IF ERROR-STATUS = 307
                MOVE CUST-FNAME-IN TO C-FNAME
                MOVE CUST-LNAME-IN TO C-LNAME
                MOVE SPACES TO C-NICKNAME
                STORE CUSTOMER
                PERFORM IDMS-STATUS
                MOVE 'YES' TO CUST-EXIST
            ELSE PERFORM IDMS-STATUS
                IF CUST-FNAME-IN = C-FNAME
                    MOVE 'YES' TO CUST-EXIST.
            OBTAIN NEXT CUSTOMER WITHIN FAMILY.

        STORE-ORDER.
            MOVE CUST-FNAME-IN TO O-FNAME.
            MOVE CUST-LNAME-IN TO O-LNAME.
            MOVE SP-NAME-IN TO SNAME.
            MOVE DATE-IN TO O-DATE.
            MOVE TIME-IN TO O-TIME.
            MOVE AMOUNT-IN TO O-AMOUNT.
            STORE L-ORDER.
            CONNECT L-ORDER TO PURCHASE.
            PERFORM IDMS-STATUS.
```

b. PROCEDURE DIVISION Code

Figure 13-33 (Cont'd)

is connected into the current PURCHASE set. A connect was not needed for the FAMILY set because FAMILY is MANDATORY AUTOMATIC. IDMS will put new CUSTOMER records automatically into the current FAMILY set. Observe in paragraphs ADD-ORDER and CHECK-ADD-CUST that if a CUSTOMER record is added, the correct FAMILY-NAME record will be current of FAMILY.

SUMMARY

To qualify as a DBTG DBMS, a system must have the five characteristics listed in Figure 13-1. There are many such systems; most are provided by hardware vendors. The grandparent of them all is IDS, a system that preceded the DBTG model.

This chapter has considered IDMS, one of the important DBTG DBMS. IDMS has eight and a half of the nine characteristics of a full-capability DBMS. Data is defined to IDMS via the Interactive Data Dictionary. Once defined, the database can be processed by application program and by query language.

IDMS has several substantial differences from the 1981 DBTG model. Major differences include support for areas, location mode of records, and the lack of CHECK and SET SELECTION clauses. Also, FIXED set members are not allowed, nor can records, data-items, or sets be renamed in subschemas. The IDMS DML conforms to a large degree with the DBTG DML discussed in Chapters 9 and 10.

Facilities for concurrent processing and recovery are provided. Locking can be done at the area and record levels. At the record level, locks can be placed implicitly by IDMS or explicitly by the application program. The term *checkpoint* is IDMS's term for transaction. IDMS produces a journal file of before and after images. Recovery can be automatic in many cases if the journal is maintained on disk.

IDMS provides facilities to control which programs can access which subschemas. Also, subschemas can define which actions can be taken with regard to areas, records, and sets. Database procedures can also be used for security.

This chapter concluded with an IDMS example for Sally Enterprises. An IDMS schema was defined, and the contents of four subschemas identified. IDMS code for one of those subschemas was illustrated. Finally, COBOL application code for three query, one modify, one delete, and one insert operation was discussed.

Group I Questions

13.1   List and describe five characteristics necessary for a DBMS to be considered a DBTG DBMS.

13.2   List four DBTG DBMS.

13.3 What facilities does IDMS have for defining and enforcing constraints?

13.4 What is a database procedure? How is it used?

13.5 Describe the five steps of defining and using an IDMS database.

13.6 Sketch the relationship of the user, IDMS, and Online Query.

13.7 Sketch the relationship of the user, IDMS, and Intellect.

13.8 Explain how the database, areas, files, pages, and records are related.

13.9 Sketch and describe IDMS page layout.

13.10 Show how linked lists are used to represent IDMS sets. Sketch an occurrence of the set between PITCHER and ORDER records. Assume the relationship has forward, reverse, and owner pointers.

13.11 Explain how IDMS area, record, and set data definitions differ from the 1981 DBTG model.

13.12 Name and describe the five sections of an IDMS schema definition.

13.13 Explain the relationship of files and areas as defined in the schema in Figure 13-14.

13.14 Explain the purpose of DMCL modules.

13.15 Define subschema inclusion rules by which IDMS will accept a STORE command.

13.16 Define subschema inclusion rules by which IDMS will accept an ERASE command.

13.17 What is the OBTAIN command? How does it differ from a FIND command?

13.18 Give an example of each of the six formats of the FIND command.

13.19 Give an example of a STORE command. Explain what actions must be taken before the STORE is issued.

13.20 Give an example of an ERASE command. Explain what actions must be taken before the ERASE is issued.

13.21 Give an example of a MODIFY command. Explain what actions must be taken before the MODIFY is issued.

13.22 Describe two levels of IDMS record locking.

13.23 What is the difference between a PROTECTED and an EXCLUSIVE lock?

13.24 Give an example of READY commands to lock AREA-B for retrieval. Assume:

    a. Other run-units can operate concurrently without restriction.

    b. Other run-units can read concurrently but not update.

    c. No other run-unit is to access the area concurrently.

13.25 What is the difference between a SHARED and an EXCLUSIVE lock?

13.26 Explain the difference between explicit and implicit locks.

13.27 Under what conditions are explicit locks used? Under what conditions are implicit locks used?

13.28 Define the term *checkpoint* as used by IDMS.

13.29 Explain how IDMS COMMIT processing differs from SQL/DS COMMIT processing.

13.30 Explain how IDMS operates to recover from (assume the journal is located on a direct access device):

   a. Unsuccessful checkpoint termination

   b. System crash

   c. Database damage

13.31 What facilities does IDMS provide to control user access?

13.32 What facilities does IDMS provide to control program access to subschemas?

13.33 What facilities does IDMS provide to control subschema activity on areas? on records? on sets?

13.34 Explain the difference between information-bearing and noninformation-bearing sets. Discuss advantages and disadvantages of each.

13.35 Explain the use of the IDMS data dictionary record prefix capability.

13.36 Explain the meaning of all entries for the definition of the PRODUCTION-UNIT record.

13.37 Explain the meaning of the differences between the location modes of PRODUCTION-UNIT and L-ORDER.

13.38 Suppose a single application program is to perform the update, deletion, and insertion operations in Figures 13-31 through 13-33. Describe the record and set contents of this subschema.

13.39 Define *logical record*. Explain the meaning of the logical path for the PITCHERS-ORDERED logical record.

13.40 Explain the functions of the code inserted by the IDMS precompiler as shown in Figure 13-29a.

13.41 Explain the functions of the code inserted by the IDMS precompiler as shown in Figure 13-29b.

13.42 Explain the functions of the code inserted by the IDMS precompiler as shown in Figure 13-29c.

13.43 Explain the use of IDMS-STATUS in paragraphs QUERY1 and Q1-SEARCH in Figure 13-30.

13.44 Suppose an instance of schema LEMONADE has three recipes: A, B, and C. Also, suppose that each recipe has three PRODUCTION-UNITS: (100, 101, 102), (103, 104, 105), (106, 107, and 108), respectively. Finally, suppose that each PRODUCTION-UNIT has generated two sales. Show

how IDMS will obtain this data using the PITCHERS-SOLD logical record.

13.45 Referring to Figure 13-33, explain why a new L-ORDER record must be connected into its set, but a new CUSTOMER record need not be connected into its set.

Group II Questions

13.46 Compare and contrast the Sally Enterprises example application program code shown for SQL/DS in Chapter 12 with the same IDMS application program code presented in this chapter. What are the advantages and disadvantages of the program interfaces of the two products? Describe a situation in which you believe that SQL/DS would be clearly superior. Describe a second situation in which you believe that IDMS would be clearly superior.

13.47 Develop a subschema definition for an application program that will accomplish the update, deletion, and insertion operations in Figure 13-27b. Integrate Figures 13-31, 13-32, and 13-33 into a single program. Specify ENVIRONMENT and DATA DIVISIONS for this integrated program. Follow Figure 13-30 as an example.

13.48 Change your answer to question 13.47 to make the program general purpose. Assume that the program will receive a transaction code and other data. The transaction code will determine whether the update, deletion, or insertion operations are to be done. The update operation will receive old and new names as input. The deletion operation will receive customer first and last names as input. The insert operation will receive the data in Figure 13-33a as input.

Projects

A. Locate a company that is using IDMS. Determine how long they have had the system, why they chose it, and how well they like it. If possible, obtain a copy of a schema or subschema. Explain the meaning of all entries in the schema and subschema. Also, if possible, obtain a copy of an application program. Explain the meaning of IDMS statements. Compare the copy of the program before precompilation with the copy afterward. How do application programs in this company do locking? Has the company ever experienced locking problems? How does the company do recovery? Is the journal on tape or disk? Have they had recovery problems? Explain whether you believe IDMS has been an effective system for that company.

B. Locate a company having a DBTG DBMS other than IDMS. Answer all questions in item A for this DBMS.

14
Database
Administration

Databases are shared resources. Since time immemorial, people have had difficulty sharing. Alternatives that are desirable to one group of users are an anathema to another group. Policies that are developed to ease the job of some people are ignored by others who cannot see the need for the policy. For these and other reasons, some people think that designing and coding the database and attendant programs is easy when compared to using the database effectively in an operational environment.

In Chapter 2, we defined five components of a business computer system: hardware, programs, data, procedures, and people. Since that chapter, we have concentrated primarily on data and program components. In this last chapter, we will focus on procedures and people. Do not believe that the concepts discussed in this chapter are unimportant because they are nontechnical. By and large, more problems arise from procedural and people issues than arise from technical ones.

To facilitate effective use of the database, most companies have staffed a position (and office) of *database administration* (DBA). This person (group) is responsible for protecting the database while at the same time maximizing benefits to users.

This position is critical. Over the years, one fact has been demonstrated again and again: when the database administration function is not established or when it is weakly established, *database processing does not succeed*. Users of the database inevitably come into conflict, and without the DBA, the ultimate result of the conflict is chaos in the database. Furthermore, the database requires considerable care. The design and implementation of recovery procedures, database documentation, performance evaluation, system tuning, and new feature evaluation are a few of the tasks inadequately performed in the absence of the DBA.

Although the DBA is often referred to as a single person, in practice the responsibilities of the DBA for any reasonably sized organization require a group of people. Thus an office of database administration is usually developed. This

536

office is managed by the individual known as the *database administrator*. The letters *DBA* refer either to the organization or to the person, depending on context.

The DBA office should evolve during the database development. Attention should be given to DBA responsibilities in the analysis stage. One approach is to draft the DBA position descriptions at that time. The database project team should continue consideration of the office throughout the evaluation of alternatives. Early in the implementation stage, the office should be established and critical positions filled. The project team should stress the importance of the position during its meetings with upper-level management and should ensure that needed positions are authorized.

The question as to who should be the DBA is as important as it is difficult. The DBA should have considerable experience in the data processing activities of the firm and should enjoy respect and rapport with the users, upper management, and the data processing staff. Generally, this means the DBA should be selected from within the organization. If no one in the organization meets these qualifications or if no one with proven database qualifications is available, then the selection may be made from outside. Under no circumstances, however, should someone be selected who is both a stranger to the organization and a stranger to database processing.

Initially, there may be resistance to the idea of a DBA. The office will seem too powerful, and users will not want to relinquish control of "their" data. Sometimes the source of the DBA is the point of contention. If the DBA is from division B, division A will object. If the DBA is from division A, division B will object. In this case, someone from division C or from outside the organization may be a good choice. In some cases, upper-level management influence may be required to soften the resistance; however, this may create anger and hostility for the new DBA.

The scope of the DBA responsibilities extends over all data in the database. Some consideration [59] has been given to the idea of extending this scope to cover all of the organization's data—whether it is in the database or not. The position might then be called *data administrator* (DA). The reasons for the DA are not as compelling as those for the DBA, and the idea does not have widespread acceptance. Initially, the DBA has quite enough to do; additional responsibilities may interfere with effective management of the database. A compromise might be to establish the DBA and, once it is effectively operating, to extend the responsibilities to that of a DA.

We will consider the organizational placement of the DBA office later in this chapter. In the meantime, Figure 14-1 shows a rough approximation of DBA organizational relationships. The DBA office interacts with users when managing both the data activity and the database structure. It interacts with the data processing staff when managing the database system. Finally, it has a responsibility to upper management to generate sufficient returns on the investment of costs of development and operation. We will consider each of these in turn.

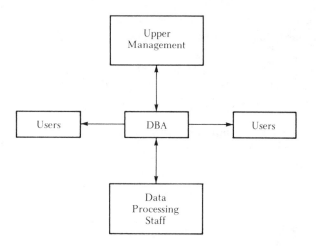

Figure 14-1   Approximate DBA Organizational Relationships

MANAGEMENT OF DATA ACTIVITY

User groups either singularly or collectively own and manage database data. Users provide the data, retrieve it, update it, and delete it. Consequently, the DBA does not manage data. The DBA does, however, manage data activity. The database is a shared resource, and the DBA provides standards, guidelines, control procedures, and documentation to ensure that users do not interfere with one another when managing the data.

Because of the inherent centralization, database processing must be standardized processing. Every field must have a standard name and format. Every database record must have a standard name, format, and standardized access strategies. Every database file must have a standard name and standardized relationships with other files. The DBA creates these standards in a manner that satisfies the majority of the collective needs of all database users.

Initially, there may be resistance to the standardization required. Users may perceive it as an unnecessary constraint on creativity or as wasted effort. User programs, operating procedures, and documentation may have to be modified. In the long run, users will gain an important side benefit of this standardization: they will be able to communicate with one another as never before. Monthly sales will mean the same thing throughout the firm. Standardization will simplify reporting and facilitate management control.

The DBMS data dictionary will be helpful in this regard. Both systems developers and users can query the dictionary to determine exactly what data is being maintained, what the name and format of data-items are, and perhaps even the semantics of the data (from stored text).

A second database concern for the DBA is data ownership, access, and modification rights. Since the data is a shared resource, problems occur regarding who can do what to which data. The DBA must consider each shared data-item and determine, in conjunction with the users, access and modification rights. The authorization facilities of the DBMS and operational policies and procedures must be established to enforce these rights.

Special problems occur when two or more user groups must be authorized to modify the same data. The simultaneous update capabilities of the database system must be documented and made well known to these user groups. Programming standards may need to be established to ensure that locks are invoked when appropriate. The consequences and procedures to be followed during concurrent processing must be documented and understood. The DBA may even restrict types of activity by different user groups to certain periods of the day. Such restrictions must be established with an eye toward successfully meeting the systems requirements, however.

Another problem occurs when users input data they do not use. For example, order entry may provide data about customer age or sex that is used by marketing. Since these data-items are not needed to process an order, there is no natural incentive to ensure that they are correct or even present. If a problem develops, the DBA and representatives from order entry and marketing should work out an acceptable solution. Such a solution may involve modifications to programs so they will accept only complete records. In any case, the DBA provides the lines of communication to solve such problems.

A third important concern for the DBA in the management of data activity is to develop recovery techniques and procedures. The DBA must anticipate failures and develop standardized methods for handling them. The DBA must establish, with the operations department, effective procedures for recovering the database. Recovery features of the DBMS should be well known and used to maximum advantage. If a communications control program is used, the recovery of its processing must be coordinated with database recovery.

Failures can be classified. Typical types are machine failure, media failure, communications failure, data user failure, and the like. For each type, the DBA in conjunction with the users must create operating instructions. The users must know what to do, how much data must be reinput, and how many reports must be redone. Also, if there will be customers standing in line, the users or user supervisors must know how to keep the organization operating and at the same time how to collect sufficient information to record transactions when the database is recovered. In a bank which did not have such recovery procedures, a new teller refused a $10,000 deposit because at the time of the intended deposit the terminals did not work!

Once policies and procedures have been established, they should be documented and users should be trained in their application. Further, the DBA has responsibility to enforce procedures. User activity should be monitored and additional training and other measures taken when personnel do not comply.

Several additional measures are available to the DBA. One, he or she can warn the user and complain to user management. If this brings no success, the

DBA can punish the user by lowering job priorities, thereby slowing turn-around. If the user persists in not following the guidelines, the user department can be charged for problems created [29]. This latter measure at least gets the attention of user management, even if no funds are ever transferred. Generally, such drastic measures are not necessary. If policies and procedures are appropriate, if they are established for the good of all, and if they are carefully explained, users will be cooperative.

Finally, the DBA is responsible for publishing and maintaining all documentation regarding data activity. This includes documentation about database standards, data ownership and retrieval and access rights, recovery procedures, and policy enforcement. Good documentation is especially important in this area because it involves diverse user groups throughout the organization. As with all documentation, keeping it current is a major and unpopular task. Allowing documentation to contain antiquated rules or incorrect information, however, degrades the user's regard not only for the documentation but also for existing policies and procedures and for the DBA itself.

Many DBMS products provide utility services to assist in the management of data activity. Some systems record the names of users and application programs that access (or are authorized to access) objects in the database. For example, the IDMS data dictionary can be queried to determine which programs access a particular record and what actions are taken.

Figure 14-2 summarizes DBA responsibilities for the management of data activity.

MANAGEMENT OF DATABASE STRUCTURE

The creation and maintenance of the database structure is perhaps the most important responsibility of the DBA. The design of the database or databases is critical. If the design adequately reflects the needs of the users, the database will be easy to use. If the design is inadequate, programmers will be forced to

Provide database standards
Establish data ownership, retrieval, and modification rights
Create and disseminate recovery procedures
Inform and train users
Enforce data activity policy
Publish and maintain documentation

Figure 14-2   DBA Data Activity Management Responsibilities

write contrived programs that are more complex than need be and difficult to debug. Query/update language users will find the database confusing and tricky.

The DBA is probably not involved in the first database design. Usually, the DBA function is developed as the first database application is developed. Thereafter, however, the DBA is intimately involved with the design of future databases. The DBA staff may perform database designs themselves, or they may assist in the design by project teams. For smaller databases utilized by only a few users, the users may design the database with guidance from the DBA staff. User design is likely for small relational databases.

Once database application systems are operational, there will be many forces for change. New requirements will develop, and users as well as the DBA staff will find better ways to accomplish goals. These forces need to be carefully managed to ensure orderly incorporation of new features. In most cases, change of the schema must be an evolutionary—not revolutionary—process.

Control of redundancy

As you know by now, database systems reduce or eliminate redundancy. At times, however, there are compelling reasons to retain redundant data. Performance is one. For example, if Customer-name, Number, and Balance must be retrieved with a 2-second response time, these items might exist alone in a single database record even though they also exist in a 6000-byte CUSTOMER record. Special programs and procedures must be designed to ensure that the redundant data are reconciled periodically.

There is another type of redundancy that the DBA must prohibit. This is the type that Charlie in sales creates when he decides he doesn't like the format of the database sales record. Charlie copies all the sales data into his own file (perhaps even in the database) and writes his programs to use the copy. Charlie doesn't design any procedures to reconcile his data with the other sales data, however, and eventually the two are in disagreement. At this point the marketing sales reports differ from the sales department's sales reports, and data integrity has been lost.

Obviously, Charlie must not be allowed to act as described above. If there are good reasons for his dislike of the sales record format, the format should be changed in the database. If this is impossible, then perhaps the redundancy should be allowed but with procedures designed to reconcile the data. In most cases, however, this compromise is not desirable, and available forces should be used to bring Charlie into line. One exception tends to breed others. Soon the DBA will spend full time reconciling data.

Configuration control

The DBA must periodically (and continually) monitor user activity on the database. Periodic reports should be generated detailing which users have been active, which files and perhaps which data-items have been used, and which access methods have been employed. Error rates and error types should also be known. This data should be analyzed to determine whether or not a change to the database design would improve performance or ease the user's tasks. If so, the DBA should instigate a design change.

User requests for change generally arise when the user finds a better way to accomplish a task or when a new requirement develops. In either case, the DBA and user should jointly agree upon a request for change to the database.

For shared public data, requests for change to database structure cannot be implemented automatically. Rather, every user or user group should have a chance to review the proposed change and to state objections to it. One way of accomplishing this is for the DBA to hold periodic configuration control meetings. Prior to the meeting, a request for change form like the one in Figure 14-3 is completed for each change. These are collected by the DBA and disseminated a few days prior to the meeting. During the meeting, each change is discussed and conflicts are worked out if possible. If not, the change is modified or additional meetings involving just the interested parties are scheduled.

In addition to discussion of changes, the configuration control meetings provide the DBA an opportunity to apprise users of pending developments such as changes to the database system or the operating system. Existing policies and procedures can be discussed and evaluated. Finally, these meetings allow users to air complaints and criticisms and to keep the DBA abreast of developments in the database user groups.

These meetings should be held on a periodic basis and should have an agenda and a specified length which are adhered to. The DBA should chair the meetings and keep them orderly and productive. Complex issues involving only a subset of users should be discussed in separate meetings. Users are busy people and often complain about such meetings. They are necessary, however, and very productive if conducted properly. Often, too, the most important communication is not on the agenda but takes place before or after the meeting. One user may ask another, "What are you people doing about-----?" and save a great deal

---

REQUEST FOR CHANGE TO DATABASE STRUCTURE

    Source:

    Description of Change:

    Justification for Change:

    Possible Adverse Impact:

Figure 14-3 Sample Change Request Form

of time. In some cases, without such meetings the users may not know or talk to one another.

Once changes have been approved, the DBA should manage a planned implementation. All users should be sent notification of the changes, perhaps in the form of modifications to documentation. Users directly impacted by the change should be allowed sufficient time to modify and test affected programs. The change should first be made to a test database so that users can verify programs against it.

The DBA should have contingency plans available for dealing with failure. The philosophy "It's not the things you know, or even the things you know you don't know; it's the things you don't know you don't know that will sink you" is appropriate here. Because of the size and complexity of a database system, changes will sometimes have an adverse impact that was not expected. Plans should be prepared to repair the database and to gather sufficient information to diagnose and correct the problem. The database is most vulnerable to failure after a change. Obviously, changes should not be implemented when half the DBA staff is on vacation in a remote wilderness area.

Change is disruptive. Neither organizations nor individuals like change. It is, however, unavoidable. There is a maximum rate at which change can be assimilated. Beyond that point, fear, anger, and frustration are the result. The DBA should keep a watchful eye toward the problems accompanying change and slow the rate if necessary and possible. Better that a part of the system runs inefficiently than that users throw up their hands in despair.

Private database data

The previous discussion does not pertain to private database data. For example, the SQL/DS user who keeps several tables of data in a private DBSPACE would find configuration control meetings unproductive and wasteful.

Instead, users of this type need to know how to manage the configuration of their own data. They should know how to access the system catalogs to determine the data they have, and to learn possible impacts of changes. Users should be able to determine, for instance, the impact on views of removing or changing a column of a base table.

The DBA operates as a consultant to private database users. The DBA provides expertise on the use of the DBMS, as well as guidance in developing procedures.

Documentation

The final responsibility of the DBA in the management of database structure is documentation. It is extremely important to know what changes have been made, how they were made, and when they were made. A change to the database structure may cause an error that does not manifest itself for six months.

Without proper documentation of the change, the diagnosis of the problem is next to impossible. Dozens of job reruns may be required to identify a point where certain symptoms first occurred. For this reason, it is also important to maintain a record of test procedures and test runs made to verify the change. If standardized test procedures, test forms, and recordkeeping methods are available, the recording of test results does not have to be time-consuming. It is an unpopular task because probably less that 1 percent of the recorded information is used. Such records can be life savers, however.

Another reason for maintaining good documentation of schema changes is so that historical data can be properly utilized. If, for some reason, marketing wants to analyze three-year-old sales data which has been in the archives for two years, a natural question is what structure was current at the time the data was last used. Records that show the changes to structure can be used to answer the question. A similar situation arises when a six-month-old save of data must be used to repair a damaged database (this ought not to occur, but sometimes it does!). The records are used to reconcile the structure of the dump and the database.

There are actually two kinds of documentation involved here. One type is user documentation, which details the database standards, policies, structure, and so on. The DBA must publish, disseminate, and maintain this documentation. The second type is documentation internal to the DBA office: how structure was changed, how it was tested, and the like. This documentation is neither published nor disseminated but it must be maintained.

Figure 14-4 summarizes DBA responsibilities for the management of database structure.

MANAGEMENT OF THE DBMS

In addition to managing data activity and database structure, the DBA must manage the DBMS itself. The DBA should compile and analyze statistics about

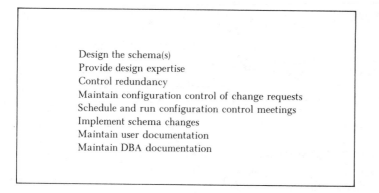

Design the schema(s)
Provide design expertise
Control redundancy
Maintain configuration control of change requests
Schedule and run configuration control meetings
Implement schema changes
Maintain user documentation
Maintain DBA documentation

Figure 14-4   DBA Database Structure Management Responsibilities

system efficiency and identify potential problem areas. All user complaints should be investigated. Analysis may indicate that a change to the DBMS is required. If so, the DBA must plan and manage the implementation of the change. Whenever the database system vendor announces new features of the database system, they must be evaluated and, if beneficial, implemented. These activities imply that the DBA must manage and control change to the DBMS as well as to the database structure.

The DBA should generate runtime statistics on database activity. These statistics include CPU time and elapsed, or clock, times (under stated background conditions) of typical database processing requests. Figure 14-5 shows an example of a statistics report for SQL/DS. This report presents time required to process the three query commands and the modify, delete, and insert commands discussed in Chapter 12. *CPU time* is the central processing unit time needed to process the requests. This time is independent of background processing conditions. *Elapsed time* is the wall clock time needed to process the activities. This time depends on other database activity. In practice the terms *moderate database* activity and *peak load* would be specifically defined.

The DBA may wish to run the sample program many times and compute averages. Also, the DBA may determine the range of times (minimum and maximum) or may calculate a frequency distribution. Figure 14-6 shows a distribution of elapsed time for processing the same three SQL/DS SELECT commands.

There are basically two ways of generating such statistics. One is to run a sample program or programs as just discussed. Statistics are easily generated this way but may be misleading if the sample program does not accurately portray the user workload.

SQL/DS Command	CPU Time	Elapsed Time (seconds)		
		Stand-alone	Moderate Database	Peak Load
SELECT #1	0.31	0.61	1.23	4.72
SELECT #2	0.35	0.70	1.43	4.81
SELECT #3	1.01	1.42	2.08	7.31
UPDATE #1	.	.	.	.
DELETE #1	.	.	.	.
INSERT #1	.	.	.	.

Figure 14-5 Sample Database System Efficiency Report

DML Command	Elapsed Time (seconds)					
	Minimum	20%	40%	60%	80%	Maximum
SELECT #1	0.35	0.41	0.52	0.72	0.89	1.16
SELECT #2	0.34	0.48	0.61	0.84	1.07	2.63
SELECT #3	1.15	1.26	1.38	1.62	1.93	2.11

Figure 14-6   Frequency Distribution of SELECT Standalone Clock Time

A second approach is to record processing times for the actual workload. The operating system may do this automatically, or the DBA can modify application programs to call special timing routines (software monitors) before and after database commands are executed. These routines determine the CPU and clock times and post them in a file for later reporting. Some DBMS vendors supply software to assist in this type of analysis.

The reports generated by the DBA should be annotated if any special conditions affect the statistics. They should be saved, so that current and preceding reports can be compared to determine if performance has deteriorated on any DML commands. The results shown on a series of reports can be plotted against time to determine if there is a trend of deterioration.

Users are another source of performance information. Users may complain that certain activities seem to be taking longer or that they are being charged more for some operations. The DBA should be open to such complaints and provide time for them during configuration control meetings. To maintain user rapport and keep communication lines open, the DBA should investigate every complaint and respond to every user involved.

When a performance problem is identified by report or user complaint, the DBA must determine whether or not a modification to the database structure or system is appropriate. Examples of possible structure modifications are data splitting, new keys, data purging, deletion of keys, and new relationships between files, new indexes, and the like. Considerations for implementing such changes are the same as those discussed in Chapter 5.

The kinds of changes that can be made to a DBMS depend on the type of system. In general, they involve changing system options, changing the communications control or operating system or their interfaces with the DBMS, or obtaining additional database features.

When the database is installed, the DBA must select parameters for options of the database system. Examples are the size of pages in IDMS areas or the devices on which SQL/DS DBEXTENTs reside. The number of such options depends on the complexity of the database system.

Options are initially chosen when little is known about how the system will perform in the particular user environment. Operational experience and performance analysis over a period of time may indicate a change is necessary. Even if performance seems acceptable, the DBA may want to alter the options and observe the effect on performance. This process is referred to as *tuning* or *optimizing* the system.

Performance tuning can be viewed in terms of the responsibility continuum presented in Figure 11-5. There are some tuning features that are built-in to the DBMS. For example, the DBMS may be programmed to balance unused space throughout its files. Other parameters affecting performance are set at installation time. The size of buffers in the IDMS DMCL specification is an example. Still other parameters are controlled by the application program. The size of a transaction is an example. Furthermore, performance can be improved by cooperative effort of the users. If a particular program is known to take an inordinate share of system resources, the users might agree to submit data to this program as a unit and to run the program in off-hours such as early morning.

In addition to changes to the DBMS, other modifications can be made to the operating system, the communications network, or their interfaces with the DBMS. The operating system can be modified to keep code often used by the DBMS resident in main memory. The device and channel allocation of the database and the DBMS can be changed to balance channel utilization. Periodic discussions of performance problems with the systems staff can identify other possibilities for improvements. Outside organizations can be a good source of information about optimization. Organizations having similar hardware and programs are often willing to trade information about design and performance.

Finally, performance considerations may indicate that a database feature previously considered unnecessary is actually required. For example, in an IDMS installation, analysis might show that response times are excessive because of lengthy sequential searches. If so, the organization may want to invest in IDMS's Sequential Processing Facility. In this case, the DBA would obtain and implement this feature.

A similar situation occurs when the database system vendor announces a new feature or a major revision to an existing one. When this occurs, the DBA must evaluate the new feature and assess its impact on the database environment. Feature evaluation is accomplished the same as evaluation of alternatives except that benchmarks may be more useful. The full database exists and can be used to test the effectiveness of the feature. Also, DBA-defined (as opposed to vendor-defined) performance programs can be used to assess its impact.

When a new feature is available, the DBA should decide how it can best be used and who should use it. An assessment must be made of required changes to the database and to user programs. Features requiring large changes may not be worthwhile.

The implementation of database system changes should follow the guidelines for database structure changes. The system is most vulnerable to failure imme-

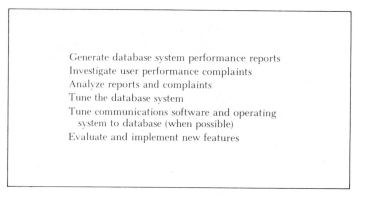

Generate database system performance reports
Investigate user performance complaints
Analyze reports and complaints
Tune the database system
Tune communications software and operating
   system to database (when possible)
Evaluate and implement new features

Figure 14-7   DBA Responsibilities for Database System Management

diately after a change, and changes should be scheduled accordingly. Documentation of all changes should be maintained, and performance should be monitored carefully. If the anticipated benefits do not materialize, it may be desirable to delete the new feature.

Figure 14-7 summarizes the DBA's responsibilities for database system management.

DATABASE ECONOMICS AND CONTROL

During database development, the cost and benefits of the system are evaluated to ensure that the project will generate the required rate of return on investment. If the project is approved, funds are provided to the DBA and other offices to design, implement, and operate the database system. At that point, funds are committed and development begins. Unfortunately, also at that point, difficult managerial dilemmas arise.

For example, one component of the database application may be more difficult to implement than anticipated. Costs in that area begin to build, and the DBA must decide whether or not the component is worth its new costs. If so, or if the component is essential, the DBA must decide how the additional costs can be met. Should more money be requested or should work on the database be adjusted to absorb the costs? If the costs are absorbed, which other database features should be delayed or canceled?

As another example, once the database applications are operational, a component may require more resources than were predicted. The inventory system may run twice as long, thereby reducing computer time available to order entry, payroll, and accounting applications. When this occurs, the DBA must decide whether the inventory system features should be reduced, the other systems should be reduced, or more computer resources should be obtained.

In theory, these kinds of decisions can be made on a cost/benefit basis. More resources should be obtained if an adequate rate of return can be generated. Or, the system that should be reduced is the one that contributes the smallest benefits. In practice, the decisions are more difficult. For one, the DBA may not have the time or resources to determine the incremental values of certain features of a system. It may be difficult to determine the benefits of half an inventory system. Second, in the database environment, systems can be highly dependent. For example, input from both order entry and inventory is required to make a shipment. Order entry supplies data about customer need, and inventory supplies data about product availability. To a shipping clerk, the fact that order entry provides customer address in 5 seconds is unimportant if inventory requires 24 hours to verify product availability. In this case, the incremental benefit of response times less than 24 hours is zero.

This is a straightforward example. In a more realistic case, order entry, production, inventory, and shipping systems may interact. The DBA may know that improving the response time for production will degrade the response time for order entry, inventory, and shipping. The DBA probably does not know by how much. Further, since order entry and inventory provide input to production, the degradation in their performance may override the performance improvement in the production system.

Finally, the DBA must contend with politics. He or she may know that the benefit of improved response time for order entry is zero, but the vice president of sales may want it improved anyway. He or she may know that there is a better return for improving shipping information used by one clerk than there is for improving production information used by 150 production foremen. Because of politics, in either of these cases the organization may be better served by taking the lower benefit alternative.

Some organizations find it beneficial to charge database users for development and/or operational costs. These charges are not actual cash transfers but transfers of funds in the accounting of the organization. For example, production may have a budget of $20,000 for database processing; it uses this sum to pay the DBA for development and operation of its applications. When users must pay for development, they may be more reasonable about requirements. They do not ask for a 10-second response time if it is unnecessary. Also, paying for operational costs encourages efficient use of the database. It focuses attention on the fact that the database is not a free resource. When the budget is overrun, users must request more funds to operate. Such requests focus management attention on the problem.

The primary disadvantage of billing is that it is difficult to be fair and equitable. Since the database is a shared resource, a change for one user can impact all others. For example, if one user requires a new relationship, the additional overhead may slow down processing for all others. This leads to the situation where a user makes two identical runs but his costs are $10.50 one week and $12.35 the next.

Another example is the user who needs straightforward sequential processing, say, for payroll. Because database processing is seldom as efficient as file processing for such applications, it may cost more to do payroll as part of the database. Further, whenever a new feature is added, payroll takes longer and the costs increase even more. Consequently, the payroll user is paying a penalty for taking part in database processing.

When billing is used, development costs are usually allocated to an overhead pool and charged back to the user using an overhead rate. Costs for the DBA office, database maintenance, recovery runs, and so on, are included in this pool. Operational costs are usually billed on an *as used* basis. In some cases, where development costs are clearly related to one user, that user can be billed directly for those costs.

DBA PERSONNEL AND PLACEMENT

By now you will probably agree that the duties of the DBA are too large for any single person to handle, at least for any but the smallest databases. Consequently, the DBA must establish a staff to accomplish these functions. Figure 14-8 lists positions on this staff. Not all DBA offices have one person for each position. In some cases, one person may handle two or more responsibilities. In others, notably in large organizations, two or more people may be involved in just one of these activities.

The database administrator

The DBA is primarily a manager. Although he or she should have a good foundation in data processing and in the business of the organization, the DBA need not be a technical giant. The DBA needs sufficient technical background to make wise decisions, but he or she does not need the experience to implement them.

```
Database Administrator
Documentation and Standards Manager
User Representative
Operations Representative
DBMS Configuration Manager
Performance Monitor
```

Figure 14-8   Positions in the DBA Office

The DBA must manage the staff to ensure orderly development of the database project, to satisfy database users, and to plan for future database requirements. The DBA must plan and budget staff, database, and computer resources. As conflicts arise, the DBA must reallocate resources to achieve maximum organizational benefits. Finally, the DBA is responsible to upper management for the database project. He or she must make periodic reports and negotiate for resources to accomplish present and planned activities.

Documentation and standards manager

The primary responsibility of this position is to create and maintain all database documentation and standards. The data dictionary is maintained by this person. The dissemination of standards and advice and training are other responsibilities. Finally, the documentation and standards manager must ensure that users comply with standards when writing new programs or converting existing ones.

User representative

The responsibilities of this position are to know the user groups, to represent their thinking, and to present their requirements to the DBA. This person serves as a point of contact with users for planning purposes. Users can state future needs to this person, and he or she in turn can assess the impacts of system changes on users. Questions requiring user responses can be channeled through the user representative. The user representative reports to the DBA, however, not to a user organization.

Operations representative

The job of operations representative is similar to the user representative position except that it relates to computer operation. This individual is the point of contact for operations planning purposes. This person states future needs of the database to operations and is available to operations to assess the impact if those needs are not fully met. The operations representative has a better understanding of the hardware and the operating system than other DBA employees. He or she works in conjunction with the performance monitor in tuning the operating system. For example, they would work together to determine the allocation of database files to disk units.

DBMS configuration manager

The responsibilities of this position are to know the database system and to maintain configuration control of it. This person works with the performance monitor in tuning the database system. He or she evaluates new features and manages feature implementation. Both this position and the operations representative position are technical in nature; they may be held by the same individual.

Performance monitor

The performance monitor obtains and analyzes statistics about system performance. He or she also investigates user complaints. The performance monitor works with the operations representative and the DBMS configuration manager in system tuning. This person may also be involved in new feature evaluation.

If the DBA positions are large enough to require at least a single person for each, the DBA personnel should be cross-trained to ensure stability. Otherwise, if something should happen to the only person knowledgeable about performance monitoring, for example, the DBA would be without that function for some time. This is similar to the cross training required for other essential positions in data processing.

DBA placement

There is considerable debate about the organizational placement of the DBA office. Professionals agree that assistant to the president is too high and assistant to data entry operations is too low. The ideal location is somewhere between these extremes and depends on the organizational structure. A large, complex manufacturing firm with many divisions has different DBA requirements than, say, a small hospital has.

Two principles are commonly accepted. One is that it is undesirable for the DBA to be organizationally below any group on which it imposes restrictions, constraints, or standards. For example, the DBA should not work for the programming staff. The second principle is that the DBA should not be more than one level above the organizations with which it interfaces. If it is, the DBA tends to be removed from important day-to-day activities and problems.

The DBA interfaces with and has impact on the classic data processing organizations of systems, programming, and operations. The DBA affects systems design, it imposes standards on programming, and it forces constraints on operations. Consequently, the lowest acceptable level would seem to be on par with these three offices. A better arrangement may be to have the DBA as a staff function to the head of data processing (Figure 14-9). Some managers say the on-par arrangement does not give the DBA sufficient power, whereas others claim the staff arrangement can give the DBA too much power and create an elitist DBA staff. The key to success is the attitude of the senior data processing manager; either organization will work if the DBA is given established and recognizable lines of authority.

SUMMARY

The database administrator is essential for success in a database project. Without a DBA, the database will be inadequately maintained and conflicting user goals will eventually result in chaos. For all but the smallest databases, the DBA responsibilities are too large for one individual, so a DBA staff must be created.

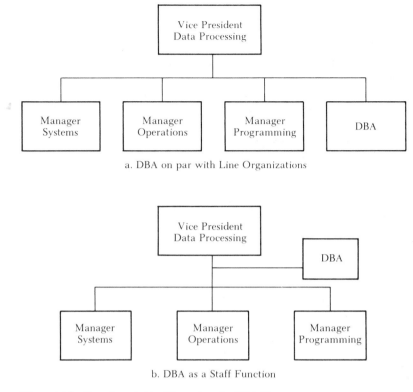

a. DBA on par with Line Organizations

b. DBA as a Staff Function

Figure 14-9   Two Acceptable Alternatives for DBA Placement

The DBA interacts with users, data processing staff, and upper management. DBA responsibilities include management of database activity, database configuration control, development and maintenance of the database system, and management of database resources. The DBA must have established and recognizable lines of authority and must be located high enough in the organization to exercise that authority.

Group I Questions

14.1   Summarize the job responsibilities for the DBA.

14.2   What do you believe is the most important DBA activity? Why?

14.3   Explain why there might be resistance to the formation of a DBA and office of database administration.

14.4   Describe three groups of people that interact with the DBA.

14.5   Summarize the DBA responsibilities for data activity management.

14.6   How can the data dictionary be used to aid database administration?

14.7   Explain the conditions in which the DBA must maintain configuration control over database structure. Under what conditions should the users maintain their own configuration control?

14.8   Describe a situation in which data redundancy is acceptable. Describe a situation in which such redundancy is unacceptable.

14.9   What types of issues should be discussed at a periodic configuration control meeting?

14.10   How can the DBA tell if configuration control meetings are being held too often? not often enough?

14.11   Why should the DBA periodically obtain performance measures? Describe data to be obtained.

14.12   Describe three different ways in which performance could be improved for an SQL/DS application.

14.13   Describe problems that can occur during and immediately after a database implementation. Why is the cost/benefit basis of decision-making difficult in these situations?

14.14   Name six different positions or roles within the office of database administration. Describe job responsibilities for each.

Group II Questions

14.15   Write a job description for the DBA office suitable for justifying the position to management.

14.16   Suppose you present a request to create a DBA office to top-level management. At the end of the presentation, the vice president in charge says that the DBA office seems to duplicate responsibilities of other offices. What would you say?

14.17   In question 14.16, suppose you are asked for the consequences of not having a DBA. What would you say?

Projects

A. Interview a DBA. Find out if his or her responsibilities correspond to those discussed in this chapter. Ask how and why the position was originated. What qualifications does the DBA have? How many people work in the DBA office? What are the major problems? What would happen if the DBA did not exist? Compare the interviewee's DBA activities with those described in this chapter.

B. Find a company whose experience with database processing has been less than successful. Does this company have a DBA? If so, interview this person. Compare his or her responsibilities with the responsibilities described in this chapter. In your opinion, are the functions and job responsibilities of the DBA related to this company's lack of success with database processing?

Appendix A
Data Language/I

The development of Data Language/I, or DL/I, was undertaken by IBM in the 1960s as an outgrowth of studies of data processing needs in the aerospace industry. A joint development project was agreed upon by IBM and North American Aviation. DL/I became the basis for the Information Management System, usually known as IMS, which is one of IBM's major DBMS products. DL/I uses hierarchical structures to represent data relationships. This means that the user's view of the data, whether it is a tree or simple or complex network, must be forced into a tree representation.

In DL/I terms, *fields* are grouped into *segments*, and segments are the nodes of tree structures. A particular tree structure is referred to as a *data base record* (**database is two words in DL/I**). An example of a STUDENT data base record is pictured in Figure A-1. The double arrow notation introduced in Chapter 4 is not part of DL/I notation, but is used here for clarity. Each STUDENT segment are a variable number of JOB HISTORY and CLASS segments. An occurrence of the STUDENT data base record is shown in Figure A-2.

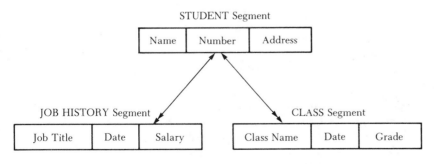

Figure A-1 STUDENT Data Base Record

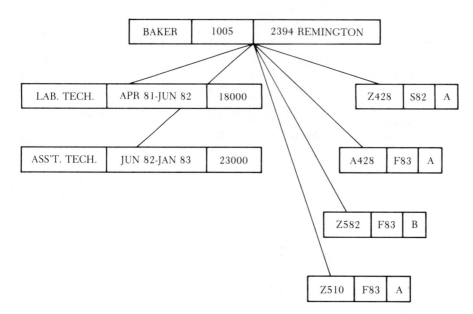

Figure A-2 STUDENT Data Base Record Occurrence

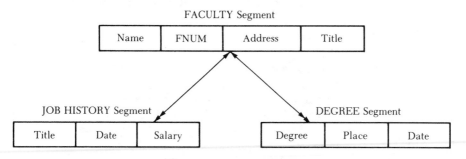

Figure A-3 FACULTY Data Base Record

In DL/I, a *data base* is composed of data base records. These records can be occurrences of the same record type or of several different record types. For example, a DL/I data base could consist of occurrences of the STUDENT data base record in Figure A-1 and the FACULTY data base record in Figure A-3. The data base would comprise all occurrences of each data base record type. Figure A-4 summarizes DL/I data structures.

Data base records are defined via a *data base description*. In the IMS implementation, a set of assembly-language macroinstructions indicates the structure of each data base record. Figure A-5 depicts a portion of the data base description for the STUDENT data base record in Figure A-1. The format of this description is unique to IMS.

Data Structure	Description
Field	Smallest unit of data.
Segment	Group of fields. Segments must be related by hierarchical structure. Each segment has a sequence field used for logical ordering.
Data base record	Hierarchically structured group of segments.
Data base	Collection of data base record occurrences of one or more data base record types.

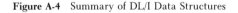

Figure A-4   Summary of DL/I Data Structures

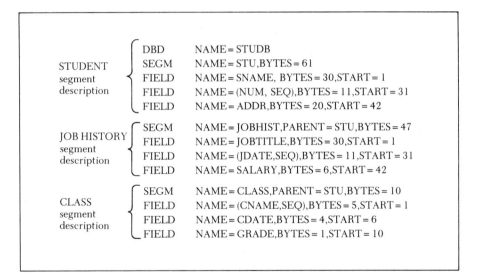

Figure A-5   Data Base Description for STUDENT Data Base Record of Figure A-1

Each segment description is headed by a SEGM macro that names the segment, shows its total length, and gives the name of its parent. The first segment, or *root*, is unique in that it has no parent. Each file within a segment is represented by a FIELD macro that indicates the field name, length, and starting position in the segment. One field within each segment is the *sequence field*. This field is used to order occurrences of a given segment type. The order is a logical one: it appears to the IMS user that segments are in order by the sequence field, but the physical ordering of segments may be different.

In Figure A-5, the STUDENT segment is named STU and is 61 bytes long. The STU record is composed of an SNAME field in bytes 1 through 30, a NUM field in bytes 31 through 41, and an ADDR field in bytes 42 through 61. (DL/I supports only capital letters, so field names are all capitals.) The sequence field for STU segments is NUM.

JOB HISTORY segments are called *JOBHIST* and are composed of JOBTI-TLE, JDATE, and SALARY fields. CLASS segments are called *CLASS* and have CNAME, CDATE, and GRADE fields.

The data base description is assembled and can be stored in object form in a library to be called into main memory when needed. Consequently, each appli-cation programmer need not go through the time-consuming process of writing the data base descriptions for his or her program.

DL/I REPRESENTATION OF RECORD RELATIONSHIPS

DL/I represents data as hierarchies. If all data relationships in a data base are hierarchical, then DL/I can be applied in a straightforward manner to represent the data base. If the data relationships involve networks, however, this is not true. In this case, the data base must be transformed into a hierarchical, or tree, structure (which can always be done) and the transformed hierarchies represented by DL/I. In this section we will show first how hierarchical, or tree, structures are represented, and then how DL/I can be used to model both simple and complex networks.

Suppose a data base consists of student data, student job histories, and stu-dent classes related as shown in Figure A-1. Since this is a tree structure, the DL/I model is straightforward. Each node of the tree corresponds to a DL/I segment, and the entire structure is a DL/I data base record.

Suppose now the FACULTY structure shown in Figure A-6a is added to the data base. Again, it is a tree, so each node is a segment, and the entire structure is a data base record.

There is considerable data duplication in the STUDENT and FACULTY data base records. Although the data could be physically represented twice, this is undesirable. To avoid such duplication, DL/I provides the logical pointer facil-ity. When this approach is used, the ADVISEE node in the FACULTY data base record contains no data, but rather a logical pointer to the STUDENT data base record (Figure A-6b). For example, if JONES advises BAKER, then the ADVISEE segment under JONES has a pointer to BAKER. DL/I logical point-ers are actually one of several types of physical pointer schemes.

In Chapter 4 we showed that any network can be represented by trees with some data duplication. Further, data duplication can be eliminated in DL/I by using logical pointers. These two facts form the basis for modeling networks using hierarchical relationships. First, we decompose the network into trees with duplication; then we represent the trees using DL/I and remove dupli-cation with logical pointers.

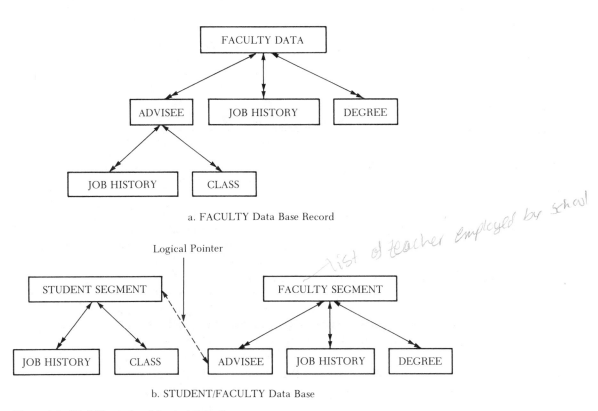

a. FACULTY Data Base Record

list of teacher employed by school

Logical Pointer

b. STUDENT/FACULTY Data Base

Figure A-6   DL/I Physical and Logical Data Structures

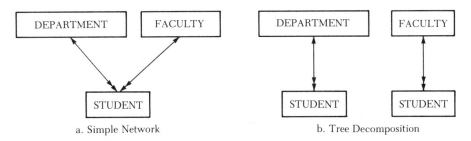

a. Simple Network

b. Tree Decomposition

Figure A-7   Decomposition of a Simple Network

To understand this process for a simple network, consider the data base in Figure A-7a. Here a STUDENT segment has two parents. One is the student's major DEPARTMENT, and the other is the student's advisor. Clearly, this network can be decomposed into the two tree structures in Figure A-7b. The STUDENT segment can be physically represented under either the DEPARTMENT or FACULTY segment, and logically represented by a pointer under the other segment.

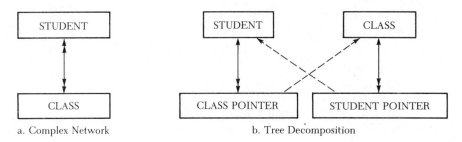

Figure A-8 Decomposition of a Complex Network

An example of a complex network appears in Figure A-8a. Here the one-to-many relationships go in both directions. A student is enrolled in many classes, and one class is composed of many students. The tree decomposition of this network results in nodes that are just pointers. Each STUDENT occurrence has a collection of CLASS pointers, and each CLASS occurrence has a collection of STUDENT pointers. The DBMS obtains all students in a given class by retrieving the CLASS segment and following the STUDENT pointers under that CLASS to the appropriate STUDENT segments. It obtains all classes for a particular student by retrieving the STUDENT segment and following the CLASS pointers under that STUDENT to the appropriate CLASS segments.

Another example of a complex network is the STUDENT/FACULTY/CLASS network in Figure A-9a. The ADVISOR relationship is one-to-many from FAC-

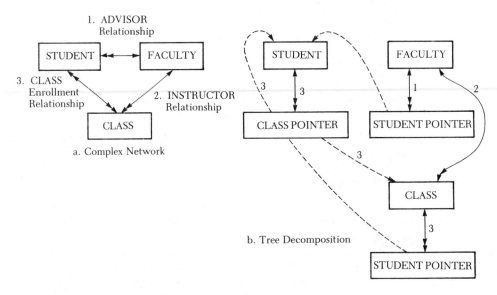

Figure A-9 STUDENT/FACULTY/CLASS Network

ULTY to STUDENT, the INSTRUCTOR relationship is one-to-many from FAC-ULTY to CLASS, and the CLASS-ENROLLMENT relationship is one-to-many in both directions. The CLASS segment can contain only general CLASS data such as Time and Location. It cannot contain a student's grade. If it did, the relationship from CLASS to STUDENT would be one-to-one.

Figure A-9b illustrates a DL/I representation of this network. The complex CLASS-ENROLLMENT relationship is modeled as in Figure A-8b, the ADVISOR relationship uses STUDENT logical pointers as shown in Figure A-6b, and the INSTRUCTOR relationship is modeled by a DL/I hierarchy.

LOGICAL AND PHYSICAL RECORDS

DL/I does not support the concept of *schemas* and *subschemas*. Instead, it divides the data base into physical and logical constructs. The terms *physical data base* (PDB) and *physical data base record* (PDBR) are used to describe the data as it exists in data storage. The terms *logical data base* (LDB) and *logical data base record* (LDBR) are used to describe the data as it appears to the application programs that process it.

LDBs differ from PDBs in either of two ways. An LDB may be a subset of a PDB, or an LDB may contain portions of two or more PDBs and have segment relationships that are not present in the PDBs.

To illustrate the first of these, consider the PDB in Figure A-10. It contains one PDBR type that has seven segment types. Figure A-11 depicts one occurrence of this PDBR. Jones has been an assistant professor and an associate professor at salaries ranging from $26,000 to $30,000 (links A and B). She is

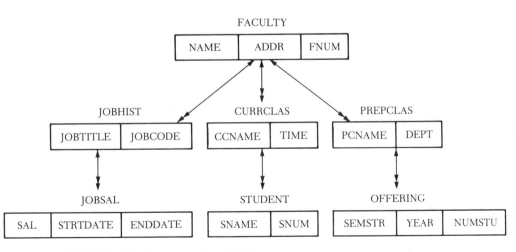

Figure A-10   FACULTY PDB Containing One PDBR Type

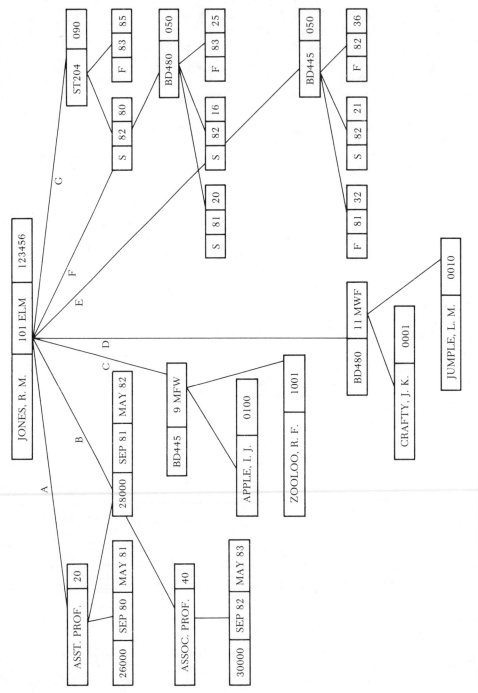

Figure A-11 Occurrence of FACULTY PDBR

```
DBD      NAME = FACULTYDB
SEGM     NAME = FACULTY,BYTES = 240
                  Faculty Field Description
                           .
                           .
                           .
SEGM     NAME = JOBHIST,PARENT = FACULTY,BYTES = 100
                  Job History Field Description
                           .
                           .
                           .
SEGM     NAME = JOBSAL,PARENT = JOBHIST,BYTES = 10
                  Job Salary Field Description
                           .
                           .
                           .
SEGM     NAME = CURRCLAS,PARENT = FACULTY,BYTES = 30
                  Current Class Field Description
                           .
                           .
                           .
SEGM     NAME = STUDENT,PARENT = CURRCLAS,BYTES = 60
                  Student Field Description
                           .
                           .
                           .
SEGM     NAME = PREPCLAS,PARENT = FACULTY,BYTES = 40
                  Prepared Class Field Description
                           .
                           .
                           .
SEGM     NAME = OFFERING,PARENT = PREPCLAS,BYTES = 60
                  Offering Field Description
                           .
                           .
                           .
```

Figure A-12   PDBR Description for Faculty PDBR

currently teaching two classes, BD445 and BD480 (links C and D). The students in each of those classes are identified in the PDBR occurrence. Further, Jones has taught (or prepared) classes ST204, BD480, and BD445; and, for example, she taught BD445 in the fall of 1981 and in the spring and fall of 1982 (links E, F, and G).

The PDBR description for this structure is presented in Figure A-12. Again the format of this description is unique to IMS. The DBD macro names the PDBR. Following it are SEGM macros, one for each segment defined in the

```
PCB        DBDNAME = FACULTYDB
SENSEG   NAME = FACULTY,PROCOPT = G
SENSEG   NAME = CURRCLAS,PROCOPT = G
SENSEG   NAME = STUDENT,PROCOPT = (G,R,D,I)
```

Figure A-13   LDBR Description for a Grade Posting Program

PDBR. FIELD macros are required to describe each segment, but for brevity are not shown here.

Suppose a program is designed to record current class grades. The program needs to reference only the FACULTY, CURRCLAS, and STUDENT segments of the PDBR. An appropriate LDBR is said to be sensitive to the FACULTY, CURRCLAS, and STUDENT segments. A program that references this LDBR need not be aware that other segments exist.

Figure A-13 shows a program communication block (PCB) that details the correspondence between the LDBR to be created and the PDBR that already exists. Several IMS-related features have been omitted for simplicity. The PCB is a collection of assembly-language macros. The first of these, a PCB macro, names the data base description (FACULTYDB) on which this LDBR is based. A series of SENSEG macros lists the segments of the FACULTYDB to which the LDBR will be sensitive. The values of the SENSEG PROCOPT parameter indicate the processing options available to users of this LDBR. Users can retrieve (G for Get) the FACULTY, CURRCLAS, and STUDENT segments. Further, they can replace (R), delete (D), and insert (I) STUDENT segments. IMS offers other processing options as well.

All PCBs for an LDB are assembled and stored in a library. To use a particular LDB, a program need only name the member of the library containing the PCBs.

This approach has several advantages. First, the LDBR user is protected from some changes in the PDBR. If a new segment is added anywhere in the FACULTY-JOBHIST-JOBSAL path or the FACULTY-PREPCLAS-OFFERING path, for example, programs using the LDBR in Figure A-13 are not affected. Also, modifications to segments in a PDBR but not in an LDBR do not impact users of the LDBR. For example, adding a field to a segment not in an LDBR does not affect users of the LDBR.

A second advantage of the LDBR is security; segments not appearing in the LDBR are protected. A program cannot modify a segment that is unknown to it. One exception to this is that a program can delete a segment and, as a consequence, delete subordinate segments to which it is not sensitive.

The second way an LDB can differ from a PDB is that it may define rela-

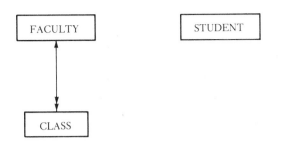

Figure A-14 Two Physical Data Base Records

tionships and structures combining several PDBs. These structures do not exist physically but appear to exist to users of the LDB. The applications involving logical pointers in Figures A-6 through A-9 fall into this category. In particular, look again at the structure in Figure A-9b. This structure could be an LDB constructed from the two PDBs in Figure A-14. One PDBR contains FACULTY and CLASS segments, while the other contains only a STUDENT segment. A description would be constructed for each of these PDBRs. Then the LDBR representing the structure in Figure A-9b would be generated by creating a third description that references the FACULTY and STUDENT descriptions. This third description will cause the student and class pointers in Figure A-9b to be generated. The process for doing this is quite complex. See reference [64].

DL/I DATA MANIPULATION LANGUAGE

DL/I manipulates data in segments. Commands are available to retrieve, update, insert, and delete segments. The application programmer defines an I/O work area that is shared between the user and the data base system. For inserts or updates, the user puts new data in the I/O work area and the data base system takes it from there. For retrievals, the DBMS puts information in the I/O work area for the user to access. Status data is also kept there.

To illustrate the DL/I data manipulation commands, consider the LDBR in Figure A-15. This LDBR is based on the FACULTY PDBR in Figure A-10. It is not sensitive to the CURRCLAS and STUDENT segments.

Get Unique (GU)

This command is used to read a particular segment into the I/O work area. For example, the statements

```
GU    FACULTY
      PREPCLAS (PCNAME = 'BD480')
```

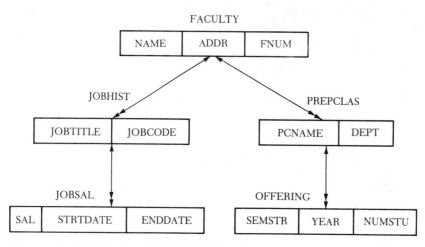

Figure A-15 LDBR Based on FACULTY PDBR in Figure A-10

will cause the first PREPCLAS segment with the name BD480 to be placed into the I/O work area. Thus, if the occurrence in Figure A-16 is the first one in the data base, the segment BD480 050 will appear in the work area. The statements

```
GU    FACULTY
      PREPCLAS (PCNAME = 'ST204')
      OFFERING (SEMSTR = 'F')
```

will cause the first OFFERING segment of ST204 in the fall to be placed in the work area. If no such segment exists, the system will set an appropriate return code in the work area.

The data base system will search for the desired segment by starting at the first occurrence of the LDBR, at the first ST204 occurrence of the PREPCLAS segment, and at the first fall occurrence of the OFFERING segment. The order of the segments is determined by the sequence fields in each segment. For this LDBR, assume the following sequence fields:

Segment	Sequence Field
FACULTY	NAME
JOBHIST	JOBCODE
JOBSAL	STRTDATE
PREPCLAS	PCNAME
OFFERING	YEAR

Thus, to find the first occurrence of a fall offering of ST204 in the Jones occurrence, segments will be examined in the following order: JONES, R.M. (FACULTY segment), BD445, BD480, ST204 (PREPCLAS segments), and finally 82, 83 (OFFERING segments). The segment read will be F 83 85.

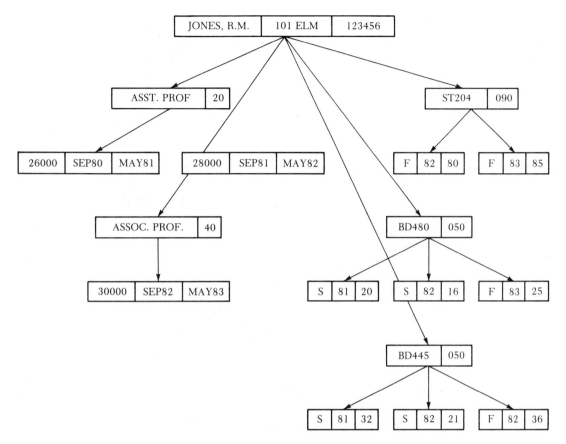

Figure A-16 Portion of Occurrence in Figure A-11 Available to User of LDBR in Figure A-15

The qualifying data after the GU command is called a *segment search argument* (SSA). In general, an SSA is the name of a segment, optionally followed by a condition. As shown, there can be one SSA for each segment in the hierarchical path for the segment to be retrieved.

Get Next (GN)

This command is used to read the next segment. NEXT implies that there be a current segment to start from, so it is necessary to indicate a current segment before issuing the GN command. For example, the statements

```
GU        FACULTY
          JOBSAL (SAL = 26000)
GN        JOBSAL
```

will cause the first JOBSAL segment in the data base with SAL field equal to 26000 to be placed in the I/O work area. This establishes a current position. Then the next JOBSAL segment is read. For the occurrence in Figure A-16, the segment 26000 SEP80 MAY81 will be read, followed by the segment 28000 SEP81 MAY82. If a subsequent GN JOBSAL command is executed, the DBMS will attempt to find another JOBSAL segment under the current JOBHIST segment. There is none for this occurrence, so it will search under the next JOBHIST segment (ASSOC. PROF 40) and read the segment 30000 SEP82 MAY83. A third GN JOBSAL command will cause the system to look for the next JOBSAL segment. Since there are no more in the Jones LDBR occurrence, the DBMS will search the next LDBR occurrence for a JOBSAL segment and place it in the work area if found. The search will continue to the end of the data base if necessary. If no JOBSAL segment remains in the data base, appropriate status information will be set.

When GN statements are executed, the system selects the next occurrence of the segment named. If there is no such occurrence under the current parent, the DBMS switches to the next parent. The application program may need to know, however, when the DBMS selects a segment from a new parent. For example, when the second GN JOBSAL statement is executed as discussed, the program may need to know that a new JOBHIST segment has been retrieved.

To provide this information, when a segment is read, data about the path leading to the segment is placed in the work area. The product IMS places the *fully concatenated key* of the retrieved segment in the work area. This key is the concatenation of all sequence fields of segments leading to the segment. For example, the fully concatenated key for the 28000 SEP81 MAY82 segment is JONES, R.M., 20 SEP81. After the second GN JOBSAL command is executed, the system will return the key JONES, R.M. 40 SEP82 and the user will be able to detect the new JOBHIST segment by the change in key.

The commands

```
GN        FACULTY
          OFFERING (SEMSTR = 'F')
GN        OFFERING (SEMSTR = 'S')
```

will cause the segment F 81 32 to be read, followed by the next OFFERING segment taught in the spring. Consequently, S 82 21 will be read next. The important point here is that sequential retrieval can be either *qualified* (GN OFFERING (SEMSTR = 'S')) or *unqualified* (we could have requested simply GN OFFERING).

Another type of sequential retrieval command requests the next segment regardless of its type. For example, the commands

```
GU        FACULTY
          JOBHIST (JOBCODE = 40)
GN
```

will cause the segment ASSOC. PROF 40 to be read, followed by the segment 30000 SEP82 MAY83. A subsequent GN command will read the BD445 050 segment. Note that all data in the PDBR (Figure A-10) but not in the LDBR (Figure A-16) is skipped. That is, all data on current classes and students in the PDBR is omitted from consideration for the GN because it is not defined in the LDBR.

Get Next within Parent (GNP)

This command sequentially retrieves segments under one parent. When all segments under that parent have been read, end-of-data status is returned to the program. For example, when the commands

```
GU        FACULTY
          JOBSAL (SAL = 26000)
GNP       JOBSAL
GNP       JOBSAL
```

are executed, the segments 26000 SEP80 MAY81 and 28000 SEP81 MAY82 will be read. The second GNP JOBSAL command will not return data; rather, it will cause the end-of-data status to be set. Contrast this with the statements

```
GU        FACULTY
          JOBSAL (SAL = 26000)
GN        JOBSAL
GN        JOBSAL
```

Here the second GN JOBSAL will retrieve the segment 30000 SEP82 MAY83.

Get Hold commands

The three commands Get Hold Unique (GHU), Get Hold Next (GHN), and Get Hold Next within Parent (GHNP) operate exactly as the Get counterparts except that they inform the system to prepare for a change or deletion of the retrieved segment. They are used in conjunction with Replace or Delete commands. When the application programmer replaces or deletes a segment, he or she must first issue one of the forms of the Get Hold commands for that segment. The system will retrieve the segment and "hold" it. Then the Replace or Delete command can be issued.

Replace (REPL)

The Replace command is used to modify data within a segment. For example, the commands

```
GHU      FACULTY (FNAME = 'JONES, R.M.')
         JOBSAL (SAL = 26000)

         (Here, application program changes STRTDATE field to OCT80)

         REPL
```

will cause the DBMS to modify the date in the first JOBSAL segment having a SAL field of 26000 in the Jones LDBR.

(The DL/I syntax we have been using is general; it could apply to any programming language. DL/I commands are actually implemented by calling a DBMS subroutine. IMS does not have a precompiler like SQL/DS and IDMS do. In the last example above, as well as in several that follow, we will need to refer to language-unique activities. When this need arises, the language-unique commands will be printed in lowercase letters and shown in parentheses.)

As another example, suppose it is desired to add 100 to the DEPT code of every PREPCLAS segment in the FACULTY data base. The commands

```
     GHU FACULTY
     PREPCLAS
LOOP (Add 100 to DEPT field)
     REPL
     GHN
     (If not end-of-data, repeat loop.)
```

will do this. The GHU command will obtain the first PREPCLAS segment, and the GHN command will obtain every PREPCLAS segment after that.

Another example is to add 1000 to the SAL field of every JOBSAL segment under a JOBHIST segment with JOBCODE = 20. This requires the use of GHN and GHNP commands as follows:

```
     GU       FACULTY
NEXT GHN      JOBHIST (JOBCODE = 20)
              JOBSAL
     (If none, stop)
LOOP Add 1000 to SAL field
     REPL
     GHNP JOBSAL
     (If not end-of-data, repeat LOOP; else repeat NEXT.)
```

The GHN command will locate a JOBSAL segment under a JOBHIST segment with JOBCODE = 20. Then the modification will be made and the segment replaced. The GHNP command will retrieve the next JOBSAL segment under the same JOBHIST segment. If there are no more, control will go to NEXT, where the next appropriate JOBHIST segment is found. Otherwise, control will go to LOOP, where the next modification is made.

Delete (DLET)

Delete operates in conjuction with the Get Hold commands in a manner similar to Replace. The commands

```
GHU       FACULTY (FNAME = 'JONES, R.M.')
          PREPCLAS (PCNAME = 'BD480')
          OFFERING (SEMSTR = 'S', YEAR = 81)
DLET
```

will delete the segment S 81 20 from the data base. When a segment is deleted, any subordinate segments are also deleted (including invisible ones). Thus the commands

```
     GHU   FACULTY (FNAME = 'JONES, R.M.')
           PREPCLAS
LOOP DLET
     GHNP
     (If not end-of-data, repeat LOOP.)
```

will delete every PREPCLAS segment *and* every OFFERING segment. Even subordinate segments to which the program is not sensitive will be deleted. Assuming our same example,

```
GHU       FACULTY (FNAME = 'JONES, R.M.')
          DLET
```

will delete all segments pertaining to Jones, including the CURRCLAS and STUDENT segments in the Jones occurrence of the FACULTY PDBR but not mentioned in the LDBR.

Insert (INSRT)

Insert is used to create a new segment. For example, the statements

```
          (Fill JOBSAL fields in the work area.)
INSRT     FACULTY (FNAME = 'JONES, R.M.')
          JOBHIST (JOBCODE = 40)
          JOBSAL
```

will insert a new JOBSAL segment into the data base. Since the JOBSAL sequence field is STRTDATE, the new segment will be inserted in order on that field.

Name	Function
Get Unique (GU)	Retrieve a particular segment
Get Next (GN)	Retrieve the next segment
Get Next within Parent (GNP)	Retrieve the next segment under a particular parent
Get Hold Unique (GHU) Get Hold Next (GHN) Get Hold Next within Parent (GHNP)	Similar to above commands, but used to obtain a segment to be modified or deleted
Replace (REPL) Delete (DLET)	Used in conjunction with Get Hold commands to modify or delete a segment
Insert (ISRT)	Insert a new segment

Figure A-17   Summary of DL/I Data Manipulation Commands

For example, the JOBSAL segment 32000 SEP83 MAY84 will be inserted after the segment 30000 SEP82 MAY83 in Figure A-16. If the STRTDATE field of the new segment were JUN82, the segment would be inserted before 30000 SEP82 MAY83.

SUMMARY

Figure A-17 summarizes the DL/I data manipulation commands. All of these commands operate on the logical structure of the data as seen by the application program. Since the physical structure of the data may be quite different from the logical structure, the commands must translate the logical activity into actions on the physical data structures. The application program is independent of the physical structure and is freed from maintaining any physical structures such as linked or inverted lists.

Questions

A.1   Consider the following organizational chart:

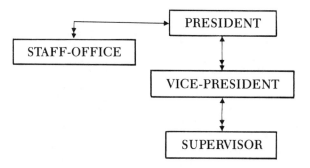

a. Sketch an occurrence of this structure.

b. What in this example constitutes a DL/I segment? a data base record? the data base?

A.2   Assume each segment in question A.1 has Name, Address, Employee-number, and Salary fields. Write a data base description similar to the one in Figure A-5 for this data base.

A.3   Sketch the hierarchical structure and logical pointers necessary to model the following data base records in DL/I.

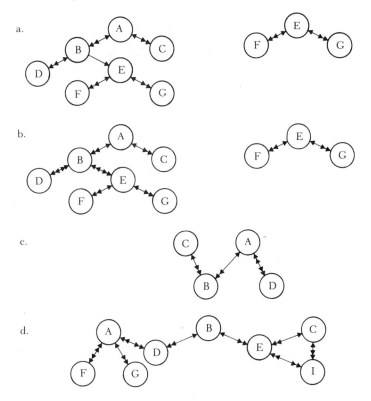

a.

b.

c.

d.

A.4   Write a data base description for the following data base. Assume each node contains a 10-character field.

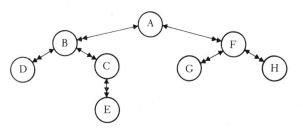

A.5 Write the LDBR description for the logical record in question A.4 that contains nodes A, B, C, E, and F only. This description should be similar to the LDBR.

A.6 Assume a data base consists of three separate PDBs as follows:

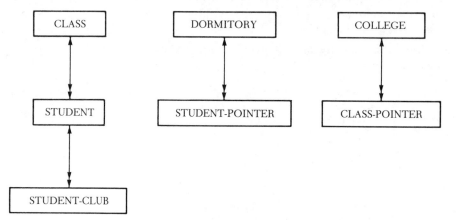

Describe the LDBR required to be able to respond to the following requests:

a. Obtain the names of all students in a class taught by the College of Business.

b. Obtain the name of every student club that has at least one member living in Green Dormitory.

The data shown on the next page pertains to questions A.7 through A.11. Sequence fields are underlined.

A.7 Describe the results of the following retrievals:

a.	GU	FACTORY
		PRODUCT (COST = 40)
		PART
b.	GU	FACTORY
		WREHOUSE (NAME = 'W2')
		DISTRBTR
c.	GU	FACTORY
		PRODUCT (COST = 40)
		PART (NUM-REQ = 24)
	GN	PART
	GN	PART
	GN	PART
	GN	PART

d. GU   FACTORY
              PRODUCT (COST = 40)
    GNP   PART
    GNP   PART

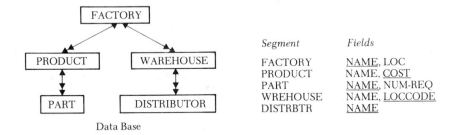

Segment	Fields
FACTORY	NAME, LOC
PRODUCT	NAME, COST
PART	NAME, NUM-REQ
WREHOUSE	NAME, LOCCODE
DISTRBTR	NAME

Data Base

A.8   What will happen when the last GN PART statement is executed in A.7c? How will the user be able to detect this?

A.9   What will happen if another GNP PART statement is executed immediately after those in A.7d?

A.10   Show the DL/I statements needed to specify the following actions.
   a. Delete the | PRT6 | 24 | segment under PRD2.
   b. Delete all data about warehouse W3.
   c. Delete all data about factory F1.
   d. Delete all products costing more than $45.

A.11   Show the DL/I statements needed to perform the following modifications and additions. In doing so, explain actions that must be performed by language-unique commands as well.
   a. Modify PRD2 to show a cost of $85.
   b. Modify the cost of all products to be 10 percent greater.
   c. Add distributor D11 to warehouse W2 and distributor D14 to warehouse W3.
   d. Add to factory F1: PRD4, COST $105, with parts PRT2, 26 required, and PRT4, 31 required.
   e. Change the cost of PRD1 to $45 and add PRT6, 21 required to it.

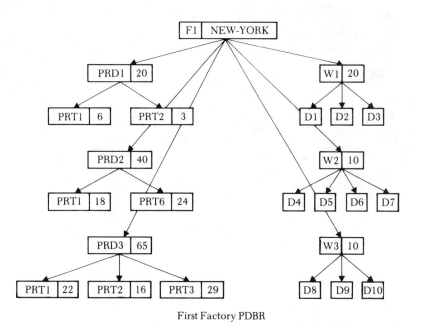

First Factory PDBR

Appendix B
TOTAL/IMAGE

TOTAL and IMAGE are two DBMS products which are based on the same database model. TOTAL is marketed by CINCOM Systems and has been available on both mainframe and minicomputers since the early 1970s. TOTAL operates on a very wide variety of computers. IMAGE is marketed by Hewlett-Packard and currently operates on the HP3000 series of computers. Although this appendix will focus on TOTAL, and use the TOTAL vocabulary, realize that most concepts pertain to both IMAGE and TOTAL.

The smallest addressable data unit is a *data item*, which corresponds to what we have called a *field*. Data items can be grouped into *data elements*. An address is an example of a data element; it is composed of street, city, state, and Zip Code data items. Data items and data elements are grouped into *data records*, which are in turn grouped into *data files*. A collection of data files that relate to one another is referred to as a *data base*.

TOTAL has two functionally different types of files. *Master files* are composed of nonvolatile, homogeneous *master records*. These records can exist independently of any other file records and can be related to one or more variable files. A *variable file* contains volatile *variable records*, which must be directly related to at least one master file.

As an example of these two file types, consider the database containing STUDENT and GRADE files in Figure B-1. The STUDENT records can be loaded on a master file and the GRADE records on a variable file. (TOTAL documentation shows master files in squares and variable files in circles.) Master records can be related to corresponding variable records by student number. This permits the master record for a particular student to be retrieved from the master file, and then all variable records containing the student's grades to be found by following the relationship (really a linked list) that starts at the STUDENT master record and extends through the GRADE variable records for the student.

Master and variable records are processed in different ways. Each master record has a unique primary key. In many versions of TOTAL, and in IMAGE, master records cannot have more than one key. Variable records may have

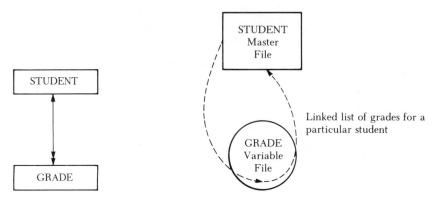

a. STUDENT/GRADE Relationship   b. TOTAL Master/Variable File Representation

Figure B-1   Examples of TOTAL File Types

multiple keys, and these keys are usually not unique. Variable record keys must be associated with a master record. In Figure B-2, GRADE variable records have Student-number as a secondary key, and a set of GRADE variable records for a given student is associated with the STUDENT master record having the matching Student-number. To access the GRADE variable records by key value, the STUDENT master record must first be accessed (this is done automatically by TOTAL). Then all variable records associated with that master record can be processed.

To illustrate a case where two keys are required, suppose there is a CLASS master file as well as a STUDENT master file. Both CLASS and STUDENT records have one-to-many relationships to GRADE records. Assume that each GRADE record has a Class-name field. To retrieve all grades given in a class, the CLASS master is read, followed by all GRADE records having matching Class-name values. In this case, GRADE records have relationships via both the Student-number and Class-name fields. In a sense, these fields can be considered nonunique secondary keys.

Two or more such key fields can refer to the same master file. For example, suppose there is a key from CLASS master records to GRADE variable records using Class-name as described. Further, assume it is also necessary to have a GRADE key on Class-number. In this case, the developers can define two relationships from CLASS to GRADE. One relationship is based on matching Class-names and the other is based on matching Class-numbers. Both keys will refer to the same master file.

Master files contain fixed-length records, and every record has the same format. Variable files have fixed-length records, but record format may vary within a file. Records whose format varies are called *coded records*. For example, suppose the GRADE file has two types of records: those for grades trans-

TR	Student-number	Class-name	Grade	Hours	SEM or Quarter	Institution-code

a. GRADE Record for Transferred Grade

← —————— Base Data —————— → ← — Redefined Data — →

HI	Student-number	Class-name	Grade	Hours	Instructor	Unused

b. GRADE Record for Grade Earned at Host Institution

Figure B-2 TOTAL Coded Records

ferred and those for grades earned at the host institution. GRADE records have the two formats shown in Figure B-2. Each record has a code indicating its type (TR for transfer, or HI for host institution). The base data portion is identical in the two types of records. The redefined data area differs.

REPRESENTATION OF RELATIONSHIPS

The representation of single-level tree and simple network relationships is straightforward. Figure B-3a shows a tree having two one-to-many relationships. In Figure B-3b, each relationship has been replaced by a TOTAL master to variable file linked list. Figure B-4 shows a similar transformation for a simple network. Each one-to-many relationship is represented with a master to variable file linked list.

Complex networks cannot be represented directly. Instead, the complex net-

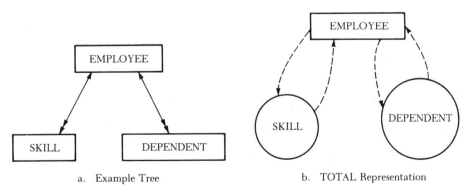

a. Example Tree

b. TOTAL Representation

Figure B-3 TOTAL Tree Representation

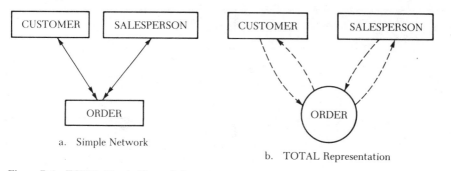

a. Simple Network

b. TOTAL Representation

Figure B-4 TOTAL Simple Network Representation

work must be reduced to a simple network by defining intersection data. This technique is similar to that used with the CODASYL DBTG model.

The relationships in Figures B-3 and B-4 are single-level. No record is both a child and a parent. Consider Figure B-5, which is a portion of the database designed for Sally Enterprises. PITCHER records are children to RECIPEs and parents of ORDERs. Also, CUSTOMER records are children to FAMILY-NAMEs and parents to NICKNAMEs. Because TOTAL will not allow variable records to be linked to other variable records, two-or-more-level structures cannot be represented directly. Instead, the multilevel relationships must be redefined to be several single-level relationships.

Figure B-6 shows such a transformation of the database structure in Figure B-5. RECIPEs are linked to a variable file containing PITCHER numbers, and FAMILY-NAMEs are linked to a variable file containing CUSTOMER names. Unfortunately, the burden for processing this structure falls on the application program. To obtain all ORDER records for a given RECIPE, for example, the

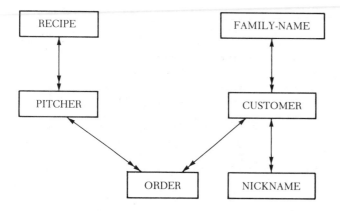

Figure B-5 A Portion of the Sally Enterprises Database

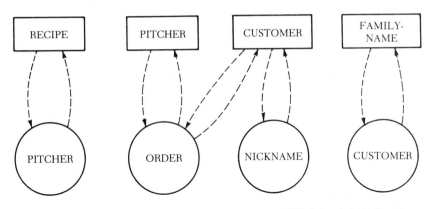

Figure B-6 Transformation of Structure in Figure B-5 to TOTAL Single-level Structure

program must FIND the desired RECIPE record, and follow the linked list to the PITCHER number file. Then, using the Pitcher number obtained, it must read the PITCHER master file and read the variable ORDER records that it owns. As compared to the DBTG model, the PITCHER number file is extraneous.

TOTAL DATA AND FILE STRUCTURES

TOTAL has one internal structure for master files and another for variable files. Each master file must be allocated to a separate physical file. These files are processed using direct file organization and relative block addressing.

TOTAL supplies a hashing scheme to convert master record keys to relative block addresses. Synonyms are processed by a two-way linked list as follows: When loading, if the location calculated by the identified address is full, the record is inserted in the physically next available location. A pointer to this record, or synonym, is inserted in the record at the calculated address. If there is a second synonym for the record at this address, it is inserted in the physically next available location and a pointer to the second synonym is inserted in the first synonym. A pointer in the second synonym is set to point to the first one. That is, two-way pointers are established. Figure B-7 illustrates this process, assuming records are unblocked. In actuality, TOTAL blocks records so the situation is more complex. The hash record number is the block address calculated from the hashing scheme. Letters after hash record numbers identify synonyms.

Chaining records together reduces the amount of I/O necessary for locating records. For example, to find hash record 1c without the linked list, all eight records would have to be read.

As we have seen, master records can be linked to variable records. When this is done, the master record has pointers to the first and last records in the

Block Number	Prior/Next	Master Record Data
1	0/4	Hash record 1a
2	0/0	Hash record 2
3	0/0	Hash record 3
4	1/8	Hash record 1b
5	0/7	Hash record 5a
6	0/0	Hash record 6
7	5/0	Hash record 5b
8	4/0	Hash record 1c
9	0/0	Unused
10	0/0	Unused

Figure B-7 TOTAL Chained Hashing Scheme

linked list of variable records. Because the linked list is two-way, the variable records can be processed in the forward or reverse direction. Since the master file must be on a separate physical file, the pointer is a relative block number on a different physical file. The name of this physical file is specified during schema definition.

Variable records also reside on directly organized physical files using relative block addressing. Since variable records have no primary key, no hashing is necessary. Instead, the pointers to the start and end of a variable record chain are stored in the master record pertaining to that chain.

Variable records have the format shown in Figure B-8. The values for all secondary keys occur first in the record, followed by the data, followed by the link fields. Each link has forward and reverse pointers. There is one link for each secondary key. Secondary-key values are stored in the record for two reasons. If the linkage paths are destroyed by accident or malfunction, they can be repaired using the key values. Also, variable records can be processed without using the linkage paths; when this is done, the user may need the values of secondary keys.

When inserting variable records, TOTAL searches for unused space as close to the point of insertion as possible. The new record is inserted in the available space, and the links in the prior and next records are set to point to the new

| KEY1 | KEY2 | KEY3 | ::: | DATA | LINK1 | LINK2 | LINK3 | ::: |

Figure B-8 TOTAL Variable Record Format

record. The first record on each cylinder is reserved for unused space management. Unused records are marked, and TOTAL searches for such marked records when it needs space.

More than one variable record type can exist on a physical file. However, all physical records on a file must have the same length. This length is that of the longest variable record block on the file. Unused and unavailable space exists in physical records holding shorter variable records. For example, if two variable record blocks of length 100 and 800 bytes exist on the same physical file, the length of the physical record must be 800 bytes. Physical records holding 100-byte variable record blocks have 700 bytes of unused space that is also unavailable because there can be only one variable record per physical record. To minimize wasted space, variable record blocks existing on the same physical file should be about the same length.

Figure B-9 shows a sample database having two types of master records, A and B, and three types of variable records, C, D, and E. Master record A has links to variable records C and D, and master record B has links to variable records D and E. Each of the master records must exist on a separate physical file. The variable files may reside on the same physical file. Since variable records C and D have about the same length, they are allocated to the same file. Variable record E has a much shorter length, so it is allocated to a separate file.

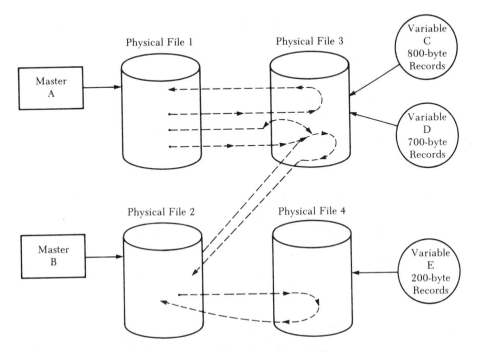

Figure B-9 TOTAL Assignment of Logical Records to Physical Files

TOTAL DATA DESCRIPTION

TOTAL data description is accomplished by providing statements defining the formats of all master and variable files to the TOTAL database generation program. The output of this program is assembler-language statements, which are assembled into a database description module. This module is required whenever the database is processed.

The input to the database generation program consists of four sections. The prologue section names the database and specifies certain options. The master file section describes the format and physical file characteristics of each master file. The variable file section describes the format and physical file characteristics of each variable file. The epilogue section terminates the database description.

An abbreviated database description for the database in Figure B-9 is shown in Figure B-10. The first master file is named MSTA in the statement labeled A (these labels are for discussion only; they are not part of the TOTAL description). The statements labeled B define the primary key as the MSTACTRL field whose length is 10 and two link fields: VARCLK01 will link to C variable records, and VARDLK02 will link to D records. The statements labeled C describe the record format. The numbers are COBOL-like level-numbers. They are followed by data item names and length specifications for the items. The statements labeled D describe characteristics of the file on which MSTA records will reside. Entries for variable files are similar except that there is no primary-key entry. Also, there are special statements for coded records (variable records with varying formats). The statement labeled E defines one link field for variable record C (VARC), which is MSTALK01 from master file A. If there were more links in variable record C, they would be named here.

The database description does not specify the names of physical files. Rather, the name as defined in the description is taken as the DDNAME of a JCL card that defines the particular physical file (name and volume).

TOTAL DATA MANIPULATION

TOTAL DML is implemented by call statements issued from a host language such as COBOL, PL/I, or assembler language. The parameter list for a call specifies the operation to be performed plus other information depending on the operation. Parameter lists for typical TOTAL commands are as follows:

A. Read Master

"READM", status, file, control-key, data-list, data-area, "END".

The control-key specification is the primary-key value of the master record to be read. Data items named in the data-list parameter are placed in the data-area.

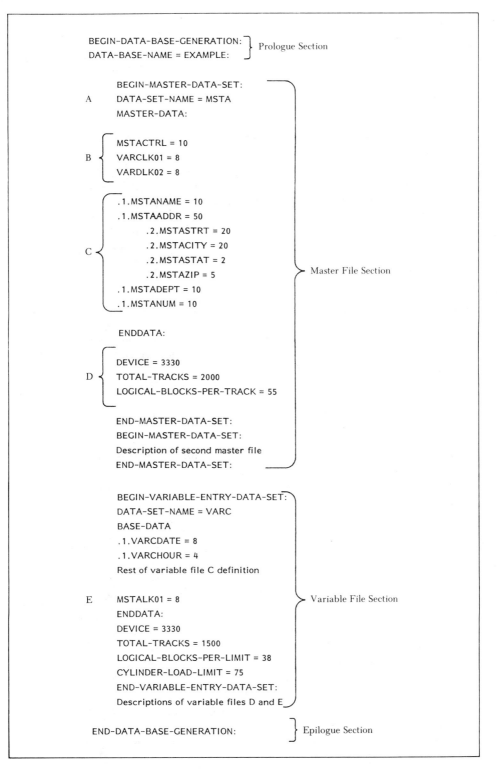

```
        BEGIN-DATA-BASE-GENERATION: ⎫
                                     ⎬  Prologue Section
        DATA-BASE-NAME = EXAMPLE:   ⎭


          BEGIN-MASTER-DATA-SET:           ⎫
    A     DATA-SET-NAME = MSTA              │
          MASTER-DATA:                      │


          MSTACTRL = 10                     │
    B     VARCLK01 = 8                      │
          VARDLK02 = 8                      │


          .1.MSTANAME = 10                  │
          .1.MSTAADDR = 50                  │
              .2.MSTASTRT = 20              │
              .2.MSTACITY = 20              │
    C         .2.MSTASTAT = 2               ⎬  Master File Section
              .2.MSTAZIP = 5                │
          .1.MSTADEPT = 10                  │
          .1.MSTANUM = 10                   │


          ENDDATA:                          │


          DEVICE = 3330                     │
    D     TOTAL-TRACKS = 2000               │
          LOGICAL-BLOCKS-PER-TRACK = 55     │


          END-MASTER-DATA-SET:             │
          BEGIN-MASTER-DATA-SET:           │
          Description of second master file │
          END-MASTER-DATA-SET:             ⎭


          BEGIN-VARIABLE-ENTRY-DATA-SET:   ⎫
          DATA-SET-NAME = VARC             │
          BASE-DATA                        │
          .1.VARCDATE = 8                  │
          .1.VARCHOUR = 4                  │
          Rest of variable file C definition │

    E     MSTALK01 = 8                     ⎬  Variable File Section
          ENDDATA:                         │
          DEVICE = 3330                    │
          TOTAL-TRACKS = 1500              │
          LOGICAL-BLOCKS-PER-LIMIT = 38    │
          CYLINDER-LOAD-LIMIT = 75         │
          END-VARIABLE-ENTRY-DATA-SET:     │
          Descriptions of variable files D and E ⎭


        END-DATA-BASE-GENERATION:   ⎫
                                     ⎬  Epilogue Section
```

Figure B-10 Abbreviated TOTAL Data Description for Database in Figure B-9

B. Read Variable

"READV", status, file, reference, linkage-path, control-key, data-list, data-area, "END".

The reference field indicates which record in a link chain should be read. This parameter can contain either a flag that indicates start at the first record in the chain or the relative record number of the record preceding the one to be read. Linkage-path names the link chain to be used. Control-key is a primary-key value identifying a particular instance of that chain. After the READV, TOTAL returns the relative record number of the record just read in the reference field. Thus, to process sequentially along a chain, the user does not modify the reference field. When end of chain is reached, TOTAL returns "END" in this field.

C. Add Master

"ADD-M", status, file, control-key, data-list, data-area, "END".

This command creates a new master record and fills it with the data items named in the data-list parameter. Values for the items are taken from data-area.

D. Add Variable After

"ADDVA", status, file, reference, linkage-path, control-key, data-list, data-area, "END".

This command inserts a variable record into a variable file and links it on all chains defined for that file. For the chain specified by the linkage-path parameter, the insert is immediately after the record specified by the reference parameter. On other chains, the record is added at the end.

E. Delete Master

"DEL-M", status, file, control-key, data-list, data-area, "END".

This command deletes the master record whose primary key is specified by control-key. The unused space is available for other uses.

F. Replace Data in Variable

"WRITV", status, file, reference, linkage-path, control-key, data-list, data-area, "END".

This command replaces existing data in a variable record with data from data-area. Reference has the relative record number of the master record which points to the variable record containing data to be replaced. Only the items in the data-list parameter are replaced.

G. Read Record with Qualifications

"FINDX", status, file qualifier, argument, data-list, data-area, "END".

This command searches either master files or variable file chains for a record that meets the qualifications specified in the argument parameter. The search starts with the record specified by the qualifier parameter. The argument parameter has the following format:

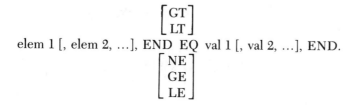

$$\text{elem 1 [, elem 2, ...], END } \begin{bmatrix} GT \\ LT \\ EQ \\ NE \\ GE \\ LE \end{bmatrix} \text{ val 1 [, val 2, ...], END.}$$

where each *elem* is the name of an element in the record, and each corresponding *val* is a value that the element may have. The FINDX command can be used in conjunction with replace or delete operations.

A summary of important (but not all) TOTAL DML commands appears in Figure B-11.

Command	Function
ADD-M	Add a master record.
ADDVA	Add a variable record after a specified record.
ADDVB	Add a variable record before a specified record.
ADDVR	Move a variable record from one chain to another.
DEL-M	Delete a master record.
DELVD	Delete a variable record direct, i.e., using relative record number.
FINDX	Read a record with qualifications.
RDNXT	Read master or variable records sequentially (in physical order).
READD	Read a variable record direct.
READM	Read a master record using primary key.
READR	Read variable records in reverse order.
READV	Read a variable record in a chain.
WRITM	Replace data in a master record.
WRITV	Replace data in a variable record.

Figure B-11   Summary of Important TOTAL DML Commands

Questions

B.1 Define the TOTAL terms *master file* and *variable file*.

B.2 Explain how TOTAL master and variable files can be used to represent single-level trees, and simple and complex networks.

B.3 Show how TOTAL master and variable files can be used to represent two-level trees.

B.4 Describe a process for representing *n*-level trees using TOTAL master and variable file structures.

B.5 Show how TOTAL can represent the following network. Which data resides in master files necessary to represent the relationships? What links are required?

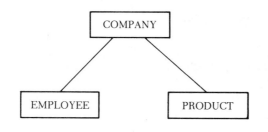

Record	Fields
COMPANY	NAME, ADDRESS, ANNUAL-SALES
EMPLOYEE	NAME, NUMBER, ADDRESS
PRODUCT	NAME, SALES-PRICE

B.6 Repeat question B.5 for the following network:

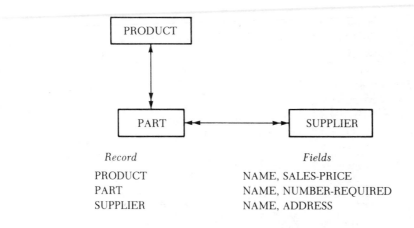

Record	Fields
PRODUCT	NAME, SALES-PRICE
PART	NAME, NUMBER-REQUIRED
SUPPLIER	NAME, ADDRESS

Appendix C
MicroRIM

MicroRIM is a relational DBMS for microcomputers vended by the MicroRIM Corporation. MicroRIM defines data as relations and supports relational data manipulation. SELECT, PROJECT, and unrestricted JOIN operations are supported by MicroRIM, and thus this system meets Codd's criteria for a minimal relational system (see Chapter 12). MicroRIM uses a combination of the terms you have learned. Tuples of relations are called *rows*, as with SQL/DS, but attributes of relations are called *attributes*, not columns. (Once more we see the challenge of terminology in the database field!)

In some ways, MicroRIM can be thought of as a scaled-down version of SQL/DS. Data definition and query/update facilities are quite similar. The program interface, however, uses subroutine calls instead of a precompiler. Also, MicroRIM is oriented toward single-user micro applications and does not, as in SQL/DS, provide control over concurrent operations, definition of logical transactions, or backup and recovery. (Data can be backed up by copying diskettes. There is no log of before and after images for rollback and rollforward, however.)

SYSTEM REQUIREMENTS

MicroRIM operates with any of the following processors: Intel 8080 and 8085, Z-80, or Apple with Z-80 card. The CP/M operating system is required and 52K bytes of user-addressable memory are needed. Also, a minimum of one diskette drive with 152K bytes of storage or two drives with at least 120K bytes of storage each is necessary. Two drives are strongly recommended by the vendor. MicroRIM is priced at typical micro software levels, and is therefore considerably less expensive than mainframe or mini DBMS products.

DATABASE DEFINITION

A MicroRIM database is a collection of relation definitions and data. A DEFINE processor is provided to build database structures. Using this processor, the database is named and (optionally) a database password is specified. The user of this password is authorized to perform any data manipulation commands and also can modify portions of the database structure.

Next, all attributes of all relations are described. Figure C-1 lists allowed attribute data types. Once attributes are described, then relations are defined by listing the name of a relation followed by the names of the attributes to be contained in the relation. Finally, optional read and update passwords can be specified.

Figure C-2 presents define commands to construct a database of RECIPE, PITCHER, and ORDER relations. The structure of these relations conforms to that presented for SQL/DS in Figure 12-22. Attribute names must be eight or fewer characters, so some of the names have been shortened.

MicroRIM will build inverted lists for any attribute identified as a KEY. The inverted list will improve the performance of SELECT, JOIN, and other operations. These operations, however, do not require inverted lists.

QUERY COMMANDS

MicroRIM query commands are very similar to SQL commands. To illustrate these commands, we will consider the same query examples as those discussed in Chapters 12 and 13.

Data Type	Format
DATE	jj/kk/ll, where j, k, and l are decimal digits. Thus DATE attributes can be mm/dd/yy, dd/mm/yy, or yy/mm/dd.
DOLLAR	range of plus or minus 9,999,999.99
INTEGER	range of plus or minus 999,999,999
REAL	range of 0 plus or minus 10 to the 38th power
TEXT	1 to 254 bytes
TIME	hh:mm:ss representing hours, minutes, seconds

Figure C-1 Summary of MicroRIM Data Types

```
DEFINE      SALLY-DB
OWNER       SE-DBA
ATTRIBUTES
R-NAME      TEXT 10     KEY
SUGAR       REAL
LEMON       INTEGER
WATER       REAL
NUMBER      INTEGER     KEY
P-DATE      DATE
R-USED      TEXT 10
C-F-NAME    TEXT 10     KEY
C-L-NAME    TEXT 20     KEY
PITCHER     INTEGER     KEY
SP          TEXT 20
O-DATE      DATE
O-TIME      TIME
AMOUNT      REAL
RELATIONS
RECIPE WITH R-NAME SUGAR LEMON WATER
PITCHER WITH NUMBER P-DATE R-USED
ORDER WITH C-F-NAME C-L-NAME PITCHER SP O-DATE O-TIME AMOUNT
PASSWORDS
MPW FOR RECIPE IS RC-SUPV
END
```

Figure C-2   MicroRIM Define Commands for Relations RECIPE, PITCHER, and ORDER from Figure C-1

To obtain the names of all RECIPEs having exactly two lemons, the following command would be issued:

SELECT R-NAME FROM RECIPE WHERE LEMON EQ 2

MicroRIM will display the names of the qualifying RECIPEs. Commands can be listed on one line, or they can be continued over several lines. If continued, the last character of the line must be a plus sign. Thus the command above could be put into more typical SQL format as follows:

```
SELECT      R-NAME          +
FROM        RECIPE          +
WHERE       LEMON EQ 2
```

From now on, we will show MicroRIM commands in this second format.

MicroRIM does not allow built-in functions to be part of a WHERE clause. Therefore, to determine the name of the RECIPE having the most sugar, the following two operations would be needed:

```
COMPUTE      MAX SUGAR          +
FROM         RECIPE
SELECT       R-NAME             +
FROM         RECIPE             +
WHERE        SUGAR = (value from COMPUTE above)
```

In the COMPUTE statement, MicroRIM will determine the largest value of the Sugar attribute. Then, the name of the RECIPE having that largest value is printed in the next query.

The third query example from Chapters 12 and 13 is to print the name of all recipes and the total amounts sold for each. To answer this query, RECIPE rows must be joined with PITCHER rows, which in turn must be joined with ORDER rows. Then, the joined relations are processed.

The following MicroRIM commands will perform the joins:

```
JOIN RECIPE USING R-NAME WITH PITCHER USING R-USED
FORMING TEMP
JOIN TEMP USING NUMBER WITH ORDER USING PITCHER
FORMING R-ORDERS
```

The first command joins the RECIPE and PITCHER relations. With MicroRIM a name must be provided for the relation that is formed as part of the join. In this example, the newly formed relation is called *TEMP*. In the second command, TEMP is joined with ORDER, based on the pitcher number attributes (Number in PITCHER and Pitcher in ORDER). The result is the relation R-ORDERS.

MicroRIM does not support the SQL GROUP BY operation. Consequently, to obtain the total sold for each RECIPE, we must determine the names of all recipes and then total the amount sold for each. The following command will produce the names of all RECIPEs:

```
TALLY R-NAME FROM R-ORDERS
```

In response to this command, MicroRIM will display two columns similar to the following:

R-NAME	NUMBER OF OCCURRENCES
A	25
B	19
C	32

The amount ordered for each can be obtained as follows:

```
SELECT      SUM AMOUNT          +
FROM        R-ORDERS            +
WHERE       R-NAME EQ (names from TALLY command above)
```

UPDATE COMMANDS

MicroRIM provides commands for data modification, deletion, and insertion. The CHANGE command alters the value or values of rows in a relation. For example, the following command will change the name of RECIPE A to the value Z:

```
CHANGE      R-NAME TO Z         +
IN          RECIPE              +
WHERE       R-NAME EQ A
```

This command will change values in all qualifying rows. If more than one row had the value A in R-NAME, then all such rows would now have the value Z in R-NAME.

MicroRIM provides two different DELETE commands. The command,

```
DELETE      DUPLICATES          +
FROM        R-ORDERS
```

will cause all duplicate rows to be consolidated into one row. This is similar to the SQL SELECT UNIQUE command.

The DELETE command can also be used more generally. The following command will eliminate all PITCHER rows based on RECIPE A:

```
DELETE      ROWS                +
FROM        PITCHER             +
WHERE       R-USED EQ A
```

Finally, rows can be added using the MicroRIM LOAD command. The following commands add two new rows to the PITCHER relation:

```
LOAD    PITCHER
100 12/25/82 A
110 12/31/82 B
END
```

Attribute values can be delimited by either spaces or commas. The LOAD command can be used to load one or more commands. MicroRIM expects the load process to be terminated with the keyword END.

ADDITIONAL FACILITIES

This discussion is a quick overview of MicroRIM capabilities. In addition to features presented here, MicroRIM provides a subroutine-call program interface, a report writer, a facility for storing query and update command sequences, and a separate mass data entry and edit program. Additionally, MicroRIM can interface with a mainframe DBMS product called RIM. Since these two systems can accept files from one another, the combination of products provides data transportability between micro and mainframe computers. For more information about these features, see reference [61].

Questions

C.1   Show MicroRIM data definition commands to define two relations. The first is an OWNER relation having attributes Name, Address, City, State, Zip, and Age. The second relation is an AUTO relation having attributes O-name, Make, Color, and Year. Make appropriate assumptions regarding attribute formats.

C.2   For the relations in question C.1, show MicroRIM commands to:

  a. Present all owners who live in DENVER.

  b. Compute the average age of owners in Zip Code 98040.

  c. Determine the number of RED autos.

C.3   Show MicroRIM commands to join the OWNER and AUTO relations on owner names. Call the new relation AUTO-OWN.

C.4   For the relation AUTO-OWN from question C.3, show MicroRIM commands to:

  a. Count the number of autos owned by each person.

  b. Compute the average age of RED auto owners.

  c. Compute the average age of FORD auto owners.

C.5   For the OWNER relation, show MicroRIM commands to:

  a. Add three new rows. Provide data in accordance with your definition of attribute formats.

  b. Change all BLUE autos to SEASIDE FROST.

  c. Delete all autos that were made prior to 1974.

Bibliography

1. ANSI X3H2. *Overview of DBCS/Programming Language Interface*. American National Standards Institute, 1982.

2. ANSI X3H2. *Proposed American National Standard for a Data Definition Language for Network Structured Databases*. American National Standards Institute, 1981.

3. Astrahan, M.M., et al. "A History and Evaluation of System R," *IBM Research Report* RJ2843, June 1980.

4. Astrahan, M.M., et al. "System R: Relational Approach to Database Management." In *Transactions on Database Systems*, Vol. 1, No. 2, June 1976.

5. Astrahan, M.M., et al. "System R, a Relational Database Management System." In *Computer*, Vol. 12, No. 5, May 1979.

6. Atre, S. *Data Base, Structured Techniques for Design, Performance, and Management*. John Wiley, 1980.

7. Bernstein, Philip, and Goodman, Nathan. "Concurrency Control in Distributed Database Systems." In *Computing Surveys*, Vol. 13, No. 2, June 1981.

8. Bernstein, Philip A.; Rothnie, James B.; and Shipman, David W. *Distributed Data Base Management*. IEEE Catalog No. EHO 141-2, 1978.

9. Blasgen, M.W., et al. "System R: An Architectural Overview." In *IBM Systems Journal*, Vol. 20, No. 1, January 1981.

10. Boehm, Barry W. *Software Engineering Economics*. Prentice-Hall, 1981.

11. Bohl, Marilyn. *Introduction to IBM Direct Access Storage Devices*. Science Research Associates, 1981.

12. Boyce, R.F., et al. "Specifying Queries as Relational Expressions: SQUARE." In *Communications of the ACM*, Vol. 18, No. 11, November 1975.

13. Bray, Olin H. *Distributed Database Management Systems*. Lexington Books, 1982.

14. Britton-Lee Corporation. *IDM 500*. Britton-Lee, 1982.

15. Cardenas, Alfonso F. *Data Base Management Systems*. Allyn and Bacon, 1979.

16. Chamberlin, D.D., et al. "SEQUEL 2: A Unified Approach to Data Definition,

Manipulation, and Control." In *IBM Journal of Research and Development*, Vol. 20, No. 6, November 1976.

17. Chen, Peter. *The Entity-Relationship Approach to Logical Data Base Design*. QED Information Sciences, Data Base Monograph Series No. 6, 1977.

18. Chen, Peter. "The Entity-Relationship Model: Toward a Unified View of Data." In *ACM Transactions on Database Systems*, Vol. 1., No. 1, March 1976.

19. Chorfas, Dimitris N. *Databases for Networks and Minicomputers*. Petrocelli, 1982.

20. Chu, Wesley W., and Chen, Peter P. *Centralized and Distributed Data Base Systems*. IEEE Catalog No. EHO 154-5, 1979.

21. CINCOM Systems Incorporated. *TOTAL Reference Manual*. CINCOM Systems, 1982.

22. CODASYL. *Data Base Task Group Report, 1971*. Association for Computing Machinery, 1975.

23. CODASYL COBOL Committee. *COBOL Journal of Development*, 1978.

24. CODASYL Data Base Administrators Wroking Group. *Data Structure Definition*, 1978.

25. CODASYL Data Description Language Committee. *DDL Journal of Development*, 1978.

26. Codd, E. F. "Extending the Relational Model to Capture More Meaning." In *Transaction on Database Systems*, Vol. 4, No. 4, December 1979.

27. Codd, E. F. "Relational Database: A Practical Foundation for Productivity." In *Communications of the ACM*, Vol. 25, No. 2, February 1982.

28. Codd, E. F. "A Relational Model of Data for Large Shared Databanks." In *Communications of the ACM*, Vol. 13, No. 6, June 1970.

29. Cortada, James W. *EDP Costs and Charges*. Prentice-Hall, 1980.

30. Cullinane Corporation. *IDMS Logical Record Facility*. Cullinane Corporation, 1981.

31. Cullinane Corporation. *IDMS Sequential Processing Facility*. Cullinane Corporation, 1979.

32. Cullinane Corporation. *IDMS Systems Overview*. Cullinane Corporation, 1979.

33. Date, C.J. *An Introduction to Database Systems*, Third Edition. Addison-Wesley, 1981.

34. DeMarco, Tom. *Structured Analysis and System Specification*. Yourdon Press, 1978.

35. Dolan, Kathy. *Business Computer Systems Design*. Mitchell Publishing, 1983.

36. Ellzey, Roy S. *Data Structures for Computer Information Systems*. Science Research Associates, 1982.

37. Elson, Mark. *Data Structures*. Science Research Associates, 1975.

38. Fagin, Ronald. "Multivalued Dependencies and a New Normal Form for Relational Databases." In *Transactions on Database Systems*, Vol. 2, No. 3, September 1977.

39. Fagin, Ronald. "A Normal Form for Relational Databases That Is Based on Domains and Keys." In *Transactions on Database Systems*, Vol. 6, No. 3, September 1981.

40. Fernandez, Eduardo B.; Summers, Rita C.; and Wood, Christopher. *Database Security and Integrity*. Addison-Wesley, 1981.

41. Flavin, Matt. *Fundamental Concepts of Information Modeling*. Yourdon Press, 1981.

42. Freedman, Daniel P., and Weinberg, Gerald M. *Walkthroughs, Inspections, and Technical Reviews*, Third Edition. Little, Brown, 1982.

43. Gray, Jim, et al. "The Recovery Manager of the System R Database Manager." In *Computing Surveys*, Vol. 13, No. 2, June 1981.

44. Hammer, Michael, and McLeod, Dennis. "Database Description with SDM: A Semantic Database Model." In *Transactions on Database Systems*, Vol. 6, No. 3, September 1981.

45. Hubbard, George U. *Computer Assisted Data Base Design*. Van Nostrand Reinhold, 1981.

46. IBM. *SQL/Data System Application Programming*. IBM Document SH24-5018-1, 1982.

47. IBM Corporation. *SQL/Data System General Information*. IBM Document GH24-5012-0, 1981.

48. IBM Corporation. *SQL/Data System Planning and Administration*. IBM Document SH24-5014-1, 1982.

49. IBM Corporation. *System/38 Control Program Facility Concepts* IBM Publication Number GC21-7729, 1982.

50. IBM Corporation. *System/38 Installation Manual-Conversion Planning*. IBM Publication Number GC21-7732, 1982.

51. Inmon, William H. *Effective Data Base Design*. Prentice-Hall, 1981.

52. Jackson, M.A. *Principles of Program Design*. Academic Press, 1975.

53. Johnson, Leroy F., and Cooper, Rodney H. *File Techniques for Data Base Organization in COBOL*. Prentice-Hall, 1981.

54. Kapp, Dan, and Leben, Joseph F. *IMS Programming Techniques*. Van Nostrand Reinhold, 1978.

55. Kim, Won. "On Optimizing an SQL-Like Nested Query." In *Transactions on Database Systems*, Vol. 7, No. 3, September 1982.

56. Knuth, Donald E. *The Art of Computer Programming: Fundamental Algorithms*. Addison-Wesley, 1968.

57. Knuth, Donald E. *The Art of Computer Programming: Sorting and Searching*, Addison-Wesley, 1973.

58. Lum, V.Y.; Yuen, P.S.T.; and Dodd, M. "Key to Address Transform Techniques: A Fundamental Performance Study on Large Existing Formatted Files." In *Communications of the ACM*, Vol. 14, No. 4, April 1971.

59. Lyon, John K. *The Database Administrator*. John Wiley, 1976.

60. Martin, James. *Computer Data-Base Organization*. Prentice-Hall, 1975.

61. MicroRIM. *MicroRIM User's Manual*. MicroRIM Corporation, 1982.

62. Nolan, Richard L. *Managing the Data Resource Function*. West Publishing, 1974.

63. Orr, Kenneth T. *Structured Requirements Definition*. Ken Orr and Associates, 1981.

64. Orr, Kenneth T. *Structured Systems Development*. Yourdon Press, 1977.

65. Page-Jones, Meilir. *The Practical Guide to Structured Systems Design*. Yourdon Press, 1980.

66. Palmer, Ian. *Data Base Systems: A Practical Reference*. QED Information Sciences, 1975.

67. Peters, Lawrence J. *Software Design: Methods and Techniques*. Yourdon Press, 1981.

68. Putnam, Lawrence H. *Software Cost Estimating and Life-Cycle Control: Getting the Software Numbers*. IEEE Catalog No. EHO 165-1, 1980.

69. Reisner, Phyllis. "Human Factor Studies of Database Query Languages: A Survey and Assessment." In *Computing Surveys*, Vol. 13, No. 1, March 1981.

70. Relational Software Incorporated. *ORACLE*. Relational Software Incorporated, 1982.

71. Schaeffer, Howard. *Data Center Operations*. Prentice-Hall, 1981.

72. Stonebreaker, M.R., et al. "The Design and Implementation of INGRES." In *Transactions on Database Systems*, Vol. 1, No. 3, September 1976.

73. Tsichritzis, Dionysios C., and Lochovsky, Frederick H. *Data Models*. Prentice-Hall, 1982.

74. Tufts, Robert J. Private correspondence, April 1982.

75. Ullman, Jeffrey D. *Principles of Database Systems*. Computer Science Press, 1980.

76. Vetter, M., and Maddison, R.N. *Database Design Methodology*. Prentice-Hall International, 1981.

77. Warnier, Jean-Dominique. *Logical Construction of Systems*. Van Nostrand Reinhold, 1981.

78. Weinberg, Victor. *Structured Analysis*. Yourdon Press, 1978.

79. Welty, Charles, and Stemple, David W. "Human Factors Comparison of a Procedural and a Nonprocedural Query Language." In *Transactions on Database Systems*, Vol. 6, No. 4, December 1981.

80. Yourdon, Edward, and Constantine, Larry L. *Structured Design*. Prentice-Hall, 1979.

81. Zaniolo, Carlo, and Melkanoff, Michel A. "A Formal Approach to the Definition and the Design of Conceptual Schemata for Database Systems." In *Transactions on Database Systems*, Vol. 7, No. 1, March 1982.

82. Zloof, M.M. "Query by Example." In *Proceedings of the National Computer Conference*, AFIPS, Vol. 44, May 1975.

Index